CHILIMANIA!

To Steve and Sharon
a chilihead at heart
Herb

CHILIMANIA!

HERB & CHRIS GELTNER

G.S.C. BOOKS
MERRITT ISLAND, FL.

CHILIMANIA!

by Herb and Chris Geltner

Published by:
G.S.C. Books
Post Office Box 452333
Merritt Island, FL 32954-2333

First edition July 1992

Library of Congress Catalog Card
Number: 92-72453

ISBN 0-9632262-0-7: Softcover

Printed in the United States of America

10 9 8 7 6 5 4 3 2 1

Matthew Rossi

CHILIMANIA!

DEDICATION

To those who originated the food which we call chili, and for their tremendous challenges and efforts in helping to mold and develop this Nation, this book is to them. To the cattlemen, their women, and the cowboys of yesterday, as well as those presently, whose hard working and living has made America's livestock raising into what it is today, the world's best, CHILIMANIA! is dedicated.

PREFACE

Multi millions of books are published each year, and probably millions of cookbooks are among them. Of these how many were purchased in hope of duplicating a beautiful photograph of a recipe, no one knows.

But how many are produced with recipes on chili and related dishes? Very few indeed. It appears that there are many in the publishing business who have never tasted or know what chili is all about. The only reference they have for "chili" is of the South American country that sounds about the same.

How many never-opened cookbooks decorate and fill bookshelves. What are given as gifts to friends and relatives, or to charities, book drives, etc., no one knows. One thing that we haven't seen being passed around is a good cookbook, with hundreds of ways of preparing chili.

We believe that CHILIMANIA! is a cookbook that a lot of people have been searching for. It seems that every cookbook with a chili recipe or two, repeat the same recipes from one book to another.

The explosion of chili as a main meal in homes and restaurants, has fast become a "food style". Chili has made a definite foothold into the food preference of millions of people. A recent study has shown, salsas were outselling catsup. This is one indication that the eating preferences are swaying "our" way.

CHILIMANIA! is self-published. From the gathering of recipes from relatives, friends, to the Gannett News Service and The Associated Press who ran articles of our recipe quest, doing the computer work (it may not be the best), finding a terrific artist in Matt Rossi, locating a printer, working out and attempting to solve the problems of distribution, sales promotion, and including the headache and numerous other etcs., it's our baby.

We have had a few Dutch ovens full of headaches. Re-reading recipes a few times too many, labored, sweated, lost much sleep, we have toiled harder on this project than we did at our full time business. A slight delay of about 21 months in getting CHILIMANIA! out was due to a severe heart attack requiring open heart surgery. But with a good, healthy diet of chili, a full recovery came about.

Several firms and organizations believed in our idea of creating the definitive cookbook on chili, and supplied us with recipes and other material to use. The McIlhenny Company, producers of the Tabasco Hot Sauce, instructed us to use their material as we wished. Woman's Day, Jarlsburg Cheese Company, Pace Foods Inc., and Geo. Hormel Co., supplied us with recipes to use.

The American Chemical Society's section of CHILIMANIA! contains material from their National Chemistry Week Chili Cookbook. We have never heard or seen of anyone being required to use hard hats when preparing or eating chili. But you really do not know the ways chemists do their thing behind the DO NOT ENTER lab doors.

By doing all the work, we have undoubtedly over proof-read, under proof-read, used wrong abbreviations and punctuations, misspelled simple words that may be found within, and generally have did things that should not have been done. But nowhere have we found it written that one must be a qualified book editor, publisher, or distributor to do what they wanted to do.

Our only interest was to create THE cookbook on chili. But to stay on just one subject, as is in the of case chili, it was rather difficult. Many contributors felt that other recipes, including salsas and various Southwestern dishes were just as important as chili, and should very well be included. So that is why CHILIMANIA! is a larger book than we intended, and why it is not strictly on chili.

Ms. Toni Cashnelli Food Editor of The Cincinnati Enquirer, was instrumental in the eventual size of the book. From an article that ran in her column, and picked up by The Gannett News Service wires, she has given us much encouragement. Our thanks to Toni is especially acknowledged.

From the amount of recipes received, we have concluded that, there are two major chili areas of the U.S.: the City of El Paso, Texas, and the City of Cincinnati, Ohio. This is not to down play the chili in other parts of the country, and there are some heavy chili centers, but it appeared that these two cities have more chiliheads per square mile than anywhere else.

No matter who said what about their chili or the other guy's chili, people prepare, eat and love their own dishes. And in the long run, isn't that what really counts when chili is concerned?

We hope that we have not embarrassed or disappointed anyone who's recipe or recipes we used, but if we have, please forgive us and accept our sincere apology. And we also hope that you will tell your relatives and friends if you like CHILIMANIA!, but please, inform us if for some reason you do not. If we're lucky with this project, maybe there will be a enough new recipes and material for CHILIMANIA!II

Herb & Chris

DISCLAIMER

Due to the specific nature of ingredients used in recipes described in CHILIMANIA!, it is only proper that this disclaimer is stated. It is not only for our own protection and peace of mind, but for a detailed warning to those who are not fully aware on what can constitute a very real and hazardous situation in food preparation and consumption.

It must be fully understood by all, and impressed upon all, especially the novices chilitis, that during any attempt to duplicate particular recipes contained herein, hazards may exist. The possibility of positive chemical reactions may be the cause of conditions creating such health hazards. Qualified medical assistants, totally familiar with chili, or a good friend, whichever the case, shall be within yelling distance or a phone call away.

First, as CHILIMANIA! is a collection of recipes contributed by many chili aficionados, we take no responsibility for any physical, mental, or other problems too numerous to mention which may arise from preparing, inhaling, or intimidating others into consuming these preparations, without their express knowledge and consent.

NO actions, we repeat NO ACTIONS shall be taken against any contributors, as their own stomachs may have been "put into shape" to tolerate their exclusive mixtures by continuous consumption. Some stomachs may very well be fitted with lead-lined stainless steel inserts. Just from reading some of the recipes, we would never attempt to make, let alone taste them. Even after many years of consuming chili, we can generally eat a pretty "favorable" dish.

These recipes, whether they be of chili or salsa, chili pies or pizzas, soups, or whatever, are dishes used by the contributors. We have not attempted to alter them in any way. Other than in presenting a more uniform appearance, balancing layouts, correcting some spelling, recipes are they were submitted.

Some recipes are, or should be listed with local 911 exchanges as they appear to approach the brink of requiring definite medical assistance to relieve discomfort. Some reactions may only require the basic home remedies for the alleviating a night destined to be one of some real bad sleep. Others are easy-eatin' dishes that can be used by those whose systems can not take too spicy foods, especially younger children.

The chiliheads of tomorrow are thè kids of today. They should not be discouraged from eating chili by being given poor quality and bad tasting examples of chili. Chili is a food that can be a very pleasant eating experience for people of all ages.

It has been impossible to check the reliability of sources for the recipes sent, as they are from near and far. We feel that any recipe contributed is used, or has been collected by those who remitted them for this book. All recipes are considered to be the property of the contributors unless otherwise specified.

Recipes taken from magazines, newspapers, and given to us without indicating their origin, the credit for the recipe has been given to it's donor. We have attempted to indicate sources of all material in CHILIMANIA! as best possible.

To the manufacturers of chili products: we hope that CHILIMANIA! is a satisfactory vehicle for the use of their products.

Livestock symbols were drawn from material sent by states' branding officials or other offices involved with Animal Industry and the livestock profession. All brand symbol information used in CHILIMANIA! was specifically requested for the purpose of being used in CHILIMANIA! as recipe dividers. Other than for symbols with dates indicating "Old Florida" and Western and Central American Spanish brands, all remaining brands were supplied to us.

It is hoped that the brand owners accept CHILIMANIA!, not only as a book on recipes, but as a source that may enlighten others, about the cattle industry of our Nation, past and present, and it's importance in our economy.

We would appreciate your comments on CHILIMANIA!

Herb & Chris

ACKNOWLEDGEMENT

It would have been virtually impossible to compile as many recipes as we have to create CHILIMANIA!, if it were not for the generous assistance of the following. The newspapers ran articles, telling their readers of our recipe quest. Contributors mentioned where they saw the articles, but there are undoubtedly additional publications who aided us, but who's names we were not given along with the recipes.

The remaining acknowledgements are to other organizations and companies who offered us material, including WFTV for giving us "air time." But, to those who sent us recipes of their chili and other favorites dishes, we thank you the most.

To the States and organizations who were generous in furnishing us with livestock and brand material, through either public records or freedom of information statutes, those sources are acknowledged in the CATTLE BRANDS Chapter.

American Chemical Society
Associated Press, The
Cincinnati Enquirer, The
Courier-Post, Cherry Hill, PA
Daily Reporter-Herald, Loveland, CO
Democrat-Chronicle, Rochester, NY
Desert Sun, Palm Springs, CA
El Paso Times, TX
Erie Daily Times, Erie, PA
Florida Today
Gannett News Service
Gary Collins' Home Show, ABC
Great Bend Tribune, Great Bend, MS
Guam Pacific Daily News
Houston Post
Kansas City Missouri
McIlhenny Co.
Merritt Island Press, FL
Montgomery Advertiser
National Enquirer
Orlando Sentinel
Pensacola News Journal
Philadelphia Enquirer
Port Huron Times Herald
Regis and Kathie Lee, With,
San Bernadino Sun
St. Petersburg Times
Wenatchee World Daily
West Hawaii Daily Today
WFTV Channel 9, ABC, Orlando
Woman's Day

Matthew Rossi

CHILIMANIA!

TABLE OF CONTENTS

CHEESE and CHILI QUESADILLAS

1 C. grated Cheddar cheese
¼ C. finely chopped scallions
1 can (4 oz.) green chiles, drained and chopped
4 flour tortillas

Preheat oven to 350 degrees.

Divide the cheese, scallions and the chiles between tortillas, placing it on one half of each. Fold over the tortillas to make half-moon shapes and place on a baking sheet.

Bake for 10 to 15 minutes or until piping hot and the cheese has melted. Serve hot.

Ben C. Seltzer
Cincinnati, OH

CIVI

Abner J. Thompson, 1882
Brevard County, FL

CHILI and MUSHROOM OMELETTE

8 eggs
2 T. diced canned green chilies
1 T. finely chopped scallion
1 T. water
1 C. thinly sliced mushroom
Salt and pepper
several drops hot sauce
4 T. butter
½ C. grated Monterey Jack cheese

Combine the eggs, chilies, scallions, water, hot sauce and salt and pepper to taste, in a bowl, and lightly beat together.

Melt half of the butter in a large skillet, and saute the mushrooms until they have softened and have turned brown. Maintain sauteing till all the liquid has evaporated. Set the mushrooms aside and keep them warm.

Melt the rest of the butter in the same skillet and pour in the egg mixture. Cook, stirring occasionally, until the omelette has started to set on the bottom. Continue cooking until the omelette is set, but moist in the middle.

Scatter the mushrooms and cheese over half of the omelette and fold over to enclose the filling. Cook for a few minutes more, then slide onto a warmed serving plate. Cut in half and serve hot, with a salsa.

Shane T. McCoy
Cincinnati,OH

A-2

Steve A. Amalong
Willcox, AZ

HOT CHILI SALSA

2 C. diced ripe beefsteak tomatoes
⅓ C. finely chopped onion
¼ C. minced seeded hot fresh chilies, or more to taste
Salt and pepper
2 T. fresh lemon juice
¼ C. finely chopped fresh parsley
Dash or two Tabasco hot sauce (optional)

In a small mixing bowl, combine all of the ingredients at one time, and stir to mix together. Cover the bowl, or place in a jar, until ready to use. Makes approximately 3 cups.

Jacob R. Hatfield
Cincinnati, OH

A

A. E. Cloar
Paris, TN

HORNY TOAD CHILI

6 Lbs. lean beef, cut into ¼-inch cubes
1 Lb. beef suet
3 or 4 onions, chopped
1 can (28 oz.) tomatoes, cut up, undrained
1 can (7 oz.) diced chilies
3 cloves of garlic, minced
6 to 8 T. paprika
7 to 8 T. chili powder
6 T. chili paste
2 T. cumin
1 T. salt
1 can (12 oz.) beer

Render the beef suet in a large skillet, or Dutch oven; drain off the fat, and discard waste. Divide the beef into portions and cook it evenly until brown. Continue cooking until all is prepared. Saute the onion and garlic.

Combine everything, including all the ingredients into the skillet or Dutch oven; cover, bring to a boil, reduce the heat, and simmer, stirring occasionally, for about 3½ to 4 hours.

As a garnish, sprinkle some shredded cheese and onion over each bowl before serving.

Frank & Helen Ruben
Cincinnati, OH

B4

S. Berthelsdorf
Portland, OR

La CASA SENA'S RED ONION SALSA

6 Ozs. fresh plum tomatoes, pureed
1½ red onion, minced
2 cloves garlic
1 T. cracked red pepper
2 Ozs. fresh lemon juice with pulp
3 T parsley, minced
½ T. salt
½ T. oregano
½ T. cumin
2 T. olive oil

Mix together all ingredients and cook, for 30 minutes on a medium heat. Serve hot.

Florida Today

Charles M. Hill
Duncan, AZ

CHILI-CORN SOUFFLE

3 T. butter
1 small onion, peeled and finely chopped
1 clove garlic, minced
¼ C. all-purpose flour
1 C. milk
2 T. canned green chilies, diced
¾ C. canned or frozen, and thawed whole kernel corn
½ C. grated Cheddar cheese
4 eggs, separated
Salt and pepper to taste

Preheat oven to 375 degrees.

Melt the butter in a saucepan and cook the onion and garlic until softened, but not brown. Stir in the flour and cook for one minute, then add the milk. Bring to a boil, stirring well until thickened.

Remove from the heat and add the chilies, corn, cheese and salt and pepper. Lightly beat in the egg yokes.

Beat the egg whites until stiff. Add 2 or 3 tablespoons of the egg white to the corn mixture, and whisk in lightly, then fold in the remaining egg white using a large metal spoon.

Spoon the mixture into a 1½-quart dish. Bake for 20 to 25 minutes, or until it has risen and is golden brown on top. Serve immediately.

Florida Today

E. Dale Doak
Knoxville, TN

LaSENA'S POBLANO SALSA

8 roasted, peeled, seeded poblano chile pods
2 red onions, minced
¼ C. cilantro leaves, minced
4 plum tomatoes, diced
3 T. olive oil
1 t. salt

Mix together all ingredients, and cook for 30 minutes on a medium heat. Season with salt to taste.

Florida Today

Steve & Betty Ann Heydon
Madras, OR

GREEN CHILI CASSEROLE

2 T. vegetable oil
1 small onion, finely chopped
1 clove garlic, minced
½ C. beef stock, preferably homemade
½ C. tomatoes, peeled, seeded and chopped
½ C. canned green chilies, chopped
Salt and pepper
8 corn tortillas
Vegetable oil for deep frying
1½ t. cornstarch
2 C. grated Monterey Jack cheese
Black olives, halved for garnish

Preheat oven to 350 degrees.

Heat the 2 tablespoons of oil in a saucepan and cook the onion and garlic until softened but not brown. Add the beef stock, tomatoes, chilies, and salt and pepper to taste. Simmer for 10 minutes, stirring occasionally.

Meanwhile, cut the tortillas into halves, then into quarters and finally, into eights. Fry the pieces lightly in one (1) inch of hot oil until just wilted but not brown. Drain well on paper towels.

Mix the cornstarch to a paste in a little water and stir into the chili sauce. Simmer, stirring until thickened.

Make alternate layers of tortillas, sauce and cheese in a casserole, ending with cheese. Bake for 25 minutes or until piping hot and bubbling. Serve hot, garnishing with the halved olives.

Florida Today

Benjamin & Evelyn Stillman
Vale, OR

LaCASA SENA'S PINEAPPLE SALSA

1 pineapple, minced
1 red bell pepper, minced
2 red onion, minced
4 jalapenos, seeded and minced
2 jalapenos, pureed with seeds
1 bunch cilantro leaves only, chopped
2 ounces pineapple juice

Mix together all ingredients, and cook for 30 minutes on a medium heat, or to taste.

Florida Today

Beef City, Inc.
Carlton, OR

PARTYTIME MEATBALL CHILI

This is an excellent appetizer for a party or get-together. Make small meatballs so that they can be picked up with toothpicks,and leave out the beans. Perfect for a fondue dish.

2 onions, finely chopped
1 green pepper, cored, seeded and chopped
1 can (24 oz.) stewed tomatoes
1 can (12 oz.) tomato paste
1 or 2 tablespoons mild chili powder (or more to taste)
Salt and pepper
1 Lb. lean ground round
1 Lb. lean ground pork
2 or 3 T. vegetable oil
1 can (16 oz.) red kidney beans, drained and rinsed

Combine the onions, green pepper, tomatoes, tomato juice, chili powder and salt and pepper to taste, in a large saucepan. Bring to a boil, stirring well. Then cover, and simmer for 2 hours, stirring occasionally.

Mix together the beef and pork by hand, and shape into 1-inch balls. Heat the oil in a skillet, and fry the meatballs until they are browned on all sides. Drain meatballs on paper towels to absorb as much of the grease as possible.

Add the meatballs to the tomato sauce and simmer for an additional 25 minutes.

Stir in the kidney beans and cook for 10 minutes more. Taste and adjust the seasonings before serving. Serves 4 to 6.

Martin & Shirley Ruben
Cincinnati, OH

T. A. Johnson, 1872
Brevard County, FL

MARTY'S CHILI con CARNE

1 C. dried red kidney beans, soaked overnight and drained
4 T. vegetable oil
2 Lbs. lean chuck beef, cut into ¾-inch cubes
2 Lg. onions, chopped
2 green peppers, chopped
2 cloves garlic, minced
1 can (16 oz.) whole tomatoes, cut-up, undrained
1 can (6 oz.) tomato paste
¼ t. cayenne pepper
2 T. mild chili powder
1 T. hot chili powder
1 C. water
1 t. dried oregano
1 t. ground cumin
¼ t. coriander
2 T. chopped parsley
¼ t. cinnamon
Salt and pepper

In a saucepan, put the beans and cover with fresh water. Bring to a boil. Boil briskly for 10 minutes, then reduce the heat and simmer for 30 to 40 minutes, or until beans are tender. Drain and set them aside.

Heat half of the oil in a large saucepan or flame-proof casserole. Add the beef cubes, in batches, and brown on all sides. As the cubes are browned, remove them from the pan, and continue browning the remaining beef.

Add the remaining oil to the pan and heat it. Then add the onions, garlic and green pepper, and cook them until lightly browned, stirring occasionally. Add the tomatoes and their juice, tomato paste, water, seasonings, including oregano, parsley, salt and pepper to taste.

For ease use a Dutch oven, and a put the browned and cooked beef cubes in it. Add the beans, mix well, then cover, and simmer on top of the range, or in a 325 degree oven, for about 2 hours, or until the beef is very tender. Stir occasionally during the cooking, and taste to change seasonings to achieve the desired flavor, if necessary.

Don't forget to have bowls of extra chopped onions, shredded cheese, chopped black olives, and chips for side dishes to be used as desired.

Martin & Shirley Ruben
Cincinnati, OH

B8

Leonard & Virginia Hitchcock
Merrill, OR

QUICK GREEN CHILI DIP

1 can (4 oz.) green chilies, drained and chopped
1 C. dairy sour cream
1 ripe avocado, peeled and diced
Salt to taste
few drops of Tabasco sauce (optional)

Combine all of the ingredients in a bowl, and fold together gently, but thoroughly. Cover and chill. Serve with tortillas or corn chips. Serves about 8.

Ms. Julian O'Neill
Cincinnati, OH

James T. Beavers, Sr.
Collinwood, TN

CHILI RICE

1 T. butter
1 T. Oil
1 small onion, chopped
1 clove garlic, minced
1 C. long-grain rice
2 C. water, or half chicken broth and half water
1 C. tomatoes, peeled and diced
1 T. tomato paste
1 to 2 t. chili powder
⅛ t. cumin
Dash of Tabasco hot sauce (more if you can go for it)

Heat the butter and oil together in a saucepan, and cook the onion and garlic until soften but not brown. Add the rice and stir to blend with the vegetables, and coated with the butter and oil mixture. Add the remaining ingredients.

Bring the saucepan to a boil, stirring well; reduce the heat, cover, and simmer for 20-30 minutes, or until all the liquid has been absorbed and the rice is tender. Serve hot.

Carl & Joyce DeStiacco
Scottville, NY

Bradley A. Seaton
Lakeview, OR

TORTILLA CHILI PIE

5 flour tortillas
quick beef filling
1 can (16 oz.) chili beans
1 C. whole kernel corn
½ C. grated Cheddar cheese
melted butter

Preheat the oven to 350 degrees.

Use four of the tortillas to line a 8- to 9-inch pie pan, overlapping them slightly. Mix together the beef filling, chili beans, corn and cheese. Pour into the tortilla case.

Cut the remaining tortilla into quarter and arrange on top of the filling. Brush the tortillas with the melted butter.

Bake for 30 minutes or until bubbling and piping hot. Serve immediately. Serves 4 to 6.

Jack & Eileen Cooney
Cincinnati, OH

B+

Betty Bunch
Heppner, OR

CHILI OLIVE DIP

¼ C. beer
½ C. pimento-stuffed olives
¼ C. mayonnaise
1 can (4 oz.) diced mild green chilies, drained
1 8-ounce container dairy sour cream
½ t. salt
½ t. chili powder
¼ t. ground oregano

Put mayonnaise, beer, chilies, and olives in the container of an electric blender or processor. Cover and whirl on medium until smooth. Spoon the sour cream into a small bowl and stir in the mayonnaise mixture, salt, chili powder and oregano. Cover, and refrigerate for at least one hour before serving, to chill.

Jeff Digulla
Merritt Island, FL

Moses Tindall, 1878
Brevard County, FL

CHILI TOMATO CHEESE DIP

2 T. butter
1 onion, finely chopped
1 clove garlic, mince
2 T. canned green chilies, diced
1 C. tomatoes, peeled and diced
Pinch of ground coriander
1 C. grated Monterey Jack cheese
1 C. grated Cheddar cheese
1 T. cornstarch
½ C. dairy sour or heavy cream

Melt the butter in a sauce pan and cook the onion and garlic until softened but not brown. Add the chilies, tomatoes, coriander and salt and pepper to taste. Cook gently for 5 minutes, stirring from time to time.

Add the cheeses and stir until they have melted and mixed well. Blend the cornstarch with a little of the cream and add the remaining cream. Stir into the cheese mixture and cook, stirring, until thickened.

Serve the dip in a cheese fondue pot or similar dish over a flame to keep it hot. Serve with tortilla or corn chips, and with baked potato skin as a second serving idea.

Ms. Jo Horstman
Britt, IA

Fred & Maureen Jensen
Klamath Falls, OR

FRESH SALSA

½ C. tomatoes, peeled, seeded and diced
¼ onion, finely chopped
1 green pepper, finely chopped
1 canned pickled jalepano pepper, seeded and chopped
1 T. finely chopped parsley
½ t. dried oregano
1 T. olive oil
1 T. fresh lime juice
¼ t. cumin seed
Pinch of brown sugar
Salt and pepper

Combine all the ingredients into a bowl and mix thoroughly. Place in a tight-lid storage container, place in refrigerator, and chill until ready to serve.

Jeff Digulla
Merritt Island, FL

Diwan Ranches Inc
Coolidge, AZ

MARY'S SALSA

2 ripe tomatoes (about ½ pound), quartered
½ C. scallions, coarsely chopped
¼ C. canned green chilies, chopped
Juice of one lime
1 T. fresh parsley, coarsely chopped
1 T. fresh coriander, coarsely chopped
¼ t. tomato paste
Salt to taste
Dash of Tabasco sauce

Place all of the ingredients into a food processor or blender, and process until the mixture is quite smooth. Put salsa into a serving bowl, cover, and place in refrigerator to chill before it is to be served.

NOTE: If the tomatoes that are to be used, have a coarse or heavy skin, it may be best to blanch them in boiling water for a few minutes, than doused with cold water. They then can be peeled easily before quartering. Makes about 3½ cups.

Don & Mary Ballentine
Cincinnati, OH

Kirby Brush
Paso Robles, CA

BEER CHILI SAUCE

½ C. beer
½ C. chili sauce
1 t. Worcestershire sauce
1 t. sugar
Dash hot pepper sauce

Combine all the ingredients in a sauce pan. Simmer, uncovered, for 5 minutes. Serve over hamburgers, frankfurters, bratwurst, or other link sausages, in buns or rolls.

Bradley McKee
Cincinnati, OH

Ellen Colier, 1875
Brevard County, FL

EASY SALSA

1 T. fresh lime juice
3 T. parsley, finely chopped
½ C. red pepper, diced
¼ C. cucumber, diced
1 T. tomato puree
¼ t. dried hot red pepper flakes
Salt to taste
¼ t. dried oregano
Dash of paprika

In a bowl, combine all of the ingredients. Mix thoroughly to blend spices. Place into a serving bowl, cover, and chill in the refrigerator until ready to serve. Makes about 1½ cups.

Suzie Zimmerer
Cincinnati, OH

Bryant Colier, 1875
Brevard County, FL

CHILI with BEER

2 Lbs. dried kidney beans
T. salt
2 Lbs. lean ground beef
4 Med. onions, (about 1 pound), chopped
¼ C. sugar
3 cloves garlic, minced
3 T. chili powder
1 T. dried mustard
3 C. (24 oz.) beer
2 cans (6 oz.) tomato paste
2 Med. green peppers, chopped

Soak the kidney beans in water, adding more water if necessary to keep covered. In the same water, simmer the beans with one (1) tablespoon of salt, covered, for about 1 hour or until they are tender to a fork. Add more water as needed to keep the beans covered during simmering.

Brown the beef and onions in a skillet, using a little oil if the meat is very lean. Pour off drippings. Add sugar, chili powder, dry mustard, and the other tablespoon of salt, and stir together well.

Add 1½ cups of beer. Cover, and simmer for 40 minutes. Stir in the tomato paste. Add the green pepper and the meat mixture. Cover, and simmer for 30 minutes. If the chili is too thin, keep the cover off. Add the rest of the beer during the past few minutes of cooking. If desired, adjust seasonings to taste.

Bill & Gail Warren
Merritt Island, FL

FL

Isaac Laners, 1878
Brevard County, FL

CHILI TIME CHILI

½ Lb. ground beef
¼ C. onion, chopped
2 T. green pepper, chopped
1 can (16 oz.) whole tomatoes
1 can (8 oz.) red kidney beans, drained
2 T. tomato paste
4 drops red pepper sauce
1½ t. sugar
1 T. chili powder
1 t. salt
⅛ t. ground black pepper

Crumble the ground beef in a 2-quart casserole. Add the onions and green pepper; cover. Microwave at High for 4 to 5 minutes, or until the meat is no longer pink, and the vegetables are tender. Stir to break up the meat after half the cooking time. Drain off grease. Stir in remaining ingredients. Microwave at High 14 to 18 minutes, or until flavors are blended and the mixture is at the desired consistency. Stir 3 or 4 times during the second cooking period.

VARIATION: Chili-Mac; prepare one serving of elbow macaroni, using 2 ounces of macaroni; in a casserole with ¼ teaspoon salt, 2 cups water, cook for 3 to 5 minutes at Medium-High setting. Makes about 2 servings.

Leonard & Hazel Bass
Las Vegas, NV

Roxanne & Jack Vine
Cottonwood, CA

CHILI BEEF SOUP

1 can (15 oz.) chili without beans
1 can (15 oz.) kidney beans, drained
1 can (10¾ oz.) condensed tomato soup
1 C. water
½ C. frozen green pepper, chopped
¼ to ½ t. chili powder

Combine all of the ingredients in a 2-quart casserole; cover. Microwave at High 8 to 10 minutes, or until heated, stirring 2 or 3 times during cooking, as well as giving the casserole dish a ¼ turn when stirring. Makes 6 servings. Have some nacho chips handy to eat with the soup.

Leonard & Hazel Bass
Las Vegas, NV

Don L. & Marguerite Thomas
Snowlake, AZ

SHORT CHILI DIP

1 T. chili sauce
1 T. yogurt or dairy sour cream
1 package (3 oz.) cream cheese
⅛ t. chili powder

Place cream cheese in 10-ounce custard cup or small bowl. Microwave at 50% (Medium) for 30 to 60 seconds, or until softened. Blend in yogurt. Blend in remaining ingredients, cover with plastic wrap.

Increase power to High. Microwave for 30 seconds. Serve hot or cold with chips, or celery and carrot sticks, if desired. Refrigerate this dip no longer than 2 days.

Ms. James Smith
Britt, IA

Asbry Sellers, agent for
Sarah R. Sellers, 1877
Brevard County, FL

MUSTARD and SWEET PEPPER SALSA

2 T. olive oil
1 T. wine vinegar
1 clove garlic, minced
1 C. sweet or green pepper, chopped
¼ C. scallions, chopped
1 T. Jijon mustard
Salt

Combine all of the ingredients in a blender or food processor, and process until quite smooth. Turn into a serving bowl, cover and chill until ready to use. Makes ¾ cup.

Jay & Joan Lowenstein
Worthington, OH

Alice Colier, 1870
Brevard County, FL

RANCHERO CORN CHILI

1 Lb. lean ground beef
1 C. green pepper, chopped
1 C. onion, chopped
2 cloves garlic, minced
1 can (17 oz.) Del Monte Whole Kernel Golden Sweet Corn
1 can (16 oz.) kidney beans (low sodium)
1 can (14½ oz.) Del Monte Original Style Stewed Tomatoes (no salt)
2 T. Chili powder
1 C. cooked rice

In a large skillet, brown the beef with the green pepper, onion and garlic, drain off drippings. Drain corn, reserving ⅓ cup of the liquid. Add reserve liquid, corn, beans, tomato and chili powder.

Bring to a boil. Reduce the heat; cover and simmer for 10 minutes. Serve with rice. Top with shredded cheese, if desired. Makes 6 servings.

Rosie & Shannon Allen
London, KY

Minor Jones, 1874
Brevard County, FL

RADISH AND WATERCRESS SALSA

½ C. radishes, chopped
1 C. watercress leaves
1 can (16 oz.) tomatoes, chopped in puree
½ C. onion, chopped
½ T. wine vinegar or lemon juice
Few drops of Tabasco sauce
Salt and pepper

Put all of the ingredients into a blender or food processor, and blend until contents are quite smooth. Taste, and add more Tabasco sauce or seasonings is desired. Spoon into a small serving bowl, and place in refrigerator covered until you are ready to serve. This will give you about 2½ cups of salsa.

Mrs. James Kastens
Cincinnati, OH

Debra & Samuel Baker
Union, OR

GREEN CHILE SALSA

1 can (4 oz.) green chiles, drained
2 or 3 canned pickled jalapeno peppers, drained, cored and seeded
3 T. scallions, chopped
2 T. parsley, chopped
2 T. fresh coriander, chopped
2 T. fresh lime juice
½ t. dried oregano
¼ t. ground cumin
Salt and pepper
Tabasco sauce as desired

Combine all of the ingredients into a blender or food processor, and process until the mixture is quite smooth. Taste, and add more Tabasco sauce or other seasonings if you desire. Spoon salsa mixture into serving bowl, or in refrigerator container and allow to chill until it is ready to serve. Makes about one (1) cup.

Mrs. Paul Horstman
Britt, IA

J. Summerling, 1875
Brevard County, FL

MEXICAN CHILI SKILLET

1 Lb. lean ground beef
1 Med. onion, chopped
1 Med. green pepper, chopped
1 clove of garlic, minced
3 C. cooked rice
1 t. salt
1¼ T. chili powder
1 can (8 oz.) tomato sauce
¾ C. beer
1 C. cubed Cheddar or Monterey Jack cheese

Saute the ground beef in a large skillet until it is browned, crumbling with a wooden spoon to break up beef chunks as it cooks. Drain off excess drippings. Add the onion, green pepper and garlic, and saute with the meat until they are tender.

Add the seasonings, and mix to blend completely with the meat and vegetables. Stir in the cooked rice, tomato sauce and beer.

Heat the chili mixture thoroughly, and let simmer for at least 30 minutes. Fold in the cheese cubes, and allow to melt. Makes enough for 6 servings.

Richard A. Walsh, MD,
Cincinnati, OH

Lewis H. Parker, 1879
Brevard County, FL

CHILI CON QUESO DIP

1 Med. onion, finely chopped
3 T. butter
3 T. flour
1 C. heavy cream
1 can (16 oz.) tomatoes, drained and coarsely chopped
1 can (4 oz.) mild green chiles, drained and diced
1 package (8 oz.) Monterey Jack cheese, cubed
½ C. beer
1 t. salt

In a medium-size saucepan, saute the onions in the butter until they are tender. Stir in the flour, mixing constantly to eliminate lumps. Add the salt. Cook until the mixture is just bubbly.

Remove from the heat, and stir in the heavy cream slowly. Return mixture to the heat, and continue cooking and stirring until the sauce thickens, and begins to bubble.

Stir in the beer, tomatoes and chiles; cook one minute. Add the cheese, stirring constantly, until melted. Serve warm with corn chips. Makes about 3 cups of dip.

Troy Govig
Cincinnati,OH

Stephen Drone
Pulaski, TN

DAD'S FAVORITE CHILI

½ Lb. pork sausage, crumbled
1½ Lb. ground beef
1 Lg. onion, chopped
2 C. tomato juice
2 C. (16 oz. can) beer
1 clove garlic, whole
2 C. cooked pinto beans
3 whole cloves
1 t. paprika
3 T. chili powder
1 bay leaf
Salt to taste
Cayenne pepper to taste

Cook the sausage over medium-high heat until done, but not brown. Add the ground beef and onion; cook slowly until the meat is no longer pink, and the onion is tender. Use a fork to further crumble the beef during cooking.

Place cooked meats, onion, and whole garlic clove into a large pot, kettle, or Dutch oven; add all of the remaining ingredients, except the beans, and simmer for one (1) hour. Add the cooked pinto beans, and simmer for another 10 minutes.

Remove the bay leaf and garlic clove before serving. Serves about 12, and for garnish to each bowl of Dad's "best", sprinkle with grated cheese and chopped onions.

Andrea Sedgwick
Cincinnati, OH

John & Mary Smith
Independence, CA

MILD TOMATO SALSA

½ C. tomatoes, seeded and diced
½ C. onion, finely chopped
1 clove garlic, minced
½ C. water
1 t. tomato paste
½ t. dried oregano
¼ t. ground cumin
Salt to taste

Combine all of the ingredients into a blender and process until the mixture is smooth. Pour into a saucepan and simmer for about 10-15 minutes, stirring constantly. As the water evaporates from the saucepan, the sauce will thicken to your desired consistency. Serve this sauce either cold or hot. It will give you about 1 cup.

Ms. Virginia Wheeler
Cincinnati, OH

Walter J. Thomson Co., Ltd.
Santa Ynez, CA

CHILI CON CARNE and CORN BREAD CASSEROLE

1 can (24 oz.) chili con carne
1 Pkg. (8½ oz.) corn bread mix
1 egg
⅓ C. milk

Follow the directions on the box to mix the corn bread batter. Use a 1½ to 2-quart microwave oven proof dish. Spread the canned chili con carne over the dish evenly. On top of this, spread the corn bread batter with a spoon, so that it is also over the chili con carne evenly. Cover, and microwave for 9 minutes on High.

After this cycle of cooking, uncover, and let brown at Medium heat for about 8 minutes, or as needed to set the degree of browning that is desired. This will give about 4 to 6 servings.

Al & Sarah Maupin
Cincinnati, OH

Nancy & Harold Carter
Maupin, OR

ARUGULA SALSA

Arugula (also called rocket) is a peppery green that's a member of the mustard family. Watercress is a very good substitute. Serve this delicious meal with crusty rolls, Italian bread or breadsticks.

2 T. olive oil
1 T. red wine vinegar
¼ t. black pepper
1 Lg. ripe tomato (8 oz.)
½ C. (3 oz.) arugula, loosely packed

Mix the oil, vinegar and pepper in a medium-size bowl. Core and coarsely chop tomato, and add to the bowl. Cut tough stems off of the arugula; rinse, drain and coarsely chop the leaves (you should have about 1¼ cups). Add this to the bowl also; toss to mix and coat leaves.

This salsa can be used to coat chicken prior to frying, broiling or other forms of preparation.

Cincinnati Enquirer

Robert M. Newman
Indian Summer Ranch
Fayetteville, TN

TOMATILLO CHILI SAUCE

2 T. vegetable oil
1 Med. onion, chopped
1 garlic clove, chopped
1 can (13 oz.) tomatillos, drained
1 can (4 oz.) green chilies, drained
1 canned pickled jalapeno pepper, cored, seeded and chopped
½ C. chicken broth
2 T. fresh lime juice
1 t. dried oregano
1 t. sugar
½ t. ground cumin
Salt to taste

Heat the oil in a saucepan and saute the onion and garlic until softened but not completely cooked. Add all of the remaining ingredients to the saucepan, and bring to a boil. Reduce the heat to a simmer, and gently cook for about 20 minutes, stirring occasionally.

After the sauce has cooled, place it in a blender and run until it is smooth. Reheat the sauce before serving. Makes about 2 cups.

Joey Sedgwick
Cincinnati, OH

Wayne Mixson
Marianna, FL

CHILI CORN BREAD CASSEROLE

1 Lb. ground chuck beef
½ C. onion, chopped
2 cans (16 oz.) stewed tomatoes, drain the liquid from can, and keep it from second
1 can (6 oz.) tomato paste
¼ t. dried oregano
1 T. rounded, chili powder
1 t. sugar
½ t. salt (or to taste)
½ t. fresh ground black pepper
2 eggs
2 pkgs (8½ oz.) corn muffin mix
⅔ C. milk

Combine the ground beef and onions in a 10-inch x 2-inch microwave safe dish. Spread out the meat in the dish, and break it up with a spoon or with fingers so that it will cook evenly. Cook with the microwave on High for 4 minutes. During the cooking period, stop to crumble the beef further.

If you are using chuck, do not discard the grease drippings, but if you use ground beef, pour off as much of the fat as desired.

Stir in the stewed tomatoes, tomato paste, chili powder, salt and pepper, and sugar. Cover the dish with a plastic wrap, turning back one corner, or poking a few holes with a fork to allow the built up steam to escape. Microwave for 15 minutes at 70% power, or Medium-High.

At the end of the cooking time, remove the plastic wrap, without burning yourself. Stir the chili mixture to get the consistency and flavor melded, then spoon the corn bread muffin batter over the bubbling hot chili. Spread it evenly so that the chili is completely covered evenly with the batter.

Place the dish back into the microwave, and cook for 9 minutes, or so on High, uncovered. It may take more time to get the desired brownness that you want. This casserole will serve about 8 people. It freezes quite well, and is ideal for a cold snack.

Joni & Joe Aden
Cincinnati, OH

William Meagher
Hardwick, SD

CHILI-CHEESE POLENTA with SALSA

Chili-Polenta:

4 C. skim milk
1 C. yellow corn meal
1 t. salt
¼ t. freshly ground black pepper
1 can (4 oz.) green chilies, chopped
4 ozs, coarsely shredded Monterey Jack cheese (about 1 cup)
½ C. grated Parmesan cheese

In a heavy 2-quart saucepan, mix the milk, cornmeal, salt and pepper. Bring this to a boil over a Medium-High heat, stirring often with a wooden spoon. Reduce the heat to low and simmer, uncovered, for 5 to 6 minutes, stirring until smooth and thick. Lightly grease a 13x9-inch baking pan. Remove the corn meal mixture from the heat, and stir in the chilies. Spread this mixture evenly into the greased baking pan. Refrigerate, after the mixture has cooled sufficiently, for about an hour, or until the mixture is set and firm. Cover the pan, if you think that you may cool it longer or may forget it is in the refrigerator. This will keep the mix from drying out.

To assemble: Heat your oven to 400 degrees. Using a 9 or 10-inch baking dish, lightly grease it. Cut the chilled polenta into 24 2-inch squares, and arrange them in the greased dish. You can stagger them in overlapping rows. Sprinkle the dish with the two cheeses.

Cover the dish loosely with foil, and bake for 15 minutes. After this baking, take off the aluminum foil and bake for an additional 10 to 15 minutes or until the edges start to brown.

Cook in the pan for about 10 minutes before serving with the salsa spooned over it. This will give about 6 to 8 helpings.

MICROWAVE: Increase cornmeal to 1¼ cups. In a 2-quart microwave safe bowl, microwave, uncovered for 10 to 12 minutes on High, and stirring every 3 to 4 minutes, until the mixture is smooth and thick.

Stir in the chilies as directed, and cut into pieces and lay out as shown above. Microwave, uncovered, on High for about 6 minutes, rotating the dish every few minutes till the polenta is hot and the cheese shreds just begin to melt. Let stand for 5 minutes.

Salsa for above:

1½ C. coarsely chopped ripe fresh tomatoes
¼ C. green onion, sliced thin
¼ C. cilantro leaves, chopped
1 T. lime juice
1 t. jalapeno pepper, minced
¼ t. salt

Mix all of the above ingredients in a small bowl. Cover bowl and refrigerate. Before serving, take it from the refrigerator and let stand to room temperature. Makes about 1½ cups.

Dave & Stevie Marks
Cincinnati, OH

O. F. Adams
Fannett,
Jefferson County, TX

BEAN and CHEESE CHILI

1 T. olive oil
2 C. onion, chopped
1 Lg. green bell pepper, chopped
1 can (28 oz.) tomatoes, broken up, undrained
1½ T. ground cumin
1 T. dried oregano leaves
1 t. minced garlic
½ t. salt
¼ t. granulated sugar
1 can (16 oz.) pinto beans, or red kidney beans, drained
¼ t. freshly ground black pepper, or to taste
4 ounces shredded Monterey Jack cheese (about 1 cup)
¼ C. loosely packed, snipped fresh cilantro
Sour cream (optional)

Heat the olive oil in a 2 or 3-quart saucepan over a medium-high heat. Add the onion and green pepper, and saute for 5 to 6 minutes or until onion is transparent, stirring often to get an even doneness.

Stir in the tomatoes, cumin, oregano, garlic, salt and sugar.

Bring the saucepan to a boil; reduce the heat to medium-low, uncovered, for about 15 minutes to blend the flavors. Add, stirring, the beans; simmer for 15 minutes or longer until the beans are hot and the chili has thickened slightly.

Mix in the black pepper. Taste, and if needed, add more ingredients to bring the flavor to your likes.

Ladle the chili into bowls or onto soup plates; sprinkle with the shredded cheese and cilantro. Serve with the sour cream, letting each person spoon on their own amounts. Makes about 5 servings.

MICROWAVE: Reduce cumin to 1 tablespoon and oregano to 2 teaspoons. Microwave the onion and pepper uncovered in a 3-quart microwave-safe bowl, on High for 5 to 6 minutes, or until the onions are transparent and the green pepper is crisp-tender. Stir in the tomatoes, cumin, oregano, garlic, salt and sugar.

Microwave, uncovered, on High for 5 to 7 minutes or until beans, are hot. Proceed as directed.

General serving suggestions: Spoon a thicker chili or con carne mixture into cored, seeded green or red bell peppers, which have been softened in the microwave. If desired, sprinkle cheese over each of the pepper.

Pour some of the mixture over corn bread which has been heated.

Mary Ann Hardini
Cincinnati, OH

John Rawlinson, 1882
Brevard County, FL

CHILI CHEESE BALLS

3 C. grated Monterey Jack cheese
1 C. grated Fontina cheese
1 Pkg. (3 oz.) cream cheese, at room temperature
4 t. prepared mustard
1 t. Worcestershire sauce
½ t. garlic powder
4 t. chili powder

Combine first 6 ingredients with two teaspoons chili powder and shape into bite-size balls. Sprinkle remaining chili powder in a large bowl, add cheese balls and roll gently to coat each completely.

Refrigerate and serve chilled. Makes 3½ to 4 dozen balls.

Cincinnati Enquirer

Bill Dougherty
Sante Fe, NM

ALL-AMERICAN CHILI DOGS

½ Lb. lean ground beef
1 small onion, chopped
1 small green pepper, chopped
1 clove garlic, crushed
1 T. chili powder
1 can (16 oz.) tomatoes, undrained
1 T. tomato paste
⅛ T. ground red pepper
1 Pkg. (16 oz.) frankfurters (8)
8 frankfurter rolls
½ C. shredded extra-sharp Cheddar cheese

In a large skillet, over a medium-high heat, saute the ground beef for 3 minutes, or until browned. Crumble the beef with a fork or wooden spoon to eliminate the large chunks. Drain off any excess fat drippings.

Add the onion, green pepper, garlic and chili pepper ingredients. Cook, stirring often until the vegetables are tender.

Stir in the tomatoes and their liquid, tomato paste, red pepper, and the salt. Bring the mixture to a boil. Reduce the heat, and simmer, uncovered, for about 10 minutes.

Prepare the barbecue grill. With a knife, score the frankfurters crosswise about ⅓ through each. Grill about 6 inches from the heat, 5 minutes, turning each frankfurter occasionally so that it is completely grilled. Place open rolls on grill to get them lightly toasted. Place frankfurters in rolls; spoon some of the chili mixture onto each one; sprinkle with cheese, and chopped onions if desired.

Scott Geltner
Cincinnati, OH

Eugene Norris
Luttrell, TN

CHILI NUGGETS

3 T. vegetable oil
2 T. Worcestershire sauce
1 T. chili powder
1 t. garlic powder
1 t. onion powder
2 bags (9 oz.) salted bite-size pretzel nuggets (about 9 cups)
1 jar (16 oz.) unsalted dry-roasted peanuts (3½ cups)

Heat your oven to 375 degrees. Line 2 jelly pans with foil (for easy cleanup). In a large bowl, mix the oil, Worcestershire sauce, chili powder, garlic powder, and onion powder. Add the pretzels and peanuts, tossing to thoroughly mix and coat. Spread coated pretzels and peanuts evenly in the prepared pans.

Back 8 to 10 minutes or until lightly toasted, stirring once to move contents around a little. Cool completely, then store in air-tight containers. Makes about 10 cups. Mixes well and keeps at room temperature for about one (1) month.

Cincinnati Enquirer

Alonzo Allen
Beaumont,
Jefferson County, TX

DAD'S FAVORITE CHILI

2 Lbs. ground beef
1 C. onion, chopped
1 green pepper, chopped
1 clove garlic, minced
1 can (15 oz.) tomato sauce
1 can (12 oz.) beer
1 Pkg. Carroll Shelby's Original Texas Brand Chili Mix
1 C. (4 oz.) 100% Natural Kraft Shredded Sharp Cheddar Cheese

Brown meat in a large saucepan; drain off fat drippings. Add the onions, green pepper, garlic, and cook until the vegetables are tender. Add the tomato sauce and one (1) cup of the beer. Add the large spice packet from the Chili Mix, salt and cayenne pepper to taste; mixing well. Bring the mixture to a boil; reduce heat, and simmer for 15 minutes.

Gradually add the remaining beer to the Masa Flour Packet, stirring until it is well blended with no lumps. Add to the meat mixture, simmer for 5 minutes longer. Serve with shredded cheese. Makes 6 one-cup servings. Prep time: 10 minutes - Cooking time 30 minutes.

Variation: Substitute 1½ cups of cold water for the beer.

Skip & Paulette Busam
Milford, OH

Edwin L. Luke
Tolleson, AZ

EASY KID'S SALSA

- 1 can (28 oz.) tomatoes, crushed
- ½ C. onion, finely chopped
- 1 clove garlic, minced
- ½ t. salt
- ½ C. tomato juice
- 1 t. vinegar
- 1 C. ice water

Add all ingredients in a mixing bowl. Place mixture into a refrigerator container, and let the children go for this salsa, which is not too uncomfortable for them to eat. Good with all kinds of chips, or burritos, tacos, or whatever is handy. Makes about 4 cups.

From a friend

Stanley Patch
Hi-Lo Farm
Bethpage, TN

I'M IN A HURRY SAUCE

- ½ C. pure ground red chile powder (no spices)
- 1 C. boiling water
- 1 clove garlic, mashed
- ¼ C. vinegar
- 1 t. oregano leaves, crushed
- 1 t. sugar
- 1 T. chile seeds for garnish

Soak chile powder in boiling water until it doubles in bulk. Add the vinegar while stirring, and if the mixture is too thick, add some more of the boiling water until the consistency is like that of cream.

Add the oregano, sugar, mashed garlic and salt. Let set before putting into a serving bowl. Sprinkle the chile seeds on top of sauce before serving for garnish.

This sauce is very good on steaks and pork chops, and well as on other types of dishes. This is one sauce that you can experiment with. Makes 2½ cups.

Old newspaper recipe

Bill F. Brooks
Tazewell, TN

CHILI DIP

2 cans (15 oz.) chili without beans
1 can (14½ oz.) tamales, mashed
1 Lb. process cheese spread, cut into 1-inch cubes
1 T. Worcestershire sauce
¼ t. Tabasco sauce
Sprinkle of chili powder for added flavor

In a double boiler, mix together all ingredients, and cook over a low heat, stirring frequently until the cheese is melted. Serve with warm taco chips, corn chips or other dipping material. Makes about 1½ quart of dip.

Ms. William Spencer
Cincinnati, OH

Richard J. Cabral
Newman, CA

MEATY CHILI

3 Lbs. ground beef
1 Med. onion, chopped
1 green pepper, chopped
3 cloves garlic, minced
1 can (15 oz.) tomato juice
5½ C. water
¼ C. plus 2 T. chili powder
1 T. paprika
1 T. cumin seeds
1 t. salt

In a Dutch oven, combine the beef, onion, green pepper and garlic. Cook until the beef is browned, crumbling with a wooden spoon to break into smaller chunks, and the vegetables are tender. Drain off any excess fat or grease that may be in the pot.

Add the remaining ingredients, mixing into the meat well. Bring to a boil; reduce the heat, and simmer for 3 to 4 hours, or until the flavor of the chili and the consistency is to your desired degree. If a thinner chili is desired, add more of the tomato juice. Stir while cooking to prevent any sticking to the pot during the simmering.

Ruth Goodstein
Cincinnati, OH

John R. Whitmer
Gilbert, AZ

HOT SALSA

1 C. chopped fresh jalapeno peppers, seeds and all
¾ C. of chopped onion
1 t. salt
1 T. vinegar
1 t. crushed garlic
½ C. ice water
½ C. tomato juice
½ t. chili powder
¼ t. crushed oregano

Combine all ingredients in a tightly sealed jar, and keep in a refrigerator until ready to serve. Makes about 3 cups of salsa.

Sam N. Geltner
Miami, FL

J. A. Condrey
Florida, 1853

CHILI RIO GRANDE

1 T. vegetable oil
1 Lg. onion, chopped
1 Lb. lean ground beef
1 Lb. lean pork, ground
1 can (28 oz.) tomatoes, including liquid
1 can (15 oz.) tomato puree
3 T. Worcestershire sauce
1½ C. beef broth
3 cloves garlic, crushed
1 t. crushed red pepper flakes
1 T. chili powder
1 t. cumin
1 t. dried thyme
1 t. dried oregano
1 t. dried basil
Grated Cheddar cheese
Sliced scallions (green onion)

Heat oil in a heavy 5- to 6-quart pan or Dutch oven. Add the onion and cook over moderate heat until softened. Add beef and pork and cook over a medium-high heat, stirring constantly, until browned, and meats are crumbled. Cook for 15 to 20 minutes. Discard fatty drippings from the cooking container.

Stir in tomatoes and their liquid, breaking them up with a spoon. Add tomato puree, Worcestershire sauce, beef broth, garlic, red pepper flakes, chili powder, cumin, thyme, oregano and basil.

Bring to a boil; then lower heat and simmer, uncovered, for about 2 hours, stirring occasionally until the chili is thick and the flavors are well blended.

Skim the surface of the pot and discard fat. Ladle chili into individual serving bowls and sprinkle with grated Cheddar cheese and sliced scallions before serving. Makes 4 to 6 servings.

Cincinnati Enquirer

J. F. Gillett & D. F. Gillett
Brevard County, FL 1877

CHILI with NOODLES

3 Lbs. ground beef
1 Med. onion, chopped
1 Pkg. (1¼ oz) chili seasoning mix
1 Pkg. (5 Oz) fine egg noodles
1 can (46 oz) tomato juice
1 can (6 oz) tomato paste
2 cans (15½ oz) chili beans
1 T. Worcestershire sauce
½ t. salt
¼ t. onion salt
¼ t. ground black pepper

In a Dutch oven, saute the ground beef, onion, and chili seasoning mix, stirring to crumble the meat with a wooden spoon, cooking until the beef is completely browned, and the onion is tender. Drain off any excess fat that has accumulated in the pot.

Add all of the remaining ingredients, stirring to mix all contents in the pot. Cover, and simmer over a low heat for about one (1) hour, stirring occasionally, (and tasting along the way). Makes about 12 cups.

Dan & Colleen Healy
Cincinnati, OH

Joseph Harley
Florida, 1825

CHUNKY CHILI

1 Lg. onion, finely chopped
1 green pepper, finely chopped
1 Lb. lean beef for stewing, cut into ½-inch pieces
1 can (16 oz.) red kidney beans, drained
1 can (16 oz.) tomatoes, undrained
1 can (8 oz.) tomato sauce
1 can (4 oz.) chopped green chiles, drained
2 T. chili powder
¼ t. garlic powder
¼ t. ground cumin
¼ t. ground black pepper
Dash or two Tabasco sauce
Shredded Cheddar cheese (optional)

In a 5-quart casserole or bowl, combine the ground beef, onion and the green pepper. Cover with casserole lid or with heavy duty plastic wrap. Microwave at High for 6 to 7 minutes, or until the beef is browned and the vegetables are crisp-tender. After a few minutes of cooking, stir and crumble the meat in the casserole. Again, at High, cook for 10 minutes more.

Stir in remaining ingredients except the cheese. Cover and again microwave at Med. (50% power) for 30 to 45 minutes, stopping every 5 minutes to stir to blend ingredients as well as further crumble beef more.

Sprinkle individual servings with cheese, and chopped onions, if desired. Make 10 cups.

Dan & Colleen Healy
Cincinnati, OH

S. T. Thomas
Florida, 1853

3-BEAN CHILI

½ C. onion, chopped
½ C. celery, chopped
⅓ C. green pepper, chopped
1 T. olive oil
1 can (28 oz.) whole tomatoes, cut up
1 can (15 oz.) tomato sauce
1 can (26 oz.) Great Northern beans, rinsed and drained
2 t. chili powder
1 can (15½ oz.) kidney beans, rinsed and drained
1 can (15 oz.) garbanzo beans, rinsed and drained
1 t. ground cumin
1 t. sugar
½ t. salt
¼ t. garlic powder
⅛ t. black pepper
⅛ t. cayenne pepper

In a 3-quart microwave-safe casserole, combine onion, celery, green pepper and oil. Cover. Microwave on High for 5 to 8 minutes,or until the vegetables are tender, stirring once or twice during the cooking period. Add the remaining ingredients. Mix well; recover, and microwave on High for 20 to 35 minutes, or until the mixture is hot and flavors are blended, stirring 3 or 4 times more, as well as giving the casserole a ¼ turn every time you stir to evenly cook the chili. Makes about 8 cups.

Dr. Donald & Beth Messersmith
Merritt Island, FL

Jack Longmoor
Mesa, AZ

HOMINY CHILI BAKE

1 Lb. ground beef
½ C. onion, chopped
1 can (14½ oz) hominy, undrained
1 can (16 oz) tomatoes, undrained and cut-up
2 T. all-purpose flour
¼ C. (1 oz) shredded Cheddar cheese
1 t. salt
1 t. chili powder
¼ t. ground oregano

Combine the ground beef in skillet, and cook until the beef is browned, and the onions are softened. Stir the beef to crumble with a fork or wooden spoon. Drain off fat drippings.

Add remaining the remaining ingredients except the cheese. Stir in well. Spoon mixture into a greased 2-quart casserole dish. Bake, uncovered at 350 degrees for 25 minutes. Sprinkle the Cheddar cheese evenly over the mix, and bake for an additional 5 minutes. Serves 4.

Ruth Goodstein
Cincinnati, OH

Joseph D. Marco
Tucson, AZ

OREGONIAN TURKEY CHILI

2 Lg. onions, finely chopped
3 T. salad oil
1 C. green bell pepper, chopped
2 cloves garlic, minced
2 Lbs. ground turkey
1 can (14½ oz.) tomatoes, with their liquid
3 cans (15 oz.) red kidney beans, drained
3 cans (15 oz.) tomato sauce
¼ C. soy sauce
3 T. chili powder
1 t. ground cumin
1 t. dried sage
1 t. dry thyme
2 limes, cut into wedges (for garnish)

Set aside ½ cup of the chopped onion for garnish.

Heat the oil in a 6- to 8-quart pan over a medium-high heat. Add bell pepper, garlic and remaining onions. Cook, stirring often, until the onions are softened.

Increase heat to high; crumble turkey into pay and cook, stirring gently until drippings begin to brown. Add tomatoes (break up with a spoon) and their liquid, beans, tomato sauce, soy sauce, chili powder, cumin, sage and thyme, stirring to scrape up browned bits.

Reduce heat, cover and simmer for 30 minutes. To serve, garnish with reserved onions and offer lime wedges to be squeezed over chili to taste. Makes 6 to 8 servings.

Cincinnati Enquirer

Aubrey & Mary Caruthers
Oxford, FL

CHILI MEAT LOAF

2 Lb. ground chuck
1½ t. salt
¼ t. black pepper
1 can (16 oz.) whole tomatoes, chopped
¼ C. onion, finely chopped
1 t. chili powder
½ C. cracker crumbs
½ t. celery seed
¼ t. ground oregano
1 C. (15 oz.) red kidney beans, drained and mashed

Combine all of the ingredients into a large mixing bowl, and mix thoroughly, but lightly. Place mixture in a 9x5x3-inch loaf pan, and shape into a loaf. Bake at 350 degrees for 1½ hours, or until it is done. Makes about 6 to 8 hearty servings.

Connie Hayes
Merritt Island, FL

Molokai Ranch Ltd.
Honolulu, HA

SIMPLY QUICK CHILI

1 Lb. lean ground beef
1 C. onion, chopped
1 clove garlic, crushed
1 can (8 oz.) tomato paste
Salt and pepper to taste
2 to 4 T. chili powder
2 C. water

In a large saucepan, brown the beef in a little oil, crumbling with a fork breaking the beef into smaller pieces. Drain off excess fat drippings. Add the onion and garlic to the meat, and sauce till the onions are softened. Add the remaining ingredients, and simmer for 45 minutes to an hour. Makes about 6 cups.

Mrs. Taylor Smith
Cincinnati, OH

Randall J. Marchese
Prescott, AZ

HEARTY CHILI

1 Med. green pepper, chopped (about 1 cup)
2 Med. onions, chopped
1 clove garlic, minced
1 T. vegetable oil
1 Lb. beef stew meat, cut into ½-inch pieces
3 T. flour
2 T. vegetable oil
2 cans (16 oz.) whole tomatoes, drained and cut into ¼ths
1 can (8 oz.) tomato sauce
1 to 2 t. chili powder
2 t. salt

Cook and stir the green pepper, onions and garlic in one (1) tablespoon of the oil in a Dutch oven over a medium heat until the onions are tender, about 5 minutes; remove the vegetables from Dutch oven. Coat beef stew meat with the flour; brown in 2 tablespoons of the vegetable oil.

Stir in the tomatoes, beans with their liquid, tomato sauce, chili powder, green pepper mixture and salt. Heat to a boil. Reduce the heat, cover, and simmer, stirring occasionally, for 30 minutes.
Makes 10 servings.

NOTE: If a thinner consistency is desired, do not drain tomatoes.

Cincinnati Enquirer

Violet Killebrew
Cornville, AZ

CHILI-TAMALE PIE

1 can (25 oz.) chili with beans
1 can (14½ oz.) tamales, cut into thirds
1 Med. onion, chopped
1 avocado, peeled and sliced
1 or 2 jalapeno peppers, seeded and finely chopped
1 C. crushed corn chips
1 C. (4 oz.) shredded Cheddar cheese

In a lightly greased 1¾-quart casserole, combine the first four ingredients; chili with beans, tamales, onion and peppers. Bake at 400 degrees for 25 minutes or until the mixture is bubbling.

Combine corn chips and cheese; sprinkle over top of casserole, and bake for 5 additional minutes or until the cheese melts. Top the casserole, when it cools, with the sliced avocado. Makes 6 servings.

Barbara Henry
Cincinnati, OH

Charlotte Aldrich
& Thomas Fraser
Stockton, CA

CINCINNATI-STYLE CHILI

"The recipe for Cincinnati-style chili throws cooks for a loop because you boil the beef instead of browning it. What makes this unique - terrific to some, odious to others - is the addition of cinnamon, vinegar and allspice".

Serve the chili alone or ala Skyline: with cheese (4-way); or with chili, spaghetti, onion, chili beans and cheese (5-way)."

3 C. water
2 Lbs. ground beef, crumbled
1 can (15 oz.) tomato sauce
1 Med.-size onion, chopped
1 bay leaf
¼ t. garlic powder
1 t. ground cinnamon
1 T. chili powder
2 t. cumin
½ t. red pepper
1 t. Worcestershire sauce
1½ t. vinegar
1½ t. allspice
1½ t. salt

In a large saucepan over a medium heat, combine water and ground beef; stir and mash the beef until mixture is soupy. Bring to a boil; stir in tomato sauce, onion, bay leaf, garlic powder, ground cinnamon, cumin, salt, chili powder, red pepper, Worcestershire sauce, vinegar, and allspice. Reduce the heat and simmer, uncovered, for 2½ to 3 hours.

Cincinnati Enquirer

B. H. Griffin, Jr.
Frostproof, FL

HOME-STYLE SALSA

1 Lb. ripe tomatoes, peeled and chopped
2 crispy fresh serrano chilies, stemmed, partially seeded & chopped
½ C. green onions, chopped (some of the green ends also)
½ C. cilantro leaves, chopped (or more if you desire)
¼ C. ice water
½ t. salt
1 T. freshly squeezed lime juice

Bruise the ingredients by hand, and if too dry, add more ice water. Combine all the ingredients in a medium-sized bowl and allow flavors to ripen for 30 minutes before serving.

Do not substitute and ingredients, although fresh jalapeno pepper will work in a pinch (but just 1, not 2). Canned tomatoes will not do. Makes 3 cups.

Cincinnati Post

Mrs. D. R. Daniel
Okeechobee, FL

SALSA SAUCE

4 T. vegetable oil
8 ancho chiles, washed and dried with paper towels
1 T. garlic, mashed
1 C. cold water
1 can (12 oz.) stale lager beer
1 t. sugar
1 t. oregano
1 T. vinegar
Salt
1 C. cold water
½ C. dry sherry
½ C. grated Parmesan cheese
6 or more pickled canned serrano chiles

In a large skillet, heat the vegetable oil, and pan-fry the ancho chiles over very low heat. Do not allow the chiles to scorch.

In boiling water in pot, place the chiles for about 20 to 30 minutes, until they become plump and soft. Let stand until cooled.

Remove the stems and place in blender with water and garlic. Run the blender until the mixture is a smooth puree. Strain the liquid into a container. Add the oil that the chiles were pan-fried in, vinegar, sherry, beer, salt, oregano and sugar. Place container into the refrigerator for about 20 minutes.

Before serving, mix the two cheeses in the sauce. Place the pickled serrano chiles around the serving bowl as garnishing accompaniment. Makes about 4 cups.

Marla Geltner
Miami, FL

Homer D. Parker
Shelbyville, TN

HOT TEXAS CHILI

1½ Lb. lean ground beef
½ Lb. bulk pork sausage
2 Med. onions, chopped
1 green pepper, chopped
1 can (8 oz.) tomato sauce
1 jalapeno pepper, seeded and chopped
1 clove garlic, minced
1 T. salt
2 T. chili powder
¼ t. dried whole oregano
1 C. beer
¼ C. instant corn Masa, divided
¼ t. cumin seed
¼ red pepper
chopped onion (optional)
commercial sour cream (optional)

In a large Dutch oven, combine both the ground beef and the pork sausage, breaking up roughly with a wooden spoon; cook over a medium heat, stirring more to crumble the meats. Brown the meats, and pour off fat and grease, and discard.

Add the onions, green peppers, and the garlic to the Dutch oven, and cook until the vegetables are tender. Add the tomato sauce and a cup of water.

Add the jalapeno pepper, chili powder, salt, oregano and beer, blending into the rest of the Dutch oven mixture. Bring to a boil; reduce heat, and allow to simmer. With a little of the chili mixture, make a little bowl of the two tablespoons of Masa flour into a paste.

Add this to the pot and stirring constantly, thoroughly mix the flour into the chili.

Cover, continue simmering for 30 minutes, stirring occasionally to prevent stock from sticking to pot.

Gradually add ½ cup of water to the remaining Masa, stirring until smooth. Add to chili mixture, and stir well. Add an additional 1 cup of water and red peppers; simmer 15 minutes. Serve with the additional chopped onion and sour cream if desired.

CSG

Joe M. & George W. Newman
Ardmore, TN

TEXAS CHAMPION CHILI

3 Lbs. boneless chuck roast, finely diced
1 T. peanut oil
2 Lg. onions, chopped
3 cloves garlic, minced
1 jalapeno pepper, finely chopped
1 t. cumin seeds
1½ T. whole oregano leaves
1 T. chili powder
1 can (28 oz.) whole tomatoes, undrained
3½ C. water
1½ t. instant corn masa (optional)
Shredded Cheddar Cheese (optional)

In a Dutch oven, saute the onion, garlic and jalapeno pepper in the oil until tender; set aside when done. Combine the meat, cumin, and oregano in the pot, and cook until the meat is browned, crumbling as it is cooking. Add the onion mixture, chili powder, tomatoes and water. Bring to a boil; reduce heat, cover, and simmer for 2 to 3 hours, stirring occasionally.

For a thicker chili, combine corn masa with a small amount of cold water to make a paste. Add this to the chili, stirring constantly to prevent lumps. Top each serving with some shredded cheese if desired. Yields about 5 to 7 servings depending on hunger of those being served.

Marvin & Maida Belkin
Cincinnati, OH

6

W. Harris
Florida, 1825

CHILI BUTTER

¼ C. butter or margarine,melted
2 T. lemon juice
1 T. minced fresh parsley
1 small clove garlic, minced
1 t. chili powder
Dash Tabasco sauce
½ t. salt
¼ t. fresh ground black pepper

In a small mixing bowl, combine all of the ingredients and stir well to blend smooth. Makes about ⅓ cup.

Marian Kohn
Cincinnati, OH

A

Jimmie B. Adcock
Readyville, TN

ENCHILADAS SALSA

1 can (28 oz.) tomatoes, drained
4 T. olive oil
3 T. flour
1 bay leaf
1 t. garlic, mashed (optional)
¼ t. chili powder
Salt and pepper to taste

In a blender, puree the tomatoes. In a saucepan, heat the oil and mix in the flour to a paste, and brown flour lightly. Add this to the strained tomatoes. Add all ingredients, and bring to a boil for about 5 minutes, stirring constantly. Cover, as the sauce will tend to spatter.

When mixture is starting to thicken, taste and correct seasonings as desired. Remove the bay leaf. This salsa can be used in place of any chile sauce. Makes about 3 cups.

Cincinnati Enquirer

John & Susanne Verretto
Cottonwood, AZ

OPEN-FACE CHILI BURGERS

1½ Lb. ground beef
½ C. chopped onions
1 can (8 oz.) tomato sauce
1 Pkg. (1¼ oz.) taco seasoning mix
6 hamburger buns
1 tomato sliced
1 C. shredded Cheddar cheese
¼ C. chopped black olives
1 C. shredded lettuce
1 onion, sliced thin

In a large skillet, brown the meat, crumbling to reduce the size of the chunks. Drain off all the fat drippings before adding any of the ingredients. Stir in the tomato sauce and taco seasonings, simmer for 5 minutes.

Split the hamburger buns and lightly toast each. Spread the meat mixture onto the buns. Place a tomato slice on each and them sprinkle each with a little of the shredded cheese.

Bake at 400 degrees for 4 minutes, or until the cheese begins to melt. Top with some shredded lettuce, olives, and onion slices.
Makes 12 servings.

Ms. Blanche Haviland
Rochester, NY

Dorothy Jean Platt, 1942
Bar D
Brevard County, FL

CHILI-CHICKEN KEBABS with PINEAPPLE SALSA

- 8 chicken thighs (about 2½ lbs.)
- 1 t. chili powder
- 1 t. paprika
- ¼ t. cayenne pepper
- 2 T. salad oil
- 2 t. Dijon mustard
- 2 ears of corn
- 1½ C. medium red onions

Skin and bone chicken thighs. Cut into 1-inch chunks. In a bowl, combine chili powder, paprika, cayenne pepper, oil and mustard. Add the chicken chunks and stir to coat evenly. Cover and marinate 30 minutes or even might.

Shuck the corn and cut ears into ¼-inch chunks. Cut onions into small wedges. Alternate chunks of chicken (two at a time), corn and a wedge of onion on six skewers, using two pieces of corn and two pieces of onion per skewer. Rub onion and corn with the remaining marinade.

Grill over medium-hot coals for about 10 minutes, or until the chicken is cooked through. Serve with the pineapple salsa. Makes 6 servings.

Cincinnati Enquirer

Joe Poe
Pope Farms
Yorkville, TN

PINEAPPLE SALSA for above as well

- 1 pineapple (about 3 Lbs.)
- 1 Med. red onion, chopped
- ¾ C. fresh cilantro leaves, minced
- 1 T. white wine vinegar
- ¼ t. Tabasco hot sauce

Cut tops from pineapple and slice away rind. Coarse-chop pineapple, and discard wood core. Place in a colander to drain, reserving juice for another use. Combine drained pineapple with remaining ingredients and mix well. Serve as a relish with Chili-Chicken Kebabs.

Cincinnati Enquirer

Dorothy & Raymond Geer
Sierra Vista, AZ

CHUCK WAGON CHILI

2 T. vegetable oil
1 C. onions, chopped, reserving ¼ C. for garnish
1 Lg. green pepper, diced
1 2-Lb. boneless chuck blade steak, cut into ½-inch cubes
2 cloves garlic, crushed
1 can (28 oz.) whole tomatoes, undrained and chopped
1 can (6 oz.) tomato paste
1 C. water
3 T. chili powder
1 T. salt
1 t. dried whole oregano
½ t. pepper
¼ t. cumin
½ C. (2 oz.) shredded Monterey Jack cheese

Brown the meat in a Dutch oven. When all the meat is done, remove from the pot and put into a bowl. Reserve drippings. Saute ¾ of the onion, green pepper and garlic in the reserved drippings. Saute until the vegetables are tender.

Add meat and the next 7 ingredients to the Dutch oven, mixing well. Bring to a boil, stirring occasionally. Reduce heat; cover, and simmer for 1½ hours, stirring occasionally to keep chili from sticking to bottom of pot.

When serving, transfer chili hot to bowls, and sprinkle with the onion and shredded cheese. Makes about 9 cups.

Scott Geltner
Cincinnati, OH

Armondo & Pamela Verdugo
Tucson, AZ

CHILI DIP

2 cans (15 oz.) chili without beans
1 can (14½ oz.) tamales, mashed
1 Lb. process American Cheese, cut into 1-inch cubes
1 T. Worcestershire sauce
¼ t. hot sauce
¼ t. chili powder
¼ t. ground cumin

In a double boiler, combine all the ingredients. Cook over a low heat, stirring frequently until the cheese melts. Serve warm with chips of your choice.

Cheryl Rossi
Merritt Island, FL

D. S. Allen
Nolensville, TN

COMPANY CHILI

1 Lb. ground chili beef
1 Lb. hot smoked sausage, sliced
1 green pepper, chopped
1 can (28 oz.) pinto beans, undrained
1 can (28 oz.) whole tomatoes, undrained
½ C. catsup
¼ t. oregano
1 T. chili powder
2 t. brown sugar
1 t. Dijon mustard
½ t. salt
¼ t. cumin seed
¼ t. ground black pepper
1 bay leaf

Combine ground beef, sausage, onion, and green pepper in a Dutch oven; over a medium-high heat, cook the meats until they are browned, stirring to crumble. Drain off all fat, as more will accumulate during the cooking.

Drain the pinto beans, reserving the liquid. Add liquid to the Dutch oven, stir in remaining ingredients, except the pinto beans. Cover and simmer for 45 minutes. Now add the pinto beans, and cook for an additional 15 minutes. Remove the bay leaf prior to serving. Makes about 3 quarts of chili.

CSG

DB

Daniel Bell
Florida, 1828

TEXAS STYLE CHILI

3 Lb. ground chuck
1 Lb. hot bulk sausage
3 Med. onions, chopped
4 cloves garlic, minced
¼ C. chili powder
2 T. all-purpose flour
1 T. sugar
1 T. ground oregano
¼ t. ground cumin
1 T. brown sugar
1 t. salt
2 cans (28 oz.) whole tomatoes, undrained and chopped
1 can (6 oz.) tomato sauce
1 bay leaf

Combine ground chuck, sausage, onions and garlic in a Dutch oven; and cook until the meats are browned; stirring often with a wooden spoon to crumble and break meats into smaller pieces. Drain off fat and excess grease from pot. Stir in the remaining ingredients; cover, and simmer for one (1) hour, stirring occasionally, and sampling the chili for the flavor that you're looking for. This recipe will provide about 5 quarts of chili.

Emmett E. Stone
Cincinnati, OH

J

J. Bryan
Florida, 1828

LUNCH TIME CHILI

3 Lbs. ground beef
6 Med. size onions, chopped
3 cans (16 oz.) whole tomatoes, undrained and chopped
2 cans (15 oz.)red kidney beans, drained
1 can (6 oz.) tomato paste
3 to 4 T. chili powder
¼ t. oregano
¼ t. salt
¼ t. ground pepper
½ t. Tabasco hot sauce

In a Dutch oven, cook the ground beef and chopped onions until the beef is browned, stirring to crumble meat. Drain fat from meat well of all excess drippings.

Add the remaining ingredients; simmer for one (1) hour, uncovered, stirring occasionally for that the contents of the pot are cooked evenly, and none has been sticking to the bottom.

Taste, and change with additional spices if desired, but what is shown in this recipe should be just right for a good hearty chili.

Serve with shredded cheese, chopped onions, crushed red pepper sprinkled over bowl, or other types of garnishing that you generally use on your table. Makes about 5 quarts of chili, which also can be frozen satisfactory.

Miami Herald

John Pledger
Florida, 1836

CHILI OIL "Hot Ingredient!"

This is a very hot ingredient. It is an orange-red oil, and is used in firing-up stir-fry cooking, as well as being added to chilies and standard mild to hot dishes.

Chili Oil can be purchased as a condiment.

Greg & Sandie McKee
Cincinnati, OH

David Bugg
D. B. Livestock
White Pine, TN

CHILI-CHEESE DOGS

*This can be used with any chili mixture that you prepare.

8 got dog buns
Spicy brown mustard
1 can (15 oz.) chili with beans
8 frankfurters
1 C. (4 oz.) shredded Process American cheese

Spread each hot dog bun with a little mustard and set aside. Place chili into a small bowl; cover with a plastic wrap, and microwave at High for 3 to 4 minutes, or until it is thoroughly heated, stirring and giving the bowl a half-turn after two minutes of cooking time. Set the bowl of chili aside and keep it warm.

Pierce each frankfurter with a fork several time, and place them on a glass pizza plate or a microwave-safe platter. Cover the franks with a paper towel, and microwave at High for 2 or 3 minutes, or until hot.

Place a frankfurter into each bun, spread with a little of the shredded cheese, and return to the microwave for just a few minutes, or just until the cheese begins to melt.

*See Cincinnati Chili Coneys

Bob & Evelyn Dodson
Cincinnati, OH

Gary Yamagata
Oahu, HA

EASY MADE CHILI

1 Lb. ground beef
1 onion, chopped
1 green pepper, chopped
1 clove garlic, minced
1 can (8 oz.) tomato sauce
1 C. water
½ t. salt
1½ to 2 T. chili powder
¼ t. black pepper
Dash of dried ground oregano
2 cans (16 oz.) red kidney beans, undrained
¼ t. celery seed

Combine ground beef, onion, and green pepper in a Dutch oven, and cook until the beef is browned and the vegetables are tender, stirring with a wooden spoon to break up and crumble meat. Drain off all pan drippings.

Add all of the remaining ingredients, except the beans, and continue cooking, covered for about 45 minutes longer. Remove cover, add the kidney beans, mix in well with the contents, and cook for a additional 15 minutes. Makes about 2 quarts of good chili.

Florida Today

Warren G. Allbritton
Beaumont,
Jefferson County, TX

CHILI SAUCE

4 Qts. of ripe tomatoes, peeled, cored and chopped
2 C. onions, chopped
2 sweet red peppers, chopped
1 hot red pepper, minced
1 C. sugar
2½ T. pickling salt
3 T. mixed pickling spices
1 T. celery seed
1 T. mustard seed
2 C. vinegar

In a heavy 10-quart Dutch oven, combine the tomatoes, onions, red peppers, hot red pepper, sugar and pickling salt. Heat to a simmer, and cook on a medium heat for 45 minutes.

Tie the pickling spices, celery seed, and the mustard seed in a cheese cloth enclosure, and add to the tomato mixture. Simmer, uncovered, for about 1½ hours or until the mixture becomes thick. Stir in the vinegar, and simmer for an additional hour, or until the desired sauce thickness is reached.

Remove the spice bag and discard.

Pour the chili sauce into hot sterilized jars, leaving about ¼-inch headspace. Cover at once with metal lids, and screw bands tightly. Process in boiling water bath for 15 minutes, or as directed.

Makes about 4 quarts of salsa.

CSG

Shiloh Perry
Melbourne, FL

CHILI CON CARNE

1½ Lbs. boneless round steak, cut into ½-inch cubes
2 T. vegetable oil
1 can (15 oz.) tomato sauce
1½ C. water
1 beef-flavored bouillon cube
2 T. chili powder
2 T. dried whole oregano
1 t. salt
¼ t. black pepper
1 t. ground cumin seed
1 t. minced garlic
¼ t. Tabasco sauce
2 T. corn meal
2 cans (16 oz.) dark kidney beans, undrained
1 can (6 oz.) tomato paste

Brown the meat in the vegetable oil using a Dutch oven or large cooking pot. Add the tomato sauce, 1½ cups of water, and bouillon cube; cover and simmer for 30 minutes, or to taste, stirring occasionally.

Stir in the kidney beans and corn meal; cover, and simmer for 30 minutes, adding additional water if necessary for the desired consistency. Makes about 2 quarts of quite freezable chili.

CSG

V. D. Aubey
Beaumont,
Jefferson County, TX

CHILI with RICE

1 Lb. lean ground beef
½ Lb. Italian sausage,cut into ½-inch pieces
1 Med. onion, coarsely chopped
1 green pepper, coarsely chopped
1 stalk celery, coarsely chopped
1 clove garlic, minced
1 can (16 oz.) stewed tomatoes, undrained
1 can (6 oz.) tomato paste
1 can (8 oz.) tomato sauce
¾ C. water
2 t. chili powder
½ t. dried whole oregano
½ t. salt
¼ t. black pepper
½ t. red crushed pepper
¼ t. ground cumin
Dash of Tabasco sauce (optional)
½ C. uncooked rice

Combine the first 6 ingredients, in a 3-quart casserole or other type of microwave-safe container. Cover, and microwave at High for 10 minutes, stirring to break up meat every few minutes.

Mix in the uncooked rice, and a little additional water if mixture is too dry, and microwave at Medium-(50% power) for 15 minutes or until rice is done and tender.

Herman & Eileen Fogel
Cincinnati, OH

G. V. & J. E. Cooper
Circle C Bar
Florida, 1915

BASIC CHILI

1 Lb. ground beef
1 onion, coarsely chopped
1 green pepper, coarsely chopped
1 clove garlic, minced
1 can (16 oz.) tomatoes, undrained
1 can (16 oz.) red kidney beans, drained
1 can (6 oz.) tomato sauce
1 can (6 oz.) tomato paste
½ C. water
2 T. chili powder
½ t. ground cumin
½ t. salt
¼ t. ground fresh black pepper
Dash of Tabasco sauce (optional)

In a 3-quart microwave-safe casserole, combine the beef, onion, and the green pepper. Cover with a casserole lid, or heavy duty plastic wrap, with one corner opened to permit built up steam to escape.

Microwave at High for 6 to 9 minutes, giving the casserole a half turn every few minutes, and also using this time, to stir and break up larger pieces of beef. If additional cooking time is needed, make sure that beef is browned before taking from microwave.

Stirring will also allow the beef to be cooked more evenly and faster. Drain off all beef grease well.

Add the remaining ingredients, mixing them well into the meat well. Cover, and microwave at High for 10 minutes longer, stirring occasionally. Cover and further microwave at Medium (50% power) for 30 to 35 minutes. Yields about a quart and a half. Can be frozen.

CSG

Julia Roberts, 1900
Brevard County, FL

CHEESE-TOPPED CHILI

1 Lb. ground beef
1 Med. onion, coarsely chopped
1 green pepper, coarsely chopped
1 stalk celery, coarsely chopped
1 clove garlic, minced
1 can (16 oz.) stewed tomatoes, undrained
1 can (6 oz.) tomato paste
¾ C. beef broth
2 t. chili powder
½ t. dried whole oregano
½ t. salt
¼ t. black pepper
1 bay leaf
¼ t. ground cumin seed
¼ t. red crushed pepper
1½ C. (6 oz.) shredded Sharp Cheddar cheese

Combine the first 5 ingredients in a 3-quart casserole, stirring to break up and crumble the meat. Cover with a casserole lid or heavy duty plastic wrap, leaving one corner open to allow steam to escape while cooking.

Microwave at High for 6 to 9 minutes, or until the beef is browned. Pour off as much of the fat as possible.

Add all of the remaining ingredients, except the cheese, mixing well. Cover and microwave at High for 10, minutes, stirring after several minutes to crumble meat more and to move contents of casserole around for more evenly cooking. Cover, and microwave for 35 to 40 minutes at Medium (50% power).

Spoon into serving bowls, and immediately sprinkle with the shredded cheese so that it becomes partially melted prior to eating.

Makes about 7 or 8 cups of chili.

CSG

Elbert Knight, 1905
Brevard County, FL

BEEFY SAUSAGE CHILI

½ Lb. ground beef
½ Lb. hot bulk pork sausage
1 Med. onion, sliced and separated into rings
1 clove garlic, minced
1 C. celery, chopped
2 cans (10¾ oz.) tomato juice, undiluted
1 can (16 oz.) kidney beans, drained
½ C. water
1 t. chili powder, or more to taste
½ t. dried whole oregano
¼ t. red pepper
¼ t. dried cumin seed

In a 3-quart microwave-safe casserole, combine the beef, pork, onion and celery, breaking up the beef into smaller pieces before cooking. Cover with a casserole lid, or heavy duty plastic wrap, leaving one corner free to vent steam as it builds from being cooked.

Microwave on High for 6 to 9 minutes, or until beef is browned. Drain off the beef drippings from the casserole.

Add the remaining ingredients, mixing them with the meat and vegetables well. Cover and microwave at High for 10 more minutes, stirring after several minutes to break up the beef lumps further, as well as giving the casserole dish a half turn every few minutes to have the meat evenly cooked.

Cover, and microwave at Medium-(50%) power for 30 to 35 minutes.

A fine garnish for this casserole dish, is to sprinkle shredded Cheddar cheese over each portion as it is dished out, and it has a chance to melt before eating.

Tom D. Ivey, MD,
Cincinnati, OH

Chambers Farms
CC Bar
Florida, 1941

VENISON CHILI

2 Lbs. venison, cut into ½-inch cubes
1 Lb. ground beef
2 Lg. red onions, chopped
1 can (15½ oz.) red kidney beans, undrained
3 cans (8 oz.) tomato sauce
1 can (6 oz.) tomato paste
¼ t. cumin seeds, crushed
⅛ t. hot Tabasco sauce
1 clove garlic, minced
1 C. water
3 to 4 T. chili powder
1 t. Worcestershire sauce

In a Dutch oven or other large cooking pot, combine the venison, ground beef and onions; cook until the meats are browned; stirring to crumble into smaller pieces with a wooden spoon. Drain off all fat and grease from the pot.

Stir in all remaining ingredients; cover and simmer for 1½ hours, or until venison is tender, adding more water if necessary for the desired consistency.

Mrs. Cheryl Haak
Ontario, NY

LC

L. Cowart
Florida, 1856

NO MEAT CHILI

1 C. dried kidney beans
1 C. dried pinto beans
1 C. dried black beans
5 stalks celery and leaves, chopped
1 Lg. carrot, shredded
3 Lg. tomatoes, peeled & cubed
1 Lg. green pepper, chopped
1 Med. onion, chopped
½ C. raisins
2 cloves garlic, minced
2 T. chili powder
2 bay leaves
¼ plus 2 T. fresh minced parsley
1 t. dried whole dill weed
1 t. dried whole basil
1 t. dried whole oregano
¼ t. hot sauce
1 t. unsalted sunflowers kernels
1 t. ground cumin
1 t. ground allspice
1 t. freshly ground pepper
½ C. unsalted dry roasted cashews
bean sprouts (optional)

Sort and wash beans, removing stones and bad ones. Place them in a large Dutch oven. Cover with water 2 inches above level of beans, and let soak overnight.

Drain beans and replace with fresh cold water. Cover, and bring to a boil, reduce the heat, and let simmer for one (1) more hour.

Add the remaining ingredients except the cashews and the sunflower kernels; simmer for 30 minutes or until the beans are tender and the chili is thickened.

Remove and discard the bay leaves. Stir in the cashews and sunflower kernels.

Serve chili topped with bean sprouts if desired, or sprinkle with chopped onions, and if asked for, have some shredded cheese on hand.

Adam & Sonja Strumpf
Columbia, MO

Lesley, 1850(?)
Florida

CHILI SAUSAGES with CHEESE RICE

2 T. vegetable oil
1½ to 2 pounds pork link sausages, pricked
1 onion, sliced thin
2 cloves garlic, cut into thin strips
1 T. all-purpose flour
1½ C. hard cider or red wine
1 C. tomatoes, peeled and diced
1 to 3 T. chili powder
1 t. dried oregano
1 t. ground cumin
1 t. brown sugar
1 C. grated Cheddar cheese
¼ C. finely chopped fresh parsley
Salt and pepper
2 T. finely chopped fresh coriander
⅛ t. paprika

Heat the oil in a large skillet or wide flame-proof casserole. Add the sausages and brown on all sides. Remove the sausages as they are browned, and continue with the remaining links until all have been cooked.

Add the onion, garlic and red pepper to the pan and cook until softened. Add the flour, stir in well. Next add the cider or red wine, tomatoes, chili powder, oregano, sugar, cumin, salt and pepper to taste, and the remaining ingredients. Bring to a boil, stirring occasionally during cooking.

Return the sausage links and coat thoroughly with the sauce. Simmer for 20-25 minutes, stirring occasionally, moving the links within the sauce.

Meanwhile, cook the rice in 3 cups of boiling water, covered, for about 20 minutes or until tender. Drain if necessary.

Add the cheese and herbs to the rice and blend well. Serve the cheese rice with the sausages.

Lee Ann Taylor
Springfield, VA

Marcelino Amaral
Stevinson, CA

CHILI CON QUESO

1 can (16 oz.) tomatoes, coarsely chopped
1 T.bacon drippings or 1 T. vegetable oil
1 Lg. onion, finely chopped
1 can (4 oz.) whole green chiles, drained and coarsely chopped
1 Lb. processed American cheese, cut into ½-inch cubes
½ t. salt
¼ t. cumin
¼ t. garlic powder
⅛ t. black pepper

Drain the tomatoes, reserving the liquid; and set aside. Heat the bacon drippings or either the vegetable oil, in a large skillet. Add the onions and saute until they are tender.

Add the tomatoes and chiles, and cook over a low heat for 15 minutes. Add the reserved tomato juice, cheese, salt and pepper and the rest of the ingredients.

Cook over a low heat, stirring frequently until the cheese is melted. Serve warm with tortilla chips, corn chips or tacos.

This recipe makes about 4 cups of dip.

Elaine Jones
Cincinnati, OH

Randy Adams
Cookeville, TN

BULL'S-EYE* CHILI SANDWICH

2 Lbs. Ground beef
1 (18 oz.) bottle BULL'S-Eye Original Barbecue Sauce
1 (8 oz.) can tomato sauce
1 C. water
1 Pkg. CARROLL SHELBY'S ORIGINAL TEXAS BRAND Chili Mix
Hamburger buns

* Brown beef in large skillet or dutch oven. Drain.
* Stir in barbecue sauce, tomato sauce and water.
* Add Lg. Spice Packet; season with Salt & Cayenne Pepper to taste.
* Cover, simmer 30 minutes or until desired thickness, stirring occasionally.
* For thicker meat mixture, stir in Masa Flour packet mixed with ⅓ cup water during last 15 minutes of cooking.
* Fill buns with meat mixture. 10 to 12 servings.

Carroll Shelby's Chili Mix

Pakoon Ranch
Mesquite, NV

HOT TEXAS CHILI

2 Lbs. ground beef
2 Lg. onions, chopped
2 cloves garlic, minced
1 Lb. dried pinto beans
1 jalapeno pepper, seeded, rinsed and chopped
3 to 5 T. chili powder
1 T. cumin
1 t. ground oregano
1 t. celery salt
1 can (15 oz.) tomato sauce
1 can (28 oz.) tomatoes, with juice, chopped
1 can (4 oz.) green chiles, undrained and chopped
4 C. cocktail vegetable juice
¼ to ½ t. crushed red pepper
Tabasco sauce, several good shakes

Sort and wash beans and place in a Dutch oven. Cover with water, and bring to a boil; uncover and cook for 2 more minutes. Remove from the heat and simmer for an hour or until the beans are tender. Drain the beans, and set aside in another container.

In the Dutch oven, combine the beef, onion, garlic and jalapeno pepper, and cook over a medium heat, stirring to crumble and break up the beef. Cook until the beef is browned, and the onion is tender. Drain all fat drippings from the pot.

Add the pinto beans and remaining ingredients, stir in with the meat well. Cover, and simmer for one (1) hour, stirring occasionally, and sampling for taste during this period of cooking.

Morry & Carol Klimboff
Cincinnati, OH

Bent River Ranch
Cottonwood, AZ

CHEESY CHILI DIP

1 Med. onion, diced
1 clove garlic, minced
1 can (10 oz.) tomatoes and green chiles
1 T. corn starch
1 t. salt
¼ t. ground black pepper
¼ t. crushed red pepper
¼ t. chili powder
¼ t. cumin
1 bay leaf
1 C. (4 oz.) diced Colby cheese
1 can (4 oz.) green chiles, chopped
Tortilla chips

Drain the tomatoes and chopped green chiles; reserving the liquid. Set vegetable mixture aside.

Combine reserved liquid and corn starchin a 1-quart saucepan, and cook over a medium heat, stirring constantly, until the mixture is thickens.

Stir in the tomatoes, chiles, onion, garlic, and the rest of the seasonings. Cook, stirring constantly until the onion is tender. Stir in the Colby cheese, cook over a low heat until it melts.

Serve with warm tortilla chips. Makes about 2½ cups of dip.

Morry & Carol Klimboff
Cincinnati, OH

Don O. Newman
Hereford, AZ

LAZY DAY CHILI

- 2 Lbs. lean ground beef
- 1 Lb. dry pink beans
- ¼ C. vegetable oil
- 2 Lg. onions, chopped fine
- 2 cloves garlic, minced
- 1 can (16 oz.) whole tomatoes, undrained, chopped up
- 3 T. chili powder
- ¼ T. cayenne pepper
- 2 T. dried oregano
- 1 T. cumin
- 1 t. salt
- ¼ t. black pepper
- 1 bay leaf

Soak the beans overnight. Drain and with fresh water, in a large kettle or Dutch oven, bring to a boil, reduce heat and allow to simmer until the beans are tender. Set aside.

In a large skillet, brown the beef, onion, and garlic, until the onion is transparent but not browned. Discard all fat drippings from pan.

Into the Dutch oven or large chili kettle, add the meat mixture, and all of the remaining ingredients including the chopped up tomatoes.

Mix well to blend, cover, and bring to a boil; reduce heat to a simmer and cook for 1 to 1½ hours. Remove bay leaf before serving, and let individual diner garnish their own bowls of a good chili with either shredded lettuce, shredded cheese, chopped onions, sour cream, black olive slices, or chopped jalapeno pepper.

Jay & Sandy Hatfield
Cincinnati, OH

Dr. Jeff Hodges
Ocean Springs, MS

AVOCADO CHILI DIP

1 avocado, peeled, and sliced
1 t. instant minced onion
¼ C. milk
1 t. salt
2 or 3 T. fresh lemon juice
½ t. chili powder
¼ C. commercial sour cream
1 clove garlic, minced
1 t. dried cilantro leaves, or
1 T. fresh cilantro
¼ t. dried oregano
¼ t. Tabasco hot sauce

Using an electric blender, combine all of the ingredients into the container, and blend until the mixture is smooth. Place into a serving dish, and display with taco,corn or tortilla chips.

Victoria Teubner, MD
Marysville, TN

Wandel Mackelprang
Camp Verde, AZ

MEXICAN CHILI SAUCE

2 T. vegetable oil
5 stalks celery, chopped
2 Med. onions, chopped
1 Med.-size green pepper, chopped
2 cans (4 oz.) green chiles, chopped
1 can (28 oz.) whole tomatoes
2 t. chili powder, or more to taste
¼ t. sugar
¼ t. ground cumin
¼ t. garlic powder
¼ t. hot sauce
Dash of salt
Dash of pepper

Preheat the vegetable oil in a large skillet, and saute the onion, green pepper and celery until they are softened.

Drain the tomatoes, reserving their liquid. Using a sharp knife, chop the tomatoes. Add the tomatoes, reserved liquid, and chiles to the skillet.

Stir occasionally to keep the mixture from sticking to the pan.

Makes about 5 cups of good chili sauce.

Cheryl Rossi
Merritt Island, FL

Allen B. Smith
Valleydale Packers
Bristol, VA

RANCH CHILI with BEANS

3 Lbs. lean ground beef
6 C. water
2 bay leaves
8 cloves garlic, crushed
4 to 6 T. chili powder
2 t. salt
1 t. ground cumin
1 t. ground oregano
1 t. allspice
2 to 3 T. paprika
¼ to ½ t. cayenne pepper
¼ t. pepper
1 T. sugar
2 cans (15 oz.) ranch-style beans
1 can (6 oz.) tomato paste
2 Lg. onions, chopped
1 Lg. green pepper, chopped

In a large Dutch oven, over a medium heat, cook the ground beef until it is all browned. Use a wooden spoon to break up and crumble the beef as it browns.

Drain the grease entirely from the meat as some will always be left behind to saute with the vegetables.

Add the chopped onions, green pepper and garlic to the browned meat, mixing together good. Cover, and simmer, stirring occasionally until the vegetables are completely done.

Add the water, bay leaves, and covered, simmer on a low heat for about an hour. Add all the remaining ingredients, except the beans, and again covered, simmer for about an hour or so, stirring and checking for taste occasionally.

Stir in the beans, simmer for an additional 15 to 20 minutes to blend and combine the flavors. Makes about 10 hearty servings.

Remove the bay leaves before serving if they can be found, or as we do, give the first second helpings to those who's bowl it's found.

Ms. Rhoda King
Chicago, IL

James & Carol Vaughn
Lyles, TN

OLD-FASHIONED SPICY CHILI

2 Lbs. ground beef
1 Med. onion, chopped
1 green pepper, chopped
4 cloves garlic, minced
4 to 6 T. chili powder
2 T. vegetable oil
¼ t. crushed red pepper
2 t. salt
2 T. all-purpose flour
1 T. ground cumin
1½ T. sugar
2 cans (16 oz.) red kidney beans, undrained
1 can (16 oz.) whole tomatoes, undrained, chopped
1 can (6 oz.) tomato paste

In a Dutch oven, brown the ground beef, stirring to crumble into smaller pieces. Drain off fat drippings. Add the chopped onions, green pepper, chopped celery and garlic to the meat, and simmer until the vegetables are tender.

Add the all-purpose flour, stirring to blend well with the mixture, along with the chili powder and sugar. Bring to a boil; reduce the heat.

Add the remaining ingredients; stir together well. Cover, and simmer for 30 minutes on a low heat. Makes about 8 to 10 servings.

We have always used as a garnish with this chili as side dishes, additional chopped onions and shredded cheese with each one eating putting on the amounts which they desire.

Bob Pratt
Cincinnati, OH

J. M. Voss
Ripley, TN

SIMPLE CHILI

2 Lbs. lean ground beef
2 Lg. onions, chopped
1 green pepper, chopped
1 clove garlic, crushed
2 T. vegetable oil
2 T. chili powder
1 t. salt
1 can (8 oz.) tomato sauce
a little crushed red pepper (opt.)
½ t. vinegar
2 whole cloves
1 small bay leaf
2 cans (16 oz.) whole tomatoes, undrained and chopped
1 can (6 oz.) tomato paste
2 cans (16 oz.) red kidney beans, undrained and mashed

In a large skillet, brown the beef over a low heat until it is completely cooked, stirring to crumble. Add and saute the onions, green peppers, and garlic until done.

Add the remaining ingredients; simmer, uncovered for an hour or more. Makes about 10 servings.

Henry Bernstein
Chicago, IL

Ed Nieira
Nolichucky Dairy Farm, Inc.
Morristown, TN

DOUBLE-MEAT CHILI

2½ Lbs. ground beef or venison
1 Lb. lean ground pork
1½ Lbs. (about 5 Lg.) onions, chopped
1 Lb. (about 4 Lg.) green peppers, chopped
3 cloves garlic, crushed
½ C. parsley, chopped
1½ T. vegetable oil
½ C. butter or margarine
½ C. chili powder
2 T. salt
1½ t. ground black pepper
1½ t. cumin seeds
1½ t. monosodium glutamate (MSG)
1 Lb. dried pinto beans
2 cans (28 oz.) whole tomatoes, undrained and chopped
1 can (6 oz.) tomato paste
1 can (15 oz.) tomato sauce

Sort and wash the pinto beans. Place then in a 6-quart Dutch oven, and cover with water until it is 2 inches above beans. Let soak overnight.

Drain the beans, and replace with fresh cold water. Cook them over a medium heat until they are tender, or about one (1) hour; reduce the heat, add the tomatoes and simmer for 5 minutes.

Add the onions and green peppers; cook about 10 minutes, or until they are tender, stirring often. Stir in the crushed garlic and parsley.

Cook the beef and pork in either the butter or margarine, crumbling it with a wooden spoon as it browns. After both meats have been browned completely, pour off all of the grease and discard it properly (and in accords with the local EPA specs).

Stir in the beef/pork mixture into the beans. Add the remaining ingredients; cover, and let simmer for one (1) hour, stirring occasionally. Uncover and simmer for an additional 30 minutes. Makes about 15 helpings.

Don & Sally Miller
Largo, FL

William E. Nichols
Woodbury, TN

ROUND-UP CHILI

2 Lbs. ground beef
3½ C. water
1 Lg. onion, chopped
1 Lg. green pepper, chopped
3 stalks celery, chopped
1 T. chili powder
1 t. cayenne pepper
1 clove garlic, chopped fine
1 can (28 oz.) tomatoes, undrained and chopped
1 can (16 oz.) red kidney beans, undrained
1 can (6 oz.) tomato paste
Salt and pepper to taste

Cook the ground beef in a Dutch oven until it is browned. Use a fork to break up and crumble meat. After meat has been browned, add the onion, green pepper, celery and garlic to the meat, and simmer until they are softened and tender.

Drain off all pan drippings. Stir in the remaining ingredients, except the beans, and simmer for 2 or 2½ hours, stirring occasionally.

Add the beans mixing thoroughly into meat mixture, and continue simmering for an additional 15 minutes to allow all ingredients to blend together. Makes approximately 8 servings.

Ann Taylor
Fairfield, OH

J. Michael Patterson
Patterson Farms
Cookeville, TN

CAMP CHILI with JERKY

6 Ozs. beef jerky
3 T. rendered suet, drippings or oil
1 t. whole cumin seed
1 t. onion flakes
1 t. oregano
4 to 6 T. unsalted Chili powder
¼ t. garlic powder
Water
Flour for thickening (optional)
¼ t. cayenne pepper
½ t. brown sugar

Cut the beef jerky into small bite-size pieces, remembering that it swells in liquid. In a pot or Dutch oven, simmer the jerky and cumin seeds gently in moderately hot fat for a minute or two, stirring steadily to prevent any sticking or burning.

Add the chili powder and continue stirring until it is well mixed. The amount of chili powder will depend on the hotness of the jerky, and your taste.

Add the remaining ingredients with enough water to cover the contents thoroughly and generously, stirring to completely blend, and let simmer for 1 to 1½ hours, adding additional water as the jerky will absorb it up.

Add chili to cook, and reheat if necessary before serving. If a thicker chili is desired, add a little of the all-purpose flour, mixed to a paste with a little of the contents of the pot. Add the flour to the chili, blending it in good. The thickness of the chili can be reached this way so that it can be just the consistency you want.

Ann Taylor
Fairfield, OH

P-D

Duffy Baudoin
Lynnville, TN

LBJ PEDERNALES RIVER CHILI

- 4 Lbs. bite-size or chili ground venison, if available, or well trimmed chuck
- 1 Lg. onion, chopped
- 2 cloves garlic, minced
- 1 t. ground oregano
- 1 t. cumin see
- 2 C. hot water
- 6 T. chili powder, or to taste
- 1½ C. canned whole tomatoes
- 2 to 6 generous dashes of liquid hot pepper sauce

Place meat, onion and garlic in a large, heavy skillet, or Dutch oven. Cook until lightly-colored. Add oregano, cumin, water, chili powder, tomatoes, hot pepper sauce and salt.

Bring to a boil. Lower heat, and simmer for about an hour. Skim off fat during cooking.

Cincinnati Enquirer

33

Edward L. Yates, 1880
Orlando, FL

LYNDON JOHNSON'S PEDERNALES RIVER CHILI

2 Lbs. coarsely ground beef
1 Med. onion, chopped
1 clove garlic, minced
1 t. cumin seed
3 to 6 t. chili powder
1 t. dried oregano
1 can (16 oz.) sliced stewed tomatoes, with liquid
1 can (12 oz.) beer
2 dashes Tabasco sauce
1 can (16 oz.) kidney beans, drained (optional)
Salt to taste

Crumble the beef into a dishwasher-safe plastic colander. Sprinkle onion on top. Set colander in a 4-quart pot, and microwave on High for 4 minutes.

Stir to break up cooked beef and redistribute uncooked areas. Microwave on High for 4 minutes, or until all the beef is no longer pink.

Pour the grease into a can; refrigerate and discard when it solidifies.

Transfer beef to the same pot.

Stir in the chili powder, garlic, oregano, cumin seeds with the beer. Add the canned tomatoes including it's liquid. Pour ¾ cup of beer into the pot and drink the rest.

Add the Tabasco sauce and salt to taste, stirring well. Do not cover the pot. Microwave on High for 12 minutes, or until the chili is to your likin'.

It reported in the newspaper article that this was taken from, that President Johnson did not put any beans in his chilies, but we use them, mixed thoroughly with the chili, and microwave on High until they have heated completely.

Kathy Stuhlbarg
Cincinnati, OH

22

W. Starling
Florida, 1856

GENERAL SALSA

½ C. onion, finely chopped
1 T. olive oil
1 clove garlic, crushed
2 T. tomato paste
1 t. sugar
½ t. salt
1 t. vinegar
1 T. flour
1 T. water
1 can chicken broth, regular strength
1 C. canned, peeled tomatoes, chopped

In a small saucepan, saute the onion and garlic in the olive oil, until they are lightly browned. Add the chopped tomatoes, tomato paste to the saucepan, stirring well to blend together.

Add the chicken broth, sugar, salt and vinegar. Simmer on a very low heat for one to one and a half hours, or until the tomatoes have become soft.

Force the mixture through a sieve or place in a blender and whirl until it is smooth. Place back into the saucepan, and reheat it almost to a boil. Turn off heat and set saucepan aside to cook.

Julie Ross
Cincinnati, OH

Adin Waterman
Florida, 1844

MEXICANA SALSA

1 small onion, chopped
1 clove garlic, minced
1 t. chili powder
½ t. oregano
¼ t. cumin seeds
Several drops of hot sauce
1 can (16 oz.) whole tomatoes, undrained, and chopped
Dash or so of salt

Combine all the ingredients in a blender container, blend until smooth. Pour into a small saucepan, simmer on low for about 30 minutes. Can be used on top of taco filling, or other dishes.

Makes 2½ to 3 cups of salsa.

Florida Today

Dave Young
Double D Ranch
Loxahatchee, FL

CINCINNATI CHILI

2 Lbs. ground beef
3 Lg. onions, chopped
3 cloves garlic, minced
1 can (15 oz.) tomato sauce
1 C. beef broth
2 T. chili powder
2 T. semi-sweet chocolate pieces
2 cans (15 oz.) red kidney beans
4 C. shredded American cheese
2 T. honey
1 T. pumpkin pie spice
1 t. salt
1 t. ground cumin
½ t. ground cardamon
¼ t. ground cloves
1 Pkg. (16 oz.) fettuccine, broken into 4-inch lengths
2 T. vinegar

In a 4½-quart Dutch oven, cook the beef, onions and garlic until the beef is brown and the onion is tender. Drain off fat from the pot. Stir in remaining ingredients except the fettuccine, beans and cheese.

Bring to a boil, stirring often. Reduce the heat, cover, and simmer over a low heat for an hour. Skim off the fat from the surface of chili during the cooking period.

Cook the fettuccine cheese in boiling fresh water and drain when soft to taste. Drain. Keep the beans warm as well. To serve, divide fettuccine among 8 main-dish servings. Make indentation in centers. Top with meat sauce, beans, and remaining onions and cheese.

MICROWAVE DIRECTIONS: Crumble the meat in a 3-quart microwave-safe casserole. Add 2 cups of onions and the garlic. Micro-cook, covered, on High (100% power) for 9 to 11 minutes, or until the meat is browned, and the pink color of the meat is gone, stirring twice.

Drain off excess fat.

Stir in the tomato sauce, ½ cup of beef broth, chili powder, cumin, chocolate pieces, vinegar, honey, pumpkin pie spice, salt, cardamon, and cloves. Cook; covered, on High for 5 minutes, stir.

Reduce the heat to Medium (50% power). Cook covered, 20 minutes, stirring twice. Cook fettuccine and beans, and serve chili as directed above.

Shannon Combs
Cincinnati, OH

Six Fleur-De-Lis
Joe Marlin Hilliard
Clewiston, FL

PANHANDLE CHILI

3 Lbs. chuck steak, cut into cubes
1 Med. onion, chopped
1 green pepper, chopped
3½ T. chili powder
4 cloves garlic, minced
2 T. oregano
2 T. cumin seed
3 T. sugar
1 t. salt
½ t. cayenne pepper
1 can (8 oz.) tomato sauce
2 C. water
3 t. paprika
2 T. corn flour
1 can (16 oz.) whole tomatoes, drained, chopped, reserve liquid

In a large Dutch oven, cook the meat, onion, green pepper and the garlic until the beef is browned and the vegetables are tender. Add the water, and simmer for 30 minutes.

Add the remaining ingredients, except the corn flour, and simmer for about 2 hours, stirring occasionally during cooking to insure even cooking. Sample for taste, flavor and consistency.

If a thicker chili mixture is desired, make a paste with the flour and a little water, and add slowly while stirring so that the chili is thoroughly blended. If too thin, use some of the reserved tomato liquid to thin the consistency.

Ms. Rhona King
Chicago, IL

George Kemper
Florida, 1915

QUICK CHILI CASSEROLE

8 eggs
1 Lb. sharp Cheddar or Monterey Jack cheese, grated
1 can (40 oz.) whole green chiles, undrained

Preheat the oven to 325 degree. Grease a shallow 1½-quart baking dish and set aside.

Place grated cheese in a large mixing bowl. Combine the eggs and the undrained chiles in a blender and whirl on High until well blended. Now, combine the egg mixture and the cheese, and stir until it is well blended.

Pour into the prepared grease dish, and bane 50 to 60 minutes, or until top is buffed and golden brown, and when a knife is inserted into the center and comes out clean.

A tossed green salad and warm corn or flour tortillas are excellent compliments to this light supper or brunch dish. Makes 4 to 6 servings.

Ginny Price
Cincinnati, OH

D Ranch
John G. DuPuis, Jr.
Canal Point, FL

CHICKEN and VEGETABLE CHILI with CORN

2 C. onion, chopped
2 cloves garlic, minced
2 T. vegetable oil
1 can (16 oz.) whole tomatoes
2 cans (16 oz.) pinto beans, drained
½ C. taco sauce
½ C. water
1 t. salt
1 t. ground cumin
½ t. oregano
1 green pepper, diced
3 T. catsup
4 T. grated Cheddar-flavored Formagg cheese
2 C. diced cooked chicken or turkey breast (optional)

This dish is something kids will love, and it's good for them. You can leave out the chicken, and it will have zero cholesterol. With the chicken, it has about 40 mg of cholesterol per serving.

In a large saucepan, heat the vegetable oil, and in it saute the onion, green pepper and garlic until the onion is lightly browned. Drain the tomatoes and chop them, reserving one cup of the juice in the can.

Combine the liquid from the tomatoes with one of the cans of drained beans in a blender or food processor, and process until it is smooth and thick.

Add beans, juice mixture to the saucepan, along with the remaining ingredients, except the cheese. Serve in bowls, sprinkled with the Cheddar-flavored Formagg cheese.

Florida Today

EMS Ranch Bar S
William D. Stark III
Florida

CHILI and CHEESE DIP

1 Med. onion, finely chopped
2 T. olive oil
1 can (16 oz.) whole tomatoes, drained and chopped up
1 can (4 oz.) green chiles,chopped

Heat oil in a medium-sized skillet; sauce the onions until they are golden; adding the tomatoes and chiles; reduce the heat, and simmer until the mixture becomes nearly dry, stirring occasionally.

Meanwhile, melt the cheese over hot water in a double boiler. Combine the melted cheese and tomato mixture.

Serve dip in a chafing dish or fondue pot, as that the dip will remain either warm or hot. Serve with corn chips or tostadas. Makes 8 to 10 servings.

Don & Verna Leach
Cincinnati, OH

Owen W. Marr, Jr.
Mims, FL

REAL GOOD TURKEY CHILI

2 Lbs. ground turkey
1 Med. onion, chopped
1 green pepper, chopped
2 cans (16 oz.) tomatoes, chopped
1 can (15½ oz.) red kidney beans, drained
1 can (8 oz.) tomato sauce
1 can (4 oz.) tomato paste
¼ C. dry red wine
1½ to 2 T. chili powder
1 t. dried parsley flake
¾ t. dried basil, crushed
¾ t. dried oregano, crushed
½ t. black pepper
½ t. ground cinnamon
2 cloves garlic, minced
¼ to ½ t. red pepper flakes
1 bay leaf

In a Dutch oven, spray the bottom with Pam to prevent the initial contact of the turkey meat from sticking to the pot. Cook the ground turkey, breaking up with a spoon as it starts to loose it's color, so that it is evenly done. Drain off the watery liquid after browning is completed.

Stir in the undrained tomatoes, drained kidney beans, tomato sauce, tomato paste, onion, green pepper, wine, chili powder, parsley flakes, basil, oregano, black pepper, red pepper flakes, cinnamon, garlic, and the bay leaf.

Bring to a boil, stirring occasionally to keep the ingredients evenly heated and blended. Reduce the heat, and simmer, covered, for about 2 hours, stirring occasionally. Remove the bay leaf.

Garnish the chili in bowls with either shredded cheese, chopped onions, oyster crackers, or some of each. Makes about 10 servings.

MICROWAVE DIRECTIONS: In a 2-quart microwave-safe casserole, cook the ground turkey covered, on High (100% power) for 8 to 10 minutes, or till the meat is no longer pink, aiding the cooking by crumbling the turkey every few minutes, and giving the dish a ¼ turn so that a more evenly cooking is done.

Add all the ingredients and microwave on High 7 to 8 minutes, stirring contents every 2 or 3 minutes, or until vegetables are tender and softened.

Serve chili as described above.

Adam & Sonja Strumpf
Columbia, MO

Don Enrique Valeriano
Honduras(1838)

HOT CHILI DIP

1 C. scallions, chopped, onions and green stems
1 can (16 oz.) tomatoes, drained and chopped
1 t. salt
1 can (4 oz.) green chili sauce
¼ t. Tabasco sauce
¼ t. chili powder

In a small mixing bowl, combine all ingredients and blend well. Check for taste, and chill before serving. Makes about 3 cups of tasty dip.

Allen Jordan
London, KY

Jean Arriaga
Williams, AZ

PORK IN RED CHILI SAUCE

1½ Lbs. lean pork, cut into 1½-inch cubes (reserve the fat)
2 T. lard, (optional)
1 Med. onion, chopped
1 clove garlic, minced
1½ to 2 T. chili powder
1½ C. canned tomatoes, broken up with a fork
1 small cinnamon stick
½ t. salt
½ t. crumbled oregano
¼ t. ground cumin
1 can (5 oz.) tomato paste

Render strips of pork fat or heat lard in a Dutch oven over a moderate heat. Remove strips of fat, if used; add onion, and garlic, and brown lightly. Add the chili powder, and stir in well. Push the vegetables to the sides of the pan and brown the meat on all sides.

Add tomatoes, salt, oregano, cumin, cloves, cinnamon stick, salt, and tomato paste, stirring well to mix thoroughly with the meat.

Bring the chili mix to a boil; reduce the heat, cover and simmer on a low heat for 2 hours or until the pork is very tender. Stir pot occasionally while it is cooking.

If the chili sauce is too thin, cook, uncovered for about 15 to 20 minutes, or until the consistency is what you want. Serve pork sauce with rice and tortillas. Makes 4 hearty servings.

Shannon Combs
Cincinnati, OH

Morgan Blasingame
Clovis, CA

VEAL WITH TEXAS CHILI SAUCE

1 Med. onion, chopped
1 green pepper, chopped
2 cloves garlic, minced
2 C. canned tomatoes, peeled and chopped, or
1 can (16 oz.) whole tomatoes, undrained
4 cubed veal steaks
1 C. dried bread crumbs
2 eggs, beaten
1½ T. chili powder
½ t. oregano
¼ t. dried cumin seeds
1 t. salt
Few drops of hot sauce
½ C. butter or margarine
¼ t. ground black pepper
½ C. shredded Monterey Jack cheese

Into a blender container or food processor, combine all of the ingredients except the butter or margarine, and the cheese. Blend until the mixture is quite smooth, then pour it into a medium size preheated saucepan. Simmer for 30 minutes. Makes about 2½ to 3 cups of chili sauce.

Dip each veal steak into the sauce, coat with the bread crumbs, salt and pepper each, then fry until browned. Drain the steaks on paper towels to remove as much as possible of the frying liquids.

Put prepared veal in a baking dish, cover with the chili sauce, and top with the shredded Monterey cheese. Bake at 350 degrees for about 20 minutes, and serve hot. Makes 4 servings.

CSG

Wallace G. Bidwell
Bieber, CA

CHILI and CHEESE APPETIZERS

12 6-inch corn tortillas
Oil for frying
6 pickled jalapeno peppers
1 C. refried beans (homemade or canned)
Dash of hot sauce
¼ t. oregano
¼ t. cumin seeds
½ C. shredded Sharp Cheddar cheese

Cut each tortilla into quarters. Heat 1-inch of oil in skillet to 360 degrees. Fry tortillas until crisp; drain thoroughly on paper towels.

Carefully stem and seed jalapeno peppers, cutting each into 6-inch strips. Spread each chip with 1 teaspoon of refried beans.

Top with ½ teaspoon of shredded cheese and a thin strip of the jalapeno pepper. Broil until the cheese melts. Serve immediately while hot. Makes approximately 48 appetizers.

Steven M. Slaman
Delray Beach, FL

Jim & Nancy Foster
Igo, CA

CARROLL SHELBY'S GOURMET CHILI

1½ Lbs. lean beef
½ Lb. lean pork
1 Lg. brown onion
1 Lg. clove garlic
1 Lg. green bell pepper, or
½ green and ½ red pepper
1 can (15 oz.) tomato sauce
1 can (12 oz.) Mexican beer (Cervaza)
1 Pkg. Carroll Shelby's original Texas Chili Preparation
4 Ozs. diced green chiles

Cut beef and pork into small pieces. Pound meat with a meat mallet. Chop onion and peppers, whether green or red. Run garlic through a press. Put these ingredients into a Dutch oven or heavy deep pot with a little bacon grease or oil.

Cook until the meat is brown. Add the tomato sauce and beer. Simmer 30 minutes. Add remaining ingredients except masa flour. Simmer 1 hour, stirring occasionally. If more liquid is needed, add beer as desired.

Mix masa flour with a little beer to make a thin paste and stir mixture into the chili.

Now add the beans if desired. Simmer another 30 minutes. Check taste and add the cayenne pepper, if you dare.

Carroll Shelby's
package recipe

Old Spanish
Florida early 1600's

GRILLED CHICKEN with CHILI HOLLANDAISE and ROASTED PEPPERS

3½ Lbs. chicken pieces, excess fat trimmed
½ C. fresh lemon juice
4 t. coarsely ground black pepper
2 t. Dijon mustard
¾ t. salt
1 C. olive oil
3 garlic cloves, crushed
Lg. red bell peppers, quartered and seeded
Lg. green bell peppers, quartered and seeded
leaves (optional)
Chili Hollandaise*

Place the chicken in a large non-aluminum bowl or baking dish. Mix lemon juice, lemon peel, pepper, mustard and salt in a medium size bowl.

Slowly whisk the oil in with a thin stream. Mix in garlic. Pour marinade over the chicken, turning to coat pieces evenly. Cover and refrigerate over night.

Prepare barbecue grill with gray coals. Oil grill rack to aid in chicken not sticking, and allowing easy clean-up.

Remove chicken from marinade. Arrange chicken and peppers on the grill rack. Grill until the chicken is crisp and juices run clear when pierced with a knife, about 10 minutes per side.

Cook peppers on both sides until slightly charred, peeled if desired. Set lemon leaves on serving platter. Top with grilled chicken and peppers. Ladle some hollandaise sauce over chicken. Pass the remaining sauce around after the chicken is served for individuals who would like more.

Charles 'Chip' Colburn
Hamilton, OH

Gregory & Lynn Brown
Brawley, CA

CHILI HOLLANDAISE SAUCE

3 egg yokes, room temperature
4½ t. fresh lemon juice
½ C. (1 stick unsalted butter or margarine
2 T. plus 1½ t. minced fresh cilantro
1 to 2 serrano or cayenne chiles, seeded and minced
Salt

Combine yokes and lemon juice in a food processor. Heat the butter or margarine in a heavy small saucepan over a low heat until it is bubbling.

With the processor running, slowly add the melted butter or margarine through the feed tube.

Transfer sauce to a bowl. Mix in the cilantro, chiles and the salt. Hollandaise sauce can be prepared 2 hours ahead of time to grill. Place sauce in vacuum bottle or set bowl into container with hot water, but not boiling water, before using.

crumbled magazine recipe

Charles D. Hansen
& June Audrey
Fresno, CA

BETSY'S NEW MEXICAN CHILI CON CARNE

This recipe won first prize red chili con carne 1983 Santa Fe's Mayor's Chili Challenge.

- 1 Oz. red chile pods
- 3 cloves garlic
- ½ t. ground oregano
- ½ t. crushed coliander
- ½ t. crushed basil
- 2 C. shredded pork rinds, cooked
- Salt to taste

Remove stems from red chile pods and shake out most of the seeds. Place pods in a bowl and cover with cold water; rinse, repeat. The third time you cover with cold water, let it stand for one hour. Then whiz chile pods and cold water in a blender in three portions, adding one clove of garlic to each portion.

Let the blender run for 10 minutes for each portion to ensure a fine grind. Pour chile from blender through strainer to remove fiber. Mix in spices and boil chile on medium heat for 30 minutes.

Then take cooked pork and remove visible fat. Add to chile and simmer for 10 minutes more. Salt to taste. Serves 8.

Florida Today

DS

A.Duda & Sons, Inc.
Cocoa, Fl

FRANCISCO'S GREEN CHILI

2 Med. onions, chopped
2 Lbs. Hatch chili
1½ Lbs. red potatoes, cut in 1½-inch cubes
2 Lbs. beef rump roast, cut in 1-inch cubes
6 carrots, sliced, and par boiled
1¼ t. oregano
3 t. salt
2 t. powdered chili
2 cloves garlic, minced
1 gallon beef broth
1 T. chicken soup base
1¼ t. tomato puree
1¼ t. white pepper

Saute onion, green chili and beef. Add beef stock and all of the remaining ingredients except potatoes and carrots. Let simmer for an hour or longer depending on toughness of the beef.

Add the carrots and potatoes during the last 30 minutes of simmering.

Florida Today

HK

Tim & Kay Preston
Davie, FL

CHILE CHEESE SANDWICHES

¼ C. butter, softened
2 t. Lawry's Garlic Spread Concentrate
8 Med. size slices French bread
Thick slices Monterey Jack cheese
whole green chiles

Blend butter and Garlic Spread Concentrate. Spread mixture evenly on one side of each slice of bread. Place cheese and chile on unbuttered side of four sliced of bread, top with remaining four slices, buttered side out. Grill until golden brown.

LAWRY'S mag. ad.

◇R

Coleman Dyess
Beaumont,
Jefferson County, TX

SANTA FE CHILI BURGERS

1 small onion
1 small bell green pepper
2 T. fresh lime juice
5 red radishes, trimmed and chopped
¼ t. salt
1 T. fresh coliander, chopped
¼ t. ground black pepper
1½ Lbs.lean ground beef
1 small avocado
1 small Boston head lettuce
4 Ozs. jalapeno Jack cheese
4 Kaiser rolls
1 C. whole corn kernel, thawed frozen or canned, drained

Combine the corn, radishes, lime juice, coliander, salt and pepper in a mixing bowl, and stir to blend the ingredients. Cover, and let the mixture stand for at least 30 minutes.

Shape the beef into four (4) patties. Cut the cheese into 4 slices, as well as slicing the onion, bell pepper and avocado. Place into a separate bowl.

Rinse and dry the lettuce leaves and set aside. Broil hamburgers 4 to 5 inches from heat, turning once. Eight to 10 minutes total broiling time should give a medium-rare hamburger. Top with cheese about 1 minute before taking burgers from the heat.

Cut Kaiser rolls in halves, and place burgers on each. Roll halves may be placed on heat is a light toasting is desired prior to placing burgers on them.

Serve with sliced onions, avocado, bell pepper, lettuce and corn relish.

Marvin & Maida Belkin
Cincinnati, OH

Gill Cattle Co.
Exeter, CA

PARSLEY SALSA

1½ C. fresh parsley, chopped
6½ T. olive oil
¼ C. of wine vinegar
1 t. salt
Freshly ground black pepper

In a small pot, using about one and a half cups of water, blanch the parsley over a low heat until tender. Drain in strainer, and add to the ingredients. Mix to blend well, put in container and serve with all kinds of dishes.

If desired, do not blanch parsley, but chop fine, and do not use as much water in mixture.

Woman's Day

A. J. Davis, Jr.
Nederland, TX

RED MEAT CHILI

2 Lbs. chuck beef or pork, cut into ¾-inch pieces
2 C. water
4 T. red chili powder, more or less to your preference, or,
8 small red chiles
3 cloves garlic
2 T. vegetable oil
1¼ t. ground oregano
2 T. all-purpose flour
½ t. cumin seeds
1 T. parsley flakes
½ C. dry sherry
Salt

Using a large skillet, cook the cubed meat in two cups of the lightly salted water, for about 30 minutes. Save the liquid.

While the meat is simmering, prepare the chiles as normally done, if prepared ones are not on hand.

Grind the chiles, garlic and the oregano into a paste. Add the wine and saved cooking liquid, into a blender. Strain.

In the vegetable oil, brown the flour, and slowly stir into the broth along with the cumin, parsley and a little salt to taste.

Combine with the meat and simmer for about 1½ hours or until the meat is tender.

If you like beans, you can add two cups to the skillet at the end of the cooking time, but with enough time to allow them to get hot before serving. Pinto or kidney beans go well.

Jean Chandler
Suntree, FL

Old Spanish
Florida early 1600's

TEXAS PANHANDLE CHILI

3 Lbs. chili-ground beef
3 Lg. onions, chopped
½ C. all-purpose flour
1 can (10½ oz.) beef consomme, undiluted
¼ C. plus 2 T. chili powder
1 T. salt
1½ t. ground oregano
1 T. ground cumin
1 can (6 oz.) tomato paste
Shredded Cheddar cheese

Combine the beef and onions in a large Dutch oven, and cook until the meat is browned. Stir to crumble the beef into smaller pieces and to ensure complete cooking. Drain off the grease and fat drippings.

Make a paste of the flour with a little water, and mix in with the meat and onions; cooking for 2 minutes or so stirring constantly to blend the flour into the mixture.

Add the consomme, stirring constantly. Stir in the chili powder, salt, cumin seeds, and the oregano. Simmer; uncovered, for 30 minutes or until contents have thickened to the desired consistency, stirring occasionally.

Ladle the chili into individual serving bowls, allowing each person to sprinkle as much shredded cheese, extra chopped onions, crushed red pepper flakes, or hot sauce, as they desire.

Sharon Geltner
Boca Raton, FL

Arizona Registered

A FAST SALSA

1 onion, chopped
2 cloves garlic, minced
3 tomatoes, medium, peel and chopped
1 red hot pepper, finely chopped
4 sprigs fresh parsley
½ t. salt
½ t. ground coriander
½ t. oregano
¼ t. crushed basil
Dash of ground cloves
Dash or two hot sauce
Salt to taste

Mix all of the vegetables together, and then add the remaining ingredients, in a small mixing bowl. Makes about 1½ cups of sauce that can be used on meats and it is generally a good all-around salsa.

Judy & Leon Seltzer
Cincinnati, OH

Dr. Joseph L. Willoughby
Franklin, TN

CHILI SALSA

1 Lg. onion, chopped
3 cloves of garlic, minced
½ C. of olive oil
1½ Qts. of chicken stock
½ C. tomato puree
½ C. all-purpose flour
7 T. red chili powder
Salt to taste

In a large skillet, saute the onion and garlic in the olive oil until tender. Add the flour and make a thick paste. To this, add the hot chicken stock, salt, and the tomato puree.

Mix the chili powder in a little water before adding to the skillet and the ingredients. Simmer for about 40 to 50 minutes.

NOTE: You can add more ingredients such as finely chopped green or red bell pepper, chopped hot peppers, as this is a sauce that can take anything you have to offer. Good on all sorts of dishes that you prepare.

Woman's Day

Conrad A. Flowers
Hankamer, TX

TOMATO CHILI SAUCE

1 red onion, chopped fine
1 clove garlic, minced
6 to 8 ripe plum tomatoes, chopped
3 scallions, finely chopped
2 T. chopped fresh parsley leaves
1 bell pepper, either red or green, diced fine
1 to 2 pickled jalapeno peppers, minced or,
2 to 3 T. drained canned chopped jalapeno
Juice of one small lime
Ground black pepper to taste
1/4 t. chili powder
dash or two of Tabasco sauce

Sprinkle salt over the chopped tomatoes in colander, and toss gently. Let tomatoes drain as much liquid as possible, for 10 minutes. Rinse gently, and let drain.

Combine the bell pepper, jalapenos, onion, chili powder, Tabasco sauce, garlic, pepper, scallions, parsley and lime juice in a mixing bowl. Toss gently and stir in the chopped tomatoes. Let stand at room temperature before serving.

Cal & Trudy LeCompte
Harbana, LA

Drinkwater Ranch
Prairie City, OR

ROCHESTER CHILI

2 Lbs. stewing beef, lean, cut into small pieces
3 T. all-purpose flour
1 Lg. onion, chopped
1 Lg. bell pepper, chopped
2 stalks celery, chopped
2 T. chili powder
2 cloves garlic, minced
2 T. vegetable oil
1 Qt. hot water
1 can (15 oz.) chili beans, undrained
1 t. salt, or to taste
¼ t. fresh ground pepper

Combine the beef, flour, chili powder, black pepper, and garlic in a mixing bowl, and mix together. Set aside.

In a Dutch oven, saute the chopped vegetables in the oil. When they are nearly completely cooked, slowly add the meat mixture, and using a wooden spoon, crumble the beef as it cooks into smaller pieces. Continue until the beef is completely cooked.

Gradually add the water, stirring constantly, salt to taste, and simmer, uncovered for 1½ hours or until the beef is tender. Add seasonings if desired. Stir in the beans; heating them thoroughly.

Ladle into serving bowls while piping hot. Extra bowls of chopped onions, shredded cheese, oyster or other types of crackers, all add to your diners getting the best from your efforts.

Les & Eileen Slocum
Fairport, NY

JSK

J.S. Kilgore
Florida 1853

MEATY CHILI

2 Lbs. lean ground beef
2 stalks celery, chopped
1 Lg. onion, chopped
1 Lg. bell pepper, chopped
2 cans (16 oz.) red kidney beans, undrained
2 cans (10¾ oz.) tomato sauce
3 T. chili powder
¼ t. cumin seed
¼ t. ground oregano
2 t. salt
1 t. sugar
½ t. garlic salt
¼ t. thyme

Combine the ground beef, onion, bell pepper, celery and garlic in a large pot or Dutch oven, cooking over a medium-heat until the meat is done, and the vegetables are tender. Stir with a wooden spoon to break up the beef as it browns. Drain off any excess fat that has accumulated.

Stir in all of the remaining ingredients, mixing them thoroughly into the meat mixture. Bring to a boil, then reduce your heat to a low simmer, and cook for 2 hours longer, or until the chili is what you desire. Stirring occasionally will keep the chili cooking evenly and lessen the chance of sticking and burning on the bottom of the pot.

This recipe will give you about 2 quarts of solid chili.

Glen & Ruth Roth
Cleves, OH

W.W. Murphy
Florida 1853

EASY WHITE WATER CHILI

The White Water River runs near us, and this recipe has been passed around and through many households. It's probably has had a 100% change from the original.

- 2 Lbs. lean ground beef
- 1 Lg.-size onion, chopped
- 3 cloves garlic, minced
- 4 C. water
- 1 can (16 oz.) whole tomatoes, undrained and chopped
- 1 can (8 oz.) tomato sauce
- 1 can (6 oz.) tomato paste
- 2 T. all-purpose flour
- 1½ t. salt
- ½ t. sugar
- 3½ t. chili powder
- 1 t. ground cumin
- ½ t. dried whole oregano
- ½ t. dried whole basil
- Dash hot red pepper sauce
- 1 can (16 oz.) pinto beans, undrained

In a large Dutch oven, combine the ground beef, chopped onions and the minced garlic. Cook until the meat is browned. Stir with a large spoon to break up the beef, so to have it brown evenly. Drain off any grease which is drawn from the meat during cooking.

Add the water, tomatoes, tomato sauce, tomato paste, sugar, salt, chili powder, cumin, oregano, basil and black pepper, mixing well to blend spices into the meat mixture.

Make a paste of the flour with a little water, and mix thoroughly into the chili.

Bring to a boil; reduce heat, and simmer for 1½ hours, stirring occasionally. Add the pinto beans, and simmer for an additional 30 minutes. This recipe will give you about 3 quarts of chili.

Glen & Ruth Roth
Cleves, OH

B128

Donald & Virginia Wilton
Foresthill, CA

COLD WEATHER CHILI

1 Pkg. (16 oz.) dried pinto beans
2½ Lbs. lean ground beef
1 Lb. lean ground pork
3 Med.-size green peppers, chopped
2 Med.-size onions, chopped
2 cloves garlic, crushed
5 cans (16 oz.) whole tomatoes, undrained, cut up
1½ Qts. water
4 T. parsley, freshly chopped
4 T. chili powder
1½ t. cumin seeds
1½ t. salt
1 t. pepper, freshly ground
Dash or two hot sauce

Sort and wash the pinto beans; placing them in a large Dutch oven. Add enough water so that the beans are covered by about 2 inches of water. Let them soak overnight. Next Day, rinse beans, change the water, and bring to a boil. Reduce the heat, cover, and let simmer until beans are tender, about 2 hours or so. Check for tenderness after an hour, and govern additional cooking time.

Saute the ground meats, onions, green pepper and garlic in a large skillet with a little oil, until the meats are done and the vegetables are tender.

Stir with a wooden spoon to break and crumble the meats as they cook. Drain excess fat from skillet, and mix in the parsley and chili powder, and simmer for 15 minutes.

Add the meat mixture to the Dutch oven as well as all remaining ingredients. Bring to a boil; reduce the heat to simmer, cover, and cook for an additional 1 hour, stirring occasionally. Uncover, and check for taste and desired consistency.

If too thick, add a little water. If your chili is too thin, mix a little all-purpose flour with some water into a paste, and add to the chili, mixing thoroughly to blend.

Leave pot uncovered, and cook over a medium heat for an hour longer. Makes about a gallon of chili.

Glen & Ruth Roth
Cleves, OH

Bud & Diana Alexander
Redmond, OR

JOE'S CHILI BREW

2 lbs. chili ground beef
1 Lg. onion, chopped
3 cloves garlic, chopped fine
2 t. ground cumin
1 t. salt
½ t. black pepper
3 T. chili powder
4 T. all-purpose flour
1 can (6 oz.) tomato paste
4 Qts., more if necessary, boiling water

In a heavy skillet, brown meat, onion and garlic until the pink color is gone from the meat. Add the ground cumin, salt, pepper, chili powder and tomato paste to the meat. Cover, and bring to a boil.

Reduce the heat, and set on simmer. Make a paste of the flour with a little water, and blend into the meat. Have the water boiling and stir into the meat mixture. Simmer for 5 to 6 hours, or until the chili has the consistency you want.

Dennis & Tina Lamb
Withamsville, OH

Rancho Los Cerritos Inc.
San Juan Capistrano, CA

CHILI SEASONING STOCK

1 C. sweet green pepper flakes
¾ C. chili powder
¼ C. ground cumin
½ C. onion flakes
¼ C. parsley flakes
1 t. garlic flakes
1 T. oregano
¼ t. crushed basil
¼ t. celery seed
½ t. crushed red pepper flakes

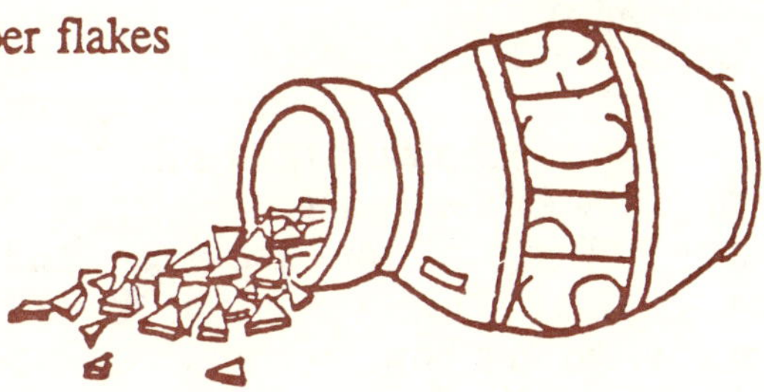

Place all ingredients into a 1-quart jar; cover tightly, and shake well to mix and blend the spices. Store in a cool, dry, dark place for up to 2 months. Makes approximately 2¾ cups.

Ellie S. Bentz
Cincinnati, OH

Forty-Four
Luther D. Crews
Lake Wales, FL

KRIS' SPICY CHILI

1 Lb. lean ground beef
1 Lb. bulk pork sausage
1 Lb. Chuck roast, cut
⅜-inch cubes
2 Med. onions, chopped
2 Med. green peppers, chopped
1 or 2 jalapeno peppers, finely chopped
2 T. minced garlic
1 t. salt
¼ t. black pepper
1 small bunch scallions, (green onion), chopped
½ t. ground cumin
2 t. cocoa
1 bay leaf
1 can (16 oz.) red kidney beans, drained
1 C. beer
2 cans (10½ oz.) beef broth, undiluted
3 cans (6 oz.) tomato paste
Sour cream
1 zucchini, medium size, chopped
Shredded Cheddar cheese

Combine the meats in a large Dutch oven, and cook over a medium heat, stirring frequently to crumble. Cook until the meats are browned and colors indicate that they are done.

Pour off the pan drippings, but reserve them. Set meat mixture aside in another container, replacing part of the grease drippings back into the Dutch oven.

Saute the vegetables and garlic in the drippings, and stir until they are tender. Drain the grease completely from the cooking vessel, and discard properly.

To the vegetables, add the meat mix, jalapeno pepper, chili powder, salt, pepper, cumin, cocoa, and the bay leaf to the pot, and stir until well blended together.

Add the beef broth, tomatoes,and the tomato paste, again stirring well to blend ingredients.

Cover, and bring the pot to a boil. Reduce the heat to a simmer, cook, uncovered, for 25 to 30 minutes or until chili has thickened. Stir occasionally to keep chili from sticking and burning to bottom.

Add the kidney beans, simmer, uncovered, for an additional 15 minutes. Remove from the heat, and cool to room temperature; discarding the bay leaf, if it can be found. If not located, it will probably be discovered in a bowl of chili along the way.

Cover, and refrigerate overnight to allow be flavors to mellow together. I always like to serve the chili the second day.

Next day, reheat over a medium heat uncovered until it is thoroughly heated, again stirring occasionally to prevent chili from sticking to the bottom of the pot. Stir in the beer, continuing to heat.

Ladle chili into individual serving bowls. Garnish with green chopped scallions, extra chopped onions, a dollop of sour cream and shredded cheese if desired. Also sprinkle chopped zucchini on top for color and flavor.

Makes about 3 quarts of fine chili.

Brian & Kris Anten
Cincinnati, OH

Wing Ranch Inc
Redmond, OR

VENISON CHILI

1 Lb. venison, ground for chili
1 Lb. ground chuck
1 Med.-size onion, chopped
2 cloves garlic, minced
3 T. chili powder
¼ t. ground cumin
1½ C. catsup
1 can (8 oz.) tomato sauce
1½ t. salt
½ t. ground fresh pepper
Red crushed pepper, if desired
1 Qt. water

Combine the venison and chuck, onion and garlic in a small Dutch oven; cook over a medium heat until the meats are done and the vegetables are tender. Drain off any pan drippings.

Add the remaining ingredients, mixing well to blend. Cover, and simmer for 3 hours, stirring occasionally, and sampling to check on flavor and consistency you desire. Makes about 2 quarts.

Rob & Debbie Coughlin
Ft. Wright, KY

Markay Corp.
Ridgewood, NJ

SPEEDY CHILI

1 Lb. ground beef, crumbled
1 Med. onion, finely chopped
2 stalks celery, chopped
2 cans (10¾ oz.) condensed, tomato soup
1 can (6 oz.) tomato paste
1 can (16 oz.) red kidney beans
1 T. chili powder
1 t. Worcestershire sauce
½ t. salt
⅛ t. cayenne pepper

Combine the onion and celery in a 3-quart casserole. Cover; microwave at High for 4 to 6 minutes, or until the vegetables are tender; stirring once during cooking time to redistribute contents.

Stir in the ground beef, mixing with the onion and celery. Microwave at High for 4 to 7 minutes, or until the meat is no longer pink, stirring to break apart meat once during cooking. Drain off any fat that has accumulated in the casserole.

Stir in the remaining ingredients, mixing to blend with the meat mixture. Microwave at Medium (50% power) for 20 to 30 minutes, or until flavors are blended and the mixture is hot. Stir every 5 minutes, as well as giving the casserole dish a quarter turn every few minutes to ensure even cooking.

Total cooking time: 28 to 43 minutes. Makes 4 to 6 servings.

Josh Hatfield
Cincinnati, OH

Kenneth & Carmel Birdwell
Birdwell Ranch
Coalinga, CA

ITALIAN CHILI

½ Lb. ground beef
1 Pkg. (3½ oz.) pepperoni, chopped, chopped
1 medium-size onion, chopped
2 stalks celery, chopped
1 green bell pepper, chopped
¼ t. chili powder
1½ T. Italian seasoning
1 can (28 oz.) whole tomatoes, cut up
1 can (15 oz.) red kidney beans, drained
1 can (12 oz.) tomato paste
1 can (8 oz.) sliced mushrooms, drained
½ t. salt
¼ to ½ t. crushed red pepper flakes

In a 3-quart casserole, combine the ground beef, onion, green pepper, celery and garlic powder. Cover, and microwave at High for 5 to 8 minutes, or until the meat is no longer pink and the vegetables are tender-crisp.

Stir to crumble and break up beef, once or twice during the cooking time.

Stir in the remaining ingredients; recover, and continue cooking on High for 20 minutes, stirring every few minutes as well as giving the casserole a half turn to evenly cook chili.

Microwave, uncovered, at High for 10 to 15 minutes, or until chili has reached the desired consistency and the flavors are blended to taste. Makes 8 to 10 servings.

Edward & Judi Ruben
Cincinnati, OH

Armando Chávez
Wittman, AZ

BEN'S CHILI BURGERS

1 Lb. ground beef
2 stalks celery, chopped
1 Med. onion, chopped
1 green pepper, chopped
1 t. parsley flakes
1 can (15 oz.) chili w/beans
½ C. catsup
1 t. chili powder
¼ t. oregano
½ t. dry mustard
½ t. salt
⅛ t. cayenne pepper
¼ t. black pepper
¼ t. garlic powder

In a 2-quart casserole, combine the ground beef, onion, celery and the green pepper. Cover; microwave at High for 5 to 8 minutes, or until the meat is no longer pink and the vegetables are tender-crisp.

Crumble the beef every few minutes during microwaving, as well as giving a quarter to half turn to the casserole. Drain off meat grease.

Add the remaining ingredients, stirring to further break up meat, and to fully blend ingredients into the chili mixture. Recover; and microwave at High for 15 to 20 minutes, or until mixture is hot and the flavors are to desired taste.

Serve chili mixture on hamburger buns and garnish with lightly sprinkled chopped onion, shredded lettuce or cheese. Makes 8 to 10 hamburger servings.

Edward & Judi Ruben
Cincinnati, OH

Lewis Dean Wallace
Cedar Hill, TN

CHEDDAR CHEESE PIE

1 Lb. lean ground beef, or veal
1 Lg. onion, chopped, or
4 green onions, chopped
2 cloves garlic minced
1 can (28 oz.) tomatoes, whole, chopped, undrained
1 can (15 oz.) kidney beans, undrained
1¼ C. corn meal
1 c. grated Cheddar cheese
2 T. chili powder
1 t. ground cumin
¼ t. cayenne pepper
½ t. freshly ground black pepper
Dash Tabasco sauce or two
2 eggs, lightly beaten
Salt and pepper to taste
½ C. milk

Saute beef (or veal), onion, and the garlic in a large skillet or Dutch oven, until the meat is browned. Drain off any fat and grease that has cooked from the meat, and discard.

Add the tomatoes, beans with it's liquid, ¾ cup of corn meal, ½ cup of cheese, and all the remaining spices except for the milk, salt and pepper. Cook over a low heat, stirring occasionally, for about 15 minutes. Pour mixture into a casserole dish.

In same saucepan, combine the milk, remainder of the corn meal, salt and pepper to taste.

Stir over a low heat until the mixture thickens a little. Add the rest of the shredded cheese and beaten eggs, stirring until smooth.

Pour this over the ground meat mixture. Bake uncovered, at 375 degrees for 30 minutes or until the crust is lightly browned. Makes 8 servings of about 308 calories per.

Ruth Geronimo
Cocoa, FL

D. Thompson
Waco 1889
McLennen County, TX

CHILI DIP with FRESH VEGETABLES

1 Med. bunch celery
3 Med.-size zucchini
1 bunch broccoli
1 Lb. large mushrooms
1 Med. onion
¼ t. ground cumin mustard seed
1 T. vinegar, white
¼ t. basil
¼ C. mild green chiles
½ t. salt
¼ t. ground black pepper
1 clove garlic
¼ C. lightly packed parsley
1 can (28 oz.) tomatoes, drained
Dash of Tabasco sauce
1 t. crushed oregano leaves

Cut the celery stalks and zucchini into sticks. Prepare the broccoli by cutting into florets. Cut the mushrooms into halves. Using plastic wrap, or baggies, store the vegetables separately in the refrigerator.

Put the remaining ingredients into a blender container, and at a low speed, blend ingredients until they are smooth. Pour prepared dip into a small bowl, cover and refrigerate as well.

About 15 minutes before serving, set bowl of dip into a basket with the vegetables lining it. Use foil to display vegetables on.

Stanley & Frieda Aaron
Cincinnati, OH

Bob Sexton
Willows, CA

TEXAS CHILI

2 Lbs. lean, lean ground round
1 small can Ortega Diced Chiles
1 green bell pepper, chopped
1 red bell pepper, chopped
1 to 2 Med. tomatoes, chopped
2 C. tomato sauce
1 or 2 stalks celery, chopped

* for extra hot add:
¼ t. cayenne pepper
¼ t. chili powder

In a large saucepan, or heavy skillet, brown meat, crumbling as it cooks. Drain pan drippings. Add remaining ingredients and simmer 30 to 60 minutes.

Gary Collins
HOME SHOW on TV

Rafter GC

LONE STAR CHILI

2 Lbs. beef chuck, cut into ½-inch pieces
2 cans (16 oz.) tomatoes,
or 4 C. peeled, fresh tomatoes, chopped
1 Med. onion, chopped
1 small green pepper, chopped
2 Lg. cloves garlic, minced
1 t. salt
¼ t. cayenne pepper
¼ t. black ground pepper
1 T. vegetable oil

In a large Dutch oven, saute the beef, onion, green pepper, and garlic over a medium-high heat for about 10 minutes, or until the meat is done and the onions and the peppers are tender. Stir the mixture occasionally to crumble meat so that it cooks evenly, but does not burn.

Add all remaining ingredients, including the tomatoes and their liquid, to the Dutch oven. Bring to a boil; reduce heat, and simmer, covered, for about 1½ hours or until it has cooked enough for your personal satisfaction. Stir occasionally while cooking. You'll end up with a perfect pot of chili that will feed 8 to 10 people just right.

Garnish with your normal side dishes of chopped onion, shredded cheese and the like if you desire.

Jan S. Cleary
Cincinnati, OH

William & Marion Collins
Gold Hill, OR

CHILI BUTTER for corn flavoring

In a small bowl, with a wooden spoon, beat ½ cup of butter, or margarine, softened, 1 tablespoon salt, 1 teaspoon chili powder, ¼ teaspoon oregano, ½ teaspoon garlic powder, ¼ teaspoon fresh ground black pepper and ⅛ teaspoon parsley flakes, well until the ingredients are well blended.

Either spread with a knife over corn, or melt mixture and brush onto the ears.

Rose B. McKenzie
Ft. Lauderdale, FL

Raymond Cattle Co.
Boston, MA

GERI'S CHILI CON CARNE

½ Lb. very lean ground beef
½ Lb. bones and skinned chicken breast, chopped fine
1 Lg. yellow onion, chopped fine
1 Med. green pepper, chopped
2 cloves garlic, minced
1 T. chili powder
1 T. ground cumin
1 can (16 oz.) low-sodium tomatoes, pureed with their juice
1 C. low-sodium beef broth
1 T. low-sodium tomato paste
1 t. crushed red pepper flakes
1 t. ground coriander
1 t. ground dried oregano
1 t. basil, crumbled
1 bay leaf
1 C. cooked and drained kidney beans
¼ C. shredded sharp Cheddar cheese (optional)

Lightly coat a heavy 10-inch skillet with a non-stick cooking spray, and set over a moderate heat for 30 seconds. Add the ground beef and chopped chicken breast; cook, stirring often, until the meat is no longer pink, about 5 to 7 minutes.

Push the cooked meat and chicken mixture to one side of the skillet.

Add the onion, green pepper, garlic, chili powder, and cumin to the skillet. Cover, and cook until the onion is soft, about 5 minutes. Add the tomatoes, beef broth, tomato paste, red pepper flakes, basil, coriander, oregano, and the bay leaf; simmer, uncovered, for about 20 minutes, stirring occasionally.

Add the kidney beans and simmer, also uncovered, for about 5 more minutes, again, stirring occasionally to keep the mixture evenly cooking.

Discard the bay leaf, ladle the hot chili mix into serving bowls, garnish with the shredded cheese, and chopped onions if desired. This can be served over rice or spaghetti. Serves 4.

Ruth Geronimo
Cocoa, Fl

Ms. D. A. Posey
Fayetteville, TN

CHILI SPUDS

¼ Lb. Velveeta Process cheese spread, cubed
¼ C. salsa, flavored to your taste
4 hot baked potatoes, split in half lengthwise

Using a 1-quart microwave-safe bowl, heat the cheese and salsa on High for 3 to 5 minutes, or until smooth, stirring every minute to insure even cooking.

Scoop a little of the potato to form a slight pocket. Spoon some of the cheese mixture over each potato half.

For garnish and color, sprinkle finely chopped green or red peppers over the cheese.

This dish can become a main-stay with guest, and you can use a variety of garnishing to alternate servings.

Woman's Day

Old Spanish
Florida early 1600's

BARBECUE CHILI SAUCE

2 T. Worcestershire sauce
1 T. vinegar
1 T. cooking oil
1 t. instant beef bouillon granules
1 clove garlic, minced
¼ to ½ t. ground red pepper
¼ t. chili powder
1 T. brown sugar
¼ t. dry mustard
1 t. cornstarch
¼ C. catsup
¼ t. crushed cumin seed

For use in brushing on ribs or chicken parts:

In a small mixing bowl, combine the Worcestershire sauce, garlic, vinegar, oil, bouillon granules, red pepper, mustard, chili powder, cumin and ⅓ cup of water.

For serving sauce:

In a small saucepan, combine brown sugar and cornstarch.Stir in reserve sauce and catsup.Cook and stir until thickened and bubbly. Cook and stir for an additional 2 minutes. This can also be used as a sauce for grilling.

Jack Morris
Palm Bay, FL

Moody & J. B. Hendry
Florida 1899

THE CHILI'S BED

9 Ozs. of spaghetti noodles, cooked and buttered
1 can (16 oz.) red kidney beans, heated
1 Lg. onion, chopped
Options:
Shredded Cheddar cheese
Sour cream
Oyster Crackers

To assemble dish: Arrange noodles on 4 to 6 serving platters. Top noodles with kidney beans (drained of all liquid). Sprinkle chopped onions over beans. Ladle on chili with as much of it's oil as you like.

Top chili with choice of shredded Cheddar cheese, sour cream, or oyster crackers, or some of each for an extra filling meal. Makes 4 to 6 servings.

The Chili Bowl
Milwaukee, WI
Cinincinnati Enquirer

Rattlesnake Creek, Inc
Bainbridge Island, WA

JUST OLE CHILI

2 Lbs. lean chuck, chili ground
1 Lg. bell green pepper, chopped
2 Lg. onions, chopped
2 cloves garlic, crushed
1 can (28 oz.) whole tomatoes, peeled, undrained, chopped
1 bay leaf
1 can (25 oz.) red kidney beans, rinsed and drained
1 can (6 oz.) tomato paste
3 T. chili powder
2 t. cumin
1½ t. salt
Fresh ground black pepper

In a preheated large skillet or Dutch oven, brown the beef until the pink is cooked from the meat.Stir to crumble the meat as it is cooking.Drain off all fat and grease that is cooked from the beef. Add the onions, green pepper, garlic and saute until the vegetables are tender.

Drain the liquid from the tomatoes, and add to the pot. Add the remaining ingredients, and simmer for one hour, uncovered. Stir the pot occasionally to keep mixture from sticking.

Taste while cooking for flavor, and adjust if necessary.

For a garnish, you may try shredded Cheddar cheese, as well as sprinkling extra chopped onions on top of each serving.

Arnold & Susan Levine
Cincinnati, OH

Walking Rocker
Ronald Wilson
Tampa, FL

PAUL'S CHILI

1 Lb. lean ground beef
2 Lg. onions, chopped
2 cans (15½ oz.) red kidney beans
2 cans (15½ oz.) dark red kidney beans
1 can (28 oz.) Italian tomatoes, cut up
1 can (14½ oz.) stewed tomatoes
2 cans (4 oz.) diced green chile peppers
¼ C. chili powder
1 t. garlic powder
1 t. dried oregano, crushed
¼ t. ground red pepper (optional)
⅛ t. black pepper
1 t. parsley flakes

In a large Dutch oven, cook the ground beef and the chopped onions until the meat is brown and the onion is tender. Spoon or drain off the pan drippings.

Stir in the undrained kidney beans, tomatoes, and green chile peppers. Bring to a boil; reduce the heat and the remaining ingredients, and simmer, uncovered, for about an hour and a half, or until the desired consistency is reached.

Add a little water if a thinner mixture is desired. Makes about 12 servings.

Arnold & Susan Levine
Cincinnati, OH

C. D. Eddy
Iron City, TN

GEBHARDT'S CHILI CON CARNE

1 Lb. ground beef
½ small onion, chopped (optional)
⅓ C. flour
1 t. salt
3¼ T. Gebhardt's Original Eagle Brand Chili Powder
1 can (15 oz.) Gebhardt's Mexican-style beans (optional), or
1 can (15 oz.) Gebhardt's Pinto Beans (optional)

Brown ground beef (and onion, if used). Drain off excess fat. Add flour, salt and chili powder. Mix well. Pour water or tomato juice over seasoned beef. Stir and bring to a boil. Add the optional beans if desired, and simmer gently for 20 minutes.

GEBHARDT'S recipe

Tom & Daisy Franklin
Kaibeto, AZ

GREEN BAY-STYLE CHILI

½ C. chopped onion
2 cloves garlic, minced fine
2 T. vegetable oil
2 Lbs. ground beef
1 t. salt
½ t. black pepper
1 t. Worcestershire sauce
5 to 10 drops Tabasco sauce, to taste
1 C. barbecue sauce of choice
⅓ C. olive oil
1 t. chili powder
½ t. ground cumin
¼ t. ground coriander
¼ t. ground cardamom

In a large skillet or Dutch oven, saute the onion in the vegetable oil until they are softened. Add the ground beef, stirring often to crumble meat. Drain off excess fat. Season with salt, black pepper, Worcestershire sauce, and Tabasco; and simmer over a medium low heat for about 5 minutes.

Combine the olive oil with the chili powder, cumin, coriander and the cardamom. Heat this mixture to a simmer in a skillet. Stir in the garlic and cook until the garlic is softened.

Stir this into the meat mixture. Bring to a boil; reduce the heat, and simmer for an hour and a half, or until desired consistency is reached.

The Chili Bowl
Milwaukee, WI
Cincinnati Enquirer

David Pickens, Jr.
DDT Ranch
Nashville, TN

FLORIDA LONGHORNS

CHILI MACARONI

2 C. Lg. elbow macaroni
2 T. vegetable oil
1 can (25 oz.) chili with beans
4 scallions, chopped
¼ t. chili powder
1 can (15 oz.) chili without beans
Shredded Cheddar cheese

Cook the macaroni in boiling water for 4 minutes or until tender. Drain. Toss with oil in crock pot. Layer ingredients as follows:

Chili with beans, half of the chopped scallions, macaroni, chili without beans, rest of scallions, rest of cheese.

Cover, and cook for 4 hours on low or 2 hours on high. Serves 4 to 6.

Abe & Tarin Fischer
Cincinnati, OH

Donald Le Fils & Family
Osteen, FL

CHILI POLENTA DEEP-DISH PIE

¾ C. corn meal
¾ C. cold water
2 C. boiling water
1 can (15 oz.) chili with beans
1 can (7½ oz.) chili with beans
1 can (16 oz) red kidney beans, drained
¼ C. minced dried onion
1 t. paprika
¼ t. dried oregano
¼ t. curry powder
¼ t. cumin

In a saucepan, mix together the corn meal and cold water. Add the salt, and gradually add in the two (2) cups of boiling water, stirring constantly. Cook until mixture thickens, stirring frequently. Cover, cook over a low heat for 10 to 15 minutes.

Cool slightly. Pour into a 1½ quart casserole, pushing up the sides to form a shell. Cover the casserole dish with wax paper, and chill.

Combine the chili with beans, kidney beans, onion, paprika, cumin, and curry powder, and spoon into the corn meal shell.

Bake, covered, in a 400 degree oven for 30 minutes; uncover and bake 10 to 15 minutes or until it is thoroughly heated. Makes 5 servings.

Sue McCormick
Cincinnati, OH

Robert S. Magill
Pleasant Grove, CA

CHILI CORN CHOWDER

3 slices bacon
1 Lb. mild Italian sausage, thinly sliced
1 Lg. onion, chopped
1 Lg. white thin-skinned potato, peeled and diced
1 C. water
2 cans (15 oz.) cream-style corn
1 can (4 oz.) diced green chiles
1 jar (2 oz.) sliced pimentos, drained
2 C. half-and-half light cream
1 clove garlic, whole
salt and pepper to taste

In a saucepan, cook the bacon over a medium heat until it is crisp. Remove bacon from the pan, drain off the drippings, and crumble, setting aside. Discard all but 2 tablespoons of the bacon fat.

In a 4-or 5-quart pot add the sliced Italian sausage, onion and the whole clove of garlic, to the reserved bacon drippings, stirring occasionally until the onion is softened and the sausage slices are browned. Discard the garlic.

in the diced potatoes and water. Bring to a boil over a high heat, cover with lid, and simmer until the potatoes are tender when pierced with a fork.

Stir in the corn, chiles, pimento, and light cream. Heat, stir occasionally, just until the chowder is beginning to steam. Do not let the chowder reach a boil.

Season to taste with salt and pepper. Garnish with the crumbled bacon bits. Makes 4 to 6 servings.

Sharon Combs
Cincinnati, OH

Old Spanish
Florida early 1600's

LOW-CALORIE CHILI

2½ Lbs. lean coarse-ground beef
2 T. chili powder
1 clove garlic, chopped fine
1 can (16 oz.) tomatoes, mashed
½ C. diced dried chile pods, stems and seeds removed
1 Lg. onion, chopped

Cook the meat in a heavy saucepan until browned, crumbling during cooking, to make smaller chunks. Add the chili powder, garlic, tomatoes and cook for 10 minutes. Add onions and cook for 10 minutes more.

Put the chile in water and boil until soft.

Pour this onto the meat mixture and cook, slowly, for 20, minutes, add more water if necessary to obtain desired consistency.

Sprinkle with low-calorie Cheddar cheese to garnish individual servings. This chili recipe will provide 8 to 10 servings.

Brooke J. Ruben
Cincinnati, OH

A3

Cindy & A.W. Grimm, II
Nogales, AZ

WILD DOGS' CHILI

3 Lbs. chuck, trimmed and cut into ½-inch cubes
2 T. vegetable oil
3 Med. onions, chopped
5 cloves garlic, finely chopped
1 T. chili powder
½ t. dried oregano
½ t. paprika
2 t. salt
Pepper as needed
2 cans (16 oz.) whole green chiles, seeded, drained and cut into 1-inch pieces
2 cans whole tomatoes, cut up
1 can (6 oz.) tomato paste
4 C. water

In a heavy skillet or Dutch oven, heat the oil, and saute the onion and garlic until the onion is transparent but not browned. Add the meat and using a wooden spoon to break up large pieces, cook until it is browned.

Add rest of ingredients, stirring to mix well. Cover, bring to a boil; reduce heat, and let simmer, uncovered, for about ½ to 1 hour.

Adjust flavor if desired, and mix in well.

Spoon off meat fat that has risen to top of chili and dispose of. If possible, allow chili to cool, and refrigerate overnight. It is much easier to remove fat when it has solidified.

When serving, place bowls of chopped onions, shredded cheese, chips and other condiments for added ingredients by your family members or guests.

CSG

D/S

Ellis P. Umberger
D/S Brahman Farm
Grand Junction, TN

LEMON-CHILI BROTH

3 C. chicken broth, or
regular-strength canned chicken broth
1 small dried hot red chile
1 strip lemon peel (about 3-inches long, yellow part only)
1 thin slice, 1"x3" fresh ginger
1 clove garlic, minced
1 T. lemon juice
fresh cilantro (corinader) sprigs
thin lemon slices

In a 2-quart saucepan, combine the chicken stock, or broth, chile pepper, lemon peel, ginger and garlic. Bring to a boil over a high heat; reduce the heat, cover and simmer for 20 minutes; stirring in the lemon juice.

Garnish individual servings with the cooked shrimp, cilantro sprigs and lemon slices. Makes about 4 to 5 servings depending upon serving sizes.

David Levine
Cincinnati, OH

St

Leroy Bass
Florida 1879

CHILI CON PILLO

2 Lbs. broiler-fryer chicken parts
¼ t. ground black pepper
1 T. salt
1 Med.-size onion, chopped
1 green pepper, chopped
1 clove garlic, minced
1 can (16 oz.) whole tomatoes, drained and chopped
1 can (16 oz.) red kidney beans, drained
1½ t. chili powder
¼ t. cumin

In a large baking dish, arrange the chicken, skin side up. Season with the salt and pepper, and place in a preheated 350 degree oven for 30 minutes, or until browned.

Remove from the oven, and pour off any accumulated drippings before continuing any further.

Add the rest of the ingredients in a mixing bowl to mix well. Then pour over the chicken; cover, and continue cooking for 30 minutes or until the chicken is tender.

Karen Furr
Cincinnati, OH

$

Chuck & Kay Barnhart
Redmond, OR

CHILI BEEF and CORN SOUP

1 Lb. lean ground beef
1 Lg. onion, chopped
1 can (16 oz.) tomato puree
½ Lb. mushrooms, sliced
1 T. chili powder
½ t. oregano
½ t. ground cumin
1 t. salt ½ C. shredded Cheddar cheese
½ t. black ground pepper
2 cans (16 oz.) red kidney beans drained
1 clove garlic, minced
1 can (12 oz.) Mexican-style corn, drained
3 C. beef stock, or regular-strength canned beef broth

In a 4-to 5-quart pot, or Dutch oven, cook the beef over a medium high heat, stirring to crumble, until it looses it's pinkness. Add the onion, garlic and mushrooms; cook, stirring occasionally until the onion is tender. Discard any fat drippings that form.

Add the chili powder, oregano, cumin, beans, tomato puree and liquid stock. Bring to a boil over a high heat; reduce the heat, cover, and simmer for 20 minutes. Add the corn; cover and simmer for an additional 10 minutes.

Season to taste with more or less salt and pepper if desired. After ladling individual bowls with the chili mixture, pass around dishes with shredded cheese or extra chopped onions for each to take what they want. This makes about 4 hearty helpings.

Joseph R. Levine
Cincinnati, OH

Norris Livestock
Brokerage
Monticello, FL

TURKEY CHILI

1½ Lbs. ground fresh turkey
1 T. margarine, or non-stick cooking spray
¼ t. crushed red pepper flakes
1 red pepper, chopped
1 can (16 oz.) whole tomatoes, drained and cut up
1 t. salt
½ t. ground pepper
1 T. or more, chili powder
1 clove garlic, minced
1 can (6 oz.) tomato sauce
1 green pepper, chopped
1 Med. onion, chopped

Melt the margarine in a heavy non-stick skillet, or spray with non-stick canned liquid. Add the turkey, and cook until it is browned, crumbling with a wooden spoon; as it cooks. Add the onion, green and red peppers, and the garlic. Cover, and cook on a medium heat until the turkey is tender.

Add the tomatoes, with it's juice, and the remaining ingredients. Cover, simmer the chili for 1 to 1½ hours. Taste during the cooking time to adjust the seasonings if desired.

C. Lynn & George Grosner
Milford, MA

United Bank of Sterling
Sterling, CO

TEXAS-STYLE HOT CHILI

5 bacon slices
8 Ozs. hot Italian sausage links, sliced
1½ Lbs. beef chuck, diced
1 Med. onion, chopped
1 small green pepper, chopped
1 clove garlic, minced
3 C. water
1 can (12 oz.) tomato paste
1 or 2 dried red chile peppers, seeded and crumbled
1 t. salt
1 to 1½ T. chili powder
1 can (16 oz.) pinto beans, drained
¼ t. dried oregano, crushed
¼ t. cumin seed
¼ t. paprika
¼ t. fresh ground black pepper
1 or 2 jalapeno peppers, seeded and chopped

In a Dutch oven, over a medium-high heat, cook the bacon until it is crisp; drain drippings. Set the bacon on paper towels, and drain off as much of the fat as possible. Crumble when is has cooled, and set aside.

In the Dutch oven, cook the sliced Italian sausage until it is lightly browned. Stir in the beef, onion, green pepper and garlic. Continue cooking until the beef is browned and the vegetables are tender. Drain off all excess grease drippings.

Stir in the crumbled bacon bits, water, tomato paste, chili powder, jalapeno peppers (chopped), chile peppers, salt, pepper, oregano, cumin and the paprika.

Bring the mixture to a boil; reduce the heat, cover, and simmer for 2 hours, stirring occasionally. After this cooking time, stir in the beans. Cover, and simmer an additional 20 minutes more, or until the beans are heated through. Makes 8 to 10 servings.

Zane B. Ruben
Cincinnati, OH

Jack & Gloria Gardella
Columbia, CA

CHILI MAC

¾ Lb. ground beef
1 Med. onion, chopped
1 green pepper, chopped
2 C. water
1 Pkg. (8 oz.) protein-enriched elbow macaroni
1 can (16 oz.) red kidney beans
1 t. chili powder
1 t. salt
¼ t. fresh ground pepper
¼ t. cumin
¼ t. oregano
½ C. shredded Cheddar cheese
2 cans (8 oz.) tomato sauce

Brown the ground beef, onion, and green pepper in a large non-stick skillet, or in a Dutch oven. Add no oil to the cooking as the meat will release a sufficient amount of grease for browning.

After the meat and vegetables are browned, add one (1) cup of water and let the mixture come to a boil.

Drain off all excess liquid from the skillet or from the Dutch oven. This will remove all the fatty drippings from the meat. Add the remaining cup of water to the cooking, as well as the remaining ingredients, except the cheese. Simmer for 20 minutes, stirring occasionally, or until most of the liquid has evaporated.

Sprinkle the shredded cheese over the top of the meat, and continue heating until it has melted. Makes about 8 servings.

C. Lynn & George Grosner
Milford, MA

A7

Riley West Inc.
Tucson, AZ

UNSER'S 500 CHILI

1 Lb. lean pork shoulder, cut into ¾-inch cubes
2 T. flour
2 T. lard, vegetable oil or oleo
½ C. onion, chopped
1 clove garlic, mince
1 green pepper, chopped
1 can (16 oz.) whole tomatoes, coarsely chopped
2 cans (7 oz.) Ortega Diced Green chiles, or more to taste
¼ t. oregano
2½ t. salt
¼ t. cumin seeds

Dredge meat cubes in the flour. Melt browning ingredient in a large deep skillet or medium-size Dutch oven. Brown the meat thoroughly. Add onion, green pepper, and garlic, and cook until the onion is soft.

Add all remaining ingredients. Simmer, covered, for 1½ to 2 hours, stirring occasionally. Remove cover, simmer, uncovered, 5 to 15 minutes to obtain the desired consistency.

Alan & Donna Routt
Cincinnati, OH

Norman Johnston, 1898
Brevard County, FL

GEBHARDT'S CHILI LOVERS CHILI

1½ Lbs. lean ground beef
1 C. onion, chopped
1 Med. green pepper, chopped
1 Lg. clove garlic, chopped
1 can (28 oz.) whole peeled tomatoes, broken up
1 can (8 oz.) tomato sauce
2 C. water
2 T. Gebhardt's Chili Powder
1 T. salt
1 bay leaf
¼ t. Gebhardt's Hot Sauce
2 cans (15 oz.) Gebhardt's Mexican-style Chili Beans

Cook beef, onion, green pepper and the garlic in a large saucepan or Dutch oven until the meat looses it red color. Stir in the remaining ingredients except the beans. Cook over a low heat, covered, for 1½ hours. Add beans and cook for 30 minutes longer. Remove and discard bay leaf.

GEBHARDT'S recipe

Charles Cleveland, 1895
Brevard County, FL

CINCINNATI CHILI

2 Lbs. lean beef, chili ground
2 Med.-size onions, chopped
2 cloves garlic, minced
1 green pepper, chopped fine
1 can (8 oz.) tomato sauce
2 C. water
1 T. red wine vinegar
2 T. chili powder
1 T. paprika
2 T. freshly ground pepper
1 t. honey or ½ t. sugar
½ t. cumin
½ t. marjoram
½ t. allspice
¼ t. cinnamon
¼ t. cloves
¼ t. mace
¼ t. coriander
¼ t. cardamon
1 bay leaf, crumbled

Sprinkle some salt over the bottom of a hot skillet or Dutch oven and add the beef, onion, green pepper, and garlic. Add the water, tomato sauce, and the remaining ingredients.

Simmer for at least 2 hours, stirring frequently.

Cincinnati style chili is made by boiling the beef, not by browning on a hot surface. The beef is often worked over with a mixer to break it us into a soupy mixture.

Craig Cunningham
Cincinnati, OH

C. S. Sharpe, 1944
Brevard County, FL

VENISON CHILI

3 T. bacon grease or butter
1 C. onion, chopped
1 clove garlic, minced
1 Lb. ground venison
3 C. tomatoes, chopped
½ t. salt
1 bay leaf
½ C. red dry wine
1 T. sugar
½ to 2 T. chili powder, or to your taste
1 can (6 oz.) tomato sauce

In a large skillet or medium-size Dutch oven, melt the bacon grease or butter over a moderate heat. Add the onion and garlic, and stir until fragrant.

Add the venison and saute until just brown. Stir in tomatoes, tomato sauce, salt, bay leaf, sugar, red wine, and chili powder, blending to mix well.

Reduce the heat to low, cover, and simmer for 1 hour, or until the venison is tender and the chili consistency is thick and tasty.

Garnish should include shredded cheese and sour cream, along with some additional chopped onions.

Robin Cunningham
Cincinnati, OH

Pete Clemons
Okeechobee, FL

CONEY ISLAND CHILI SAUCE

½ C. olive oil
¾ Lb. lean ground beef
1 can (8 oz.) tomato sauce
4 dried chile pods, finely ground
3 cloves garlic, mashed
1½ t. sugar
½ t. turmeric
½ t. oregano
½ t. paprika
½ t. cumin
1½ T. cornstarch
¼ C. water

Heat the olive oil in a skillet, and fry beef for three minutes, breaking it up well during cooking. Add remaining ingredients, except the cornstarch and water. Cover, and simmer for 20 minutes, stirring frequently to prevent sticking or burning.

Add just enough water to keep mixture flowing, if necessary. Mix cornstarch with ¼ cup of water. Add to meat mixture and simmer, stirring, for about 10 minutes or until desired thickness is achieved.

For Cincinnati Coney dogs, put in blender and run for just a second to eliminate meat chunks, and then ladle sauce onto hot dogs nestled in buns.

Cincinnati Enquirer

Dave Wortham, 1889
China Springs
McLennan County, TX

C.V. WOODS JR'S CHILI

1 3-Lb. stewing chicken, cut up
1½ quarts water
½ Lb. beef kidney suet
4 Lbs. flank steak
5 Lbs. center-cut pork chops
¼ C. finely chopped celery
7 C. tomatoes, chopped
2 T. sugar
6 long green chiles, Anaheim Green or New Mexico No.6
8 Oz. good light beer, preferably, Mexican
3 T. oregano
3 T. ground cumin
½ T. MSG (optional)
3 T. fine ground black pepper
4 T. salt
5 T. chili powder
1 T. fresh cilantro, chopped
1 T. thyme
2 cloves garlic, finely chopped
2 C. onions, cut into ¼-inch pieces (diced)
1 green pepper, cut into ⅜-inch pieces
1 Lb. Jack Cheese, grated
1 Lg. lime

In a 2-gallon pot, simmer the chicken parts in water for two hours. Strain off the broth and discard the chicken. Let broth simmer while preparing remaining ingredients. Render suet to make 6 to 8 tablespoons of oil. Throw fat away and save the oil.

Trim all fat from flank steak. Cut the meat into ⅜-inch cubes. Do the same with the pork chops, after trimming the fat and the bones completely.

In a 2-quart saucepan, combine the celery, tomatoes, and the sugar. Simmer one and a half hours, or until all the ingredients are completely tender. Prepare green chiles as previously described, and cut each into ¼ inch squares.

Into 8-ounces of light beer, mix until dissolved, the oregano, cumin, MSG, black pepper, salt, chili powder, cilantro, and thyme.

Add the tomato mixture, chiles, beer mixture, and garlic to the chicken broth in the 2-quart gallon pot. Stir with a wooden spoon, bring to a low simmer.

Brown the cut up pork in a skillet with about one-third of the oil from the suet. Pork should become white on all sides, and fully broken apart. Add the pork to the 2-quart pot, and bring to a low boil for about 30 minutes. Pork will require about a half-hour start in cooking ahead of the beef.

With the rest of the oil, brown the beef. Once it becomes white, add the beer to the pork in the 2-quart pot, and cook at a low boil for about an hour.

Add the remaining ingredients except the Jack Cheese, and bring the mixture to a low boil for about 2 or 3 hours, stirring with a wooden spoon every 15 to 20 minutes.

Add the grated cheese to the chili in individual serving bowls about 5 minutes before serving. Stir until completely dissolved. Just before serving, add the juice of the lime to the mixture.

Justin Fischer
Cincinnati, OH

Larry K. Lantz
Pierre, SD

CHILI STEW

- 2½ Lbs. boneless chuck cut into 1-inch cubes
- ¼ C. vegetable oil
- 1½ t. salt
- 1⅛ t. garlic powder
- 2 onions, chopped fine
- 2 cloves garlic, minced
- 2 cans (14½ oz.) stewed tomatoes, cut up, broken
- 1 can (12 oz.) tomatillos Senteros (whole green Spanish tomatoes), drained, coarsely chopped
- 1 can (4 oz.) mild green chiles, chopped
- 1 C. chopped parsley
- ⅓ C. lemon juice
- 2 t. oregano
- 1½ t. ground cumin
- 1 t. ground coriander
- ⅛ t. ground allspice
- Cooked rice
- Sour cream or yogurt

Brown the meat in a skillet using the vegetable oil, and salt and pepper. Place in slow cooker, sauce onions and garlic in 2 tablespoons of the oil, until soft.

Mix in the tomatoes, and juice into the onions. Add tomatillos, chiles, parsley, lemon juice, oregano, coriander and allspice. Mix into the beef, cover, and cook for about 7 hours on low or until tender.

Adjust seasonings if desired. Serve this over cooked rice for a hearty meal, adding either the sour cream or yogurt for appearance and an extra flavor.

Ted & Ann Swinarski
Cincinnati, OH

W. Bruce Lehrke
Longhorn World
Championship Rodeo, Inc
Nashville, TN

FINNEYTOWN'S HILLTOP CHILI

2 Lbs. lean ground beef
1 Lg. onion, chopped
1 green pepper, chopped
2 cloves garlic, chopped
1 can (28 oz.) tomatoes, undrained
1 can (10½ oz.) red kidney beans, undrained
1 can (10½ oz.) Campbell's Beef Broth
2 cans (10½ oz.) Campbell's Chili beef Soup
½ C. Open Pit Barbecue Sauce
1 T. Worcestershire sauce
¼ C. corn meal
½ t. garlic salt
1½ t. cumin powder
1 t. paprika
1 T. chili powder
1 bay leaf
1 can (16 oz.) chili beans in hot chili gravy

In a 6-quart kettle, saute the beef, stirring with a wooden spoon to break up meat into smaller chunks as it cooks and browns. Drain off all the fat that is cooked from the meat. Add the chopped onions, green pepper and garlic and simmer with the beef until they are soft.

Add all the remaining ingredients except the beans, and cook on a simmer, covered, for about an hour or so. Add the beans, and cook, uncovered on low simmer for 2 to 2½ hours, stirring occasionally.

If chili is too thin, mix the corn meal with a little water, and add to the chili. If it is too thick, add just sufficient water or tomato juice to bring it to your desired consistency. Discard the bay leaf before you serve.

Sandy & Kim McCoy
Cincinnati, OH

H6

H. F. Osteen
Florida, 1856

RIVERFRONT TAILGATE CHILI

2 Lbs. lean meat, ground or finely chopped
1 T. cooking oil
1 Med. onion, chopped
1 green pepper, chopped
1 T. all-purpose flour
6 T. chili powder
1 T. MSG (optional)
1 T. cayenne pepper
1 bay leaf
2 T. garlic powder
1 can (28 oz.) tomatoes, finely chopped
2 cans (8 oz.) green chile salsa
Dash of Tabasco sauce
1 can (15 oz.) pinto beans, drained
¼ t. paprika
1 t. cumin

Saute meat and onions with the green peppers in a large skillet or a Dutch oven, until the beef begins to brown and the onions and peppers are soft. Blend together the flour, chili powder, MSG (if used), cayenne pepper, garlic powder, oregano, paprika, and cumin.

Combine these dry ingredients with water and some of the fat from the meat drippings, then add to the meat mixture.

Add the tomatoes, chili salsa and the pinto beans along with the bay leaf, to the meat.

Simmer the chili for one hour or more, adjusting the taste and the consistency if desired. Discard the bay leaf.

Serve with chopped onions, and, or shredded Cheddar cheese, that can be sprinkled onto each serving bowl of chili as preferred.

Sandy & Kim McCoy
Cincinnati, OH

Harold Conger
Honolulu, HA

NOTHIN' BUT EASY CHILI

- 1 Lb. lean beef, coarsely chopped
- 6 Med.-size onions, chopped
- 6 green peppers, chopped
- 1 or 2 cloves garlic, minced
- 1 can (15 oz.) red kidney beans, undrained
- 1 can (28 oz.) whole tomatoes, cut up
- 4 T. chili powder
- ¼ t. oregano
- Salt and pepper to taste

Brown beef, onions and peppers in a large skillet. Stir in the tomatoes, chili powder, garlic, oregano, salt and pepper. Bring to a low simmer for 20 minutes. Add the beans and simmer for 2 to 2½ hours.

Serve in individual bowls, with chopped onions, shredded Cheddar cheese, oyster crackers or any other type of side condiments you have.

Wayne Vice
Cincinnati, OH

Bar U Ranch, Inc
Wauchula, FL

SOUTHERN CHILI SUPREME

3 Lbs. lean round steak cut into ⅜-inch cubes
3 Lbs. lean pork shoulder, finely chopped
3 Med. onions, chopped
1 green pepper, chopped
1 red pepper, chopped
7 cloves garlic, minced
1 can (16 oz.) tomato paste
2 C. white wine
1 C. water
1½ t. salt
1 t. black pepper
1 T. sugar
6 to 7 T. chili powder
3 T. ground cumin
1 T. thyme, ground
1 T. ground coriander, or
1 T. oregano may be subbed
5 T. Masa Harina flour
2 bay leaves
1 C. orange juice
1 t. garlic powder
1 4-Oz. stick butter or margarine

In a Dutch oven, brown the meat, with the onions, peppers, garlic, salt, and pepper until the meat is done and the vegetables are soft. Reduce heat, simmer on a very low heat for about an hour. Add the wine, water, orange juice, and the sugar and cook approximately an additional hour.

Carefully skim off the fat from the pot. Add hot water, if necessary to cover the meat to make skimming easier.

Add the chili powder, cumin, thyme, coriander, or oregano if used, and the bay leaves to the Dutch oven, which would be discarded after cooking and before serving.

Mix the Masa Harina flour in a small amount of water, and once it is a smooth paste, add to the meat mixture. Then add the tomato paste, garlic powder and butter or margarine. Check and adjust the seasonings if necessary, and consistency of mix.

Miami Herald

Dick C. Hoch
Seal Rock, OR

CHARLES WILLEFORD'S TEXAS CHILI

4 Lbs. chuck roast, cut into ½x'-inch chunks
3 Med. onions, chopped into ½-inch pieces
2 to 3 T. oil
Salt and pepper to taste
2 heaping T. cumin seed
1 clove garlic
1 can (16 oz.) whole tomatoes
2 Pkgs. chili seasoning
1 T. chili powder
1 can (6 oz.) Mole paste
Tabasco sauce to taste
3 to 4 C. water
3 jalapeno peppers, seeded and stems removed, chopped
⅔ C. Masa flour
1 t. sugar

Brown meat and onion together in oil in an iron skillet. It is not necessary to cook the meat thoroughly. Onion should be browned, but not caramelized. Season meat and onions with the salt and pepper to taste, and dump the skilletfull into a large pot or Dutch oven.

Grind the cumin seed in a mortar. Using the same pestle, mash the garlic. Add a little water. Remove the cumin and garlic to the meat.

In a blender, combine, the tomatoes, sugar, chili seasonings, and the chili powder. Open a can of 12-ounce cold beer and pour 6 ounces into a glass. Drink the glassful and then pour the remaining 6 ounces from the can into the blender.

Blend with tomato mixture, and add to the meat. Add mole paste, Tabasco sauce and salt, along with about a quart of water, to the meat mixture. Add the chopped jalapenos. Simmer for about 2½ hours, stirring occasionally to prevent sticking or burning.

At the end of the cooking time, make a runny paste of the Masa flour and water. Stir very fast as you add it to the chili, or it will be lumpy. Cook for 30 minutes longer, stirring often. Serve hot.

Miami Herald

J. L. Mahon
Fannett, TX

CHILI MENDOW

- 2 Lbs. ground lean beef
- 3½ Lb. Kosher salami, cut into small pieces
- 7 Med. onions, finely chopped
- 2 cans (16 oz.) whole tomatoes
- 2 cans (16 oz.) red kidney beans
- 1 Lg. T. butter or margarine
- 2 t. fresh ground black pepper
- 1 t. salt
- 3 T. paprika
- 2 T. sugar
- 2 to 3 T. chili powder
- ½ t. oregano
- ½ t. cumin seed, ground
- ½ Lb. wide noodles

Do not brown meat. Put all but the noodles and the salami in a heavy kettle or Dutch oven, and cook for not less than two hours. About 30 minutes before serving, add the salami and the noodles.

This chili is to cook down so that it can be eaten with a fork...no lapping up from bowl with a spoon. Pumpernickel is passed with the chili.

David Painter
Gary, NC

Brooke Allison Holve
Springville, CA

BLACK BEAN CHILI

2 Med. onions, coarsely chopped
2 cans (16 oz.) tomatoes in juice, undrained and coarsely chopped
2 C. zucchini, chopped
2 cans (16 oz.) black beans, drained
¼ C. vegetable oil
1 T. chili powder
1 t. ground cumin
1 shredded carrot
1 t. dried oregano
2 t. hot pepper sauce (Tabasco)
1½ t. paprika
¼ t. thyme
1 can (6 oz.) tomato paste
4 cloves garlic, minced
½ t. salt
¼ t. black pepper
Shredded Cheddar or Monterey Jack cheese
Sour cream, optional

In a Dutch oven or a large skillet, heat the oil over a medium heat. Add the chili powder, paprika, oregano and cumin. Increase the heat to high; cook for one minute, stirring frequently.

Add the onion and garlic. Reduce the heat to medium, cook for five (5) minutes, again stirring occasionally.

Add the tomatoes and their liquid, zucchini, carrots, hot pepper sauce and remaining ingredients except the cheese and the sour cream. Cook for 5 to 10 minutes, again stirring occasionally to keep blended.

Add the canned black beans, and bring the mixture to a boil; reduce the heat, and simmer on low for one (1) hour.

Garnish with the shredded cheese and a dollop of sour cream to top each serving bowl.

Sharon Geltner
Boca Raton, FL

B/I

William E. Bublitz
DePere, WI

GERMAN CHILI

1½ Lbs. lean stewing pork, cut into bit-size pieces
1 Med. onion, chopped
1 green pepper, chopped
3 cloves garlic, minced
2 T. olive oil
1 can (15 oz.) red kidney beans, drained
2 T. chili powder
½ t. oregano
½ t. crushed dried Japanese chiles
½t. ground cumin
1 beef bouillon cube, crumbled
1 can (6 oz.) tomato paste
1 can (12 oz.) beer
2 C. sauerkraut, drained
⅛ t. black pepper
Dash (2 or 3 drops) Tabasco hot sauce

Heat the olive oil in a large saucepan or cooking pot. Brown the pork pieces and saute the onions and garlic, along with the green pepper, until they are tender.

Add all remaining ingredients, except the beans and the sauerkraut. Stir well to mix thoroughly.

Cover and simmer for about an hour, or until the meat is tender. Add the beans and sauerkraut, and heat through before serving.

Elka Woebbeking
Pollhagen, W. Germany

C.H. & Helen Prude
Cochise, AZ

Peppers Burn Calories

Eager to melt away those holiday pounds? Try sprinkling your diet with hot peppers. The substance in peppers that make them hot -- capsaicin -- causes the body to burn up to 25 percent more calories a day than it would otherwise, according to the January issue of Self magazine. The hotter the pepper, the greaterits capsicin. There's even a scale, called the Scoville Count, that rates hotness. Bell peppers rate a 0, jalapenos rate between 2.5 and 5, and cayennes between 30 and 50.

Boca Raton News, FL 1/7/92

PANHANDLE CHILI

5 Lbs. ground beef
3 onions, chopped
3 stalks celery, chopped
1 green pepper, chopped
6 cloves garlic, minced
3 jalapeno peppers, chopped
1 T. oregano
1 T. Tabasco Hot Sauce
3 Qts. beef broth
1 can (16 oz.) tomato paste
1 can (16 oz.) tomatoes, chopped
⅓ C. olive oil
2 T. seasoning salt
5 T. paprika
½ t. celery seed
1 t. sugar
1 t. ground coriander
1 bay leaf
¾ C. Masa flour
1 can (12 oz.) beer
1 T. salt
1 t. black pepper
3 T. chili powder
2 t. cayenne pepper
3 t. corn meal

In a large Dutch oven, brown the meat with the onions using the olive oil. Add sugar, salt, pepper and garlic to mixture. Crumble the meat as it browns to form smaller pieces other than large clumps. Cover, and simmer for 2 hours on a low heat.

Drain off pan drippings, reserving one cup of the liquid. Add the beer, tomatoes, chili powder, Tabasco sauce, cumin, and oregano to the Dutch oven. Mix well to blend the ingredients. Continue simmering.

Combine the Masa flour with a little water to form a paste, and then add to the cooking mixture, stirring in well. Add all the remaining ingredients, again stirring well.

Pour the reserved beef broth into the pot, stirring. Reduce the heat, cover, and simmer for an additional 2½ to 3 hours.

NOTE: With the large portions of hot spices, it may be best to reserve adding all of them at one time, and taste as cooking proceeds, and add to pot enough to satisfy the individual taste and flavor. Makes about 15 or so servings.

Try placing bowls of chopped onions, shredded cheeses, and chips on the table for those being served to garnish their individual bowls.

Michelle B. Geltner
Streamwood, IL

Magic Valley Brahmans
Athens, TN

NOT HARD CHILI

1 Lb. ground beef
2 stalks celery, chopped
2 Med. onions, chopped
2 green or red peppers, chopped
2 cans (15 oz.) red kidney beans
1 can (4 oz.) jalapeno bean dip
2 cans (6oz.) tomato puree
Dash Tabasco sauce
Dash chili powder
Salt and pepper to taste

In a large skillet, brown the beef, crumbling as it cooks. Add the chopped onions, peppers and celery. Cook the vegetables until they are done and tender to taste.

Add the remaining ingredients, and simmer for about 2 hours. Add water if necessary to reach the desired consistency.

Seasonings can be added to chili as it cooks slowly to taste, as some people can not take too highly spiced foods, and this is an easy recipe to change to personal flavoring.

Wilson Williams
Cocoa, FL

John Reed, 1898
Brevard County, FL

GREEN GARLIC CHILI

2 Lbs. beef
½ C. olive oil
3 cloves garlic, whole
6 fresh green chiles
½ t. salt
½ t. white pepper
1 Lg. onion, chopped
3 Lg. green tomatoes, diced

Cut beef into ½-inch cubes. In a skillet, heat the oil and cook the beef until it is well-done and tender. Add whole garlic cloves and cook till tender.

Add the green chiles and onions, diced green tomatoes, to the skillet. Add the remaining ingredients, and cook, uncovered, until the chili is done and seasoned to taste.

Stanley & Annie Minor
Cincinnati, OH

B.J. Alderman
Florida, 1857

ZUCCHINI CHILI

2 Lbs. ground chuck
1 Med. zucchini, chopped
1 Med. onion, chopped
½ C. green pepper, chopped
½ C. olive oil
2 t. apple cider vinegar
1 t. sugar
1 can (8 oz.) whole kernel corn, drained
1 can (16 oz.) pinto beans
1 can (6 oz.) tomato paste
¼ C. chili powder
¼ t. oregano
¼ t. dried cumin

Saute the zucchini in the olive oil until it is transparent; remove and set aside. Brown the beef and vegetables in the same oil, and liquid from the zucchini.

Return cooked zucchini to the beef-vegetable mixture, and add the remaining ingredients except the beans. Stir well to blend the mixture.

Cook on a low heat at simmer for a full 2 hours. Add more liquid if necessary for the desired thickness. Serves 4 to 6 helpings.

Skye Fischer
Cincinnati, OH

Jerry D. Medlin
Lyles, TN

MACARONI CHILI

2 Lbs. ground beef
2 Lg. onions, chopped
1 green pepper, chopped
½ C. macaroni
2 C. beef broth
3 T. olive oil
1 can (16 oz.) tomatoes, chopped
1 can (16 oz.) kidney beans
¼ t. garlic powder
2 T. chili powder
1 t. paprika
1 t. salt
¼ t. fresh ground black pepper

In a large skillet or Dutch oven, brown the onions until they are transparent. Add the ground beef, stirring to crumble while it cooks. Add the beef broth, and tomatoes. Stir in well. Add the beans, garlic powder, pepper, paprika, salt, and the chili powder.

Cover, simmer at low heat for 3 hours, stirring occasionally. Serve with hot corn bread and a salad. Serves 4 to 6.

Nicole Layne
Merritt Island, FL

Calvin P. Turner
Mt. Juliet, TN

GULF COAST CHILI

3 Lbs. beef, chili ground
¼ c. olive oil
1 t. salt
3 C. water
½ t. ground black pepper
1 t. oregano
Few drops Tabasco sauce
1 t. paprika
2 C. beef broth
1½ T. chili powder
¼ t. crushed red pepper
¼ C. Masa flour
1 T. cumin powder
½ t. ground black pepper
¼ C. cornmeal
3 cloves garlic, finely chopped
2 Med. onions, chopped
2 Med. onions, chopped
2 Lg. green peppers, chopped

In a large skillet, saute the vegetables in 2 tablespoons of the olive oil until the onions are transparent. Add the meat, and brown, crumbling as it cooks. Drain off all of the oil and meat drippings and discard.

Add the remaining ingredients, cover, and bring to a boil; then reduce to simmer, and cook at the low heat for about 2 hours. Stir the mixture occasionally to keep from sticking and burning to the bottom of the pan.

David Hoffman
Cincinnati, OH

L & J Cattle, Inc
Carthage, TN

GILROY CHILI

3 cloves fresh garlic, minced
2 Lg. onions, finely chopped
2 Lbs. ground beef
2 T. olive oil
1 can (4 oz.) green chiles
1 C. canned stewed tomatoes
2 C. beef broth
1 T. ground cumin
1 T. chili powder
1½ t. MSG (optional)
1 t. salt
¼ t. pepper

In a large skillet slowly brown garlic and onions in the olive oil; stir and cook until tender. Heat skillet to hot, add meat and cook until done.

Add all other ingredients. Cover and reduce heat. Cook about 45 minutes more. Either remove grease or add a little cornstarch to absorb it.

Cincinnati Enquirer
from cookoff: David B. Swope
Redondo Bch, CA

Triangle Cattle Co
Orlando, FL

ELECTRONIC CHILI

1 Lb. ground beef
1 Med. onion, chopped
1 green or red pepper, chopped
2 cloves garlic, crushed
½ t. salt
¼ t. black pepper
1 can (16 oz.) whole tomatoes, drained, chopped
1 can (16 oz.) red kidney beans, undrained
2 T. tomato paste
½ t. cumin powder
¼ C. green chile peppers, seeded, chopped
2 T. chili powder

In a microwave-safe casserole, crumble the beef as much as possible. Add the vegetables, garlic, salt and pepper; mixing well to blend the spices with the meat.

Cover with microwave lid, or heavy duty wax paper, and cook at the Medium-High setting for about 8 minutes. It is important that you stir the mixture every few minutes during the cooking time and give the dish a half turn to insure even cooking of ingredients.

Stir in the tomatoes, chiles, tomato paste, chili powder, and cumin, stirring well to blend with the meat and vegetables.

Recover casserole, continue cooking on Medium-High for 8 to 10 minutes, again stirring and giving the dish a half turn every few minutes.

Let casserole stand for several minutes after removing from the microwave, covered, prior to serving. Makes about 4 to 5 servings.

Elyce Remick
Dublin, OH

Mildred Major
Beaumont, TX

CHILI SAUCE DIP

1 bottle (12 oz.) chili sauce
1 T. lemon juice
¼ C. celery, finely chopped
¼ C. onion, finely chopped
1 T. fresh parsley, minced
1 small clove garlic, crushed
1 T. horseradish
4 drops Tabasco sauce
¼ t. oregano

In a mixing bowl, combine all ingredients, and transfer to salad dish. This can be served with celery, zucchini, carrot sticks, or with cauliflower and broccoli sections.

Woman's Day

H.O. Partin, 1918
Brevard County, FL

CHILI BARBECUE SAUCE

3 T. olive oil
¼ C. vinegar
½ C. water
½ C. chili sauce
1½ T. dry mustard
½ T. chili powder
¼ t. oregano
3 T. onion, finely chopped
¼ t. fresh ground black pepper

In a sauce pan, combine all the ingredients, and simmer for about 20 minutes to blend. Cook until ready to use, and apply to any types of meat that is to be grilled.

Also a good sauce to spread over prepared dishes at the table. Makes about 2 cups of sauce.

Jeff Boyd
Cocoa Beach, FL

B.S. Parker, 1882
Brevard County, FL

CHICAGO LOOP CHILI

1 Lb. lean ground beef
1 Med. onion, chopped
1 green pepper, chopped
2 cloves garlic, minced
2 T. olive oil
2 t. salt
1 can (16 oz.) tomato paste
½ t. ground black pepper
1 can (16 oz.) seasoned stewed tomatoes
dash (only) cayenne pepper
1 t. Tabasco sauce
2 cans (15 oz.) red or dark kidney beans, drained, reserve 1 cup of liquid
¼ t. paprika
1 can (12 oz.) whole kernel corn, drained
2 t. chili powder
1 t. sugar

In a large skillet, cook the onion, green pepper and garlic until the onion become transparent, but not browned. Add the ground beef, salt, pepper, paprika and chili powder. Mix well, breaking and crumbling the beef with a wooden spoon during the browning. Cook the meat until it is brown and the pinkness has been cooked out.

Stir in the reserved liquid from the beans, tomatoes, tomato paste, sugar and Tabasco sauce. Cover, and simmer for about 30 minutes, stirring frequently.

Add the kidney beans, and remaining ingredients, including the kernel corn. Cover, and simmer for an additional 20 minutes, stirring occasionally. Makes 6 to 8 servings.

Bernie & Gail Geltner
Boynton Beach, FL

Mark & Eddie Bundy
St. George, UT

QUICK CHILI

1 Lb. ground beef
1 T. all-purpose flour
1 can (15½ oz) chili with beans
½ C. chili sauce
1 C. evaporated milk
½ C. fine chopped onions
1 T. margarine

In a heated skillet using the margarine, brown the beef, stirring with a spoon to break it into smaller chunks. Add the chili and beans with the onions. Saute until the onion is softened but not browned.

In a mixing bowl, blend the chili sauce, flour and milk. Add the mix to the meat mixture, stirring constantly, until the chili thickens and becomes smooth. Makes about 4-5 servings.

Woman's Day

Willow Ranch at Indian Ford
Sisters, OR

BORDER CHILI

3 Lbs. round steak, cut into ¾-inch cubes
2 T. cooking oil
6 T. chili powder
1 T. ground oregano
1 T. salt
½ t. black pepper
½ to 1 t. cayenne pepper
1 t. Tabasco sauce
1½ C. corn meal
1½ Qts. water

In a large heavy skillet or Dutch oven, brown the cubed steak meat in the oil, so that all sides are done. Add the water and all of the ingredients except the corn meal. Cover, and bring the mixture to a boil; reduce the heat, and simmer for 1½ hours.

Skim off the excess fat and discard. Stir in the corn meal. Continue to cook, uncovered, for 30 to 45 minutes, stirring occasionally.

Chili can be served with beans, chopped onions, or shredded cheese sprinkled; on top of individual serving bowls.

David & Sharon North
Merritt Island, FL

Bryce Mountain Ranch
Blythe, CA

RIVERBEND CHILI

2 Lbs. lean ground beef
2 Lg. onions, finely chopped
3 cloves garlic, minced
2 T. salad oil
1 green pepper, chopped
1 can (4 oz.) green chiles, chopped
1 t. salt
¼ t. black pepper
1 T. chili powder
1 T. ground cumin
1 t. oregano
¼ t. cinnamon
dash of hot sauce
2 C. beef broth
1 can (15 oz.) stewed tomatoes, chopped up

In a Dutch oven, slowly brown the beef, breading up with a spoon as it browns. Push the meat to the sides of the pot as it browns. Add the salad oil, as well as the chopped onions, peppers and garlic.

After a few minutes of simmering, add the remaining ingredients except the beans. Cover, and simmer for about 1½ hours.

Skim off excess fat. Add the beans, stirring in well, and cook at simmer for about 20 minutes, before serving hot.

Bert Dryfoose
Cincinnati, OH

O.C. Robertson, 1880
McLennan County, TX

NEW ENGLAND CHILI

1½ Lbs. ground beef
1 Lb. ground pork shoulder
1 Lg. onion, chopped
3 T. vegetable oil
1 green pepper, chopped
2 stalks celery, chopped
2 cloves garlic, chopped
¼ t. paprika
2 cans (8 oz.) tomato sauce
3 C. water
4 T. chili powder
1 t. salt
¼ t. white pepper
2 t. cumin powder
1 T. oregano
¼ t. cayenne pepper

In a Dutch oven, brown the meats using the vegetable oil. Add the onion, green pepper, celery and the garlic to the meats, and cook until the vegetables are tender.

Add the rest of the ingredients, cover, and simmer on a low heat for about 2 hours or until you feel the chili is what you're after. Stir the mixture occasionally while cooking, and check and adjust seasonings if desired. Serves 6 to 8.

Jordyn Fischer
Cincinnati, OH

Lykes Bros., Inc.
Tampa, FL

KENDALL CHILI

3 Lbs. lean ground beef
2 Lg. onions, chopped
2 Lg. green peppers, chopped
2 stalks celery chopped
2 carrots, chopped
3 cloves garlic, minced
1 can (10 oz.) tomato juice
¼ t. cumin
1 can (16 oz.) red kidney beans
½ t. parsley flakes
½ t. saffron
¼ t. rosemary
1 t. chili powder
¼ t. Tabasco sauce
¼ t.black pepper
1 t. salt
1 can (16 oz.) whole tomatoes, chopped up

Saute the beef in a Dutch oven or large skillet, crumbling it as it cooks. Add the chopped onions, green peppers, carrots and garlic. Saute the mixture until the vegetables are tender. Cover and simmer for one hour.

Add the remaining ingredients and cook on simmer, for another 3 hours. Add additional water if the chili is too thick.

Marla Geltner
Miami, FL

Gordon Ferguson
Roseburg, OR

CHILI BEAN RICE CASSEROLE

1 Lb. dried red kidney or pinto beans
1 t. chili powder
½ t. sugar
Med. onion, chopped
1 t. salt
1 green pepper, chopped
¼ t. black pepper
6 T. cooking oil
2 cans (16 oz.) tomatoes
4 C. cooked rice
2 T. Worcestershire sauce
⅓ C. parsley, chopped
¼ t. oregano

Sort and wash beans, and soak overnight, covered with 2 inches of water. Rinse and simmer slowly until tender and skins have opened.

Saute the onion and pepper until tender. Combine beans with rest of ingredients in a mixing bowl and blend together.

Pour mixture into a 4-quart baking dish and bake for 30 minutes at 350 degrees. Makes 12 to 14 servings.

Jean Bush
Merritt Island, FL

Ridge-Vue Stock Farm
Sardis, TN

COLORADO, EL CHILI

3 Lbs. chuck beef, cut into ½ to ¾-inch pieces
1 Lb. fresh ham steak, trimmed and cut as above
4 T. olive oil
1 t. cayenne pepper
1 Qt. water
2½ T. paprika
2 onions, chopped
1 T. sugar
2 green peppers, chopped
3 T. Masa flour
7 T. chili powder
5 to 6 T. cornmeal
1 bay leaf
¼ t. chopped cilantro
2 t. salt
¼ t. pepper, freshly ground
8 cloves garlic, chopped fine
1 t. ground cumin

Saute the onions, peppers, and garlic in the olive oil until the onion is transparent. Add the cubed meats, and cook, stirring occasionally until they are no longer pink.

In a mixing bowl, add water Masa flour and the cornmeal and mix until it is smooth and pasty. Mix this well and fast into the meat mixture to prevent the lumping that occurs when the Masa flour is added.

Simmer, covered, for 45 minutes, with an occasional stirring. Add the remaining ingredients, mixing them well into the pot to blend. Uncovered, let the chili cook at the low simmer heat for 1 to 1½ hours, stirring occasionally. Discard the bay leaf before serving.

Dennis & Colleen Wilhoite
Cincinnati,OH

Cynthia D. Wilkinson
Prescott, AZ

DIAL 911 CHILI

3 Lbs. chuck beef, cut
1 can (7 oz.) diced green chiles
¾-inch pieces
6 T. chili powder
2 Lg. onions, chopped
2 T. Tabasco sauce
1 green pepper, chopped
1½ t. cayenne pepper
3 cloves garlic, minced

8 jalapeno peppers, chopped
1 can (6 oz.) tomato paste
½ C. white vinegar
1 can (8 oz.) tomato sauce
½ t. oregano
1 can (16 oz.) whole
¼ t. crushed red pepper flakes
tomatoes, chopped
1 Qt. water

In a Dutch oven, brown the beef with the onions, peppers and garlic, over a medium heat until the beef is no longer pink and the vegetables are tender.

Add the remaining ingredients; stir to mix and blend well. Bring the pot to a boil. Reduce the heat to simmer, and let the mixture settle into an hour and a half of pure mellowing. Only disturb the bubbling with an occasional stirring.

After the cooking is over, skim off the excess fat before serving. Makes 7 to 9 servings.

For "added" flavoring, have extra bowls of chopped onions, maybe some shredded cheese, a Tabasco bottle, and an assortment of chips to pass around at the table.

T. O. Lowenstein
San Francisco, CA

Guy Purinton
Tipton, CA

RIVERBOAT CHILI

3 Lbs. lean beef, grounded
or chopped
4 T. olive oil
1 Lg. onion, chopped
1 green pepper, chopped
2 stalks celery, chopped
4 to 6 cloves garlic, minced
2 C. water
2 t. fresh oregano
1 bay leaf

1 t. ground cumi
¼ t. allspice
½ t. ground cinnamon
1 C. red chile pulp
6 T. chili powder, more or less
to taste
1 t. salt
½ t. black pepper
¼ t. cayenne pepper
1 T. sugar
6 Oz. cold beer

Using a 6-quart Dutch oven or other large pot, sear the meat in the olive oil, stirring to crumble as it cooks. Cook until the pink has disappeared, and the meat is grayish-brown. Do not brown completely. Add water and mix well with the meat.

Add the onions, green pepper, celery and garlic at this time to the meat mixture and bring to a boil. Reduce the heat to a simmer, and add all remaining ingredients, and let simmer, stirring occasionally, for 1 to 1½ hours.

Skim off fat from the surface of the chili as it simmers, and discard the bay leaf.

Adjust the seasoning if needed, cover, land allow chili to simmer on a low heat for at least an additional 30 minutes. Skim off any more fat that may have accumulated on surface.

T. O. Lowenstein
San Francisco, CA

ADA

Mrs. A.J. Boggess, 1880
10 miles W. of Waco
McLennan County, TX

FROZEN CHILI

- 1 Pkg. basic beef mix, defrosted
- 1 can (16 oz.) tomato sauce
- 1 can (16 oz.) kidney beans, drained
- 1 can (6 oz.) tomato paste
- 1½ to 2 t. chili powder
- ¼ t. dry mustard
- ¼ t. crushed red pepper
- Dash of cayenne pepper (optional)

In a 2-quart casserole, combine all the ingredients. Mix to blend, cover, and microwave at High for 6 to 10 minutes, or until the contents are hot and bubbly. Stir often and rotate the casserole ½ turn every few minutes to evenly cook.

Serve with chopped onions, or shredded cheese, or both if desired, sprinkled over serving bowls. Microwaving time: 6 to 10 minutes. Serves 4 to 6.

Fred Tracy
Deer Park, OH

G.S. Bell, 1886
Brevard County, FL

SCOTT'S HAMMER HEAD CHILI

3 Lbs. lean beef, chili ground
½ t. Tabasco sauce
2 green bell peppers, chopped
2 T. cumin powder
2 Lg. onions, chopped
½ t. paprika
1 Lg. carrot, shredded
1 T. celery seed
3 cloves garlic, minced
1 can (16 oz.) dark kidney beans, drained
1 can (16 oz.) tomatoes, chopped, undrained
1 can (16 oz.) pinto beans, drained
1 can (6 oz.) tomato paste
1 can (8 oz.) tomato sauce
½ t. allspice
2 jalapeno peppers, seeded, and chopped fine
½ t. coriander
¼ t. crushed thyme
¼ C. olive oil
¼ t. sage leaves, crushed
1 t. oregano
1½ t. salt
5 T. chili powder
½ t. fresh ground pepper

In a Dutch oven, saute the onion, peppers, celery and the garlic, until the onion is golden, but not brown. Remove the vegetables from the pot and set aside.

Brown the beef crumbling with a fork, or better, a wooden spoon, to break up beef lumps smaller. After the meat has been cooked, return the vegetables to the Dutch oven, and add the remaining ingredients except the beans and shredded carrots.

Cover, and simmer for two to three hours, stirring occasionally to prevent sticking to bottom of pot. Add additional water to mixture to obtain your desired consistency. Add the beans, and allow chili to further simmer for a few minutes to heat them. Serves 6 to 8 with a little left over for seconds.

NOTE: Reserve some of the chopped onions to sprinkle onto the chili if desired. Also, sprinkle the shredded carrots over the chili for a little color, and a different eating texture.

Scott Geltner
Cincinnati, OH

M

Paul McCormick
Florida, 1825

CHILI POT PIE

1½ Lbs. lean ground beef
1 t. salt
1 onion, chopped
¼ t. ground black pepper
1 clove garlic, minced
Few drops Tabasco hot sauce
1 green pepper, cut in strips
1 T. chili powder
3 T. olive oil
1 t. Worcestershire sauce
1 can (16 oz.) red kidney beans, drained
Sliced, pitted black olives
Shredded Cheddar cheese
1 can (16 oz.) whole tomatoes, undrained
corn meal biscuit mix topping
1 can (10 oz.) whole kernel corn, drained

Combine the beef, salt, pepper and Worcestershire sauce in a bowl and mix well. Shape into 12 balls. Cook the onion, green pepper and garlic in little olive oil, and saute until the onion is tender, and the beef is browned and done. Remove and set aside.

Mix the chili powder in the used oil, adding the kernel corn, kidney beans, tomatoes, and black olives, in a saucepan, and simmer for 5 to 10 minutes. Stir in the onion, green pepper, garlic mixture in a 2-quart casserole; pour over the meat balls.

Prepare the corn meal biscuit topping, and arrange on top of the meatballs. Bake at 425 degrees for 20 to 25 minutes, or until biscuits are done. Makes 6 to 8 servings.

Ms. Heide G. Bowman
Merritt Island, FL

William P. Barnes
Mililani, HA

AVOCADO CHILI DIP

2 Lg. ripe California avocado, or 1 standard Florida avocado
1 t. mashed garlic
1 Lg. fresh tomato, chopped fine
1 Med. onion, chopped fine
1 T. fresh lime juice
¼ C. cilantro leaves, chopped
1 fresh jalapeno pepper, seeded and chopped fine
½ t. salt
¼ t. cayenne pepper
Dash or two Tabasco Hot Sauce

Peel avocado(s) and mash in a large bowl. Add ingredients, and mix lightly with the avocado but thoroughly.

Taste and change flavor of dip if desired, and serve immediately with corn or taco chips. Makes 2½ to 3 cups of dip.

NOTE: To keep the dip from browning before being served, keep the pit (s) in the mixture.

Andy & Lynn Fogel
Cincinnati, OH

Alfred Wakefield
Lewisburg, TN

CHILI CORNED BEEF

8 slices bacon, diced
1 t. salt
2 onions, sliced
¼ t. black ground pepper
2 green peppers, chopped
1 T. brown sugar
4 cans (16 oz.) kidney beans, drained

¼ t. Worcestershire sauce
Dash Tabasco sauce
2 cans (8 oz.) tomato sauce
2 Pkgs. (8 oz.) sharp Cheddar cheese, grated
2 cans (12 oz.) corned beef, cut in cubes
English muffins
4 T. chili powder

Fry the bacon until it is crisp; drain on paper towels, and set aside. Drain off all but two tablespoons of the bacon grease, and saute the onions and green peppers until the onions are soft but not browned.

Add the kidney beans, tomato sauce, chili powder,Worcestershire sauce, Tabasco, salt, pepper and the brown sugar; stirring well to mix the ingredients thoroughly. Add the cheese and cook, stirring over a low heat until the cheese melts.

Add the corned beef cubes. Heat and serve on toasted English muffins topped with the bacon bits.

Al & Linda Merkel
Merritt Island, FL

George & Denise Biely
West Union, OH

MY CHILI

3½ Lbs. lean beef, cut into small pieces
2 Med.-size onions, chopped
3 cloves garlic, minced
Vegetable oil
6 T. chili powder
2 T. paprika

2 C. water
1 T. cumin
1 can (16 oz.) tomatoes, whole, drained, chopped
1 can (6 oz.) tomato paste
1 can (15 oz.) kidney beans
Salt and pepper to taste

Saute the onions and garlic in a skillet using a little of the vegetable oil, until they are transparent. Add the meat to the onion and garlic mixture, and cook until the meat has a grayish color.

Add the remaining ingredients to the meat mixture except the beans. Stir to fully mix chili. Add sufficient water to cover all ingredients; cover, and simmer for about 1 to 1½ hours, stirring occasionally.

Add the kidney beans when there's about 30 minutes left in the cooking time, and the chili can be checked to any adjusting with the spices at this time.

Skim off fat that has been cooked to the surface of the chili, as some people can't really enjoy a good tasting bowl of chili that has a sea of grease on it. Besides, it a lot healthier not consuming too much fat.

Easy garnish for this chili, extra chopped onions, shredded cheese, and corn and other chips that you have around.

Woman's Day

Kauai Invest.Inc.
Prescott, AZ

FARMER'S TURKEY CHILI

4 Lbs. ground turkey
4 T. vegetable oil
4 Med. onions, chopped
3 green bell peppers, chopped
4 fresh tomatoes, diced
2 cloves garlic, chopped
3 T. chili powder
1 T. oregano
½ T. ground cumin
¼ t. paprika
½ t. salt
¼ t. pepper
1 can (16 oz.) tomato juice
1 can (6 oz.) tomato paste
2 cans (16 oz.) whole tomatoes, cut up, reserve all liquid

Saute the onions, peppers, garlic and diced tomatoes, in a small amount of the oil using a Dutch oven. Saute until the ingredients are done and the onions are transparent. Remove and set aside.

Brown the turkey in the same oil, till the pinkish color has been cooked away. Add the vegetables to the meat; cover, and bring to a boil. Reduce the heat, add remaining ingredients to the pot, except the cut up whole tomatoes.

Cook on simmer for 2½ to 3 hours. During the last 30 minutes of the cooking time, add the cut up tomatoes. If the mixture is too thin, add a little of the reserved liquid from the tomatoes.

Woman's Day

Greg & Patricia Brown
Cottage Grove, OR

WAYCROSS CHILI

1½ Lbs. coarsely ground beef
3 to 4 cloves garlic, minced
3 T. ground cumin
1 T. garlic powder
2 cans (16 oz.) whole tomatoes, chopped, undrained
1 Qt. water
2 Med. onions, chopped
1 Lb. coarsely ground beef suet
4 T. cornmeal
2 T. flour
¼ t. oregano
1 T. chili powder
Salt and pepper to taste

Saute beef and garlic until the meat is thoroughly cooked, about 20 to 30 minutes on medium heat. Add cumin and chili powder with the remaining ingredients except the flour and the cornmeal.

Make a paste of the flour with a little water, and add to the chili mixture, as a thickening agent if desired. Cornmeal can be added if desired, and simmer, covered for 2 to 2½ hours.

NOTE: When substituting turkey for beef, use more water, and add salad oil in place of the suet.

Edward Chnapko
"The Tomato Man"
Cocoa Beach, FL

Joe & Jan Power
Cookeville, TN

CHILI RICE

1 Lb. ground beef
1 Med. onion, chopped
1 green pepper, chopped
2 cloves garlic, chopped
1 can (16 oz.) whole tomatoes, chopped up
1 can (15 oz.) kidney beans, drained
1 C. instant rice
1½ t. salt
¼ t. black pepper
1 t. sugar
1 T. chili powder
½ t. cumin
½ t. oregano
1 C. shredded Cheddar cheese

Crumble beef in a 2-quart casserole. Add onion, pepper and garlic; cover, and microwave at High for 4 to 6 minutes, stirring once during the cooking time. Add additional cooking time at High if the beef is not completely cooked and has lost it's pink color. Stir to break up beef occasionally during cooking.

Add the remaining ingredients except the cheese. Cover, and microwave for 16 to 20 minutes on Medium (50% power), or until the rice is tender, stirring after half of the time to further crumble the meat.

Sprinkle cheese over mixture in casserole, and let stand for 5 minutes prior to serving, so that the cheese is slightly melted. Serves 4 to 5.

Prep time: Microwave 20-26 minutes/standing time 5 minutes.

Woman's Day

Don Bartolome Tapia
California (1804)

CHICKEN CHILI BUNS

- 8 chicken thighs and drumsticks
- 1 can (16 oz.) red kidney beans, drained
- ¼ C. vegetable oil
- ½ t. salt
- 1 can (16 oz.) whole tomatoes, cut up
- 1 small onion, chopped
- ¼ t. fresh ground pepper
- 1 can (8 oz.) tomato sauce
- 2 t. chili powder
- 1 can (6 oz.) tomato paste
- 1 small clove garlic, minced
- 8 split hamburger buns, toasted

Brown the chicken parts well in the hot oil over a hot heat. Sprinkle parts with salt. Set chicken aside after it has browned.

Saute the onion, and garlic in the skillet until they are tender. Drain pan of oil. Add beans, tomatoes, tomato sauce, tomato paste to the skillet. Add chili powder and pepper.

While the pan is simmering on a low heat, strip off as much of the chicken meat from the bones and cut up into medium-sized pieces.

Cook the mixture until it thickens, about 5 to 10 minutes. Replace the chicken meat to the skillet, reduce the heat and simmer for about 5 minutes longer until the chicken pieces are tender.

Serve on the toasted buns. Garnish with reserved chopped onions, or other accompaniments which you have available.

Albertine Eschbach
W. Germany

Running H
William Haynie
Groveland, FL

QUICK CHILI with CORN CAKES

½ C. yellow corn meal
½ C. sifted all-purpose flour
2 t. sugar
1 small egg
3 T. soft shortening
¼ t. salt
2 t. baking powder
½ C. milk
2 cans (16 oz.) chili con carne

Mix and sift dry ingredients. Add the egg, milk and two tablespoons of the shortening. With a rotary blender, beat until well mixed.

Melt the remaining shortening in a skillet. Make the corn cakes by using ¼ cup batter for each cake, fry in the hot skillet, two at a time. When cakes are browned on both sides, remove and set aside.

Add the chili con carne to the same skillet, and heat to serving temperature, stirring often to prevent sticking or burning. Just before serving, place the corn cakes on top; cover and heat them thoroughly. Serve the chili over the cakes. Makes 6 servings.

Johanna Moretti
Cocoa Beach, FL

John Yates, 1886
Brevard County, FL

CHILI CHEESE DIP

1 Pkg. (16 oz.) process cheese loaf, cut into 1-inch cubes
1 can (16 oz.) hot chili with, or without beans
1 can (4 oz.) green chiles, chopped

Place all ingredients into a 1-quart casserole dish. Microwave at Medium (50% power) for 12 to 15 minutes, or until the cheese has melted, stirring every 4 to 5 minutes.

Garnish with shredded lettuce, chopped onions, chopped tomatoes, or black sliced olives, if desired.

NOTE: Other spices such as paprika, garlic powder, chili powder, oregano and the like can be added to give different flavors from time to time. It is a good party dip for when guest are over.

Fred Tracy
Deer Park, OH

J.E. Thibedeaux
China, TX

TEXAS CHILI CORNBREAD CASSEROLE

½ Lb. ground beef
½ Lb. ground sausage
1 Med. onion, chopped
1 Med. green pepper, chopped
1 T. brown sugar
2 t. white vinegar
1 can (10¾ oz.) condensed tomato soup
1 t. Worcestershire sauce
1 Pkg. (8½ oz.) cornbread mix
¼ t. salt
¼ t. garlic powder
⅛ t. paprika
⅛ t. fresh ground black pepper
Dash of cayenne pepper
¼ t. oregano

In a 8x8-inch microwave baking dish, combine the beef, sausage, onion and green pepper. Cover with wax paper, and microwave at High for 3 to 5 minutes, or until the meat is no longer pink, stirring to break up and crumble meat after half of the cooking time. Stir to mix; drain off accumulated drippings.

Mix in the remaining ingredients except the cornbread mix and paprika. Microwave at High for 3 to 4 minutes, or unit bubbly. Stir to blend ingredients. While microwaving, prepare the cornbread as directed on package.

Spread the cornbread over the hot meat mixture. Sprinkle evenly with the paprika. Microwaye at High for 6 to 7 minutes, or until the cornbread is set, rotating the dish ½ turn after half the cooking time.

Let the dish stand for 2 to 3 minutes before serving. Serves 4 to 5. Microwaving time: 12 to 16 minutes.

Johanna Moretti
Cocoa Beach, FL

Diamond X
Manuel Peterson, 1926
Brevard County, FL

CHILI BURGERS

1 Lb. ground lean beef
¼ t. oregano
2 stalks celery, chopped
1 t. sugar
1 green pepper, chopped
⅛ t. black pepper
1 Med. onion, chopped
⅛ t. cayenne pepper
1 can (10¾ oz.) condensed tomato soup
⅛ t. garlic powder
1 T. cornstarch
5 T. catsup
1 T. brown sugar
1 can (15 oz.) kidney beans, drained
1 t. chili powder
¼ t. Worcestershire sauce
½ t. dry mustard

In a two-quart casserole, combine the ground beef, onion, celery, green pepper; cover and microwave at High for 5 to 6 minutes, or until the meat is no longer pink, stirring after half the cooking time to break up and crumble the meat. Drain off excess fat from casserole.

Stir in the remaining ingredients. Cover, and microwave at High for 5 minutes. Stir; reduce heat to Medium (50% power), rotate casserole ½ turn, and microwave 7 to 10 minutes or until the dish is fully cooked and the flavor have melded.

Serve on toasted hamburger buns. Microwave time: 17 to 21 minutes. Serves 4 to 6.

Woman's Day

John McLaughlin, 1884
Brevard County, FL

ALA MICROWAVE CHILI

2 Lbs. lean ground beef
1 Lg. onion, chopped
1 green pepper, chopped
2 cloves garlic, minced
1 can (16 oz.) whole tomatoes, chopped
2 cans (8 oz.) tomato sauce, or
1 can (8 oz.) tomato sauce and
1 C. beef broth
2 T. chili powder
2 t. cumin seed
1 T. brown sugar
¼ t. Tabasco sauce
¼ t. cayenne pepper
1 t. dried oregano

In a 2-quart casserole, combine the beef, onion, green pepper and garlic. Cover, and microwave at High for 10 minutes, or until the meat has lost it's pinkness, stirring once or twice during cooking.

Add the remaining ingredients, mixing thoroughly. Cover the casserole and microwave at High for 15 minutes, or until the mixture comes to a boil, again stirring the contents every few minutes for an even cook, and giving the dish a ½ turn at the same time.

Reduce microwave temperature to low or defrost, and cook for about one hour, stirring often and giving ½ turn to casserole.

After cooking, allow the casserole to stand a few minutes before serving.

Woman's Day

Darren D. Padget
Grass Valley, OR

SMITH'S PERFECT CHILI

4 Lbs. trimmed sirloin or tenderloin tips, coarsely ground
5 T. olive oil
1 or 2 cans (6 oz.) tomato paste
1 Qt. water
4 Med. onions, chopped
2 bell green peppers, chopped
6 cloves garlic, finely chopped
1 T. oregano
¼ t. basil
1 T. cumin seed, crushed
4 or 5 T. chili powder, to taste
½ t. cayenne pepper, (optional)
2 cans (15 oz.) pinto beans

In a Dutch oven, cook the meat with the onions, peppers and garlic in the oil until the pink color has been cooked from the meat. While cooking, use a wooden spoon to break up and crumble the meat to a more suitable eating size. Drain off all excess fat before proceeding further.

Add the tomato paste and water, stirring to mix. Then add the remaining ingredients except the pinto beans. Cover, and simmer for 2 to 3 hours, stirring occasionally, and checking for taste.

Correct the seasonings if desired. Add the pinto beans during the last 10 or 15 minutes left of the cooking time.

Shannon Combs
Cincinnati, OH

Tommy Perry
Moore Haven, FL

CINCINNATI CHILI

- ½ Lb. lean ground beef
- 1 can (8 oz.) tomato sauce
- 1 can (14½ oz.) whole tomatoes, chopped
- 1 small onion, chopped
- ½ t. cinnamo
- ½ t. allspice
- 1 T. white vinegar
- 1 T. chili powder
- 1 clove garlic, minced
- 3 bay leafs
- ½ cube unsweetened chocolate

In a skillet, or large pot, brown the meat and onion. Drain pan of excess drippings. Place meat in a large crock or Dutch oven.

Add the remaining ingredients to the meat mixture. Cook slowly, on low heat for 4 to 5 hours, covered, stirring occasionally to avoid sticking of meat to the pot.

Remove the bay leafs and discard before serving. Serve on a bed of spaghetti, and top with onions, cheese or kidney beans. Serves 6 to 8.

Cincinnati Enquirer

LaGrande Livestock
Exchange, Inc
LaGrange, OR

CINCINNATI CHILI BY NUMBERS

1 Way or just chili
2 Way with spaghetti added
3 Way with cheese added to above
4 Way with chopped onions added to above
5 Way with red kidney beans added to above

Cincinnati Enquirer

Frank L. Calhoun
Buckeye, Az

CHILI PARLOR CHILI

4 Lbs. lean beef, cut into ¾-inch cubes
¼ C. vegetable oil
1 Lg. onion, minced
1 green pepper, chopped fine
3 cloves garlic, crushed
1 can (15 oz.) tomato sauce
1 can (12 oz.) beer
5 T. chili powder
1 T. cumin seed
2 T. oregano
1 t. salt
¼ t. pepper
¼ t. cayenne pepper
1 t. paprika
1 t. brown sugar
2 T. Masa flour, or,
1 T. flour mixed with 1 T. corn meal
Shredded Monterey Jack, or, Cheddar cheese (optional)

In a large Dutch oven, cook meat in some of the oil, stirring with a wooden spoon to break up beef as it cooks. Let it get just grayish in color, but not brown. Drain off oil and drippings from meat, before adding the onions, green pepper, and garlic.

Cover, and simmer for 10 minutes. Add the tomato sauce and beer. Bring to a boil; reduce to simmer.

In a small bowl, mix the chili powder, cumin, oregano, salt, pepper, cayenne pepper, paprika and sugar. Add this spice mixture to the kettle, stirring thoroughly into the meat.

Cover, and on a low heat, let the chili just bubble gently for an hour or so, stirring occasionally.

If necessary to thicken mixture, just before serving, mix the Masa flour, or flour and cornmeal with enough water to make a thick paste. Stir this mixture rapidly into the chili a little at a time, to prevent lumping. Add enough to reach the consistency wanted.

Sprinkle chopped onions, and, or shredded cheese over each serving bowl.

Andy & Lynn Fogel
Cincinnati, OH

Geo. C. Burrell
Beaumont,
Jefferson County, TX

RED RIVER CHILI

3 Lbs. beef round, or chuck cut into ½-inch cubes
1 Lg. onion, chopped fine
1 bell pepper, chopped fine
2 cloves garlic, minced
¼ C. vegetable oil
1 t. salt
1 C. beef broth
¼ t. freshly ground pepper
1 can beer
1 can (4 oz.) diced green chiles, drained
1 t. celery seed, crushed
1 t. cumin seed, crushed
1½ to 2 T. chili 1 (35 oz.) plum tomatoes with liquid
2 cans (16 oz.) red kidney beans, drained

In a large skillet or Dutch oven, brown the beef, doing only part at a time so that all will be cooked evenly. Remove the beef when it has finished browning, and set aside. Drain off the beef fat from the Dutch oven.

Saute the onion, green pepper and the garlic until the onion is tender but not browned. Again, drain off any excess drippings. Return the browned beef to the kettle; add the tomatoes with it's liquid, beef broth, beer, chiles, celery seed, cumin seed, chili powder, salt and pepper. Mix thoroughly with the meat mixture.

Bring the pot to a boil; reduce the heat, and simmer, stirring occasionally, for 2½ hours, or more until meat is tender and the flavor is what you want.

Add the kidney beans, and simmer for about 15 minutes longer. Makes about 12 servings.

Jay & Sandy Hatfield
Cincinnati, OH

Carl Twisselman
McKittrick, CA

CHILI CON CARNE

1 Lb. ground beef chuck
1 Lg. onion, chopped
2 stalks celery, chopped
1 green bell pepper, chopped
1 can (16 oz.) whole tomatoes, with liquid, chopped
1 can (16 oz.) tomato paste
2 cans (16 oz.) Mexican-style chili beans, or red kidney beans
1 C. hot water
1 C. beer
2 to 3 T. chili powder
1 t. salt
2 t. sugar
1 t. garlic powder
¼ t. ground cinnamon
Shredded Monterey Jack or Cheddar cheeses, grated, (optional)

In a 3-quart skillet or saucepan, brown the beef, onion, celery and green pepper, stirring to crumble beef as it cooks. Drain pan drippings.

Stir in other ingredients except the beans, cheeses and some reserved onion, and simmer for 1½ hours, stirring occasionally.

Serve topped with reserved chopped onions, and shredded cheeses, if desired. Provides chili enough for 4 to 5 hearty servings.

Jay & Sandy Hatfield
Cincinnati, OH

Dewey H. Lane
Pascagoula, MS

CHILE CON QUESO

- 1 Lg. onion, chopped
- 1 clove garlic, minced
- 1 can (10 oz.) tomatoes and green chiles
- 1 canned jalapeno pepper, seeded, and chopped (optional)
- 1 T. all-purpose flour
- 1 T. vegetable oil
- 1 T. chili powder
- ¼ t. oregano
- 1 Lb. process cheese spread, cut into ½-inch cubes
- ¼ t. onion salt

Saute onion and garlic in the vegetable oil using a saucepan; cook over a low heat for one (1) minute, stirring constantly. Add the tomatoes and green chiles; again cooking over a low heat, and again, stirring constantly, until the mixture thickens and is bubbly. Add the remaining ingredients, stirring well to blend.

Add the cheese, if desired; cooking over a low heat, stirring frequently, until the cheese is melted.

This is an ideal dish to have at a party or get together using a fondue dish, with either tacos, corn chips or tortilla chips as mode of "transportation".

Joe & Joanne Kucklick
Merritt Island, FL

William M. Carpenter
Marana, AZ

GOOD CHILI

2 Lbs. lean chuck, coarsely ground
¼ Lb. beef suet
1 Med. onion, chopped
1 green pepper, chopped
1 T. chili powder
1 T. flour
1 t. powdered cumin
¼ t. cayenne pepper
1 t. salt
¼ t. pepper

In a large skillet, melt down the suet, and discard. Add onions and brown. Add the ground chuck and green peppers, stirring to crumble the beef until it has turned gray but not brown. Drain off excess drippings and cooking remains of suet.

In a small mixing bowl, add rest of ingredients, and with a little water, make into a thick paste. Add this paste to the meat, mixing thoroughly. Add enough water gradually;, to cover the meat, and let simmer on a low heat for approximately 45 minutes to 1 hour.

Stir frequently to keep mixture from sticking, using a wooden spoon. If chili is still too greasy, mix a little flour to thicken, or skim off additional grease with a spoon. Taste and correct flavor if desired.

Sandy & Kim McCoy
Cincinnati, OH

F.M. Platt, 1882
Brevard County, FL

COOKED SALSA

1 Lb. ripe tomatoes, or 1 can (28 oz.) Italian-style tomatoes
2 cans (4 oz.) green chiles, chopped
½ t. oregano leaves, crushed
¼ t. cumin
¼ t. chili powder
1 t. salt
1 t. mashed garlic

Chop the tomatoes, and mix with rest of ingredients, except the garlic and oregano. Cook, cover for 3 to 4 minutes. Season with salt the garlic and oregano leaves. Makes 3 to 4 cups.

Laurie A. Seltzer
Cincinnati, OH

George Bend
Nome, TX

CHILI con QUESO

½ C. onion, sliced
2 T. vegetable oil
1 can (4 oz.) green chiles, chopped
1 Lb. Monterey Jack cheese, or Wisconsin White Cheddar,cubed
1 small can evaporated milk, diluted with 1 C. warm water

Saute the onions in the hot oil until transparent, but not browned. Add the chopped chiles, being sure to remove any blackened peel often found in this type of canned pepper. Add diluted canned milk and season with salt and pepper to taste.

Bring the saucepan to a simmer; do not allow mixture to come to a boil.

Place cubed cheese in a serving bowl. Pour the hot chile and milk mixture over the cheese. Allow to set 2 or 3 minutes before ladling into cereal bowls. Serve as a side dish to eat with grilled steak strips, corn tortillas and cold slaw.

AS A DIP: Do not dilute the canned milk. Correct seasonings is desired. Serve in a shafing dish or over a candle warmer. Use tortilla chips.

Emily Routt
Cincinnati, OH

Don Juan Revelle
Eduador (1585)

SPANISH SALSA

1 Med. onion, chopped
1 can (28 oz.) Italian-style tomatoes, crushed
2 T. olive oil
1 C. tomato juice
½ can (6 oz.) tomato paste
1 t. mashed garlic
1 bay leaf

Heat oil in a skillet, and saute the chopped onion for only a few minutes to barely soften. Stir. Add the crushed tomatoes, tomato juice, and the tomato paste to the pan and mix well to blend.

Add the remaining ingredients to skillet, stirring. Cover and simmer for 5 minutes. Remove the bay leaf, and store in a tight sealing jar in the refrigerator. Sauce will keep for at least 2 weeks and will also freeze well. Makes 3 to 4 cups of salsa.

Emily Routt
Cincinnati, OH

Arnold Brothers
Antioch, TN

ROSALYN CARTER'S CHILI

1 Lb. round steak, cut into small pieces
1 small onion, chopped
1 can (4 oz.) green chiles, chopped
1 can (8 oz.) tomato paste
3 T. olive oil
1½ C. water
2 T. chili powder
3 cloves garlic, minced
½ t. cumin powder
½ t. oregano
¼ t. black pepper
1½ t. sugar
1½ t. salt
4½ t. flour

In a heavy skillet, cook the meat in oil until it has turned grayish. Add the remaining ingredients and simmer for about an hour, or until meat is tender. Serves 4 to 6.

Cincinnati Enquirer

Ms. Belle Cason 6/1880
16 miles SE of Waco
McLennan County, TX

HEARTBURN CHILI

4 Lbs. coarsely ground chuck
3 Lg. yellow onions, chopped
1 green bell pepper, chopped
1 red bell pepper, chopped
2 stalks celery, chopped
5 cloves garlic, minced
4 T. oregano
1 t. cayenne pepper
2 T. paprika
3 T. vegetable oil
3 T. cumin powder
2 T. chili powder
3 cans (8 oz.) tomato sauce
1 can (6 oz.) tomato paste
1 can (28 oz.) whole tomatoes, undrained, chopped up
4 or 5 dashes Tabasco sauce
½ t. red crushed pepper
3½ T. Masa or all-purpose flour
Water if necessary

In a large Dutch oven, saute the onions and green peppers, until the onion is softened but not browned. Add the beef and cook until the grayish appearance is reached. Crumble the meat with a spoon as you stir the mixture to break up large chunks.

Add remaining ingredients except the Masa or all-purpose flour. Bring to a boil. Add sufficient water to cover mixture, stirring to mix chili thoroughly. Reduce the heat to simmer and cook, covered, for 2½ to 3 hours, stirring occasionally.

If a thicker chili is desired, mix the flour with a little water into a paste, and add, stirring constantly, to the chili, but not before bringing the pot to a boil. Makes 8 to 10 hearty servings.

Sandy & Kim McCoy
Cincinnati, OH

Don Jose Antonio Chirino
Texas (1806)

BILLIE'S CHILI

8 Lbs. coarsely ground round steak
2 stalks celery, chopped fine
2 green peppers, chopped
2 Med. onions, chopped
2 cans (14½ oz.) tomato sauce
3 cloves garlic, minced
2 cans (14½ oz.) stewed tomatoes, undrained, cut up
3 T. vegetable oil
1 can (16 oz.)tomato paste
½ C. commercial salsa
½ C. chili powder
1½ t. cumin powder
1 t. oregano
1½ t. salt
1 t. ground black pepper
½ t. crushed red pepper
2 bay leaves
¾ t. allspice
shake or two Tabasco sauce

Saute the onions, green peppers, celery and the garlic in a large Dutch oven, using a little of the cooking oil. Cook the vegetables until they are soft and the onions are transparent but not brown.

Remove and set aside when they are done, trying to drain as much of the oil from them back into the kettle with which to do the meat.

In doing this much meat, only cook about two (2) pounds at a time so that you can cook and break up the beef quite a bit into more workable pieces. In the left over oil from the vegetables, cook the meat until the color has turned somewhat gray. Do not brown completely, as it will become overcooked with all the simmering that will be done later on.

As the meat is cooked, drain good using a slotted spoon, and set aside in another container. Cook all the meat as indicated. Once you have prepared the meat enough, pour off all the grease and fat from the cooked meat.

Put the vegetables and meat back into the pot, and put in all the other ingredients, making sure that they are mixed and blended well with each other and the meat. Add just enough water to cover the mixture, so that while it simmers, it will not become too dry and thick.

Cover, and bring the kettle to a boil. Reduce the heat, and let simmer for about 2½ to 3 hours, stirring every so often to keep the mixture from sticking or burning to the bottom of the kettle.

After cooking, remove the bay leaves. Taste the chili, and if you like, play with the flavor and change it if necessary. You may not want to use as much ingredients as called for in this recipe, but it's one heck of a start to a swell bowl of chili.

This makes about 16 to 20 helpings, that has to be set off with some extra bowls of chopped onions, shredded cheese, and an assortment of chips styles that you may like to serve to family and guests.

Laurie A. Seltzer
Cincinnati, OH

J.H. Wilson, 1896
Brevard County, FL

CHILI BEANS

1 Lb. pinto beans
1 T. chili powder
1 clove garlic, minced
1 onion, chopped fine
¤ t. salt
Lg. pinch black pepper
Dash or two hot sauce
¼ t. allspice

Wash and sort beans, cover with extra water, and soak overnight. Drain. Rinse. In kettle, place beans and add chili powder, onions, garlic, pepper and Tabasco sauce. Cover, and simmer for about 2 hours or until beans are tender to taste.

Add remaining ingredients, cover, and simmer for another 30 minutes longer. Makes 8 to 10 servings as a side dish.

Sara Geltner
Miami, FL

Edward Ayres
Fayetteville, TN

GUNSMOKE CHILI

(Festus's-Ken Curtis)

4 Lbs. coarsely ground lean beef or venison
1 Lg. onion, chopped
2 t. MSG
2 T. parsley flakes
1 t. ground black
1½ t. basil leaves, crushed by hand
4 T. chili powder
1 can (28 oz.) beef broth
1 t. cayenne pepper
2 cans (10½ oz.) tomato sauce
1½ t. oregano leaves, crushed
½ t. cumin seed
¼ t. thyme
1 t. salt

Mince the meat, crumbling it good while browning. Add all ingredients, in a large Dutch oven. Mix to blend together well. Cover, and simmer for 2½ to 3 hours. Serves 8 to 10.

Michael C. Giannotta
Cincinnati, OH

T.C. Hager 12/1880
Crawford
McLennan County, TX

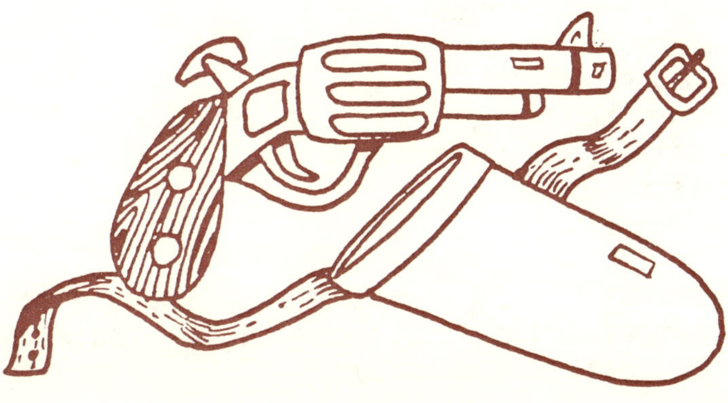

LONG LIST CHILI

1 Lb. filet minnon, cut into ½-inch cubes
1 Lb. flank steak, cut into ½-inch cubes
1 Lb. top sirloin, cut into ½-inch cubes
1 Lg. red onion, chopped
1 Lg. white onion, chopped
6 or so green onions, chopped
2 fresh tomatoes, chopped
2 stalks celery, chopped
3 cloves garlic, minced
2 cans (15 oz.) tomato sauce
1 can (6 oz.) tomato paste
1 can (26 oz.) whole tomatoes, cut up, undrained
2½ t. chili powder
½ t. onion powder
½ t. garlic powder
½ t. cumin seed
½ t. parsley flakes
½ t. tarragon leaves, crushed
½ t. celery seed
¼ t. turmeric
¼ t. herb seasoning
1 t. salt
½ t. black pepper
½ t. thyme
1 t. oregano
½ t. paprika
3 whole cloves
2 bay leaves
½ t. savory leaves, crushed
¼ t. allspice
1 T. prepared mustard
¼ t. crushed basil
few drops of Tabasco hot sauce
1 t. cayenne pepper
3 T. olive oil

In a Dutch oven, heat the olive oil, add and saute the meat pieces; brown only, do not cook completely through; remove and set aside. Do the same with the flank steak and sirloin.

In a heavy saucepan, saute the vegetables and garlic until the onions are transparent. Add the cooked vegetables to the meats in the Dutch oven and simmer for 20 minutes.

Add all of the remaining ingredients, mixing well to completely blend the meat and the spices. Cover, simmer on low heat for 1½ to 2 hours, stirring occasionally to avoid burning and sticking of chili to pot.

Orlando Sentinel

Hawkins
Florida (1858?)

HOTTERN' CHILI

- 2 Lbs. lean chuck, chili ground
- 1 Lb. pork shoulder, cut into bite-size pieces
- 1 Lb. lamb, cut into bite-size pieces
- 3 Med. onions, chopped
- 2 green peppers, chopped
- 3 stalks celery, chopped
- 4 cloves garlic, minced
- 4 T. chili powder
- 1 t. cayenne pepper
- 1 T. dry mustard
- 1 T. paprika
- ¼ t. thyme
- ¼ t. basil, crushed
- 1 t. hot sauce
- 1 can (16 oz.) whole tomatoes, crushed, undrained
- 1 can (12 oz.) beer
- 2 cans (8 oz.) tomato sauce
- 1 can (6 oz.) tomato paste
- 2 cans (4 oz.) green chiles, chopped fine
- 1 T. cumin seed
- 1 t. marjoram

Saute the vegetables in a little oil until the onions are transparent. Set aside. Cook each of the meats separately, starting with the pork as it will take longer to do. Break up the meats as they are cooking, stirring with a wooden spoon. Set aside each as they are done, draining the grease and fat as you transfer them. Discard all of the drippings.

Combine all the meats into a large kettle, add the ingredients reserving the whole-cut-up tomatoes, mixing well. Cover, and bring to a boil. Reduce the heat, and simmer for about 45 to 60 minutes, or longer depending upon the tenderness of the meat desired. Add the tomatoes during the last 20 minutes of simmering. Serves 10 to 12 with enough for seconds.

Ms. Gloria Mejia
Merritt Island, FL

J.B. Murphy
Beaumont, TX

VULTURE'S BREATH CHILI

4 Lbs. flank steak, cut into small pieces
3 Lg. onions, chopped
2 green peppers, chopped
3 cloves garlic, chopped
1 Qt. water
1 can (8 oz.) tomato paste
8 fresh tomatoes, chopped
½ C. chili powder
1 T. crushed red pepper
1 t. oregano
1 t. coriander
2 T. Masa flour
8 chile pods, chopped

In a large skillet, or Dutch oven, cook the meat over a medium heat until it browns. Add the remaining ingredients, except the Masa flour, stirring well to mix and blend spices and ingredients with the meat.

Bring the cooking vessel to a boil; reduce the heat, and simmer, stirring frequently, uncovered for 2 hours, or until it's taste is what you are searching for.

Make a paste of the Masa flour and a little water, making surè that all the lumps have been eliminated, and blend well into the chili mixture. This will thicken your chili if necessary.

Simmer, uncovered for an additional 15 to 25 minutes. Makes 8 to 10 servings.

Scott Geltner
Cincinnati, OH

Jodi & Marti Anderson
Eagle Point, OR

ROMA CHILI

1½ Lbs. ground beef
½ Lb. pepperoni, ground
½ Lb. Italian sausage, ground
2 cloves garlic, chopped fine
2 Med. onions, chopped
1 Med. zucchini, chopped
1 green pepper, chopped
1 stalk celery, chopped
1 Lg. eggplant, peeled and cubed
1 can (16 oz.) whole tomatoes, chopped
1 can (15 oz.) tomato sauce
1 can (6 oz.) tomato paste
2 t. oregano
2½ t. chili powder
½ t. thyme
½ C. freshly chopped parsley
½ C. white wine
½ C. Parmesan cheese

In a large Dutch oven or kettle, brown the meats. Stir to crumble. Cook, covered at a low heat for 20 minutes. Drain all the pan drippings, and discard. Set aside cooked meats.

Saute the vegetables in kettle until done. Add all remaining ingredients, and bring to a boil; reduce heat, and simmer for 2 hours, except for the parsley, cheese and wine.

Add the reserved ingredients just before serving in individual bowls, or hold out to sprinkle the parsley and cheese over each serving. Serves 6 to 8.

From an old recipe box

Donald Struckmeyer
Yuma, AZ

FAR EAST CHILI

- 2 Lbs. pork, cut into ½-inch pieces
- 1 Lb. lean ground round, cut into ½-inch cubes
- 2 Lg. onions, chopped
- 2 Lg. green peppers, chopped
- 1 can (28 oz.) beef broth
- 1 can (8 oz.) water chestnuts, sliced
- 1 can (8 oz.) bamboo shoots
- 1 t. black pepper
- 3 T. chili powder
- 3 Ozs. soy sauce
- 1 Pkg. bean sprouts
- 1 Pkg. (6 oz.) white rice noodles
- 10 fresh mushrooms, sliced
- ¼ t. oregano
- ½ t. cumin seed
- 4 dashes hot sauce

Brown the pork in a Dutch oven or large kettle. It can be done in a wok with care. Add beef and cook till done. Drain off all grease formed from the cooking. Add vegetables and cook until they are done and onions are tender.

Add beef broth, bamboo shoots, water chestnuts, pepper, chili powder and salt. Mix to blend well. Cover, and bring to a boil; reduce the heat and add all of the ingredients except the white rice noodles, and bean sprouts. Let simmer for 1½ to 2 hours or until the meat is tender and flavor is as desired.

When serving, ladle into serving bowls, and let diners have the side bowls of white rice noodles, and bean sprouts to garnish their individual servings. Makes 6 to 8 servings.

House of Ming
Miami, FL

Ricky Haskins
Lebanon, TN

DEVIL'S SWEET CHILI

3 Lbs. chuck steak, coarsely ground
2 Lg. onions, chopped
2 green peppers, chopped
2 stalks celery, chopped
3 cloves garlic, minced
3 T. vegetable oil
1½ t. salt
¾ t. black pepper
3½ T. + or - chili powder
2 t. Tabasco sauce
3 T. cumin powder
1½ T. oregano
2 cans (4 oz.) green chiles, chopped
1 can (12 oz.) beer
2 cans (12 oz.) beef broth
1 can (28 oz.) stewed tomatoes, chopped up
4 T. Masa flour
1 can (16 oz.)tomato sauce
1½ T. paprika

In a large skillet or Dutch oven, brown the beef in the oil. Drain off excess pan drippings. Add the onions, green peppers, celery and garlic, and saute until the onions are softened but not done to a browning.

Add all ingredients except the tomatoes, and bring to a boil. Reduce heat, and simmer for 1 to 1½ hours. Add tomatoes during the last 15 minutes of simmering.

If the chili is too thin, make a paste of the Masa flour and a little water, and mix into the chili. Only use a little at a time so that it isn't thicker than you want.

Bernie & Gail Geltner
Boynton Beach, FL

W.V. Rogers, 1897
Brevard County, FL

WABASH CHILI MARINADE

3 T. olive oil
3 T. onion, finely chopped
2 t. chili powder
½ t. salt
¼ t. fresh ground pepper
½ C. catsup
½ C. vinegar
¼ t. oregano
Few drops hot sauce

Blend all of the ingredients together and allow to set for 2 or 3 hours before using. Use to marinate any type of meat or poultry before grilling. The marinade can also be used to baste food while on the grill. Makes about 1½ cups of sauce.

Kelly Wilhoite
Cincinnati, OH

Jerry and Margaret Koile
Laveen, AZ

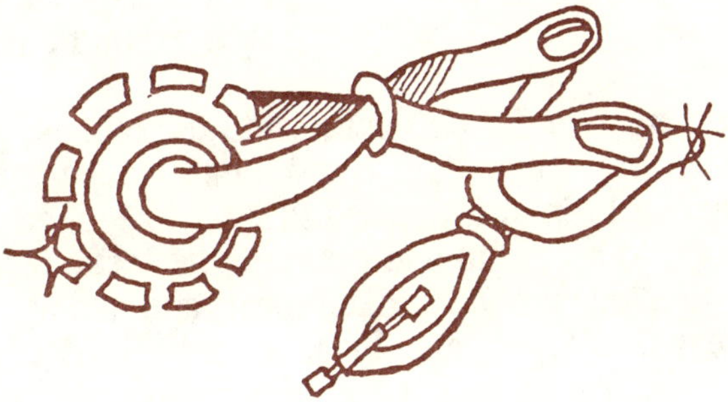

FOSTER'S FRIENDLY CHILI

- 2 Lbs. ground lean chuck, cut into ⅜-inch cubes
- 1 Lb. coarsely ground pork
- 1 Lb. lamb, cut into ⅜-inch cubes
- 2 Lg. onions, chopped
- 2 green peppers, chopped
- 1 stalk celery, chopped
- 1 can (6 oz.) tomato paste
- 1 can (16 oz.) whole tomatoes, chopped, undrained
- 1 t. marjoram
- 2 t. Tabasco sauce
- 1 T. dry mustard
- 1 t. cayenne pepper
- ¼ t. cumin seed
- ½ t. oregano
- 2 T. chili powder

Saute vegetables in a large skillet until onions are done. Add meats to skillet and brown evenly. Add all ingredients and mix well to blend. Cover; bring to a boil, stirring frequently.

Reduce heat, simmer, stirring occasionally, for 1½ to 2 hours, or until meats are tender. Taste during cooking time to alter or change flavors if desired. Makes 8 to 10 servings.

Robert Foster
Milford, OH

Two D Cattle Co.,Inc
Wauchula,FL

DEER PARK CHILI

6 Lbs. lean ground beef
3 Lg. onions, chopped
5 cloves garlic, minced
2 Lg. bell peppers, chopped
2 cans (28 oz.) whole tomatoes, chopped up
3 cans (4 oz.) green chiles, diced
2 cans (16 oz.) pinto beans, drained
1 can (16 oz.) red kidney beans, drained
3 bay leaves
4 T. chili powder
1 t. oregano
1 t. basil leaves, crushed
¼ t. allspice
½ t. cumin seed
1 Oz. unsweetened chocolate
¼ t. ground cinnamon

In a large skillet or Dutch oven, saute the onions, peppers and garlic until the onions are tender and transparent. Set vegetables aside, and brown the beef, a little at a time so that all is cooked evenly. Stir with a wooden spoon to break up and crumble the meat as it is being cooked.

Add the vegetables to the cooked meat, and add all of the ingredients, except the beans. Cover, and bring to a boil. Reduce the heat to a simmer and cook for an hour or until the desired consistency has been achieved.

To thicken, add a little flour paste, or thin with water or if you want, keep some of the bean liquid in reserve and thin with it.

Josh Hatfield
Cincinnati, OH

Donna Vickery
Murfreesboro, TN

WESTERN HILL TURKEY CHILI

1 t. vegetable oil
1 onion, chopped
3 cloves garlic, minced
1 red bell pepper, finely chopped
1 green bell pepper, finely chopped
2 C. chicken broth
1½ Lbs. turkey breasts, coarsely ground
2 T. flour
2 T. chili powder
2 T. ground cumin
2 T. powdered cocoa
1 to 2 t. cayenne pepper
¼ C. tarragon vinegar
2 T. strong brewed coffee
2 cans (14 oz.) plum tomatoes, crushed
¼ t. salt
2 C. cooked, black beans

Heat the oil in a heavy skillet or Dutch oven. Add the onion, bell peppers, garlic, sauteing, stirring to cook the onion until they are transparent but not brown. Drain from cooking utensil, and set aside.

Cook the turkey in the remaining oil until it is grayish in color and not browned. Stir to break up turkey while cooking.

Add the vegetables to the turkey, and simmer, while adding the chicken broth, after which the dry ingredients can be added. Add in the coffee, plum tomatoes except the black beans and flour.

Bring the kettle to a boil; reduce the heat, and simmer for 40 to 50 minutes. Stir in the flour if the chili mixture is too thick, or either a little water or tomato juice if it is necessary to thin the consistency.

Add the beans a few minutes before preparing to serve and heat them through.

Pat & JoAnn Sedgwick
Cincinnati, OH

Z

George E. Bryant
Beaumont, TX

CHILI CHEESE DIP

3 slices bacon, crisp and chopped
1 small onion, chopped fine
1 can (10 oz.) tomatoes with hot peppers, chopped
1 can (15 oz.) chili without beans
1 Lb. Velveeta cheese, cubed
Corn or taco chips

Saute the onions and bacon until the onion is tender, and the bacon is crisp. Mix in remaining ingredients, except of course, the chips, heat until bubbly, stirring well and frequently to keep the mixture from burning or sticking to the saucepan.

Pour prepared dip into candle warmer type dish, and serve with either type of chips.

Woman's Day

Hooker
Florida 1850(?)

MEATY CHILI SAUCE

3 Lbs. lean ground beef
2 Med. onions, chopped
2 Med. green peppers, chopped
1 Lb. fresh sliced mushrooms
2 cans (16 oz.) whole tomatoes, chopped up
1 can (10 oz.) condensed tomato soup
2 T. Worcestershire sauce
¼ t. Tabasco sauce
1 t. oregano
1 t. garlic powder
1 t. salt
½ t. black pepper
¼ t. cinnamon
½ t. thyme
2 T. olive oil

In a large Dutch oven or cooking kettle, heat the oil and sauté the meat with the vegetables until both the meat and vegetables are done. Drain off the grease and fat that is cooked from the beef.

Add all remaining ingredients, mixing in well. Cover, and bring to a boil. Reduce heat to simmer, and cook, stirring often, for about 3½ to 4 hours.

Check for desired consistency, and either add a little more water to thin the chili, or a little all-purpose flour, mixed into a paste, and then blended into the chili, to thicken.

Andy Oliver
Cocoa Beach, FL

<->

William & Juanita Marchek
Harper, OR

SHOE BOX CHILI

1 Lb. lean beef, cut into pieces
1 Lg. onion, chopped
3 T. cooking oil
1 green pepper, chopped
2 cloves garlic, crushed
2 or 3 T. chili powder
½ t. ground cumin
1 can (16 oz.) whole tomatoes, chopped up, undrained
1½ T. all-purpose flour
Salt and pepper to taste
Dash or two Tabasco sauce
Dusting of red crushed pepper flakes

Heat oil in skillet or large saucepan, and blend in the flour, and brown slightly. Saute the onions and green pepper until the onion is transparent. Set aside, or push to one side of the skillet while cooking the meat.

Add the meat, crumbling with a large fork or a wooden spoon, and saute until done. Drain excess fat formed, and discard properly.

Add in the ingredients except the tomatoes, and simmer, covered, for 1 hour to blend spices and flavors with meat.

Add the tomatoes and sufficient water to mixture to allow easy stirring while cooking, and simmer for an hour longer, stirring occasionally.

If chili is too thin, using a little of the flour, mixed with a cup of water, will thicken chili. Makes 4 to 6 servings.

Bob Pratt
Cincinnati, OH

PI Cattle Co.
Blythe, CA

S.R.'S CHILI con CARNE

3 Lbs. boneless trimmed beef,
 cut into ½ inch pieces
1 Lb. dried pinto beans
4 T. chili powder
10 cloves garlic, finely chopped
1 T. sugar
3 T. all-purpose flour
1 t. ground cumin
¼ t. hot sauce
1 t. ground red pepper
1 t. salt
¼ t. black pepper
1 Qt. water
1 t. ground marjoram
¼ t. basil, crushed
2 T. paprika
⅓ C. corn meal

Sort and wash beans, and soak them overnight in sufficient water to cover top of beans by two (2) inches.

In vegetable oil, saute the beef in a heavy skillet or Dutch oven, doing a divided portion at a time to cook all the beef evenly. Do not brown, but cooked enough to remove the pink shade.

Add water, and cover. Simmer over a low heat for 30 to 45 minutes. Add all seasonings, stirring frequently to mix with meat. Keep pinto beans and corn meal out of mixture. Simmer for an additional 35 to 50 minutes, or until meat is tender and flavor is to the desired taste.

If chili is too thin, mix a little flour in a cup of water, and add to meat mixture, stirring constantly, until the consistency is what you want. Add the pinto beans, and simmer for just 15 minutes. Makes 10 to 12 servings.

NOTE: Garnishes of chopped onions, shredded cheese, of your choice, oyster crackers, or chips, helps this recipe to become a real meal pleaser.

Sid & Adele Bernstein
Chicago, IL

Rim Ranch
Hickey, AZ

WINDY CITY CHILI

3 Lbs. lean beef, chili ground
1 Lg. onion, chopped
1 green pepper, chopped
2 cloves garlic, crushed
3 to 4 T. chili powder
2 jalapeno peppers, diced
2 T. A-1 sauce
1 T. soy sauce
1 t. paprika
1½ t. cumin powder
1 t. sugar
½ can beer
1½ t. salt
½ t. ground black pepper
½ C. white vinegar
½ t. cayenne pepper
few shakes of hot sauce
2 cans (16 oz.) whole tomatoes chopped up, undrained
1 can (7 oz.) green chiles, diced
1 can (10 oz.) tomato sauce
1 can (6 oz.) tomato paste
Water

In a large skillet, heat some cooking oil, and saute the vegetables until they are nearly done. Add the ground beef, and saute until mostly done, breaking up and crumbling. Spoon off excess fat from the skillet.

Add all remaining ingredients, stirring to mix. Cover; and bring to a boil. Reduce heat and simmer for about 2 hours or until thoroughly cooked to your satisfaction. Stir occasionally during cooking. Makes 6 to 8 servings.

Bernie & Gail Geltner
Boynton, Beach, FL

Velma & Harry Wilcoxson
Buckeye, AZ

CHILI-ON-A-BUN

1½ Lbs. lean ground beef
1 small onion, chopped
1 can (8 oz.) tomato sauce
1 Pkg. (1¼ oz.) taco seasoning mix
1 tomato, cut into 12 slices
1 small onion, cut into rings and separated
½ C. chopped black olives
Shredded Cheddar cheese
Shredded lettuce
Few drops of hot sauce (optional)
6 hamburger buns, split

In a large skillet, brown beef and onions, stirring to crumble the meat as fine as possible. Drain off fat drippings. Stir in all ingredients except cheese, sliced onions and tomatoes, chopped olives, and shredded lettuce.

Toast the buns, and spread with chili mix. Sprinkle with cheese on top. Either place tomato slices on top of cheese topped chili, or after they have been baked at 400 degree for 5 minutes, or until the cheese has melted. Top with the shredded lettuce and sliced tomatoes and onions. NOTE: Tomato may be diced and added as a topper if it would be easier to eat. Yields 12 servings.

Ms. Anita Smith
Cincinnati, OH

MB

J. Mathews
Florida 1855

CHILI PUFFED EGGS

10 eggs, beaten to blend
1 Lb. Monterey Jack Cheese, grated
2 C. (1 stick) butter, melted
½ c. all-purpose flour
1 t. baking powder
½ t. salt
2 cans (4 oz.) diced green chiles, drained

Preheat oven to 350 degrees. Lightly butter a 9x13-inch baking dish. In a large mixing bowl, combine all the ingredients except the diced green chiles. After blending well, stir in the chiles.

Pour the mixture into the baking dish, and bake until the top is lightly browned and tester comes our clean when stuck into eggs.

Time to bake is about 30 to 45 minutes. Serve this dish as soon as it is taken from the oven, as it should be eater warm. Sprinkle with paprika for added color when serving.

Bernie & Gail Geltner
Boynton Beach, FL

AJ

A.J. McGeehee 2/1881
N. of Waco about 15 miles
McLennan County, TX

TURKEY CHILI DIP

1 Lb. ground turkey
1 small onion, chopped
1 green pepper, chopped
2 C. catsup
3 t. chili powder
½ t. ground oregano
¼ t. cumin
1 clove garlic, chopped
1 t. salt
¼ t. pepper
1 can (16 oz.) refried beans
Pam non-stick spray cooking oil
½ C. chopped black olives
1 C. shredded Cheddar or Monterey Jack cheese
Corn or taco chips

In a skillet, coated with a spray oil, cook the ground turkey, onion, pepper and garlic until done. Drain off liquid from cooking the turkey... very little if any fat, it will mainly be water.

Add all remaining ingredients except the cheese; cover, and simmer for 20 to 30 minutes, stirring frequently. If chili dip is too thin, uncover and let simmer, mixing occasionally to allow evaporation of more liquid.

Pour into a fondue server. Sprinkle with reserved onion, if desired, with shredded cheese and chopped olives on top.

Keep the fondue warm so that cheese will melt, and serve with corn or taco chips. This is a real party pleaser.

David & Sheryl Geltner
Streamwood, IL

ALV

Alva H. Storrs 2/1881
8 miles below Waco
McLennan County, TX

TEXAS CHILI

1½ Lbs. ground chuck
½ Lb. hot sausage
2 Med. onions, chopped
1 green pepper, chopped
2 cloves garlic, crushed
2 T. chili powder
1 T. all-purpose flour
½ t. salt
1 t. oregano, ground
1 t. cumin, ground
1 t. sugar
Dash or two Tabasco Hot sauce
2 cans (16 oz.) kidney beans, drained
1 can (28 oz.) whole tomatoes, drained and chopped

In a Dutch oven or a large skillet, combine the meats with the onions, pepper and garlic; cook until the meats are browned, stirring occasionally to crumble meat. Drain pan grease.

Add remaining ingredients except the beans, stirring to mix well. Cover, and simmer for 1 hour, or until meats are tender. Stir often to prevent burning or sticking.

Add beans, cover, and simmer for an additional 30 minutes. Makes about 1½ to 2 quarts, depending on the consistency you want. Add a little water for a thinner chili, or add a little of the flour mixed in a small amount of water, blended into the chili to thicken if you desire a thicker recipe.

Ms. Gloria Mejia
Merritt Island, FL

LeRoy H. Bauer
Nome, TX

CHILI and SQUASH CASSEROLE SOUFFLE

1½ Lbs. zucchini, thinly sliced
1½ Lbs. yellow squash, thinly sliced
1½ C. dry bread crumbs
1½ t. salt
1¼ t. dried oregano, crushed
¼ t. fresh ground black pepper
1 C. freshly ground chili strips with tomatoes
¼ t. cumin powder
¾ Lb. Muenster cheese, grated (3 c.)
8 eggs, separated, room temperature
Pinch of cream of tartar

Toss squash, zucchini and salt in a colander. Place a heavy plate atop the vegetables to supply weight. Let drain for 1½ to 2 hours. Rinse salt from vegetables; drain, and rinse a second time to wash as much salt as possible away. Use paper towels to extract additional water.

Preheat the oven to 350 degrees. Generously butter a large souffle baking dish. Combine the bread crumbs, salt, oregano, and pepper. Spread ½ cup of the mixture in the dish, and shake off excess that does not adhere to the butter.

Spoon ⅓ of the vegetables into the dish. Top with ⅓ cup of chili stirps with tomatoes. Sprinkle with ⅓ of remaining bread crumbs. Cover with ⅓ of the grated Muenster cheese.

Whisk eggs yokes until thick and pale.

Using a electric mixer, beat eggs whites with cream of tartar until stiff, but not dry. Spread ⅓ of the egg mixture over the cheese. Repeat layering with remaining ingredients, ending with egg mixture.

Bake souffle until it is slightly puffy and golden brown, about 40 to 50 minutes. Serves 6.

CSG

Dona Juana De Figueroa
Ecuador (1593)

GREEN CHILE ANCHILADES

1 can whole long green chiles, mashed
1 C. milk
1 T. flour
Salt to taste
1 Doz. tortillas

Cook above ingredients until thickened. Dip tortillas into mixture one at a time and roll. After sprinkling with grated cheese and chopped onion, put into a baking pan and pour the remaining sauce over all the tortillas in the pan.

Bake about 15 minutes at 350 degrees.

Carmen L. Caruso
El Paso, TX

Don Miguel Hernandez
De Hoyos, Texas(1765)

CHILI STRIPS with TOMATOES

3 T. peanut oil
6 Lg. pasilla or poblano chiles, roasted, peeled, seeded, deveined and cut into thin strips
4 Med. tomatoes, peeled, seeded and chopped
1 Lg. onion, halved and thinly sliced

Heat the oil in a heavy skillet over medium heat. Add chiles, tomatoes and onion, and cook until softened, stirring occasionally, about 10 minutes.

Reduce heat to medium-low and cook until liquid has evaporated, stirring occasionally, about 20 minutes. Makes 2 cups of mix.

CSG

Old Spanish
Florida early 1600's

MY MOM'S CHILI

1 Lb. beef, chili ground
1 Lg. onion, chopped
1 Med. green pepper, chopped
2 cloves garlic, crushed
1 can (16 oz.) whole tomatoes, cut up and undrained
1 can (16 oz.) red kidney beans
1 can (16 oz.) tomato sauce
½ t. dried basil
1 T. chili powder, or to taste
¼ t. cumin powder
¼ t. oregano
½ to ½ t. Worcestershire sauce
Salt and pepper to taste

In a large heavy skillet or Dutch oven, simmer beef, onion, green pepper and garlic until meat is browned; drain off any fat liquid that may have accumulated from the cooking.

Stir in the remaining ingredients including the tomatoes and it's liquid. Bring to a boil, stirring occasionally. Reduce heat, cover, and simmer for about 30 to 45 minutes longer. Makes about 8 servings.

Natalie Pratt
Cincinnati, OH

Len G. Hofer
Meadow, SD

MRS. G'S CHILI

2 Lbs. lean beef, chili ground
2 small onions, chopped
1 green pepper, chopped
2 stalks celery, chopped fine
1 Med. carrot, shredded
1 can (10 oz.) condensed tomato soup
1 can (16 oz.) red kidney beans, undrained
1 T. chili powder, or more to taste
½ t. oregano, ground
1 bay leaf
1 t. salt
¼ t. black ground pepper
¼ t. crushed red pepper
2 cloves garlic, chopped fine
¼ t. ground cumin seed

Combine meat with the vegetables in a Dutch oven or a large skillet; cook over a medium heat, crumbling beef until it is cooked, but not browned. Drain off pan drippings.

Add the remaining ingredients, cover, and bring to a boil; reduce heat and simmer for at least one hour, stirring occasionally.

Don't forget garnishing of chopped onions and shredded cheese can be used on this dish, or just about any chili that is created.

CSG

D. Glenn Hawkins
Provo, UT

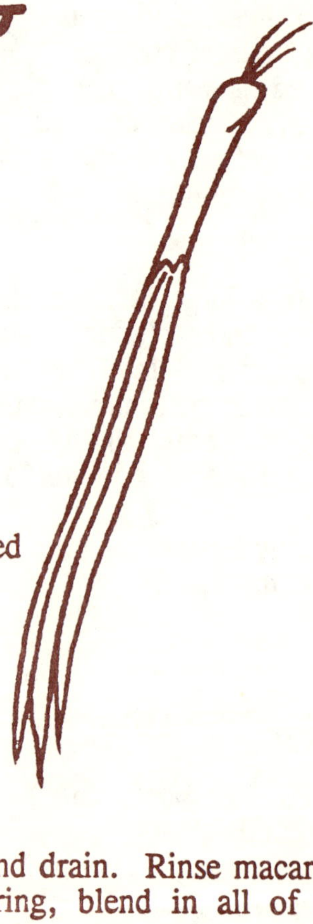

MacCHILI SALAD

- 3 T. onions, finely chopped
- 2 Med. carrots, shredded
- 2 stalks celery, chopped
- 1 C. green pepper, chopped
- 1 C. elbow macaroni
- 1 can (15 oz.) red kidney beans, drained
- 1½ t. chili powder
- Dash of garlic powder
- ⅔ C. mayonnaise
- ½ t. salt
- Several drops hot sauce
- ½ t. dried oregano, crushed
- ⅛ t. or less, cayenne pepper

Cook macaroni as directed on package, and drain. Rinse macaroni with cold water, drain. While gently stirring, blend in all of the ingredients.

Cover, and refrigerate at least overnight, before using.

Lettuce and bell pepper rings can ge used for garnish with this salad.

Chris Sayer
Cincinnati, OH

L. Dean Anderson
Glendale, UT

JEANETTE'S CHILI

1 Lb. ground beef
1 Lg. onion, chopped
1 can (16 oz.) whole tomatoes, cut up
1 can (16 oz.) kidney beans

Brown the meat and onions in a skillet until done. Drain off what dripping is form. Add the remaining ingredients, mixing in well with the meat. Simmer for one hour.

Option: Cook approximately 4 ounces of dry spaghetti. Drain and add to the chili before serving, or spread the chili over the spaghetti if desired.

Garnish this chili with extra chopped onions, and shredded cheese for extra tastes.

Jeannette Sheffield
Cincinnati, OH

Cow Creek Ranch
Tom Sloan
Ft. Pierce, FL

MEX-CHILI

2 Lbs. round steak, cut into ¾-inch cubes
2 cloves garlic, minced
1 T. cooking oil
1 Lg. onion, chopped
2 T. chili powder
1 t. dried oregano
1 t. crushed red pepper
2 cans (16 oz.) whole tomatoes, chopped, undrained
2 cans (16 oz.) kidney beans
2 C. water
1 T. all-purpose flour
1 can (6 oz.) tomato paste

Combine, in a Dutch oven, meat, onion and the garlic. Cook until the beef is browned. Crumble the meat during the cooking. Drain the pan drippings.

Add all the ingredients except the beans; cover, and bring to a boil. Reduce the heat and simmer for 1½ to 2 hours, stirring occasionally.

Add the beans after this cooking time, recover, and simmer for 30 minutes longer. Makes about 2 quarts of chili which can be frozen well.
NOTE: When freezing, it is not a good idea to use plastic containers without a liner as the spices will tend to etch themselves into the material and leave a stain that can not be scrubbed, washed, or cursed off.

Use a plastic bag such as used in produce departments to put your selections in. They're large enough, and if they're good enough to put your food into, they should be ideal to use as liners to freeze your chili in.

Heath Smith
Cincinnati, OH

Seymour Shingle
Honolulu, HA

NIPPY CHILI

2 Lbs. lean ground beef
2 Med. onion, chopped
2 cloves garlic, minced
3 T. chili powder
1 t. allspice
1 T. cider vinegar
1 t. salt
¼ t. fresh ground black pepper
1 T. dry mustard
1 T. Worcestershire sauce
½ t. Tabasco Hot Sauce
½ t. cinnamon, ground
¼ t. red pepper flakes
1½ t. cumin, ground
4 bay leafs
1 can (6 oz.) tomato paste
1 can (10 oz.) tomato sauce
1 can (16 oz.) whole tomatoes, chopped

In a large Dutch oven, combine and cook the beef, onion and garlic, until the meat is evenly cooked. Use a wooden spoon to move and crumble the meat as it is browning. Drain off the grease from the cooked meat and discard.

Add remaining ingredients; cover, and bring to a boil, stirring occasionally. Reduce heat, and simmer over a low heat for 1½ to 2 hours, stirring frequently.

Remove the bay leafs before serving. This recipe will yield about 2½ to 3 quarts of rich, flavorful chili, that when garnished with chopped onions, shredded cheese, a dollop of sour cream and the like, will make Nippy Chili the center of any meal.

Cal & Trudy LeCompte
Harban, LA

EL Cattle Company Inc
El Paso, TX

3-BEAN CHILI

½ Lb. dried pinto beans
½ Lb. dried red Kidney beans
½ Lb. dried garbanzo beans
3 Lbs. lean beef, coarsely ground
3 Med. onions, chopped
3 Med.green peppers, chopped
3 cloves garlic, minced
⅓ c. chili powder
½ t. ground oregano
½ t. pepper
1 can (6 oz.) tomato paste
1 can (12 oz.) tomato sauce
1 t. cumin seed, crushed
1 can (16 oz.) whole tomatoes, with liquid, chopped
1 t. sugar
1 t. Worcestershire sauce
½ t. cinnamon
¼ t. Tabasco sauce

In a large Dutch oven, sort and wash the beans. Cover with at least 2 inches over top of beans, and allow to soak overnight. The following morning, drain. Rinse with fresh cold water, and in a large container with again, water to cover top of beans, place on low heat and simmer for one hour, or until beans are tender.

While the beans are simmering, in the same Dutch oven, combine the beef and vegetables, and sauce until both are cooked, with the meat crumbled, and the vegetables are tender. Dispose of the fat that will be cooked from the meat.

Stir in rest of ingredients with the meat mixture, cover, and simmer for an additional hour or so, stirring occasionally.

Add the beans, and simmer for an additional 30 minutes. With a good consistency, 3½ to 4 quarts of chili will be "created".

Woman's Day

John Powers, 1903
Brevard County, FL

BEARNAISE CHILI SAUCE

½ C. dry white wine
¼ C. fresh lemon juice
¼ C. minced green onion
2 T. minced shallots
1 T. fresh tarragon, chopped
1 T. fresh chervil, chopped
3 cloves garlic, minced
½ t. Tabasco hot sauce
¼ t. ground black pepper
¼ t. oregano
¼ t. cumin
6 egg yokes, room temperature
1 t. coarse-ground mustard
¼ t. cayenne pepper
1 C. (2 sticks) unsalted butter

Boil the white wine and the lemon juice in a heavy saucepan until the liquids have been reduced to about 2 tablespoons. Strain, and set liquid aside.

Whisk the egg yokes, mustard, oregano, cumin seeds, and cayenne pepper in a large mixing bowl, and place it over a pan with gently simmering water until it becomes thick and pale in color, about 6 to 10 minutes.

Whisk the butter, softened to room temperature, in a steady stream. Remove from the simmering water. Add the reduced liquid from the white wine and lemon juice from the first part of the recipe, and whisk the mixture until it is glowy, about 2 to 3 minutes. Serve immediately.

U.Skip Cleland,
Merritt Island, FL

William Travis Pittman
Drummonds, TN

NO MEAT CHILI

2 Med. onions, quartered
2 Med. green peppers, cut into large pieces
1 C. pinto beans, dry
2 Lg. cloves garlic, minced
1 can (15 oz.) kidney beans, drained
1 can (6 oz.) tomato sauce
2 T. chili powder
1 T. ground cumin
1 t. salt
¼ t. ground black pepper
⅛ t. ground cinnamon
¼ t. thyme

Wash and sort the beans. Cover with 1½ inches of water and let soak overnight. Drain. Rinse with cold water, cover, and with 2 inches of water covering the beans, bring to a boil. Add the onion and garlic. Reduce the heat. Add the green pepper and simmer for one hour.

Add the kidney beans, tomato sauce and seasonings. Simmer for an additional hour and a half, stirring occasionally. If needed, add more water.

Let mixture cook until the beans start to break down and form a gravy with the water. Adjust the seasonings to taste. Serves 6 to 8.

from a friend's
recipe box

Mitchell Armes
Lancing, TN

ALBUQUERQUE CHILI CAULIFLOWER

1 cauliflower, steamed, or parboiled in milk,
1 Med. onion, chopped
3 tomatoes, finely chopped
1 T. cooking oil
1 clove garlic, crushed
1½ T. chili powder
1 T. parsley flakes
½ t. cloves
Dash cinnamon
½ t. salt
¼ C. bread crumbs
½ C. cheddar cheese, grated
½ C. pimento-stuffed olives, sliced

Preheat the oven to 350 degrees. Drain the cauliflower and place in an oven-proof casserole dish. Set aside. Heat the oil in a heavy skillet and saute the onion, and garlic until the onion is transparent. Add the chili powder, and cook for 2 minutes, stirring.

Add tomatoes, parsley flakes, spices and the remaining seasonings to the skillet, and cook for about 7 minutes or until the sauce thickens.

Pour the sauce over the cauliflower and sprinkle with the breadcrumbs, on top of the cauliflower. Spread the sliced olives on top, and if desired, add more sprinklings of breadcrumbs.

If the dish looks a little too dry, add a little more oil. Bake for about 30 minutes, or until the casserole has a toasted-breadcrumb appearance.

friend's recipe given to Laurie A. Seltzer

Paul D. Dyck
Rimrock, AZ

SPICY CHILI SAUCE

1 Med. onion, chopped
2 cloves garlic, minced
1 C. hot vegetable oil
2 T. chili powder
1 can (8 oz.) tomato sauce
½ C. brown sugar
¼ C. white vinegar
1 T. Worcestershire sauce
2 t. salt
1 t. dry mustard
Dash hot sauce

In a 2-quart skillet, mix all ingredients, and bring to a boil. Reduce the heat, and simmer until the mixture has thickened slightly.

Makes about 2½ cups.

CSG

LeRoy Carpenter, 1943
Brevard County, FL

DAVID'S CHILI

½ Lb. lean ground beef
1 C. of white beans
½ C. black beans
1½ Qts. water
5 cloves garlic, minced or crushed real fine
2 T. salad oil
2 Med. onion, quartered
1 t. salt
¼ C. uncooked brown rice
¼ C. lentils
2 T. chili powder
1 T. red pepper flakes, (optional)
½ t. oregano
1 Med. green pepper, chopped

Wash and sort the beans. Place then in a 2½-quart saucepan with about 1½ quarts of water. Bring to a boil; then reduce the heat to low and simmer for about 1½ hours, or until then are tender. Stir to insure against sticking and burning of beans in the saucepan.

Add the garlic, salt, oil, onion and green pepper. Cover, and simmer for about 2½ hours, stirring occasionally. Then add the rice and lentils, along with an additional cup of water if necessary to keep the beans covered.

Brown the beef in a skillet, and drain off any excess fat, and stir in the tomato puree. Simmer for about 15 to 20 minutes, stirring.

When most of the liquid has cooked away from the beans, add the meat sauce and mix together well.

Laurie A. Seltzer
from a friend

Red Cattle Co.
Immokalee, FL

CHEDDAR CHILI PIE

1 Lb. lean ground beef
1 Lg. onion, chopped
1 green pepper, chopped
2 stalks celery, chopped fine
2 or 3 cloves garlic, chopped fine
1 can (28 oz.) whole tomatoes
1 can (16 oz.) red kidney beans, undrained
1¼ C. cornmeal
1 C. Cheddar cheese, grated
1 t. cumin
¼ t. cayenne pepper
¼ t. red pepper flakes
¼ t. fresh ground black pepper
¼ t. thyme
Dash or two Tabasco Hot Sauce
½ t. Worcestershire sauce
2 eggs, lightly beaten
1¼ C. skim milk
Salt to taste
2 T. chili powder

Saute the beef, onion, green pepper and the garlic in a Dutch oven or a large skillet using a little cooking oil, stirring with a wooden spoon to break up the beef as it cooks into smaller pieces. Drain pan of excess grease and fat.

Add tomatoes, beans, ¾ cup of the cornmeal, ½ cup of Cheddar cheese, and rest of ingredients. Cook over a medium heat, stirring occasionally for about 15 to 20 minutes.

Pour into a casserole dish, spread the remaining ½ cup of cheese over the casserole evenly, and bake in a preheated 350 degree oven for about 25 to 30 minutes or until the cheese is lightly browned.

from a friend's recipe box

Steven & Nancy Albertson
Lakeview, OR

BOW'S CHILI DIP

- 2 Lbs. ground beef
- 1 small onion, finely chopped
- 2 cans (10½ oz.) condensed tomato soup
- 1 Pkg. Lipton Onion Soup mixture
- ⅛ t. fresh ground black pepper
- 2 T. chili powder
- 2 t. oregano
- ⅛ t. garlic salt
- 2 t. cumin seed, crushed
- 1 T. olive oil
- 1 Lb. Velveeta Processed Cheese

Saute the beef in a large skillet, using little oil. Stir to break up beef while browning. Add all ingredients except the cheese at this time, mixing together good.

Bring to a boil, then reduce the heat to a simmer, and cook with the cover on, for about 40 minutes. If mixture is too thick, add some additional water.

Pour into chafing dish, and serve with taco chips, tostados. Makes about 2 quarts of dipping dip.

NOTE: If candle heater is too heat, the chili dip may require a little more water to be added from time to time so that is does not get completely too dry.

Greg Bower
Cincinnati, OH

Don Aleyo Sierra
Texas (1765)

ROADSIDE CHILI

3 Lbs. ground chuck
3 cloves garlic, minced
2 Med. onions, chopped
2 bell peppers, chopped
1 can (10 oz.) tomato sauce
1 can (6 oz.) tomato paste
1 can (28 oz.) whole tomatoes, cut or chopped up, undrained
1 Qt. water
3 t. cinnamon
1 t. allspice
3 T. chili powder
1½ T. vinegar
1 t. sugar
Salt and pepper to taste
1 bay leaf
2 dashes Worcestershire sauce
Little Tabasco sauce
Spaghetti
Grated sharp cheese

Brown the meat in a large skillet, or a Dutch oven. Add the onion and garlic, and green pepper. Cook, stirring the meat, until it is browned evenly, and the vegetables are done.

Add rest of the ingredients, except the cheese and the spaghetti. Put on a simmer heat, covered, for 2½ to 3 hours, adding more water if necessary to keep the chili loose and not too dry and stiff. Stir occasionally. Remove the bay leaf upon end of cooking.

Serve this chili ladled over cooked spaghetti, with some chopped onions and the shredded or grated cheese sprinkled on top. Serves 8.

Charles & Helen Mathiason
Cape Canaveral, FL

Old Spanish
Florida Early 1600's

NO-BEAN BEEF CHILI

½ C. olive oil
3 Lg. onion, chopped
6 cloves garlic, minced
5 Lbs. lean chuck, cut in ½-inch cubes
½ C. flour
2½ C. canned tomatoes
3 green bell peppers, seeded and chopped
3 C. beef stock
2 t. celery seed
4 T. chili powder
2 t. ground coriander
2 t. ground cumin
2 t. dried oregano
2 C. prepared picante sauce
Salt and ground black pepper, to taste

Heat oil in large saucepan or Dutch oven. Add onions and garlic. Saute until golden brown. Add beef. Cook, stirring, just until meat loses red color. Sprinkle flour over meat, stirring constantly, so that the beef cubes are evenly coated.

Add tomatoes, bell peppers, beef stock, celery seed, chili powder, coriander, cumin, oregano, picante sauce and salt and pepper, mixing well.

Bring to a boil. Lower heat. Simmer, uncovered, until sauce thickens, approximately 3 to 4 hours. Makes 12 servings.

Bernie & Gail Geltner
from Pioneer Press
Rolling Meadows, IL

Lloyd, Rose & Vard Heaton
Alton, UT

SET N' EAT CHILI

2½ Lbs. beef, pot roast, leftover roast beef, or hamburger meat will do
2 small onions, chopped
2 green peppers, chopped
2 or 3 cloves garlic, chopped
1 C. water
¼ C. catsup
2 or 3 T. chili powder
1 T. salt
½ t. black pepper
1½ t. Worcestershire sauce
½ t. paprika
1 T. cumin seed, crushed
⅛ t. garlic salt
2 bay leafs
1 can (8 oz.) pinto beans, drained
1 can (8 oz.) chili beans, drained
1 can (8 oz.) small red beans, drained
1 can (10 oz.) tomato sauce
1 can (16 oz.) whole tomatoes, chopped up, undrained
1 can (4 oz.) green chiles, diced

Cut precooked beef into small pieces. Combine beef with all other ingredients in a large Dutch oven or large skillet; cover, and simmer for about 45 minutes, stirring occasionally. Remove bay leafs and serve hot.

If fresh hamburger meat is used, it should be completely cooked before using with rest of ingredients.

Pat Sedgwick
Cincinnati, OH

Darrell & Norma Rysdam
Aumsville, OR

RED BEAN CHILI

2 Lbs. lean ground beef
1 Lg. onion, chopped
1 Lg. green pepper, chopped
2 cloves garlic, minced
1 t. ground allspice
4 t. dry oregano leaves
½ C. ground New Mexican chili
2 t. ground cumin
2 t. ground coriander
2 jars (7 oz.) roasted red peppers, or canned pimentos
3½ C. beef broth
1 can (28 oz.) tomatoes
3 cans (16 oz.) red kidney beans, drained

Cook beef in a Dutch oven, crumbling to reduce sizes of pieces, until it is well done. Pour off pan drippings. Save about 3 tablespoons of fat, and discard the remainder. Set cooked beef aside, and saute the onion, green pepper and garlic until the onions is soft.

Puree the jar peppers and their liquid in a blender until smooth. Put cooked beef back into large pot, combine vegetables, and the remaining ingredients. Cover, and bring to a boil. Reduce the heat to simmer, and cook for about one hour.

To thicken mixture, uncover and simmer for more time until part of the liquid has steamed off sufficiently to get the consistency you want. Makes 8 to 10 servings.

Bertram Rudolph Jr.
Pebble Beach, CA

RED BEAN CHILI with TURKEY

Follow the directions as given in RED BEAN CHILI, substituting ground turkey for the beef, and use chicken broth instead of the beef broth. Use some vegetable oil to cook the turkey in, as there is no fat that is extruded from the turkey as is in beef, pork or other types of meats.

Jacob R. Hatfield
Cincinnati, OH

Vern & Cheryl Howard
Friendswood, TX

WHITE BEAN CHILI

3 Lbs. boneless pork shoulder or butt, trimmed and cut into ½-inch pieces
2 Lg. green peppers, chopped
2 C. green onions, sliced including the tops
3 T. vegetable oil
8 cloves garlic, minced
4 t. ground cumin
4 t. dried oregano leaves
½ t. cayenne pepper
½ C. fresh cilantro leaves, crushed
6 cans (13 oz.) tomatillos
4 cans (7 oz.) diced green chiles
6 cans (15 oz.) Italian White Beans, cannellini drained, or
9 C. cooked small white beans, drained

Thinly slice the green peppers crosswise, and in a heated kettle or Dutch oven, saute the peppers, onions, garlic and cumin. Cook, stirring over a medium-high heat for about 5 minutes, or until the onion is tender,

Mix in the tomatillos and their liquid, breaking up with a spoon, and the rest of the ingredients including the cut up pork pieces.

Bring to a boil; reduce heat, and simmer until the pork is tender, about 1½ to 2 hours. Stir occasionally. Makes 10 to 12 servings.

Teri Wells
Cincinnati, OH

Half Circle L
Lynn Henderson
Wauchula, FL

TURKEY CHILI

3 Lbs. ground turkey
Vegetable oil
2 Lg. onions, chopped
2 green peppers, chopped
2 cloves garlic, minced
3 T. chili powder
1 t. oregano
¼ t. cumin
1 t. salt
5 cans (14 oz.) red kidney beans, drained
1 can (28 oz.) tomatoes, with liquid, chopped
2 cans (4 oz.) mild green chiles, drained, chopped

In an 8-quart Dutch oven, saute the ground turkey until cooked, stirring to crumble as it cooks. Add onions, peppers and garlic and simmer until the vegetables are soft. Stir in chili powder, oregano, and cumin, and cook for about 2 minutes.

Add in remaining ingredients including beans, cover, and bring to a boil; reduce heat, and simmer for 1 hour, stirring occasionally.

Garnishes of chopped onions, shredded cheese, black chopped olives and sour cream, will set off each serving bowl just right. Makes 6 to 8 servings.

Jack & Teresa Dawson
Cincinnati, OH

A+

A.P. Smith 4/1881
China Springs
McLennan County, TX

RIO GRANDE CHILI

8 Lbs. beef chuck
4 Lg. onions, chopped
3 green peppers, chopped
1 head (15) cloves garlic, minced, or pressed
4 Oz. dried red New Mexican or California chiles
2 cans (12 oz.) beer
4 t. ground cumin
1 T. dried oregano leaves
1½ T. chili powder
1½ T. paprika
1½ t. sugar
1 t. ground coriander
1 bay leaf
½ t. cayenne pepper
¼ t. allspice
1 can (14½ oz.) chicken broth
1 can (8 oz.) tomato sauce
2 T. bourbon Whiskey (optional)
Salt and pepper to taste
Cooked pinto beans, 1 Lb. dry

Prepare beans as directed on package. Prepare chiles as methods as shown on other recipes requiring discarding of stems and seeds.

Combine beer and chiles in Dutch oven, and bring to a boil; then reduce heat, cover, and simmer until chiles are soft, about 30 minutes. Place chiles in a blender or food processor, and whirl until smooth. Press puree through fine strainer and discard residue. Set aside.

Cut beef into ¾ to 1-inch pieces, discarding fat and excess gristle. Cook the meat in the Dutch oven until well browned on all sides. Set aside.

Add onions, pepper and garlic to the pot and cook over a low heat until the onions are soft. Add the cumin, chili powder, paprika, oregano, coriander, allspice, red pepper and sugar. Cook stirring, for about 2 minutes.

Add the cooked meat and any liquid that may come from the beef, chile puree, broth, tomato juice, and whiskey, if desired. Stir well. Bring to a boil; reduce heat, and simmer until the meat is tender, stirring occasionally, for about 2 hours.

Combine the beans with about 8 cups of water, the bay leaf in 6-quart pot. Bring to a boil; reduce heat, cover, and simmer until the beans are tender to eat. Season beans to taste, drain, and discard the before serving.

Heath Smith
Cincinnati, OH

G.W. Smith 6/1880
7 miles from Waco
McLennan County, TX

CHILI (3 servings)

1 T. oil
½ Lb. ground beef
1 small onion, chopped
2 pieces celery, chopped
1 t. salt
¼ t. pepper
¼ t. sugar
½ t. chili powder (or to taste)
¼ t. cayenne pepper or hot pepper sauce
1 #300 can Bush's Best Chili Hot Beans (16 oz.) can
¼ C. catsup
1 C. water

Heat oil in frying pan. Cook beef until lightly browned. Push to one side of pan. Add onion and celery. Cook until soft. Drain excess fat. Add remaining ingredients. Mix well. Simmer 30 to 45 minutes. This is very good reheated.

Bush's Best Chili Hot
Beans container recipe

Noble Enterprises Inc
Alpine, AZ

CINCINNATI RECIPE CHILI MIX

Combine the contents of this package with:

1 can (6 oz.) tomato paste
6 cups water
1½ pounds of lean ground beef. Do not brown.

Beat mixture with a fork and bring to a boil. Reduce heat and simmer (slow boil) uncovered, stirring occasionally, until desired thickness (approximately 1 to 1½ hours).

Cincinnati Favorites:

Two Way: Spaghetti topped with chili
Three Way: Spaghetti topped with chili, and grated cheddar cheese
Four Way: Spaghetti topped with chili, grated cheese and chopped onion
Coneys: Frankfurter on bun topped with, chili, onions and grated cheese. A mild cheddar cheese is recommended.

If beans are desired, heat favorite chili or kidney beans separately, then add to prepared Cincinnati Recipe Chili Mix.

CinRecipe Chili Mix
container recipe

Rising M
Melissa Howell
Okeechobee, FL

WESTERN STYLE CHILI MIX

1. Measure 1 tablespoon oil or shortening into a large skillet.
2. Add 1 Lb. ground beef and cook until lightly browned (about 10 minutes).
3. Skim off grease.
4. Add an 8 oz. can tomato sauce and one can of water.
5. Blend in Kroger Western Style Chili Mix.
6. Bring to a boil; reduce heat; simmer covered for 20 minutes.

Yields: 5⅔ cups.

Kroger Western Style
Chili Mix container recipe

Zeb L. Adcock
Smithville, TN

CHILI-MAC CASSEROLE

Prepare chili as instructed with Western Style Chili Mix.

Macaroni- add 1½ cups macaroni to 6 cups boiling salted water. Stir. Boil rapidly, stirring occasionally 7 to 10 minutes or until desired tenderness is reached. Drain.

In buttered 2 quart casserole layer half of the macaroni and chili. Top with a layer of grated/sliced cheese.

Repeat, ending with another layer of cheese. Bake in preheated 350 degree oven 25 to 30 minutes.

Kroger Western Style Chili
Mix container recipe

Clarence B. Canada
Orlando, FL

SCHNURR'S CHILI

- 1 Lb. fresh ground beef or turkey
- 4 green onions, chopped
- 1 T. salad oil
- 1½ C. water
- 1 No. 2 can pinto beans
- 1 can (8 oz.) tomatoes
- 1 can (4 oz.) chopped green chile peppers
- 1 t. salt
- 1 t. black pepper
- 1 T. chili powder

Cook meat and onions with fat in a heavy skillet. Add one cup of water when cooking turkey in place of ground beef. Add remaining ½ cup of water with tomatoes to keep the turkey from sticking.

Add remaining ingredients. Simmer until serving time. Serve as chili or over pasta. Serves 6.

Don Schnurrenberger
Milford, OH

Allan R. Inman
Black Canyon City, AZ

LENNICE'S CHILI

1 Lb. ground beef
1 Lg. onion, chopped
½ green pepper, chopped
1 C. celery, chopped (optional)
2 cloves garlic, minced
1 can (16 oz.) whole tomatoes, mashed
1 can (8 oz.) V-8 Juice
1 can (8 oz.) tomato sauce
1 to 3 T. chili powder, to taste
1 C. water
1 t. basil
1 t. salt
1 t. paprika
1 can (14 oz.) kidney beans, drained

Cook beef, onion, pepper, celery and garlic in water soaked clay dish. * Cover and microwave 7-10 minutes on HIGH. Drain off excess liquid. Add remaining ingredients except beans.

Recover and cook 90 minutes at 50% power. Add beans and stir well.

Continue to cook 10 minutes at 50% power. Let stand 5 minutes.

* A 6 quart liner of a large crock-pot may be used and fits well in a large microwave oven.

Mrs. Lennice C. Warren
Cincinnati, OH

Boteilho Hawaii
Enterprises, Inc.
Honolulu, HA

KIMMERS CHILI

This is my son's favorite chili recipe. It is also a favorite of Shebougan, Wisconsin where they live. It does make a large amount.

1 Lb. ground beef
1 Med. onion, chopped
1 Pkg. elbow macaroni
1 can (16 oz.) tomato sauce
1 can (12 oz.) tomato paste
1 can (16 oz.) pork & beans
1 can (16 oz.) kidney beans

Brown ground beef and chopped onions in a large pot. Add 6 to 8 cups of water, bring to a boil. Cook macaroni until it is tender. Add undrained pork and beans, and kidney beans. Add tomato sauce and the tomato paste.

If not "tomato-e-e" enough, add catsup to taste. Simmer at least ½ hour and serve.

Mrs. Lucille D. Roebuck
West Union, OH

H.F. Brinkley, 1889
Waco,
McLennan County, TX

CHARLIE'S CHILI

I used to work for Charlie Ashcraft who created this recipe. I named it "Charlie's Chili" when he gave it to me in 1970. Charlie died over 10 years ago, but his chili lives on!

Everyone has asked for a copy of this recipe and I've given it to countless people over the years.

2 Lbs. ground chuck
1 C. chopped onions
1 green pepper, chopped
1 can (15 oz.) stewed tomatoes
1 can (16 oz.) fancy red kidney beans
1 can (6 oz.) tomato paste
2 T. Frank's chili powder (now Frank's French Foods)
2 t. garlic powder
2 t. salt
1 t. cumin
1 t. pepper
½ t. allspice

Brown ground chuck over medium high heat in large pot. Put browned chuck in a colander to drain, leaving about one tablespoon of meat grease in pan.

Saute onion and green pepper until soft. Add meat and mix well. Add tomato paste, stewed tomatoes, chili powder, garlic powder, salt, pepper, cumin and allspice. Mix well, turn heat down to medium and cook for 15 minutes.

Add kidney beans (do not drain) and continue to cook for an additional 15 minutes. Serves 6.

Marcia Hauenstein
Fairfield, OH

Garey & Judy Fischer
Chino, CA

CHILI DIP

15 oz. can chili-no beans
1 Lb. Velveeta cheese- in chucks
1 can green chiles-cut up
1 small onion-cut up

Put into a casserole dish. Bake at 350 degrees for 45 minutes. Serve with taco chips.

Ms. Lynn Wallenhorst
Cincinnati, OH

Andrew Adams 5/1881
McLennan County, TX

PEACHTREE HILLS PUB CHILI

This recipe was developed by my son Dennis when he was the proprietor of the Peachtree Hills Pub in Atlanta, and used at the Rib Shak he and his sister Peppy owned in Cunning/Davisville, off Rt. 400 in the Greater Atlanta area. The recipe won prizes in Southern Chili contests.

1 #10 can tomato paste
1 #10 can diced tomatoes
1½ gal. water
4 Med. sized onions
10 pieces bacon (save bacon grease)
2 oz. chili peppers (if using jalapenos, 10 peppers)
12 oz. red wine vinegar
4 oz. Tabasco hot sauce
10 bay leaves
3 oz. chopped garlic
3 oz. salt
2 oz. black pepper
3 oz. chili powder
2 oz. cumin
⅛ oz. oregano
⅛ oz. thyme
⅛ oz. sage
5 oz. brown sugar
5 oz. beef base
15 Lbs. ground beef

In a 5 gallon pot, heat the tomato paste and diced tomatoes in water. When heated, add the bay leaves, garlic, salt, pepper, cumin, chili powder, oregano, thyme, sage, brown sugar and beef base.

Cook bacon until crisp. Chop bacon into bits, and add with grease to sauce.

Brown the ground beef. Drain off grease, and add to pot. Chop the onions and add also to pot. Simmer for 30 minutes.

Mrs. George Costello
Cincinnati, OH

J.E. & Ray Sharp
Hermiston, OR

VENISON CHILI

2 Lbs. ground venison (not too fine)
2 Med. onions, chopped
1 Lb. can red kidney "chili" beans
1 Lb. can tomatoes, crushed
Tomato or V-8 juice added for desired thickness
Chili powder to taste
Salt, pepper and garlic salt to taste

Method: Cook venison, then grind in food processor, careful not to grind too fine. Remove to chili pot, add onions, and chili powder, salt and pepper. Add a small amount of juice to prevent sticking, venison is not a "greasy" meat.

Simmer until the onion is tender. Add beans, tomatoes and remaining juice if needed. Cook until well blended.

Olive Gillies
Georgetown, OH

Don Benito Camalluclla
Ecuador (1594)

GRAMPA BROWN CHILY

1 Lb. ground beef
2 cans tomato soup
1½ cans water
1 can (15 oz.) pork & beans
1 can (16 oz.) tomato paste,
+ 1½ cans of water
1 can (8 oz.) tomato sauce,
+ ¾ can of water
1½ T. chilly powder
¾ t. pepper
¾ T. salt
1 Med. onion, chopped

Brown beef and chopped onions in a skillet. Drain off excess grease. In a Large pot, add meat, onions and all the other ingredients. Bring to a boil - simmer for 1 hour.

Sharon Brown
Williamsburg, OH

K-Bar
W.G. Kowalski, 1941
Brevard County, FL

CHILI CON TURKEY (Mild)

This chili calls for turkey instead of beef. Top with minced onions and grated Cheddar cheese, served with crackers or over plain rice.

- 2 T. vegetable oil
- 1 C. chopped onions
- 1 C. chopped celery
- 1 clove garlic, minced
- 1¼ Lb. ground turkey
- 1 can (15 oz.) tomato sauce
- 1 t. chili powder
- 1 t. ground cumin
- 1 can (15 oz.) pinto or red kidney beans
- Salt and pepper to taste

In a medium skillet, over low heat, heat oil and saute onion, celery, and garlic until onion is golden. Add turkey, raise heat to medium and saute until turkey is no longer pink. Stir to break up meat into small pieces.

Add tomato sauce, chili powder and cumin; stir. Bring to a boil, reduce heat to low, cover and simmer for 20 minutes. Stir occasionally.

Mix in beans, salt and pepper to taste. Cover and simmer 30 minutes longer. Let rest 5 minutes before serving.

El Paso Times

Wes Smartt
Eugene, OR

MEXICAN CHILI

2 cans (15½ oz.) red kidney beans, drained
1 can (28 oz.) tomatoes, cut up
1½ C. chopped celery
1 C. chopped onion
1 can (6 oz.) tomato paste
½ C. chopped green pepper
1 can (4 oz.) green chile peppers; drained, rinsed, seeded and chopped
2 T. sugar
1 bay leaf
1 t. salt
Dash of pepper
1 Lb. ground beef or ground turkey

Brown either ground beef or turkey whichever you desire; drain the beef grease, and put into a crock pot with the rest of ingredients. Cover and cook on low heat setting for 8 to 10 hours.

Remove bay leaf and stir before serving.

Elsie Grebe
Cincinnati, OH

Carolyn B. Ballard
Hurricane, UT

GARLIC CHILI

2 Lbs. ground beef
2 cans (28 oz.) whole tomatoes, chopped, cut or smashed
2 cans (6 oz.) tomato paste
1 onion, chopped
½ green pepper, chopped
1 whole, large bulb (about 15 cloves) of garlic, sliced, chopped, crushed, or smashed
2 to 3 T. chili powder
2 cans (15 oz.) kidney beans (rinsed) or I recommend Joan of Arc Chili Beans (don't rinse! Use the sauce they're packed in!) yum yum

Brown and drain the ground beef in a big pot. Add everything but the beans and gently bubble for 1 to 1½ hours.

Add the beans at the end. I serve this with a glob of sour cream in the bowl.

This chili is rich and savory. No one will ever guess - or believe - the amount of garlic in it. THIS IS TO DIE FOR.

Susan Burns
Cincinnati, OH

O. W. Booth
Florida 1870

CHICKEN CHILI

Here is my recipe for a terrific chicken chili:

4 chicken thighs, cut into bite size pieces
2 T. vegetable oil
½ C. chopped onion
1 Lg. garlic clove, minced
1 green pepper, chopped
1 can (16 oz.) tomatoes, chopped with liquid
1 can (16 oz.) kidney beans, drained
2 T. chili powder
Salt and freshly ground pepper to taste
Tabasco to taste

Heat the oil in a Dutch oven and add chicken, onion, garlic and green pepper. Cook over a medium high heat stirring until chicken loses its pink color. Add remaining ingredients and stir.

Simmer, covered for 30 minutes, or until chicken is tender.

Serve chicken with hot cooked rice and cheese nachos.

My husband has had by-pass surgery and his diet is limited. He can eat this with the salt omitted, and he loves it.

Ms. Betty Gottschalk
Rochester, NY

Jaymes M. Spurlock
Elk Grove, CA

GREEN CHILI CON CARNE

2 T. cooking oil
2 Lbs. green chili (if used canned (diced) make sure skins are removed
3 cloves garlic, diced
2 t. flour
2 C. beef broth
2 C. water
1 Lb. stewing beef
1 Lb. pork loin cubed
1 can tomatoes, chopped well

Brown cubed pork in 1 tablespoon oil and 1 teaspoon flour, remove. Brown beef in 1 tablespoon oil and 1 t. flour. Return pork in pan with beef.

Add diced chile and garlic to meat. Add water and broth and simmer 1½ to 2 hours until meat is tender. Add tomatoes to heat.

Serve with flour tortillas for dipping.

Debbie Waters
Cincinnati, OH

Peter W. Lockwich
Piedra, CA

CHILI POT ROAST

4 to 5 Lbs. beef pot roast
2 T. flour
1 T. paprika
1 t. chili powder
2 t. salt
3 T. cooking oil
2 Med.-sized onions
8 whole cloves garlic
⅓ C. water
1 cinnamon stick
2 T. flour
¼ C. water

Combine 2 tablespoons flour, chili powder, paprika and salt. Dredge pot roast in seasoned flour. Brown roast in oil. Pour off drippings.

Stud each onion with 4 cloves of garlic. Add water, onions and cinnamon stick to meat. Cover, and cook slowly for 2½ to 3 hours, or until tender.

Remove meat to platter. Discard onion and cinnamon stick. Measure cooking liquid and add water to make two cups. Mix flour, 2d 2 tablespoons, with ¼ cup of water. Add to cooking liquid and cook, stirring constantly until thickened.

Debbie Waters
Cincinnati, OH

Janaro Calle
Rio Rancho Corp.
Okeechobee, FL

GRANDMA'S BEST CHILI CON CARNE

1½ Lbs. cubed round steak
Garlic powder
Salt
1 C. celery with leaves, chopped
½ C. chopped onion
Margarine
3 cans (16 oz.) tomatoes, undrained
2 cans (6 oz.) tomato paste
1 Lb. pinto beans, cooked
1 T. sugar
Dash of oregano
½ C. parsley
1 T. Worcestershire sauce
1 can pitted ripe olives, quartered
1 bay leaf
¾ T. chili powder
Cayenne pepper
Tabasco sauce

Coat beef with garlic powder and salt. Saute beef, onion and celery in margarine. Add one cup of water, cover, and simmer for 30 minutes.

Add tomato paste, tomatoes with juices, pepper, sugar, beans, oregano, parsley and Worcestershire sauce. Simmer for 15 minutes.

Add remaining ingredients and simmer for 10 minutes. Remove from heat remove bay leaf, and when at room temperature, refrigerate overnite for best flavor.

Debbie Waters
Cincinnati, OH

Caliso Blanchard
Neches,
Jefferson County, TX

CHILI CON QUESO

1 T. bacon grease
1 T. Crisco
1 onion, chopped
2 fresh tomatoes, chopped
7-9 long green chiles, roasted, peeled and chopped
1 Lb. Monterey jack cheese, grated
½ C. milk

Saute onion, chopped tomatoes and chopped chiles in the bacon grease until the onions are tender. Drain off grease.

Mix in the Monterey Jack cheese and milk. Let simmer until the cheese has melted. This is very good on steak, vegetables, baked potatoes, or just as a dip.

Joyce Benortham
El Paso, TX

Ms. Alice Robinson
Watertown, TN

GREEN ENCHILADAS

20 roasted long green chilies
2 Lg. cans of Pet milk
2 cans of Campbell's Chicken Soup
1½ Lbs. hamburger beef
1 onion, chopped
Garlic salt to taste
Pepper to taste
2 Dz. corn-tortillas
Crisco oil
1 Lb. Cheddar cheese, grated

Fry tortillas in Crisco oil on each side for a few seconds. Fry your meat, mixed with the chopped onion, salt and pepper until the meat is done.

Mix in the milk and chicken soup, and let simmer.

Chop your chilies, mixing with meat sauce "make sure you peel the chiles". Put cheese in each tortillas roll. Put in pan. Pour sauce over each enchiladas. Bake at 350 degrees till hot.

Joyce Benortham
El Paso, TX

John Hall & Alice Anderson
Bowie, AZ

CHILE QUESO

2 Lbs. Velveeta Cheese
1½ onions, 3" diameter, chopped
1 fresh tomato 4" diameter, chopped
1 can condensed Cream of Mushroom Soup
2 cans (4 oz.) peeled green chilies, chopped
5 T. butter

Saute chilies, onion and tomatoes in butter while the cheese and the mushroom soup are melting in a fondue dish or simular container.

Saute until the onions are transparent. Add all ingredients to the cheese and soup mixture. Serve with chips.

Lori Cooper
El Paso, TX

Marvin & JoAnn Arruda
Honolulu, HA

TONGUE IN SPANISH SAUCE

1 4-5 Lb. tongue
1 can (15 oz.) tomatoes
2 cans (8 oz.) tomato sauce
1 Lg. can green chilies, (mild, medium, or hot) (if using fresh green chilies, roast and peel the green chilies and cut up or shred)
1 whole onion, sliced
1 C. diced parsley, fresh or dried
1 jar (8 oz.) pitted green olives, with pimento
1 can garbanzos (chick peas)
Dash of garlic salt
Salt and pepper to taste

Cook the tongue in water with onion (to be discarded later), until skin can be peeled off. When cooked, swet tongue aside.

Fry onions in two tablespoons of cooking oil (preferably sunflower or corn), add tomatoes and tomato sauce, and let simmer for a few minutes.

Add chilies, parsley, olives, garbanzos, salt and pepper to taste, and last, add sliced tongue.

Add as much tongue as tomato sauce allows. Simmer approximately 10 to 15 minutes.

Serve with a salad of your choice.

Mrs. Robert Duran
El Paso, TX

Slash A
Abby Schloot
St. Cloud, FL

LAUREEN'S ENCHILADAS

This can be enchiladas with or without an egg on top.

12 tortillas
1 Lb. ground round meat
½ Lb. cheese (Longhorn) grated
1 Med. onion
½ chopped lettuce
2 cans (8 oz.) chili (red)

Fry tortillas very lightly. Set aside to drain on paper towels. After frying tortillas, take one, put a little meat on top of it. Then top with grated cheese, then onion, then the lettuce, and on top of it all, put some red chili on top.

Repeat this as many times as you wish. Men usually eat three, women eat two.

After stacking as many as one wants, you fry an egg on both sides, and place on top of it all. Pour red chili over it all, and sprinkle a little cheese and enjoy! It's out of this world.

Laureen Butler
El Paso, TX

Donald Dunlap
Covelo, CA

CHILI el VERA

This recipe has been in my family for over 40 years. When we lived in Dalhart, Texas, (the coldest place in Texas) it was given to me, by our friend Tommy Tomlinson, who passed away several years ago. Now we live in El Paso, Texas, and you are nobody unless you like chili, so it has been used in this town for 23 years-hope you enjoy it.

- 1 Lb. hamburger or chili meat
- 1 Med. size onion, chopped
- 1 Lb. red beans, cooked (Pintos)
- 2 T. chili powder
- 1 t. salt
- 1 can tomatoes
- ½ bottle catsup
- 1 pint water

Brown meat. Add onions, chili powder and water. Bring to a boil, and add tomatoes. Let simmer for 4 hours. Add cooked beans and catsup during the last hour. I always add hot chili peppers to mine.

Mrs. Vera Garrison
El Paso, TX

ICU

W.D. Yates, 1911
Brevard County, FL

PICO de GALLO

2-4 sprigs cilantro-stems removed
7 fresh jalapeno peppers, stems removed
1 Lg. green chile-stem removed
1 clove garlic, minced
¼ Med. onion, chopped fine
½ t. oregano
1 t. vegetable oil
¾ C. water
1 tomato

Mince cilantro, peppers; chop vegetables and combine all ingredients. Let stand to blend before serving.

Mary Rey
El Paso, TX

EW

E. Ward
Florida 1888

PICANTE CINCINNATI-STYLE CHILI

2 Lbs. ground pork
2 Lg. onions, chopped
2 cloves garlic, minced
1 can (15 oz.) tomato sauce
1 C. prepared picante sauce
2 T. chili powder
1½ t. cinnamon
1 t. ground cumin
1 t. salt
¼ t. allspice
2 bay leaves

In large saucepan or Dutch oven, brown meat with onion and garlic. Drain. Add tomato sauce, picante sauce, chili powder, cinnamon, salt, allspice and bay leaves. Cover.

Simmer 1 hour, stirring occasionally. Remove bay leaves. If desired, serve over cooked thin spaghetti and accompany with toppings: shredded Cheddar cheese, sour cream, chopped raw onions, heated cooked red or kidney beans, oyster crackers etc. Makes 8 servings.

Bernie & Gail Geltner
from Pioneer Press
Rolling Meadows, IL

Richard & Stephen Hoyt
Burns, OR

WEST TEXAS CHILI

This is my famous "West Texas Chili" recipe. I used to live in Cincinnati from 1965 to 1983 in Mt. Washington. I now reside here in El Paso, Texas. I saw a blurb in the El Paso Times regarding your book and couldn't resist sharing this recipe with you!

I learned this recipe from an old Mescalero Apache in Cloudcroft, New Mexico. Please don't take any "short-cuts" or the true flavor will evade you.

Serve hot tortillas with the chili and I assure your satisfaction.

1 Lb. lean ground beef
3 cans "Old El Paso" pinto beans
3 Lg. russet potatoes-diced
3 cloves fresh garlic-diced
2 Lg. fresh tomatoes-diced
2 Lg. fresh jalapeno peppers-diced
1 Lg. red onion-diced
1 Lg. carrot-diced
2 cans "Old El Paso" enchilada sauce (medium hot)
3 T. virgin olive oil
1 T. salt
1 T. lemon pepper
½ bunch fresh parsley-very finely diced

Dice red onion and mix (knead) into ground beef. Barbecue meat over open flame over mesquite wood or charcoal.

Saute diced carrot, potatoes, garlic, jalepeno peppers, tomatoes, salt and lemon pepper in olive oil for 30 minutes on medium low heat.

In a large stew pot, mix everything together (sauted vegies and meat and beans); add 2 cans of "Old El Paso" Enchilada sauce. Cover pot and simmer for at least 2 hours.

After 2 hours let chili sit for 2 more hours in fridge. Re-heat and serve. Add fresh parsley before serving.

Steve Snyder
El Paso, TX

Y.M. Sawyer 12/1881
McLennan County, TX

CHILAQUILES

24 tortillas
1 C. oil
12 red chili pods
6 cloves garlic
2 C. water
Oregano
2 C. grated Muenster or Monterey Jack cheese, shredded

Cut tortillas in small pieces. Fry in oil. Boil chili pods. Turn off heat. Let steam for 10 minutes. Remove stems and seeds.

Liquify in blender with garlic and water. Strain. Add sauce to fried tortillas in pan. Season. Top with cheese.

Mary Rey
El Paso, TX

J. B. Sharkey, Sr.
Pinellas County, FL

RED CHILI CHEESE ROLL

3 oz. Philadelphia cream cheese
4 oz. Velveeta cheese
4 oz. Med. sharp Cheddar cheese
1 C. chopped nuts
1 t. Lee & Perrins sauce
1½ t. red chili powder
1 t. fresh onion juice
Finely chopped parsley
Garlic

Rub the garlic on sides of mixing bowl. Mix all ingredients except the nuts and chopped parsley. Roll into a log, then roll in the chopped nuts and parsley.

Wrap in foil and refrigerate overnight.

Carmen L. Caruso
El Paso, TX

Roy Dale Foster
Brawley, CA

BLACK BEANS 'N VEGETABLE CHILI

Bright, fresh vegetables blend with black beans and savory seasonings in this satisfying, meatless meal-in-bowl that's ready to serve in about half an hour.

1 Lg. onion, coarsely chopped
1 T. vegetable oil
1 can (28 ozs.) whole tomatoes, undrained, coarsely chopped
⅔ C. Pace Picante Sauce
1½ t. ground cumin
1 t. salt
½ t. basil leaves, crushed
1 can (16 oz.) black beans, rinsed and brained
1 green pepper, cut into ¾-inch pieces
1 red bell pepper, cut into ¾-inch pieces
1 Lg. yellow squash, or zucchini, cut into ½-inch chunks (2 C.)

Toppings: Rice, chopped cilantro, sour cream, shredded cheese

In large saucepan or Dutch oven, cook onion in oil until tender. Add tomatoes, Pace Picante Sauce and seasonings. Cover and simmer 5 minutes. Stir in beans, peppers and squash; cover and simmer until vegetables are tender, about 15 minutes. Ladle into bowls; top as desired and serve with additional Pace Picante Sauce. Makes 8 servings, about 8 cups chili.

Pace Foods, Inc.

S.A. Tucker, Jr.
Gallatin, TN

BAKER'S CHILI

Even in out hot climate, this recipe is always requested and enjoyed by our party guests, as it makes servings for 24 people.

4 T. fat
6 C. onions, diced
3 green peppers, diced
Garlic powder to taste, or
1 garlic clove, minced
5 Lbs. ground beef
6 cans, large tomatoes
4 cans tomato paste
4 to 6 T. chili powder, mix with 6 T. cold water
4 t. salt
6 t. sugar
8 cans kidney beans, or to your liking

Procedure is standard from browning beef through adding all ingredients, and simmer for 2 hours.

Arlene Baker
Palm Springs, CA

Carl V. Negranti
Cayucos, CA

ORIGINAL TEXAS STYLE CHILI

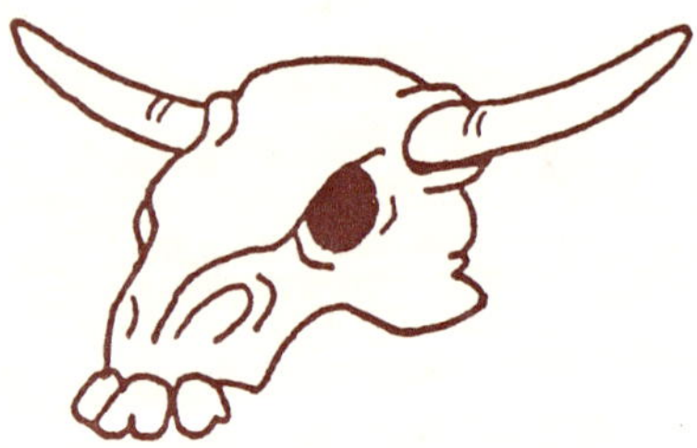

3 Lg. onions, chopped
1 t. oregano
3 cloves garlic, chopped
1 t. ground cumin
4 T. chili powder
1 T. sugar
2 T. paprika
2 t. cayenne pepper
3 t. salt
1 can (8 oz.) tomato sauce
3 Lbs. ground lean chuck

Put 2 tablespoons of oil into a large pot, then add the ground chuck. Cook while stirring until meat is browned. Add enough water to cover meat, then add remaining ingredients.

Mix all and simmer 1½ hours.

Ms. Bernice Taylor
South Point, OH

Trudy Feiteira
Maui, HA

MEXICAN SCRAMBLED EGGS

1 can (15 oz.) tamales
6 eggs
2 T. milk
2 T. margarine
Salt and pepper to taste
½ C. Cheddar or longhorn cheese, grated
1 can (4 oz.) green chilies, or
3 or 4 frozen green chilies, chopped
1 C. sour cream
Note: fresh tamales can be used

Remove wrappings from tamales. Cut each tamale into 3 equal pieces, and arrange in a 9-inch glass pie pan. Cover. Microwave at full power for 4 minutes. Break eggs into microwave-safe bowl. Add milk, margarine, salt and pepper. Beat.

Microwave on 70% power for approximately 4 minutes, or until almost set. Stir several times during cooking time. Spoon eggs over tamales. Sprinkle cheese evenly over eggs. Cover. Return to microwave for one minute on full power.

Top with sour cream and green chilies. Serves 4.

Mary Rey
El Paso, TX

Jean Allen
Beaumont,
Jefferson County, TX

CHILI CON QUESO

1 Med. onion, chopped
1 C. green chilies, chopped
1 C. taco sauce
1 C. tomatoes, chopped
1 can evaporated milk
1 Lg. package, Velveeta cheese

Saute the onion in a large skillet. Add the green chilies, taco sauce, and the tomatoes. Simmer until dry.

Add the evaporated milk and cheese. Simmer until the cheese has melted.

Carmen L. Caruso
El Paso, TX

Joe Miller, Jr.
Ft. Meyers, FL

CHILI BARBECUE-STYLE TORTILLAS

1 lb. beef flank steak
½ C. chopped onion
¼ C. chopped celery
1 T. water
1 T. vinegar
1 t. dry mustard
1 t. chili powder
½ t. dried basil, crushed
¼ t. salt
¼ t. garlic powder
1 T. cold water
2 t. corn starch
1 can (8 oz.) tomato sauce
1 t. brown sugar
4 7-inch flour tortillas

Partially freeze beef. Thinly slice across the grain into bite-size strips. In a microwave-safe casserole, stir together onion, celery, 1 tablespoon water, vinegar, dry mustard, chili powder, basil, salt and garlic powder. Stir in beef. Cook, covered, on 100% power (High) 6 minutes, stirring once. Cook, covered, on 50% power (Medium) 20 minutes more or until meat is tender, stirring every 7 minutes.

Stir together 1 tablespoon cold water and corn starch. Stir into meat mixture along with tomato sauce and brown sugar. Cook, uncovered, on High 3 to 4 minutes, or until bubbly, stirring after every minute. To assemble, spoon about ⅓ cup meat mixture down the center of each tortilla and roll up. Place, seam side down, on microwave-safe serving platter. Spoon remaining meat mixture over tortillas. Cook, uncovered, on High 1 to 2 minutes or until heated through, rotating platter a half-turn once.

Makes 4 servings.

Test kitchen notes: Beef is easier to slice thinly when it is partially frozen. That takes about 45 minutes in the freezer. Serve the tortillas with tomato slices and shredded lettuce for a 1-plate meal.

Orlando Sentinel

Markwood Enterprises Ltd
Chandler, AZ

BUDGET CHILI BEAN BAKE

This is a family favorite with us, especially when we are feeding a crowd.

2 cans (15 oz.) pinto beans
1 can (15 oz.) black eye peas
1 can (15 oz.) lima beans
3 Lbs. ground beef
2 cans (15 oz.) kidney beans
2 Lg. onions, chopped
1 green pepper, chopped
3 T. oil
2 C. catsup
1½ C. Burgundy wine (or apple juice)
½ C. honey
2 or 3 T. chili powder
Parsley

Drain beans and combine. Brown the beef with onion and green pepper in oil and add to beans. Add remaining ingredients, except parsley, and place in 2 casserole dishes. Bake 1 hour at 350 degrees. At serving time, garnish with parsley. Makes 16 servings.

NOTE: Good served with a green salad and corn bread. Also good for making ahead and freezing.

Mary Alice Hardin
Loveland, OH

Don Nicolas Saez
Texas (1742)

HOT CHILI VINEGAR

To each quart jar, add:

3 hot peppers which have been slit open, (use rubber gloves if necessary)
2 cloves garlic

Pour white grain vinegar into each jar almost to the brim. Cap, and let steep about 3 weeks.

Mint vinegar is good made with either dicer or white wine vinegar; spearmint is my first choice here. However, any mint will make a flavorful vinegar.

Cincinnati Enquirer

One Bar
Horace Prescott
St. Cloud, FL

CHILI BEEF PIE

2 Lbs. ground beef
1 Lb. ground turkey
½ C. oatmeal
1 egg
3 T. dry onion, or
1 small fresh onion, diced
2 T. dry parsley

1 t. garlic powder
½ t. seasoned salt
½ t. Taco or chili powder
½ t. pepper
¼ Lb. American cheese, grated
¼ Lb. Colby cheese, grated
¼ Lb. Mozzarella cheese, grated

Mix ground beef and ground turkey; add the remaining ingredients except the cheeses. Divide meat mixture into halfs. Spread on pizza pan. Top with two cups of chili and cheese.

On wax paper, roll other half of meat mixture; press on top to flatten, seal around edges well. Bake in pre-heated oven at 350° for 1½ hours.

NOTE: Use chili filling of Chili Crepe Pie.

Judith E. Agar
Jeddo, MI

Crescent H Ranch
Lebanon, TN

CHILI CREPE PIE

(This recipe is good with left over chili)

Chili Filling

3 Lbs. ground beef
½ C. dry onion or 1 onion diced
2 green peppers, diced
2 ribs of celery, diced
3 cans tomatoes, crushed
1 T. sugar
Pinch of hot pepper seeds
½ Lb. Cheddar cheese, grated
½ Lb. Mozzarella Cheese, grated

Crepes

2 C. flour
4 eggs
2 T. butter, melted
1 C. water
1 C. milk
2 T. chili powder or hot sauce

Make crepe mixture: Mix all ingredients together for 1 minute. Let set at room temperature. Next, brown beef, onion, green pepper and celery. Add 1 cup of water; cook until meat is brown. Drain off drippings; add crushed tomatoes, sugar, chili powder, hot pepper seeds. Stir well; let simmer to flavor for 30 minutes.

In a large hot skillet, lightly melt the butter; add ½ cup batter to pan. Tilt pan to cover bottom with batter until browned and dry looking; flipping over and cook till brown on both sides.

Remove; put in lightly greased pie pan or 9x13-inch casserole dish. Make up all batter into crepes. Bake in 350 degree oven for 30 to 40 minutes till heated thoroughly. Cut in serving pieces. Top with diced tomatoes, cheese and sour cream.

Judith E. Agar
Jeddo, MI

Lazy L Bar
Louis N. Lowery
Laurel Hill, FL

CHILI CHEESE DIP

1 Pkg. (8 oz.) Philadelphia Cream Cheese
2 cans (4 oz.) chopped chilies
¼ C. mayonnaise
¼ t. salt
¼ t. garlic powder
2 or 3 drops green food coloring

Soften the cream cheese at room temperature. Mix all ingredients until well blended.

Serve with crackers, potato or corn chips. Makes 2½ cups.

It is best to make this at least 24 hours ahead so that the flavors can blend!

Carmen L. Caruso
El Paso, TX

Ms. Betty Auls
Hamshire, TX

CHILI CON CARNE

3 Lbs. pork shoulder or combination of beef and pork
1 t. salt
2 T. oil
1 Lg. onion, chopped
6 clove garlic, minced
1 T. red pepper, crushed
4 T. Red chili powder
1 t. ground cumins
Water

Season meat with salt and boil, with water to cover, until very tender. Remove meat from pot and dice. Skim fat from broth and set aside.

Heat oil in a large Dutch oven and saute onion and garlic until soft. Add meat, red pepper, cumins and chili powder. Cook over medium heat about 5 minutes.

Add enough water to reserved broth to make 6 cups, then add to meat mixture. Cover and simmer 1 hour. Adjust seasonings before serving.

Mary Rey
El Paso, TX

Roy A. Tyrer, M.D.
Franklin, TN

CHILI COWBOY CASSEROLE

1 Lb. beef, ground or cubed
2 T. chili powder
1½ t. salt
¼ t. pepper
1 clove garlic, minced

2 T. salad oil
2 Med. onions, chopped
1 Lb. red beans
1 can (16 oz.) whole kernel corn
1 green pepper, chopped

Sprinkle beef with chili powder, salt and pepper. Brown very slowly with garlic in salad oil in a large skillet. Add the onions, and green peppers; cook over a low heat, stirring often for 10 minutes.

Drain the beans and corn, adding the liquids to the meat mixture. Cover, and simmer for 45 minutes or until the meat is tender.

Add the beans and corn, and heat thoroughly. Serve garnished with avocado slices.

Carmen L. Caurso
El Paso, TX

Mark Killian
Gooding, AZ

PINTO CHILI

- ½ Lb. dried pinto beans
- 1 Lb. lean ground beef, browned
- 2 Med. onions, coarsely chopped
- 1 green onion, coarsely chopped
- 1 t. pepper
- 2 cans (16 oz.) tomatoes
- 2 cloves garlic, crushed
- ⅔ t. chili powder
- 1 t. cider vinegar (optional)

Soak beans in water overnight; drain. Place all ingredients in crock-pot. Add 2 cups of water, stir once. Cover; cook on LOW for 10 to 12 hours, or on HIGH for 5 to 6 hours.

Ms. Brenda S. Allen
Maryville, TN

Brian Tuggle
Circle T Ranch
Lebanon, TN

CHILI HOT TAMALES

2 Lbs. hamburger
1 T. salt
1 t. ground red pepper
1 Lg. box chili powder
2 T. shortening
onions (optional)

Mix well. To make hotter, add more red pepper.

6 C. self-rising meal
1 t. salt
1 T. shortening

Add water slowly and mix well. Should be on dry side. Let stand for five minutes.

Roll meat out in hand and pat meal around. Wrap in tamale paper (which you put in water and squeeze out first), and tie, (cut strips out of tamale papers), wetting them also.

Cook in water about 30 to 45 minutes. Cool. Freeze. Cook 10 minutes when remove from freezer before eating.

Serve with chili over them..."Delicious."

Linda Braden
Knoxville, TN

Bar HD Joined
F.J. Heider
Cocoa, FL

CHILI CORN BREAD

Mix:
½ t. baking soda
1½ t. salt
3 t. baking powder

Add:
1 C. corn meal
1 C. buttermilk
1 C. cream style corn
2 eggs, beaten
1 Med. onion, chopped
¼ C. melted shortening
1 small can green chilies, peeled

Put half of the batter in a buttered baking dish. Cover with one small can of peeled chilies. Sprinkle ½ cup grated cheese. Pour on rest of the batter.

Bake 35 minutes in 400 degree oven. Be sure and cook in a large pan (12"x15").

Carmen L. Caruso
El Paso, TX

Santos Aguilar
Honduras (1838)

MEXICAN MEATLOAF

2 Lbs. hamburger meat
½ C. green chile, chopped
½ C. onion, chopped
1 C. cracker crumbs
1 egg, slightly beaten

½ C. milk
½ C. ripe olives, chopped
1 C. tomato sauce
1 T. chili powder
⅛ t. ground cumins
½ C. Cheddar cheese, grated

Combine hamburger meat, chili, onion, cracker crumbs, egg, milk, and chopped olives and form a loaf.

Bake in a 350 degree oven for 1 hour. While meat is cooking, combine tomato sauce, chili powder and cumins; mix well and set aside to let flavors blend.

Remove meatloaf from oven and spread tomato mixture over it.

Mary Rey
El Paso, TX

Robert & Nina Renz
Hollister, CA

"SURE FIRE" CHILE Con CARNE QUESO

1 T. butter
2 C. Velveeta cheese, cubed

½ C. chopped green chile
2 T. milk
1 t. garlic salt

Melt butter in double boiler; add cubed Cheddar cheese to butter and blend. Stir in chopped green chile, milk and garlic salt to butter-cheese mixture. Heat but do not boil. Serve with tastados.

Carl F. Tarlowski, MD
Las Cruces, NM

J.R. Healer, 1899
near Rosa,
McLennan County, TX

CHILI MY WAY

1 salsa Casera
1 salsa veboe
3 T. cooking oil
2 Lg. onions, coarsely chopped
3 green chiles, cut ¼-pieces
5 Med. cloves garlic, coarsely chopped
1 stalk celery, coarsely chopped
1 green pepper, coarsely chopped
8 jalapeno peppers, finely chopped
¼ Lb. shredded sharp cheese
1 Lb. hot country-style pork links sausage, cut to ½ sections
2 Lbs. beef, coarse chili grind
2 center cut pork chops, cut to ½-inch cubes
2 Lbs. top beef sirloin, cut to 1-inch cubes
2 t. fresh ground pepper
5 T. ground hot red chili powder
3 T. ground mild red chili powder
1 T. Mexican dried oregano
2 T. Worcestershire sauce
3 t. ground cumin
2 t. salt
2 T. brown sugar
2 bay leaves, crumbled
1 t. ground cayenne
2 T. chili caribe (Mexican)
3 Med. tomatoes, coarsely chopped
1 can (28 oz.) whole tomatoes
1 can (6 oz.) tomato paste
3 cans chicken broth
1 lime
3 cans (12 oz.) beer

1. Place 3 tablespoons cooking oil into frying pan and saute onions and garlic over medium heat for five minutes, then place into a large soup pot.
2. Cook link sausage in frying pan. Pour grease out and place into large soup pot.
3. Cook pork chops in frying pan. Pour grease out and place into large soup pot.
4. Place beef sirloin into frying pan, brown evenly, pour grease out and place in large soup pot.
5. Brown the 2 pounds of beef in frying pan, eliminating grease and pour into large soup pot.
6. Add and stir in all other ingredients - except - 4 jalapeno peppers, including 2 cans of the beer. Bring to a boil then lower and simmer for 4 hours.
7. Allow to age overnight in the refrigerator then add the 4 jalapeno peppers and bring to a boil, then lower heat and simmer for 30 minutes.

Stir occasionally and add lime juice 10 minutes before serving.

NOTE: Any time chili needs thinning - add beer. When you re-heat always add beer.

With Beans:

3 C. pinto beans
1 cans (12 oz.) beer

1. Place the rinsed pinto beans in a bowl, add water and soak overnight.
2. Pour water from beans, add two cans of beer, put into large frying pan, bring to a boil, then lower heat and simmer, partially covered, for about 60 minutes, until beans are cooked, but still firm. Check occasionally and add beer if necessary.
3. Pour entire contents in with chili and cook for 30 minutes more. Stir occasionally and test for firmness of beans and palate.

Don E. Harding
Palm Springs, CA

Y H Ranch
Youell B. Harvey
Titusville, FL

CHILI DIP CON QUESO

Prep time: 10 minutes
Microwave cooking time: 7 minutes

1 (8 oz.) pkg. Philadelphia Brand Cream Cheese, softened
2 C. prepared Carroll Shelby's Original Texas Brand Chili Mix
1 (4 oz.) can chopped green chilies, drained
1 (4 oz.) can chopped pitted ripe olives, drained
2 T. chopped green onion
1 C. (4 oz.) Velveeta Mexican Shredded Pasterized Process Cream Food

Spread cream cheese over bottom of 9-inch pie plate.

Layer remaining ingredients over cream cheese.

Microwave on HIGH 5 to 7 minutes or until thoroughly heated. Serve with tortilla chips.

8 to 10 servings.

Carroll Shelby's recipe

Ralph Fukushima
Ewa Beach, HA

CHILE CHEESE PIN WHEELS

- 2 C. Cheddar cheese (I prefer sharp), grated coarsely
- 1 C. all-purpose flour
- ¼ Lb. butter
- 2 C. green chile, chopped
- 1 T. Brandy

Mix cheese into flour well. Melt butter, and blend into cheese-flour mixture, thoroughly. Roll out mixture in rectangular shape about ⅛-inch thick. Spread chopped green chile over dough.

Roll dough up like a jelly roll. Slice into rounds and bake in degree oven for about 10 minutes or until lightly browned.

Carl F. Tarlowski, MD
Las Cruces, NM

Don Baltasar Dela Garza
Texas(1806)

CHILI Con CARNE el ARLENE

This is my favorite chili recipe.

- 1 Lb. ground beef
- ¾ t. salt
- 1 Med. onion, chopped
- 1 can (14 oz.) tomatoes
- 1 can (16 oz.) red kidney beans, drained
- 2 t. chili powder
- 2 cloves garlic, crushed
- ½ t. cumin seed, ground
- ¼ t. oregano
- ½ t. basil
- 2 T. tomato paste
- 1 C. water

Brown beef in frying pan. Discard fat. Add other ingredients to pan with the beef. Simmer uncovered; stir to break up tomatoes. Cover and cook on Low for 1 hour or more. Makes 4 servings.

Ms. Arlene H. Verstringhe
Palmyra, NY

Gunsight
Oppenheimer Inds. Inc.
Kansas City, MS

BETTY'S CINCINNATI PARLOR CHILI

6 Lbs. hamburger, browned and completely drained of grease
4 Qts. tomato juice
6 Oz. dehydrated onion, or
3 C. raw, chopped onions
4 cans (6 oz.) tomato paste
3 Qts. water (if dehydrated onions are used; otherwise 1½ Qts.)

Spices:

2 t. garlic powder
6 T. chili powder
6 T. white vinegar
1 T. ground cinnamon
6 t. brown sugar, loosely packed
1 T. dried mustard
2 T. cumin seed
3 T. Worcestershire sauce
1 T. basil leaves
1 t. sage
1 t. marjoram
1 t. thyme
1 t. allspice, ground
1 t. ground cloves
1 t. rosemary leaves
2 t. oregano leaves
1 T. crushed red pepper
10-15 bay leaves
1 t. instant beef bouillon, or equivalent bouillon cubes
1 T. salt
1 T. coarse ground black pepper

Simmer all for 2 to 3 hours to completely blend flavors. Adjust seasonings after one hour. If too thick, add tomato juice or water.

NOTE: I rarely add beans or anything else to this chili. Part of the fun of having chili at our house or for guests is to let everyone fix his/her own way they like it.

Serve on the side: Beans, spaghetti, or macaroni, rice, crackers, grated cheese, onions, hot sauce or red peppers, or whatever else you like with chili. Enjoy!

Ms. Gertrude Ponder
Cincinnati, OH
This recipe from Wayne County Outlook, Monticello, KY

Eldon & Cordelia La Rue
Hermiston, OR

CHILI Con QUESO

Chili and cheese are popular items often paired up to produce some of the most delicious and entertaining menus found on the border.

Cheese is a very important item in Mexican cookery. The favorite native cheese called asadero, is a white cheese finished in flat thin cakes, and said to be best for chili rellenos.

The popular Mexican dip called, chili con queso, is prepared in a variety of ways.

My mother-in-law, Margaret Munoz, is one of the few people I know that continues to prepare this popular dip in this traditional manner. The authentic recipe calls for green chile pods that have been roasted, peeled and sliced, then mixed in with melted asadero cheese.

The white cheese has been replaced with yellow cheese in most kitchens. Here are some of the recipes I have obtained from friends and family members. Some are easier to prepare than others. But trust me, they are all delicious.

OLD-FASHIONED CHILI Con QUESO

6 green chile pods
1 t. oil
½ Pt. fresh milk
3 Oz. finely chopped asadero cheese
Dash of garlic
¼ t. salt

Roast, then peel chile pods. Cut chile into long strips. Remove seeds and veins. Fry in a teaspoon of hot oil with a little garlic. Add the milk and slowly begin to add the cheese. Stir constantly. When the mixture boils, add a fourth teaspoon of salt and remove from heat. Dish is ready to serve.

Water can be substituted for milk and more cheese added, if desired.

South of the Border
with Mexican Recipes
by Carol DeSantis-Munoz
El Paso Herald-Post

Dona Maria Josefa
De Farza, Texas(1813)

submitted by
Carl F. Tarlowski, MD
Las Cruces, NM

GOURMET CHILI Con QUESO

1 stick of margarine
2 Lb. box Velveeta cheese
1 Med. onion, diced
1 small can tomatoes (drained)
2 cans (7 oz.) chopped green chile
1 t. garlic salt

In a skillet, melt butter. Add garlic salt. The add onions and saute for about 10 minutes. Break-up tomatoes with a fork, then add to onions and let simmer for about 10 minutes. Cut block of cheese into small cubes. Add to onions and tomatoes one cube at a time, allowing cheese to melt. Can substitute Monterey Jack cheese for a different taste.

South of the Border with
Mexican Recipes
by Carol DeSantis-Munoz
El Paso Herald-Post
Carl F. Tarlowski, MD
Las Cruces, NM

Luther H. Sutton
Melbourne, FL

PINTO BEAN DIP

4 C. cooked pinto beans
1 T. Worcestershire sauce
¼ t. celery salt
½ t. garlic powder
1 C. diced green chiles

Mash pinto beans thoroughly. Add remaining ingredients to beans, stir to blend mixture.

Carl F. Tarlowski, MD
Las Cruces, NM

Gary F. Byers
Taft, TN

Two big sellers in any bookstore are the cookbooks and the diet books. The cookbooks tell you how to prepare the food, and the diet books tell you how not to eat it.

--And More by Andy Rooney (Atheneum)

SALSAS de CHILE (Chile Sauces)

Since many New Mexican dishes require a little chili sauce, it is appropriate to explain it's preparation first. Ground or powdered chile may be purchased, but care must be taken that the product is pure. Sauce prepared from chile pods is more satisfactory.

Chili Sauce -1

(a) 3 T. fat
2 T. flour
1 clove garlic, chopped
8 T. chili powder
1 t. salt
2 C. hot water

Melt fat, add flour and garlic. Brown well. Add chili powder and blend. Slowly add water. Salt and cook until thick.

(b) 24 chile pods
1 Qt. boiling water
1 t. salt
1 t. oregano
1 T. fat
1 T. minced onion
1 clove garlic, chopped

Wash chile pods; remove stems, seeds, and white veins. Put in a kettle and pour boiling water over them. Cook until tender. Pass through a food mill or fruit press until all the pulp has been removed from the skin. Add as much of the water which it was boiled as is needed for desired consistency. (A good; consistency for chile is that similar to tomato sauce.) Put on stove; add salt, fat, garlic, onion and oregano. Bring to a boil.

The use of your electric blender for making chile sauce will save you time, and you will get more sauce from the pods than by any other method.

To make: Remove stems, seeds and veins from pods. Place pods in warm oven (200 degrees) being careful that chile pods do not scorch, for about 10 minutes, stirring often and leaving oven door open. Remove chile pods from oven, add enough waster to cover, and let soak for 15 minutes.

Place chile pods and seasoning in the blender and add enough water to cover, leaving about an inch space or more in the glass container. Blend for 2 minutes. If sauce is too thick, add more water, if there is space, and blend one minute longer or until skin disappears completely. Remove from container and add enough water to give it the desired consistency.

Sixteen large chile pods will yield about 1 quart of sauce. For this amount, use 1 clove garlic, 1 tablespoon chopped onion, 1 teaspoon salt, and 1 teaspoon oregano for seasoning.

Chile Sauce with Tomatoes - II

3 T. olive oil or fat
1 T. chopped onion
2 cloves garlic, chopped
6 Med.-size fresh tomatoes
1 t. vinegar
8 T. powder chile, or
1 C. green chile
1 T. oregano
1 t. salt

Fry onion and garlic in oil or fat. Add tomatoes; cook until thick. Add chile and seasonings. (1 cup chile sauce No. 1-b may be used instead of powdered chile) Cook for 5 minutes.

Carl F. Tarlowski, MD
Las Cruces, NM

John B. Armstrong
Kingsville, TX

QUICK CHILI Con QUESO

1 can of cheddar cheese soup
1 can of cream of mushroom soup
1 can (7 oz.) chopped green chile

In a saucepan, combine cheddar and mushroom soups. Simmer for about five minutes. Add the chopped green chile. When dip is warm, it is ready to serve.

South of the Border
with Mexican Recipes
by Carol DeSantis-Munoz
El Paso Herald-Post
Carl F. Tarlowski, MD
Las Cruces, NM

Compania De Mon Clava
Texas(1817)

CHEEZ-WHIZ QUESO

1 Lg. bottle Cheez-whiz
3 jalapenos, roasted, peeled and chopped
water

Add one tablespoon of water directly in bottle of Cheez-Whiz. Mix slowly, continue to add water until you come up with a consistency you like. Do not warm this cheese up in a pan and then add water. It will quickly harden. Just add water. Stir in chopped jalapenos, or substitute green chile. Remember to serve dip as is. Do not heat.

South of the Border
with Mexican Recipes
by Carol DeSantis-Munoz
El Paso Herald-Post
Carl F. Tarlowski, MD
Las Cruces, NM

Matt A. Swift
Houston, TX

CHILI NIGHT CHILI FOR TWO

Dear Herb-

Thought you'd like to try my 2 recipes: Chili Night Chili For Two came from my art teacher, Joan Orrclle in high school (1966). She was a newly wed and thought recipes for two were so cute. For the novice cook (that I was)- it was a real achievement.

My chili recipe, Carolyn's Chili,suits us fine - it is not loaded with rattlesnake or gizzards (which are popular here in the West as chili additives). However, everyone who has ever had it is wild for the recipe. XLNT Chili Con Carne comes in a plastic peel top square package and is found either in refrigerated or freezer area of your supermarket. The success of this recipe IS dependent on that ingredient - I do suppose that any "chili brick" on the market will do quite nicely.

I am surprised that I am actually sending these recipes. It is not my norm to mail recipes to names in the newspaper - I have a feeling I'm a sucker for people who live on such a lovely sounding street as Blue Ash Road - makes me want to go antiquing.

1 Lb. hamburger
1 Med. onion, chopped
1 can (12-14 oz.) kidney beans
1 can tomato soup
1 t. chili powder
½ bell pepper, chopped
Salt and pepper to taste

Saute onion and pepper to taste. Brown hamburger beef, and drain off grease. Add beans including liquid, and the soup. Add chili powder. Bring to a boil. Reduce heat to Low and simmer for ½ to 1 hour.

It's quick, and hits the spot on cold nights. This is my very first chili recipe 20 years ago.

Ms. Carolyn Earsom
Bloomington, CA

James R. Hudgens
Rocking H Farms
Warren, MI

CAROLYN'S CHILI
(20 years in the making)

- 1½ Lbs. Hamburger meat, (coarse grind)
- 1 Lg. Bermuda or Mavi onion, chopped
- 1 or 2 bell peppers, chopped
- 1 small "XLNT" Chili Brick (it's chili con carne)
- ½ or 1 can beer (if you only use ½, then feel free to drink the rest)
- 1 Lb. can Hunt's Chili Beans, with liquid
- 1 small can kidney beans, drained
- 1 Lb. can whole tomatoes, squashed

Saute meat and veggies - combine all ingredients in a large pot and bring to a boil - turn to low and simmer up to half a day.

It is great spooned over a hunk of corn bread and topped with chopped onion and shredded cheese!!

Ms. Carolyn Earsom
Bloomington, CA

Double Barred S
Saxon Groves, Inc.
Avon Park, FL

CHILI LINDA

- 2 Lbs. ground beef
- 1 Lg. onion, chopped
- 1 green pepper, chopped
- 1 can (8 oz.) tomato sauce
- 1 can (8 oz.) water
- 1 T. chili powder
- ¼ t. cayenne pepper
- ½ t. black pepper
- ½ t. oregano
- 1 t. ground cumin
- 2 cloves garlic, finely chopped
- 1 t. salt
- 1 can (16 oz.) kidney beans, drained and rinsed

Increase cayenne or chili powder for hotter chili.

Brown beef and saute onion and green pepper. Mix all ingredients well, and proceed as normal.

Linda Braden
Knoxville, TN

Thomas W. McClure & Son
Amanda, OH

CHILI HOMINY CASSEROLE

- 2 Lg. cans hominy
- 1 Pt. sour cream
- 1½ small cans green chile
- ½ to ¾ Lb. Monterey Jack cheese, grated
- 1 Med. onion, chopped
- Salt to taste

Mix all ingredients, and pour into baking dish. Top with bread crumbs. Bake at degrees for 30 minutes.

Ora Maye Casgrove
Carlsbad, NM

F. M. Esplin
St. George, UT

CHILI CORN BREAD

- 1 C. corn meal
- ¼ t. salt
- ¼ Lb. Longhorn cheese, grated
- 1 can (16 oz.) whole kernel corn
- 1 C. sour cream
- ⅔ C. butter or oleo
- 2 eggs
- 1 C. green chilies, chopped

Mix all ingredients together and bake, 350 degree for one hour.

Carmen L. Caruso
El Paso, TX

Hank & Mae Dean Fehn
Benson, AZ

FRIDAY NIGHT CHILI

Here is a recipe that I use that is easy, good the first time, even better the next day when re-heated, and also freezes well.

2 Lbs. ground beef
1 Med. onion, chopped
2 cans (16 oz.) kidney beans, drained
2 C. water
2 cans (16 oz.) tomatoes, chopped and undrained
1 can (8 oz.) tomato sauce
1 T. chili powder
2 t. garlic salt
1 t. whole dried oregano
1 t. black pepper
½ t. red pepper
1 t. ground cumin (increase the amount for more "heat")

Combine beef and onions, brown. Drain off drippings. Add all other ingredients. Simmer, uncovered, for at least one hour, or longer. Makes 2 quarts, and freezes quite well.

Ms. Pat Richards
Pensacola, FL

WT

Ms. Violet T. Medeiros
Kailua, HA

CHILI GLACAMOLE

1 can chopped green chile
2 ripe avocados, mashed
1 t. salt
1 small tomato, chopped fine
2 drops lemon juice
Garlic to taste

Combine all ingredients, mixing well. Bury avocado bits in the glacamole to prevent discoloration, then cover and chill until served. This is a super dip!

NOTE: Glacamole is typically served with New Mexican food as a salad... place a scoop of Glacamole on a bed of shredded lettuce, top with a dollop of sour cream and garnished with crisp corn tostadas.

Mary Rey
El Paso, TX

F

Old Spanish
Florida early 1600's

GREEN CHILI CASSEROLE

In a baking dish arrange:

1 layer of Fritos or tostados
1 layer of canned chili con carne, without beans
1 layer of canned whole kernel corn
1 layer of canned tomatoes with green chili cooked with chopped onions
1 layer of grated cheese

Bake in moderate, 350 degree oven.

Carmen L. Caruso
El Paso, TX

Ernest Wineman
Santa Maria, CA

FAJITAS

2 Lbs. flank steak
1½ C. red wine vinegar
2 t. salt
½ t. pepper
2 cloves garlic
4 green chilies
1 t. oregano
1 t. cumin
1 t. paprika
½ C. red wine

Combine all ingredients. Pour over meat. Let marinate over-night. Wrap meat in heavy duty foil, and grill 15 to 20 minutes. Remove the meat from the foil and brown on each side.

Serve with warm flour tortillas, guacamole and pico de gallo.

Mary Rey
El Paso, TX

Mary Bass Minor, 1877
Brevard County, FL

CHILI CON QUESO

1 Lb. Velveeta cheese
2 cans (4 oz.) roasted and peeled green chilies (Old El Paso/ Mountain Pass)
1 small onion, finely chopped
Dash of garlic salt
a few drops of Tabasco sauce to taste
2 or 3 T. milk or cream to thin

Combine all ingredients and heat slowly until the cheese melts. Serve with chips as a dip, or on other foods as a sauce. Delicious!

Carmen L. Caruso
El Paso, Tx

Manuel Amoral, Sr.
Maui, HA

CHILI CON QUESO SUPREME

1 Lb. chile California, peeled
1 can evaporated milk, (fresh milk if necessary)
1 Lb. Monterey Jack cheese
Garlic powder, salt and pepper to taste
1 Med. onion
3 Med. tomatoes

Chop onion, tomatoes and chilies. Heat oil in a frying pan and fry the onion and chilies until the onions are tender; then add the tomatoes and fry a little more.

Pour the can of evaporated milk and grated cheese into pan. Add spices and cook slowly until cheese melts.

Carmen L. Caruso
El Paso, TX

United States Sugar Corp
Clewiston, FL

BAKED CHILI CON QUESO SQUARES

1 can (8 oz.) whole green chilies
1 Lb. Monterey Jack cheese
6 eggs

Cut the green chilies open and remove seeds. Line the chilies on bottom of greased 9½x9½-inch pan (skin side down). Sprinkle grated cheese over chilies.

Beat eggs and pour over chilies and cheese. Salt lightly on top. Bake at 275 degrees for 45 minutes. Cool and cut into 2x2" squares.

Makes about 16 squares.

Carmen L. Caruso
El Paso, TX

David & Dona Tullis
West Liberty, OH

BAKER'S MEXICAN CHILE Con CARNE

This is another recipe that goes good even in the hot weather we have here. Good chili is a "for all seasons" enjoyment.

1 Lb. ground beef
2 T. fat
2 onions, chopped
1 can (28 oz.) tomatoes
2 cans tomato sauce, or
1 can (10 oz.) tomato puree
2 bay leaves
2 t. salt
¼ t. pepper
1 T. chili powder
1 can (15 oz.) red kidney beans
⅛ t. cayenne pepper

Brown beef in fat, and all remaining ingredients, but the beans. Simmer for 2 hours. Add beans and it's ready to eat.

Arlene Baker
Palm Springs, CA

Robt. & Mary K. Campbell
Chino Valley, AZ

BULLOCK'S CHILI

For each pound of ground beef, use:

1 onion, quartered
1 bell pepper, quartered
1 can 16 oz.) VanCamp's New Orlean Style Red Beans
1 can DeMonte Whole Tomatoes
1 T. chili powder
Salt and pepper to taste

Brown beef in a little oil. Add other ingredients, cook and simmer for an hour. Just before serving, sprinkle with grated Cheddar cheese.

Ms. Ellis W. Bullock, Jr.
Pensacola, FL

R-D Livestock
Aumsville, OR

JALAPENO CHILI CHEESE OMELETTE

2 eggs
3 T. water
½ t. salt
dash pepper
1 T. butter
1 C. Jalepeno cheese (grated)

Mix eggs, water, salt and pepper with a fork. Heat butter in a 8" skillet until hot enough to sizzle a drop of water.

Pour the mixture and reduce the heat. When eggs are set and surface still moist, add 1 cup of grated cheese. Fold in half and serve. Serves 2 or 3.

Carmen L. Caruso
El Paso, TX

Howard J. De Rego, Sr.
Honolulu, HA

MEXI-CHILI CASSEROLE

1 Pkg. (16 oz.) corn chips
2 C. shredded Sharp American cheese
1 can (15 oz.) chili with beans
1 can (15 oz.) enchilada sauce
1 can (8 oz.) seasoned tomato sauce
1 T. instant minced onion
1 C. sour cream

Reserve one cup corn chips and ½ of the cheese. Combine remaining chips and cheese with all ingredients, (except sour cream), in a bowl; mix well. Pour into a casserole dish. Bake at 375 degrees for 10 minutes. Top with sour cream. Arrange remaining corn chips around the edge. Bake for 5 minutes longer. Yields 6 servings.

Ms. Brenda S. Allen
Maryville, TN

PA Joined
Margaret Ann Hartwell
Gaithersburg, MD

CHILI TORTA

4 C. chilies (cleaned and chopped)
1½ C. Parmesan cheese
1½ C. Longhorn cheese, grated
¼ C. Wesson oil
5 eggs
Dash of salt
2 onions, chopped

Mix the above ingredients well and then pour into a greased oblong pan. Bake at 350 degrees for 45 minutes.

Carmen L. Caruso
El Paso, TX

Henry E. Brown
Mesa, AZ

MONTANA HELL

This recipe was given to me by a group of cowboys from Montana several years ago, and is my family's favorite. We call it, for reasons you will discover, "Montana Hell", but it has the best overall flavor of any chili we've ever tried. Hope you like it. Bon Appetit!

3 Lbs. finely chopped steak (or pork)
1 bottle dark Mexican beer
3 Oz. chili powder
1 Lg. chili pepper, peeled and finely chopped
1 Med. jalapeno pepper, minced
1 t. salt
1 Qt. chopped canned tomatoes
2 Lg. onions, chopped
16 Oz. tomato sauce
2 cans (16 oz.) pinto beans

In a large pot, brown the meat in a little oil; add all other ingredients, except the beans. Cook over low heat for 2 hours, adding the beans during the last half hour.

Serve with lots of bread or crackers to soothe your mouth!

Jane Taylor
Yucaipa, CA

Tom L. Hayford
Black, AL

CHILI TWIST

- 2 C. egg noodles, cooked
- 2 cans (15½ oz.) chili con carne
- 1 t. parsley flakes
- ¼ t. oregano
- ½ t. sweet basil
- 2 cans (8 oz.) tomato sauce

Combine all ingredients in large sauce pan, mix well. Cook until heated through. Yields 4 to 6 servings.

Ms. Brenda S. Allen
Maryville, TN

Robert Godwin
Prescott, AR

CHILE CHEESE MEAT ROLLS

- 5 thinly cut steaks
- 4 strips bacon, in sections
- 4 California green chilies, (roasted and peeled) in strips
- ½ Lb. Cheddar cheese, in strips
- 1 can mushrooms (optional)
- 1 can consomme

Cut the meat in long strips about 2 inches wide by 6 inches long. Place chile and cheese strips on a strip of meat crosswise and make small rolls.

Place bacon around the rolls and fasten with toothpicks.

Heat a skillet and fry the rolls to an even brownness. Pour the consomme over then, and let simmer for about 40 minutes. Top with the drained mushrooms, and serve very warm.

Carmen L. Caruso
El Paso, TX

Old Spanish
Florida early 1600's

FIVE WAYS TO MAKE QUICK CHILI TAMALE PIE

In almost every city I have visited, your mothers say the casserole of tuna, mushroom soup and potato chips is their favorite quick dish.

Not so in Texas where Tamale Pie takes the honors. Here it's made of corn chips and canned chili (chili con carne) and the variations are legion.

These five call for either 15 ounce or 1 pound cans of chili.

Take your Pick!!

#1 Place 2 cups of corn chips in a casserole, add chili, with or without beans. Top with 1 cup of crushed corn chips. Bake at 350 degrees for 25 to 30 minutes. Serves 4.

#2 Spread 2 cups of corn chips in a baking dish. Unwrap and arrange 6 canned tamales on top. Add 1 large chopped onion, pour a can of chili without beans. Crown with 1 cup grated cheese and 1 cup of crushed corn chips. Bake at 350 degrees for 25 to 30 minutes. Serves 6.

#3 Put 2 cups corn chips in a baking dish. Add 1 can chili, 1 minced onion, and top with 1 cup of corn chips. Heat 1 can undiluted condensed tomato soup, stir in 1 cup of grated American cheese and heat to melt cheese.

Pour over the chips in baking dish and bake at 350 degrees 25 to 30 minutes. Serves 6.

#4 Divide 2 cups crisp corn chips equally in 4 soup bowls. Heat a can of chili without beans, and pour over the chips. Serve at once without baking.

#5 Pour 1¾ to 2 cups canned Spanish rice into a greased casserole. Sprinkle on ½ cup grated cheese and ½ cup crushed corn chips measured after crushing. Bake at 350 degrees for 20 minutes. Serves 5.

Carmen L. Caruso
El Paso, TX

Garate Ranch
T.J., Donald & Faye Garate
Ravendale, CA

CHICKEN-CHILI-CHEESE CASSEROLE

12 corn tortillas
1 C. milk
1 can green chile sauce
1 onion, chopped
1 can cream of mushroom soup
1 can chicken soup
1 Lb. Cheddar cheese, grated
Melted butter

Cut each tortilla into 8 wedges. Combine soups, milk and chile sauce. Layer tortillas, chicken, cheese, onion and soup mixture into greased baking dish until all ingredients are used, ending with tortillas. Drizzle butter over top. Refrigerate for 24 hours. Bake at 300 degrees for 1½ hours. Yields 8 servings.

Ms. Brenda S. Allen
Maryville, TN

WH Bar
Mitchell Harris
Rockledge, FL

CHILI-O-CHEESE DIP

1 Lb. American cheese, cut in chunks
1 Lb. can chili without beans
2 T. minced onion

Combine all ingredients in 1½ quart glass casserole. Microwave on Roast for 4 to 6 minutes, or until cheese is melted. Serve with chips.

Ms. Brenda S. Allen
Maryville, TN

N Over W
NuWay Accept. Corp.
Menton, IN

PICANTE CINCINNATI-STYLE CHILI

This far-from-the-ordinary spicy-sweet chili is traditionally served over spaghetti with help-yourself toppings and oyster crackers.

2 Lbs. ground pork or beef
2 Lg. onions, chopped (2 cups)
2 cloves garlic, minced
1 can (15 oz.) tomato sauce
1 C. Pace Picante Sauce
2 T. chili powder
1 to 1½ t. cinnamon, as desired
1 t. ground cumin
1 t. salt
¼ t. ground allspice
2 bay leaves
1 Lb. thin spaghetti, cooked
Toppings: Shredded cheddar cheese, chopped onion, red beans or kidney beans (heated), oyster crackers

In large saucepan or Dutch oven, brown meat with onion and garlic; drain. Add remaining ingredients except spaghetti and optional toppings; cover and simmer 1 hour, stirring occasionally. Remove bay leaves. Serve chili over spaghetti with optional toppings and additional Pace Picante Sauce. Makes 8 servings, about 6 cups chili.

Pace Foods, Inc.

Jose Escalada
Nogales, AZ

CHILI CON CARNE CON MAIZ

1 C. day old bread cubes
4 T. bacon drippings
1 No. 2 can yellow kernel corn
1 No. 2 can chili con carne, without beans
1 can (4 oz.) chopped green chiles

Saute the bread cubes in the bacon drippings. In a quart casserole, place the corn, chili con carne and chopped chile.

Add half of the sauteed bread cubes and mix. Top with remaining bread cubes and bake at 350 degrees for about an hour. Serves 4.

Good as a leftover, too! Cold slaw or tossed salad, celery and carrot sticks, hot French rolls or garlic bread are good with it. Top it off with pineapple sticks and cookies.

Carmen L. Caruso
El Paso, TX

Don & Rose Marie Coops
Cedarville, CA

SURF CHILI

(minus 1 or 2 secrete ingredients)

Herb- Read an article on your new cookbook in the El Paso Times... What a great idea! I have just received enough points to cook and show in the World's Championship Chili Cookoff in Terlinqua.

3 Lbs. chuck, sirloin, or round steak cubed
1 can (8 Oz.) tomato sauce
1 Med. onion, chopped
Water to cover
3 T. chili powder
1 t. garlic powder
1 t. paprika
2 t. salt
2 T. ground cumin
½ t. cayenne pepper
½ t. oregano
1 t. MSG
1 t. black pepper

Place meat, tomato sauce and onion in pot. Add water to cover. Bring to a boil, cover, reduce heat and cook till meat is tender- 2 to 2½ hours. Check and stir occasionally. Add water as needed.

When meat is tender, stir in chili powder, garlic powder, paprika, salt, cumin, cayenne, oregano, MSG, and black pepper. Cover and cook for 30 minutes.

Jason Douglass
El Paso, TX

Don Juan Joseph
Flores. Texas(1762)

CHILI-IN-A-HURRY

6 to 8 slices bacon, diced
1 C. rice
4 C. tomatoes
¼ Lb. Cheddar cheese, grated
1 T. chili powder
½ t. salt

Saute bacon in skillet until tender but not crisp. Stir in remaining ingredients with ½ cup of hot water. Simmer, covered, until rice is tender.

Ms. Brenda S. Allen
Maryville, TN

Veith H. Herre
Morrow, OH

CALDILLO

Mexican Stew

1 Lb. lean round steak, cut in 1-inch cubes
½ C. water
1 garlic clove, chopped
½ C. onion, chopped
½ t. whole cominos, crushed
½ t. dried leaf oregano, crushed
2 C. diced potatoes
½ C. diced green chiles
½ t. salt
½ C. water
1½ T. all-purpose flour

If using a covered dish, combine beef, ½ cup of water, onion, cominos and oregano in a 2-quart casserole. Cover with a lid; microwave on 50% (Medium) for 10 minutes. Add potatoes, chiles and salt. Cover and microwave on 70% (Medium-High) for 15 to 20 minutes, stirring after 8 minutes.

Combine ½ cup of water and flour in a small bowl, stirring until smooth. Stir into meat mixture. Cover and microwave on 100% (High) 2 to 3 minutes, or until tender; stir mixture. Let stand 5 minutes before serving.

Carl F. Tarlowski, MD
Las Cruces, NM

Flying A
J.R. Anderson
Wimauma, FL

CHILI PEPPER SOUFFLE

1 can (7 oz.) green chile
1½ Lbs. grated Monterey Jack cheese
1 C. milk
1 egg
1 t. salt

In a well-greased souffle dish (or casserole), place green chiles. Add grated cheese - pack down to fit well; mix remaining ingredients and pour over cheese. Bake for 1 hour at 350 degrees (should be golden and bubbling).

Carmen L. Caruso
El Paso,TX

Terry F. Neff
Napa, CA

RICE and GREEN CHILE CASSEROLE

1 C. raw white rice
2 C. sour cream
½ C. Longhorn cheese, grated
1 6-oz. can whole, roasted and peeled green chile

Add sour cream and cooked rice, blend. Butter a Pyrex dish; place ½ of rice mixture in dish, cover with green chile and ½ of the grated cheese. Place the remaining rice over the cheese, top with the rest of the cheese. Bake for 30 minutes at 350 degrees. Serves 6. Cheese lovers - use more cheese.

Carmen L. Caruso
El Paso, TX

Don Francisco Zangotasi
Ecuador (1594)

CHILI FOR A CROWD

3 Lbs. hamburger
1 onion, chopped
Salt and pepper
1 can (46 oz.) Hunt's Tomato Juice
1 1-Oz. bottle Mexican chili powder
4 cans (16 oz.) kidney beans, or half pinto beans, undrained

Put hamburger in large skillet, salt and pepper to taste. Add the chopped onions. Fry and crumble meat until done. Drain.

While hamburger is cooking, put into a large pot the tomato juice, chili powder, salt and pepper to taste. Stir well, then add all of the beans. Simmer. When hamburger is done, add it to the tomato juice and simmer a couple of hours to blend flavors.

This recipe is how my Mom and Dad always made chili and I've made it the same way for years, and it is always a real crowd pleaser.

Nancy V. Blazon
Pensacola, FL

Standing T Bar
Troy R. Story
Chulota, FL

CHILE COLORADO Con CARNE DE PUERCO
(Pork in Red Chile Sauce)

4 T. powdered red chile (Chimayo or Chiquita brands if possible)
4 T. flour
1 t. level, garlic salt
2 Lbs. pork (round steak may be substituted)
2 Lg. potatoes
Salt to taste

Dissolve powdered chile in 3 cups of water. Brown flour in about 1 tablespoons of oil, lard, shortening, add chile and stir constantly until it comes to a boil; simmer until it thickens (approximately 10 minutes). If a thinner consistency is desired, add water. Cube meat and potatoes. Brown the meat. Add meat and potatoes to chile, simmer until potatoes are tender.

Carmen L. Caruso
El Paso, TX

Dennis Whitaker, 1890
McLennan County, TX

CHILES RELLENOS EN CREMA

10 chiles, roasted and peeled
2 Lbs. ground beef
Raisins
1 onion, chopped
1 Lg. tomato, chopped
1 8-oz. container sour cream
Salt and pepper to taste
Cooking oil
Chopped pecans to taste

Fry the ground beef in the oil. Add the chopped must, raisins, onion and tomato. Cook this mixture well, and when it is done, stuff the chiles one by one. The stuffed chiles are placed in a Pyrex dish and the sour cream is poured over them.

Bake in the oven at 350 degrees for 30 minutes.

Carmen L. Caruso
El Paso, EX

Ralph Holmes, 1900
Brevard County, FL

BASIC RED CHILI SAUCE

18 chile pods, half hot, half mild (Las Cruces type)
6 garlic cloves, small
1 t. white vinegar
1 t. oregano
1 T. salt
½ onion, if desired

Soak the chile pods in hot water until they are soft. Drain the water; wash out the seeds and remove the stems. Place chile pods in a blender, and add 2 cups of water, the garlic cloves, onion if desired, the oregano and salt.

Blend until completely pureed. Taste-more salt can be added depending on individual preference. Put through a fine sieve for a beautiful pureed chile sauce.

Excellent for chile con carne, enchiladas, and chile beans.

Carmen L. Caruso
El Paso, TX

ALK Joined
Archie Lee Kelly
Kissimmee, FL

RANGER REDEYE
(A.K.A. YELLOWSTONE COCKTAILS)

There was a recent article in the Guam Pacific Daily News concerning contributions on chili recipes. As the only two National Park Rangers in the Western Pacific, we would like to contribute our recipe. We have organized several chili cookoffs here on Guam and this recipe has garnered the most attention. As a native Texan an a native Guamanian, we have teamed up to combine the best of Texas with the best of the tropics.

Best of luck from the tropics.

If the truth be known, it was a drop of Ranger Redeye that was accidently spilled to the ground from a park ranger's dinner that actually started the fires in Yellowstone National Park, several years back.

½ Lb. beef or kidney suet, or
 1 C. corn oil
4 Lbs. lean beef chuck, cut into
 ½-inch cubes
2 Lbs. lean pork shoulder, cut into
 ½-inch cubes
5 Lg. white onions
7 cloves garlic
5 Lg. tomatoes
6 long green peppers, or
 2 cans of chiles
6 celery stalks
1 can beef broth, or
 6 beef bouillon cubes
4 cans Mansfields Best Bitters
 British Beer or Long Star Beer
1 8 Oz. can tomato paste*
5 T. fresh chili powder
2 t. paprika*
1 t. cayenne pepper*
3 t. oregano
3 t. cumin
1 t. cilantro
1 T. coriander*
1 t. thyme
2 t. sugar
1 t. Masa Harina*
2 jalapeno peppers*
3 t. coarse ground black pepper
4 t. smoked salt seasoning
10 dashes of Tabasco sauce*
1 Lg. lime
1 Lb. smokey cheddar cheese
5 dashes Worcestershire sauce*

* if needed and to taste

Mixing and Cooking Directions:

CLASSIFIED!!! On orders from J&R Rustproofing & Chili, Co.

WARNING

Preparation and/or consumption of this product without professional training could be hazardous to your health. Keep out of reach of small children and politicians. Highly flammable, keep away from open flames. Use only under the direction of a professional National Park Service Ranger.

This product has been found to be environmentally safe and does not cause damage to the ozone layer, or is it responsible for acid rain or the "greenhouse" effect. It has been approved by the EPA, NPS, and CIA.

Other Texas recipes:

"Put a pot of chili on the stove to simmer. Let it simmer. Meanwhile, boil a sirloin steak. Continue to simmer the chili and eat the steak. Ignore chili."

Allan Shivers, Ex-Texas Governor

"Get yourself a big black pot.
Turn the stove on High.
Set the pot on the stove.
Wait 'till the black pot glows red.
Stick your head inside...and Dream."

Good ol' boy, Terry Allen, musician

(1) Fry suet until crisp, or oil, until it is hot.
(2) Then add beef one pound at a time, stirring as it cooks until brown. Remove each pound as it is browned.
(3) Add pork, cook until white on all sides and then remove.
(4) Drain all fat/oil except 2 tablespoons.
(5) Add onions and garlic; cook and stir until tender.
(6) Now add one can of beer and let it warm.
(7) Add browned pork and cook it for thirty minutes.
(8) In a sauce pan, mix chopped tomatoes, chopped celery and sugar, and simmer until tender.
(9) Blister green chiles over an open flame. Remove skins and seeds; boil in a small amount of beer. Cut into ¼-inch squares.
(10) Put oregano and thyme into 8 ounces of beer and stir until lumps dissolve.
(11) Add the tomato mixture, the cut up chiles, and the beer mixture to the cooking pot. Stir with a wooden spoon and bring to a low simmer.
(12) Add beef to the pot, cook on low heat for one hour.
(13) Add more chopped onions and jalapeno peppers, continue to cook for two hours.
(14) Stir together Masa (1 teaspoon) and warm beer (1 teaspoon). Mix well. Stir into chili mixture about twenty minutes before serving. ADD only if needed to thicken.
(15) At this point the remaining ingredients -may- be added depending on one's taste. You -may- add liquid smoke, Tabasco, Etc. DON'T add it if you don't think it needs it.

(16)Five minutes before serving, add grated cheese; stir until it is melted.
(17)About one minute before serving, add lime juice, stir with wooden spoon and serve.

DON'T LET IT BURN, ROSE!!!!

James E. Miculka
& Rose SN Manubusan
U. S. National Park Service
Agana, Guam

Charles K. Chapman
Mobile, AL

JALAPENO CHILE SAUCE

24 Lg. green jalapenos, roasted and peeled
1 small onion
1 Med.-size tomatoes, (an 8-oz. can of tomatoes may be substituted)
2 small tomatillos (green tomatoes)
1 8-oz. can tomato sauce
1 t. garlic salt
½ t. salt
Fresh coriander is recommended for extra flavor

Finely chop chile, onion, tomatoes, tomatillo and coriander; add tomato sauce, garlic salt and salt; mix thoroughly. If a thinner consistency is desired, water or more tomato sauce may be added.

Carmen L. Caruso
El Paso, TX

VonTrapp Family Lodge
Stowe, VT

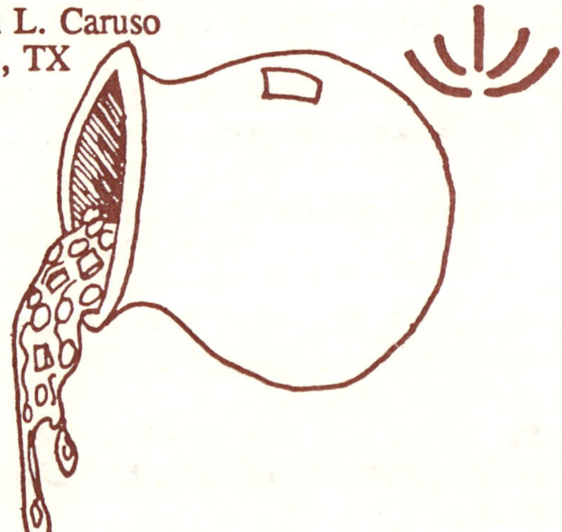

CHICKEN-CHILI CASSEROLE

1 Med. onion, chopped
1 clove garlic, minced
3 C. white sauce
1 or 2 cans green chile
1 doz. corn tortillas, torn into strips
1 chicken, cooked, boned, chopped
¾ Lb. Cheddar cheese, grated

Saute onion and garlic in skillet until golden. Add white sauce and green chile, mixing well. Alternate layers of chicken, tortillas, sauce and cheese in buttered casserole dish until all ingredients are used. Bake at degrees for 35 minutes or until bubbly. Yields 10 servings.

Ms. Brenda S. Allen
Maryville, TN

John Philips Broadcasting
Tallahassee, FL

HOT GREEN CHILE SAUCE

Hot green chile sauce is popular in both New Mexico and California, when so many green chiles are grown. At it's best when made with freshly parched green chiles, it is a great sauce with pork, chicken, or seafood, and with traditional dishes such as enchiladas, chimichangos, burritos, and eggs. Canned green chilies can be substituted, but the effect will be less pronounced.

Yield: 3 pints

¼ C. lard
½ C. finely chopped Spanish onion
½ C. flour
1 Qt. rich chicken broth
2 C. chopped green chiles which have been parched, peeled, and seeded
2 garlic cloves, minced
Pinch of ground cumin
½ t. salt

Melt the lard in a heavy saucepan. Stir in the onion and cook until it becomes clean. Stir in the flour.

When mixture becomes lightly golden, gradually add broth, cooking and stirring until the sauce slightly thickens. Add the remaining ingredients and simmer over a low heat for about 30 minutes, until the flavors blend and the sauce is thickened. Taste and adjust flavor if desired.

Carmen L. Caruso
El Paso, TX

Jernigan, 1869
Florida

BLACK BEAN CHILI

1 Lb. dried black beans
3 onions
2 cloves garlic
1 or 2 bay leaves
3 Lbs. ground beef
2 green pepper, chopped
2 or 3 cloves garlic, pressed
4 T. heaping, chili powder
½ t. cayenne pepper, or to taste
Salt
1 t. black pepper
2 t. ground cumin
2 t. ground coriander
2 bay leaves, crumbled
3-4 tomatoes, peeled and chopped
1 t. cinnamon
2 t. dry mustard

Wash the beans, cover with water, and soak overnight. Cook beans in soaking water, or drain and cover with fresh water. Add 1 whole onion, garlic, cloves and bay leaves to beans. Bring to a boil, then reduce heat and simmer, uncovered, about 1 hour or until tender. Remove garlic cloves and bay leaves. Leave onion. Add about 1 tablespoon salt when the beans are tender.

Meanwhile, cook beef in skillet until it looses color, stirring to keep crumbly. Drain off fat. Chop remaining onions, green peppers, and pressed garlic, and cook until tender. Add meat, chili powder, cayenne pepper, salt, pepper, cumin, coriander, bay leaves, cinnamon and mustard.

Add tomatoes and simmer until cooked. Add to beans, cover, and simmer for 1 hour. Serve with chopped onions and hot pepper sauce on side.

Post marked:
Pensacola, FL No name

James B. Baxter
Albany, NY

CHILI SPAGHETTI SAUCE

1½ Lbs. ground beef
1 T. oil
1 onion, minced
Salt and pepper to taste
½ t. chili powder
½ t. Tabasco sauce
1 t. oregano
1 can tomato soup
1 can mushroom soup

Brown meat; singe it for better flavor. Add onion, salt and pepper,Z and seasonings. Add soups with 1½ can of water. Let simmer and enjoy over spaghetti.

Ms. Marge Pung
Lansing, MI

Terrell & Beverly Bounds
Camarillo, CA

MARIAN'S CROCKPOT CHILI

There is no one-bar none-who is a bigger "chili" nut than me be he Mexican or Texan. That is my playtime, when I make a big batch of chili in my crockpot. Just throw it all in and slow cook for hours and hours.

1¼ Lbs. coarse chili grind beef
1 Lg. onion, chopped
olive oil
¼ c. chili powder
3 or 4 T. cumin
3 or 4 T. Tequila
8 fresh tomatoes
1 can light red kidney beans
1 Pkg. unsweetened chocolate
¼ C. corn meal
1 can pinto beans

Brown the meat with the onion along with the chili powder and cumin. When browned, dump into crockpot. Pour Tequila in a pan and scrape the "brown" into pot. Peel the tomatoes and chop fine. Put into pan with minced garlic and chopped parsley - a dash of olive oil and cook. Add salt and pepper. Throw into pot.

Add 1 package of unsweetened chocolate - stir up pot. Add enough corn meal to thicken. After 10 to 12 hours, add the kidney beans and pintos. Stir frequently as the "brown" will gather on the sides - scrape back into chili-brown is the secret-like with good gravy.

Serve with Mexican hot cornbread and jalapeno relish. You can add more spices or salt. Keep tasting it to make sure that it's just the way you want it. It will thicken, if so add more Tequila or water.

Marian Sakolinsky
Binghamton, NY

Courtesy Leasing, Inc.
Montgomery, AL

CHILE RELLENO PIE

2 cans of roasted and peeled whole green chiles
6 eggs
1 Lb. shredded Monterey cheese

Line a 8- or 9-inch pie plate with the chiles. Beat the eggs and add cheese. Pour the mixture over the chiles. Bake at 350 degrees for 20 minutes or until the top begins to turn brown.

Carmen L. Caruso
El Paso, TX

V-F

William Carpenter
Marana, AZ

CHILE RELLENO CASSEROLE

1 Lb. hamburger meat (browned)
½ Med. onion, chopped
1 can (4 oz.) chile, whole
1½ C. Cheddar cheese
4 eggs
½ C. milk
¼ C. flour
Salt to taste
Pepper to taste
Garlic to taste
Cumin to taste
Oregano to taste

Spray casserole dish with Pam, then line with chile. Spread the meat and onion on top of chile layer. Sprinkle 1 cup of Cheddar cheese over meat and onions. Blend 4 eggs, milk and flour. Add salt and pepper and other spices to taste.

Pour egg mixture on top of the meat, then place another layer of chile. Sprinkle ½ cup of cheese on top and bake 25 to 30 minutes at 375 degrees.

Gloria C. Fernandez
El Paso, TX

HB

Herbert J. Bock
Elmhurst, IL

VIVIAN'S EASY CHILI

2 Lbs. lean ground round
3 cloves garlic, finely chopped
1 Lg. onion, chopped
2 bell peppers, chopped
2 cans (28 oz.) tomatoes, chopped coarsely
1 can (40 oz.) pinto beans
2 cans (10¾ oz.) tomato soup
2 T. green chile peppers-from a jar, or can-finely chopped
2 T. chili powder
1 t. salt or to taste
½ t. pepper or to taste

Brown ground beef. Add garlic, onion, peppers, tomatoes, pinto beans and tomato soup. Add green chile peppers, chili powder, salt and pepper.

Simmer on low to medium heat about 4 hours or until it reaches your desired consistency.

Vivian Richardson
San Bernardino, CA

Harrel Cross
Limon, CO

CHILI FOR A CROWD

2 Lbs. lean ground beef
2 Lg. onions, chopped
2 Lg. bell peppers, chopped
1 can (6 oz.) tomato paste
3 cans water
3 cans (15 oz.) dark red kidney beans (or a 40 oz. can)
1 Pkg. French's Chili-Seasoning
1 t. salt
1 t. pepper

Brown meat, onions and pepper in a large skillet, breaking meat up as it browns. When it is brown, drain with a slotted spoon and put into a crockpot or large soup pot. Add remaining ingredients and let come to a boil. Turn on low and let it cook 1½ to 2 hours, or longer.

This will fill a crockpot. Serve with crackers and corn chips. You may like it hotter, so add more chili seasoning or hot sauce to taste. If you are going to be gone all day, if the crockpot is on low, it will be fine until you get ready to serve it.

You can brown meat, onions and peppers the night before, refrigerate and the next morning put everything in the crockpot and it will be all right all day. This recipe is great for church suppers, especially for teenagers.

If you are serving fifty or more have several ladies make a pot full and bring it to the church or school, ready to serve. We often did this when my two sons were growing up. You might like to have grated cheese to sprinkle over it.

Ms. Evelyn S. Salter
Niceville, FL

Joseph Bellino
Yonkers, NY

MEXICAN WHITE CHILI con QUESO

- 2 T. butter or margarine
- 1 Lg. onion, chopped fine
- 2 Med. tomatoes, peeled, seeded and chopped (mild or hot as you prefer)
- 2 cans (4 oz.) diced chiles
- Salt and freshly ground black pepper to taste
- 1 Pkg. (8 oz.) cream cheese
- ¾ C. heavy cream

Heat butter or margarine in skillet and saute onions until transparent. Add tomatoes, chiles, salt and pepper. Simmer for 15 minutes. Break cheese into pieces and add to hot mixture. When cheese begins to melt, add cream and stir until smooth and heated through.

Serve with tastadoes or warm flour tortillas. Serves 4 to 6.

Cay Mangold
El Paso, TX

Troy L. Powell
Mt. Juliet, TN

WEST COAST TURKEY CHILI

- 1 C. green pepper, cut in ¼-inch cubes
- 1¼ C. onion, chopped
- 2 cloves garlic, minced
- 3 T. oil
- 2 cans (15½ oz.) kidney beans, drained
- 1 can (28 oz.) stewed tomatoes, crushed

1 C. red wine
3 C. cooked turkey, cut in ½-inch cubes, or
1½ to 2 Lbs. browned ground turkey
1 T. fresh cilantro, chopped, or 1 t. dried
1 t. crushed red pepper
½ t. salt
1 T. chili powder

In a 3-quart saucepan, over medium-high heat, saute green pepper, onion and garlic in oil about 5 minutes, or until vegetables are tender crisp.

Add beans, tomatoes, wine turkey, chili powder, cilantro, red pepper and salt. Increase heat and bring mixture to a boil; reduce heat and simmer uncovered for 25 minutes.

To serve, garnish with onion and fresh cilantro, if desired.

NOTE: Approximate nutrient contents per serving: 356 KCAL; 30 gm protein; 11 gm fat; 35 gm carbohydrate; 1094 mg sodium; 54 mg cholesterol.

National Turkey Federation
Reston, VA

Richard E. Millage
Burbank, WA

AQUACATE (AVOCADO) DIP FOR CHRISTMAS

2 C. aquacate, mashed well
2 t. lemon juice
¼ C. sour cream
½ t. Tabasco
1 t. salt
Canned red pimento

Mix all ingredients together (except the pimento). It will be a creamy and soft paste. Serve in a dip dish and decorate with the pimento to give it a Christmas decoration. Serve with crackers or small pieces of toast.

Carmen L. Caruso
El Paso, TX

J.F. Banks
Nashville, TN

MARY'S BASIC CHILI

Use one pound of browned chopped lean sirloin to a one pound can of tomato sauce, and a one-pound can of red kidney beans. Season with chili powder to taste. Mix ingredients and simmer about 15 to 20 minutes, stirring occasionally. If too thick, thin with tomato juice. Serves 4.

NOTE: Basic recipe may easily be doubled, or increased to any size needed. Sauteed chopped onions and/or green peppers may be added, if desired.

Chili Variations: When making chili, prepare enough to freeze in one pint plastic containers for simple but tasty meals in the future. It's like having money in the bank! Here are some recipes for those meals:

CHILI-MAC

Heat chili. Serve over hot boiled macaroni.

CHILI-SPUDS

Serve generous amounts of hot chili as a topping for baked potato halves.

CHILI con CORN

Serve hot chili over cooked canned, frozen or fresh corn kernels.

CHILI-CORNBREAD PIE

Baked cornbread batter in well-greased, preheated iron skillet or round, shallow pan. Split horizontally, after removing from pan. Spread bottom layer thickly with hot chili. Place top layer of cornbread on chili. Press down lightly but firmly. Cut into wedges and serve.

CHILI DIP

Serve a bowl of hot chili (without beans) as a dip for hot crisp French fries.

Ms. Mary Curtis
Pensacola, FL

Charles Chesnut
Pineland, FL

CROCK POT CHILI CON CARNE

2 Lbs. ground beef
2 T. shortening
2 C. chopped onion
2 cloves garlic, crushed
3 T. chili powder
1 t. salt
1 t. paprika
1 t. oregano
1 t. ground cumin
½ t. cayenne pepper
½ C. beef stock
1 can (28 oz.) tomatoes
3 cans (16 oz.) red kidney beans

Heat the shortening in a skillet and brown the beef; discarding the fat.

Combine all ingredients in a cooker, stirring well. Cook on a low heat 8 to 10 hours; on High 5 hours, or on automatic for 6 hours. This recipe yields 8-10 servings.

Mary D. Wallace
Pensacola, FL

Henry Levi, Jr.
Pearl City, HA

MARGE'S CHILI

1½-2 Lbs ground beef
1 Med. onion, sliced
1 C. celery, chopped
2 cans (10¾ oz.) tomato soup
1 can (16 oz.) chili beans (Bush)
¼ C. water
1½ to 2 t. chili powder
1 t. brown sugar
1 t. Worcestershire sauce
½ t. salt - optional
⅛ t. pepper
⅛ t. cayenne pepper

Combine beef and onion; cook in skillet until browned. Add celery, soup, water and seasonings. Simmer as long as you like to blend the mixture. Add beans the very last and simmer 30-45 minutes.

MICROWAVE: Combine beef, onion and celery in a 3-quart microwave casserole. Cook on High 6 to 9 minutes. Drain fat, and break up meat. Stir in soup, beans, water, chili powder, brown sugar, Worcestershire sauce, salt, pepper and cayenne. Cover Microwave on High 5 minutes.

Remove cover and stir. Cook, uncovered, 50% Medium power for 30-35 minutes. Stir twice during cooking. Makes 2 quarts.

Ms. Marge Pung
Lansing, MI

Mision De La
Espada De Bexar
Texas(1817)

PABLO'S - "HOT STUFF" - CHILI

- ¼ C. diced bacon pieces
- ½ C. olive oil
- 1 Lb. beef cut into ¾-inch cubes
- ½ white onion, chopped
- 6 cloves garlic
- 2½ T. chili powder (see below)
- 1 T. garlic powder
- 1 T. cumin, roasted and ground
- 1 T. coriander, roasted and ground
- 1 T. Mexican oregano
- 1 T. fresh ground pepper
- 1 C. Roma tomatoes, peeled
- 1 can (10 oz.) beef bouillon
- 1 can (12 oz.) beer
- ½ C. Tequila
- ¼ C. Masa flour
- 2 ground chili pequin
- ½ jalapeno chili, fresh
- ½ fresh wax chili
- ½ fresh serrano chili

Cut meat into ¾-inch cubes. Brown bacon, then add olive oil and heat. Saute onions and garlic in the hot fat and bacon until soft. Add meat and saute until grey. Add balance of dry ingredients to meat and vegetables to season. Can use 2 tablespoons chili powder for less hot.

Add beer and bouillon, Tequila if desired. Add tomatoes. Simmer 2½ hours; stirring frequently. Add fresh chilies, finely diced. Simmer another 15 minutes. Check for flavor. Add Masa and simmer another 15 to 30 minutes.

Add beer or water if additional liquid is needed during cooking.

Lots of work but worth it when you are done. ENJOY!! Makes 2 quarts.

CHILI POWDER: @ Type Ground Together As Many As needed

New Mexico Chili Pepper	1@
California Chili Pepper	1@
Pasilla Chili Pepper	1@
Guajillo Chili Pepper	1@
Arbol Chili Pepper	2@
Japanese Chili Pepper	2@

Paul W. Englund
Salinas, CA

Bruce & Elizabeth Beckway
River Forest, IL

RED CHILI SAUCE

This sauce-sometimes called enchilada sauce-is probably the most frequently served sauce in the Southwest. Although it is sold canned, which is always dreadful, and frozen, which is barely acceptable, you can easily whip up a homemade version in 5 minutes, with another 15 to 30 minutes of simmering.

The critical ingredient is pure, ground red New Mexico or California chile. The best color and texture comes from blending the two. The California Anaheims have a higher starch level, which acts as a thickener, and are a deeper, almost bluish red color, which blends beautifully with the orange-red New Mexico chile, which supplies the heat.

You can easily adjust the piquancy to taste-even at the meal itself- by making a mild sauce and providing a bowl of ground, pure, hot New Mexico chile at the table. Don't even make this sauce with commercial chile powder, as it will be briny, dark, and stale-tasting due to the salt and the chemicals that have been added.

You'll find this sauce terrific over enchiladas, burritos, chimichangos, eggs, hamburgers, pork chops, and rellenos. For convenience, freeze in 1- to 2- cup portions, which keeps well up to 8 months. Yield: 3 pints

¼ C. lard
¼ C. flour
¼ C. ground pure mild California chile powder
¼ C. ground pure hot New Mexico chile powder
¼ t. ground cumin
1 Qt. well-flavored beef stock
1 t. salt, or to taste
2 garlic cloves, minced

Melt the lard in a heavy saucepan over low heat, then stir in the flour. When it is lightly browned, remove from heat. When the pan has cooled slightly, thoroughly stir in the chile powders.

Add the cumin, then stir in about 1 cup of the beef stock; when well blended, return to the heat and cook and stir, adding a little more stock at a time until all has been added. Season to taste with the salt and the garlic; simmer for at least 10 minutes--up to 30 minutes over low heat--until the sauce thickens and the flavors blend. Use as desired, or freeze.

Variation: For beef enchiladas, brown 2 pounds of hamburger beef first, omitting the lard. Then add the flour and proceed with recipe.

Carmen L. Caruso
El Paso, TX

Robert Louis Randall
Bonanza, OR

CHILI NIGHTS CHILI Con CARNE

This mild chili can be everyone's favorite. If you like it spicier, add more red pepper or a chopped jalapeno to suit your taste.

¼ t. corn oil
½ Lb. very lean ground beef
½ Lb. boned and skinned chicken breast, finely chopped
1 Lg. yellow onion, finely chopped
1 Med.-sized sweet green pepper, cored, seeded and chopped
2 cloves garlic, minced
1 T. chili powder
1 T. ground cumin
1 can (16 oz.) low-sodium tomatoes, pureed with their juice
1 C. low-sodium beef broth
1 T. low-sodium tomato paste
1 t. red pepper flakes
1 t. ground coriander
1 t. dried oregano
1 t. basil, crumbled
1 bay leaf
1 C. cooked and drained kidney beans
¼ C. shredded sharp Cheddar cheese (optional)

In a heavy 10-inch skillet, heat the corn oil over a moderate heat for 30 seconds. Add the beef and chicken; cook, stirring often, until no longer pink color, about 4 to 5 minutes. Push meat mixture to one side of the skillet.

Add onion, green pepper, garlic, chili powder, and cumin; cover and cook until the onion is soft, about 5 minutes. Add the tomatoes, beef broth, tomato paste, red pepper flakes, coriander, oregano, basil, and bay leaf. Simmer, uncovered, stirring occasionally for 20 minutes.

Add the kidney beans; simmer, uncovered, stirring occasionally, five minutes longer. Discard the bay leaf before ladling into bowls. Top with shredded cheese if desired.

Jay & Sandy Hatfield
Cincinnati, OH

Lazy TK
Tammi Kelley
Kissimmee, FL

CHILE RELLENO CASSEROLE

- 12-15 long green chiles, roasted and peeled
- 1 Lb. ground meat
- 1½ C. shredded cheese
- 4 eggs, beaten
- 1½ C. milk
- ¼ C. flour
- Salt

Brown the meat, and salt to taste. Grease a 13-inch oblong pan. Open the chiles and line the bottom of the pan. Alternate layers of ground meat, cheese, and remaining chiles. Mix eggs, milk, flour and 1 teaspoon salt. Pour mixture over casserole. Bake at 350 degrees for 45 minutes.

Carmen L. Caruso
El Paso, TX

Joan W. Meininger
Woodside, CA

HEALTHY, LOW FAT CHILI

½ onion, chopped
½ green pepper, chopped
2-3 cloves garlic, minced
1 Lb. ground turkey breast, uncooked
2-3 T. hot chili powder
Pepper to taste
2 ripe tomatoes, chopped
1 small can tomato paste
1½ C. cooked kidney beans

Spray pan with cooking spray and saute the onion, green pepper and the garlic for about 3 minutes. Add the turkey and brown completely.

Mix in chili powder and pepper. Next stir in chopped tomatoes and the tomato paste, adding water for the desired consistency. Let simmer for 45 minutes. Add more water if necessary and stir in beans.

OPTION: Add 1-2 cups cooked elbow macaroni. It's great!!

Kelli Hibberd
Olympia, WA

D.B. Suffolks, Unltd.
Dallas, OR

CHILI VERDE

An historical dish that goes back to the Southwestern Indians.

3 Lbs. boneless pork
4 T. salad oil
1 yellow onion, chopped
4 cloves garlic, chopped
1 can (12 oz.) chicken stock/ broth (not dried bouillon
3 stalks celery, chopped
2 cans (4 oz.) diced green chiles
½ t. crushed red pepper
1 t. ground cumin
1 T. coarse ground pepper
Water
4 T. Masa (or flour)
Jalapeno salsa (optional)

Dice pork into ¾-inch cubes, trim off any excessive fat. Brown pork in salad oil, using heavy (black if you have) frying pan. Do it in several batches so all will be browned evenly.

Remove meat with slotted spoon, to drain off excess fat, and place in a 4-quart pot. Reserve 2 tablespoons fat, and then add onions and garlic.

Saute for a couple of minutes. Then add chicken broth to deglaze pan. Scrape pan and pour liquid into pot.

Add remaining ingredients (except Masa and salsa), and water to cover meat. Simmer, covered for 1½ hours or until meat is tender.

Remove cover, add Masa or flour to thicken, simmer for 20 minutes more. Check seasonings, add salt if needed, or more thickener if desired. Add jalapeno salsa if adventurous, simmer for an additional 10 minutes. Serve in bowls, over plain boiled rice, or in flour tortillas as burritos.

ENJOY!!! Makes 2 quarts.

Paul W. Englund
Salinas, CA

Lawrence C. D'Angelo
Apalachin, NY

CHILI CON QUESO

- 10 green chiles (long) roasted and peeled. Discard seeds
- 1 fresh ripe tomato, chopped
- 1 onion, chopped
- 1 button garlic, chopped fine
- 8 Oz. mild Longhorn Cheddar cheese. Cut into small cubes
- 1 can chicken broth
- 2 C. water

Saute onion in 2 tablespoons of Wesson oil. Add tomatoes and chiles and cook a little longer. Add the can of chicken broth and water, and simmer for 20 minutes.

Add cheese and cook until the cheese has melted. Season to taste.

Elsie Salome
El Paso, TX

Charles McDonald
Prescott, AZ

MERLINE'S VENISON CHILI

2 Lbs. venison, cubed
1 Lb. pork sausage
1 C. chopped onion
3 T. green peppers
1 can (12 oz.) tomato paste
24 Oz. water or chicken broth (-divide)
1 can (22 oz.) chili beans, do not drain
1½ t. garlic powder, or fresh garlic
2 t. chili powder
1 t. cumin powder
1 C. oat bran
Dash Tabasco (optional)

Brown sausage; drain and set aside. In a Dutch oven, using 2 tablespoons of sausage fat, brown the venison, adding 12 ounces of water or chicken broth. Cover; simmer 2 hours; meanwhile, saute onions and green pepper in 1 tablespoon of butter or margarine.

After venison has simmered 2 hours, add sausage, onions, green pepper, tomato paste, 12 ounces of remaining water or chicken broth, chili beans, garlic, chili powder, cumin and one cup of oat bran.

Cover and cook another 40 minutes; if you need more water, add a little at a time.

You may spoon this into tortillas and eat as finger food or in bowls with corn bread and cheese on the side.

Merline McKenzie
Lansing, MI

R. L. & Susen Hewitson
Avenal, CA

PINTO BEAN CHILI

1 Lb. ground beef
1 Lg. onion, chopped
1 green pepper, chopped
2 cans (16 oz.) whole tomatoes, chopped, undrained
1 C. water
2 T. chili powder
1 t. sugar
1 t. salt
1 can (15 oz.) pinto beans, undrained

Combine first 3 ingredients in a Dutch oven; cook until meat is browned, stirring to crumble. Drain off drippings. Stir in remaining ingredients except beans; cover, bring to a boil, reduce heat, and simmer 1 hour, stirring occasionally. Add beans and simmer, 5 minutes.

Yield: 7 cups.

John G. Wright
Warsaw, KY

Dean Cobb Nichols
Brentwood, TN

TURKEY CHILI

2 t. oil
2 Lbs. ground turkey, defrosted
½ C. onion, chopped
2 cloves garlic, minced
2 T. chili powder (or to taste)
1 T. paprika
1 t. cumin
1 t. salt
Fresh ground pepper (to taste)
1 can (28 oz.) tomatoes, drained
2 cans (15 oz.) red kidney beans, drained

Over medium heat, in a large skillet, heat the oil. Add turkey and onions, cook and stir about 4-5 minutes or until turkey is no longer pink.

Stir in garlic, chili powder, paprika, cumin, salt, pepper and tomatoes; cover. Over high heat, bring to a boil; reduce heat and simmer for 1 hour.

Add beans, cook until heated through.

May be prepared a day ahead. Simmer 1 hour.

NOTE: Approximate nutrient content per serving: 334 KCAL; 28 gm protein; 16 gm fat; 24 gm carbohydrate; 914 mg sodium; 76 mg cholesterol.

Serves 8.

National Turkey Federation
Reston, VA

HJW

Harry Wilfong
Buffalo, TX

SUPER CHILI

3 Lbs. ground meat
2 C. coarsely chopped onion
4 cloves garlic, minced
3 T. chili powder
1½ t. oregano
1½ t. ground cumin
1 t. crushed red pepper
2 C. beef broth
1 can (25 oz.) whole tomatoes
1 can (6 oz.) tomato paste
1 t. salt
1 t. sugar

Brown the meat. Saute the onions and garlic until soft. Stir in the chili powder, oregano, cumin and crushed red peppers and mix well. Add broth, tomatoes, juices and all, tomato paste, salt and sugar, mixing well.
Break up tomatoes. Cover and simmer for 1 hour. Uncover and simmer 40 to 50 minutes. Cool. Cover and refrigerate overnight.
To serve, bring slowly to a boil. Red beans may be added.

Gloria Ford
Apalachin, NY

Donald N. Pence
St. Paris, OH

GREEN CHILE AZTEC PIE

1 Lb. corn meal tortillas
1 Pt. heavy cream
Cheese (fresh, or may be Monterey Jack)
Roasted and mashed tomato
Strips of green chile
Slices of onion

Fry the tortillas and drain. Meanwhile, prepare the sauce with the tomato and onion slices, salt and pepper to taste. Fry the strips of green chile separately. Butter an oven dish and sprinkle with bread crumbs. Pour part of the tomato sauce on the bottom, then a layer of tortillas, a layer of chile strips, slices of cheese and some cream. Repeat layers. Bake at 350 degrees, moderate oven, for 20 to 30 minutes.

Carmen L. Caruso
El Paso, TX

Fredric & Barbara Nagel
Happy Valley Ranch
Susanville, CA

JICAMA En ESCABECKE de CHILE

Over the 20 years of living in El Paso, I have collected many recipes from my many Mexican friends. I am enclosing several of them for your use.

3-4 carrots
1 C. vinegar
1 C. water
½ C. salad oil
3 white onions, sliced
6 clove garlic
2 Med. peeled, sliced jicamas
¼ C. sugar
¾ t. salt
2 t. oregano
3-4 bay leaves
1 can (4 oz.) jalapeno chiles or
3 fresh jalapenos, sliced

Cut carrots into small chunks, cook in slightly salted water until tender. Drain and cool. In a large pan combine vinegar, water, oil, onions, garlic, salt and sugar. Cook until onions are tender. Add oregano and bay leaves.

Boil about five (5) minutes and let cool. Add jalapenos, carrots, and jicamas; let set for several hours. Store in refrigerator. Serve as an appetizer with crackers.

Cay Mangold
El Paso, TX

B.A. Cattle Co.
Honolulu, HA

HOT CHILE PEPPER JELLY

¾ C. bell pepper, measured after grinding
¼ C. hot peppers, measured after grinding
1½ C. apple cider vinegar
6 C. sugar
1 bottle (6 oz.) cirto

Remove seeds and grind peppers in blender. Add vinegar and sugar. Bring to a full, rolling boil, stirring constantly. Add cirto and boil for one (1) minute, stirring.

Set aside, skim, pour into sterilized glasses and seal. Delicious with cold meats. Makes eight (8) 8-ounce jelly glasses.

Cay Mangold
El Paso, TX

Ed Aul
Harquahla, AZ

PICO de GALLO

(chile relish)

8 long green chiles, roasted, peeled, deveined and chopped
2 small yellow chiles, roasted, peeled and chopped, or
2 jalapeno chiles
5 green onions, chopped (including tops)
5 Med. tomatoes, peeled and chopped
¼ C. chopped fresh cilantro leaves
2 T. salad oil
1 t. vinegar
Salt to taste

Combine all ingredients; chill. Will keep at least two (2) weeks in refrigerator. Serve with meats, chicken, hamburger, etc. Makes about 2 cups.

Cay Mangold
El Paso, TX

Agri-Tech Services, Inc.
Ft. Morgan, CO

MEXICAN BAKED POTATOES with CHILE

6 Lg. baked potatoes
1 can (4 oz.) chopped green chile
3 hard cooked eggs, chopped
½ C. butter or margarine, softened
1 C. sour cream
Shredded Longhorn cheese
Salt to taste

Mix mashed potatoes, chile, chopped eggs, butter or margarine, sour cream and salt. Fill shells with this mixture. Top with shredded cheese and heat in oven for 15 minutes.

Cay Mangold
El Paso, TX

Jim, Judy Woods & Daughters
Carroll, OH

CHILE CALDILLO

Mexican stew

3 Lbs. cubed meat
1½ C. onion, diced
Cooking oil or bacon fat
3 C. tomatoes, diced
1½ C. green chile strips
½ C. beef stock
1 T. salt
1 t. pepper
2 t. garlic salt
1 t. cumin
2 Lbs. cubed cooked potatoes

Saute beef and onions in cooking oil or bacon fat. Add tomatoes, chile strips, beef stock and seasonings. Cook over low heat until the meat is tender. Add cubed potatoes during the last 30 minutes. Caldillo may be frozen after preparation.

Serve with hard rolls. Makes one (1) gallon.

Cay Mangold
El Paso, TX

Hidden Springs Ranch
Hopewell, OH

CHILE COLORADO

Red chili with Pork and Beef

An authentic American original dish from the days of the old West.

2 slices bacon, diced
¼ C. olive oil
1 yellow onion, diced
4 cloves garlic, minced
1 Lb. beef, cut into ¾-inch cubes
1 Lb. pork, cut into ¾-inch cubes
3 T. chili powder
1 T. garlic powder
1 T. ground cumin
1 T. oregano leaves, crushed
1 T. coarse ground pepper
1 can (16 oz.) peeled tomatoes
1 can (10 oz.) beef bouillon
1 can (12 oz.) beer
¼ C. Masa or flour

Cut beef and pork into ¾-inch cubes. Heat oil in a heavy 8-quart pot, (black if you have), saute bacon until brown. Saute onions and garlic until transparent. Add meats and saute until grey and somewhat browned. Cook out all liquid from meat.

Add chili powder and spices to season meats. Add bouillon and beer. Add additional water to cover meat. Simmer, uncovered, 2½ hours, stirring occasionally. Add water if needed.

Mix Masa or flour with water to thin paste, and add to meats and simmer an additional 30 minutes. Check for salt and seasoning after Masa has simmered for 20 minutes. Add additional Masa if needed and simmer an additional 15 minutes. Add additional chili powder or salsa as desired to taste.

Serve in bowls, over rice or pasta, or as burritos. Makes 2 quarts.

Paul W. Englund
Salinas, CA

J.E. Dalton Jr.
Arlington, TX

McKENZIE'S UNFORGETTABLE CHILI For A Crowd

This recipes requires 2 large soup pots, with tight lids.

- 3 Lbs. chuck roast, cubed 1" pieces
- 3 Lbs. ground chuck
- 2 Lg. yellow onions, diced
- 6 stalks celery, diced
- 2 cans (28 oz.) tomatoes, chopped
- 2 cans (12 oz.) tomato paste
- 48 Oz. chicken broth (home made)
- 8 Lg. cloves garlic, crushed
- 3 T. chili powder
- 1 T. salt (more if needed)
- 1 T. cumin
- ½ C. dark molasses
- 2 cans (4 oz.) green chile peppers
- 1 can (48 oz.) red kidney beans
- 4 T. Worcestershire sauce
- Several shakes Tabasco
- Enough flour for dusting cubes of beef

Dice chick roast-separate fat-saute fat use for browning meat. Toss meat with flour and brown, using a large soup pot. Add 24 ounces of chicken broth. Cover; simmer 1 hour. Meanwhile brown ground chuck, and set aside.

Saute onions and celery in 1 tablespoon oil until tender. After 1 hour simmer time, add all the remaining ingredients, both meats, all the tomatoes and paste, remaining chicken broth, spices and chiles. Stir well. Cover and simmer for another 2 hours. Stir often. During the last 15 minutes of cooking time, add molasses, beans, Worcestershire sauce and Tabasco.

Serve with lots of corn bread, nachos, diced cheese, Cheddar or Monterey Jack. Put the Tabasco bottle on the table for those people that may want a little more.

Merline McKenzie
Lansing, MI

Spur, 1937
Sargent & Camerer, Inc
Brevard County, FL

GREEN CHILE SAUCE CHICKEN ENCHILADAS

Tortillas (as many as you need)
Shredded chicken (or cheese)
1 pint cream (whipping cream)
4 California chiles, roasted and peeled
1 Pkg. Philadelphia Cream Cheese (small)

Roll up the tortillas with chicken, or cheese. Fasten each with a toothpick. In a mixer, place the cream cheese, diced green chiles, and cream; mix well. Salt and pepper to taste. Pour the cream mixture over the rolled tortillas and bake in oven at 350 degrees for 30 minutes.

Carmen L. Caruso
El Paso, TX

Bar Diamond I
S.M. Mercer
Sebring, FL

FIESTA CHILI SOUP

1 C. onion, coarsely chopped
1 C. green pepper, chopped
2 T. olive oil
1½ t. chili powder
1 clove garlic, minced
1 can (14½ oz.) ready to serve chicken broth
1 jar (12 oz.) medium flavored salsa
1 can (10¾ oz.) condensed tomato soup
1 C. (8 oz.) kernel corn, drained
1 C. fully cooked deli juienna turkey thick slices, ¾" squares

In a 2-quart casserole, combine onion, green pepper, oil, chili powder and garlic. Cover. Microwave at HIGH 5 to 7 minutes, or until vegetables are tender, stirring once during the cooking time.

Stir in remaining ingredients. Recover. Microwave at HIGH 7 to 9 minutes, or until the soup is hot, stirring once or twice during cooking.

Garnish with sour cream and chopped black olives. Serve with corn chips.

This recipe can easily be doubled, with cooking time extended, and made spicier with a shot or two of Tabasco.

This recipe is one that has been given to me by someone who it was passed to by a friend of a friend. It has probably been passed around so many times that it has been slightly altered each time, but it undoubtedly tastes very close to the original. We use it all the time.

Don & Sally Miller
Largo, FL

Michael J. Vidinha
Kawai, HA

QUICK-COOK CHILI

1 Lb. ground beef
½ C. onions, chopped
1 can (16 oz.) pinto beans
1 can (10¾ oz.) condensed tomato soup
1 T. chili powder, or as desired to taste

Heat beef and onion in a fry pan until beef is browned and the onion is tender. Drain off excess fat. Stir in remaining ingredients.

Cover. Simmer for 30 minutes, stirring occasionally.

Makes 6 servings, about ¾ cup each; about 270 calories per.

Mary D. Wallace
Pensacola, FL

Robert C. Rogers
Hillsboro, OH

BABB'S TAMALES w/CHILI GRAVY

Dough:

1 C. sweet milk
10 T. chili puree
½ C. sugar
1 C. lard
1 t. salt

Kneed above good with mesa prepared dough, (fresh better at any Mexican factory or prepared package.

2 Lbs. lean stew pork
2 Lbs. lean beef, cut in very small pieces
2 onions, chopped
4 fresh tomatoes
4 cloves garlic, minced
1 C. raisins
3 whole cloves garlic
1 t. thyme
1 t. salt
1 t. pepper (red one only)
1 t. pepper
1 T. tamale flour

Get tamale leaves spread with dough-big leaf only (6). On another big leaf center fill with stew and tie each end with a strong string. Put in large kettle with bottom lined with tamale leaves to 2 inches thick. Put a lot of water, and cover leaves. Steam several hours.
Make sure bottom and top get rotated once.

Chili Gravy:

8 C. pure chili (Los Palmos)
1 cube butter
6 minced garlic
2 t. oregano
6 T. cornstarch, dissolved

Mix well and make smooth gravy.

Mrs. Paul Babb
Salinas, CA

Levi Kapahulehua, Jr.
Kawai, HA

TURKEY VERDE CHILI

A variation of a historic dish that goes back to the Southwestern Indians.

3 Lbs. boneless, skinless turkey
4 T. olive oil
1 yellow onion, chopped
4 cloves garlic, chopped
1 can (12 oz.) chicken stock/broth (not dried bouillon)
3 stalks celery, chopped
2 cans (4 oz.) diced green chiles
½ t. crushed red pepper
1 t. ground cumin
1 T. coarse ground pepper
Water as needed
4 T. Masa (or flour)
Jalapeno salsa as desired

Cut turkey into ¾-inch cubes. Can be thighs, breasts or combination. Brown turkey in oil, using heavy (black if you have) frying pan. Do it in several batches so it will brown evenly.

Remove beat with slotted spoon, drain, and place in a 4-quart pot. Drain all but 2 tablespoons of fat from the pan, and then add onions and garlic. Saute onions and garlic for a couple of minutes. Then add the chicken broth to deglaze the pan. Scrape pan and pour liquid into pot.

Add remaining ingredients (except Masa and salsa), add water to cover meat. Simmer, covered for 1½ hours or until meat is tender. Remove cover, mix Masa or flour into a thin paste, and add to pot to thicken. Simmer, uncovered, for an additional 20 minutes.

Check seasonings, add salt if needed, or more thickener if desired. Add jalapeno salsa if adventurous, simmer for an additional 10 minutes. Serve in bowls over plain boiled rice or in flour tortillas as burritos. Makes 2 quarts.

Paul W. Englund
Salinas, CA

William & Sandra DeJong
Bonanza, OR

JALAPENO CHILE MARTINIS

For this recipe, simply prepare your favorite martini, substituting a round of pickled jalapeno for the lemon twist, olive, or pickled onion. If you don't usually make martinis, then get a shaker or nice glass or silver pitcher and a long-handled spoon.

For 6 generous drinks, put several ice cubes in the shaker and add half a bottle of at least 80-proof gin or vodka (measures 24 ounces, or 3 liquid measuring cups) and a generous optional splash or tablespoon of dry vermouth.

Some omit the vermouth and a splash of periemced with this! You may want to sample the proportions ahead of time. Mix vigorously or shake to mix well. Serve garnished with a round of pickled jalapeno. For an added tough, place the glasses in the freezer about 30 minutes before making the drinks.

Carmen L. Caruso
El Paso, TX

Circle J Farms
Marianna, FL

HOT CHILI NUTS

1 dried large red chile such as ancho, chipotle, or guajillo (wear rubber gloves), ground about 1 tablespoon
½ stick (¼ C.) unsalted butter
3 C. unsalted raw nuts such as cashews or peanuts, about ¾ cup

In a large heavy skillet cook the chile in the butter over a moderate heat and add the nuts, stirring constantly for 10 minutes, or until they no longer taste raw, and transfer them with a slotted spoon to paper towels to drain.

Sprinkle the chili nuts with salt to taste and serve them warm or at room temperature. The nuts keep in a tightly covered container for 3 or 4 days. Makes 3 cups.

Jay & Sandy Hatfield
Cincinnati, OH

Padre Thomas Estenage
Mission San Gabriel,
California (1842)

ANCHO CHILE FUDGE PIE

2 eggs
½ C. sugar
½ C. packed brown sugar
½ C. plus 2 T. flour
2 T. ancho chile paste*
1 C. butter, melted and cooled
½ C. chopped walnuts (roasted in 400° oven for 3 to 5 minutes)
1 C. semisweet chocolate chips
1 T. vanilla extract
1 (9-inch) unbaked pastry shell
whipped cream for garnish

Preheat oven to 350 degrees. In a large bowl, beat eggs until foamy; add sugar and brown sugar and beat until well blended. Beat in flour and ancho chile paste. Blend in melted butter and mix until thick and smooth. Fold in roasted nuts, chocolate chips and vanilla.

Pour into pie shell, bake one (1) hour until firm and set. Serve with a dollop of whipped cream. Makes 6 to 8 servings.

Cay Mangold
El Paso, TX
see ANCHO CHILE PASTE recipe

James N. Gaskin
Satellite Bch, FL

ANCHO CHILE PASTE

use with ANCHO CHILE FUDGE PIE recipe

Roast 4 to 5 large ancho chiles in a large iron skillet or a griddle, turning frequently until the dry chiles puff slightly. Drop into a saucepan filled with boiling water. Cover and remove from heat. Let steep for 20 minutes.

Remove stems, skin and seeds. Blend in food processor until smooth and thick. Use some of the soaking liquid to thin puree, if needed.

Cay Mangold
El Paso, TX

Sims Cattle Co.
Bonifay, FL

TWO-BEAN CHIRIZO CHILI

Great in-front-of-the-television football fair, this spicy, quick-to-fix chili has complex flavors that make it taste as if it simmered all day.

1 Lb. chorizo (Mexican sausage)
3 Med. onions, cut into ½-inch pieces (1-1½ cups)
1 can (16 oz.) black beans, undrained
1 can (16 oz.) kidney beans or pinto beans, undrained
1 C. beef broth
1 can (8 oz.) whole kernel corn, drained
¾ C. Pace Picante Sauce
1 green pepper, cut into ¾-inch pieces
1 red pepper, cut into ¾-inch pieces

Toppings: Sour cream, shredded cheese, chopped cilantro

Remove sausage from casing. In large saucepan or Dutch oven, brown sausage with onion until onion is tender; drain. Add remaining ingredients except optional toppings. Bring to a boil; reduce heat. Simmer uncovered about 15 minutes, stirring occasionally, or until chili is desired consistency. Ladle into bowls; top as desired and serve with additional Pace Picante Sauce. Makes 6 servings, about 6 cups chili.

Pace Foods, Inc.

Algee Ranch
Madeline J. Algee
Creston, CA

CHILI a la DUFF

Brown:

1 Lb. hamburger
2 Lg. onions

Mix in pot:

1 Lg. can (32½ oz) tomatoes
1 can #300 red kidney beans, 2½ C. and liquid
1 C. water
1 t. salt
1 healthy T. chili powder

Add onion and hamburger. Cover and simmer for 2 hours. Stir every 15 minutes. Makes 4 medium servings. This is really easy - anyone can throw it together.

Mary M. Pratt
Lansing, MI

Lazy S
Robert W. Gould
Merritt Island, FL

RED CHILE ENCHILADA BAKE

1 Lg. onion
1¼ Lb. ground round
1 Lg. can (28 oz.) red chile sauce
12 tortillas
1 can (15 oz.) chile con carne with beans
1 can (6 oz.) tomato paste
1 C. water
1 Lb. grated Cheddar cheese
1 can (16 oz.) black olives, sliced

Chop onion and add to ground round. Brown in skillet until crisp. Combine with tomato paste, water, and chile sauce. Bring to a boil. Put a layer of sauce in greased casserole. Cover with 3 tortillas. Cover with ¼ of the grated Cheddar cheese and sliced olives. Repeat for 4 layers, then pour the can of chile con carne with beans over the tortillas and top with the remaining cheese and olives. Bake at 325 degrees for 1 hour. Serves 12.

(There is a difference of opinion as to the number of servings-some say it only serves 6 to 8. I would say the number of servings depends on how well it is received).

Carmen L. Caruso
El Paso, TX

Davis Norwood, 1892
McLennan County, TX

TURKEY COLORADA CHILI

Red Chili with Turkey

Low-calorie and low cholesterol. A Version of an American original.

½ C. olive oil
1 yellow onion, diced
4 cloves garlic, minced
3 Lbs. boneless turkey, uncooked, cubed
3 T. chili powder
1 T. garlic powder
1 T. ground cumin
1 T. oregano leaves, crushed
1 T. coarse ground pepper
1 can (16 oz.) peeled tomatoes
1 can (10 oz.) beef bouillon
1 can (12 oz.) beer
¼ C. Masa or flour

Cut skinned, boneless turkey (thighs, breast, or combination) into ¾-inch cubes. Heat olive oil in heavy 8-quart pot, (black if you have).

Saute onions and garlic until transparent. Add turkey meat and saute until grey and somewhat browned. Cook out all liquid from the turkey.

Add chili powder and spices to season turkey. Add bouillon and beer. Add water to cover meat. Simmer, uncovered for 2½ hours, stirring occasionally. Add water as needed.

Mix Masa or flour with water to thin paste. Add and simmer an additional 30 minutes. Check for salt and seasoning after Masa has simmered for 20 minutes. Add additional Masa if needed, and simmer for an additional 15 minutes. Add additional chili powder or salsa as desired to taste. Serve in bowls, over rice or pasta, or as burritos. Makes 2 quarts.

Paul W. Englund
Salinas, CA

James M. Barnsley
Olney, MD

TURKEY CHILI TACOS

1 Lb. ground turkey, defrosted
2 T. dried onion
1 T. chili powder
1 t. paprika
½ t. cumin
½ t. dried oregano
½ t. salt
¼ t. garlic powder
⅛ t. pepper
10 Taco shells
1-2 tomatoes, chopped
2-3 C. lettuce, shredded
2-3 C. Cheddar cheese, grated

In a 1-quart microwave-safe container, combine turkey, onion, chili powder, paprika, cumin, oregano, salt, garlic powder and pepper. Cover.

Microwave at 100% power (High) for 5 to 6 minutes, or until meat is no longer pink, stirring one or two times during cooking.

Spoon into taco shells; top each taco evenly with tomatoes, lettuce and cheese.

Other optional toppings include, salsa, taco sauce, sour cream, guacamole, chopped or sliced olives and chopped onions.

NOTE: Approximate nutrient content per serving: 357 KCAL; 21 gm protein; 21 gm fat; 21 gm carbohydrate; 429 mg sodium; 77 mg cholesterol.

Serves 5.

National Turkey Federation
Reston, VA

Latt Maxcy Corp.
Frostproof, FL

COAST TO COAST CHILI

1 Lg. onion, diced
1½ Lbs. ground meat, coarse grind
1 T. oil/fat
1 Lg. can tomatoes, blended
1 Med. can, tomato puree
4 cans dark kidney beans with juice
2 jalapeno peppers, 1 green, 1 yellow
1 square baking chocolate, melted
Fresh cilantro, minced
⅓ C. cider vinegar
⅓ C. red wine
1 T. cumin
2 T. chili powder
1 T. oregano, ground
1 t. seasoned salt
1 t. garlic powder or to taste

Brown onion is oil or fat, adding remaining ingredients, cover and simmer 30-40 minutes. Remove lid, simmer 20-30 minutes longer.
Serve with grated sharp Cheddar cheese.

Joan A. Leavitt
Highland, CA

Joseph M. Dalton
Franklin, TN

GRANDMA KONEMANN'S CHILI

This recipe is the only way I know how to make chili until I got married. Grandma died in 1948, so this is her recipe. Hope that you will like it as we do.

- 2 Lbs. chop suey meat (beef pork and veal)
- 1 T. salt or to taste
- 6 8 red peppers (chiles)
- 1 t. chili powder (more if desired)
- 6 8 potatoes (cubed)
- 3 T. molasses
- 2 cans tomato soup
- 2 cans kidney beans

Just cover meat with water and cook until tender adding salt, red peppers, chili powder and potatoes.
Let potatoes get nearly done, then add molasses, soup, and beans. Thicken mixture with 2 tablespoons of flour and ½ cup of water.
P.S. This was often served as a company meal and the guests were served beer to drink.

Barbara Poitra
Melvin, MI

L. M. Hegner
Beaumont,
Jefferson County, TX

TED'S FAMOUS WINDBREAKER CHILI

(Stolen from friend, Ken, in Okemos - slightly modified after many batches)...

1 gal. tomatoes, chopped
6 oz. tomato juice
8 4" onions, chopped fine
2 or 3 ribs celery, chopped fine
6 bay leaves
4 chili peppers, red, and
2 chili peppers, green, remove seeds and mince. For more zesty, slightly spicier taste, substitute "Pregresso" hot peppers, (6), seeded and minced
6 T. chili powder
3½ T. salt
Ground black pepper to taste
Pinch of oregano, cayenne pepper, cumin and caraway

Dice 1½ pounds lean ground steak, brown, and add all juices plus 2 ounces water to pot.

Cook well... allow to cook down, about 3-3½ hours.

If onions aren't sweet, add ½ cup of sugar.

Add 4 pounds of lean ground round. Do NOT brown. Stir in and save all the meat flavor. Cook another 2 hours.

This makes about 8 quarts. No flavor lost if frozen.

Optional: We add 3 cans of kidney beans after the chili is cooked and spaghetti broken into one-inch lengths for added body.

Ted J. Madzia
Detroit, MI

Boy Scouts of America
Explorer Post 636
Milwaukie, OR

MARY D'S CHILI

3 Lbs. ground beef
1 Lg. onion, chopped
2 cans Mexican chili beans
1 Med. can tomatoes
1 can tomato sauce
1 small can or jar taco hot sauce or picante sauce
1 T. chili powder
3 beef bouillon cubes

Brown ground beef and chopped onion in a skillet. In a separate large pan, combine the other ingredients. After browning the meat and onions, drain excess grease off, and mix this with the other ingredients, and bring to a boil. Turn down the heat to a simmer, and cook for 30 or 40 minutes longer.

Mary D. Wallace
Pensacola, FL

Larry C. Knighten
New Market, TN

CHILI Con CARNE

- 2 Lbs. lean ground beef
- 4 T. chili powder
- 2 t. salt
- 1 t. sugar
- 1 Lg. onion, chopped fine
- 1 green pepper, coarsely chopped
- 1 C. water
- 2 cans (15 oz.) tomato sauce, or tomato sauce w/tomato bits
- 1 bay leaf
- 2 T. vegetable oil
- 2 T. flour
- 2 cans (16 oz.) red kidney beans, undrained

In a large saucepan over a moderate low heat, brown the beef, crumbling with a fork. Push beef to one side and spoon off fat. Sprinkle the meat with chili powder, salt and sugar, mixing well. Add the onions, green pepper, tomato sauce, water and bay leaf.

Cover, and simmer, stirring occasionally for one hour. Remove the bay leaf. In a small bowl stir together the oil and flour until smooth. Stir in the beans; add to meat mixture. Cover and simmer, stirring occasionally, until thoroughly heated and slightly thickened-about 30 minutes.

Makes about 3 quarts - 8 to 10 servings.

The amount of chili powder called for gives the recipe character; if you like a milder chili reduce the amount; if you want it even hotter, add more chili powder or Tabasco sauce, or cayenne pepper to taste. My own personal preference is about 3 tablespoons of chili powder.

This chili freezes well and may be kept for several months.

Marie Yachwan
Niagara Falls, NY

Roy Claude Titus
Cloverdale, CA

GREEN CHILE CHILAQUILES

2½ Doz. corn tortillas
shortening
2 cans cream of chicken or mushroom soup
1 soup can milk
8 chopped long green chiles, roasted and peeled)
1½ C. shredded Monterey Jack cheese

Tear the tortillas into 1½ inch pieces. Fry lightly. Drain on paper towels. Place in a 9x13-inch baking dish. Combine soup, milk and green chiles; pour over tortillas. Top with cheese. Bake at 350 degrees for about 25 minutes or until bubbly. Serves 6 to 8.

Carmen L. Caruso
El Paso, TX

W.G. Dement, Jr.
Jackson, TN

VENISON CHILI

This is my favorite chili recipe. I live in New York, but an a transplant from Houston, TX, where we think of Chili as a contest!

1 Lb. dried pinto beans
¼ C. salad oil
3 Lbs. venison roast, in bite size chunks
3 Lg. onions, chopped
3 Lg. green peppers, cut in large pieces
3 stalks celery, cut in bite size pieces
3 garlic cloves, crushed
⅓ C. chili powder (you might add more)
Cayenne pepper to taste (BE CAREFUL)
1 T. salt
1 t. paprika
1 t. cumin
1 t. oregano
3 C. boiling water
3 bouillon cubes
1 Lg. can whole tomatoes with juice, chopped
1 can tomato paste
Crushed red pepper to taste

Soak beans overnight, drain, cover with water, cook with water only until tender, adding one salt at end of cooking time.

Cook venison in oil till just brown. Add onions, peppers, garlic and celery. While steaming, boil water for bouillon. Dump all the spices on top of the steaming vegies. Dissolve the bouillon cubes in water and add tomato paste, mixing well. Pour bouillon and canned tomatoes in, stir and cover. Cool til? You may add crushed red pepper then or individually later. Chili is always better the second day - if you can wait. Serve with chopped onions, corn chips and grated or sliced cheese.

Janice Anderson
Nineveh, NY

James E. Dunning
Roseburg, OR

CHILI SANDWICHES -Cathy Pfeil's

* Lightly toast rye party size bread on both sides under broiler
* Spread with mayo, them cream cheese
* Spoon chopped green chiles and cover top
* Layer swiss cheese over chiles
* Broil until cheese melts

Cathy Pfeil
Olympia, WA

James B. Henson
Pullman, WA

FINE CHILI

1 Lb. coarse ground beef
1 Lb. dry pinto beans *
1 can (6 oz.) tomato puree
2 C. onion, chopped
3 T. chili powder
1 T. cumin
Salt to taste
Water to desire consistency

Saute beef and drain off excess fat. Add onions, puree and beans. Mix chili powder, salt and cumin; add to mixture. Bring to a boil, turn down the heat and cook slowly until the onions and beans are tender, adding water to reach your desired consistency.

* Beans can be soaked overnight, or if added dry, chili must cook long enough for them to become tender. Serves 4 to 6.

Mary D. Wallace
Pensacola, FL

Tony & Helen Gregory
Lemmon, SD

SOUTHWESTERN CHILI CHEESE GRITS

3 C. water
½ t. salt
1 C. quick grits
2 eggs, beaten
¼ C. milk
1¾ C. shredded sharp Cheddar cheese
2-3 T. drained, chopped mild green chiles
2 large cloves garlic, minced

Heat water to boiling in a saucepan. Add salt and pour grits in slowly, stirring continually. Reduce heat to low, cover pan and cook for 4 to 5 minutes, stirring occasionally. Remove from heat and transfer to a mixing bowl.

Add eggs, 1 cup of the cheese, milk, chiles and garlic. Mix well and transfer to a buttered 2-quart casserole. Top with the remaining cheese, and bake in a preheated 350 degree oven for 45 to 60 minutes or until set in the middle and lightly browned.

Makes 6 servings.

Test kitchen note: Once grits are prepared for baking, then can sit until you want to put them in the oven.

Nutrition information per serving: Calories, 273; fat, 13.5 grams; carbohydrates, 23.4 grams; cholesterol, 147 mg; sodium, 440 mg.

Orlando Sentinel
Orlando, FL

John W. Wilke II
Maricopa, CA

CHINESE CHILI

"Greetings! We're on the same wave length as I too have a collection of chili recipes. Chili is a fun food, delicious, a conversation piece, economical and popular.

On weekends furloughs from West Point our son typically had friends drop in. My favorite crimson colored cast iron enameled pot became a tradition on the stove filled to the brim with chili, bowls, crackers, cheese and pepper flakes (AKA Hot Shakes) on hand. Word went out among the boys that "Mom has a 'missionary pot' of chili on the stove".

A wonderful memory in the art gallery of my mind".

2 Lbs. cubed chuck meat
½ C. vegetable oil
2 onions, chopped
4 cloves garlic, chopped
1 can (6 oz.) tomato paste
1 can (8 oz.) tomato sauce
4 chile peppers
1 t. cayenne pepper
2 T. paprika
2 t. oregano
4 t. cumin
2 Lg. cans red beans

In a large skillet, heat the oil to smoking hot. Brown beef on all sides. Drain oil. Cover beef with water, cover skillet and simmer for 90 minutes.

Add onions, simmer for 30 minutes, covered. Add the remaining ingredients and simmer for another 30 minutes, uncovered.

Serve over your favorite red beans, heated. Makes 4 servings.

Ms. Flo Ottman
Johnson City, NY

Cherokee Cattle Co.
Gustine, CA

SOMEONE ELSE'S CHILI CON CARNE

This is a mild, very good and easy chili recipe to prepare.

2 T. butter, or margarine
1 Lb. ground beef
½ C. chopped onion
½ clove garlic, chopped
1½ C. canned tomatoes
2 cans (16 oz.) red kidney beans
2 t. to 2 T. chili powder, depending on flavor desired
¾ t. salt, more or less to taste

Melt butter or margarine, sauce onion and garlic until the onion is tender. Add the beef and saute until it is well done. Add the remaining ingredients, cover and cook slowly for 1 hour.

Mark & Stacy Sayer
Cincinnati, OH

Marvis T. Hogen
Former Secty. of Agric.
Kadoka, SD

FESTIVE CHILI con CARNE

1 Lb. ground beef or pork
1 Med. onion, chopped
1 Med. green bell pepper, chopped
1 clove garlic, minced
2 to 4 t. chili powder
1 t. salt
½ t. dried oregano, crumbled
¼ t. cumin
1 can (16 oz.) whole tomatoes, undrained
1 can 8 oz.) tomato sauce
1 can (15 oz.) red kidney beans, drained
1 T. red wine vinegar
1 bay leaf
Tortilla chips or crackers

Crumble meat in microwave-safe plastic colander. Place colander in a 2-quart casserole, at High, microwave covered casserole for 4 to 6 minutes, or until meat is no longer pink. Stir with a fork to break up meat every 2 minutes during the cooking period. Also give casserole a half turn once during cooking.

Discard meat drippings from casserole. Transfer the meat from the colander to the casserole, and break up meat even further into smaller pieces. Stir in the onion, green pepper and garlic. Uncovered, microwave at High for 4 to 5 minutes or until onion and pepper are tender.

Add the chili powder, salt and oregano to meat mixture; mixing together well. Drain the juice from the whole tomato can into the casserole. Chop tomatoes in the can, and add then to the casserole. Add the tomato sauce and beans; mixing well into dish. Microwave, covered, at High for 5 minutes.

Add the vinegar to the chili; stirring to mix well. Microwave, uncovered, 20 to 25 minutes, at medium power, until mixture is slightly thickened and to allow flavors to blend together. Stir several times during the cooking time. Serve with chips or crackers. Remove bay leaf before serving.

Makes 4 servings.

Note: Keep a bottle of hot sauce and crushed red peppers on the table for those wishing for a peppier tang.

Laurie A. Seltzer
Cincinnati, OH

K6

Deseret Farms of FL
Melbourne, FL

DIETER'S TURKEY CHILI

3 Lbs. ground turkey
2 T. cholesterol free oil
2 Med. yellow onions, diced
2 stalks celery, diced
½ green pepper, diced
1 Lg. can tomatoes, chopped
1 can (6 oz.) tomato paste
12 Ozs. chicken or turkey broth (fat removed)
2 t. chili powder
1 t. cumin powder
4 packets, Nutra Sweet
2 t. salt (optional)
½ t. black pepper, freshly grated
1 T. Worcestershire sauce
1 Med. can red kidney beans (optional)
Tabasco sauce (optional)

In a Dutch oven, heat the oil. Brown turkey and drain and discard oil except for 2 teaspoons. In a sauce pan, put reserved oil and saute onions, celery and green pepper. Cook until tender. Mix vegetables, tomatoes, tomato paste, broth, salt, pepper, chili powder and cumin with turkey in the Dutch oven. Cover, and simmer for 45 minutes.

Add Nutra Sweet, Worcestershire sauce and beans. Use a little Tabasco if you want a hotter chili. Top with Lite cheese or turn in to a casserole. Add 2 cups of cooked macaroni. Top with cheese, bake long enough to melt the cheese. This can be done in a microwave.

Merline McKenzie
Lansing, MI

Lazy E
Maxwell C. King
Melbourne, FL

GREEN CHILE ENCHILADAS

1 Med. onion, chopped
1 Lg. can tomatoes
1 can tomato paste
2 C. diced Velveeta cheese (1 Lb.)
2 C. chopped green chiles
1 Lb. ground meat
1 Pt. sour cream
Grated Monterey Jack cheese
1 Doz. tortillas

Cook the meat until it is gray. Add the rest of ingredients (except sour cream and Monterey Jack cheese), and simmer. At the last minute, add sour cream but do not let mixture boil. A little water may be added if this is too thick. Fry tortillas and layer in stacks of 2 or 3 with sauce, chopped onion and grated Jack cheese between each layer. Top with Jack cheese and place in oven until cheese is melted. This sauce freezes well.

Carmen L. Caruso
El Paso, TX

Melissa Martinique
Boynton Beach, FL

JOHNNYCAKE CHILI

1 Med. onion, chopped
2 Med. carrots, thinly sliced
1 Lb. ground beef
2 t. chili powder
1 can (28 oz.) tomatoes, drained and chopped
1 can (16 oz.) red kidney beans, drained
1 Pkg. (10 oz.) frozen whole-kernel corn
1 t. sugar
1 t. oregano
1 Pkg. (8½ oz.) corn muffin mix

Cook the onion and carrots in 2 tablespoons of water, covered, on High 3 to 5 minutes. Drain.

Add ground beef and chili powder. Cook, loosely covered with wax paper, on High 3 to 5 minutes, stirring once.

Add tomatoes, beans, corn, sugar and oregano. Cook, loosely covered with wax paper on High 7 to 9 minutes, stirring once.

Prepare muffin mix according to directions on the package. Spoon batter onto chili mixture in casserole, making decorative design. Cook on medium power 12 to 14 minutes, or until topping is slightly firm to the touch. Rotate casserole dish twice for even cooking.

Ms. Flo Ottman
Johnson City, NY

Bell Ranch
Chowchilla, CA

CHILI BEEF

8 slices bacon, diced
2 Med. onions, chopped
2 green peppers, chopped
4 cans (15 oz.) red kidney beans
2 cans (8 oz.) tomato sauce
¼ C. chili powder
1 t. salt
2 T. brown sugar
1 Lb. sharp Cheddar cheese, grated
1 cans (12 oz.) corn beef
12 English muffins, or more if desired

Fry the bacon and drain grease; cook the onions and green peppers in 1 tablespoon of bacon drippings. Add kidney beans, tomato sauce, salt, chili powder and brown sugar. Stir to mix well. Add cheese. Cook and stir over a low heat until the cheese has melted. Add corned beef and mix well. Heat through. Yields 12 servings.

Mary D. Wallace
Pensacola, FL

NY9

Robert Day
Bloomingburg, NY

CHILI CASSEROLE

Happened to catch your note in our newspaper, the Pensacola News Journal. Having been born in Texas, I love chili. My Grandma swore I was weaned on it.

#1. This is a quick, easy recipe. I love the tamales in it. My grandmother used to make her own.

#2. Sheriff "Smoot" Schmid was the Sheriff of Dallas, Texas, I think in the 30's. It used to be said, "Felons would try to break into his jail just for his chili".

#3. This is very good. I make it for dyed-in-the-wool real Texans-not the Austex eaters (canned chili).

#4. Just thought I'd throw this in for fun.

#5. Can't give you this one-it's going into My cookbook!

1 small package Fritos
2 C. chili con carne
1½ C. grated cheese
1 C. finely chopped onions
2 cans tamales

Arrange broken Fritos in bottom of a 2-quart casserole. Pour warmed chili over Fritos. Add layer of onions. Remove husks from tamales and place over onions. Cover with cheese. Bake covered in a 350 degree oven till cheese melts.

Serve with an avocado salad.

Bernidine P. Brown
Pensacola, FL

A.R. Hendrix
Titusville, FL

SHERIFF "SMOOT" SCHMID'S JAILHOUSE CHILI

2 C. ground beef suet
3 cloves garlic, diced
3 T. garlic powder
2 t. salt
1½ ground chili pod
2 Lbs. coarse ground beef
1½ T. paprika
1 T. cumin seed
1 t. pepper
3 C. water

Saute suet lightly, add beef and seasonings. Cover, cook slowly 1 hour, stirring occasionally. Add water and continue cooking until slightly thickened-about 4 hours.

Bernidine P. Brown
Pensacola, FL

George O'Neill, Jr.
New York, NY

CHILI CON CARNE

3 Lbs. top round - cut into ½-inch cubes
6 T. vegetable oil
2 C. coarsely chopped onions
2 T. finely chopped garlic
4 T. chili powder
1 t. oregano
1 t. ground cumin
1 t. red pepper flakes
1 can (6 oz.) tomato paste
4 C. beef stock
1 t. salt
Freshly ground black pepper

Pat the meat dry with paper towels. Then, in a heavy 12-inch skillet, heat 4 tablespoons of the oil until a light haze forms above it. Add the meat and cook over a high heat for 2-3 minutes, stirring, until the meat is lightly browned.

With a slotted spoon, transfer the meat to a 4-quart flame-proof casserole. Add the remaining 2 tablespoons of oil to the skillet and in it cook the onion and garlic for 4-5 minutes, stirring frequently.

Remove the skillet from the heat, add 4 tablespoons of chili powder, oregano, cumin and pepper flakes, and stir until the onions are well coated with the mixture.

Then add the tomato paste, pour in the beef stock and with a large spoon, mix the ingredients together thoroughly before adding them to the meat in the casserole. Add the salt and a few grindings of black pepper.

Bring to a boil, stirring once or twice, then half cover the pot, turn the heat to low and simmer for 1 to 1½ hours, or until the meat is tender. Skin off the fat before serving.

Bernidine P. Brown
Pensacola, FL

Harold L. Dyke
Maupin, OR

AUSTRALIAN CHILI

1 Emu, diced in ½" cubes
1 t. salt
1 Qt. chili powder
Water to cover
1 C. cumin seeds
1 Lg. rock

Place diced emu, spices and rock in a large pot. Add water to cover. Simmer for one week. Drain water. Discard emu. Eat rock.

Bernidine P. Brown
Pensacola, FL

Rex & Lauras Glenn
Douglas, AZ

FAMILY CHILI SAUCE

This recipe was given to me by a friend from a family recipe box.

12 to 14 tomatoes
1 Lb. celery, about 2 bunches
1 Qt. small onions
3 green peppers
¼ C. salt
2 T. chili powder
1 t. nutmeg
½ t. ground cloves
1 T. dry mustard
2 sticks cinnamon
2 Lbs. brown sugar
1 Qt. cider vinegar
1 T. oregano
Dash or two Tabasco sauce

Scald and peel tomatoes, and cook for 15 minutes. Drain off half of the liquid. Chop remaining vegetables; and add to tomatoes and simmer for about 1½ hours. Tie spices in cloth bag; and add with remaining ingredients to tomato mixture. Continue cooking for 1½ hours, or until vegetables are soft. Remove spice bag; seal in hot, sterilized jars. Makes 6 pints.

Jay & Sandy Hatfield
Cincinnati, OH

Wm. F. Nobles
Titusville, FL

RED BELL PEPPER-CORN SALSA

2½ Lbs. red bell peppers, halved and seeded (about 5 large)
1 ear fresh corn
2 T. plus 1 t. minced jalapeno pepper
½ C. chopped onion
½ C. loosely packed fresh cilantro, chopped
1 t. sugar
1 t. lime juice
¼ t. salt

Place peppers in a 3-quart microwave-safe casserole, cover, and vent. Microwave at High for 20 minutes; drain and set aside.

Microwave corn in husk at High for 2½ minutes. Let it cool, and remove husk and silk; cut corn from cob.

Place jalapeno pepper in container of an electric blender or food processor; cover and process until minced. Add peppers; cover and blend until smooth. Place the mixture in a bowl. Add corn, onion, and remaining ingredients; stir together well.

Serve warm or chilled with chicken or seafood. Yields about 3 cups.

Gordon DeDevgd
Merritt Island, FL

Minto Ranch Inc
Chico, CA

JALAPENO CHILE PICO DE GALLO

"Cock's Comb" is the literal translation of this Southwestern Texas border sauce borrowed from northern Mexico. The traditional accompaniment to Fajitas, it is also an excellent spicy red table sauce. Although traditionalists use chipotle (smoked Jalapenos) for the sauce, they are often difficult to find, so I have substituted a combination of familiar Texas chiles--the jalapeno and some pequinor caribe. (If you do have access to chipotles, use them for part or all of the jalapenos).

Many recipes also call for serrano chiles, which I eliminated from my lexicon of ingredients quite some time ago. To me, their only reason for being is to create undiluted pain without pleasure, and they offer very little flavor in contrast to the jalapenos and other American chiles.

Yield: 6 to 8 servings

- 3 fresh jalapenos, finely chopped (to equal ½ cup)
- 1 Lg. red ripe unpeeled tomato, coarsely chopped (to equal ½ cup)
- 1 Med. white Spanish onion, coarsely chopped (to equal ½ cup)
- 2 garlic cloves, minced
- ½ t. salt
- ½ t. peqin or caribe (or to taste)
- 3 T. coarsely chopped fresh cilantro

Combine all ingredients and allow to marinate and develop natural juices for at least 1 hour before serving. Serve with tostados.

Carmen L. Caruso
El Paso, TX

Bogle Farms Inc
Chandler, AZ

CHILI SAUCE

16 Qts. (½ bushel) tomatoes
14 Lg. green peppers, finely chopped
12 Lg. white onions, finely chopped
2 bay leaves
1 C. sugar
1 t. ground cloves
¼ C. celery seeds
½ C. coarse salt
2 C. cider vinegar
1 t. cinnamon

Peel tomatoes and slice. Bring tomatoes to a boil; reduce heat, and add remaining ingredients. Return to a low rolling boil, and cook until the sauce becomes thick, about 3 hours or so. Stir the sauce while cooking frequently.

Taste sauce while cooking, and add more spices if desired. Bottle sauce in the prescribed directions. Makes about 5 quarts.

Scott Geltner
Cincinnati, OH

P. G. Noble
Beckwourth, CA

CHILI-CHEESE SALAD

1 T. (1 envelope) unflavored gelatine
½ C. cold water
1 C. chili sauce
1 C. dry cottage cheese
½ C. mayonnaise
½ t. salt
1 C. heavy cream, whipped

Soften gelatine in cold water; dissolve over hot water. Combine chili sauce, cheese, mayonnaise and salt; add gelatine; fold in whipped cream. Chill in oiled mold until firm. Unmold on crisp lettuce and garish with tomato wedges. Serves 6.

Jay & Sandy Hatfield
Cincinnati, OH

Puu Waa Waa Ranch
Kawai, HA

CHILI BURGERS

2 Lbs. lean ground beef
1 small onion, chopped
1 C. celery, chopped
1 can (8 oz.) tomato sauce
1 t. garlic salt
⅛ t. dry mustard
10 to 12 sandwich buns
¼ t. hot pepper sauce
1 C. catsup
¼ C. Worcestershire sauce
1 t. sugar
½ t. chili powder
Pkg. shredded Cheddar cheese (optional)

In a 2-quart casserole, combine ground beef, onion and celery. Microwave on High for 7 to 8 minutes or until beef is no longer pink. Stir after half way of cooking to crumble beef into smaller pieces for burgers.

Drain off all excess fat drippings as it will only soak into buns and it is not necessary to eat more fat than is left in the meat mixture.

Stir in remaining ingredients; cover, and microwave on High for 9 to 10 minutes, or until mixture is bubbly.

Open end of plastic bun package, and microwave on High for 35 to 40 seconds, or until buns are warmed.

Spoon chili mixture onto heated buns, sprinkle shredded Cheddar cheese on top, if desired, and serve. Makes 10 to 12 Chili Burgers.

Bernie & Gail Geltner
Boynton Beach, FL

Spencer B. Jones
Dayton, TN

TIMOTHY'S WHITE CHILI

1 Lb. Lg. white beans
6 C. chicken broth
2 cloves garlic, minced
2 Med. onions, chopped
1 T. oil
2 cans (4 oz.) mild green chilies, chopped
1½ t. oregano
¼ t. ground cloves
¼ t. cayenne pepper
4 C. diced cooked chicken breast
3 C. Monterey Jack cheese, grated
Salsa
Sour cream

Combine beans, chicken broth, garlic and half of the onions, in a large soup pot. Bring to a boil; reduce heat, and simmer until the beans are soft (3 hours or more), adding more broth if necessary.

In a skillet, saute remaining onions in oil until tender. Add chilies and seasonings and mix thoroughly. Add to bean mixture. Add diced chicken and simmer for 1 hour.

Serve topped with grated cheese, salsa and sour cream.

Serves 8 to 10.

SALSA: You can use store-brought chunky Mexican tomato or make you own with peeled tomatoes, green chilies, onion, garlic and fresh cilantro.

P.S. I have made this several times using ground turkey, not chunks of chicken breast. The dark turkey meat plus the oregano makes the soup brown, not white. But, the taste is tremendous. The recipe multiplies well - I use 3 pounds turkey and 2 pounds beans, adding enough chicken broth, or bouillon, to cook the beans. Freezes well. SUBSTITUTE PLAIN yogurt for sour cream. Good health-healthy dish.

John G. Wright
Warsaw, KY

Stoney Point Ranch
Ronald L. White
Zanesville, OH

GREEN CHILE ENCHILADA CASSEROLE

1 Doz. corn tortillas
½ C. shortening
½ C. finely chopped onion
2 C. grated Cheddar cheese
1 C. milk
1 can (10¾ oz.) cream of chicken soup
¼ C. chopped green chiles, roasted and peeled

Fry tortillas in hot fat until they bubble. Drain on paper towels. Place a layer of tortillas in shallow, 3-quart casserole. Top each tortilla with onion and cheese. Continue until all tortillas are used. Combine milk, soup and chiles. Pour over tortillas. Bake at 350° for 30 minutes.

Carmen L. Caruso
El Paso, TX

Circle H Ranch, Inc.
Immokalee, FL

BEN'S HOT & SPICY CHILI

2 Lbs. lean ground beef
1 Lg. onion, chopped
1 Med. green pepper, seeded, chopped
2 stalks celery, chopped
1 clove garlic, minced
2 cans (16 oz.) cut up tomatoes, save juice
1 can (15 oz.) tomato sauce
1½ C. water
4 to 6 pickled jalapeno peppers, rinsed and chopped, ½ C.
1½ t. ground red pepper
½ t. black pepper
2 bay leaves
1 can (16 oz.) red kidney beans, drained
Dash salt (optional)

In a large saucepan or Dutch oven, cook the ground beef, onions, green peppers, celery and garlic until the meat is brown and the vegetables are tender. Do not drain. Stir in undrained tomatoes, tomato sauce, water, jalapeno peppers, chili powder, ground red pepper, salt, bay leaf and black pepper.

Bring mixture to a boil; reduce heat, and simmer uncovered for 2 hours, stirring occasionally. Stir in kidney beans, and cook 30 minutes longer. Remove bay leaves before serving. Makes 8 to 10 servings.

Ben C. Seltzer
Cincinnati, OH

KK

King Ranch
Bradenton, FL

CHILI BALLS

1 Lb. ground beef
1 Lb. ground lean pork
2 t. chili powder
1 t. vinegar
1 T. prepared mustard
¾ C. uncooked rice
½ C. milk
1 can (12 oz.) tomatoes
2½ C. water
3 t. salt (adjust to taste)
1 t. sugar
2 T. chopped onions
1 beaten egg

Mix meats; add egg, milk, rice and 1 teaspoon chili powder, and 2 teaspoons of salt. Form in 1½-inch balls. Brown evenly in hot oil. Combine tomatoes, water, onion and remaining seasonings. Bring to a boil; drop in meat balls. Cover, and cook slowly for 1½ hours. Chili powder may be reduced if desired. Makes about 20 meat balls with enough sauce to spread around on each serving dish.

Jay & Sandy Hatfield
Cincinnati, OH

TIV

George Tivis
Faith, SD

SCOOTER'S CHILI CON CARNE

1 Lb. lean ground beef
1 Lg. onion, sliced
1 green pepper, chopped
3 T. cooking oil
1 can (15 oz.) tomatoes
1 can (16 oz.) kidney beans, or 1½ C. red chili beans
3 cloves garlic, whole
1 to 2 T. chili powder
¼ t. cayenne pepper
1 t. salt
1 bay leaf
¼ t. paprika

In a large skillet, brown the meat, using a fork to crumble meat into smaller pieces. Move cooked beef to side of pan, and saute the onion, green pepper and whole cloves of garlic, until onions are transparent but not browned. Discard the garlic cloves.

Add the tomatoes, cut up, with its liquid, and rest of ingredients to the meat mixture. Bring to a boil; reduce heat and simmer for 1½ to 2 hours. If necessary to keep consistency, add water, or canned tomato juice. Stir occasionally. Add beans and allow to heat thoroughly before serving.

Serve hot into bowls, and provide your guests with assorted bowls of chopped onions, shredded Cheddar cheese, crackers and other things that just go good with chilies.

Scott Geltner
Cincinnati, OH

"Elkhorn" was recorded by early day rancher and later President of the United States, Theodore Roosevelt on July 17, 1884.

GREEN CHILE STEW

2 T. olive oil
2¼ Lbs. bone-in pork loin, cut into ¾-inch cubes
3 garlic cloves, finely minced
28 green chiles, parched, peeled and cut into 1-inch lengths (fresh, canned or frozen)
2 C. Spanish onion, chopped
1 can (28 oz.) peeled whole tomatoes
½ t. Mexican oregano
½ t. cumin
¼ t. whole coriander, crushed
3 C. water, rinsed in can
1 t. salt

In a large stewing pot, at least 5 quart capacity, heat the olive oil until it almost begins to smoke. Add the pork cubes and lightly brown. Add the remaining ingredients. Cook for about 1 hour. Taste and adjust the seasonings if desired.

Carmen L. Caruso
El Paso, TX

DEN

Dennis McIntyre, 1890
McLennan County, TX

CHRIS'S BLISS CHILI

3 Lbs. lean ground beef
2 Lg. onions, sliced
2 Med. green peppers, cut in slices
1 C. celery, coarsely chopped
2 cloves garlic, minced
3 cans (16 oz.) tomatoes
3 cans (20 oz.) kidney beans
oil
1 t. hot sauce
1 T. salt
2 T. chili powder
2 t. MSG
¼ t. thyme
1 t. oregano
2 cans (6 oz.) tomato paste
2 cans (12 oz.) tomato sauce

In a large pot or Dutch oven, saute the onions, peppers, celery and the garlic until tender. Do not brown. Add the beef and cook until the redness is gone, using a wooden spoon to break up and crumble the beef as it browns.

Add the rest of the ingredients except the beans; cover, and bring to a boil. Reduce the heat, and simmer for one (1) hour. Add the kidney beans, and simmer for an additional 30 minutes.

This recipe will make about 12 normal sized servings, or less if your family and guests like a good tasting brew.

Marty Hollander
Cincinnati, OH

YL

Burl Little III,
Sequin, TX

FAIRGROUND CHILI

3 Lbs. chuck or round steak
2 Lg. onions, chopped
2 green peppers, chopped
3 cloves garlic, finely chopped
2 jalapeno peppers, finely chopped
½ t. thyme
½ t. freshly ground pepper
3 C. water
2 to 4 T. chili powder
2 T. salt
2 T. olive oil
1 t. oregano
2 t. ground cumin
½ t. hot sauce

Heat the oil in a skillet or Dutch oven. Cut the meat into small cubes, and brown evenly. Add the onion, green pepper, garlic and water. Cover; and simmer for one hour or until the meat is tender.

Next, add remaining ingredients; cover, and cook for an additional hour on low simmer. If consistency is to be changed, add more water. Also, if you wish to alter the flavor and taste, now is the time to do it so that there is enough cooking time to allow the spices to be blended into the chili. Makes 9 to 10 servings.

Al & Bernice Shawn
Peoria, AZ

B.L. McMullen
Florida, 1885

CHILES RELLENOS JOS'E

1 can (26 oz.) whole green chiles (not hot ones) or,
18 whole green chiles, roasted and peeled
1 Lb. Monterey Jack cheese strips about
1-inch wide, 3-inches long,
¼-inch thick
½ Lb. Cheddar cheese, grated
5 Lg. eggs
¼ C. flour
1¼ C. milk
½ t. salt
Black pepper to taste
Liquid red pepper to taste
Paprika

Carefully rinse seeds from the chiles with cold water. Spread chiles in single layer on paper towels. Pat chiles with another towel until they are dry. Split a sheet of cheese into each chile. Beat eggs, gradually add flour beating until smooth. Add milk, salt, pepper and liquid red pepper. Arrange half the stuffed chiles in a well greased, shallow baking dish about 7x13-inches.

Sprinkle with half the Cheddar cheese and paprika. Repeat layers ending with cheese. Carefully pour egg mixture over all. Bake uncovered in a preheated oven at 350 degrees for about 45 minutes, or until a knife, inserted between chiles in the custard, comes out clean. Serves 6 to 8.

Carmen L. Caruso
El Paso, TX

H. Crum, 1844
Florida

C

CHILI VIA SLOW COOKER

1 Lb. Italian sausage, casings removed
1 Lb. ground beef
3 C. tomatoes, undrained, cut up
1 clove garlic, chopped fine
1 Lg. onion, chopped
½ t. sugar
½ t. salt
1½ t. chili powder
1 t. cumin seeds
1½ t. oregano leaves, crumbled
1 can (15 oz.) chili beans, undrained
1 can (15 oz.) garbanzo beans
dash or two Tabasco sauce

In a large skillet brown the sausage and the ground beef. Drain off excess drippings. In a slow cooker, combine browned meats, tomatoes, tomato sauce, onion, garlic, sugar, salt, chili powder, cumin and oregano.

Cook on Low for 3 to 4 hours, to allow flavors to mell. Add chili beans, garbanzo beans, and cook on Low for 45 minutes longer, or until beans are heated through, and done to desired taste. Add additional ingredients to adjust if needed. Makes 6 hearty servings.

Laurie A. Seltzer
Cincinnati, OH

Jack H. Kelley
Cocoa, FL

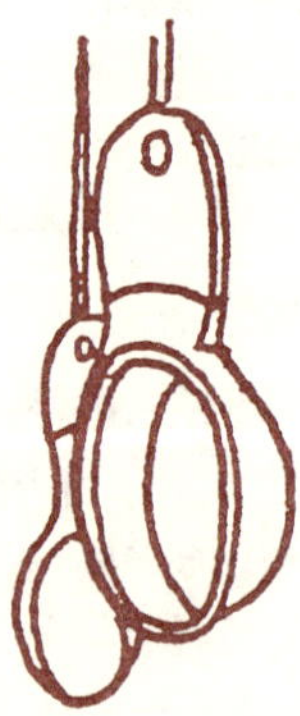

COTTONWOOD CHILI SUPREME

1 Lb. lean beef, chili ground
1 Med. onion, chopped
1 can (10½ oz.) condensed beef broth
1 can (8 oz.) tomato sauce
1 can (6 oz.) tomato paste
1 can (15 oz.) chili beans, undrained
1 Pkg. frozen baby lima beans
1 t. chili powder
½ t. oregano leaves
¼ t. salt (optional)

Brown beef and onion in large skillet. Drain excess drippings. Combine beef, onion, beef broth, tomato sauce and tomato paste. Stir occasionally, bring to a boil. Reduce heat. Add chili beans, frozen lima beans and seasonings. Cover, and let simmer 20-30 minutes or until lima beans are tender. Makes 4-5 servings.

Laurie A. Seltzer
Cincinnati, OH

Ohia Ranch
Honolulu, HA

CHILI SAUCE

36 Lg. tomatoes, peeled
12 Lg. green peppers, seeded
12 Lg. white onions
3 small hot red peppers, seeded
1 t. allspice
1 T. chili powder
2 Lbs. brown sugar
1 Qt. cider vinegar
1 t. ground cloves
1 T. black pepper
½ C. coarse salt
1 t. minced garlic

In a food processor or blender, process onions, green peppers and hot red peppers. Add the tomatoes and sugar, and remaining ingredients.

Pour the ingredients as they are ground up into a large soup pot, and slowly cook the sauce until it thickens, or about 3½ hours. Stir the sauce frequently to prevent the stock from sticking, and burning.

Taste the sauce during cooking, and adjust seasonings if desired. This makes about 5½ quarts. Seal the sauce in sterilized jars as directed.

Dan & Robin Broaddus
Cincinnati, OH

Foxley Cattle Co.
Omaha, NE

CINCINNATI CHILI NO. ???

2 Lbs. ground beef
2 Med. onions, chopped
1 Qt. water
1 can (16 oz.) tomatoes
1½ t. vinegar
1 t. Worcestershire sauce
1½ t. allspice
1 C. chopped onions, Optional
1 can (16 oz.) kidney beans, heated (optional)
1 t. ground cinnamon
½ t. garlic powder
2 bay leaves
6 servings hot, cooked spaghetti
1½ C. shredded Cheddar
1 box 11 or 12 ozs. Oyster crackers
1½ t. salt
1 T. chili powder
2 t. ground cumin
1 t. cayenne pepper

Combine beef, onions and water in a saucepan. Simmer until beef turns brown. Add tomatoes with liquid, vinegar, Worcestershire sauce, chili powder cumin, allspice, salt, cayenne pepper, cinnamon, garlic powder and bay leaves. Cover and simmer for 3 hours. (Fat from the meat will float on the liquid. Skim it, or if there's time, chill it and lift off fat layer).

3-way chili: serve meat sauce over cooked spaghetti and top with cheese. Pass oyster crackers. Serves 6.

4-way chili: serve meat sauce over cooked spaghetti and top with cheese, but this time, sprinkle; with chopped onions.

5-way chili: repeat above, but this time, add heated kidney beans on top of 4-way.

John G. Wright
Warsaw, KY

7 Hat
A. S. Holst, 1936
Brevard County, FL

CHILI TOPPING

1 Med. onion, chopped
1 small green pepper, chopped
½ t. salt
1 C. sliced ripe olives
¼ t. fresh ground pepper
1 can (16 oz.) red kidney beans
1 can (16 oz.) stewed tomatoes
1 t. chili powder
Dash Tabasco sauce
2 T. olive oil

Saute onions and green pepper in the olive oil along with the chili powder, until the vegetables are soft. Stir in the remaining ingredients except the sliced olives. Cover, simmer for 30 minutes to blend flavors.

Stir several times to prevent burning and sticking. Stir in olives.
Makes about 4 cups.

Jay & Sandy Hatfield
Cincinnati, OH

Alberta & Marion Bonnifield
San Miguel, CA

ST. LOUIS CHILI

1 Lb. ground beef
1 Lg. onion, chopped
1 small green pepper, chopped
1 can (8 oz.) tomato sauce
1 can (16 oz.) tomatoes, undrained, chopped
1 can (16 oz.) kidney beans,
1 t. salt
½ t. paprika
Dash cayenne pepper (optional)
1 clove garlic, minced
¼ t. fresh ground pepper
¼ t. oregano
Dash or so Tabasco sauce

In a 3-quart casserole, combine ground beef, onion and celery. Microwave on High for 7 to 8 minutes or until beef is no longer pink. Stir halfway during cooking tome to crumble meat. Drain off excess fat drippings.

Stir in remaining ingredients and microwave on High for 25 to 30 minutes, or until mixture is thoroughly cooked. Stir every fine minutes, and rotate casserole for even cooking.

Bernie & Gail Geltner
Boynton Beach, FL

Calyxta Lacayo,
Honduras (1845)

CHILI BURGER BALLS

2 Lbs. ground beef, or ground turkey
½ C. bread crumbs
1 egg
1 t. prepared mustard
1 bottle (12 oz.) chili sauce
2 T. oil
1 C. water
1 T. brown sugar
¼ C. milk
2 t. salt
1 t. paprika

Mix meat lightly with the egg, bread crumbs, milk, salt and paprika until well blended. Form mixture into 16 or 17 balls. In a hot skillet, brown meat balls in oil. Remove and set aside. Pour off fat dripping that may accumulate.

Stir the chili sauce, water, brown sugar and mustard in the skillet. Return the meat balls; cover, and simmer, stirring occasionally, for 30 minutes or longer until meat is cooked thoroughly through.

Serve the meat balls with mashed potatoes, hot rice, or noodles. Makes enough for 8 or so mouths.

Dawn Smeltzer
Melbourne, FL

Peter & Etta Massaro
Chowchilla, CA

AROMATIC CHILI CON CARNE

1 Med. onion, chopped
1 green pepper, chopped
1½ Lbs. ground beef
¼ Lb. butter
1 clove garlic, minced
2 cans (16 oz.) kidney beans
2 T. angostura aromatic bitters
2 T. flour
1 can (16 oz.) tomatoes
1 can (8 oz.) tomato sauce
2 t. salt
1 T. chili powder
¼ t. oregano

Saute the onions, green pepper and garlic in the butter. Add the beef and brown. Place this into a large skillet, and add the remaining ingredients. Cover, and simmer for 30 minutes stirring occasionally. Add more water or tomato sauce if liquid is needed. Makes 6 servings.

Bernie & Gail Geltner
Boynton Beach, FL

Fred G. Myers
Brawley, CA

CHILI BARBECUED PORK CHOPS

6 pork loin butterfly chops
½ C. onion, chopped
½ C. chili sauce
⅛ t. oregano
1 T. brown sugar
1 t. Olive oil
¼ C. orange juice
½ t. salt
Dash Tabasco sauce
¼ t. shredded orange peel
1 clove garlic, minced
Pinch fresh ground black pepper

In a skillet, saute the onion and garlic in the oil until they are tender. Do not brown. Stir in the orange peel, orange juice, chili sauce, Tabasco sauce, brown sugar, salt and mix together well. Bring mixture to a boil. Remove skillet from heat.

Sprinkle pork chops with a little salt and pepper. Grill over a medium bed of coals for 15 minutes. Turn meat and brush with the mixture. Grill 15 to 20 minutes longer. Brush on remaining sauce and grill just a few minutes longer. Makes 6 servings.

Andy & Lynn Fogel
Cincinnati, OH

Ernest S. Texeir
Honolulu, HA

STOLEN RECIPE CHILI

3 Lbs. ground beef
1 Lg. onion, chopped fine
2 cloves garlic, minced
½ can (3 oz.) tomato paste
1 T. salt
3 T. chili powder
Salad oil for cooking
1 t. white pepper
1 T. cumin seed
1½ T. finely ground dried chile pepper
1½ T. sugar or corn syrup
3 C. water

Saute the beef in some oil, and add onions and garlic. Drain off excess fat. Add all seasonings. Bring to a boil, stirring to keep the mixture from sticking or burning to pot. Add the water, and simmer for 3 to 4 hours. If chili is too thick, add more water, or some tomato juice if desired.

Taste for flavor, and alter it if desired with additional spices. Let the chili set before serving, or if time allows, let it cool and refrigerate overnight for a more mellow taste. Makes 6 to 8 servings.

Mike White
Cincinnati, OH

Pare Cline
Simi Valley, CA

NOT MUCH BUT GOOD CHILI

1 Lb. ground beef
½ C. chopped onion
Pinch of red pepper flakes
4 t. chili powder
1 green pepper, chopped
1 can (16 oz.) red kidney beans, undrained
1 t. salt
⅛ t. black pepper
1 can (10½ oz.) condensed tomato soup
Salad oil
1 clove garlic, crushed
Dash or two hot sauce

In a heavy skillet, saute the onion, pepper and garlic, adding the beef after the vegetables are tender. Brown the beef, and drain off fat. Stir skillet to break up beef, and keep any from sticking to bottom of pot.

Add rest of ingredients, holding the beans out until the last 30 minutes of the 2 to 2½ hour cooking time. Stir occasionally to evenly cook chili. Heat thoroughly and serve with sprinkled cheese on top, and crisp crackers on the side. Makes about 6 servings.

Ms. Maria E. Valle
Miami, FL

Yutaka Nakashima
Honolulu, HA

CHILI-SPAGHETTI w/TURKEY

1 Lb. ground turkey
2½ C. tomato juice
½ C. onion, chopped
½ C. carrot, chopped
Pinch black pepper
1 can (16 oz.) red kidney beans
1 t. salt
1 C. uncooked spaghetti, broken
1 t. chili powder
Water if need to cook turkey

In a saucepan, saute ground turkey, onion and carrot until the meat is no longer pink. Stir in rest of ingredients except the spaghetti. Simmer, covered, for 30 minutes to blend contents of mixture.

Put uncooked spaghetti in a 1-quart casserole; add meat mixture, and bake at 375 degree oven for 1 hour or till spaghetti is tender. Stir casserole occasionally during cooking. Makes 5 to 6 servings.

Don Greenslade
Cocoa, FL

Everett Palmer
Shelbyville, TN

WESTERN CHILI

1 Lb. ground lean beef
1 Lb. chili beans
1 Lg. onion, chopped
1 green pepper, chopped
1 can (16 oz.) tomatoes, cut up
1 t. paprika
1½ t. chili powder
¼ t. black pepper
2 C. tomato puree
Salt to taste
Red pepper flakes, if desired
1 T. olive oil

Wash the beans, and soak overnight. Drain and put into a large saucepan and cover with water. Add salt. Cook slowly until the beans are tender.

In a large skillet, heat the olive oil; add beef, onions and green pepper. Cook until the meat is browned, stirring often with a fork to break up beef while it is cooking.

Add the remaining ingredients including the beans cover, and simmer for about 30 to 45 minutes, mixing occasionally to well blend the chili. Taste, and if necessary add spices to get the desired flavor you want.

Serve with chopped onions, shredded Cheddar cheese, and crackers.

Jordan M. Geltner
Streamwood, IL

John & Betty Jamison
O'Neals, CA

WELCHE'S BELCHES CHILI

3 Lbs. chuck roast
5 Lg. onions, finely chopped
3 Lg. green peppers, chopped
14 cloves garlic, finely chopped
10 C. hot water
¼ C. oil
2 T. ground cumin
1 bay leaf
1 T. ground oregano
6 T. salt
6 jalapeno peppers, finely chopped
2 T. Masa flour
½ C. cold water
¾ C. chili powder
1 t. thyme
½ t. ground black pepper
½ t. cayenne pepper

Cut the chuck steak into small pieces and place in a Dutch oven; brown the meat in the oil until it is done. Drain or spoon off any excess oil or grease from the meat. Add the onion, green pepper, garlic; cover, and simmer for 1 hour or until the meat is tender.

Add remaining ingredients, except the flour, and cook on low, for an additional hour. Add water if necessary for consistency, and stir occasionally. During the cooking, taste and add more seasonings is desired.

Stir the Masa, or cornmeal if on hand, in a little cold water to form a paste. Add to chili, stirring constantly to avoid lumps, and until the mixture has thickened. Remove the bay leaf before servings. Makes about 14 to 16 helpings.

Scott Govig
Cincinnati, OH

Kempfer Cattle Co.
Melbourne, FL

SPEEDY CHILI

1 Lb. ground beef
1 Med. onion, chopped
1 Med. green pepper, chopped
1 t. paprika
1 clove garlic, minced
2 t. salt
2 t. chili powder
2 C. water
1 can (16 oz.) red kidney beans
1 can (16 oz.) tomatoes, chopped

In a skillet, saute the beef and vegetables in a little oil, until the beef is brown and the vegetables are tender. Add the remaining ingredients, and let simmer for one (1) hour, or until it's to your taste.

If you like shredded cheese and onion sprinkled over you cheese chili, use Cheddar as it seems to go better with chili than other types. For an extra tangy mixture, keep a bottle of hot sauce on the table for those who like a dash or two to liven up their meal.

Laurie A. Seltzer
Cincinnati, OH

University of Florida
Gainesville, FL

CHILI con ELOTE

Chili with corn is a hearty, meatless soup, ideal for chilly-day lunches or suppers. Top with cheese and sour cream and serve with tortilla chips.

- 1 C. chopped onion
- 1 garlic clove, minced
- 2 T. vegetable oil
- 1 can (15 or 16 oz.) kidney beans or pinto beans, drained
- 1 can (8¾ oz.) whole kernel corn, drained
- ½ C. Pace Picante Sauce
- ½ C. water
- 1 t. salt
- 1 t. ground cumin
- 1 t. oregano leaves, crushed
- 1 green pepper, diced
- Shredded Cheddar cheese and dairy sour cream (optional)

Cook onion and garlic in oil in a large saucepan until onion is tender but not brown. Drain and coarsely chop tomatoes, reserving juice. Combine juice and 1 can beans in work bowl of food processor or blender container. Process with steel blade until fairly smooth.

Add bean mixture to saucepan with remaining beans, reserving tomatoes, corn, picante sauce, water, salt, cumin and oregano. Bring to a boil, reduce heat. Cover and simmer 30 minutes. Add green pepper; simmer 5 minutes. Ladle into soup bowls; top with cheese and sour cream, if desired. Serve with additional picante sauce. Makes 6 servings, about 6 cups of soup.

Pace Foods, Inc.

Seventeen
George R. Kempfer
Melbourne, FL

ZESTY CHILI

- 1 Lb. stew meat, cut ¾-inch cubes
- 2 T. oil
- 4 to 6 t. chili powder
- 1 C. water
- 1 clove garlic, minced
- 2 Med. potatoes, 1-inch cubed
- Drop or two Worcestershire sauce

In a saucepan, brown the meat. Drain off drippings. Stir in water and remaining ingredients except the potatoes. Cover and cook for 30 to 35 minutes.

Stir in the cubed potatoes and simmer, covered, for 25 to 30 minutes or until potatoes are tender. Serves 4.

Bernie & Gail Geltner
Boynton Beach, FL

Rafter 85
Dr. Claude Godwin
Titusville, FL

HASTY TURKEY CHILI

1 Lb. ground turkey
2 T. salad oil
1 Lg. onion, chopped
1 green pepper, chopped
2 stalks celery, chopped
¼ t. paprika
1 can (16 oz.) tomatoes
1 can (10½ oz.) black bean soup
1 soup can of water
1 t. salt
½ t. oregano
4 t. chili powder

In a skillet, cook the turkey until the pink color is gone, crumbling with a wooden fork to break up meat as it cooks. Push the cooked turkey to one side and saute the onions, green pepper and celery until tender.

Add all remaining ingredients to the skillet and mix through. Bring the chili to a boil; reducing the heat to simmer and let cook for 30 minutes.

Serve with chopped onions, shredded cheese, crackers or chips.

Al & Bernice Shawn
Peoria, AZ

Stewart Brothers
Pangle Stewart
Fayetteville, TN

PINTO CHILI

This has been a steady chili recipe in our family for many years, and has been passed around to relatives and friends for some time. Hope that it is accepted by other chiliheads.

2 Lbs. ground beef
2 onions, chopped
1 green pepper, chopped
4 stalks celery, chopped
3 cloves garlic, minced
2 T. salad oil
1 Lb. dried pinto beans
1 to 2 T. chili powder
1 t. ground cumin
2 cans (6 oz.) tomato paste
6 C. water
2 T. salt
6 C. tomato juice
1 bay leaf

Wash and sort the beans and place in a heavy kettle. Cover them with water, and bring to a boil for 3 minutes. Remove from heat and let soak for one hour. Add tomato juice, and cook over a low heat while preparing the meat.

Saute the meat, onions, green pepper, celery and garlic. Cook, crumbling meat with a fork until it is brown. Add rest of the ingredients, mixing well to blend with meat and vegetables. Cover and simmer for 3 to 3½ hours, or until the beans are tender. Taste for flavor, and add more seasonings if wanted. Makes 10 to 12 servings.

Mike White
Cincinnati, OH

Alfredo Ahumada
Tucson, AZ

BORDER CHILI BEEF SOUP

We have been serving this soup for many years, and each time, there's a little something added or taken away just to have a variety of flavors and ingredients in it. Any number of vegetables can be put in, and none will do any harm to the chili if used.

3 Lbs. ground beef
1 Lg. onion, chopped
1 green pepper, chopped
3 stalks celery, chopped
* 2 carrots, sliced
2 Med. potatoes, diced
Mushrooms, sliced, optional
* 1 Pkg. frozen mixed vegetables instead of carrots
1 can (16 oz.) tomatoes, chopped
1 can (10 oz.) whole kernel corn
1½ to 2 t. chili powder
½ t. oregano
Salt and pepper to taste
1 can (12 oz.) tomato sauce
1 C. uncooked rice or macaroni
10 to 12 C. water
¼ t. cumin powder

Saute the ground beef with the onion, pepper and celery in a large skillet or Dutch oven, until the meat is done and the vegetables are tender. Drain off fat. Add all remaining ingredients to the Dutch oven; cover, and simmer for about 2 hours. Stir occasionally and check for consistency. During the 2 hours of cooking, the rice should be fully cooked.

This soup should be solid and not too "watery". Taste while cooking, and add more seasonings if necessary.

Jan & Sandy Hatfield
Cincinnati, OH

Lone Pine Ranch
Richard Gomer
Hollister, CA

CHILLY NIGHT CHILI

1 can (15½ oz.) Hanover Kidney beans
1 Pkg. (1¼ oz.) McCormick/ Schilling Chili Seasoning Mix
1 Lb. ground beef
1 cans (8 oz.) tomato sauce, or
1 can (15½ oz.) tomatoes

Brown ground beef, drain fat. Stir in Seasoning Mix, two 8 ounce cans tomato sauce (or one pound can tomatoes broken into pieces) and one 15½ ounce can Hanover Kidney Beans, cover and simmer 10 minutes. Yields five 1 cup servings.
MICROWAVE DIRECTIONS: Microcook beef on High 3-5 minutes, drain fat. Stir in ingredients as directed above. Microcook on High 6-8 minutes. Rotate bowl once during cooking.

McCormick/Shilling

J. D., H. D.,
Jimmie W. Estes
Laton, CA

CHILI-CHICKEN STEW

A light yet satisfying stew-like variation of 'Texas' favorite food-chili. The do-it-yourself toppings add to the casual fun of this crowd pleaser.

3 whole chicken breasts, split, boned and skinned
1 C. chopped onion
1 medium green pepper, chopped
2 garlic cloves, minced
2 cans (14½ oz.) stewed tomatoes
1 can (15 oz.) pinto beans, drained
⅔ to ¾ C. Pace Picante Sauce, if desired
1 t. chili powder
1 t. ground cumin
½ t. salt
Optional toppings:
Shredded Cheddar cheese, Green onion slices, diced Avocado, dairy sour cream
2 T. vegetable oil

Cut chicken into 1-inch pieces. Cook chicken, onion, green pepper and garlic in oil in a Dutch oven until chicken looses it pink color.

Add remaining ingredients; simmer 20 minutes. Ladle into bowls; top with cheese, onion, avocado, sour cream and additional picante sauce, as desired. Makes 6 to 8 servings, about 9 cups stew.

Pace Foods, Inc.

David Fischer
Hamshire,
Jefferson County, TX

CHICKEN-ON-THE-RUN CHILI

1987 winner of Deer Park, Ohio 75th Anniversary Celebration Chili Cookoff. Served at Chicken-On-The-Run Restaurant, Deer Park, Ohio.

10 Lbs. ground beef
4 cans (46 oz.) tomato juice
½ #10 can tomato sauce
1 can (46 oz.) water
1 C. minced onion
¾ C. celery flakes
1 C. chili powder
2 T. salt
1 T. dry mustard
2 t. curry powder
2 t. garlic salt
1 t. ground cayenne pepper
1 Qt. fresh canned mixed chili pepper, chopped and drained
1 can (16 oz.) pinto beans
1 T. garlic powder
1 T. cumin

In a large skillet brown beef, drain and place in large heavy pot. Add all ingredients except the beans, stirring as you add. Cook at a simmer for about an hour, stirring often. Add beans and cook till heated through. Makes approximately 5 gallons.

Dan Bachman
Cincinnati, OH

7 Seven Up
J.L. Drawdy, 1935
Brevard County, FL

TURKEY CHILI PICANTE

Virginia T. DuKet of Oceanside, California, sent us her recipe for delicious, spicy chili the morning she created it. Chock-full of healthy ingredients, it's high in taste appeal and low in fat and cholesterol.

1 Lb. ground turkey
1 large onion, chopped
2 garlic cloves, chopped
2 cans (16 oz.) red kidney or pinto beans, rinsed and drained
1 can (16 oz.) tomato sauce
1 large green pepper, coarsely chopped
½ t. oregano leaves, crushed
¼ t. pepper
¼ t. basil leaves, crushed
1 C. thawed frozen corn, or 1 can about 8 oz. whole kernel corn, drained
½ C. chopped cilantro
2 t. ground cumin

Cook turkey, onion and garlic in Dutch oven or large saucepan until the turkey is no longer pink. Add beans, tomato sauce, Pace Picante Sauce, green pepper and seasonings; bring to a boil.

Reduce heat and simmer uncovered 25 minutes. Stir in corn and cilantro; simmer 5 minutes. Serve with additional Pace Picante Sauce. Makes 6 to 8 servings, about 8 cups.

Pace Foods, Inc.

Lorain L. Laughlin
Memphis, TN

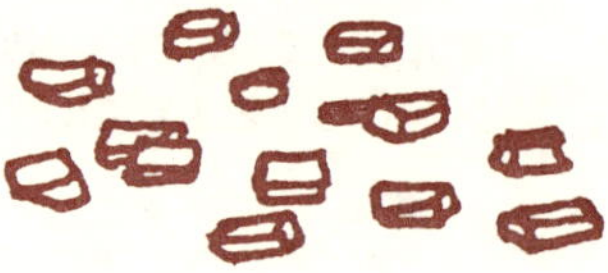

CRAZY MARY'S CHILI

2 T. chili powder
1 t. salt
½ t. freshly ground pepper
¼ C. (½ stick) butter or margarine
2 C. sliced fresh mushrooms (7 or 8 large)
1 C. chopped onion
1 c. chopped celery
1 Lb. lean ground beef
2 cans (28 oz.) crushed tomatoes in tomato puree
¼ C. water
1 T. sugar
1 t. Worcestershire sauce
2 C. canned kidney beans, drained
Shredded Cheddar cheese
Sour cream

Combine chili powder, salt and pepper in cup; set aside. Melt butter or margarine in heavy large saucepan over medium heat. Add mushrooms, onion and celery, and cook, stirring occasionally, until the onion is transparent, about 10 minutes. Add ground beef and about ¼ of the chili powder mixture. Cook, breaking up meat with a fork, until browned. Stir in remaining chili powder mixture, tomatoes, water, sugar and Worcestershire sauce. Cover partially and simmer 15 minutes. Add beans and simmer 10 minutes more.

Ladle chili into broiler-proof serving bowls. Sprinkle each serving with about 2 tablespoons shredded Cheddar cheese. Broil just until cheese melts. Top each with dollop of sour cream. Serve immediately.

Ms. Betsy Young
Cincinnati, OH

G.A. Tucker & Sons
Rockledge, FL

CHILI with CHOCOLATE

1 onion, chopped
1 green pepper, chopped
3 T. vegetable oil
1 garlic clove, minced
1 Lb. ground beef chuck
1 Lb. ground pork
3 T. chili powder
1 T. ground cumin
1 28 oz. can tomatoes, chopped including juice
1 C. beef broth
1 bay leaf
¾ t. cayenne pepper
½ t. Tabasco sauce
½ t. dried oregano
¾ t. salt
¼ t. pepper
1 Oz. semisweet chocolate, grated
Pinch of cinnamon
Sour cream and minced onion as accompaniments

In a kettle cook the onion and the green pepper in the oil over a moderate heat, stirring, for 4 minutes. Add the garlic and cook the mixture for 1 minute.

In a large skillet brown the chuck and the pork over a high heat and transfer the meats with a slotted spoon to the kettle.

Add to the kettle the chili powder and the cumin and cook the mixture over moderately low heat, stirring, for 1 minute. Add the tomatoes, the beef stock, bay leaf, cayenne pepper, Tabasco sauce, oregano, salt and the pepper, bring the liquid to a boil, stirring, and simmer the chili for 2 hours.

Remove the kettle from the heat and stir in the chocolate, cinnamon and salt and pepper to taste. Serve the chili with the sour cream and minced onion. Serves 4 to 6.

Ms. Betsy Young
Cincinnati, OH

William Chard,
California(1845)

SMOKY SAUSAGE CHILI

1 Lb. ground beef
1 Lg. onion, coarsely chopped
2 t. chili powder
2 t. ground cumin
½ Lb. smoked sausage or kielbasa, sliced ¼-inch thick, each slice halved
1 can (16 oz.) red kidney beans, drained
1 C. Pace Picante Sauce
1 C. vegetable juice cocktail
1 can (8 oz.) tomato sauce
Toppings: Sour Cream, shredded cheddar cheese, diced avocado

Brown ground beef with onion in large saucepan or Dutch oven; drain. Sprinkle chili powder and cumin over meat; cook and stir 1 minute. Add remaining ingredients except optional toppings; bring to a boil. Reduce heat; simmer uncovered 20 minutes, stirring occasionally. Ladle into soup bowls; top as desired. Serve with additional Pace Picante Sauce. Makes 6 servings, about 7 cups chili.

Pace Foods, Inc.

George Kahalekomo, Jr.
Waipahu, HA

BILTMORE CHILI con CARNE

¼ Lb. kidney fat, diced
1 Lb. lean beef, diced
2 C. water
1 small onion, chopped
3 T. chili powder
1 C. solid packed tomatoes
½ T. paprika
salt to taste
6 ripe avocados
3 small, hot chile peppers
1 Oz. finely chopped onion
1 t. Mexican lime juice
1 dash Tabasco sauce

Melt kidney fat in heavy skillet, then add meat and water. Cook 1 hour slowly; in fact, cook the whole batch slowly. Add onion; cook ½ hour. Stir in chili powder and cook another ½ hour. Add tomatoes; cook 1 hour, seasoning with paprika and more salt, if needed. Top chili with guacamole made by blending peeled avocados with finely diced hot peppers, onion, lime juice, and Tabasco.

Serve with tamales and fresh hot tortillas or crisp corn tortilla wedges.

John G. Wright
Warsaw, KY

Jay Baird Stock Farm
Pataskala, OH

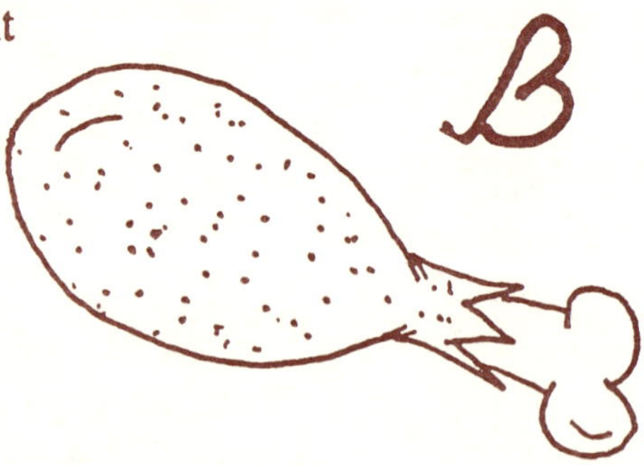

DEEP-DISH LENTIL CHILI PIE WITH CORN BREAD CRUST

For the lentil chili:

2 C. coarsely chopped onion
¼ C. vegetable oil
2 garlic cloves, minced
2 T. powder
2 t. ground cumin
1 t. dried oregano, crumbled
1 t. dried thyme, crumbled
1 t. paprika
3 ribs of celery, strings discarded and the celery chopped coarse
4 C. chicken stock, canned chicken broth, or water
2 C. lentils, picked over and rinsed
1 can (14 oz.) plum tomatoes, chopped coarse, including the juice
2 green bell peppers, chopped coarse
⅛ t. cayenne, or to taste

CHILI: In heavy kettle cook the onion in the oil over moderately low heat, stirring, until it is softened, add the garlic, chili powder, cumin, oregano, thyme, paprika, cayenne and bay leaf, and cook the mixture, stirring, for 3 minutes. Add the stock and 2 cups of water and bring the liquid to a boil. Reduce heat. Add the lentils and simmer the mixture, covered partially, and stirring occasionally, for 40 minutes.

Add the tomatoes with the juice, bell peppers, celery and salt and pepper to taste, simmer the mixture, uncovered, for 15 to 20 minutes or until it is thickened. Transfer chili to a 3-quart casserole, discarding the bay leaf. The lentil chili may be made 3 days in advance, cooled to room temperature, and kept covered and chilled.

CRUST:

½ C. yellow cornmeal
½ C. all-purpose flour
1½ t. double-acting baking powder
¼ t. baking soda
½ t. salt
1 Lg. egg, beaten lightly
2 T. unsalted butter, melted and cooled
¼ C. milk
¼ C. sour cream
2 t. honey

In a bowl, combine well the cornmeal, flour, baking soda, baking powder, salt, egg, butter, milk, sour cream and the honey. Stir the batter until it is just combined.

Drop the batter by spoonfuls over the lentil chili and bake the pie in a preheated 400 degree oven for 30 minutes, or until a tester inserted in the corn bread comes our clean. Serves 6.

TB

Ms. Betsy Young
Cincinnati, OH

TB

Horace N. Sharp
Titusville, FL

BENNY'S CHILI

- 4 T. olive oil
- 3 Lbs. ground hamburger
- 2 t. chili powder
- ½ C. sliced onion
- 1 t. cumin powder
- 1½ t. salt
- 2 cans (8 oz.) tomato sauce
- 3 cloves garlic, minced

Heat oil in large skillet. Sauce onions for about 3 minutes. Add the minced garlic and saute until lightly browned. Push onion and garlic to one side of skillet, or remove and set aside.

Add hamburger to skillet in one flat piece, and as it browns, slowly break it up, so that the juices are retained.

When meat is slightly browned, add tomato sauce, cumin, chili powder, salt, and simmer for 15 minutes or so. Check for flavor, adding more if you desire, and add enough water to chili for consistency.

Laurie A. Seltzer
Cincinnati, OH

6T

Helen Jenkins
State Brand Clerk
Phoenix, AZ

MY CHILI

- 3 C. dried kidney beans
- 9 C. water
- 1 Lg. onion, chopped
- 1½ Lbs. hamburger
- 6 C. sliced stewed tomatoes, or 2 cans (28 oz.)
- 3 C. tomato puree, or 1 can (28 oz.)
- 2 C. diced green chilies
- 3 T. crushed dried red chilies
- ¼ C. whole cumin seed, toasted
- 3 cloves garlic, finely minced
- ⅛ C. parsley
- 2 T. oregano
- Salt and pepper to taste

Bring 3 cups of dried kidney beans to a boil in 9 cups of water. Turn heat down and simmer 1½ to 2 hours, or until tender. Drain. (Yields about 6 cups of beans).

In a large skillet, brown hamburger and chopped onions. In kettle, combine drained beans, hamburger and onions, spices and remaining ingredients. Simmer for about an hour.

John G. Wright
Warsaw,KY

Horseshoe-One
Livestock Co.
Honolulu, HA

NORTHERN MICHIGAN VENISON CHILI PASTIES

2 large pasties-serves 4-

1½ to 2 Lbs. venison steak, cut in small pieces
Marinate overnight (see below)
3 slices bacon, cut and fry (not crispy)
2 T. flour
2 cloves garlic, minced or crushed
2 T. chili powder
Tabasco - if desired
1 t. ground cumin
1 T. salt (optional)
1 t. pepper
2 small potatoes - diced small
2 small carrots - diced small
1 rib celery - diced small
1 small onion, diced
2 Med. tomatoes, (blanched, skinned, seeded and chopped

Marinate:

2 C. pineapple juice
1 envelope meat marinate
2 T. lemon juice
¼ t. dried basil
1 t. garlic powder

Combine meat and marinate in bag or covered bowl.Refrigerate overnight. Double marinate for 4 pasties.

Pastie Dough:

2 C. all-purpose flour
scant C. Crisco
1 t. salt
6 T. cold water, add ½ then small amounts as needed to make a pliable dough.

Roll out on floured board.

Drain and reserve marinate. Pat meat dry with paper towels. Fry the bacon; using fat for sauteing meat.Add 2 tablespoons flour, stir then gradually add marinate.Stir in potatoes, carrots, celery, onions, and tomatoes. Now add the spices: garlic, chili powder, cumin, salt and pepper. Cover, simmer about 8 to 10 minutes.

Place one 9" crust pie place, fill ½ with meat mixture (if too soupy, use a slotted spoon). Fold over and crimp edges.Do the same with the other half of the pan. DO NOT SLIT DOUGH. Bake at 325 degrees for 45 minutes. Pierce crust to check on vegetables. Cut pie in half. Serves 4. Serve with tossed salad.

Merline McKenzie
Lansing, MI

Inverted Bar M
James B. Martin
Melbourne, FL

PALM CHILI

2 Lbs. hamburger beef
1 Lg. onion, chopped
2 cans (10½ oz.) condensed tomato soup
3 cans (10½ oz.) water
2 cans Brooks Chili Beans
1 C. Catsup
1 T. chili powder

Saute beef and onions until done, and drain off excess grease.Add rest of ingredients and cook for 90 minutes on low heat.Serve hot.

Mrs. Joe Osborne
Palm Bay, FL

Wayne & Lucille Carlin
Stryker, OH

QUICK-AND-EASY CHILI

1¼ Lbs. ground beef
1 Lg. onion, chopped
1 can (16 oz.) whole tomatoes, undrained and chopped
1 can (16 oz.) pork and beans, undrained
1 can (15 oz.) kidney beans, undrained
2 T. chili powder
1 t. salt
1 clove garlic, minced
1 can (11 oz.) zesty tomato soup

Combine ground beef and onion in a Dutch oven; cook until meat is browned, stirring to crumble. Drain off drippings. Add remaining ingredients; bring to a boil and cook 3 minutes, stirring occasionally. Yield: 2 quarts.

John G. Wright
Warsaw, KY

Burton French
Beaumont,
Jefferson County, TX

TEXAS-STYLE CHILI

- 3 T. oil
- 1½ Lbs. round steak, cut into ½-inch cubes
- 1½ C. water
- 4 T. chili powder
- 2 heaping T. Masa harina (or yellow cornmeal)

Brown cubed meat in oil in large skillet. Add water, stir in chili powder and cornmeal, and simmer until liquid is reduced to half.

John G. Wright
Wasaw, KY

Baker Valley Packing
Baker, OR

N.Y. CHILI con TURKEY

- ½ Lb. ground turkey
- 2 Med. onions, chopped
- 1 green pepper, chopped
- 1 clove garlic, minced
- 1 can (16 oz.) tomatoes, chopped, undrained
- 3 C. cooked kidney beans, drained
- 2 t. chili powder, more or less to taste
- 1 t. cumin seed (optional)
- salt to taste

Brown ground turkey lightly in a non-stick skillet. Do not use any oil or grease. The turkey will release sufficient water for cooking and browning.

Stir in remaining ingredients; cover, and simmer for 25 minutes. Uncover and continue cooking on a low heat until mixture has thickened to the desired consistency. If a thinner chili is desired, use a little tomato juice.

Makes 6 servings.

Sanford G. Slocum
Rochester, NY

Rocking Arrow T
A.C. Tedford
Melbourne, FL

PIZZA CHILI STYLE

12 tortillas
1 can (19 oz.) Wolf brand Chili With or Without Beans
1 Med. green pepper, cut into strips
1 small onion, chopped
½ Lb. Kraft Jalapeno Pepper Process Cheese Spread, cubed

Cover bottom and sides of lightly greased 14-inch pizza pan with tortillas.Spread the chili mix evenly over tortillas to the edges.Top with strips of green pepper, and sprinkle onions over the spread.

Bake at 350 degrees for about 20 minutes then top with the Process Cheese Spread cubes, and cook for 5 minutes longer.

This recipe states that this is to serve 6 people, but it does not indicate how many you need to serve a troop of kids.

Kim Orosco
Cincinnati, OH

"Mission Cross" used at St. Mary's Mission near Stevensville during the 1840's. Montana

MEXI CHILI

1½ Lbs. ground beef
1 Med. onion, chopped
2 cans (16 oz.) chili beans
1 can (16 oz.) whole tomatoes, undrained and chopped
1 can (10 oz.) enchilada sauce
1 can (10 oz.) tomatoes with green chiles, undrained
¼ t. salt
¼ t. pepper
¼ t. garlic powder

Combine ground beef and onion in a Dutch oven; cook until meat is browned, stirring to crumble. Drain off drippings. Add remaining ingredients; cover, bring to a boil, reduce heat, and simmer for 30 minutes, stirring occasionally to blend. Uncover and simmer 156 minutes or until thickened. Yield: about 2½ quarts.

John G. Wright
Warsaw, KY

Amon English
Phoenix, AZ

CHILI SAUCE - CANADIAN STYLE

1 C. celery, chopped
1 C. onion, chopped
1 can (17 oz.) S&W sliced Cling Peaches, drained
1 can (17 oz.) S&W Bartlett Pears, drained and chopped
4 cans (16 oz.) S&W Stewed Tomatoes
1 Rd. T. whole pickling spices (tied in a cheese cloth bag)
1 C. brown sugar
½ C. garlic flavored red wine vinegar
1 t. seasoned salt
Dash dill weed
Dash or two Tabasco sauce
¼ t. cumin seed, crushed

Cook the first 6 ingredients in a large saucepan or soup pot for 15 minutes. Add the remaining ingredients and cook until the mixture thickens and the contents are tender.

Remove the spice bag and discard. Pour the chili mixture into pint jars and seal according to the bottle's manufacture instructions.

This can be served with meat, poultry or with eggs. Makes 4 to 6 pints of sauce.

Ms. Andy Holland
Goshen, OH

Fort Baker Ranch
John C. Rice
Kneeland, CA

MARVE'S CHILI con CARNE

4 Lbs. dry uncooked beans
8 C. tomato sauce or tomato paste and water
1⅓ C. onion, chopped
1⅓ C. green pepper, chopped
2 Lbs. ground beef (very lean or defatted) browned
⅓ C. chili powder
4 t. Lite salt
1 t. garlic powder
½ t. ground bay leaf
2 t. cumin
3 T. whole wheat flour (in cool liquid)

1. Soak beans 12-hours or overnight in water to cover, plus 6-inches over.
2. Pour off soak-water, then rinse in fresh water.

3. In a pressure cooker, cover beans with enough water to 2-inches above level of beans. Cook at 15-pounds pressure for approximately 20 minutes, (or simmer until almost done, 1½ to 2 hours).

4. Break up cooked meat in food processor. Add tomato sauce, onions, green peppers, chili powder, salt, garlic powder, bay leaf and cumin. Transfer to large pot, and bring to a boil, then cook for 10-minutes or until vegetables are tender.

5. Add flour-liquid; cook until mixture thickens.

6. Add cooked beans; bring back to a boil, then lower heat and simmer approximately 20 minutes until beans and vegetables are tender and flavors are blended.

Marve H. Lavin
FOOD CRAFTERS
Iowa City, IA

Fannie D. Crow
Dallas,
Jefferson County, TX

BEEFY CHILI

2 Lbs. ground beef
½ C. chopped onion
1 clove garlic, minced
2 C. cola-flavored beverage
1 C. water
1 can (6 oz.) tomato paste
2 T. chili powder
1 T. paprika
1 t. salt
1 t. pepper
⅛ t. dried whole oregano
1 can (16 oz.) kidney beans, undrained

Combine first 3 ingredients in a Dutch oven; cook until meat is browned, stirring to crumble. Drain off drippings. Add remaining ingredients except the beans. Bring to a boil; reduce heat and simmer, uncovered, 30 minutes or until thickened. Add the beans, cover and simmer 10 minutes. Yield: 7 cups.

John G. Wright
Warsaw, KY

Square M Ranch Arizona
Kirkland, AZ

KARZ'S CHILI

½ Lb. ground beef
½ Lb. ground turkey
3 onions, chopped
1 Lb. pinto beans
(dried preferred)
½ C. crushed soy bean flakes
Salt and pepper to taste
pinch (?) sugar (I use ¼ cup)
2 Lg. cans tomatoes
2 cans (12 oz.) tomato sauce
2 cans (6 oz.) tomato paste
Dried garlic or fresh, to taste
Chili powder of choice

Cook the dried pinto beans with ½ cup of crushed soy beans. Add the chopped onions and garlic powder. Salt and pepper to taste.

While the above is cooking till done, put your meats in a large skillet. Cook to done, then add tomatoes, tomato sauce and tomato paste, sugar.

When all is cooked... mix together and simmer 1 to 2 hours or until it's ready.

Walter Karczewski
Leesburg, FL
Sent in by
Beverly Fullerton
Grand Island, FL

Frank Gaulding
Beaumont,
Jefferson County, TX

GOURMET CHICKEN CHILI

3 T. oil 2 jalapeno peppers, minced
1 Lg. onion, chopped
6-8 chicken breasts, halves,
boned, and cubed
1 can (28 oz.) sliced stewed
tomatoes
8 oz. pitted black olives
2 T. whole cumin seeds
½ t. ground cinnamon
1 C. dark beer
1 sweet red pepper, chopped

Brown chicken in oil in a large skillet. Remove and set aside. Saute onion and chopped red pepper. Replace chicken, and add tomatoes, olives, jalapeno peppers, spices and beer. Simmer about 30 minutes.

John C. Wright
Warsaw, KY

Pete Pascoe
El Paso, TX

ARNOLD'S CHILI

MICROWAVE OR FRY:

1 Lb. bacon, cut into squares
Drain bacon on paper towels and reserve
Brown in bacon grease; and remove to large kettle:
2 Lbs. coarsely ground hamburger
Saute until beginning to brown; remove to large kettle:
5 onions, chopped
Add and stir to blend:
1 2.5 Oz. hot chili powder
1 t. seasoned salt
1 t. paprika
1 T. fresh minced oregano, or
1 t. dried oregano
1 T. fresh minced basil, or
1 t. dried basil
5 fresh garlic cloves, minced
1 T. dried cumin
1 T. Worcestershire sauce
6 whole dried red chilies, or to taste
Combine in a saucepan, bring to a boil and pour over mixture:
2 cans (16 oz.) tomatoes, from blender or processor; undrained
½ t. baking soda
Add and mix in:
2 cans (15 oz.) pinto beans, undrained
Turn heat to low and cover.
Simmer 3 hours, stirring occasionally.
Add and blend in:
Reserved bacon
Cook, cover and refrigerate overnight.
Return to very low heat and simmer, covered, stirring occasionally, 3 hours longer.
Ladle into bowls.
Garnish each bowl with:
1 thin slice green pepper
grated extra sharp Cheddar cheese, mounded inside the pepper slice.

Serves 10 to 12.

Jo Ann Maywald
Satellite Beach, FL

Borg-Warner Leasing
Dallas, TX

DENTON'S CHILI

1 Lb . ground beef
2 cans (16 oz.) kidney beans
1 small onion, chopped
1 small green pepper, chopped
1 can (6 oz.) tomato paste
½ t. garlic salt
2 T. chili powder

Mix chili powder with garlic salt in cup with ¼ cup flour until mixed.

Brown ground beef in a small amount of oil, season to taste with salt and pepper. Add onion and green pepper, cook for about 3-5 minutes. Add the tomato paste and enough water to enable it to cook. Add kidney beans.

Simmer for 30 minutes, then add mixture of chili powder, garlic salt flour that has been smoothly mixed. Cook 30 minutes longer. Very Good!!

To cook for larger amount:

3 Lbs. ground beef
6 cans of kidney beans
3 onions
3 green peppers
3 cans tomato paste
triple garlic and chili powder
water amounts, etc.

Serves 4

Our family has enjoyed this chili recipe for more than 30 years.

Ms. Marion Denton
Palm Bay, FL

John Roen
Waterford, CA

CHILI-O-MEAT LOAF

1 Lb. ground beef
1 Lb. ground veal
½ Lb. ground ham
1 envelope French's Chili-O
½ C. bread crumbs
1 egg, beaten
1 C. water

Combine all ingredients, mixing with a fork. Pack lightly in well greased 9x5x3-inch loaf pan. Bake in moderate oven (350 degrees) for 1 hour. Serve with tomato sauce, if desired. Makes 8 to 10 servings.

Durkee French Foods

I X I
Richard Llewellyn
Christmas, FL

RICE'S CHILI

¼ to ½ Lb. suet, ground
1½ Lb. beef - ground at least twice
1 clove of garlic
1 onion, size of tennis ball, chopped fine

Render suet in heavy skillet or Dutch oven, add garlic and onion. Fry until transparent, add beef and brown.

Add:
1 can tomato pate
4 cans water..if using puree, use less water
1 t. ground mixed spices
1 t. salt, dash of pepper, white or black
1 T. ground cardamon or ground cumin seed
1 T paprika
4 dried red peppers
1 t. pickling spices

Tie spices in cloth bag..simmer for about 4 hours stirring occasionally. If too thick, add tomato juice.

Walter Rice
Umatilla, FL
Sent in by
Beverly Fullerton
Grand Island, FL

Geo. F. Bixy
California (1870

EARLY CHILI or PICADILLO

1 Lb. beefsteak, raw or cooked
1 onion, diced
2 T. lard
1 T. flour
Salt and pepper to taste
1 T. chili powder
1 Pt. boiling water
½ C. tomatoes, if desired

Grind raw or cooked meat with the onion. Have the lard very hot in a heavy skillet. Add meat and sprinkle at once with flour, salt, and pepper. While this is browning on medium heat, combine chili powder with boiling water and let boil. When meat is brown, add chili water and stir.

Reduce heat to low and let stew until ready to heat, adding the tomatoes if this flavor is desired. In either case, Picadillo is good with beans or rice in the bowl. Serves 4 with beans or rice.

John G. Wright
Warsaw, KY

Cow Track
Wayne T. Wade
Plant City, FL

HIMALAYAN CHILI

1 C. dried kidney beans
3 T. unsalted butter
½ t. tumeric
1 t. ground cumin
1 t. cumin seed
1 t. coriander
2 stalks celery (leaves removed) chopped
1 C. broccoli stems, trimmed and cut into 1" lengths
½ Lb. mushrooms, stems removed, tops chopped
1 Lg. onion, coarsely chopped
1 Lg. green pepper, chopped
1 C. carrots, cut into ¼" rounds (scrub but do not peel)
1 6" to 8" zucchini, cut into circles, then into quarters
1 can (6 oz.) tomato paste I prefer Contadina
¼ t. cayenne pepper
1 t. leaf oregano

In a pressure cooker, cover the cup of beans with 3 to 4 inches of water. When cooker comes to pressure, time cooking for 25 minutes. Remove from heat and let pan cool. Drain beans and reserve the cooking liquid.

While the beans are cooling, prepare the vegetables and melt the 3 tablespoons of butter in a Dutch oven. Add the tumeric, ground and seed cumin, and the coriander. Slowly brown the spices. When browned lightly, add the mushrooms, onion, green pepper, carrots, celery, zucchini, beans, and the broccoli.

Pour in 1 cup of the bean cooking liquid. Stir well and bring to a simmer. Cover and cook for 10 minutes, stirring occasionally.

Now add the tomato paste and 1 to 1½ cups more of the bean cooking liquid. Stir well. Sprinkle in the vegies, salt, cayenne pepper, chili powder, oregano and the garlic powder. Stir well again. Adjust the consistency of the chili if necessary by adding more of the bean cooking liquid. Cover and simmer 25 to 35 minutes or until the vegetables are cooked and the spices have blended. During this cooking time, check the pot for liquid and stir every 5 to 8 minutes. Add salt as desired.

Serve on tortillas, sprinkle with grated cheese and bake in oven at 350 degrees until hot and cheese bubbles. Served this way, makes a thick chili. Or serve with whole grain rolls.

Although this is a vegetarian recipe, it is very satisfying and always brings requests for seconds.

Carol Hinckley
Melbourne Beach, FL

Dewey K. Knight
Carthage, TN

SEA BREEZE CHILI

1 Lb. lean coarse ground beef
1 C. diced onion
1 C. diced green pepper
1 can (16 oz.) whole kernel corn in water with liquid
1 can (16 oz.) dark red kidney beans with liquid
1 can (28 oz.) peeled, crushed tomatoes with liquid
1 T. salt (optional)
½ t. coarsely ground black pepper
½ t. red chili pepper
½ t. cumin seed
½ t. ground allspice
½ t. garlic powder
1 t. oregano
¼ t. ground cloves
¼ t. ground coriander
½ C. Old Fashioned Oatmeal

Brown meat in skillet. Place browned meat in a crock pot or slow cooker. Add all other ingredients, except the oatmeal, and enough water to fill the pot. Simmer for 6 hours or more. Stir in the oatmeal during the last 60 minutes; (more or less oatmeal may be used to thicken to desired consistency).

Serve into microwave-safe bowls. Top with sharp cheddar cheese. Microwave to melt the cheese, and garnish with raw onion ring.

Jim Gifford, Owner
Breeze Boat Rental
Port Canaveral, FL

The No Brand
Nina Ortiz
Mims, FL

BARRY GOLDWATER'S ARIZONA CHILI

1 Lb. dried pinto beans, soaked overnight
1 Lb. coarse-ground beef
6 Oz. tomato puree
Water, if needed
2 C. chopped onion
3 T. chili powder
1 T. cumin
Salt to taste

Saute beef and drain off excess fat, leaving a little for flavor. Add beans, puree, and onion and stir well. Mix the chili powder, cumin, and salt (about 2 teaspoons to his taste), and add to chili. Bring to a boil, stirring. Turn low and cook slowly until onions and beans are tender, adding water to desired consistency as needed. Serves 4 to 6 guests who know beans about chili.

John G. Wright
Warsaw, KY
from the Arizona Highway Heritage Cookbook

Old Woman Ranch
Texas (1868)

WILLIAMS' CHILI FROM W. VA.

I enjoyed your request for recipes in the food section of our newspaper. It made me think back to my father who passed away 9 years ago. He and my mom owned a Dairy Queen and he made (W. Va.) his own chili. He wouldn't even give the recipe to us kids, (six girls and 2 boys in family).

After he passed away, mom sent the recipe to the whole family. It was dad's secret and when we would ask him, he would grin and say 'a little of this - a little of that - a dab of that - - - -'

My dad's name was William Boswell, and mom called it his chili.

2½ Lb. ground chuck
⅛ t. black pepper
¼ C. sugar
¼ C. salt
Small dash of garlic salt
¼ t. Italian seasoning
¼ C. chili powder
⅛ t. red pepper
1½ T. paprika
2½ C. dried onions, let soak in water for 20 minutes
¼ Gal. tomato catsup
½ Gal. Castleberry Hot Dog Chili or any kind
13 cans (46 oz.) tomato juice

Brown chuck in a large pot or Dutch oven. Add just about remaining ingredients, and cook 5 to 6 hours on low heat. Stir every now and then. It really is good!!

Mrs. Betti Pratt
Cocoa, FL

JO

J.G. Hinton, 1901
Valley Mills,
McLennan County, TX

MARGO'S CHILI

3 Lbs. cubed (or coarsely ground) tri-tip cut beef
3 Oz. sausage
2 T. kidney suet or Wesson
½ Oz. salt
2 Oz. Gebhardt's Chili Powder
½ Oz. cumin
½ t. Hot New Mexico Chili Powder
Oregano tea (1 T. oregano leaves in ½ cup of hot water, let steep)
white pepper to taste
5 to 7 cloves garlic
2 Med. onions, chopped fine
½ t. coriander (optional)
4 to 6 Ozs. Hunts Tomato Sauce
½ Pt. beef broth, add water if necessary
1 Med. Ortega pepper (minced)
¼ t. cayenne pepper
Dash of Tabasco brand pepper sauce

Saute onions and garlic in suet about 3 minutes. Add Gebhardt's and chili powder; mix well. Brown beef in separate pan a pound at a time. Pepper while browning. Add onions and spices. Use a little beef broth to keep from sticking. Saute sausage and ortega pepper together (about 2 minutes). Add to pot and cook about 15 minutes.

Add remaining spices, Hunts tomato sauce, water or broth, mix well. Cook about 30 minutes. Add oregano tea. Cook about 2 hours or until meat is tender, stirring occasionally. During last 20 to 30 minutes add salt and cayenne pepper if desired.

John G. Wright
Warsaw, KY

H Bar
James H. Hendrie, Sr
Venus, FL

TURKEY CHILI

1 Pkg. (1 Lb.) Louis Rich Ground Turkey, 90% Fat Free
1 Med. onion, chopped
½ Med. green pepper, chopped
¼ C. sliced celery
1 can (15½ or 16 oz.) kidney beans, with liquid
1 can (14½ oz.) stewed tomatoes
1 can (12 oz.) tomato juice
1 can (6 oz.) tomato paste
1 T. Worcestershire sauce
1 t. ground cumin or chili powder
½ t. salt
¼ t. garlic powder

Place turkey and fresh vegetables in large skillet. Cook on medium heat for 10 minutes, stirring and separating turkey as it cooks. Add the remaining ingredients. Bring to a boil; turn down heat. Simmer 5 minutes, stirring occasionally. 6 servings. 241 calories per serving.

Louis Rich Company

Bar D
Bennie L. Whaley
Melbourne Bch, FL

CHICKEN, TURKEY OR DUCK CHILI w/ CORN MEAL DUMPLING

2 Lbs. skinless fowl, cut in ½ x 2-inch strips
2 T. peanut oil
1 C. chopped onion
1 Lg. can tomatoes
1 t. cumin
1 can (22 oz.) chili beans
3 T. chopped green peppers
1 t. garlic powder or,
2 cloves garlic, crushed
1 T. chili powder

Heat peanut oil and saute meat, chopped onion, and green pepper.Add omatoes, beans, garlic powder or garlic cloves, chili powder and cumin.Bring to a boil; reduce heat and simmer for 30 minutes.If needed before adding dumplings, add can of chicken broth.

CORN MEAL DUMPLINGS:

In a sauce pan, combine 1 cup of water, ½ cup yellow corn meal, and ½ teaspoon salt.Bring to boiling, cook and stir until thickened.Remove from heat, and stir moderate amount of hot mixture into a bowl and beat in one egg.Return the mixture to sauce pan.Mix together ½ cup of flour, 1 teaspoon baking powder, and a dash of pepper.Blend well then add to cornmeal mixture.

Stir in one 7 ounce can of whole kernel corn, drained.Wet spoon in chili, dip dumplings.Add one at a time to chili mixture.

P. S. I would call this Fowl Chili, but it just doesn't sound right.

Merline McKenzie
Lansing, MI

John L. & Dolly Costa
Pearl City, HA

CHILI-CHICKEN STEW

3 whole chicken breasts, split
1 C. chopped onion
1 Med. green pepper, chopped
2 garlic cloves, minced
2 T. vegetable oil
2 cans (14½ oz.) stewed tomatoes
1 can (15 oz.) pinto beans, drained
Dairy sour cream
⅔ to ¾ C. Pace Picante Sauce, as desired
1 t. chili powder
1 t. ground cumin
½ t. salt
Optional toppings:
Shredded cheddar cheese
Green onion slices
Diced avocado

Cut chicken into 1-inch pieces. Cook chicken, onion, green pepper and garlic in oil in a Dutch oven, until chicken loses it's pink color. Add remaining ingredients; simmer 20 minutes. Ladle into bowls; top with cheese, onion, avocado, sour cream and additional picante sauce as desired. Makes 6 to 8 servings, about 9 cups of stew.

PACE Picante Sauces

Don Juan Sepulveda
California (1855)

STAGECOACH CHILI

The famed Butterfield Stage offered the cold and weary or hot and jittery some form of chili year around during trips through Southern Arizona. If game or beef was at hand, it was Chili con Carne. If not, Chili Beans at worst, Chili Soup; Historians Roscoe Wilson and Will James both wrote colorfully of those fly-infested, open-air stations. This chili is not for sissies or children.

10 dried red chiles
2 cloves garlic, diced
4 C. water
2 onions, chopped fine
1 T. salt pork, diced
½ t. oregano
2 or 3 C. chopped game or beef
1 C. chopped tomatoes, if available
Salt and pepper
1 t. cumin powder

Toast chiles in hot skillet. Then boil a half-hour in water with the garlic. Cool and strain through sieve, making a chili paste rather than the usual chili powder. Saute onion with salt pork. Sprinkle cumin and oregano over meat (antelope, bear, venison, or wild pig will do if beef is not available), and brown with salt pork and onion.

Add chili paste and tomatoes. Stir to blend and simmer 1 hour. Taste and add salt and pepper if needed. Simmer at least another 20 minutes before serving. It's better and hotter the second day. This recipe is why chili is called "red hot". Serve with pinto beans cooked with onion and garlic, and biscuits.

John G. Wright
Warsaw, KY

Circle Arrow L Ranch
A.W. Lee, Jr
Wildwood, FL

BLACK BEAN-TURKEY CHILI

1½ C. dry black beans
1 Med. onion, quartered
2 T. olive oil
2¼ Lbs. (3 large) turkey drumsticks
1 Lg. onion, chopped
1 green pepper, cut into squares
1 Lg. clove garlic, minced
1 C. chicken broth
2 T. chili powder, or to taste
1 T. ground cumin
1½ t. salt, or to taste
¼ t. freshly ground black pepper
Hot cooked rice, sour cream or yogurt and salsa

Place beans in large bowl, add water to 2 inches above beans. Cover and soak overnight.

Drain beans and add fresh water to cover by 1 inch. Push onion quarters into beans. Bring to a boil; lower heat, cover and simmer for 45 minutes to an hour, or until beans are tender but not mushy.

Heat olive oil in Dutch oven or large deep skillet. Add drumsticks and saute for 10 minutes, turning to brown lightly. Add chopped onion, bell pepper squares and garlic. Saute slowly until the vegetables are tender but do not let them brown. Add chicken broth, chili powder, cumin, salt and pepper. Cover, and simmer 30 minutes, until the turkey is tender.

Remove drumsticks, and let them cool until they can be handled. Cut the meat into bite size pieces, discard all skin and bones.

Return meat to vegetables mixture; stir in black beans with their liquid. Simmer for 30 minutes, adding hot water if needed to keep chili runny but not swimming in liquid.

Serve hot on rice with a dollop of sour cream or yogurt, and salsa on each serving. Serves 6 to 8.

Chris Poole
Cocoa, FL

Anton Livestock
Phoenix, AZ

SALLIE HAYDEN'S CHILI

2 C. Rose Brand pinto or red beans
1 Qt. fresh water
1 T. salt
4 slices bacon
1 Lb. chopped beef or venison
2 T. bacon drippings
2 C. chopped onion
2 cloves garlic, crushed
1½ C. tomato puree
1 C. beef broth
4 t. chili powder
½ t. oregano
¼ t. each sage and cumin seed
2 T. butter
½ green chile pepper, seeded and diced

Wash and pick over beans. Soak in fresh water overnight. Drain. Cover with 1 quart fresh water and salt, then simmer in heavy 4-quart kettle 1½ hours. Saute bacon and drain off grease on paper towels. Brown beef or venison in drippings. Add to beans with seasonings, tomato puree, and beef broth. Saute onion and pepper in butter and add to beans. Cover, simmer until beans are tender, about 3 hours. Garnish with crumbled bacon. Serves 6 to 8.

John G. Wright
Warsaw, KY

D D Ranch
Dallas Dart
Sarasota, FL

QUICK VEGETARIAN CHILI

1 can (16 oz.) dark red kidney beans
1 can (16 oz.) tomatoes, chopped
1 C. green peppers, chopped
1 C. celery, chopped
1 C. onions, white, diced
1 Pkg. (12 oz.) mushrooms, halved
2 T. corn or peanut oil
2 T. butter for sauteing or use oil
½ C. flour (for rue)
1 T. cumin
1 T. garlic powder
1 t. black pepper
½ C. molasses (dark)
2 T. Worcestershire sauce
Tabasco sauce, or green chilies to taste
V-8 juice for liquid. If final chili is too thick, use this item as last ingredient if necessary to obtain desired consistency.

Saute peppers, celery, onions in large skillet until tender but not pale. Add mushrooms; saute mixture a little longer. Set aside. In a Dutch oven or wok, but if you use a wok, set vegetables aside before continuing. Add additional oil then flour for rue.Brown flour, then add beans, tomatoes, sauted vegetables, remaining ingredients, and V-8 juice if necessary.

Cover, simmer for 20 minutes.Serves 6 to 8.

Merline McKenzie
Lansing, MI

Julian Mediano, 1912
Riesee,
McLennan County, TX

PORK and BLACK BEAN CHILI

1 Pkg. (16 oz.) dry black beans
1½ Lbs. fresh pork butt
1 Lg. red pepper
1 Lg. green pepper
1 Med. onion
3 T. salad oil
⅓ C. chili powder
1 can (28 oz.) whole tomatoes in puree
1¾ t. salt
Hot pepper sauce to taste

1. About 3½ hours before serving; rinse beans with running cold water, discarding any stones or shriveled beans. In a 4-quart saucepan, over a high heat, cook the beans with 6 cups of water and bring to a boil.Cook at a boil for 3 minutes.Remove the saucepan from the heat; cover and let stand for 1 hour. Drain and rinse the beans.

2. Meanwhile, cut the pork butt into ½-inch cubes. Cut peppers into ½-inch pieces.Dice the onions.

3. In a 5-quart Dutch oven, over medium-high heat, using the oil, cook the pork cubes, one-half at a time, until all is browned, stirring often during process. With a slotted spoon, remove pork from the pot and place in a bowl, first allowing as much of the grease and oil to drain as possible.

4. In the Dutch oven, with a little of the drippings, cook the peppers and onions over a medium heat, until they are tender crisp, stirring occasionally. Stir in the chili powder, and cook for 2 minutes. Add the tomatoes with their puree, stirring to break up tomatoes. Over a high heat, stir in the salt, beans, pork, and 4 cups more of water. Bring to a boil.

5. Leave chili in the Dutch oven or transfer to a 4-quart casserole. Cover and bake in a 375 degrees oven for about an hour and 45 minutes, or until the beans are tender, stirring occasionally. Stir in hot pepper sauce to taste. Serve chili in bowls. Makes 10 main-dish servings. About 365 calories per serving.

John G. Wright
Warsaw, KY

Cornell University
Bull Test
Ithaca, NY

NEW TWIST CHILI

Two meals in one

First: Large batch spaghetti sauce.

2 Lbs. ground beef
1 Lb. ground pork sausage, lean
1 Lg. onion, diced
1 Lg. can peeled Roma tomatoes
2 cans (18 oz.) tomato paste
72 Ozs. water, or ½ water, ½ tomato sauce
8 Lg. garlic cloves, crushed
4 t. dried basil leaves
3 T. dried oregano leaves
2 t. thyme
1 t. celery seed
2 T. salt (optional)
1 T. black pepper
½ C. brown sugar

In a Dutch oven with a TIGHT COVER, brown beef, sausage and onion. Drain off fat.Add next eleven (11) ingredients, and bring to a boil. Reduce heat; cover, and simmer for 1 hour, stirring occasionally. Serve with hot pasta and Parmasan cheese.

Second - Next day Chili
Add to left over spaghetti sauce:

- 1 Lg. can dark red kidney beans
- 1 T. chili powder
- 2 t. ground cumin (it's a must)
- 2 T. Worcestershire sauce
- ½ t. cayenne pepper or green chilies
- Tabasco sauce to satisfy your desire of hotness.

Serve with corn bread or corn bread sticks.

Merline McKenzie
Lansing, MI

TIM

Orville Long
Philip, SD

FRED'S CHILI

- 3 cans (29 oz.) tomato puree
- 1 can (30 oz.) drained, or undrained kidney beans
- 2 cans (12 oz.) tomato paste
- 1½ cans (29 oz.) water for thin style, delete water for thicker style
- 1½ to 2 Lbs. ground chuck
- 1 Lg. can chili powder (regular or Mexican style)*

Combine in frying pan:

- ½ stick butter
- 2 diced onions

To taste add: salt, garlic, pepper, meat tenderizer.

After the first four (4) ingredients have been fully cooked, add the ground chuck. When spices are done, stir into items in large pot.

After simmering for 1-2 hours, add the large can of chili powder.
*The size of the chili powder used was confirmed in a personal phone call to Mrs. Owens. She stated the amount as her husband like it HOT!!.

Fred Owens
Merritt Island, FL
from Mary Wester,
Cocoa Beach Area
Chamber of Commerce

96

Clay Ranch
Grandin, FL

CHILI GRAVY

1½ T. butter or beef drippings
2 T. flour
2 to 3 C. meat, chopped, cubed or ground
1 C. cold water
1 clove garlic, chopped or crushed
1 T. red chili powder
Salt, if needed
Hot biscuits, mashed potatoes, or rice

Melt butter or drippings in iron fry pan. Add flour and stir until rich brown. Slowly stir in cold water and continue to stir as it cooks so it won't lump up. Taste and add salt, if needed.

Brown meat with garlic and chili powder in skillet, then add to the gravy, which should be contentedly bubbling. Simmer a few minutes, then serve over fresh, hot biscuits, mashed potatoes, or fluffy rice. Makes 5 or 6 rib-sticking servings.

John G. Wright
Warsaw, KY

T2

Cecil A. Tucker II
Sanford, FL

LAMB CHILI con CARNE

A change of pace chili.

3 T. olive or peanut oil
1 C. chopped onion
3 cloves garlic, crushed, or minced
3 Lbs. lamb in ¼-inch cubed
2 T. chili powder
1 T. curry powder
2 t. salt
1 can (29 oz.) tomatoes
1 Lg. can red kidney beans
Green chilies or Tabasco sauce (optional)

Heat oil in a Dutch oven with a tight cover.Brown lamb, onions and garlic.Add tomatoes, chili powder, curry powder and salt.Cover, and cook over a low heat for 1½ hours.Add beans, cover, and cook 30 minutes longer.

Taste for seasonings.Add chilies or Tabasco sauce not if you want it hotter.

Serve with mounds of rice, shredded lettuce, minced onions, and shredded cheese, using Cheddar or Monterey Jack for best flavors with chilies...add tortillas or crackers with servings.We like a dollop of sour cream on top.Garnish with mint leaves for company.

Merline McKenzie
Lansing, MI

Laurel Leaf Ranch
Texas (1868)

YANKEE CHILI con CARNE

1 Lb. ground beef
1 can (16 oz.) whole tomatoes, drained
1 can (16 oz.) kidney beans
1 can (67 oz.) tomato sauce
½ C. onions, chopped
½ C. green pepper, chopped
¼ C. celery, chopped
¼ C. Worcestershire sauce
⅛ t. cumin, ground
½ t. chili powder, more or less to taste
Dash or two garlic salt
Dash or so onion salt

Brown the ground beef in a large skillet using a little vegetable oil, until it looses most of the pink color.Add the onions, green pepper and celery and cook until the vegetables are tender and the onion is transparent.

Add the rest of the ingredients on the list, bring to a boil; reduce the heat, and simmer until the flavors have blended, and are to your taste.

Serve plain from the skillet, or over rice or spaghetti.Makes 4 servings.

Ms. Laurie Williams
Bethel, OH

Gary & Vicky Marks
Imnaha, OR

VEAL and PORK CHILI
over homemade square noodles

1½* Lbs. boneless stewing cubed
1½* Lbs. boneless pork shoulder, cubed
3 T. butter or corn oil margarine
1 Lg. onion, chopped
2 sprigs parsley, chopped
1 C. hot water
½ t. black pepper
1 bay leaf, crumbled
2 T. chili powder
1 T. cumin
1 Lg. can tomatoes, chopped
1 can (6 oz.) tomato paste
Tabasco sauce (optional)
1 can kidney beans (optional)
1 Lb. mushrooms, halved

In a Dutch oven, with tight cover, heat butter or margarine.Dredge pork and veal cubes in flour, and brown completely.*

*I saute the meat, veal and pork separately, because the pork should require longer cooking time than the veal, but you can do it all at one time, but the veal kind a falls apart.During the last hour, add the cooked veal to the Dutch oven.

After browning the meats, add onions and brown a few minutes longer.Add the next nine (9) ingredients; cover, and bring to a boil.Reduce heat and simmer for 2 hours, maybe more.Check meat for tenderness.

When heat is tender, add the mushrooms, more water if needed.Cover, return to simmer for 20 to 30 minutes longer.You may add the beans to the pot at this point if you desire.I do not add beans, as this mixture is great when served over homemade square noodles.

HOMEMADE SQUARE NOODLES:

2 C. all-purpose flour
½ t. salt
3 eggs, beaten, or just whites (no cholesterol)
Water

Mix the flour, and salt; stir in beaten eggs, using just enough water to make a stiff dough.Roll dough out on a lightly floured surface, to 20" x 15" rectangle. Cover, and let rise for 20 minutes.Cut into 1" squares (I use my pizza cutter as it gives a crimped edge).

Allow dough to dry for a while.Drop into a large amount of boiling water or chicken broth.Boil until then are tender, 15 to 18 minutes.Drain on paper towels.Makes 6 to 8 servings.

Merline McKenzie
Lansing, MI

B-M

B bar M
Bobby R. McCormick
Cocoa, FL

THREE BEAN CHILI CHOWDER

1 Lg. onion, chopped (about 1½ cups)
2 T. vegetable oil
1 green or yellow pepper, chopped
1 can (16 oz.) kidney beans, rinsed and drained
1 can (15 oz.) pinto beans
1 can (15 oz.) black beans
2 cans (14½ oz.) stewed
1 C. chicken broth or stock
1 can (16 oz.) tomato paste
¾ to 1 C. Pace Picante Sauce, as desired
1 t. ground cumin
½ t. salt
Optional garnishes:
Shredded Cheddar or Monterey Jack cheese
Chopped fresh cilantro
Dairy sour cream
Green onion slices

Cook onion in oil in large saucepan or Dutch oven until onion is tender but not brown. Add remaining ingredients except optional garnishes; bring to a boil. Reduce heat; simmer 10 minutes.

Ladle into soup bowls; garnish with cheese, cilantro, green onion, sour cream and additional picante sauce, as desired. Makes 8 servings, about 10 cups of chowder.

Pace Foods Inc.

John T. Kihara
Honolulu, HA

HEALTHY CHILI with TURKEY

1 Lb. dried beans - mixed
1½ Lbs. turkey - shredded or ground
1 can (15 oz.) whole tomatoes
1 can (15 oz.) tomato sauce
1 small can chopped chilies
4 T. chili powder spice
1 T. salt
Black pepper, ground to taste
1 Lg. onion (Spanish) chopped
2 cloves garlic, chopped

Soak beans overnight in water to cover. Drain. Add 1 quart water, tomatoes, tomato sauce, spices, salt and pepper. Simmer for 9 hours to tenderize beans.

Shred turkey (raw) or cube, then brown in frying pan with chopped garlic and onions. Add to chili and then add chopped chilies to sauce just before serving.

This takes a while to make but is good, very good.

Norbert Violette
Satellite Beach, FL

M P
R.W. McDowell
Cocoa, FL

CHILI con ELOTE

1 C. chopped onion
1 garlic clove, minced
2 T. vegetable oil
1 can (26 oz.) whole tomatoes
1 can (8¾ oz.) whole kernel corn, drained
1 green pepper, diced
½ C. PACE Picante Sauce
½ C. water
1 t. salt
1 t. ground cumin
1 t. oregano leaves, crushed
Shredded Cheddar cheese and dairy sour cream (optional)

Cook onion and garlic in oil in a large saucepan until onion is tender but not brown. Drain and coarsely chop tomatoes, reserving juice. Combine juice and 1 can beans in work bowl of food processor or blender container.

Process with steel blade or blend until fairly smooth. Add bean mixture to saucepan with remaining beans, reserved tomatoes, corn, picante sauce, water, salt, cumin and oregano. Bring to a boil; reduce heat.

Cover and simmer for 30 minutes. Add green pepper; simmer 5 minutes longer. Ladle into soup bowls; top with cheese and sour cream, if desired. Serve with additional picante sauce. Makes 6 servings, about 6 cups soup.

Pace Foods Inc.

Palaika Ranch
Wm. Paris, Jr.
Honolulu, HA

THANKSGIVING LEFTOVER CHILI

Don't forget the fowl that's left over from the "big" dinner... the bird, or more commonly known, as the turkey, or what is left of it.

Debone the meat and any other turkey such as remaining slices, and cut into ½" or so, pieces. Use about any chili recipe you have, and sub turkey for the meat portion of it. Use the spices and other ingredients as normally done. ONLY cook onions, green pepper, garlic and other vegetables prior to adding turkey.

This is one way of eliminating a problem in the refrigerator, and it isn't bad, as you will not be able to tell the difference of using the turkey over other meats. Once you add the spices, and it's cooked....

CSG

Russell Taggart
Cadiz, OH

BUCKEYE TURKEY CHILI

2 Lbs. ground turkey
2 T. salad oil
1 Med. onion, chopped
1 green pepper, chopped
2 cloves garlic, minced
1 can (28 oz.) whole tomatoes, drained, chopped
1 can (6 oz.) tomato paste
1 can (10 oz.) whole kernel corn, drained
2 cans (15 oz.) red kidney beans, drained

2 t. cumin
1 T. paprika
2 T. chili powder (+ or -)
½ t. salt
½ t. seasoned salt
Fresh ground pepper to taste
½ t. oregano
Dash Tabasco sauce
Shredded cheddar cheese
Sour cream
Chopped onions

In a large skillet or Dutch oven, cook the turkey until it starts to loose it's pinkness. Add onions, green pepper and garlic, and cook until the vegetables are tender. Stir to crumble turkey while it cooks.

Stir in remaining ingredients except the beans and items for garnishing (last three ingredients). Bring to a boil; reduce heat to simmer and cook for 1 hour.

Add the beans, and cook until they are thoroughly heated before serving. Adjust taste with seasonings if desired. Makes 6 to 8 servings.

Al & Bernice Shawn
Peoria, AZ

Grove Farm Co.,Inc.
Kawai, HA

MARY ELLEN'S FAVORITE CHILI

1½ Lbs. ground chuck
2 Med. onions, chopped
2 cloves garlic, minced
1 Lg. can crushed tomatoes
1 can (6 oz.) tomato paste
1 can water

1 beef bouillon cube
2 cans Mexican chili beans (small beans)
2 t. salt
2 t. oregano
2 t. chili powder
1 bay leaf

Combine first two ingredients in a Dutch oven. Brown meat; drain off fat. Add rest of the ingredients; stir to blend well. Cover, and simmer for 1½ to 2 hours, stirring occasionally. Remove bay leaf. Serve with crackers. Makes 6 servings.

Mild - not too spicy - kids love it mild -

Mary Ellen Branan
Ocala, FL

Dan Scruggs, D.V.M.
Spring Hill, TN

BAYLESS' CHICKEN and CHILI STEW

8 chicken thighs
1 Med. onion, chopped
3 cloves garlic, minced
1 can (16 oz.) cooked, pinto beans (I cook my own)
salt and pepper to taste
3 T. oil
2 T. chili powder
1 Pt. cherry tomatoes
¼ C. chopped fresh coriander leaves

Sprinkle the chicken thighs with salt and pepper. Heat the oil in a 4-quart soup kettle or Dutch oven. Saute the chicken over medium-high heat until golden brown on both sides.

Reduce the heat to medium, stir in the onion, garlic and chili powder, and cook until vegetables are softened, about 5 minutes. Add the tomatoes and ¼ cup of water. Cover and simmer, stirring occasionally, until the chicken is cooked through and juices have thickened, about 30 minutes.

Drain and rinse the beans; stir beans into chicken mixture. Return stew to a simmer, and season to taste with salt and pepper. Stir in coriander.

Recipe can be made a couple of days ahead. If so, omit coriander, cool and refrigerate stew uncovered until thoroughly chilled. Reheat stew over low heat, and stir in coriander. Serves 4.

NOTE: Coriander gives this stew an authentic Mexican flavor. Dress it up with your choice of the following garnishes: sour cream, black olives, grated Monterey Jack cheese, chopped jalapeno peppers, tomato, green bell peppers, or scallions. (I particularly like sour cream, olives, tomatoes and scallions.

Ms. Doreen Bayless
Rialto, CA

Manfred & JoAnne Branco
Honolulu, HA

DALLAS CHILI

1 Lb. ground beef
1 Pkg. (1¾ oz.) French's Chili-O Seasoning Mix
1 can (16 oz.) whole tomatoes, cut-up
½ C. water
1 can (16 oz.) kidney beans, drained (optional)
1 T. Durkee Red Hot Cayenne Pepper Sauce or more to taste

In a Dutch oven, brown ground beef; drain. French's Chili-O Seasoning Mix, water, tomatoes, beans and Durkee Red Hot Sauce. Bring to boil; reduce heat and simmer covered 10 minutes. Garnish with chopped red pepper and green onion, if desired. Makes 6 servings.

Durkee-French Foods

Elgin Cattle Co.
Mesa, AZ

SPEAKEASY'S CHILI

On our traveling around the highways, we are interested in restaurants that have chilies on their menus. Speakeasy's is one that held us by the arms until they made a copy of their brew. It was one of the finest we have eaten, and if you're in the area, try them. The size of the recipe can be cut, or this would be one heck of a "batch" to freeze.

30 Lbs. ground beef
10 Lbs. onions, diced
1 C. lemon juice
4 C. chili powder
2 C. green chilies, diced
4 #10 cans, kidney beans
2 #10 cans, tomato sauce
4 bay leaves
2 #10 cans, crushed tomatoes
2 T. salt
2 T. sugar
4 Ozs. Great garlic
4 T. ground cumin
6 Ozs. paprika

Brown meat and drain well. Saute onions till wilted. Add remaining ingredients into large stockpot and simmer 2½ hours. Stir often to keep chili from burning.

This quantity is for a day's worth of customers, and it goes from what we've seen while sitting at the counter.

Arthur Frogel
Speakeasy's Restaurant
West Palm Beach, FL

Lynn R. Hansel
Titusville, FL

PATELLA'S CHILI

Brown Together:
- 2 Lbs. ground chuck
- 1 Lg. chopped green pepper
- 1 Lg. chopped onion

Add:
- 2 cans condensed tomato soup
- 1 can (6 oz.) tomato paste
- 1 lb. fresh sliced mushrooms
- 3 cans (15 oz.) kidney beans

Cook for 10 minutes.

Make into paste and add in:
- 2 T. flour
- 4 T. chili powder
- 2 t. salt
- 1 T. oregano
- 2 T. parsley flakes
- 6 T. water

Add:
- 1 C. hot catsup

Add to taste:
- Garlic powder
- Cayenne pepper (dash)
- Tabasco sauce (4 drops)

Simmer 10 minutes: Deliscioso!!

Nicholas Patella
Orlando, FL

George & Susan Andrews
Santa Maria, CA

HALF TIME CHILI

1 Pkg. Carroll Shelby's Original Texas Brand Chili Mix
2 Lbs. ground turkey or ground beef
1 Pkg. (10 oz.) Birds Eye Corn
1 can (4 oz.) chopped green chilies
Velveeta Shredded Pasteurized Process Cheese

Prepare chili according to package directions, using ground turkey or ground beef. Add corn and chilies with tomato sauce. Serve topped with shredded pasteurized Process cheese. 6 to 8 servings.

Prep time: 20 minutes
Cooking time: 25 minutes

Kraft Foods

Teichi Yamada
Maui, HA

WILD BULL CHILI or FIRE ON A FORK

2 Lbs. buffalo or ground beef
1 onion, chopped
3 cloves garlic, minced

Stir in beef or buffalo meat, and cook until bubbly. Pour off fat.
Mix in:

½ t. paprika
½ t. oregano
½ t. cumin
½ t. red pepper
1 t. chili powder
3 T. Masa flour
2 C. beer or water

Cook for 45 minutes on simmer.

Mickey Gilley's
Gary Collins' HOME SHOW

Catskill Game Farm, Inc
Catskill, NY

BURKE'S CHILI

The following recipe is one that my family has been using for years. I hope it is one of the few that seems to be unique in it's own way. Our family has enjoyed it, as well as friends who have tried it.

2 Lbs. lean ground beef
1 can (28 oz.) whole tomatoes
2 cans (8 oz.) tomato sauce
1 can (16 oz.) kidney beans
2 cloves garlic, finely cut
2 Lg. onions, finely chopped
4 stalks celery, chopped
2 T. bacon drippings
2 t. salt (or to taste)
1 T. chili powder
1 T. cumin powder
1 C. chopped green pepper
1 T. vinegar

This is not a hot chili. The secret of the flavor is the celery. It gives a subtle nutty flavor combined with the regular chili taste. The amount of celery, chili powder, onions and garlic may be adjusted to suit your taste, however, if you try to stay within the above requirements, you will be delightfully surprised.

Use a large skillet and brown the beef with the bacon drippings. Add the garlic. In a 6-quart pan, mix the tomatoes, tomato sauce, salt, chili powder, cumin and vinegar.

The tomatoes should be cut up slightly. A half teaspoon of sugar will remove some of the acid taste of the tomatoes. Add the ground beef. Put a small amount of cooking oil in the skillet, saute the onions until they are limp and transparent.

Add the green pepper and celery, and cook this mixture for about ten minutes, stirring occasionally. Combine with the ground beef mixture in the 6-quart pan. Add 1 cup of water, or enough to thin the mixture slightly and bring to a gentle boil, stirring occasionally. Simmer for 2 hours. Remove from heat and allow to cool so that the grease will accumulate on the surface. Spoon off as much of the grease as possible, and add the kidney beans. Reheat for about 30 minutes. Serves 6 to 8.

John Burke
Titusville, FL

Danny & Marla Traylor
Central, AZ

DAVE GARROWAY'S "HOMEMADE" CANNED CHILI

I wonder if you have this one, which has been in my file for years?

6 Med. onions, thinly sliced
¼ C. margarine
½ Lb. ground beef

Saute onions until soft; remove from pan. Cook ground beef with the margarine. (I use Pam instead of margarine), until brown. Add onions.

Combine with above:
2 cans (16 oz.) chili con carne with beans
½ C. chili sauce
2 cloves garlic, crushed
½ t. salt
Dash of fresh ground pepper
Few drops of hot pepper sauce

Heat, stir and blend. Cover. Heat on low 10 minutes. Serves 4.

Mrs. Berkeley E. Pickens
Cape Canaveral, FL

AN

Aaron Cherry & Sons
Lebanon, TN

CHICKEN CHILI MEXICANO

This is a chili recipe I threw together a couple years ago and has been a favorite ever since.

1-1½ Lbs. chicken breast (skinned, deboned and cut cubes)
1 Med. Red onion, diced
5-6 cloves garlic, minced
1 Med. zucchini, diced
1 Med. carrot, diced
1 C. diced cabbage, (red cabbage adds more color)
1 can (15½ oz.) garbanzo beans or chick peas
1 can (7 oz.) tomato sauce
1 can (4 oz.) green chilies
2-4 T. Mexican chili powder
Pinch of oregano
Pinch of cumin
Salt and pepper to taste

In a large pot, saute chicken, onion, carrot, garlic, zucchini, and cabbage until chicken is cooked. Add tomatoes, tomato sauce, green chilies and garbanzo beans (drained). You'll need to add from 2 to 4 cups of water depending on the consistency desired.

Add chili powder, spices and salt and pepper. Heat to almost boiling then simmer on low heat for 1 to 2 hours or longer if desired.

Then enjoy! This recipe is complimented with flour tortillas or Mexican style cornbread.

Cynthia Ferguson
Cocoa, FL

G Double Bar
Henry Goolsby, Jr.
Cocoa, FL

ISLANDER'S CHILI con CARNE

1 T. oil ½ t. cayenne pepper
½ C. onion, chopped
1 C. green pepper, chopped
1½ Lbs. LEAN boneless beef
2 T. minced garlic
3 T. chili powder
1 t. ground cumin
½ t. crushed red pepper flakes
1 t. oregano
1 bay leaf
½ t. black pepper
4 C. canned unsalted tomatoes, with juice, chopped
1 T. red wine vinegar

Heat the oil in a heavy pot. Add the onion and green pepper, cook until onion is wilted. Add the chopped meat and sprinkle with the garlic, chili powder, cumin, cayenne pepper and oregano. Stir as the meat browns.

Add the bay leaf, black pepper, chopped tomatoes and juice, vinegar and crushed red pepper. Bring to a boil; then reduce heat and simmer, uncovered, for an hour, stirring occasionally.

NOTE: Good chili must be made with chopped, not ground beef. Cut the beef into slices, cut the slices into narrow strips and cut the strips across into tiny pieces.

Mrs. Gladys A. Jeter
Merritt Island, FL

James D. Marques
Kawai, HA

MEXICAN VEGETABLE CHILI

This recipe has less cholesterol and more fiber.

1 C. dried jicama
1 C. chopped onion
½ C. chopped celery
½ C. sliced carrot
1 Med. bell pepper (green) chopped
2 cloves garlic, minced
2 t. oil
½ C. water
½ t. beef-flavored instant bouillon
½ C. (2 oz.) shredded Cheddar cheese
1½ t. cumin
1½ t. chili powder
2 cans (14½ oz.) no salt whole tomatoes, undrained, cut up
1 can (8 oz.) no salt tomato sauce
1 can (15 oz.) chili beans, undrained
1 can (15 oz.) pinto beans, undrained

In a Dutch oven, saute jicama, onions, celery, carrot, green pepper and garlic in oil until crisp tender. Stir in water, bouillon, cumin, chili powder, tomatoes and tomato sauce, bring to boil; reduce heat, cover and simmer for 20 minutes or until desired consistency, and carrots and celery are tender.

Stir in beans, simmer until heated, serve with cheese.

Only 180 calories a 1½ cup serving and 4g. fat and 6 g. cholesterol.

June Flavin
Merritt Island, FL

Ricky J. Volner
Volner Beefmasters
Scotts Hill, TN

FRAN'S CHILI con CARNE

Here is a recipe for chili that I have used for many years. I always used ground beef but have started to use ground turkey as a substitute the past couple of years and it seems to be just as good.

1 Lg. onion, chopped
1 or 2 cloves garlic, minced
1 Lb. ground beef or turkey
1 can (16 oz.) tomatoes
2 cans (16 oz.) kidney beans
1¼ T. chili powder
½ t. salt
1 bay leaf

Brown beef, crumble with a fork. Add rest of ingredients, and simmer for 1 hour.

Mrs. Francis Grisar
Merritt Island, FL

J.E. Smith, 1898
Near Bruceville,
McLennan County, TX

CHICKEN-CHILI CHALUPAS

1 4 Lbs. hen
1 Lg. onion, grated
1 clove garlic, mashed
2 C. milk
2 t. salt
¼ t. pepper
1 T. Worcestershire sauce
2 C. heavy cream
Tabasco to taste
Celery salt
1 Lb. Cheddar cheese, grated
24 tortillas
3 T. canned chopped green chilies, or to taste

In a bowl, combine the onion, garlic, milk, cream, salt, pepper, Worcestershire sauce and Tabasco. Set aside. Simmer chicken until it is tender in water to cover, seasoning to taste with celery seed. Remove from broth when cooked, saving the liquid for other use.

Remove the meat from the chicken and cut into small strips. Bone the entire chicken for meat afterwards, and use it also. Combine the chicken with ⅓ of the Cheddar cheese. Put a heaping tablespoon of the mixture on each of the tortillas, and roll up.

Arrange a layer of rolled tortillas in a buttered baking dish. Sprinkle on some of the remaining cheese and a little of the chopped green chilies until filled.

Pour on all the milk-cream mixture. Cover the dish and refrigerate overnight. If more milk is needed, add it as necessary to keep the tortillas covered in the dish. Spread with the remaining cheese and bake at 350 degrees for 40 to 50 minutes. Serves 8.

Paul Burke
El Paso, TX

Steve R. Dias
Honolulu, HA

KICK-BUTT CHILI or HOT CHILI

8 oz. slab bacon, chopped fine
2 C. chopped onion
2 T. oil
4 Lbs. boneless beef chuck, cut into ½-inch pieces
2 Lbs. boneless pork butt, cut into ½-inch pieces
1 C. water
3 C. beer
2 cans (28 oz.) crushed tomatoes in puree
⅔ C. ground pure mild red chili powder
¼ C. (3) fresh or canned jalapeno pepper chopped fine
½ C. ground cumin
2½ T. ground red pepper
2½ T. dried oregano
1 T. salt
¼ C. fresh lime juice
2½ T. minced garlic

Fry bacon in large skillet until crisp. Add onions and cook until tender. Transfer to a heavy 6-8 quart pot. Heat oil in skillet. Brown beef and pork in batches. Add to pot. Add remaining ingredients except the lime juice, to pot and bring to a boil over high heat. Reduce heat and simmer, uncovered, 2 to 2½ hours, stirring occasionally and skimming off the fat until the meat is tender.

Remove from heat and stir in lime juice.

June Flavin
Merritt Island, FL

Isaac & Squire Williams
California (1847)

CHILI PITAS

½ Lb. ground beef
2 t. chili powder
Salt and pepper to taste
2 t. vegetable oil
2 T. catsup or chili sauce
2 or 3 slices, Monterey Jack cheese

Season beef with chili powder, salt and pepper in a skillet. Brown beef in the oil. Drain off fat, and stir in catsup or chili sauce. Stuff the meat mixture into the pita pockets, adding a slice of cheese to each.

Serves 2 or 3.

Stanley Finkelstein
Palm Bay, FL

Wolf Creek Farms
Malta, OH

TWILIGHT CHILI SAUCE

This recipe for Twilight Chili Sauce was given to me many years ago (1940).

When the children were in their beds and all was quiet, I would make my chili sauce. The aroma that wafted around me was reward in itself. Hence the name Twilight.

Its my favorite because of its mild sweet taste and it rich reddish brown color.

18 Lg. ripe tomatoes, chopped
6 Lg.onions, ground
6 Lg. peppers, ground
1½ C. sugar
3 T. cinnamon
¼ T. each cloves and allspice
3 T. celery seed
3 T. mustard seed

Mix all together into a large pot and cook for one hour. Ladle into pint jars. Follow instructions of jar manufacturer. Makes 4½ pints.

Ms. Dorothy D. Snow
Satellite, Beach, FL

James E. Pratt
Alturas, CA

JUNE'S CHILI

1 C. dried pinto or red kidney beans
¼ C. olive oil
2½ Lbs. cubed beef
½ Lb. sausage, sliced
1 bay leaf
1 T. dried oregano
3 T. chili powder
1 t. cumin

Place beans in a bowl, cover with water and soak overnight. Drain beans, put in pan and cover with fresh cold water. Bring to a boil. Reduce heat and simmer for 45 minutes. Discard water.

In a large heavy pan, heat the oil. Add beef, sausage, onion and garlic. Fry for 5 minutes stirring constantly to break up beef. Add all of the other ingredients, except the beans; mix well to completely blend mixture; bring to a boil, reduce heat and simmer at least 2 hours, stirring occasionally. Add beans, stir well and reheat.

June Flavin
Merritt Island, FL

Herbert & Mamo Laranang
Honolulu, HA

CINCINNATI CHILI FIVE-WAY

You know most people think Texas is the Chili Capital of the World. WRONG!

Cincinnati is the uncontested "Chili Capital". There has been numerous articles written about it.

Having been born and raised in Cincinnati, I can vouch for it. Every suburb of Cincinnati has a "Chili Parlor". The original is the Empress Chili Parlor which dates back to early Cincinnati and can be found in a book about early historical Cincinnati.

1 Lb. ground beef chuck
1 Med. onion, finely chopped
2 cloves garlic, minced
1 C. barbecue sauce
1 C. water
1 T. chili powder
1 t. black pepper
½ Oz. unsweetened chocolate, grated
½ t. ground cumin
½ t. turmeric
½ t. cinnamon
¼ t. ground cloves
¼ t. ground coriander
¼ t. ground cardamom
1 t. salt
Tomato juice, as needed
9 Ozs. spaghetti, cooked and buttered
1 can (16 oz.) kidney beans, heated
2 onions, chopped
1 Lb. shredded Cheddar cheese

Salt a large skillet. Turn the heat to medium and add the meat, the chopped medium onion and garlic. Break up meat with a fork and cook until it is browned. Drain off fat. Add barbecue sauce and water. Bring to a boil. Add remaining spices. Cover and simmer at very low heat for ½ hour, stirring and tasting occasionally, adding tomato juice if it is getting too dry to ladle up easily. (We like this chili best when it is reheated after being allowed to "age" overnight in the refrigerator).

To construct the plate of five-way, layer the spaghetti on a plate (a small oval plate is traditional), top it with hot chili, then with a sparse layer of beans, then onions. Pat on plenty of cheese while the chili is still hot, and serve immediately, with oyster crackers on the side.

If desired, omit either the beans, or onions, or both, for four-way or three-way chili (known in Cincinnati lingo as a "haywagon").

Glenn M. Doddy
Cocoa, FL

H.A. & D.C. Vibbert
Madras, OR

NORMA'S CHILI con CARNE

1 C. dried pinto beans
3 Lbs. lean stew beef
¼ C. olive oil
1 bay leaf
2 T. chili powder
1 T. salt
4 cloves garlic, minced
1 t. crushed cumin seed
1 t. oregano
3 T. paprika
3 T. corn meal
1 T. flour

Cover washed beans with 4 cups of water, bring to a boil for 2 minutes. Cover and set stand 1 hour, then cook until tender. Drain. Cut meat in ½-inch cubes and sear in hot oil.

Add 6 cups of water, cover; bring to boil and simmer for about 1 hour. Add bay leaf and next six (6) ingredients. Simmer for an additional hour. Blend corn meal, flour and cold water to make a paste. Stir this into pot, simmer 5 minutes, then add beans and heat. Serves 6.

Norma Flavin
Merritt Island, FL

Anchor T
Monroe & Arminta Tyson
Orlando, FL

CHILI MEAT LOAF

3 Lbs. ground chuck
3 Lg. onions, chopped
1 C. fine cracker crumbs
1 Lg. egg
1 T. (rounded) chili powder, or to taste
1 T. salt
½ t. coarsely ground black pepper
2 C. canned tomatoes
Minced fresh parley

Combine beef, onions, crumbs, egg and seasoning in a mixing bowl. Blend thoroughly. Work the mixture with you hands. Form into a roll. Place in a greased baking pan. Cover with the canned tomatoes.

Bake at 350 degrees for 1¼ hours. Baste several times with the pan juices. Sprinkle with parsley before serving. For sauce, serve a tomato sauce or with a salsa of your choice. This recipe is good hot or cold.

Scott Geltner
Cincinnati, OH

C Slant Bar G
C & G Cattle Co.
Wauchula, FL

MOUNTAIN VENISON CHILI

3 Lbs. coarse ground venison
2 Lbs. coarse ground beef
4 T. vegetable oil
3 Lg. onions, chopped
2 green peppers, chopped
2 cans (16 oz.) tomatoes
1 Qt. water
3 cloves garlic, minced
1 T. salt
3 T. paprika
1 T. (level) oregano
6 T. chili powder
1½ t. cumin
1 t. pepper
⅛ t. cayenne pepper

In a large heavy pot or Dutch oven, brown the venison and beef. Use a wooden spoon to crumble meats as they are cooking. After meats are cooked, add onions and garlic and cook until onion is transparent, stirring frequently to keep meats from sticking to pot.

Add water and tomatoes and blend well. Bring to a boil; reduce heat, and simmer for 3 hours with a partially covered lid. Add remaining ingredients, and cook for 1 hour longer.

Serve right from pot, or refrigerate overnight and reheat before serving for the enhanced flavor that you get from waiting to eat this dish.

Bob & Marie Teubner
Cincinnati, OH

TP

TP Bar
Elbert & Peggy Tindall
Melbourne, FL

-20 BELOW CHILI from Wisconsin

1 Lb. ground chuck
1 Lg. green pepper
1 Lg. onion
1 box elbow macaroni
1 can (16 or 18 oz.) chili hot beans
1 can (28 oz.) peeled tomatoes
1 jar Pace Picante sauce (med)
1 T. salt, or to taste
¼ C. chili powder
1 t. cayenne pepper
1 can of tomato soup or more water to thicken
4 stalks celery, cut up

Brown ground chuck. Drain fat off. Combine all ingredients in your favorite chili kettle, cover and simmer till all ingredients are done.

Richard Olbrys
Campbellsport, WI

H.D.S.

A.J. Sewell, 1900
McGregor,
McLennan County, TX

FLAVIN'S FAVORITE CHILI

2 Lbs. ground beef
2 T. shortening
3 T. chili powder
1 t. salt
2 C. chopped onions
2 cloves garlic, crushed
1 t. paprika
1 t. oregano
½ t. cayenne pepper
½ C. beef stock
1 t. ground cumin
1 can (28 oz.) tomatoes
3 cans (16 oz.) red kidney beans

Heat shortening in large skillet, and brown beef, drain off excess fat. Combine all remaining ingredients, stirring well.

Cook on low heat 8 to 10 hours, on high for 5 hours.

Yields 8-10 servings.

Norma Flavin
Merritt Island, FL

MC

Mill Creek Farms
West Memphis, AR

AMBERELY CHILI

2 Lbs. ground beef
1 C. chopped onions
2 cans (16 oz.) kidney beans, undrained
1 can (28 oz.) whole, tomatoes, peeled, w/juice, chopped
3½ C. tomato juice
3 t. sugar
1 Pkg. chili seasoning mix
¼ t. onion salt
¼ t. garlic salt
½ C. grated Cheddar cheese

1. Brown beef in a skillet with onions and cook until the beef is done. Use a fork to break up beef as it is being cooked.

2. Drain off excess fat, and put into larger pot or Dutch oven. Add the remaining ingredients except the cheese, and bring to a boil. Reduce the heat to medium, and cook for an additional hour, stirring occasionally.

3. Reduce heat further to a simmer for ½ hour longer. Serve with Cheddar cheese and, or chopped onion, sprinkled over each serving.

This is a thick chili. To obtain a thinner consistency, add tomato juice until it is reached.

Kim Orosco
Cincinnati, OH

77

Seventy-seven
Turner Cattle Co.
Arcadia, FL

BASIC CROWD PLEASIN' CHILI #1

This is the same named recipe as #2, but different ingredients

1 Lb. ground beef
1 C. chopped onions
3 Lg. cloves garlic, minced
1 T. chili powder
1 t. ground cumin
2 C. cooked or canned beans, rinsed and drained (black, pinto, kidney or a combination
⅓ C. finely chopped mild pepper rings
Chopped avocado for garnish
Sliced pitted ripe olives for garnish
2 cans (16 oz.) tomato sauce

In a 10-inch skillet over medium heat, cook beef, onions and garlic with chili powder and cumin until beef is browned and onions are tender, stirring to separate meat. Spoon off fat.

Add tomato sauce and beans; heat to boiling. Reduce heat to low. Cover: simmer 10 minutes, stirring occasionally. Stir in peppers; heat through. Garnish with chopped avocado and sliced olives.

Makes 5 servings. Recipe may be doubled.

Medium-hot chili: Prepare chili as above but substitute ⅓d cup seeded and finely chopped red cherry peppers for the mild pepper rings. Garnish with shredded Monterey Jack cheese, chopped tomatoes and crumbled cooked bacon.

Hot Chili: Prepare chili as above but increase chili powder to 2 tablespoons. Substitute ⅓d cut seeded and chopped hot jalapeno peppers for mild pepper rings. Serve with sour cream. Garnish with sliced green onions and tortilla chips.

Vlasic Foods

Joe C. Cueto
Duncan, AZ

MY KIDS FAVORITE CHILI

1 Lb. ground round steak
1 C. diced onions
1 stick butter
2 cans fancy red kidney beans
2 cans Campbell's Tomato Soup
Chili powder to taste

Saute onion in butter. Put in large kettle. Saute meat in same skillet. Put in the onions. Add the beans, soup and 2 cans of water.

Simmer 1 hour, and add chili powder to taste. Go easy adding chili powder during the simmering.

Mrs. Dorothy Walker
Barefoot Bay, FL

George A. Will
Sulpher, LA
Jefferson County, TX

TIMOTHY'S WHITE CHILI

1 Lb. large white beans
6 C. chicken broth
2 cloves garlic, minced
2 Med. onions, chopped
1 T. oil
2 cans (4 oz.) mild green chilies, chopped
Sour cream
2 t. ground cumin
1½ t. oregano
¼ t. ground cloves
¼ t. cayenne pepper
4 C. diced cooked chicken breast
3 C. grated Monterey Jack cheese
Salsa

Combine beans, broth, garlic and half of the onions in a large soup pot. Bring to a boil. Reduce heat, simmer until beans are soft (3 hours or more), adding more broth if necessary.

In a skillet, saute remaining onions in oil until tender. Add chilies and seasonings and mix thoroughly. Add to bean mixture. Add chicken and simmer 1 hour.

Serve topped with grated cheese, salsa and sour cream.

Makes 8 to 10 servings.

Salsa: You can use store-bought chunky Mexican salsa or make your own with peeled tomatoes, green chilies, onion, garlic and fresh cilantro.

Take white beans (not red), chicken broth (not beef), and chilies that are mild (not hot). You get white chili, a dish that unites chicken and chili lovers.

Cincinnati Enquirer

Bar C
Doyle Conner
Tallahassee, FL

CHILI con CARNE

¼ Lb. ground beef
½ C. chopped onions
1 Med. clove garlic, minced
Generous dash ground cumin seed
1 can (16 oz.) Campbell's Pork & Beans in Tomato Sauce
½ C. tomatoes and green chilies

In saucepan, brown beef and cook onions with garlic and cumin until tender (use shortening if necessary): stir to separate meat. Add remaining ingredients. Bring to boil; reduce heat. Simmer 10 minutes; stir occasionally.
Makes about 3 cups.

Mrs. Joseph McWilliams
Cocoa Beach, FL

Kaneohe Ranch Ltd.
Oahu, HA

CHAMPION CHILI

1 Lb. ground beef
½ C. chopped onion
½ C. chopped green pepper
1 can (28 oz.) whole tomatoes,
1 can (15 oz.) or
2 cans (8 oz.) tomato sauce
1 Pkg. (1½ oz.) McCormick Chili Chili Seasoning Mix
2 cans (15 oz.) Van Camp's Dark or Light Red Kidney Beans, undrained
or New Orleans Style Red Kidney Beans, undrained

In a 4-quart saucepan or Dutch oven, brown ground beef with onion and green pepper, drain. Add remaining ingredients except the beans.

Bring to a boil; reduce heat. Cover, simmer 20 minutes. Add beans; continue simmering 10 minutes.
About 10-1 cup servings.

Ms. Joseph McWilliams
Cocoa Beach, FL

Tanner Farms
Zanesville, OH

CHILI-TOPPED ENGLISH MUFFINS

½ Lb. ground raw turkey
4 to 5 t. chili powder
¼ t. onion powder
1 can (15 oz.) tomato sauce with tomato tidbits
Dairy sour cream, optional
3 English muffins, split and toasted
½ (4 oz.) Pkg. (1½ C.) finely shredded Cheddar cheese
1 can (18 oz.) red kidney beans, drained

In a medium skillet, cook turkey, chili powder, and onion powder until turkey is no longer pink. Drain, if necessary. Stir in tomato sauce and beans. Bring to boiling. Reduce heat. Simmer, uncovered, for 4 minutes.

To serve, spoon turkey mixture onto muffin halves. Sprinkle with cheese. Dollop of sour cream if desired.

National Inquirer

Carl & Wanda Schnabele
Canyon City, OR

CHILIBREW

4 Lbs. ground meat, lightly browned
2 C. chopped onions
2 C. chopped green peppers
1¼ C. chopped celery
1 can (28 oz.) sliced tomatoes
1 can (28 oz.) water
2 cans (30 oz.) chili hot beans
3 cans (12 oz.) regular beer
¼ t. garlic powder
4 T. chili powder
1 T. + 3 t. salt
1 t. sugar
2 t. cumin
2 cans (12 oz.) tomato paste

Saute onions, peppers and celery in juice remaining after browning meat. Add rest of the ingredients and simmer for about 2 hours. Cool and refrigerate overnight for best flavor. Yield: 2 gallons of chili.

Recipe may be halved, quartered, etc. I serve small separate dishes each of finely chopped raw onions, shredded mild cheddar cheese, cooked small shell noodles, oyster crackers and sour cream. Everyone adds their own preference! Great for a crowd!!!

Cy & Shirley Swiecichowski
Jackson, WI

F Bar
R.E. Field
Grant, FL

POLLY BERGEN'S CHILI #1

3 garlic cloves, minced
2 T. vegetable oil
4 Lbs. round steak, ground
6 Lg. onions
4 Lg. green peppers
3 cans (16 oz.) tomatoes
4 cans (16 oz.) red kidney beans, undrained
2 cans (16 oz.) tomato paste
¼ C. chili powder
1 t. white vinegar
3 dashes cayenne pepper
3 whole cloves
1 bay leaf
Salt and pepper to taste

Cook garlic in oil until brown. Crumble ground round in pieces and cook 10 minutes, breaking up to brown evenly. Pour off some of the oil and drippings into another skillet and cook sliced onion and green peppers until tender. Add to cooked ground beef with tomatoes kidney beans, chili powder, tomatoes, kidney beans, tomato paste, vinegar, cayenne pepper, bay leaf, cloves, salt and pepper.

Cover; cook over low heat 1 hour. If too dry, add additional tomatoes. If too much liquid, uncover and simmer longer. Serve with rice.

Makes 12 servings.

I have had the Polly Bergen's recipe for many years, but never tried it. Maybe soon.

Ms. Joseph McWilliams
Cocoa Beach, FL

Howard L. Hays
Pulaski, TN

TEXAS JAILHOUSE CHILI

¼ Lb. beef suet
2 Lbs. coarsely ground beef
3 cloves garlic
1½ T. paprika
3 T. chili powder
1 T. cumin seed
1 T. salt
1 t. pepper
1½ T. diced sweet pepper
1½ to 3 C. water
½ C. kidney beans (optional)

Fry out the suet in a heavy skillet, then add the meat, garlic and other seasonings. Cook under cover slowly for four hours, stirring occasionally. Then add water depending on how thick you want it, and cook for another hour. Kidney beans can be added if desired.

Ronald W. DelPorto
Erie, PA

Merry L. Ranch
Ft. Pierce, FL

NINA'S CHILI

1 Lb. ground beef
2 Lbs. ground cajun sausage (Delchamp's carries this)
1 can (32 oz.) tomato sauce
1 can (16 oz.) whole tomatoes
1 can of rotel
1 can chili hot beans (Bush's)
1 Env. of chili seasonings
1 Lg. onion, chopped

Cook both meats, slowly, in pan with the onions. Drain off all fats and add whole tomatoes and rotel. Grind tomatoes in pan to bite-size. Add tomato sauce, beans and spices. Let simmer at least one hour.

This can be eaten with Fritos, cheese, sour cream, black olives, etc., to make a taco salad.

Ms. Nina L. Elliott
Tuscaloosa, AL

Kahua Ranch Ltd.
Honolulu, HA

REAL TEXAS CHILI

This is the recipe my mother. My 2 brothers and I have used for at least 30 years.

3 Lbs. meat (2 of chili meat and 1 ground beef)
3 chili peppers (the dried ones that come in a cellophane bag)
2 T. comino seed, toasted
1 T. paprika
2 T. oil
2 or 3 T. chili powder
1 T. garlic, minced
Salt to taste
2 T. flour
½ C. tomato paste (can use catsup
Black and red pepper to taste

To prepare comino seed:

Toast on cast iron griddle until golden (medium heat), stirring constantly. Be careful not to burn. When toasted, empty onto wax paper and grind to powder with wooden rolling pin.

To prepare chili peppers:

Put 3 dried chilies in small saucepan, cover with water, and simmer till water turns dark brown. Remove chilies from water and scrape pulp, discarding seeds and skin. Put pulp *and water* into your chili pot.

To prepare chili:

Put oil into heavy pot (cast iron works best). When oil is hot, add meat and brown, stirring occasionally. When meat is browned, remove to a bowl and add flour to oil, stirring constantly until it turns a nice medium brown.

Add meat and rest of ingredients. Fill pot with water and simmer for 1 hour. Skim grease off top if desired.

Joan Looney
Sante Fe, TX

Don Jose Tomas Talamantes
California(1848)

1984 INTERNATIONAL CHILI

2 Lbs. coarsely ground beef
1 C. water
1 can (16 oz.) tomatoes, pureed
1 onion, finely chopped
1 t. garlic powder
1 t. red pepper sauce
¼ C. chili powder
1 t. oregano
1½ t. salt
2 t. cayenne pepper
1 can (12 oz.) beer
2 t. Masa trigo or flour, dissolved in 2 T. water
2 t. ground cumin

Cook meat over high heat in a 2-quart Dutch oven or heavy pan until the meat loses color. Add water, pureed tomatoes, onion and garlic powder.

Bring liquid to a boil; reduce heat, cover and simmer for 30 minutes. Stirring occasionally, add red pepper sauce, chili powder, oregano, salt, cumin, cayenne pepper and beer; stir well. Simmer uncovered, 1 hour longer, or until meat is tender and stew is thickened. If a thicker stew is desired, stir in smooth paste or Masa flour with water. Cook several minutes longer to thicken.

Ms. Joan Smithson
Tuscaloosa, AL

Ulupalakua Ranch Inc
Maui, HA

VENISON CHILI

1½ to 2 Lbs. venison, trimmed
¼ C. beef suet
2 cans kidney beans
1½ cans (15 oz.) tomato sauce
3 T. chili powder
½ to ¾ C. water
½ t. cayenne pepper
1 t. crushed oregano
¼ t. garlic powder
1½ t. fresh ground pepper
½ C. minced onions

Chop the venison into small pieces; saute the beef suet in an iron skillet, then when the fat is hot, add the venison and saute until brown. Combine all remaining ingredients except the water in a large pot, add venison and simmer for two (2) hours, stirring occasionally. After one hour taste chili and if needed, add more cayenne pepper to taste. Continue to cook until desired thickness is reached. (If finished product is too thick, add water).

Ms. Joan Smithson
Tuscaloosa, AL

J Bar
Bennet Ballington
Mims, FL

HEARTLAND OF WISCONSIN CHILI

I like this recipe because you can put it together in the least amount of time. It's amazing the different ingredients people can use in their chilies.

2 Lbs. ground round
1 Med. onion, chopped
1 bay leaf
½ t. white vinegar
½ t. chili powder
½ t. cumin
1 t. salt
1 t. white pepper, preferable
¼ C. green pepper, chopped, (optional)
¾ C. celery, plus 1 stalk, top chopped fine
2 cans (48 oz.) whole tomatoes or, 1 Lg. can and 1 (16 oz.)
2 cans (16 oz.) drained kidney beans, chili flavored, (optional)
1½ C. cooked macaroni or noodles

Spray Pan or Mazola corn oil cooking spray, No Stick on bottom of a 10" skillet.

Crumble meat as it is browning. Drain off grease. Put meat in large kettle and fill ¾ full of water. Bring to a boil, add celery and green pepper, if used.

Add onion, bay leaf, cumin, salt, pepper and chili powder. Stir real good. Add tomatoes and vinegar. Simmer one (1) hour stirring occasionally. Add kidney beans and noodles or macaroni. Stir real good. Cook chili and taste it during simmering to way you like it.

Ms. Theresa Sternitzky
Fond du Lac, WI

Glen & Janet Flake
Snowflake, AZ

ARIZONA-TEXAS CHILI

This recipe is over 100 years old. Truly good chili should not be hurried. Beans should be soaked 6 to 8 hours and them be simmered. There is one ingredient that must be included if the end result is to be good, one that can't be found in any cookbook. That's the ingredient is "love".

Serves 10 to 12.

5 Lbs. lean beef (neck meat is possible), cubed or very coarsely ground
1 Qt. water
2 cans of tomato paste
¼ Lb. suet, ground or, 6 oz. olive oil
1 T. sugar
1½ T. salt
6 to 8 T. ground chili powder
6 cloves garlic, chopped
3 Med. onions, chopped
1 T. cumin

This is similar to chili I make, but I usually use half ground chuck and half ground round and omit the suet and use olive oil or peanut oil. Sometimes I add a pinch or two of cayenne pepper. The best beans are pinto or Mexican red. For me, kidney beans are just plain nuts. They are a sweet bean and don't belong in any chili, but there are all kinds of people and just about as many tastes.

If some people want kidney beans in their chili that's fine with me. I guess I'm a crank about chili. I like the time tested traditional chili, and the kind that can be felt all the way down and remembered a long time. Your to good eating.

P.S. Anyone who can eat my chili and survive, proves he's a man instead of a mouse.

Merrell W. Edwards
Bishop, CA

B.C. Chenault
Wellsville, NY
Jefferson County, TX

ARAGOSA'S CHILI

1½ Lbs. ground chuck
1½ Lbs. ground beef
1 can (46 oz.) tomato juice
1 can (8 oz.) tomato sauce
1 can (8 oz.) tomato paste
2 cans (15½ oz.) kidney beans, dark red, undrained
1 Lg. green sweet pepper, chopped into pieces to suit you
5 stalks celery, cut to suit you
1 Lg. or 3 small garlic bulbs, cut fine
3 T. olive oil or other kind
2 T. chili powder or more to taste
50 strands of fine (very thin) dry spaghetti

1. In a large kettle add the tomato juice, tomato sauce, tomato paste, kidney beans, chili powder and oil.

2. I use about 1 pint of water that I get from rinsing skillet. In a large skillet, I use an old fashion (cast iron), add meat and onions, chop fine and fry to a golden brown. Add celery, peppers, garlic, which is also cut fine. Cook until the vegetables are done, not mushy.

3. Add this to the big kettle, bring to a boil. Add dry spaghetti, broken once or left whole. Turn down to simmer, stirring quite often.

I have 100% praise on this recipe, not bragging.

Frank & Virginia Aragosa
Waupun, WI

San Diego County Council
Boy Scouts of America
San Diego, CA

CHILI con CARNE

1 T. olive oil
1 Lg. onion, chopped
2 cloves garlic, crushed
½ Lb. ground sirloin, or chuck
1 can (28 oz.) crushed tomatoes
3 T. chili powder
2 t. ground cumin seed
Salt and pepper to taste
1 can (19 oz.) red kidney beans

for garnish:
1 small onion, chopped
1 C. sour cream
1 C. cheddar cheese, grated
½ C. fresh cilantro, chopped

Pour the olive oil into a small fry pan and saute the onion about 5 minutes. Add the garlic and saute ¾ minute. Add the meat and brown. Place cooked items into a strainer and drain to remove as much fat as possible. Return to the pan.

Strain and wash the kidney beans and add to the meat along with the remaining ingredients.

Simmer 20 minutes. Add salt and pepper to taste for seasoning. Add more chili powder or cumin as needed.

To serve: Serve the chili and pass the bowls of sour cream, onion, cheddar cheese and cilantro. Warm some tortillas or some crusty bread and serve with the chili. Serves 2.

Miami Herald
Barry & Roberta Geltner

T Five Joined
Guy Masters
Immokalee, FL

JULIA BATCHO'S PHILLY CHILI

1 Lb. extra lean ground beef
2 cans Progresso Kidney Beans (undrained)
1 Med. onion, chopped
1 large green pepper
1 can (6 oz.) tomato paste
2 cloves garlic, chopped fine
Black pepper to taste (or cayenne if you like it hot!)
1 heaping T. chili powder

Brown beef, green pepper, onion and garlic. Drain. Add tomato paste and 3½ cans water, (paste cans). Add seasonings and simmer one hour.

Add kidney beans. Cook on medium heat for 10 minutes. Stir often. Serve over ½ cooked cup brown rice. Makes 5 to 6 good size servings.

Terri L. Brittingham
Exton, PA

Lyle Devine & Son
Miles City, MT

CHILI MARINADE

3 T. olive oil
2 cloves garlic, crushed
1 t. chili powder
½ t. sugar
½ C. vinegar
¼ t. pepper
½ C. apple juice
Dash Tabasco sauce

Prepare the marinade sauce about 24 hours before using, by first sauteing the garlic in the olive oil to golden brown. Add remaining ingredients and bring to a boil. For a stronger flavor, any meat that you plan to grill, let it cook in the hot marinade for a few minutes. Otherwise, let it cool, place meat in plastic baggies, pour liquid into container, close and place in refrigerator overnight. During grilling, pour liquid over the meat to further enhance flavor.

Barry & Roberta Geltner
Miami, FL

RTC

Ruben T. H. Ching
Alea, HA

TEXAS CHILI 1st Alarm Chili

1 can (29 oz.) Hunts Tomato Sauce
1 can (15 oz.) Hunts Tomato Sauce
3 Lbs. lean round steak
4 level T. chili powder
2 t. white sugar
1 rounded t. ground cayenne
½ t. ground oregano
½ t. ground celery seed
¼ t. ground coriander
½ t. ground cumin
1 level t. granulated garlic
1 heaping T. ham base*
1½ t. onion powder
8 Oz. good beer

Trim meat of all gristle and 90% of the fat. Brown meat in 2 tablespoons of vegetable oil. Drain off grease. Add beer and simmer until the been is almost absorbed into the meat. Add tomato sauce and bring to a boil. Reduce heat and add all other ingredients stirring in each ingredient as you put it into the pot. Simmer 1½ to 2 hours (2 hours max.).

*Add ham base first and stir in real good.

In various forms but basically the same as this recipe, I have won numerous awards with it.

I started in the chili Cookoff competition in July of 1987 in an open style Industrial Cookoff. This recipe took 1st and 2nd place. The only difference was in one batch, I used cubed moose meat and diced with leeks in one. In 1988 in another Texas Style Cookoff, I placed 2nd and in another I placed 12th. Then in 1989 I hit the big one... 1st place in the Texas Style Pennsylvania State Championship Cookoff at Camp Sherwin in Lake City, PA. ABOVE is the winner.

(Good luck with the cookbook and I'll see you along the Chili Trail as they say in Texas). 1st Alarm Chili is my logo, and is used at chili cookoffs.

G. David Frist Jr.
Meadville, PA

Hassell & Hughes
Lumber Co.
Collinwood, TN

WALT'S TEXAS CHILI

I developed this recipe by employing the best sounding ingredients of other prize-winning recipes I've collected over the years.

3 cans (10½ oz.) beef bouillon
2 C. V-8 Juice
1 Pkg. dried onion soup mix
3 Lbs. ground beef, browned and drained
3 Lbs. round steak, cubed, browned
1 Lg. onion, chopped
2 celery stalks, chopped
1 green pepper, chopped
2 pickled mild banana peppers, seeded and chopped
¼ C. banana pepper juice
¼ C. white vinegar
2 bay leaves
2 t. cumin
1 t. oregano
1 t. onion powder
¼ t. paprika
1 t. instant beef bouillon
2 t. salt
3 T. barbecue sauce
2 t. catsup
Pinch of crushed red pepper
Pinch of dried basil
Pinch of dried thyme
⅓ t. black pepper
1 t. liquid hot sauce
Beer to taste
2 cloves garlic, minced
2 Ozs. chili powder

Combine ingredients in a large pot. Simmer two hours. Add some beer for flavoring, adjust seasonings. Simmer additional hour. Makes about four to five quarts.

Walt Lehmann
Downington, PA

Valley View Farms
Sam & Bonnie Scott
Langsville, OH

BILL'S LONE STAR CHILI

2 Lbs. coarsely ground round beef
2 cans chili beans with juice
1 can tomatoes with green chilies
1 can tomato sauce
1 can or bottle beer (Lone Star preferred
½ can green chilies (optional)
½ Pkg. chili seasoning mix
½ contents of Carol Shelby's Chili Seasoning Mix
3 T. chili powder (optional)
1 T. cumin (optional)
Salt and pepper to taste
1 Lg. onion, chopped
4 cloves garlic, chopped
Olive oil
2 T. mustard or,
1 T. dry mustard

In a large pot, saute the onions and garlic in a small amount of the olive oil. Add beef and brown. Remove and drain off grease. Return pot to heat and add all other ingredients. Add enough water to cover mixture, bring to a boil, stirring frequently, then reduce heat and simmer for at least two hours, stirring occasionally.

Serve with crackers and cheese if preferred.

Bill Dyer
Merritt Island, FL

Seven Lazy Eleven
Beefmasters
Okeechobee, FL

ORCHARD'S CHILI MEATBALLS

1 Lb. ground beef
1 Med. onion, chopped fine
1 green pepper, chopped fine
1 t. ground colander
1 to 3 t. chili powder, or to taste
1 clove garlic, minced
¼ t. ground black pepper
1 t. salt
¼ C. white cornmeal
Sauce (see below)

Combine all ingredients except hot sauce. Shape into balls about ¾ to 1-inch in diameter. Place in boiling sauce.

SAUCE: In a saucepan, melt 1 tablespoon of butter, add one small onion, chopped and 1 clove of garlic, minced. Over a low heat, cook until the sauce mixture is lightly browned. Add one can (10 oz.) of tomato juice. Simmer for 10 minutes. Season with salt and pepper to taste.

Bill & Chrissy Hatfield
Cincinnati, OH

Jackson Taylor, 1898
East Waco,
McLennan County, TX

WHOLE TURKEY CHILI

Fresh ground turkey added to the remaining bird from a feast can provide a very tasty and filling chili dish. It's also a good method of disposing of a carcass of a partially carved up turkey. Follow the easy directions at the end of this recipe, and you'll have a whole turkey bowl.

2 Lbs. ground turkey
1 Lg. onion, chopped
1 green pepper, chopped
3 cloves garlic, minced
2 to 3 T. chili powder
1 t. dried whole oregano
2 cans (6 oz.) tomato paste
1 can (16 oz.) whole tomatoes, chopped up good
1 t. ground cumin seed
1 t. brown sugar
½ t. fresh ground black pepper
¼ t. Tabasco Hot sauce
1 bay leaf
1 t. paprika
2 T. olive oil

1. Prepare basic stock of meat by making soup from bones and carcass of carved up turkey, and tearing off as much of the remaining meat with either fingers or scraping with small knife. Discard bones and fat.

2. Cook soup down to a thick mixture, and set aside. Most of the liquid will evaporate, leaving the best portion.

3. In a large skillet or Dutch oven, cook the ground turkey in the olive oil, breaking up as it browns and loses it pinkness. Push the meat to one side as it is done, and saute the onion, peppers and garlic until the onion is tender, but not browned.

4. Add all ingredients to turkey and vegetables except the cooked down turkey soup. Strain liquid and transfer any meat to chili pot. Keep the liquid handy if the consistency is thicker than you like and you have to thin some.

5. Bring pot to a boil. Reduce heat, and let simmer for 30 minutes to an hour, or until it's what you like.

Kelly Haviland
Cincinnati, OH

Div. Of Animal Industry
State Of Florida
Tallahassee, FL

MOM'S CHILI!

This is a very simple recipe, but my friends like it.

1 Lb. hamburger
1 small onion, chopped
2-3 stalks of celery, chopped
1 can (16 oz.) beans in chili gravy
1 can (16 oz.) tomatoes
Salt and pepper
1 T. chili powder
(I use a tiny pinch of cumin. Mom didn't)

Brown hamburger and saute the celery and onion with the meat. Drain off excess grease.

Add beans, tomatoes, salt, chili powder and water. Cook over low heat for at least two hours. Add water as it cooks. Tomato juice can be added also. Freezes well.

Colleen Adams
Kansas City, MO

A9

Townsend
Florida, 1860

BOLANDER'S CHILI

This chili recipe is my brother-in-laws'(Dale Bolander). The recipe was Dale's mothers' relatives who ran a chili parlor in Kansas City, MO. She was the one who taught him to carry on the tradition. This recipe is special because you pour the sauce over the beans, instead of mixing it all together as most people do, he said.

4 Lbs. ground beef
1½ Lbs. suet - if none in beef
4 T. rounded, comino seed
4 T. rounded, Mexican sage (or oregano seed)
1 can (16 oz.) tomatoes
8 dry big chili peppers, coarsely
1 Lg. onion, chopped
2 T. level, chili powder
4 or 5 chopped pieces of garlic
2 cans chili beans
1 T. salt

Put comino and Mexican sage in a sack made of loose material. Tie or sew the end and put in with the rest of the ingredients and simmer for 3 or 4 hours.

Cook the beans separately, until soft.

Milroy Mitchell
Independence, MO

W.H. Shipman, Ltd
Honolulu, HA

CHILI con CARNE

1 C. dried pinto beans
3 Lbs. lean stew beef
¼ C. olive oil
2 T. chili powder
1 T. flour
4 cloves garlic, minced
1 t. crushed cumin seed
1 t. oregano, crushed
1 bay leaf
3 T. paprika
1 T. salt
1½ T. cornmeal

In a heavy pot, cover beans with 5 cups of water, bringing to a boil for 2 minutes. Place cover on pot and allow beans to stand in hot water for one hour. Again bring pot to boil with sufficient water to cover beans and cook until beans are tender. Drain off water, and allow beans to cool.

Cut meat into ½ to ¾-inch cubes and brown in hot oil. Add to the meat, 5 to 6 cups of water, cover; bring to a boil. Reduce heat, and simmer for one hour. Blend cornmeal, flour and cold water to make a smooth paste, then stir the mixture completely into the pot. Simmer for about 5 minutes or so. Add the pinto beans, and heat before serving.

Makes 5 to 6 good size helpings.

Garnish this chili dish with all, or some of the following items: shredded Cheddar cheese, chopped raw onions, black olive slices and sour cream. Don't forget oyster or regular crackers on the side.

Vic & Pauline Moore
Deer Park, OH

Rice Livestock Co.
Altoras, CA

QUICK and SPICY CHILI

1 Lb. hamburger meat
1 garlic clove, chopped
1 can DeMonte Tomatoes
1 can tomato sauce
1 can kidney beans
2 T. chili powder
1 C. onion, chopped

In a skillet brown meat, garlic and onions. Add remaining ingredients. Simmer 20 minutes. Makes 4 servings or six cups.

Mabel & Jerome Kober
Great Bend, KS

Bluehead Ranch
Edna Carlton
Arcadia, FL

CHILI con CARNE

1½ C. red beans or,
2½ C. canned kidney beans
1 Lg. onion, sliced
1 green pepper, chopped
1 Lb. ground beef
1½ t. salt
Dash paprika
Dash pepper
3 whole cloves
1 bay leaf
3 T. fat
2 T. chili powder
3½ C. tomatoes

Cook beans in boiling salted water until tender. Drain. Brown meat, onion and green pepper in hot fat. Add tomatoes and seasonings. Simmer 2 hours adding water if necessary. Add beans and heat. Serves 6.

Mabel & Jerome Kober
Great Bend, KS

Dusty R. Posey
Fayetteville, TN

CAROLYN'S CHILI

1 Lb. ground beef
1 small onion, chopped
2 cans (10 oz.) tomato soup
2 cans (16 oz.) chili beans
Salt, pepper and chili powder to taste

Brown ground beef and onion. Drain off fat and add tomato soup and chili beans. Heat through and serve.

So quick and easy this has been a 2 generation favorite of our family and friends. We usually have corn bread to go with it.

Mabel & Jerome Kober
Great Bend, KS

Quarter Circle Diamond
Ranch Inc.
Condon, OR

M & J CHILI

- 1 Lb. ground beef
- 1 small onion, chopped
- 1 can (10 oz.) tomato sauce
- 1 can (10 oz.) mushroom sauce
- 1 can (16 oz.) kidney beans
- 1½ T. chili powder
- ¾ T. garlic powder
- Salt and pepper to taste

Fry ground beef and onions for 10 minutes or till cooked. Drain fat. Add rest of ingredients. Simmer for 25 minutes.

Mabel & Jerome Kober
Great Bend, KS

Riley R. Brown
Winnemucca, NV

TEXAS RED

- 3 Lbs. top round steak, cubed
- ¼ Lb. suet
- 3 Lbs. Spanish onions, chopped roughly
- ½ C. dark red chili powder
- ½ t. oregano
- 3 cloves garlic, minced
- 1 t. salt
- 1 t. pepper
- 2 t. ground cumin seed
- 6 C. water

In a Dutch oven, render the suet over a low-medium heat. In the fat, brown the meat. Add onions and cook until they start to turn golden. Add chili powder, cumin, and the rest of the ingredients. Stir, then add the water, and cook for 4 to 6 hours, stirring occasionally.

Serve with side dishes of chopped onions, shredded cheese, sour cream, and the like if desired to add to the color and flavor of this chili dish.

Don Husman
Cincinnati, OH

C Dot
C.L. Campbell
Tallahassee, FL

PORTAGE CHILI

- 1 or 2 Lbs. hamburger beef
- 1 onion, chopped
- 1 stalk celery, chopped
- 1 can (10½ oz.) tomato soup
- 1 Lg. can tomato juice
- Salt and pepper to taste
- 1 C. approx. sugar
- 1 T. chili powder
- 1 can Mrs. Grass Chicken Soup
- 1 can (15½ oz.) chili beans
- Macaroni, uncooked

Brown hamburger, and saute onion and celery. Mix all ingredients together and simmer till the desired thickness and taste are achieved.

Ellen Richardson
Portage, WI

CH Joined
Charles Hayes
Radford, VA

KOBER CHILI

- 3 Lbs. hamburger
- 2 C. chopped onion
- 2 Lbs. pinto beans, cooked
- 2 C. cooked tomatoes
- 1 can (48 oz.) tomato juice
- 3 t. chili powder
- 1 t. salt

Brown hamburger and chopped onion. Drain off fat. Add cooked beans and other ingredients. Simmer on low heat until done. If too strong, add a little water.

Mabel & Jerome Kober
Great Bend, KS

Al Veron Ranch
Bronson, FL

YANKEE CHILI

2 Lbs. venison steak, cut in ½-inch chunks
3½ Lbs. beef sirloin, cut in ½-inch chunks
2½ Lbs. fresh ground pork
¾ C. olive oil
3½ Med. size onion, Chpd
2 cloves garlic, minced
4 jalapeno peppers, seeded and chopped
4 Med. size sweet potatoes, peeled and diced
3 green bell peppers, chopped
1 red bell pepper, chopped
2 Med. sized zucchini Squash ends trimmed, chopped small
5 fresh yellow or red hot banana peppers, seeded and chopped
2 cans (35 oz.) tomatoes plus juice
2 cans (8 oz.) tomato paste
4 bay leaves
2 T. crushed oregano
1 T. salt
2½ T. cuminos, (add during 45 minutes of cooking time)
2 T. red wine vinegar
2 T. brown sugar, packed
2 T. cinnamon
1½ T. black pepper
4½ to 6½ T. chili powder
2 t. dry prepared mustard
1 C. beef broth (from bouillon cube)
¼ C. "Crystal Louisiana's Pure
2 t. ground coriander
2 T. Tabasco sauce
¼ C. L&P Worcestershire sauce
1 can (12 oz.) beer - your choice
4 Oz. Whiskey - your choice
1 Oz. Tequila - your choice
1 - 2 cans (48 oz.) V8 vegetable Juice

Cut up meat as directed. Brown in order given using ¼ cup of the olive oil for each meat group. Preserve the meat drippings and use it to saute the peppers and onions. Put meat into a large pot and add the balance of the ingredients in order given. Simmer for 2½ to 3½ hours.

Makes approximately 2 to 2¼ gallons. Best when served the following day of course.

Note: Beans may be added to this recipe. Use 2 or 3 cans (16 oz.) Chili Hot Beans.

Ruth Ann Podoll
Gulf Breeze, FL

Teodoso Yorba
California (1851)

GREAT BEND CHILI Con CARNE

2 t. vegetable oil
½ C. chopped onion
½ clove garlic, minced
1 Lb. hamburger beef
2 C. kidney beans, cooked
2 cans (8 oz.) tomato sauce
½ t. salt
2 T. chili powder

Cook hamburger meat and onions, and add all other things stirring and mixing good. Cook for about 45 minutes. Makes 4 servings.

Mabel & Jerome Kober
Great Bend, KS

Nicolas Sanchez
Texas (1848)

MABEL'S CHILI

1 Lb. hamburger
½ C. chopped onion
1 clove of garlic
½ C. chopped celery
3 C. tomato juice
½ can red beans or kidney beans
1 C. water
3 T. flour
1 T. sugar
2 t. chili powder
1 t. salt

Cook hamburger, onion and celery until done. Put tomato juice and water in pan. Mix. Add hamburger mixture, add beans, chili powder, salt, flour and sugar. Cook 20 to 30 minutes.

Mabel & Jerome Kober
Great Bend, KS

Clyde A. Hill
Cedarville, CA

ALLEGANI JANIZ'S CHILI

2 T. vegetable oil
4 Lbs. chuck or round*, cut into 1-inch cubes
3 Med. onions, finely chopped
Garlic salt
Lemon pepper
2 Lg. cloves garlic, minced
2 t. cumin seed
1 can (16 oz.) tomatoes
1 can oz.) tomato sauce
½ C. beer
* ground beef may be substituted

1 T. oregano
1 T. paprika
1 t. ground cumin
1 t. salt
1 t. sugar
1 t. Tabasco sauce
1 square unsweetened chocolate
3 C. water
¼ C. Masa flour (available in Mexican grocery stores)
5 T. chili powder

Brown meat in hot oil on all sides over high heat. Add onion, and cook for about 3 minutes. Sprinkle with garlic salt and a little lemon pepper to taste.

In a small bowl, mash together the garlic cloves, cumin seed and a little water. A mortar and pestle is ideal for this work. Add this mixture to the browned meat.

In a blender, combine the tomatoes and tomato sauce, beer, chili powder, oregano, paprika, ground cumin, salt and sugar. Blend until smooth. Stir into meat mixture.

Add Tabasco sauce, chocolate and the three cups of water. Cover, bring to a boil; reduce the heat and cook for 2 hours. Masa flour can be used to thicken chili, by making a paste with mixing water to a little of the flour, and adding to the chili, stirring rapidly to dissolve flour. Cook at simmer for 30 minutes longer.

Robert Williams, Jr.
Milford, DE

Bar M 6
Donald T. Moore
Huntsville, AL

HEAVY METAL RED CHILI

(Mike DelReal)

3 Lbs. of top sirloin
1 C. water
1 Med. red onion
3 T. garlic
1 t. oregano
1 t. cumin
3 t. chili powder
2 cans tomato sauce
1 can red chili sauce
1 T. paprika
1 T. brown sugar
1 can (8 oz.) tomato paste
1 T. chicken bouillon
2 T. beef bouillon
½ t. ancho pepper
½ t. red jalapeno pepper
½ t. green jalapeno pepper
¼ t. black pepper
¼ t. white pepper
¼ t. crushed red pepper
Pinch of baking soda

Dice top sirloin into small pieces and brown. Add water and chopped red onion. Bring to a boil for about 20 minutes. Add garlic, oregano, cumin and 1 teaspoon of chili pepper. Let cook for another 20 minutes.

Add tomato sauce, red chili sauce, tomato paste, chicken bouillon, one teaspoon of beef bouillon and ancho pepper. Let simmer 20 minutes. Add two teaspoons chili pepper, black, white and crushed red pepper, red and green jalapeno pepper powder and paprika. Let simmer for 20 more minutes.

Add brown sugar, baking soda, hot sauce and the other tablespoon of beef bouillon. Let simmer another 20 minutes before serving.

Following from Daily Reporter-Herald, Loveland, Colorado from Cookoff of Feb 17, 1990:

'The title of "best chili in Loveland (Colorado) was given to 25-year-old Mike DelRead and his Heavy Metal Red chili in the annual cookoff... the Denver resident has only been competing in cookoffs for the past year and a half, but has attended about 50, and won several of the events in that time span DelRead said the secret to his chili is that it doesn't taste like chili powder, as he said many of the others do. it's all in the way you brew it up, DelRead explained.'

Leila Dunham
Loveland, CO

Bar H, 1944
Frank J. Heider, Cocoa,
Brevard County, FL

OLD FASHION CHILI

1 Lb. hamburger
¼ t. pepper
1 t. salt
1 large onion, chopped
1 C. water
2 C. canned tomato, or
1 can tomato juice
1 t. chili powder
1 can kidney beans

Cook hamburger and onions until done. Add all other things, but chili powder, and cook for one hour. Then add the chili powder and cook for 10 minutes longer.

Mabel & Jerome Kober
Great Bend, KS

Overlook Groves, Inc.
Ona, FL

COUNTY FAIR CHILI

2 Lbs. lamb with fat trimmed, cut into ½-inch cubes
4 cloves garlic, crushed
1 T. whole cumin seeds
3 T. vegetable oil
1 Lg. onion, chopped fine
1 t. whole oregano leaves
2 T. chili powder
2 jalapeno peppers, seeded, and chopped
2 green peppers, chopped
1 T. Worcestershire sauce
3 fresh tomatoes, chopped
1 can (8 oz.) tomato sauce
1 can (16 oz.) kidney beans
Salt to taste

In a large Dutch oven, using the vegetable oil, brown the lamb but do not overcook it. Add the onions, green peppers, garlic, chili powder and cumin. When the meat is cooked and tender, and the vegetables are softened, add the remaining ingredients. Bring the cooking vessel to a boil; reduce heat and simmer, covered, for 1½ to 2 hours, stirring occasionally.

Add water sparingly if necessary to keep to your desired consistency.

Ms. Laurie Williams
Bethel, OH

John Jerabek, 1897
McLennan County, TX

QUICK HOMEMADE CHILI

2 T. shortening
1 Lb. hamburger
½ clove of garlic
1 can red beans or kidney beans
1 can (8 oz.) Hunt's Tomato Sauce
1 t. salt
2 t. chili powder
½ C. chopped onion
½ C. green pepper, chopped

Cook hamburger, chopped onion, green pepper and garlic till done. Drain off fat. Add cooked beans and other ingredients. Simmer on low heat until cooked.

Mabel & Jerome Kober
Great Bend, KS

N. McLennan, 1850
McLennan County, TX

BLACK BEANS CHILI RICE

2 C. Water
1 C. long grain white rice
1 T. olive oil
¼ C. chopped onion
¼ C. chopped jalapeno peppers, optional
¼ t. chili powder, or to taste
2 Med. tomatoes, cut up
1 ear corn, kernels cut from cob
1 t. crushed garlic
1 can (15 oz.) black beans

Bring the water to a boil, add rice, reduce heat, cover and simmer 15 minutes.

Meanwhile, saute onion and jalapeno peppers in oil in a large, heavy skillet over a medium heat for 1 to 2 minutes or until the onions are soft, but not browned.

Add tomatoes, corn, chili powder and garlic, and cook for 3 minutes. Stir in beans and heat through. Serve immediately over rice.

Serves 4. Preparation time: 10 minutes. Cooking time: 15 minutes.

Ms. Anne Mooney
Miami Beach, FL

B. W. Wright
Port Arthur,
Jefferson County, TX

BI'S CHILI

I truly believe my recipe is one of the best. I developed it while in San Antonio, TX. It has never failed me, and I'll gladly share it with anyone interested.

It's strength improves while sitting on the fire. While I prefer it hot, I usually prepare it mild for the sake of my three children. Here Goes!!.

1½ Lbs. ground chuck
1½ Lbs. top sirloin or round steak
1 Lg. onion
2 Lg. cloves garlic
1 can (22 oz.) tomatoes
2 cans dark red kidney beans
¼ C. (or more) chili powder
¼ C. Med. to hot picante sauce
3 T. corn meal
2 T. vegetable shortening
Garlic salt
1 can (6 oz.) tomato paste

To Prepare:

Dice sirloin into small bite-size pieces, lightly season with garlic salt and set aside. Mince onion and garlic, brown in a large saucepan with the ground meat. Drain off fat, and spoon meat and vegetables into a deep heavy-bottomed pot or kettle.

In the same saucepan, melt the shortening and brown sirloin. Add to the deep pot. Add the tomatoes with juice, tomato paste and beans with juice. Stir in chili powder, picante sauce, and corn meal. Simmer for at least 2 hours. Longer low cooking is better. Serve hot as is, or over rice or pasta.

Hope you and your readers will enjoy this as much as our family has. Happy cooking!

Trudi Bils
Loveland, CO

Warren & Doris Black
Grants Pass, OR

CHUNKY CHILI

Brown one pound of hamburger in a large skillet. Add one can stewed tomatoes, one can tomato puree, one can kidney beans, 2 teaspoons chili powder, and ½ stick of butter. Bring to a boil; reduce heat and simmer stirring it. This freezes well. Serves 8.

Mabel & Jerome Kober
Great Bend, KS

John P. Norgaard
Scappoose, OR

CINCY CHILI SAUCE

2 C. canned tomatoes
⅛ t. ground cloves
Dash cayenne pepper
⅛ t. cinnamon
1 T. sugar
½ t. salt + - to taste
2 T. green pepper, chopped
1 onion, chopped
¼ C. vinegar

In a saucepan, combine the tomatoes, onion, cayenne pepper, cloves, cinnamon, sugar and vinegar. Simmer, uncovered, about 1 hour. Add the salt to taste. Chill the sauce before serving.

Grover & Sue Dudding
Cincinnati, Ohio

KP
Cecil Whaley, Jr.
St. Cloud, FL

BAKED CHILI

This recipe was given to me by my sister who had received it from a friend. I do not know whether it is an original but is a good recipe.

2 Lbs. ground meat
2 small cans Hunt's Tomato
  Sauce or,
  1 family size
2 cans Van Camp's New Orleans
Style red kidney beans
Bell pepper
Garlic
Salt
Pepper
Tabasco sauce
Worcestershire sauce
Hot cherry peppers
Cumin
½ t. sugar
Water

Brown ground meat and drain. Mix all ingredients in a baking dish, not Pyrex. Begin cooking on top of stove. Place in oven on 350 degrees for 1½ to 2 hours.

Bessie A. Bruce
Montgomery, AL

JK Joined
Jeanette Y. Korn
Louisville, KY

RANCH STYLE CHILI

1 Lb. hamburger
1 Pkg. Chili Seasoning Mix
½ C. water
½ C. onion
1 can tomatoes, stewed
1 can kidney beans

Brown hamburger in large skillet. Drain off fat. Cook onion with meat till done. Stir in chili seasoning mix and water, tomatoes and beans. Bring to a boil. Reduce heat and simmer, covered for 10 minutes. Makes 4 to 6 servings.

Mabel & Jerome Kober
Great Bend, KS

Beechwood Stock Farms
Bob Clark
Franklin, TN

GREAT BEND VENISON CHILI

2 Lbs. coarsely ground venison
¼ C. vegetable oil
2 cloves garlic
1 Lg. green pepper, cut in strips
3 T. chili powder
2 t. sugar
3½ C. whole tomatoes
1 C. tomato sauce
1 C. water
½ t. salt
1 T. flour
2 C. cooked kidney beans

Brown venison in the vegetable oil. Add onion, garlic and green pepper. Mix together, stirring constantly. Add chili powder, sugar, whole tomatoes, tomato sauce, water and salt. Simmer for 1½ hours.

If a thicker chili is desired, stir in the flour mixed with water to make a paste. Just before serving, add the 2 cups of cooked kidney beans. Makes 6 to 8 servings.

Mabel & Jerome Kober
Great Bend, KS

Six R
Cushman Radebaugh Jr.
Nashville, AK

DEVIL'S DELIGHT CHILI

3 Lbs. chuck, cut in small chunks
2 T. suet grease
4 cloves garlic, finely chopped
1 Lg. white onion, chopped
3 T. flour
4 T. hot Mexican style chili powder
2 t. ground cumin
1 T. oregano
3 cans beef broth
1 t. salt
¼ t. coarse ground black pepper
1 t. crushed red pepper
2 cans dark red kidney beans, drained (reserve liquid)

What I do is brown the meat quickly in the hot grease, add the garlic and onion; lower the heat and let it cook for 15 minutes and add the combined: flour, chili powder, cumin and oregano. Lots of stirring.

Then I add the beef broth, salt, black pepper and crushed red pepper and just let it simmer, for one 1 hour at least. Then I add the kidney beans. Stir, adding the bean liquid if needed. Let it sit for an hour before even tasting it. I call it a "get acquainted" time for the flavors.

This is the definitive chili for those who like it HOT!

John L. Ennis
Portage, WI

Cornell King
Cornersville, TN

CAREE'S COLORADO CHILI

2 Lbs. ground chuck (extra lean)
1 Lg. onion, chopped
1 can (16 oz.) tomato sauce
1 can (16 oz.) chili beans
1 can (8 oz.) tomato paste
½ t. cumin
½ t. garlic powder
½ t. chili powder
½ t. hot sauce

Saute the onions in 2 tablespoons of butter. Cook until the onions are tender. Drain off excess liquids. Add ground chuck and cook until browned. Add all other ingredients in a Dutch oven and simmer for about 5 hours.

Karee Read
Loveland, CO

Alex M. Parker
Montgomery, AL

CHILI con CARNE

This is the only chili I make. It is from Eat And Stay Slim cookbook by Better Homes & Gardens. The cookbook has a Food Exchange list, for reference.

1 Lb. lean ground beef
1 C. onions, chopped
¾ C. green pepper, chopped
1 can (16 oz.) tomatoes, broken up
1 can (16 oz.) water
1 can (16 oz.) dark red kidney beans, drained
1 can (8 oz.) tomato sauce
1 t. salt
1 to 2 t. chili powder
1 bay leaf

Cook the ground beef, onion and green pepper until the meat is lightly browned, and the vegetables are tender. Spoon off excess fat. Stir in the broken up tomatoes, 1 equal can of water, kidney beans, tomato sauce, salt, chili powder and the bay leaf.

Cover; simmer for one hour. Remove the bay leaf. Serve 4. Each serving has 4 Meat Exchanges, 2 Bread Exchanges and 1 Fat Exchange.

Leila Dunham
Loveland, CO

BR Horse Ranch
Burt Reynolds
Jupiter, FL

BEEF LOAF CHILI

2 Lbs. lean ground beef
1 t. chili powder
1 t. steak sauce
2 C. soft bread crumbs
1½ C. tomato juice
1 Med. onion, chopped
2 t. salt
½ t. dry mustard
2 eggs
2 T. quick cooking tapioca

Combine all ingredients in a mixing bowl, and blend well. Shape into a loaf about 12 inches, and put into baking pan. Bake at 375 degrees for one hour. Longer if needed.

Mabel & Jerome Kober
Great Bend, KS

Bar C
C.L. Hearndon, 1940
Brevard County, FL

CHILI.... CHILI con CARNE

INGREDIENTS	24 SERVINGS	100 SERVINGS
Onion, chopped	2 cups	2 quarts
Green Pepper, chopped	2 cups	2 quarts
Salad oil	½ cup	1 pint
Ground beef chuck, lean	5 pounds	20 pounds
Tomatoes, solid pack	1 #10 can	4 #10 cans
Red kidney beans, solid pack	1 #10 can	4 #10 cans
Chili powder	2 tablespoons	½ cup
Cumin seed (optional)	1 tablespoon	¼ cup
Tabasco	2 teaspoons	3 tablespoons
Salt	2 tablespoons	½ cup
Sugar	2 teaspoons	3 tablespoons
Cornstarch	⅓ cup	1⅓ cups
Cold water	⅔ cup	2⅔ cups

Method: Saute onions and green pepper in salad oil until tender, about 5 minutes.

Add meat and cook until lightly browned, stirring enough to break meat into small pieces. Drain excess juice from tomatoes and save for use in soups. Drain liquid from kidney beans. Add tomatoes, bean juice and seasonings to meat mixture. Stir well and cook slowly over low heat for about 1 hour. Add kidney beans, stir lightly but well and continue to cook 15 minutes longer.

Combine cornstarch and cold water, stir into chili and cook until the chili is thick and starch is cooked, about 15 minutes. Serve with crackers or rusks. Size Servings: 1 cup (about 8 ounces)

McIlnenny Co.
by Robert Williams, Jr.
Milford, DE

Gunstock Ranch
Oahu, HA

American Angus Association
St. Joseph, MO

SKILLET CHILI con CARNE

1 Lb. hamburger
1 Med. onion, chopped
2 T. chili powder
1 can (10¾ oz.) Campbell's Tomato Soup
2 cans (15½ oz.) kidney beans, undrained

In a skillet, brown hamburger and onion until it is tender, using some shortening if necessary. Stir with spoon to separate meat. Add soup and beans. Cook over low heat for 10 minutes. Stir occasionally. Serve with fried eggs if desired. Makes 5 servings.

Mabel & Jerome Kober
Great Bend, KS

Dud Whittaker, 1891
Bosquville,
McLennan County, TX

SOUR CREAM CHILI

1 Lb. ground beef
2 cans condensed chili with beef soup
2 T. dry onion soup mix
1 to 1½ t. chili powder
1 C. dairy sour cream
Grated cheese
Chopped onion

In a large saucepan, brown beef. Add soup, 2 cups water, onion soup mix and chili powder. Bring to a boil. Cover and simmer for 5 minutes. Stir some of the mixture with sour cream. Return to saucepan. Heat and stir 5 minutes more. Top with grated cheese and chopped onion. Makes 6 servings.

Mabel & Jerome Kober
Great Bend, KS

M
Henry P. Hoffstot
Pittsburgh, PA

HOOF HEARTED CHILI

This recipe is that of Don Sanders' from the Daily Reporter-Herald, Loveland, Co of Cookoff of Feb 17, 1990.

3 Lbs. chuck roast
2 onions
2 cloves fresh garlic
2 cans beef broth
2 green chilies
1 t. salt
2 C. water
6 T. chili powder
4 t. cumin
1 t. garlic powder
2 jalapeno peppers
1 can (8 oz.) low-sodium tomato sauce
¼ t. oregano

Dice the chuck roast into small pieces. Chop the onions, green chilies and garlic cloves. Place in a large pot, adding beef broth, ½ teaspoon salt, and sufficient water to cover. Boil for one hour.

Add 2 tablespoons chili powder, 2 teaspoons cumin, ½ teaspoon garlic powder, ½ teaspoon salt, and the tomato sauce. Slice jalapenos in half and add. Simmer for one hour.

Add 4 tablespoons chili powder, 2 teaspoons cumin, ½ teaspoon garlic powder and ¼ teaspoon oregano. Cook on low heat for 30 more minutes.

Leila Dunham
Loveland, CO

Louis Santiago, Jr.
Mililani, HA

REAL QUICK COWBOY CHILI

This recipe is by Mark Turner from the Daily Reporter-Herald of Loveland, Colorado of the Feb 17, 1990 area Cookoff.

1 Lb. ground beef
1 bottle (16 oz.) El Bravito salsa
1 can (12 or 16 oz.) chili beans

Brown ground beef. Drain Chili beans. Add salsa and beans, let simmer until hot. Takes about 20 minutes.

Leila Dunham
Loveland, CO

Robb Ted & Wm. Swift
Rodeo, NM

DOX

"For a real taste of homemade goodness, follow these instructions:

Brown and drain 2 Lbs. lean ground beef (hamburger)
Add: 1 can (14 oz.) beef broth, or
2 cubes beef bouillon, dissolved in 1½ cups of water
1 can (8 oz.) tomato sauce
½ C. water
Cook 20 minutes
Add: DOX Seasoning Packet
Salt or salt substitute to taste (1 t.)
For hotter chili, add desired hot sauce

Serves 4

With the above recipe, try these ideas:

* Substitute venison, or ground turkey for the beef
* Try toppings of: Chopped onion, grated cheese, sour cream, or chopped green chiles
* Add your favorite beans
* Add chili to your favorite hot cheese dip and serve with crisp tortilla chips
* Red Top - served on top of stew
* Serve over spaghetti, noodles or other pasta
* Excellent for hamburgers and hot dogs

The above recipe was sent to us with samples of the chili seasoning. This is not an endorsement, but of the many firms who we contacted for information on their products pertaining to their products for chili, DOX and McIlhenney were the only firms who requested that we try theirs.

DOX Seasoning
Company, Inc.
Davis, OK

Hamakua Sugar Co., Inc.
Honolulu, HA

CHILI SOUP

- 2½ Lbs. hamburger
- 2 cans No. 303 Van Camps Mexican Style Beans in Chili Sauce
- 1 small onion
- 1 Lg. can tomato juice

Place hamburger and onion in a large saucepan or skillet. Cook until done. Season with salt and pepper. Drain off fat, add beans and tomato juice. Let simmer.

Mabel & Jerome Kober
Great Bend, KS

Lazy H
Roy T. Mack
Mims, FL

HUNTER'S CHILI

- 2 Lbs.lean ground venison
- 1 link kielbasa (Polish sausage)
- 1 can (16 oz.) whole cooked tomatoes
- 1 can (16 oz.) red kidney, or chili beans
- 1 T. chili powder (making sure it is fresh)
- ½ t. Knorr seasoning for meat
- ½ t. salt
- 1½ C. water

Put the kielbasa sausage through a food processor to grind it. Then brown kielbasa in an electric skillet. It should have enough fat so that no extra oil is needed. Next add the venison and brown. Pour off any extra fat drippings. If you wish, the sausage can be eliminated from this recipe, but it will be necessary to use some olive oil for browning of the venison.

Now, add the chili powder and remaining ingredients, except the tomatoes. Also add the water. Cook at about 250 degrees for 15 minutes. If time is short, use less water and simmering time. Add tomatoes and chop them up while mixing them into the chili. Lastly, add the beans and turn the heat down to simmer until chili is heated through. It's is the kind of dish that can "wait" well and be improved with time if the meal is delayed, and chili reheated before serving.

Scott Geltner
Cincinnati, OH

President Ronald Reagan
Los Angeles, CA

CHILI con CARNE WITH AUTHORITY

I saw your request of recipes in West Hawaii Today and would very much like to submit an Island "Chili" recipe of mine. I have always said "anyone who eats chili, can't be all bad". Well, here we go!

2½ Lbs. lean beef, diced (any cut, any kind) in ½-inch pieces
2 Lg. onions, diced
½ C. green pepper, diced
¼ C. cooking oil
3 cloves garlic, minced, cloves, not buttons
2 cans (8 oz.) tomato sauce
16 Oz. water
* ½ Lb. pork, diced ½-inch pieces, some fat O.K.

1 T. seasoned salt
3 T. ground cumin
1 t. Tabasco or equivalent pepper sauce
2 dried cayenne peppers, or other dried hot peppers, with seeds, cut up fine
1 t. paprika
1 t. oregano
2 T. vinegar, any type

In a large heavy pot with lid, cook pork on medium-high heat in a small amount of the cooking oil, if needed, until meat is gray in color. Now add the beef, and cook until browned. This part of the cooking is done with the lid off.

Next, add onion, green pepper, garlic and cook until the onion turns clear. To this add the tomato sauce and water. Simmer for 15 minutes with the lid on.

Add the seasonings next, salt, cumin, chili powder, Tabasco sauce, cayenne peppers, paprika, oregano and vinegar.

Heat pot to a boil, reduce heat and simmer for one hour with the lid on. Stir carefully to prevent sticking, keeping the lid on as much as possible to retain liquid. Add small amounts of water as necessary to prevent mixture from burning.

If you desire beans in your con carne, cook separate pinto beans adding a pinch of salt and chili powder while cooking. I always cook my beans a day before, then reheat before adding to the chili con carne.

Salted soda crackers go well with this chili.

Thanking you very much & Aloha nui loa from Hawaii nei,

Jerry H. Ramaker
Kailua Kona, HA

One O T Bar J
J.J. Atkinson
Cocoa, FL

TI'S HOMESTYLE CHILI

2 Lbs. coarsely ground beef
2 C. onions, chopped
2 C. green peppers, chopped
5 C. tomatoes, crushed with juice
5 C. tomatoes, fresh, chopped
6 t. sugar or packs
¼ C. chili powder
1 C. (8 oz.) instant brewed regular coffee
2 t. salt
9 C. red kidney beans, cooked

In a skillet or Dutch oven, brown the beef in a little oil; drain off fat, and add the onions and green peppers. When vegetables are done and tender, again drain off fat from the meat mixture.

Add the remaining ingredients including the beans, and simmer for at least one hour, or until it's tastes and the consistency are those you desire.

Tina Tiumalu
Orlando, FL

9 R Joined
Sherrod's Heritage
Immokalee, FL

TEXAS CHILI El CASSEROLE

1½ Lbs. lean ground beef
2 T. oil
2 cloves garlic, minced
½ t. ground cumin
1 can (28 oz.) whole tomatoes
1 t. salt
½ fresh ground pepper
½ t. ground oregano
½ C. water
3 T. chili powder
½ t. sugar
2 or 3 C. cooked or canned pinto beans
½ C. onion, minced
3 C. corn chips
Shredded Cheddar cheese

In a large skillet, using the oil, brown the beef, using a wooden spoon to break up the meat as it is cooking. After browning, drain off any excess fat and oil remaining. Saute the onion with the beef until the onion is transparent and tender.

Add the garlic, tomatoes with juice, which should be broken up when mixing in the ingredients, cumin, oregano, sugar, salt and pepper. Stir in well to fully blend ingredients with meat mixture. Cover, and bring to a boil. Reduce heat and simmer, uncovered, for 30 minutes.

During final minutes of simmering, preheat oven to 350 degrees.

Mix in the pinto beans and chili powder, mixing in well. Line a 2 quart casserole with the corn chips. Pour the chili mixture over the chips. Top with the cheese, a little more chips if desired, and bake for 15 to 20 minutes until cheese melts, or to desired appearance.

For garnish, sprinkle a little chopped onions, chopped black olives, or more cheese on top of servings when offering this dish to your guests.

Michael J. Ynclan
Cape Canaveral, FL

Mauna Kea Beach Hotel
Kamuela, HA

CHILI GUMBO

¾ Lb. ground beef
1 Med. onion, chopped
2 cloves garlic, minced
1 T. olive oil
1 can (16 oz.) whole tomatoes, undrained, chpd
2 C. water
1 t. salt
1 C. dried black-eyed beans
1 or 2 t. chili powder
1 bay leaf
¾ t. fresh ground cumin
1 can (10½ oz.) beef broth
1 can (10 oz.) frozen cut okra
1 can (4 oz.) diced or chopped green chilies
½ t. gumbo file'

Sort, pick and rinse black-eyed beans. In a saucepan, combine beans, olive oil, water and ½ teaspoon salt, and bring to a boil. Reduce heat, cover, and simmer on low heat until the beans are tender, about 1½ to 2 hours. Add additional water if necessary to keep beans from becoming dried. Also, stir occasionally to keep the beans from sticking to saucepan during the long simmering time.

In a Dutch oven, brown the beef until it is done. Drain off excess fat drippings. Add the onions and garlic. Simmer until the onions look done, and mix in the tomatoes, bay leaf, chili powder, green chilies, cumin and the remaining ½ teaspoon of salt. Cover. Simmer for 15 to 20 minutes, then add the beans and okra.

In one (1) cup of the mixture, blend in the gumbo file'. Add gumbo file' to the Dutch oven, and simmer for just a few minutes. Stir constantly and serve immediately, as overcooking this soup becomes stringy from the Gumbo file'.

Gumbo file' is crushed wild sassafras. Can be found in gourmet shops.

Cheri & Joel Bobo
Cincinnati, OH

William S. Keeler
Reno, NV

POT O' CHILI SAUCE

This recipe was given to us by a former restaurateur, who said that he went through gallons of sauce daily over everything from rice to spaghetti. It's a good crowd pleaser.

5½ to 6 Lbs. beef sirloin, rough chili ground
6 Lg. onions, chopped
4 stalks celery, chopped fine, including leaves
15 or more, cloves of garlic, minced
2 bay leaves
Vegetable oil
⅛ t. ground cloves
1 T. oregano
1 T. ground cumin
1 t. salt
6 T. tomato paste
½ t. fresh black pepper
2 cans (28 oz.) whole tomatoes drained and chopped up
½ C. chili powder, or to taste
8 to 10 C. cooked or canned red kidney beans with juice

In a large Dutch oven, heat the oil and saute the beef until completely cooked, stirring to break up lumps into smaller pieces. Use the oil to sauce the onions until they are tender.

Add the onion to the meat, continuing to cook breaking up the meat further. Add the cumin, chili powder, oregano, garlic, cloves and celery. Stir the mixture and simmer for about 5 minutes. Add the salt and pepper, tomatoes and tomato paste. Cover, bring kettle to a boil, stirring as it bubbles. Reduce heat, and simmer, covered, for about a hour, stirring occasionally.

For a little different flavor, add a little beer if the chili is too thick and you like it thinner. Remove the bay leaf prior to ladling into serving bowls.

Heat the beans separately, and serve as a side dish is some do not like the beans and chili together. Have additional bowls of chopped onion, shredded cheese, chips and the like to pass around.

Frank & Helen Ruben
Cincinnati, OH

M

A.M. McMillian
Florida, 1888

DOWN HOME CHILI

1 Lb. lean ground beef
1 Med. onion, chopped
1 green pepper, chopped
1 stalk celery, chopped, with green leafs
3 C. cooked red kidney beans, or 2 cans (15 oz.) red kidney beans, drained
1 can (10½ oz.) beef broth
1 can (28 oz.) tomatoes, diced, undrained
1 can (12 oz.) V8 Tomato Juice
1 t. salt
1 to 2 T. chili powder
¼ t. cayenne pepper
2 cloves garlic, chopped

If beans are dried, prepare them by soaking overnight with sufficient water to cover, and from your previous experience with preparing beans, fix them prior to making your chili.

In a large skillet, or Dutch oven (I prefer a large pot over a skillet as the chances of splattering the range with chili is eliminated), brown meat till it is done. Pour or spoon off all unnecessary drippings. Move the cooked beef to one side of the pot, or remove completely before putting in and cooking the vegetables until they are tender. Leaving the meat in tends to overcook it.

Mix the beef with the vegetables, and combine tomatoes, V8 Juice, beef broth, cayenne pepper, salt and bring to a boil. Reduce the heat, cover, and simmer for just about 45 minutes, or until your taste buds tell you to either stop simmering or go a little longer. Spread some shredded cheese on top of chili before serving for a little color and added flavor.

Michael J. Ynclan
Cape Canaveral, FL

Bernard Galleano
Searchlight, NV

EATIN' CHILI con CARNE

2 T. fat
¾ C. chopped onion
1 or 2 cloves garlic
1 Lb. ground beef
1 T. flour
½ t. salt
⅛ t. pepper
2 T. chili powder
1 can No. 2 kidney beans
1 can No. 2 Van Camps tomatoes

Chop onion and garlic together. Cook in hot fat. Add meat and cook till done. Drain. Sprinkle with flour, salt and pepper. Then add beans and tomatoes. Simmer 2 to 3 hours.

Mabel & Jerome Kober
Great Bend, KS

University of Hawaii
Honolulu, HA

EASTERN CHILI and BEANS

2 Lbs. lean ground beef
1 Med. onion, chopped
1 Med. green pepper, chopped
2 cloves garlic, minced
1½ t. dry mustard
1 bay leaf
2 T. olive oil
Beer enough to either thin consistency or drink

2 t. ground cumin
⅛ t. crushed red pepper
1 T. salt
¼ t. oregano
5 T. chili powder
¼ t. fresh ground black pepper
1 can (6 oz.) tomato paste
2 cans (16 oz.) whole tomatoes
2 cans (16 oz.) dark red kidney beans, drained

In a large kettle or Dutch oven, heat the olive oil and saute the beef, breaking up using a wooden spoon as it cooks. Pour off all excess fat and discard. Add the onion, green pepper and garlic, and saute until they are done.

Add the remaining ingredients, except the beans, and mix thoroughly to blend the spices together. Bring the pot to a boil for 2 or 3 minutes. Reduce the heat, and simmer, covered, for about 1½ to 2 hours. Stir occasionally to keep chili from sticking to bottom and sides of pot.

This is the time to check your consistency, and add beer to thin if it is necessary. If not, open can and drink it so that it doesn't go to waste.

Ms. Anita Smith
Cincinnati, OH

Don Juan Antonio Valli
Texas (1852)

PLAIN'S CHILI con CARNE

1 can (15 oz.) Brown Beauty Mexican Style Beans
2 T. minced pimento
1 or 2 stalks celery
½ Lb. ground beef

1 T. minced onion
½ C. canned tomatoes
2 T. minced or green pepper
Salt and pepper to taste
2 t. chili powder

Fry beef, onion, pepper and celery until meat and vegetables are done. Drain off fat. Add beans, tomatoes and pimento. Cook until done.

Mabel & Jerome Kober
Great Bend, KS

Rocking H
James C. Herndon
Melbourne, FL

CHILI CORN PONE PIE

¾ Lb. ground turkey
1 small onion, chopped
1 C. whole kernel corn
1 C. canned tomatoes, cut up and drained
1 can (16 oz.) red kidney beans, drained
1 clove garlic, minced
½ t. ground cumin
1 t. chili powder
1 t. salt
1 can (8 oz.) tomato sauce
1 C. shredded Cheddar cheese
¼ t. ground oregano
1 T. vegetable oil
1 Pkg. cornbread mix

In a skillet, using the vegetable oil, saute the turkey meat until the gray has been cooked out. Pour off any water that may be drawn from the turkey. Add the onions and garlic, and saute till the onion is tender.

Prepare the cornbread mix as directed on package. Using two 9-inch pie pans which have been greased, use the fingers to press the cornbread mixture evenly into each of the pans. Pour half of the chili mixture into each pie pan.

Bake in a preheated oven of 350 degrees, for 30 minutes. After that time, sprinkle the shredded Cheddar cheese on each shell, and continue to bake an additional 5 minutes so that the cheese is partially melted.

Milt & Maxine Brant
Pompano Beach, FL

B.R. Weaver
Nome,
Jefferson County, TX

RANCHERS CHILI con CARNE

2 T. vegetable oil
½ C. chopped onion
½ clove garlic, minced
1 Lb. ground beef
2 cans (8 oz.) tomato sauce
2 C. cooked or can kidney beans
1 t. salt
2 t. chili powder

Cook beef, onion and garlic in vegetable oil. Drain off fat. Stir in undrained beans, and tomato sauce, and all other things. Simmer over low heat until chili is desired thickness, about 45 minutes. Makes 4 servings.

Mabel & Jerome Kober
Great Bend, KS

Arrow JD Joined
Joseph Walter
Christmas, FL

MEDICINE MAN CHILI

This recipe is from the Feb. 17, 1990 area Cookoff as appeared in the Daily Reporter-Herald, Loveland, Colorado. It was prepared by Hank Wedemeyer.

3 Lbs. beef (sirloin or round steak
3 t. garlic salt
1 can (8 oz.) tomato sauce
3 t. crushed garlic (6 cloves)
6 T. chili powder
2 T. cumin
1 good size onion

Note: Method of preparing this recipe were not in newspaper article. Only instructions were: "Brown beef. Chop onions, add along with other ingredients. Cook on low heat for about an hour. Add optional spices (such as oregano, basil, Tabasco) to taste."

"If you go to the cookoffs and taste the chili," said contestant Hank Wedemeyer, "you'll be surprised, because almost every one tastes a little different. Most cooks use sirloin, chuck or top round steak in their chili. The experts said that the meat should be cooked so that it is tender, but not overdone."

"You want it tender enough to crush between the roof of your mouth and your tongue without chewing", explained Bill Spooner, one of the Loveland competitors at the Cookoff.

Leila Dunham
Loveland, CO

Jerry Sans
Hollister, CA

FASTEST CHILI GOIN'

This chili can be put together pretty fast, and the ingredients are easy to use.

1 Lb. ground beef
2 T. olive oil, or any standard cooking oil
2 t. chili powder, or plus minus to suit your taste
1 can (16 oz.) whole tomatoes, chopped up with juice
½ t. salt
2 cloves garlic, minced
2 C. or
1 can (16 oz.) pinto beans, or red kidney beans

In a skillet, heat oil and brown the meat over a medium heat. Break up the meat with a fork while it is cooking to get rid of the large pieces. Mix in all of the remaining ingredients, put hold out the beans to later.

Cover, and simmer for 30 minutes. Add the beans and continue simmering for 10 more minutes or so, stirring occasionally.

Since onions are not used in the cooking of this chili, we generally have a bowl of raw chopped onions and some shredded cheese on the table for those who like some of each sprinkled on top of their servings.

Barbara Basso Scott
Cocoa, FL

"Three Christian Crosses" reportedly used by Cortez during the 1500's, Mexico.

HELEN'S CHILI

In large Dutch oven:

- 1 Spanish onion (size of grapefruit) cut up very fine
- 1 green pepper, cut fine
- 2 Lbs. ground round steak

Cook on very low heat with lid on until meat is done.

Add:

- 1 Lg. can peeled tomatoes, cut up
- 1 small can tomato paste

Still on very low burner: Add:

- 1 heaping T. chili powder
- 1 t. coarsely ground black pepper
- 1 scat t. salt
- 1 t. sugar (to cut the acid)
- ¼ t. cumin
- ¼ t. oregano
- ½ t. cayenne pepper
- ⅓ C. brandy or burgandy wine
- 1 can Brooks Spicy Beans, undrained
- 2 C. kidney beans, drained

Stir well and carefully, and simmer (very low) one hour covered. Cool in refrigerator overnight and reheat (low).

Helen Cedervall
Deerfield, IL

Tenn Tex Cattle Co.
Leslie & Ronald Cope
Springfield, TN

CHILI CHEESE DIP

½ Lb. very lean ground beef
1 small onion, chopped fine
1 t. salt + or - to taste
1 C. Pace Picante Salsa, medium flavored (HOT if you like it hot!)
2 cans (15 oz.) kidney or pinto beans, drained of liquid
1 Lb. American process cheese

In a saucepan, brown the beef with the onion until the beef is done and the onion is tender. Drain off excess liquid from pan. In a double boiler, melt the cheese, stirring occasionally.

Add the salsa, salt and beans to the meat, mixing well to blend. Cover, heat saucepan until the mixture is bubbling. Stir the mixture into the melted cheese. Serve this dip warm.

Steve Kyler
Cincinnati, OH

Maria H. Hustace
Kaluaaha Ranch
Molokai, HA

PARTY CHILI

10 Lbs. ground beef
3 Lg. yellow onions, chopped
4 Med. green peppers, chopped
3 Oz. mild chili powder, plus to taste
3½ Oz. granulated garlic
3 bay leaves
2-3 Oz. black pepper
3 Oz. salt plus to taste
1 Oz. cayenne pepper
3 cans (16 oz.) dark red kidney beans
1 can (16 oz.) tomato sauce
1 can (16 oz.) tomatoes, crushed

In a large heavy pot, cook meat and add all the ingredients, except the crushed tomatoes, tomato sauce, and beans. Simmer for 15 minutes and then add the reserved ingredients. Add 1½ cans of water. Simmer, uncovered, for 2 to 2½ hours or until you feel it is ready to serve.

Remember to stir occasionally and taste for an evenly cooked pot of terrific chili.

Serve in bowls with cornbread sticks brushed with garlic butter.

David Jamieson
Port St. John, FL

Bob Laughrin
Brawley, CA

EASY COACHES CHILI

This recipe is my own, and as school superintendent, I sent it to 90-100 coaches and their wives each February as a show and Appreciation for their year-long efforts. It is extremely well received - possibly because for its rather unique ingredients - chocolate, cinnamon and pork.

3 Lg. coarsely chopped yellow onions
3 C. coarsely chopped celery
2 C. coarsely chopped green pepper
2 Lbs. hamburger
2 Lbs. pork sausage
⅔ C. chili powder
4 T. cumin
4 T. oregano
3 T. unsweetened cocoa
2 T. cinnamon
2 T. Louisiana Red Hot
1 can (8 oz.) beef broth
1 can (32 oz.) tomatoes
1 can (16 oz.) tomato juice
6-8 thin sliced garlic cloves
2 cans (16 oz.) red kidney

Mix and cook hamburger and sausage in large skillet. Saute peppers and onions in separate pans. Drain off all juices. Mix meat and onions in 12 quart pot.

Add remaining ingredients except celery and kidney beans.

Simmer, uncovered for 1 hour. Stir occasionally.

Add chopped celery and simmer for an additional ½ hour.

Add kidney beans and simmer for an additional 15 minutes.

Serve hot with oyster crackers, grated Cheddar cheese, and coarsely chopped onions. This recipe should serve about 15.

Milton R. Herzog
Deerfield, IL

Thomas P. King
Hillmar, CA

POLLY BERGEN'S CHILI #2

This is the only duplicate recipe that has been sent in by name. The other contributor was Ms. Joseph McWilliams of nearby Cocoa Beach, Florida.

Ms. Nell Johnson
16200 Raines Road
Little Rock, Ark
72210

Orlando Trout Creek Ranch
Saratoga, CA

CHILI SOUP

1 Lb. ground beef
1 Med. yellow onion chopped
1 T. chili powder
1 can (16 oz.) dark red
kidney beans, undrained
2 cloves garlic, chopped
1 can (16 oz.) tomatoes, crushed
2 Qt. water
1 C. yellow kernel corn
1 C. green pepper, chopped
1 C. elbow macaroni, cooked

In a large soup pot or kettle, brown the beef, crumbling up very good to get rid of large pieces. Pour, or spoon off as much of the drippings as possible. Saute onion, green pepper and garlic with the meat, until they are tender and softened.

Add the two quarts of water, chili powder, crushed tomatoes with its's liquid, kernel corn and macaroni. Let the pot come to a boil, then lower heat, and simmer for 30 minutes. This chili soup should be thick and not too runny.

We use frozen corn as well as frozen chopped onions at times. There's no real difference in taste than canned corn or fresh onion.

Ron Daniel
Cocoa Beach, FL

Rocking D Ranch, Inc
Cambridge, OH

CASTLE CHILI Con CARNE

1 Lb. dried kidney beans
1½ Qt. boiling water
1 t. salt
1 bay leaf
½ C. onion, chopped
1 clove garlic, minced
2 T. salad oil
1 Lb. lean ground beef
1½ C. tomatoes, stewed
2 T. yeast flakes
1 t. salt
1 t. brown sugar
2-6 t. chili powder
1 Lg. onion, finely chopped
½ small head lettuce, shredded
1 C. pitted black olives

In the boiling water, drop washed kidney beans, not fast enough to disturb the boil. Stir in one teaspoon of salt and add the bay leaf. Reduce heat to a low boil, and cook until the skins of the beans crack when blown onto; about 1½ to 2 hours. Drain, saving the water.

In a large skillet, saute the onion and garlic using the salad oil, for about 2 to 3 minutes. Add the ground beef and brown, breaking up the meat with a fork as it cooks. Drain off fat, if any from beef. Add the tomatoes and one cup of bean cooking liquid, and blend in the yeast flakes, 2nd teaspoon of salt, brown sugar, and chili powder. Simmer for 20 minutes longer. Add the kidney beans and stir to mix well.

If the chili mixture is tool thick, add more of the water from boiling the beans.

Simmer for 30 minutes longer. This chili can be served immediately, or made ahead for reheating later on. The flavor of this chili intensifies on being allowed to stand.

If you reheat, add a little more of the yeast flakes to compensate for vitamin loss. Serve in bowls garnished with chopped black olives, chopped onion, and shredded lettuce.

Trudi Gilson
The Scent Castle
Merritt Island, FL

Kelvin L. Ferguson
Fergie's Ranch
Maui, HA

HOT CHILI

1 Med. yellow onion, chopped
1½ Lbs. lean ground beef
2 cloves garlic, crushed
2 t. chili powder
1 t. salt
2 cans (16 oz.) red kidney beans
1 hot cherry pepper, chopped, or
½ t. cayenne pepper
½ t. white pepper
½ t. coarse ground black pepper

In a heavy 3-quart pot over a medium heat, cook the beef until the red color is gone. Add the onions, garlic, chili powder, cherry pepper or the subs: cayenne pepper, white pepper, black pepper, and cook uncovered, for 8 to 10 minutes, or until the onion is soft and the meat has browned.

Stir frequently. Add tomatoes and two cans of water, bring pot to the boiling point. Cook, uncovered, stirring for 5 minutes. Add beans, cover, reduce heat and simmer for 45 minutes, stirring occasionally. Cook until the mixture becomes stiff or to the consistency desired. If thinning is needed, use some tomato juice instead of more water.

Serve in bowls and topped with sour cream and chopped green spring onions.

Jean I. Jamieson
Merritt Island, FL

John Kreuger
Myrtle Point, OR

CHILI con ELOTE

3 T. vegetable oil
1 onion, chopped
1 clove garlic, chopped
1 green pepper, diced
2 C. vegetable stock
1 C. tomatoes, chopped, or
2 T. tomato paste
1 C. fresh corn
4 C. cooked kidney or pinto beans
½ t. chili powder
¼ t. cumin
1½ t. salt
1 t. oregano

Saute onion and garlic in the vegetable oil, until the onions is soft. Add the green pepper and saute for another 2 or 3 minutes. Add the fresh kernel corn, vegetable stock and tomatoes. Stir to completely blend the mixture.

Mash 2 cups of kidney or pinto beans, and add to the mixture, along with the remaining whole beans, and seasonings. Simmer for 30 minutes. If the chili is too thin, remove the cover, and simmer an additional 10 minutes, or until the consistency is as desired. Makes about 6 servings.

Trudi Gilson
Merritt Island, FL

Last Box Ranch
James B. McReynolds
Pikeville, TN

CASTLE CHILI

4 T. olive oil
½ C. onion, sliced
2 cloves garlic, minced
3 Lbs. lean ground beef
2 cans (8 oz.) tomato sauce
2 t. chili powder
1 t. cumin
1 t. or less, salt

In a large skillet or Dutch oven, saute the onion in olive oil, until softened. Add garlic and saute until lightly browned. Push onion and garlic to one side of the skillet or pot.

Add beef in onc piece, and as it browns, slowly break it up with a wooden spoon. When beef is slightly browned, add tomato sauce, chili powder, cumin and salt. Simmer for 15 minutes.

Serve with garnishes such as chopped onion, shredded Cheddar cheese, chopped black olives and or sour cream.

Trudi Gilson
Merritt Island, FL

Andrew G. Tucker, Jr.
Brevard County, FL

CHILI STEW

1½ C. potatoes, diced
1 C. pinto beans, cooked
½ Med. onion, chopped
2 small fresh tomatoes, cut up
1 t. chili powder
1 T. vegetable powder
¼ C. bean thickened gravy

Combine all ingredients with 1½ cups of water, bringing to a boil and simmer for 45 minutes. Flavor improves with reheating. Makes about 1 quart.

Ms. Lisa Wolgamot
Cincinnati, OH

Lake Shore Longhorns
Nicholas D. Penna
Holley, NY

DIETER'S CHILI con CARNE

1 C. dried red kidney or pinto beans
½ Lb. leanest ground beef
1 Lg. onion, sliced
1 green pepper, coarsely chopped
1 can (15 oz.) whole tomatoes, cut up with liquid
2 t. chili powder
1 bay leaf
¼ t. cumin
½ t. oregano

Rinse beans. Bring to a boil in about 4 cups of water, and let simmer for about 3 minutes, and set aside for one hour. Then cook until tender about 2 or 3 hours. Drain beans, saving the liquid. Brown the meat in a large skillet. Drain off all fat.

Add remaining ingredients to the meat, stirring occasionally. Let cook on a high heat until it begins to boil. Reduce heat; add drained beans to mixture, cover and simmer on low for 1 to 1½ hours, stirring occasionally.

Add beans cooking liquid to chili if the mixture becomes too thick. If too thin, uncover, and allow to simmer until consistency is reached. Remove the bay leaf before serving. Makes 4 to 6 servings.

Chet & Jayne Wolgamot
Cincinnati, OH

D. M. Martin
Gila Bend, AZ

PALM BAY CHILI SOUP

½ Lb. lean ground beef
1 Med. onion, chopped
1 clove garlic, minced
1 can (16 oz.) pinto or kidney beans
1 can (16 oz.) tomatoes, cut up, undrained
2 C. water
2 t. chili powder
½ t. salt
¼ t. cumin
⅛ t. black pepper
1 bay leaf

In a 4-quart saucepan, over medium-high heat, brown the beef, and with using a wooden spoon, break up the meat as it is done so that the large pieces are reduced to spoon size chunks. Add the chopped onion, green pepper and garlic, and sauteing the vegetables. Drain off all excess fat and discard.

Stir in all of the remaining ingredients, and bring to e saucepan to a boil. Then reduce the heat to low. Cover, and simmer for about 15 to 20 minutes, or until the flavor is what is desired.

To thin the mixture prior to serving, use tomato juice if necessary, but allow soup to mellow for 10 minutes cooking before serving.

Carrie Hatfield
Cincinnati, OH

Tom Graves
Clark, SD

AGIES MICROWAVE CHILI

I made this recipe to our taste and tolerance. Friends that tasted it, like it, but said that is not chili without chili powder and pepper. This though agrees with us and is tasty.

1 Lb ground chuck
2 t. onion flakes
1 can (16 oz.) pork and beans
1 can (10½ oz.) tomato soup
⅓ t. salt
⅓ t. oregano
½ t. sugar
1 C. water

In a microwave-proof dish, cook chuck with 1 teaspoon of onion flakes, covered, until it is done, stopping during the cooking to mash meat into pieces with a fork and to separate for easier cooking. When no longer pink, it is cooked completely, drain fat and discard.

Add the pork and beans, tomato soup, water, salt, oregano, sugar and remaining ½ teaspoon of onion flakes. Cover, and cook for 4 minutes; stir, and continue cooking, covered, for 4 more minutes. Cook only until the chili is bubbling well.

Chili powder and pepper may be added if desired.

This recipe may be made with macaroni if you like it instead of the pork and beans. Seasonings may be altered if desired.

Mrs. Agnes Gieseking
Troy, IL

Moses & Deanna Makuakane
Honolulu, HA

TEXAS GROGGIN' CHILI

3 Lbs. good ground beef
2 buds garlic
6 T. chili powder
1 t. cumin seeds
1 huge onion, chopped
4 beef bouillon cubes
1 small can ranch style beans, optional
1 small can tomato paste
1 Lg. can tomato juice or V-8 Juice, (to make soupy)
Pepper to taste

Saute the beef and chopped onion. Add the chili powder, cumin seeds and stir to break up and crumble meat as it browns. Saute for a few minutes. Do not burn.

Add the tomato paste and mix in well, then add tomato juice (or V-8) and make soupy. Next, add beans and bouillon cubes. Simmer for several hours, stirring occasionally.

Heat should be low enough so the mixture bubbles now and then. Serve with rice scoop on top, and side dish of crushed jalapeno or red pepper for tang. The longer you cook it, the better is gets.

Serves 10 normal chili heads, or 6 Texans.

Madonna Frain
DeBuque, IA

WH
Corinne M. Hancock
Dade City, FL

TENNESSEE PRIDE CHILI #1

This is an identical recipe as submitted by Ms. E. L. Stewart of Gatlinburg, TN

1 Lb. Tennessee Pride Country Sausage
1 Lb. ground beef
1 Med. onion, chopped
1 clove garlic, minced
1 Med. green pepper, chopped
1 can (28 oz.) whole tomatoes, peeled, undrained
2 cans (16 oz.) red kidney beans
1 T. chili powder
2 t. ground cumin
½ t. salt
½ t. cayenne pepper
1 C. water

Saute sausage and ground beef, onion, green pepper and garlic in a large pot or Dutch oven until browned and crumbled to small chunks. Drain off excess fat.

Stir in remaining ingredients. Break up tomatoes with the back of a wooden spoon. Cover, and simmer 1 to 1½ hours. Additional water may be needed to get consistency you want. Yields 8 servings.

Lynnette Cholewa
Cocoa, FL

Jim Coley
Castalian Spgs, TN

DALLAS CHILI

1 Lb. ground beef
1 Pkg. (1¾ oz.) French's Chili-O Seasoning Mix
½ C. water
1 can (16 oz.) whole tomatoes, cut-up
1 can (16 oz.) kidney beans, drained, optional
1 T. Durkee Red Hot Cayenne Pepper Sauce, or more to taste

In a Dutch oven, brown ground beef; drain. Stir in French's Chili-O Seasoning Mix, water, tomatoes, beans and Durkee Red Hot Sauce. Bring to a boil; reduce heat and simmer, covered for 10 minutes. Garnish with chopped red pepper and green onion, if desired.

Susan L. Skelton
Hamilton, OH

F T X
Lawrence Lasater
San Angelo, TX

JACK'S CHILI

1 Lg. red onion, chopped
4 whole jalapeno peppers
1 green pepper, chopped
1 red bell pepper, chopped
2 cloves garlic, chopped
2 Qt. plus 1 pint, tomatoes
1 can (12 oz.) cocktail vegetable juice
¾ C. red wine
4 Lbs. ground round or chuck steak
2 cans (14½ oz.) dark red kidney beans
⅛ t. white pepper
3 T. sugar
6 T. vinegar
1 T. olive oil
½ T. hot pepper sauce
¼ t. chili powder
¼ t. celery salt
¼ t. oregano
¼ t. accent
¼ t. salt
⅛ t. cayenne pepper
⅛ t. garlic powder
⅛ t. onion salt
⅛ t. ground cumin

Mix all ingredients except beef and kidney beans, in a large pot; Cover, on medium heat. Meanwhile, brown meat in larger skillet and drain off fat.

Cook tomato mixture 1½ hours before you add the browned and drained meat. Cook 30 minutes then add drained kidney beans.

Now put the lid on and cook on low for several hours.

Freezes well. Almost better the next time. Serves 8-10 adults.

Madonna Frain
DuBuque, IA

Rocking R Ranch
Texas (1870)

CHILI

1 Lb. ground beef
½ C. chopped onion
½ C. chopped celery
1 can (46 oz.) Stokely's Finest* Tomato Juice
1 can (15½ oz.) VAN CAMP'S* Mexican Style Chili Beans
⅓ C. uncooked macaroni
1 t. chili powder

In a large saucepan, brown first 3 ingredients; drain excess fat. Stir in remaining ingredients and simmer 30 minutes, stirring occasionally. Makes 6 servings.

STOKELY'S mag ad

Walter G. Carlos
Oahu, HA

TURKEY CHILI

1 Lg. onion, chopped
2 cloves garlic, minced
¼ C. butter
1 can (14½ oz.) whole tomatoes, undrained, cut-up
2 C. turkey or chicken broth
1 can (4 oz.) green chilies, chopped
1 t. cumin powder
½ t. thyme
½ t. oregano
½ t. salt
2 C. cubed turkey
1 C. kernel corn
1 can (6 oz.) tomato paste

In a large sauce pan, saute the onion and garlic in butter until tender. Stir in tomatoes with liquid, tomato paste, broth, chilies, chili powder, cumin, thyme, oregano and salt. Cover, and simmer 10 to 15 minutes.

Ms. Nita Crosswhite
Cincinnati, OH

Gary W. Taylor
Igo, CA

VEGETARIAN CHILI

3½ Lbs. assorted hot chilies
3 green peppers, diced
2 red peppers, diced
2 yellow peppers, diced
4 Lbs. black turtle beans*
3 Lg. onions, diced
5 cans (32 oz.) tomatoes
5 cans (16 oz.) tomato sauce
5 cans (6 oz.) tomato paste
1 clove garlic, diced
2 T. rosemary
2 T. thyme
2 T. marjoram
2 T. cayenne pepper
2 T. hot sauce
1 T. cumin
6 T. chili powder
¼ C. olive oil
1 t. salt

Dice all onions, (chunky), and garlic. In large pot add: 1 cup of water, all cans of tomatoes and juices, drained black turtle beans*. To this add the peppers and heat on medium-high for 20 minutes.

While stirring, add spices and olive oil.

Turn on low-medium heat for 8 hours, stirring frequently!

*Soak beans over night, then boil for one hour, drain, then add to chili. Makes approximately 6 quarts.

Madonna Frain
DuBuque, IA

Gurrentz Int'l Corp.
Pittsburgh, PA

MAGGIE'S CHILI

2 Lbs. pork sausage
1-2 Lg. onions (3 cups), chopped
2 green peppers, chopped
2-3 cloves garlic, minced
1-2 stalks celery, chopped
1 can (6 oz.) beef broth
2 C. tomato puree
1½ T. chili powder
1¼ t. cumin
⅜ t. cayenne pepper
⅜ t. basil
¾ t. oregano
1 can (16 oz.) kidney beans, undrained

Saute sausage until well done. Remove using a slotted spoon to drain as much rendered grease as possible, and set aside. Saute the onion, pepper, garlic and celery. When tender, add the beef broth, and cook until completely softened.

Add sausage and remaining ingredients. Simmer over a low heat, stirring occasionally for ½ hour. Serves 12-15.

Ms. Barb Flannery
Hamilton, OH

J. H. Pinson, 1900
McLennan County, TX

TURKEY CHILI

1 Lb. ground turkey breast
1 Med. green pepper, chopped
1 Med. onion, chopped
1 can (16 oz.) kidney beans, or chili beans
1 can (28 oz.) tomatoes
1 Pkg. commercial Chili Mix

In a large sauce pan sprayed with Pan, brown the turkey on medium-high heat, breaking it up as it cooks.

Add green pepper and onion. Reduce heat and cover. Cook over medium heat until peppers are tender. Transfer to chili pot.

Add the beans, tomatoes, and Chili Mix.

Add water for desired thickness. Simmer for at least 10 minutes.

Serving Suggestion: As with any spicy mixture, let the chili sit overnight in the refrigerator to allow blending of the flavors.

George Bailey
Satellite Beach, FL

William Head
Florida 1878

BLACK RIVER CHILI

¼ Lb. finely chopped suet
6 Lbs. lean beef cubed, (stew size)
10 T. chili powder
2 T. ground cumin
2 T. ground oregano
1 T. salt
1 T. cayenne pepper
4 cloves garlic, minced
2 Qt. beef stock or canned beef stock
½ C. Masa harina/cornmeal
½ C. water or beer
1-2 cans pinto or red kidney beans (optional)

Fry suet in a cast iron chili kettle until crisp. Add the beef, one pound at a time, and cook until browned. Remove each pound of cooked beef as it is browned. When all meat is cooked, return it to the kettle, and add all seasonings including the beef broth, but do not put Masa Harina/- cornmeal into same kettle.

Combine Masa harina/cornmeal with cold water or beer, and stir thoroughly into chili. Simmer 30 minutes. Add beans, and simmer for 20-30 more minutes.

Serve with grated Cheddar cheese and chopped onion.

Dr. Gary Petersen
Black River Falls, WI

Craig & Judy Tolman
Palermo, CA

MICRO-CHILI BEANS

1 C. pinto or kidney beans, washed
1 t. olive or salad oil
1 Med. onion, chopped (½ C.)
1 clove garlic, minced
2 t. chili powder
½ t. salt
2½ C. beef or chicken broth, or water
½ green pepper, chopped
1 Med. tomato, peeled, coarsely chopped
1 t. cumin

Soak beans conventionally in 2 cups of water for 4 or more hours or soak by microwave method: Place 1 cup washed, drained beans and 2 cups of water in 5-quart casserole with tight-fitting lid. Microwave on High for 15 minutes; remove from oven, let stand 5 minutes, covered. Add 2 cups of hot water, recover and let stand 1 hour.

In 2-quart microwave-safe casserole, stir together oil, onion, garlic, chili powder and cumin. Microwave, uncovered, on High for 2 minutes. Drain and soaked beans and add to casserole with broth. Cover and microwave on High 45 minutes, stirring after 20 minutes.

Stir in green peppers, tomato and salt, replace cover and microwave on High for 5 minutes. Let stand, covered, 10 minutes. Serve hot over cooked rice, or chilled on shredded lettuce, one or more - tortilla chips, ripe olives, avocado cubes, sour cream, or low-fat yogurt, grated Cheddar or Jack cheese.

Makes 2 entree servings, each with 435 calories, 17 percent of calories in fat. Hands on and microwave times: 1 hour, not including presoaking time.

The following recipes are to be kept with #641 for ingredients...... or turn above into:

Chili Bean Soup: For 1 serving, puree half of the Chili Beans in blender with 1 cup of liquid (beef or chicken broth, tomato juice or water). Heat to serving temperature and top, if desired, with any of the garnishes suggested for Chili Beans.

Stove-Top Chili Beans: Pre-soak beans 4 or more hours. Drain and, in a 2-quart saucepan, combine with all ingredients listed except tomato and salt. Bring to a simmer on stove top and cook on lowest heat setting for 30 minutes. Add tomato and salt, continue to cook 30 minutes longer or until beans are tender.

St. Petersburg Times (FL)

St. Laurent Land & Cattle Co.
Eagle Point, OR

CHILI MEAT LOAF

1 can (15 oz.) NALLEY'S* Chili with Beans
2 eggs, separated
1 Med. onion, minced
½ C. diced green pepper
1 teaspoon salt
2 Lbs. lean ground beef

Pour Chili into large mixing bowl. Stir in the eggs. Add onion, pepper, salt, and meat broken into pieces. Tip bowl and cut through mixture until blended. (Tender mixing makes tender meat loaf).

Shape into loaf. Turn out on greased shallow pan; smooth into shape. Bake in 400 degree oven for 1 hour. Makes 6 servings.

NALLEY'S Foods

Patty K. Shuster
Cincinnati, OH

SAUSAGE CHILI

2 Lbs. BOB EVANS FARMS Roll Sausage (Original Recipe or Zesty Hot)
1 Lb. or 14 oz. can red kidney beans
1½ C. tomato puree
1 can (12 oz.) tomato paste
1 t. chili powder
1 t. salt
2 T. sugar
2 Med. onions, diced
3 C. water

Crumble BOB EVANS FARMS* Sausage in a skillet, cook until tender and lightly browned. Add remaining ingredients to a large Dutch oven and bring to a full boil. To enhance the flavor, let cook. Refrigerate overnight; reheat the next day. This chili will keep refrigerated for several days or if may be frozen. Yield 14 8-ounce servings.

BOB EVANS counter recipe

David Bale
New Underwood, SD

REAL TEXAS CHILI

½ Lb. chorizo
½ Lb. ground beef
1½ C. chopped onion
2 cloves garlic, minced
1 can (15 oz.) HUNT'S Tomato Sauce with Tomato Bits
½ t. salt
1 can (15 oz.) small red beans undrained
1 can (8 oz.) refried beans
3 to 4 T. chili powder
1 t. ground cumin
1 t. oregano

In a 3-quart saucepan, cook chorizo, beef, 1 cup onion and garlic until onion is soft; spoon off excess fat. Add HUNT'S Sauce, red beans, refried beans and seasonings; mix thoroughly.

Cover, simmer 10 minutes; stir once or twice. To serve, spoon chili into individual serving bowls and top with an equal amount of remaining chopped onion. Makes 5 1-cup servings.

HUNT'S label recipe

Richard Call
Willcox, AZ

CHILI SKILLET SUPPER

8 Ozs. (about 2 C.) SAN GIORGIO Short Cut Elbow Macaroni, uncooked
1 clove garlic, minced
¼ C. chopped green pepper
½ C. chopped onion
1 Lb. ground beef
1 can (28 oz.) tomatoes, cut up
1 jar (21 oz.) Italian cooking sauce
2 t. salt
2 t. chili powder
⅛ t. pepper

In a large saucepan add garlic, green peppers, onion and ground beef. Brown lightly. Drain off fat. Add tomatoes, Italian cooking sauce and seasonings, mixing well.

Bring to boiling. Gradually stir in macaroni. Reduce heat and simmer stirring occasionally, about 20 minutes or until macaroni reaches desired tenderness. Makes about 4 to 6 servings.

San Giorgio recipe

Albert J. Suncelia
Phoenix, AZ

ONE DISH RONI-MAC* CHILI

1 Lb. ground beef
½ C. chopped onion
1 can (28 oz.) tomatoes, undrained
1 can (15 oz.) kidney beans, undrained and cut up
1 C. water
1 can (6 oz.) tomato paste
1½ C. AMERICAN BEAUTY RONI-MAC
1 T. chili powder
1 t. salt
½ t. oregano

In a Dutch oven, brown ground beef with the onion; drain off fat. Add the remaining ingredients. Stirring frequently, bring to a boil over high heat. Cover and cook over a low heat, stirring occasionally, for 25 to 30 minutes or until RONI-MAC* is tender. Makes 8 servings.

RONI-MAC label recipe

L Bar F
David R. Speer
Mims, FL

IMPERIAL CHILI

2 Lbs. coarse ground chili meat
½ C. water (or beer)
1 can (8 oz.) tomato sauce
2 small onions, chopped
1 Med. green pepper, finely chopped
5-6 cloves garlic, minced
1 t. oregano
1 t. ground cumin
4 T. chili powder
1 t. salt
½ t. IMPERIAL Granulated Sugar
cayenne pepper (to taste)
4-5 jalapeno peppers, chopped

In a large skillet, braise meat in ¼ cup of oil until brown. Transfer meat to large kettle, Dutch oven or electric slow-cooker, leaving liquid in skillet.

Add water and tomato sauce to meat, cook over low heat. Saute onion, green pepper and garlic in skillet. Add remaining dry ingredients and chopped jalapeno peppers with seeds removed.

Simmer for about 30 minutes then transfer to kettle. Simmer for about 2 hours. Dip off grease that rises to top. (Cayenne and jalapeno peppers are the "zinger" in this recipe. Add both with caution). Serves 8.

IMPERIAL Product recipe

)-S

Big Island Meat
Honolulu, HA

TEXAS-STYLE CHILI

3 Lbs. beef (stew beef, round steak, etc.)
2 garlic buds, quartered
2 fresh tomatoes, chopped
1 can (8 oz.) S&W Tomato Sauce
1 T. oregano
1 t. salt
1 t. cumin
1½ t. powdered cayenne pepper
5 T. chili powder
2 cans (15¼ oz.) or
1 can (27 oz.) S&W Dark Red Kidney Beans, undrained
3 T. yellow corn meal

Cut meat into bite size pieces, about ¼-inch in diameter, trim fat-suet and save. Render suet in a 3 or 4-quart pan. Add the garlic and cook until brown. Discard excess suet pieces and garlic.

Add the meat in the fat and cook until all liquid has evaporated. Add the remaining ingredients except the corn meal and the kidney beans. Simmer at least 1½ hours adding water if necessary to keep from burning.

At the end of this time, adjust seasonings to taste. Add water to the corn meal (consistency of pancake batter), and stir into the chili. Stir in the beans, including liquid, simmer 30 minutes longer. Makes about 2 quarts.

S&W magazine recipe

Rocker G Livestock
Kailua, HA

CHILI con TURKEY

½ Lb. ground LOUIS RICH Turkey
2 peeled, chopped onions
1 seeded, chopped green bell pepper
1 minced clove garlic
1 can (16 oz.) tomatoes
3 C. canned, drained kidney beans
2 t. chili powder (or more to taste)
1 t. cumin seeds, (optional)
Salt to taste

Brown LOUIS RICH Turkey lightly in a non-stick skillet with no fat added. Stir in all remaining ingredients. Cover and simmer for 25 minutes. Uncover and continue cooking until thickened. Makes 6 servings. About 210 calories per serving.

Louis Rich Company
magazine recipe

"Ox-Yoke T" was the brand on the first herd of Texas cattle to be trailed to Montana. This was accomplished in 1866 by Nelson Story who recorded this brand in Montana on January 21, 1880.

CHILI MEAT ROLL

2 Lbs. ground chuck
½ C. fine dry bread crumbs
2 eggs
1 C. finely minced onion
1 can (15 oz.) NALLEY'S Big Chunk Chili
1 C. crushed NALLEY'S Corn Chips

Preheat oven to 350 degrees. Combine ground chuck, bread crumbs, eggs, and onion; mix well. On waxed paper, pat meat mixture to 8x14 inch rectangle. Spread NALLEY'S* Chili and Corn Chips. Roll up meat jelly-roll fashion. Place in shallow baking dish. Bake 1 hour; drain off excess fat. Bake 15 minutes more, or until done. Makes 6 to 8 servings.

NALLEY'S magazine recipe

Lazy Seventy Six
Dick Chauncey
Lockwood, NY

GREEN CHILI STEAKS

½ Lb. lean ground beef
½ t. LAWRY'S Seasoned Salt
¼ t. LAWRY'Y Seasoned Pepper
Dash LAWRY'S Garlic Powder with Parsley
1 fresh green chile, seeded and minced
3 T. chopped green onion

In a medium bowl, thoroughly combine all ingredients. Form into 2 oval steak patties or 4 hamburger patties. Cook in skillet, broiler or on barbecue until done. Makes 2 steak patties or 4 hamburger patties.

LAWRY'S store recipe

James H.Creasy
Westmoreland, TN

CHILI BEANS

1 T. butter or margarine
1 t. chopped onion
1 t. chili powder
½ Lb. frankfurts, cut into 1" pieces
1 can (28 oz.) B&M Brick Oven Baked Beans

In a skillet, melt butter or margarine and add onions, chili powder, and frankfurts. Saute frankfurts until lightly browned. In a 2-quart casserole, combine frankfurts and beans; bake at 350 degrees for 30 minutes.
Makes 4 servings.

B&M mfg's. coupon

David R. Mann
Sherve, OH

CAMPY'S TWO-BY-TWO CHILI

Here is one which I use at home in Bishop--C. Shelb's does a creditable job when we're out exploring in the desert. Recipe from Campy's great memory... all you have to do is remember "2".

2 Lbs. boneless lean beef, chili-ground or chucked
2 T. oil
2 Lg. tomatoes, chopped, or
2 #2 cans of whole toms
2 Lg. onions, chopped
2 cans (4 oz.) diced green chilies
2 T. strong prepared chili powder
2 t. dried leaf oregano
2 t. salt
2 t. ground cumin
2 t. hot pepper sauce
2 cloves garlic, crushed
2 cans (16 oz.) pinto or kidney beans, drained

In a two-quart pot over high heat, brown half of the beef in half of the oil; push to side of pot, repeat with the other half of the meat and oil. Add ingredients up to but not including the garlic, stirring as you go, and add water if the mixture is already too thick. Cook two hours. Near the end of the cooking time add the garlic and the beans, or leave the beans out altogether.

"Campy" Camphausen
Bishop, CA

W. Hawkins
Florida 1849

CHILI PIE CASSEROLE

3 C. FRITOS* Brand Corn Chips
1 Lg. onion, chopped
1 can (19 oz.) chili
1 C. grated American cheese

Spread 2 cups of FRITOS* Brand Corn Chips in a baking dish. Arrange chopped onion and half of the cheese on the FRITOS* Brand Corn Chips. Pour chili over onion and cheese. Top with the remaining Corn Chips and cheese. Bake at 350 degrees for 15 to 20 minutes until hot and bubbly. Makes 4 to 6 servings.

FRITOS package recipe

Rafter TK
Tim Kelly
Okeechobee, FL

HOT CHILI-CHEESE DIP

1 can (15 oz.) ARMOUR Star Chili without Beans
1 can (4 oz.) chopped green chilies
1 Lb. process American cheese, shredded
1 T. Worcestershire sauce
Corn chips

Combine all ingredients, except chips; heat, stirring occasionally, over low heat until cheese melts. Serve as a dip with corn chips.

Microwave instructions: Combine all ingredients, except chips, in a 1½ to 2-quart microwave-save casserole. Cook, covered, 6 minutes, stirring occasionally. Serve as a dip with corn chips.

ARMOUR'S magazine recipe

John F. McGonigle, MD
Santa Monica, CA

CHILI STUFFING

1 can (15 oz.) NALLEYS Big Chunk Chili
4 C. croutons
¾ C. chopped celery
¾ C. chopped onion

Combine all ingredients and mix well. (A good rule for poultry is 1 cup stuffing per pound.) Leftover Chili Stuffing can be baked in a greased casserole. Makes about 6 cups stuffing.

NALLEY'S magazine recipe

Bill Harnetty, D.V.M.
Athens, OH

WOLF BRAND CHILI CREPE

4 crepes
8 Oz. shredded lettuce
1 small diced tomato
1 can (16 oz.) WOLF Brand Chili
¾ C. grated cheddar cheese
¼ C. sour cream
¼ C. chopped green onions

Have crepes ready. Heat chili. Place ¼ cup plus 1 tablespoon chili in center of each crepe. Top with shredded lettuce and diced tomatoes. Sprinkle grated cheese on filling and fold sides of crepe over center of enclosure. Top crepe with one tablespoon sour cream, one teaspoon chopped green onion and one teaspoon grated cheese. Serves four.

WOLF package recipe

Solomon Barron
Texas (1860)

CHILI STYLE PIZZA

12 tortillas
1 can (19 oz.) WOLF*S Brand Chili (with or without beans)
1 Med. green pepper, cut into strips
1 small onion
½ Lb. Kraft Jalapeno Pepper Process Cheese Spread, cubed

Cover bottom and sides of lightly greased 14-inch round pizza pan with tortillas. Spread chili evenly over tortillas to edge. Top with green pepper and onion. Bake at 350 degrees, 20 minutes. Top with Process Cheese Spread, continue baking 5 minutes. Makes 6 servings.

WOLF package recipe

McCandless Ranch
Honolulu, HA

CHILI MEATBALLS

1 Lb. ground beef
1 Med. onion, chopped
2 cloves garlic, minced
1 T. chili powder
½ t. oregano
½ t. paprika
½ to 1 t. salt
¼ to ½ t. ground black pepper
Dash of cayenne pepper
1 can (10 oz.) tomato sauce
¼ C. corn meal

Mix all ingredients in a mixing bowl, except the tomato sauce. Shape the meat into small balls, and simmer slowly in skillet until they are cooked. As they are done, place in a pot with the tomato sauce, and keep them warm by lightly folding with the sauce. Heat the skillet several minutes before serving so that they are hot when dished out.

Mike & Chickie Ballentine
Cincinnati, OH

King Chevrolet Inc
Chico, CA

CHILI FOR 20

If you're in a hurry, this recipe is quick and easy!!

5 Lbs. ground beef
5 cans (28 oz.) chili beans
1 can (42 oz.) sweet beans
2 Med. onions, chopped
2 green bell peppers, chopped
2 or 3 chili jalapeno peppers (minus seeds!)
2 Pkgs. Seasonings (McCormick)
2 cans (28 oz.0 whole tomatoes
1 can (12 oz.) beer
½ clove garlic or powder
4 cans (28 oz.) tomato sauce
2 cans (28 oz.) tomato puree
1 can (12 oz.) whole kernel corn, drained

1. Brown and drain beef
2. Put everything in to pot, except beans, cook approximately 2 on medium heat. Stir frequently.
3. Add beans and cook for 1 more hour = READY!! This recipe equals 2 (16 oz.) bowls per person.

Extras:
Bowls - 20 (8 oz.)
Spoons - 20
Server - 1
Knife - 1
Lg. cooker - 1
Heat Source - 1
Aluminum foil - pot cover
Stir-stick - 1

Options:
1. Jar of dill pickles (diced for garnishments)
2. Large bowl of onions (cut up for garnishments)
3. Wendy's Chili Spice or more chili peppers to make it hotter
4. Tabasco sauce

Bill Hardy
Merritt Island, FL

Wm., S.C. & L.A. Clemons
New Pine Creek, Or

LITE BEER CHILI
(by Chef-Boy-Hardy)

2 Lbs. of lean ground beef
1 can (28 oz.) kidney beans
1 can (16 oz.) tomato sauce
1 can (8 oz.) whole tomatoes
½ C. whole corn (drained)
½ C. chopped onion
¼ C. chopped celery
¼ C. chopped green pepper
1 jalapeno pepper, chopped include seeds if you like it hot
2 T. chili powder
2 T. cumin
2 T. minced garlic
½ t. pepper
½ t. hot sauce
1 can "Lite beer"

Brown and drain beef in pan. Combine all ingredients in a large sauce pan and simmer, covered for 1 hour. Add beans and simmer for 30 minutes. If chili is too thick ADD MORE LITE BEER!!

Serve with the following condiments:
1 bowl of coarse cut onions
1 bowl of diced jalapeno peppers
1 bowl of diced pickles
2 boxes of crackers
Plenty of: Nabisco Premium Crackers!!

Bill Hardy
Merritt Island, FL

Wilbur & Michael Smith
Prineville, OR

CHANNEL 9 CHILI

To gather additional recipes for CHILIMANIA! from the Central Florida area, we appeared on WFTV Channel 9, Eyewitness Noon News, the ABC affiliate in Orlando, a short hour drive from here, to talk about the book and also bring along an example of the "goods".

We were given time and Martie Salt, the program's co-anchor, was more than helpful in promoting our quest to viewers.

After the program, the set's crew, and Channel 9 personnel did a very nice job of finishing off more than three solid quarts of chili, topped with chopped onions and shredded cheese. It was the first time that some said that they have ever eaten chili. It's hope that we have convinced some more people that chili is easy to make, and a real eatable pleasure.

2 Lbs. fresh ground turkey, not frozen
2 Pkg. (4 oz.) Carroll Shelby's Chili Mix (discard flour)
2 cans (15 oz.) tomato sauce
1½ cans water (sauce can)
1 or 2 cans Bush's Chili Beans
2 squares, Baker's Unsweetened Chocolate
1½ t. nutmeg
2 cans (15 oz.) whole tomatoes

Brown the ground turkey in a large skillet or Dutch oven. Use a wooden spoon to break up large chinks of turkey as it cooks. Drain off the liquid that will be drawn from the turkey. Add Chili Mix, tomato sauce, water, peeled cut up tomatoes with liquid, and beans.

Stir together well, crumbling to further break up cooked turkey. Cover and simmer for about 30 to 45 minutes.

Add the unsweetened chocolate and let it melt in the chili while stirring. Add the nutmeg, stirring. Season with chili powder to taste if necessary. For a hotter chili, use the cayenne pepper packet in the Chili Mix.

CSG

WFTV, Channel 9
Orlando, FL

9
WFTV

LEW'S CHILI

½ Lb. ground chuck or ground turkey
⅔ of Lg. can V-8 Juice
3 T. chili powder
1 t. oregano
2 cans kidney beans, drained
⅓ to ½ C. beer
¼ C. flour
2 tomatoes, chopped
¼ C. green pepper, chopped

Brown meat, and simmer all ingredients for ½ to 1 hour.

Michael & Patricia Lewis
Palm Bay, FL

Jerry Mann
Flintville, TN

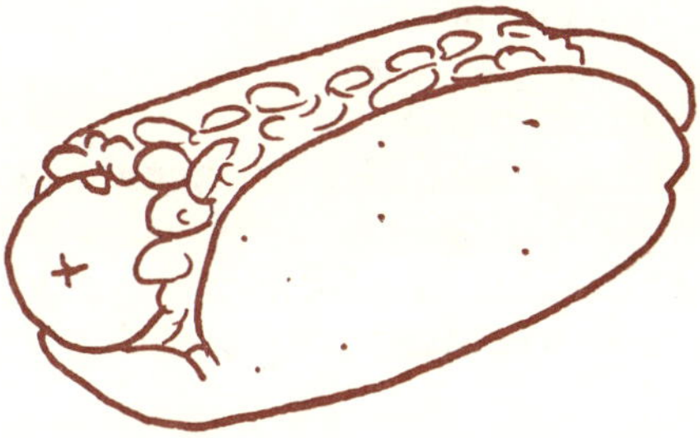

JB & VEL'S CHILI

Here's one more for your collection. Nothing special, but enjoyable.

Serves: 4

2 Lbs. ground chuck
2 Lbs. kidney beans
2 cans (14 oz.) stewed tomatoes
1 can (12 oz.) tomato sauce
4-5 T. chili powder
1 T. crushed red pepper
1 T. Worcestershire sauce

Directions: In a medium size skillet, brown the ground chuck and drain any grease.

Place all ingredients in Crock Pot; mix thoroughly.

Cook on "Low" for 8 to 9 hours, stirring occasionally.

Note: If it bring tears to your eyes, you know you overshot a mite with the red peppers!

J. B. Williams
Melbourne, FL

Agricultural Technical Inst.
Lyndon, OH

RAMON'S SALAD DRESSING

This is in no way, shape, form or color a recipe in the chili realm of food, but it is, or was one of the famous restaurants on the Space Coast, known for it's display of panels giving detailed information on every space shot flown from either KSC (Kennedy Space Center) or from the Air Force Station, Cape Canaveral. It closed 1988, leaving a true void in local eateries.

Try it. You'll keep it in the refrigerator, and in use for a long time. This is the original recipe!!

- 1 Qt. mayonnaise
- 6 whole eggs
- ½ to 1 t. curry powder
- ½ t. garlic powder
- 1 Pkg. onion soup mix
- 1¼ C. Parmesan cheese
- 2 t. anchovy paste (1 t. is enough) (2 oz. tube)

Mix all ingredients in a blender (or mixer) until it is creamy. Store in refrigerator. Serve over crisp romaine lettuce. Add croutons before serving.

Bill Hardy
Merritt Island, FL

Note: We agree with Mr. Hardy on Romon's Restaurant. As we have eaten there several times before it's closing and eventual demolishion, and to have read many of the historical panels covering space exploration, it was a fine place to have dined.

H&CG

WESTERN CHILI

- 1 Lb. dried pinto beans
- 2 garlic cloves, crushed
- 1 Lg. onion, chopped
- 2 Lbs. ground beef
- 1 can (10 oz.) tomato puree
- 1 can (8 oz.) tomato sauce
- Liquid hot sauce (optional)
- 1 t. salt
- ¼ t. ground black pepper
- 1½ t. paprika
- 2 T. chili powder
- 1 bay leaf
- Red pepper flakes (optional)

Wash and soak beans overnight. Next day, rinse and put into a skillet or cooking pot, and simmer until they are tender. Add water to keep the beans completely covered while cooking.

In another skillet, brown the beef until mostly done. Add all the rest of ingredients. Cover and simmer for about 30 to 40 minutes, or until it's good to the taste. Take out the bay leaf, and let chili cool completely. Put into the refrigerator, and keep overnight. It's really a next-day meal.

Tina & Steve Ballentine
Fenton, MI

Albert & Ruth Schenfisch
Eagle Point, OR

CHILI BEEF SOUP

2 Lbs. lean ground beef
2 Med. onions, chopped
1 Lg. sweet pepper, chopped
1 small carrot, shredded
2 cans (28 oz.) whole tomatoes, cut up, undrained
2 cans (10 oz.) tomato sauce
1 jar Pace Picante Sauce, medium
2 T. chili powder
1 t. paprika
Salt and pepper to taste
1 clove garlic, chopped fine

In a Dutch oven or large cooking pot, brown the beef, crumbling as it cooks. Add the chopped onions, peppers and garlic;, and saute until the onions are done. Drain off the excess fat liquid that forms, and discard.

Add all other ingredients, and simmer for at least 45 minutes to an hour. Season further to taste, and add additional water if necessary to get your consistency.

Serve with tortillas, taco or other cracker-like side dish.

Larry & Shellee Tyenda
Indianapolis, IN

JKL Joined
Joe K. Ligon, DMD
Venice, FL

CINCINNATI FIVE-WAY CHILI

1 Lb. ground beef chuck
1 Med. onion, finely chopped
2 cloves garlic, minced
1 C. barbecue sauce
1 C. water
1 T. chili powder
1 t. ground black pepper
½ Oz. unsweetened chocolate, grated
½ t. ground cumin
½ t. allspice
¼ t. ground cloves
¼ t. ground coriander
¼ t. ground cardamom
1 t. salt
Tomato juice, as needed
9 Ozs. spaghetti, cooked, buttered
1 can (16 oz.) kidney beans, heated
2 onions, chopped
1 Lb. shredded Cheddar cheese
½ t. turmeric
½ t. cinnamon

Salt a large skillet. Turn the heat to medium and add the meat, the chopped medium onion and garlic. Break up meat with a fork and cook until it is browned. Drain fat.

Add barbecue sauce and water. Bring to boil. Add remaining spices. Cover and simmer at very low heat for ½ hour, stirring and tasting occasionally, adding tomato juice if it is getting too dry to ladle up easily.

To construct the plate of five-way, layer the spaghetti on a plate, top it with hot chili, then with a sparse layer of beans, then onions. Put on plenty of shredded cheese while the chili is still hot, and serve immediately, with oyster crackers on the side.

Cindy Skaggs
Deltona, FL

Wesley K. Yadao
Kawai, HA

CHILI with POTATOES!

2 Lbs. ground hamburger or ground chuck, whichever you prefer. Brown in a large pan.
Add: 1 bell pepper and 1 onion. Stir together until all the meat is browned.
Then add 1 can Chili Mix (can size-2 Lbs.-8 Ozs.) or
2 cans (22 oz.) cans chili beans.
1 can (28 oz.) tomato puree
1 can (22 oz.) stewed tomatoes
3 to 4 t. chili powder, or until desire taste (not too hot, I guess it's mild)

Add: 4 to 5 potatoes, peeled and cubed.

Cook on medium to low heat, or simmer until potatoes are tender to a fork.

Add water if necessary.

Sherry Waters
Lake Wales, FL

6T

Helen M. Jenkins
State Brand Clerk
Phoenix, AZ

MARIE'S CINCINNATI CHILI (Five-Way)

1 Lb. ground beef chuck
1 Med. onion, finely chopped
2 cloves garlic, minced
1 C. barbecue sauce
1 C. water
1 T. chili powder
1 t. ground black pepper
½ Oz. unsweetened chocolate, grated
½ t. ground cumin
½ t. turmeric
1 t. allspice
½ t. cinnamon
¼ t. ground cloves
¼ t. ground coriander
¼ t. ground cardamom
1 t. salt
Tomato juice, as needed
9 Ozs. spaghetti, cooked and buttered
1 can (16 oz.) kidney beans,
2 onions, chopped
1 Lb. shredded Cheddar cheese

Salt a large skillet. Turn the heat to medium and add the meat, the chopped onion and the garlic. Break up the meat with a fork and cook until it is browned. Drain off the fat drippings. Add the barbecue sauce and water. Bring to a boil. Add remaining spices. Cover and simmer at a very low heat for 1½ hours, stirring and tasting ocassionally, adding tomato juice if it is getting too dry to ladle up easily. (We like this chili best when it is reheated after being allowed to "age" overnight in the refrigerator.

To construct the plate of five-way, layer the spaghetti on the plate (a small oval plate is traditional), top it with hot chili, then topped with a sparse layer of beans, then onions. Pat on plenty of shredded cheese while the chili is still hot, and serve immediately, with oyster crackers on the side.

If desired, omit either the beans or onions, or both, for four-way or three-way chili.

Ms. Marie Kiehborth
Cocoa, FL

→E

James K. Evans
Honolulu, HA

FAYE'S CHILI

1½ Lbs. ground chuck or steak
3 cans hot chili beans
2 small cans tomato sauce
1 Med. onion, chopped
2 jalapeno peppers, chopped
1 Pkg. chili mix
½ t. chili powder

Mix everything in a crock pot. Cook all night, or all day if you prefer.

When first turned on, put on High. After 1½ to 2 hours, turn on low for remaining cooking. Cook about 8 hours. Will serve 6 to 8.

Ms. Faye A. Stephens
Leesburg, FL

E. J. Reid
Nebraska (1870)

BONNIE'S CINCINNATI-STYLE CHILI

2 Lbs. lean ground beef
1 can (46 oz.) tomato juice
2 chopped onions
1 t. garlic powder, or, garlic salt
4 t. chili powder
1 t. cinnamon
4 t. cumin
2 t. red pepper
1 T. salt
3 bay leaves
1 t. allspice
1½ t. vinegar
2 t. Worcestershire sauce

Add the tomato juice to a large sauce pan. Separate the uncooked ground beef in small pieces and add to the heated tomato juice, and cook, stirring, until done. Add the remaining ingredients, stir to blend and bring to the boiling point.

Turn the heat down, and simmer for 3 hours uncovered.

Serve over spaghetti topped with grated sharp cheese and chopped onions.

Bonnie Van Arsdall
Casselberry, FL

Mill Iron Ranches
Wellington,
Jefferson County, TX

MAJESTIC CHILI

2 Lbs. ground turkey
2 Lg. onions, chopped
4 long celery pieces, chopped
1 T. jalapeno, diced
1 Lg. can V-8 Juice
1 C. chicken broth
1 t. cumin
2 t. salt
4 T. brown sugar
2 Oz. chili powder
1 T. garlic powder
2 cans (16 oz.) tomatoes, undrained and chopped up
1 Lg. can chili or kidney beans

Saute first four ingredients until the turkey is no longer pink. Add the rest of the ingredients and simmer, covered, for 1 hour.

Ms. Gwendolyn W. Hyde
Merritt Island, FL

John W. Patterson
Columbus, OH

ROB'S FAVORITE CHILI

2 Lbs. lean beef, cut in 1-inch cubes
⅓ Lb. JIMMY DEAN Hot Sausage
1 green bell pepper, chopped
½ red bell pepper, chopped
1 can (8 oz.) tomato sauce
1 can (8 oz.) tomatoes
1 Lg. jalapeno pepper, from jar
2 cloves garlic, minced
1 T. salt
1 T. oregano
1 T. cumin
½ t. ground red pepper

Brown sausage with chopped jalapeno pepper. Also add some juice from the jalapeno jar, about 1-2 tablespoons. Cook until the juice is absorbed.

Brown the beef, and add the chopped bell peppers and spices.

Simmer for 1½ to 2 hours.

Eat!

Robert Loucks
Orlando, FL

H.L. Craigen
Fannett,
Jefferson County, TX

JAK'S CHILI

This has been a very good recipe, and has been enjoyed by many.

1 Lb. chuck beef
¼ Lb. sausage
3 Ozs. cooking oil
1 Lg. onion, chopped well
2 t. garlic oil
2 t. oregano
2 t. cayenne pepper
2 cans (10½ oz.) tomato paste
1 t. salt
2 t. sugar
3 T. corn meal
1 can (10 oz.) beef broth

Now you're ready to make REAL CHILI:

Cut your beef in small cubes; heat oil in a large skillet and add the beef cubes.

Sear till almost BROWN, turning all the time to get it uniform. Remove the meat and, set it aside to cool off. In the oil not add the onions, garlic, oil, oregano and cayenne pepper. Saute till the onions are limp.

Shut fire off and return the meat stirring it in well. Add tow (2) cups of cool water. Now, on LOW heat, add the tomato products, salt and sugar. This MUST simmer at least ½ hour.

Remove from heat and let it cool. As it's cooling, add your beef broth cold. Let it set till really cooled off.

Return to flame and stir it well. Simmer at least thirty (30) minutes on a low flame. If it's too thin, then you may add the corn meal.

The next day is when it's really better. Serve with salad and, oyster crackers.

Serves 4.

Edmund B. Jakutis
Winter Haven, FL

Bob On The Square Ranch
Texas (1875)

KACEY'S CHILI

1 to 2 Lbs. hamburger
4 cans tomato soup
4 cans kidney beans, drained
3 to 4 cans water *use soup cans
1 onion, chopped
Chili powder - as desired

Brown hamburger and onion. Drain off fat. Add the tomato soup, beans and water. Bring to a bubbling state - turn heat to low and let simmer - add the desired amount of chili powder to taste - serve when ready and hot.

Serve chili powder on the side, so others may add to their desire and taste.

Kacey Keller
Orlando, FL

George W. Maxwell
Melbourne, FL

FAMILY'S CHILI

This was my mother's chili recipe and I have changed it a little for our family use:

3 cans (24 oz.) pork & beans
3 Lbs. ground beef - 1½ Lbs. beef, 1½ Lbs. pork or all lean meat
2 Lg. cans tomatoes
1 bottle (12 oz.) catsup
¼ Lb. bacon
4 Med. potatoes
3 green peppers
4 stalks celery
2 garlic fingers
6 T. chili powder
salt and pepper

In a large iron Dutch oven, fry the bacon and remove. Dice all the vegetables and garlic.

Add to pot and simmer, stirring often, until vegetables are done. Brown the ground meat. Crumble the bacon and add it, the ground meat and remaining ingredients to the pot.

Add water to desired consistency. Season, cover pot and simmer all day. Stir often and taste. Add additional seasonings if necessary.

Geraldine Anderson
Winter Park, FL

D Mc D Corporation
Lostine, OR

PETE'S CHILI

3 Lbs. diced beef
¼ C. olive oil
1 Qt. water
6 T. chili powder
3 T. salt
10 cloves garlic, finely chopped
1 T. oregano
1 T. red pepper
1 T. sugar
3 T. paprika
3 T. flour
6 T. corn meal

Sear meat in hot olive oil until color of meat is grey. Add water and cover. Cook for 1½ to 2 hours. Add all ingredients except the flour and corn meal.

Cook for an additional ½ hour. Mix flour and corn meal in one (1) cup of water and add to mixture. Cook for 5 more minutes.

Pete Knox
American Airlines
Cincinnati Reservations Office

David R. Durr
Halfway, OR

40 MINUTE CHILI

This is so simple it may not seem worthy-but it is very good...

2 T. fat
1 onion, chopped
1 or 2 cloves garlic, minced
1 Lb. ground meat
2 cans condensed tomato soup
2 cans (16 oz.) kidney beans
2 t. chili powder
½ t. salt
⅛ to ¼ t. red pepper (optional)
Dash pepper

Saute onions and garlic. Brown meat - stir in soup, beans and chili powder, salt and pepper. Cover and simmer 30 minutes - stirring occasionally.

Ms. Fred M. Harper
Merritt Island, FL

Nakoa Ranch
William K. Nakoa
Honolulu, HA

CHILI BEAN SALAD

This recipe can be used either for a salad or a dip that can be served in a fondue dish.

1 C. cooked or canned kidney or pinto beans
2 or 3 T. chopped celery
½ to 1 t. chili powder
1 t. vinegar
2 t. salad dressing
¼ t. onion powder, or
1 T. finely chopped onion
1 or 2 drops hot sauce (optional)
Pepper to taste
Shredded Cheddar cheese (optional)

For Salad: Mix lightly in small bowl. Taste for flavor, and alter if desired by adding more separate ingredients. Multiply ingredients if more serving are desired. This makes about 1 good size portion.

For Dip: Lightly chop and break down size of beans. Add a little V-8 or tomato juice to make a little more liquidly. Place in fondue dish and sprinkle with a little shredded Cheddar cheese so that it melts a little while being served. Makes a real party favorite.

Grover & Sue Dudding
Cincinnati, OH

Alice & Jesse James
Porterville, CA

MOM'S CHILI

3 Lbs. ground chuck
2 cans (15½ oz.) Van Camp's Chili Beans (Pinto beans)
1 can (28 oz.) crushed tomatoes
Spaghetti for two
1 T. chili powder
1 T. paprika
1 onion
3 Lg. cloves garlic

Cook ground chuck until about half done, and add thinly sliced onion, thin sliced garlic, and cook until well done.

In large pot, cook spaghetti for 8 to 10 minutes, break into ½-inch pieces. Add chili beans, crushed tomatoes, chili powder, and paprika. Cook together until very hot, add meat and simmer for ½ hour.

Ms. Alice Earle Smith
Deland, FL

Cornelius-Williams
Cattle Co.
Solvang, CA

TEXAS BEANS

¼ Lb. salt pork
3 T. cooking oil
2 onions, finely chopped
3 cloves garlic, finely chopped
Dash ground cumin seeds
½ t. oregano
3 T. chili powder
salt and pepper to taste
2 C. tomato juice
2 C. (1 Lb.) dried pinto beans

In a good pot, cook the beans until they are nearly done. Do not boil, but slowly, using very low heat. Keep enough water to completely cover beans while cooking.

In a skillet, using the cooking oil, fry the salt pork to render as much fat as possible. Discard most of the drippings, reserving enough to use for flavoring of beans. Saute the onion and garlic with the pork.

Add remaining ingredients including the beans to the skillet; cover, and simmer for about 1 hour. Adjust the seasonings if desired. Beans are ready to serve when hot and firm and not mushy.

C. Richard & Isabel Coburn
New Harbor, ME

William Farson
Barnesville, OH

EASY CHILI FLAVORING

If chili flavoring is a thing in your cooking, but you are serving chicken, either baked, grilled or broiled, melt about 4 or 5 tablespoons of butter or margarine, adding 1½ to 2 teaspoons of chili powder, mixing well.

Baste chicken with seasoning on both sides, and let brown, using as much mixture as you wish. If hotter taste is wanted, add more chili powder to the zing you want.

Patti Jo Sedgwick
Cincinnati, OH

D. Sloane
Florida 1860

POP'S QUICK & EASY CHILI

1 Lb. ground pork
2 Med. onions, chopped
1 small green pepper, chopped
1 T. salt
1 T. pepper
1 t. oregano
2 Lg. garlic cloves, minced
1 bay leaf
1 T. soy sauce
1 T. Worcestershire sauce
1 t. hot sauce
1 T. steak sauce
1 T. sugar
2 small cans, kidney beans
1 can chopped whole tomatoes
1 can (6 oz.) tomato paste
1 can (8 oz.) tomato sauce
1 can (4 oz.) mushroom pieces
Crushed pepper to taste
Chili powder to taste - start with 6 T.

Place ground pork, chopped onion and green pepper into a crock pot. Turn the heat on High and stir and chop ground pork mixture about every half-hour until meat is about done. Drain off excess fat.

Then add kidney beans, tomatoes (chopped up), tomato paste, tomato sauce and mushroom pieces. Stir.

Add remaining seasonings and cook on Low heat 4 to 5 hours, or until desired time to serve.

(This may be started the night before then placed in the refrigerator until next morning to finish cooking on Low heat).

Ms. Laralle H. Hendrix
Deltona, FL

Stewart-Gadbois Co./
Hoomau Ranch
Honolulu, HA

CHEEZY CHILI DOGS

1½ Lbs. lean ground beef
1 bottle (12 oz.) Bennett's Chili Sauce
2 T. water
1 t. chili powder
8 frankfurters, cooked
8 frankfurter buns
Fisher* Ched-O-Mate or Pizza-Mate* Shredded Cheese Substitute

In a skillet, brown meat; pour off fat. Stir in Chili sauce, water and chili powder; bring to a boil. Reduce heat; simmer uncovered 15 minutes, stirring occasionally. Serve on frankfurters in buns; top with Fisher Shreds. Refrigerate leftovers.

Borden Inc.

Seven P Bar
Donald T. Davis
Zolgo Springs, FL

SEENA'S CHILI MOLD

½ C. Kraft Mayonnaise
1 Pkg. (8 oz.) cream cheese
Chopped celery
1 Med. onion, chopped coarsely
1 T. chili sauce
Seasonings you like
Small sour cream
Caviar if desired

Blend all ingredients in a blender until well mixed. Pour and spoon into mold, sprinkle with caviar, and allow to set and chill in refrigerator before serving.

Serve with corn chips or crackers, just so long as they are strong enough to dig into the mix and not break up.

Seena Golden
Cincinnati, OH

Crescent X Bar
Agricultural Mgt. Servs.
Punta Gorda, FL

VEAL CHILI

1 Lb. ground veal
2 Lg. onions, chopped fine
2 t. dried minced garlic
1 can (28 oz.) tomato juice
1 can (15 oz.) and
1 can (40 oz.) kidney beans, drained and rinsed
4 T. chili powder
¾ t. hot pepper sauce
Pinch of cumin

Brown veal and drain. Add onions and garlic. Cook, covered, for a few minutes until onions are tender. Place remaining ingredients into a large saucepan, mix together while warming.

Once warmed, add veal, onions and garlic to skillet and simmer for about 30 to 35 minutes, or until it's what you want.

Keith & Kathy Roth
Harrison, OH

Bill & Kathy Lackner
Klondyke, AZ

FRAN'S CHILI

2 small onions, chopped
1 Med. green pepper, chopped
1 T. salad oil
1 Lb. ground turkey
1 Lb. ground chuck
2 cans stewed tomatoes
3 T. tomato paste
2½ T. chili powder
1 t. garlic powder
Scant t. salt
½ t. sugar
1 t. Worcestershire sauce
½ t. celery salt
1 can kidney beans

Saute onions and green peppers in the salad oil. Add the ground meat, brown, and drain grease. Set aside and cook the turkey. Combine meats and with a wooden spoon, break up and crumble larger pieces. Again, spoon off any fat that has been rendered from the meat.

Add the rest of the ingredients except the beans. Simmer for about 1½ hours. Then add the beans and heat for 15 minutes more.

Fran Yalch
Cincinnati, OH

WP

J.P. Pierce
Florida 1855(?)

LYNDON JOHNSON'S RIVER CHILI

2 Lbs. ground beef
1 Med. onion, chopped
3-6 t. chili powder
1 clove garlic, minced
1 t. oregano
1 t. cumin seed
¾ C.beer
1 can (16 oz.) sliced stewed tomatoes, plus liquid
2 dashes Tabasco sauce
Salt to taste
1 can (16 oz.) kidney beans, drained (optional)

Place ground beef in a plastic colander. Sprinkle onion on top. Set colander in a 4-quart pot. Microwave on High 4 minutes. Pour off grease. Transfer beef to pot.

Stir in the next four ingredients into the meat. Add tomatoes plus the liquid. Pour beer into the pot. Add the Tabasco sauce and salt; stir to blend. Do not cover pot. Microwave on High for 12 minutes.

Optional - add kidney beans. Microwave till heated thoroughly. Serves 6. 441 calories per serving.

Fran Yalch
Cincinnati, OH

S

Larry C. Steves
Whitehall, NY

CHILI con QUESO

2 Lbs. pasteurized process cheese spread
1 can (10 oz.) Old El Paso Tomatoes and Green Chilies
½ C. finely chopped onion
3 T. finely chopped fresh cilantro
Old El Paso NACHIPS Tortillas Chips

Cut cheese spread into 1-inch cubes; melt in a double boiler. Add tomatoes and green chilies, onion and cilantro. Serve warm with Old El Paso NACHIPS Tortilla Chips. Makes 5 cups.

Microwave directions: In a 2-quart casserole, microwave cheese cubes on 50% power for 13 minutes, stirring and turning every 2½ minutes. Continue as directed above.

Barry Geltner from
the Miami Herald

Katherine P. Bronson
L Fleur De Lis
Kissimmee, FL

SOUTHWEST COWPOKE CHILI

6 jalapenos, chopped
2 Lg. onions, chopped
1 clove garlic, chopped
1 can (8 oz.) tomato sauce
Salt and Pepper to taste
2 Lbs. lean beef
1 t. cumin seed
1 t. oregano
4 cases cold beer
2 Lg. roadrunners

Saute jalapenos, beef, onions and garlic until the meat loses its's red color. Add the remaining ingredients and ¼ to ½ cup of water. Bring to a boil, reduce the heat, and simmer, covered until you've finished a case of the beer.

Prepare roadrunners-let chili cool and feed it to the roadrunners. Lean back, take it easy and enjoy the rest of the beer.

Ms. Flora Martinez
Silver City, NM

3 H 3 Ranch
Texas (1875)

KOOCH'S NUCLEAR CHILI

2 Lbs. beef chuck, coarse ground
2 Lbs. venison, coarse ground
8 C. beef soup stock
2 Lg. Spanish onions, chopped
1 can (6 oz.) tomato paste
1 can (28 oz.) Italian tomatoes, chopped
2 cans (4 oz.) hot green chilies, chopped
1 can (40 oz.) Brooks Hot Chili Beans
1 T. oregano
2 T. cumin
4 T. chili powder
1 T. cayenne pepper
2 T. hot chili sauce, Chinese
6 cloves garlic, chopped
1 can (12 oz.) beer

= Brown chuck lightly. Strain off grease.
= Add soup stock and beer to large soup pot. Bring to boil.
= Add green peppers, onions, chilies, garlic, tomatoes, tomato paste and chili sauce. Stir and bring to boil.
= Add chuck and venison. Stir and bring to boil.
= Add all remaining spices. Stir. Reduce heat, and simmer with lid slightly open, for 2 hours. Stir every 20-30 minutes.
= Add beans. Stir. Simmer for 10 minutes. Turn off heat and let cool.

Notes:
= You can modify this recipe, but then you will not be eating the original Kooch's Nuclear Chili. (Hint: You can add spices, but please do not eliminate or reduce any.)
= Can be eaten immediately, but is best re-heated after cooling and aging in refrigerator for two days.
= Use lean meat and trim off all fat to reduce grease.
= Thicken to desired consistency by removing lid while simmering.
= Can be frozen for up to about one year (...but I guarantee, you won't keep it in the freezer that long!)

Dennis Kuczynski
Darien, IL
Submitted by his uncle:
Matthew B. Pisarek
Oak Lawn, IL

Walter D. Miller
Lt. Governor,
South Dakota

PORK and LENTIL CHILI

8 Ozs. lean boneless pork
Non-stick spray coating
1 can (16 oz.) tomatoes, cut up
3 stalks celery, sliced
½ C. chopped onion
1 C. dry lentils
1 C. water
1 can (6 oz.) hot-style tomato juice
2 t. chili powder
1 t. sugar
¼ t. garlic powder
¼ t. ground cumin

Trim fat from meat. Cut meat into ½-inch cubes. Spray a cold large saucepan with non-stick coating. Quickly brown meat over medium-high heat.

Stir undrained tomatoes, celery, onion, lentils, water, tomato juice, chili powder, sugar, garlic and cumin into meat in saucepan. Bring the mixture to boiling; reduce heat. Cover and simmer about 1 hour or until lentils and meat are tender.

To serve, ladle into bowls. Makes 4 servings.

Ms. E. L. Stewart
Gatlinburg, TN

H & J Longhorns
Springfield, TN

TENNESSEE PRIDE CHILI #2

This is an identical recipe as submitted by Ms. Lynnette Cholewa of nearby Cocoa, FL

TURKEY CHILI

Vegetable cooking spray
2 Lbs. ground turkey, uncooked
1 Med. onion, chopped
1 Med. green pepper, chopped
2 cloves garlic, minced
1 can (16 oz.) whole tomatoes, undrained
1 can (10 oz.) tomatoes and green chilies, undrained
2 C. tomato juice
1 to 2 T. chili powder
1 T. prepared mustard
1 t. paprika
¼ t. salt
1 can (15½ oz.) kidney beans, drained

Coat a wok, electric skillet or other cooking pan with cooking spray. Add turkey, onion, green pepper and minced garlic. Saute mixture over heat until the turkey loses it's pink color. Stir in remaining ingredients except beans, bring to a boil; cover, reduce heat and simmer 1 hour.

Stir in beans, cover and simmer an additional 15 minutes. Yield: 5 cups. Each cup contains approximately 223 calories.

Ms. E. L. Stewart
Gatlinburg, TN

Wiley Williams
Florida 1869

E. L.'S MEATLESS CHILI

2 T. corn oil
1½ C. chopped onion
3 cloves garlic, minced
2 T. chili powder
½ t. ground cumin
1 C. diced carrots
1 green pepper, chopped
2 cans (14½ to 16 oz.) cans tomatoes in juice, undrained
1 can (16 oz.) chick peas, drained
1 can (15 oz.) kidney beans, drained
1 Pkg. (10 oz.) frozen corn, thawed
1 to 2 pickled jalapeno peppers, chopped

In a 5-quart saucepan, heat the corn oil over medium heat, and add onions, garlic, chili powder and cumin; saute 5 minutes or until tender. Add carrots and green peppers; saute 2 minutes.

Add tomatoes with juice, crushing tomatoes with spoon. Stir in chick peas, kidney beans, corn and jalapeno peppers. Bring to a boil.

Reduce heat; cover and simmer 30 to 35 minutes. If desired, serve with rice. Makes 8 servings, about 1¼ cup each.

Ms. E. L. Stewart
Gatlinburg, TN

Lizard Ranch
Texas (1857)

JOYCES' CHILI

2 Med. onions, coarsely chopped
1 clove garlic, crushed
¼ C. vegetable oil
½ t. oregano
1 t. cumin seed, crushed
1 bay leaf, broken
⅛ C. chili powder
1 can (16 oz.) tomatoes, undrained
2 cans (15 oz.) kidney beans, undrained
1 t. salt
1½ T. cider vinegar
1 Lb. ground beef

In a heavy 6-quart pan, cook the onions and garlic in the vegetable oil for about 10 minutes, stirring occasionally, being careful not to burn.

Add oregano, cumin, bay leaf and beef, cook stirring until beef is browned. Add half of the chili powder; the tomatoes and one can of the beans. Heat mixture to boiling, reduce heat and simmer, uncovered, stirring occasionally, for 1½ hours.

Add the remaining chili powder, kidney beans, salt and vinegar, reheat to boiling, reduce to simmer and cook for 15 minutes longer. Taste, add more chili powder if desired. Serve in soup bowls. Chopped onions can be sprinkled on top if so wished.

Ms. Joyce Viets
Colfax, WI

Walter Dean Dennis
Buchanan Dam, TX

CHILI STRATA

1 egg, slightly beaten
⅓ C. water
1 Pkg. (12 oz.) corn chips
2 cans (15½ oz.) Armour Star Chili with Beans
1 can (20 oz.) enchilada sauce
¾ C. chopped green pepper
⅓ C. chopped onion
2 C. (8 oz.) shredded Cheddar cheese
4 C. chopped lettuce
2 C. chopped tomatoes

Heat oven to 350 degrees. Mix egg with water. Crush 4 cups corn chips to make 2 cups crushed chips. Add egg mixture to crushed chips; spread in lightly greased 13x9-inch baking dish. Combine chili, 1 cup enchilada sauce, green pepper and onion; spread over corn chips in casserole. Bake at 350 degrees for 35 minutes.

Top with cheese and remaining whole corn chips; bake 5 minutes. Top with lettuce and tomatoes. Serve with sauce. 6 to 8 servings.

Ms. E. L. Stewart
Gatlinburg, TN

Summitcrest, Inc
Summitville, OH

VEGETARIAN CHILI

1 C. tomato juice
1 C. raw bulgur
2 T. olive oil
2 Med. onions, coarsely chopped
5 Med. cloves garlic, crushed
3 stalks celery, sliced
3 carrots, coarsely chopped
1 can (16 oz.) whole tomatoes, drained (save juice)
1 T. fresh lemon juice
1½ t. ground cumin
½2 t. ground hot pepper
1 t. dried basil
1½ green bell peppers, coarsely chopped
2 cans (16 oz.) red kidney beans
1 can (4 oz.) mild green chilies, chopped

Bring tomato juice to boil over medium heat. Remove from heat and immediately add the bulgur. Cover and let stand 15 minutes.

Meanwhile, heat olive oil in large heavy pot over medium heat. Add onions and garlic and cook 5 to 10 minutes, or until onions are transparent.

Add celery, carrots, tomatoes, lemon juice and spices and cook, covered until vegetables are nearly tender, about 15 minutes. Add the bell peppers and cook another 10 minutes.

Add kidney beans, green chilies, the juice from the drained tomatoes, the bulgur and the tomato juice mixture. Stir, cover, and simmer for about 30 minutes more. Check and stir from time to time. If it gets too thick, add more tomato juice or water. Makes 4 servings.

from Cooking to
Your Heart's Content
Democrat and Chronicle,
Rochester, NY

Andiron Ranch
Texas (1875)

JEANNE JONES CHILI-BURGER SAUCE

1 C. low-calorie mayonnaise
½ C. chili sauce
⅓ C. sweet pickle relish
¼ t. salt
2 T. white vinegar
½ t. sugar
⅓ t. white pepper

Combine all ingredients and mix thoroughly. Refrigerate. Serve with low-fat beef burgers. Makes just under a pint of sauce.

From food columnist and cookbook author Jeanne Jones.

Florida Today

Thomas Rapoza
Honolulu, HA

SIX SLAVES VEGETARIAN CHILI W/CUMIN

6 T. virgin olive oil
2 onions
50 cloves fresh garlic, 6 peeled and chopped
2 jalapeno peppers, seeded and chopped
1 EACH red, green, yellow bell peppers, thinly sliced
1 Lb. whole small mushrooms
1 Med. zucchini, cut in rounds
1 C. canned garbanzo beans, rinsed
½ t. salt
½ t. crumbled basil
1 t. sugar
1 C. corn, cut from cob
1 C. canned red or pinto beans, rinsed
½ t. ground cumin
½ t. crumbled thyme
2 T. chili powder
1 C. dry white wine
1 Lb. plum tomatoes, peeled, seeded and quartered
1 can (6 oz.) tomato paste
2 C. water
½ C. minced fresh cilantro (optional)

In a large soup pot, heat olive oil, and in it saute onions, 6 cloves of garlic peeled and chopped, and jalapeno peppers (use only one, or omit, or substitute a touch of cayenne pepper, if you don't like it too hot) for 5 minutes.

Add bell peppers, zucchini, and the remaining 44 whole cloves of garlic, but not peeled. Saute another 4 to 5 minutes. Add tomatoes, tomato paste and sugar. Blend in wine, then water. Add chili powder, cumin, basil, thyme and salt. Bring to a boil, stir in mushrooms, corn, garbanzo and red beans, and half the minced cilantro.

Simmer, covered, for about an hour. Taste and adjust seasoning. Sprinkle more chopped cilantro on just before serving. It's okay; for diners to fish out the cooked garlic cloves and spread on bread, or crackers. Serves 8-10. Serve with steamed rice, if desired.

Florida Today

Babcock Florida CO.
Punta Gorda, FL

JIM and SARAH BRADY'S CHILI

March 26, 1990 Washington (AP) Former White House Press Secretary James Brady is a gourmet cook and an avid fan of chili. In fact, he makes one of the "hottest" pots of chili in town. Brady's chili has won three consecutive "Chili Bull" contests in the Washington, D.C. area, which has earned him "Lifetime Member" status with the

International Chili Society. Brady has also been recognized by the Goat Gap Gazette, a newspaper for chili-lovers, as one of Washington's leading promoters of chili.

3 Lbs. boneless beef round or chuck, cut into ¾-inch pieces
3 T. vegetable oil
1 box (2.4 oz.) hot chili powder (about ½ cup)
3 Med. onions, chopped
4 cloves garlic, minced
1 can (7 or 8 oz.) jalapeno peppers, seeded and chopped
1 can (28 tomatoes, and juice
1 T. oregano leaves
3 bay leaves
1 T. salt
1 T. ground cumin
1 T. red wine vinegar
2 T. brown sugar
1 Pt. ripe olives, drained and sliced
1 T. Masa harina
Shredded Cheddar cheese for garnish

Brown beef cubes in oil. Add chili powder to meat. Stir. Put aside in heavy iron pot or Dutch oven.

Saute onion, garlic and pepper in oil until golden. Add to meat with tomatoes and cook 20 minutes. Add remaining spices, vinegar and brown sugar.

Cook slowly, covered, 2 hours. Add Masa harina and olives. Serve with shredded cheese. Makes 6 servings (about 9 cups).

Ms. E. L. Stewart
Gatlinburg, TN

Hangin F Ranch
Phoenix, AZ

LIZ'S SPEEDY CHILI

½ C. chopped onions
¼ C. chopped green pepper
1 Lb. ground lean beef
2 cans (8 oz.) tomato sauce
1 can (16 oz.) red kidney beans
1 t. (or less) salt
1 t. chili powder

Brown beef in large saucepan, breaking up as it cooks. Drain off drippings. Add chopped onions and green peppers, and saute until they are tender. Spoon off excess fat.

Stir in tomato sauce, chili powder and salt. Cook over medium heat for 10 minutes. Stir in beans; cover and let simmer for 10 to 15 minutes.

Serve with crackers, and some shredded cheese and onions if desired for extra taste and appearance. Makes 6 servings.

Ms. E. L. Stewart
Gatlinburg, TN

Cope Ranch
Oelrichs, SD

CHILI PINTO BEANS

2 C. (16 oz.) dried pinto beans
2 C. tomato juice
¼ Lb. salt pork
3 T. grease
3 cloves garlic, finely chopped
2 Med. onion, finely chopped
½ t. oregano
Dash of cumin
3 T. chili powder
Salt and freshly ground pepper, to taste

Cook the pinto beans slowly in enough water to keep them covered, until the beans are nearly done. Fry the salt pork in a large skillet using the grease or vegetable oil. Pour off all excess fat, and add the onions and garlic. Saute the mixture together for a few minutes.

Add the remaining spices, tomato juice and beans. Cover, and let simmer for one (1) hour. Adjust the seasonings if desired. Beans are ready to serve when they are firm and not mushy.

Don Husman
Cincinnati, OH

M
Marion Canada
Osteen, FL

TOUCHDOWN CHILI

2 Lbs. chuck steak, thinly sliced
2 T. olive oil
1 T. flour
1 Lg. onion, thinly sliced
¾ C. red wine
1 clove garlic, mashed
1 carrot, thinly sliced
1 green pepper, diced
1 can (40 oz.) assorted beans, drained, rinse
2 bay leaves
½ t. cumin
1 t. oregano
¼ t. crushed red pepper
1 can (10½ oz.) minestrone soup
1 can (10½ oz.) lentil soup

In a large pot, brown the sliced beef in the olive oil. Drain off the excess liquid. Add the vegetables and saute until the onion are tender. Add the remaining ingredients except the beans. Bring pot to a boil. Reduce the heat, and add the beans, ¼ cup of red wine, cover, and simmer for 1½ to 2 hours.

Uncover for the last 30 minutes before serving.

Regis & Kathie Lee, Live With (+ Joy)

Bar RKL Bar

CINCINNATI CHILI

1 Qt. water
2 Lbs. lean hamburger
1 t. cinnamon
1 t. cumin seed or ground cumin
1 t. Worcestershire sauce
1 toe garlic
2 T. chili powder
1 t. black pepper
½ t. red pepper or chili pepper
1 T. salt
1½ t. ground allspice
1 can (6 oz.) tomato paste
1½ T. cider vinegar
3 Lg. whole bay leaves

Directions:

Crumble raw (do not brown) hamburger in water, add all ingredients. Bring to boil, then simmer for 3 hours. Remove garlic toe and bay leaves. Add whole red peppers (if desired) for spicier taste.
Serves 10-12.

2-Way: Spaghetti topped with chili.

3-way: Spaghetti topped with chili and grated cheese (a mild Cheddar is recommended.

4-Way: Spaghetti topped with chili, grated cheese and chopped onions.

5-Way: Same as 4-Way but kidney beans added to the chili.

Coneys: Frankfurter on a bun topped with chili, onions and grated Cheddar cheese.

Ms. Yvonne Wilt
Clearwater, Fl
White House Publishing
Company, Inc.
Cincinnati, OH

Ernest & Tammy Tosti
Aquanga, CA

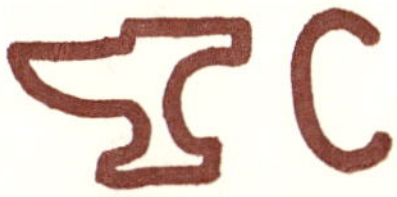

Graig Coldflesh
Grantville, PA

CHICKEN CHILI+ cardiac

½ C. chopped onion
½ C. chopped green pepper
1 clove garlic, minced
1 can (15½ oz.) kidney beans, rinsed and drained
1 can (14½ oz.) no-salt whole tomatoes
1 can (8 oz.) no-salt whole kernel corn, drained
2 T. red wine vinegar
2 T. Worcestershire sauce
1 C. cut-up chicken or turkey
1 T. packed brown sugar
1 t. chili powder
¼ t. dry mustard
⅛ t. pepper

In a 2-quart casserole, combine onion, green pepper and garlic. Cover. Microwave at High for 2 to 4 minutes, or until tender-crisp. Add the remaining ingredients, stirring to break apart tomatoes. Cover. Reduce heat power to 70% (Medium-High). Microwave for 25 to 30 minutes longer, or until flavors are blended and chili is hot; stirring twice.

Makes 6 servings, 1 cup each.

Per serving:

Calories:	187
Protein:	14 g.
Carbohydrates:	22 g.
Fat:	1 g.
Cholesterol:	13 mg.
Sodium:	75 mg.
Calcium:	--
Exchanges:	1½ bread, 2 low-fat meat

Ms. Karen Liscon, RD LD
Dietary Service
U. of Cincinnati Hospital
Cincinnati,OH

Don Jose Reyes
California (1855)

CHILI

1 Lb. ground beef
1 onion, chopped
1 can tomato sauce
1 T. catsup
1½ t. chili powder
¾ t. salt
Dash pepper
1 t. sugar
1 can red kidney beans

Saute the onion is a small amount of fat till limp. Crumble the beef and brown. Combine the beef and onion. Drain off fat. Add remaining ingredients, and simmer, covered, for about an hour.

Serve with long grain rice.

Ms. Florence R. Schultz
Cocoa Beach, FL

J.J. Parker
Florida 1888

BEEFY MEXICALI RICE with CHEESE

Chili Dish

For a delicious chili, add ground beef, chilies and cheese to this rice mix. Makes 2 servings.

- 2¼ C. water
- ½ Lb. lean ground beef
- Salt and pepper to taste
- 1 Pkg. Lipton Rice & Sauce-Spanish
- 1 can (4 oz.) chopped green chilies, undrained
- ½ C. shredded Cheddar cheese (about 2 oz.)

1. In a large skillet bring water to boil.
2. Stir in ingredients except cheese, breaking up the meat into smaller pieces.
3. Reduce heat and simmer, stirring occasionally, 12 minutes or until rice is tender and most of the liquid absorbed.
4. Top with cheese; cover and let stand 2 minutes or until cheese is melted.
5. Serve.

LIPTON recipe

Montsdeoca Ranch Inc.
Lorida, FL

CHILI BEAN SOUP

1 Lb. ground beef, coarsely chopped
2 C. onion, coarsely chopped
½ C. fresh cilantro, chopped (coriander) or parsley
2 T. minced garlic
6 C. heavy ham or meat stock, such as stew with vegetables
2 C. red beans, cooked or canned
2 C. tomato sauce
Chili powder to taste
Dash or two Louisiana Hot SAUCE
Dash cayenne pepper to taste
Salt and pepper to tastes

Brown ground beef over medium-high heat in a large pot. Break up beef quite well with wooden spoon to form small pieces. Drain off excess grease by using a slotted spoon and transferring meat to bowl until all is drained.

Return meat to pot, adding the onions, cilantro and minced garlic to the meat. Saute until the onions are tender.

Add the 6 cups of stock, beans, tomato juice, chili powder, hot sauce and salt. Stir well. Bring to a boil, then reduce heat. Cover; and let simmer for at least 2 hours or more, stirring often to keep the contents from either burning or sticking to pot.

Service with chopped onions, shredded cheese, or other types of toppings that you use.

Deb Cole,
Cincinnati, OH

Parker Ranch
Honolulu, HA

TURKEY STORE CHILI

1 Pkg. (about 1¼ Lb.) The Turkey Store Premium Fresh Lean Ground Turkey
1½ C. chopped onion
1 C. chopped green bell pepper
3 garlic cloves, minced
1 can (16 oz.) stewed tomatoes
1 can (15 oz.) tomato sauce
2 t. Worcestershire sauce
3 T. chili powder
1 t. dried basil leaves
1 t. dried oregano leaves
½ t. salt, if desired
⅛ t. cayenne pepper
1 can (16 oz.) kidney beans, rinsed, drained

Crumble turkey into Dutch oven. Add onion, green pepper and garlic. Cook and stir over medium-high heat for 5 to 7 minutes or until turkey is no longer pink. Add remaining ingredients except the kidney beans. Bring to a boil. Reduce heat. Cover; cook over low heat for 20 minutes. Stir in kidney beans. Heat 10 minutes longer. Makes 5 servings.

Madelin Streu,
Home Economist
JEROME FOODS, INC.
Barron, WI

Larry & Lonnie Work
Dunlap, CA

GATLIN TURKEY CHILI

2 Lbs. raw ground turkey
2 T. margarine
½ C. chopped onion
2 garlic cloves, minced
2 T. chili powder, or more to taste
2 t. ground cumin
1 T. paprika
1 can (28 oz.) tomatoes
1 can (15 oz.) red kidney beans
1 can (15 oz.) pinto beans
1 t. salt
Freshly ground black pepper, to taste

Cook turkey and onions in the margarine until the turkey is no longer pink. Add garlic, chili powder, cumin, paprika, tomatoes, beans, salt and pepper. Cover. Bring to a boil over a high heat, then reduce heat and simmer for 45 minutes to an hour. To cook liquid down if too thin, uncover and let simmer.

It is best when prepared a day ahead and simmered for an hour just before serving.

Yield: 8 servings, of approximately 520 calories per serving.

Note: Serve topped with grated cheese, if desired.

The liquid that comes out when browning the turkey is moisture, not grease, and doesn't have to be drained off. Serve the chili with corn or tortilla chips or corn bread and a green salad.

Ms. E. L. Stewart
Gatlinburg, TN

Bill & Dale Henceroth
Salem, OH

TEX-MEX SALSA

1 T. vegetable oil
1 Lg. onion, chopped, about 1 cup
1 Lg. clove garlic, crushed
1 can (16 oz.) whole tomatoes, well drained
1 can (4 oz.) mild green chilies, drained and chopped
¼ t. salt
¼ t. freshly ground pepper

In an 8-inch skillet over medium-high heat, heat oil; add onion and garlic and cook 1 to 2 minutes, stirring frequently, or until onion is crisp-tender. Remove from heat; cool slightly.

Meanwhile in a medium bowl, combine tomatoes, chilies, salt and pepper. Add onion and garlic to bowl; stir well to mix, breaking up any large chunks of tomato. Makes about 2½ cups.

Cincinnati Enquirer

Donald G. Zimmerman
Mt. Juliet, TN

AUTUMN CHILI VEGETABLE SOUP

2 T. unsalted butter, or margarine
1 Lg. onion, chopped
4 stalks celery, diced
3 Lg. Leeks, white parts, coarsely chopped
½ t. dried thyme
2 t. chili powder
⅛ t. ground cloves
1 or 2 cloves garlic, crushed
1 T. salt
Fresh ground pepper to taste
1 C. frozen or fresh lima beans
6 carrots, diced
1 Med.-sized sweet red pepper coarsely chopped
4 Med.-sized white turnips, diced
1 small butternut squash, peeled and diced
1 small head green cabbage, coarsely chopped
3 T. parsley, chopped, for garnish
2½ to 3 Qts. chicken stock, or more if desired

In a large pot, or Dutch oven, melt the butter or margarine over a medium-high heat. Add onions, celery, leeks and thyme and saute until the onions are transparent but not browned.

Increase heat to high and add the carrots, red pepper, lima beans, cabbage, garlic, cloves, squash, turnips, chicken stock, salt and pepper. Cover, reduce heat to low, and cook until the vegetables are tender, about one (1) hour or so. Stir several times during cooking period.

If soup is too thick, add more chicken stock or water to thin. Check the seasonings, and add additional spices if necessary.

This soup can be made several days ahead, and refrigerated. Re-heat on low heat.

This makes 8 bowls when ladled into individual servings.

Bill & Chrissy Hatfield
Cincinnati, OH

R.E. Denison
Waco, 1903
Jefferson County, TX

THREE BEAN CHILI

1 T. olive or vegetable oil
3 cloves garlic, minced
1 can (28 oz.) Italian-style tomatoes, cut up
1 can (6 oz.) tomato paste
1 can (8 oz.) tomato sauce
1 can (10 oz.) V-8 Juice
1 T. chili powder
1 T. Dijon mustard
1 t. oregano
½ t. ground cumin
1 t. basil
½ t. fresh ground pepper
1 can (15 oz.) garbanzo beans, drained
1 can (15 oz.) great northern beans, drained
1 can (15 oz.) red kidney beans, drained
1 C. carrots, chopped
1 C. zucchini, chopped
1 C. whole kernel corn
Few dashed Tabasco sauce

In a Dutch oven, cook the garlic in the oil. Add the tomatoes, V-8, tomato paste, tomato sauce, mustard, chili powder, oregano, cumin, basil and pepper. Add the three types of beans, all being drained; bring to a boil. Reduce the heat, cover, and simmer for 15 to 20 minutes.

Add the carrots, corn, zucchini, and covered, simmer for 10 minutes longer. During this simmering, add the hot sauce to your taste.

For a garnish, sprinkle top of each bowl with a little Parmesan cheese and serve with crackers, tacos, or tortilla chips. Makes 6 servings.
359 calories, 9 gm. fat, 10 mg. cholesterol, 776 mg. sodium.

Ms. Rosie Allen
E. Bernstadt, KY

Bonnie L. Webster
Payson, AZ

MEXICAN CHILI BEAN SOUP

2 T. olive oil
1 Lg. onion, chopped
2 cloves garlic, minced
1 Lb. skinless, boneless chicken breast, cubed
2 cans (14 oz.) stewed tomatoes
2 cans (15 oz.) red kidney beans, drained
1 Pkg. (10 oz.0 frozen kernel corn
1 can (7 oz.) diced green chiles
1 t. chili powder
½ t. ground cumin
½ t. oregano
Dash of hot sauce to taste
1 can (16 oz.) cling peach slices in juice or extra light syrup

In a Dutch oven or large pot, saute onions and garlic in the olive oil over a medium heat, until the onions are done. Add the cubed chicken and cook until completely done.

Stir in all remaining ingredients with the exception of the peaches, and bring to a boil; reduce heat, and simmer, covered, for about 25 to 30 minutes.

Add drained peach slices into the mixture. Makes 6 to 8 servings.

Ms. Andy Holland
Goshen, OH

Running MV
Allan H. Horton
Sarasota, FL

VEGETABLE CHILI

¾ C. olive oil, divided
2 zucchini, cut into ½-inch dice
2 onions, cut into ½-inch dice
4 cloves garlic, finely chopped
1 t. basil
2 Lg. sweet red peppers, ¼-inch dice
1 can (35 oz.) Italian-style plum tomatoes, with their juice
1½ Lbs. ripe plum tomatoes, cut into 1-inch dice
2 T. chili powder
1 T. oregano
2 t. freshly ground pepper
1 t. salt
1 t. fennel seeds
½ C. fresh Italian parsley
1 C. dark red kidney beans, drained
1 C. garbanzo beans, drained
½ C. fresh dill, chopped
2 T. lemon juice
1 C. dairy sour cream
1 Pkg. shredded Cheddar or Monterey Jack cheese
4 green onions, cut diagonally
1 T. ground cumin

In a large pot, heat ½ cup of the oil. Add the zucchini, and saute until tender. Transfer the zucchini to a large flame-proof casserole dish or another large pot or Dutch Oven.

Heat the rest of the olive oil in the pot over a low heat. Add the onions, garlic and bell pepper. Saute until the onions are nearly done. Put the vegetables into the pot with the zucchini, and place over a low heat.

Add the tomatoes, with juice, fresh tomatoes, chili powder, cumin, basil, oregano, pepper, salt, fennel seeds and the parsley. Cook, uncovered, for 30 minutes, stirring several times.

Add the kidney and garbanzo beans, dill and lemon juice. Cook for another 15 minutes or until done to tenderness and taste.

Ladle into serving bowls, garnished with sour cream, shredded cheese, and sliced green onions. Makes 8 servings.

Dorothy Borstein
Cincinnati, OH

U Cross
Curtis, Mildred,
& Jerry Skates
Ft. Myers, FL

CHILI CHEESE NACHOS

2 C. prepared Carroll Shelby's Original Texas Brand Chili Mix
1 (8 oz.) jar Cheez Whiz Pasteurized Process Cheese Spread
2 C. shredded lettuce
1 C. chopped tomatoes
½ C. sour cream
1 (8 oz.) Pkg. tortilla chips

Microwave chili and process cheese spread on HIGH 5 minutes or until thoroughly heated, stirring every 2 minutes.

Layer half of chips, half of chili mixture, remaining chips and remaining chili mixture on large serving platter. Top with remaining ingredients. Makes 8 Servings.

Prep time: 30 minutes

Judy DeProspo
Merritt Island, FL

Stanley & Maurice Weishaar
LaGrande, OR

SPICY VEGETABLE CHILI

Zesty jalapeno peppers spice this vegie-loaded chili that's cooled down with cilantro.

1 Lb. eggplant
5 T. light olive oil
2 Med.-sized onions, chopped
3 cloves garlic, minced
2 Med.-sized zucchini, diced
2 Lg. red bell peppers, diced
1 or 2 jalapeno peppers, seeded and finely minced
1 can (28 oz.) Italian-style plum tomatoes
Fresh ground pepper, to taste
5 Lg. plum tomatoes, diced
½ C. dry red wine
2 T. chili powder
1 T. ground cumin
2 t. dried oregano
1 t. fennel seeds
1 C. cooked white beans
1 C. cooked kidney beans
1 Lg. lemon, grated with juice
⅓ C. chopped fresh cilantro

Preheat oven to 350 degrees. Cut the eggplant into 1-inch chunks and place in a small, shallow roasting pan. Toss with 2 tablespoons olive oil; cover with aluminum foil and bake for 30 minutes, stirring once. Place in a bowl when done.

Heat the remaining oil in a casserole dish. Add onions and garlic; cook until onions are tender. Add the zucchini, red peppers and jalapenos; and cook for 5 minutes, stirring once.

Coarsely chop the canned tomatoes. Add them to the casserole with their juice, fresh tomatoes, red wine, chili powder, cumin, oregano and fennel seeds. Lightly stir in the remaining eggplant and let simmer on a low heat, for about 20 or 25 minutes.

Add rest of ingredients, stirring gently into the mixture, and simmer, for about 5 minutes.

For garnish on this chili dish, use sour cream, grated cheese of your choice, chopped onions or scallions.

Serves 8 to 10. Contains about 189 calories, 9g fat, and no cholesterol per serving.

Fred & Sharon Dorman
Carmel, IN

Flying B
Grant Baker
Coral Gables, FL

DOT'S VEGETARIAN CHILI

6 T. olive oil
1½ C. zucchini (about 2 small) cut into ½inch cubes
1 C. yellow onion, coarsely chopped cloves garlic, crushed
T. chili powder
1½ t. cumin
¼ C. fresh parsley, minced
Salt and pepper, to taste
2 C. canned beans (kidney and/ or garbanzo), drained
Garnish: Grated Cheddar cheese and low-fat sour cream, to taste
1½ t. dried oregano

1. Heat olive oil in a large skillet. Add zucchini, onion, garlic, and green pepper. Saute for 10 minutes or until softened.

2. Transfer vegetables to a saucepan and add tomatoes, chili powder, cumin, oregano, parsley, salt, and pepper. Cook over a low heat, uncovered, for about 10 minutes. Stir in the beans and cook an additional 10 minutes still on a low heat. If necessary, this is the time to adjust seasonings.

3. Serve chili rolled up in a warm flour tortilla or on a bed of brown rice. Garnish with the Cheddar cheese and a dollop of sour cream. Serves 4. As a sub for the zucchini, cut an eggplant into ½-inch cubes and prepare in the same manner.

Per serving: 362 calories; 10.6g protein; 21.7g fat; 0 mg cholesterol; 356 mg sodium

Dorothy Borstein
Cincinnati, OH

George T. Cobb, Jr.
Cadiz, OH

CHILI WINGS

4 Lbs. chicken wings
1 Pkg. favorite chili seasoning mix
¼ C. corn meal
½ t. salt
2 t. parsley flakes

Put all ingredients in a plastic bag. Shake wings thoroughly a few at a time to completely cover them with the spices.

Place wings, skin side up, in single layer in well buttered baking pan.

Bake at 350 degrees for 25 to 30 minutes. Turn and bake until chicken is tender, approximately 8 to 10 minutes.

Betsy Gross
Merritt Island, FL

"Square and Compass" recorded in 1872 by Pointdexter and Orr of Beaverhead County. This is the first brand shown in the book kept by the Clerk of the Supreme Court of Montana Territory.

1,2,3 CHILI W-A-L-A!!!

Fast and good chili that take no time at all to prepare....

I Pkg. Chili-O-Mix (onion)
1 Lb. ground chuck
1 reg jar spaghetti sauce - your choice (mine is garden style (chunky) Ragu
Pinch or two garlic powder
1 can kidney beans
Little pinch of chili powder for extra taste
Salt and pepper to taste

Directions:

1. Brown ground chuck, sprinkle garlic powder while browning, salt and pepper. Drain any fat.

2. Add the package of chili mix and follow directions on back of package - usually all I do is add package and one cup of water! Mix well.

3. Add jar of sauce and mix, then add your beans, mix and simmer a while. Serve over spaghetti.

John & Margie Napier
London, KY

Bar None Ranch Ltd
Ed Hedemann
Honolulu, HA

NEW ORLEANS CHILI

1 can (14½ oz.) Del Monte Cajun or Original Style Stewed Tomatoes
1 can (8 oz.) Del Monte Tomato Sauce
2 C. diced cooked beef
1 onion, chopped
1 green pepper, chopped
1 T. chili powder
½ t. cumin (optional)
⅛-¼ t. cayenne pepper
1 can (15½ oz.) kidney beans, drained

In large saucepan, combine tomatoes, tomato sauce, meat, onion, pepper, chili powder, cumin and cayenne; cover and simmer 15 minutes. Stir in beans and simmer, uncovered 10 minutes. Garnish with shredded Cheddar cheese, if desired. 6 servings.

Prep Time: 6 minutes. Cook Time: 25 minutes.

Del Monte's label recipe

Marilyn Cope
Cadiz, OH

EAST-WEST 10-MINUTE STIR-FRIED CHILI

½ Lb. lean beef round, diced or ground
1 Lg. (or 2 Med.) onions, peeled and chopped
1 (or 2) clove garlic, peeled and minced
1 T. lime juice (or vinegar)
2 fresh (or canned) red or green hot chili peppers, seeded and chopped
2 sweet bell peppers (red or green) seeded and diced
Water
2 ripe fresh unpeeled tomatoes, diced
1 C. tomato juice (or fat-skimmed beef broth)
½ C. chopped fresh parsley
1 T. minced fresh (or 1 t. dried) leaf oregano
2 t. whole cumin seeds (or 1 t. ground cumin)
Salt and pepper, to taste
Optional: 2 t. instant-blending flour and 2 T. cold
Optional: ½ of a Med. head crisp iceberg lettuce,diced
Optional: 4 T. shredded very sharp Cheddar cheese

Spray large non-stick skillet or electric frying pan with cooking spray. Spread beef in shallow layer and cook without adding fat over high heat until chunks are brown; turn to brown evenly. Drain and discard any melted fat. Stir in onion, garlic and juice (or vinegar). Cook and stir over high heat just until onion begins to brown. Stir in remaining ingredients except flour, water, lettuce and cheese. Cover and cook over low heat for 4 to 5 minutes.

Uncover and cook an additional 1 to 2 minutes, until most liquid evaporates. (If desired, combine flour with cold water, stir into skillet and simmer until sauce is thick, stir in lettuce and heat through, then sprinkle with shredded cheese.) Serve from skillet. Makes 4 servings, 165 calories each; with all optional ingredients, 205 calories per serving.

A word about fresh hot peppers; There are close to 60 varieties of them, in varying flavors, colors, size and "heat." If you are new to using fresh hot peppers, it's best to err on the side of caution. You can cut the BTU's by soaking diced fresh peppers in cold water for a few minutes before adding to the skillet. (This cuts the heat in half.)

One further caution: Wash your hands with soap and water after handling fresh hot peppers because if you inadvertently wipe your eyes with peppery fingers, the volatile oils will do the same to you eye membranes that they do to your tongue. Ouch!

Cincinnati Enquirer

Douglas M. Horn
Wooster, OH

TEXAS CHILI VIA CINCINNATI

This is my recipe for "Texas Chili". It is a hand-me-down which I added a couple of ingredients is well worth the time to prepare one's own pinto beans (no substitutes).

- 1½ Lbs. lean ground beef
- ½ C. chopped bell pepper
- 1 t. salt
- ½ t. prepared mustard
- 1 t. heaping chili powder
- 5 dashes Tabasco sauce
- 2 T. olive oil
- 1 can (6 oz.) tomato sauce
- 1½ C. water
- ½ C. chopped onion
- 2 Lg. cloves garlic, minced
- ¼ t. black pepper
- 2 T. tomato catsup
- 1 small jalapeno, seeded & minced
- 1 Lg. fresh tomato, chopped
- 2 C. freshly cooked pinto beans with juice
- 1 can (16 oz.) stewed tomatoes

Directions: Brown meat in olive oil. Add onion, and bell pepper. Saute one minute then add fresh tomato and stir. Add remaining ingredients and slowly simmer for 2 hours, stirring every 20 minutes. Check if too thick and add small amount of water while cooking. Use heavy-duty container to prevent sticking.

Ms. Mabel Meeks
Administrative Secretary
Univ. of Cincinnati
College of Medicine,
Division of Cardiology
Cincinnati, OH

Douglas Vance
Sanger, CA

JUST EATIN' CHILI

- 2 Lbs. ground round, or lean chuck
- 1 Qt. + 1 C. tomato juice
- 1 t. ground cinnamon
- 1 t. ground cumin
- 1 Lg. whole onion
- 2 Lg. dashes Worcestershire sauce
- ⅛ t. garlic powder
- 1 t. ground allspice
- 4 T. chili powder or to taste
- 1 t. fresh ground pepper
- 1 t. red pepper
- 1½ t. salt
- 1½ t. vinegar
- 5 whole bay leaves

In a large saucepan or Dutch oven, combine all of the ingredients, and cook, uncovered, for about 2 hours. Stir occasionally for even cooking. After time, remove onion and bay leaves.

For removal of all grease from cooked meat, allow to cook, and refrigerate overnight. Skim off solidified grease. Reheat and serve as desired.

This chili can be used with spaghetti for Cincinnati style chilies, or add beans for chili with beans, or put on hot dogs for chili coneys.

Ms. Margie Napier
E. Bernstadt, KY

79

Montana Cattle Co. 1879
John T. Murphy, Mgr.
Ryegate Area, Powder River

MY FAVORITE CHILI

½ Lb. dry pinto or kidney beans
2 C. water
1 cans (16 oz.) tomatoes
1 Lb. chuck, coarsely ground
2 Med. onions, coarsely chopped
2 stalks celery, chopped
1 green pepper, coarsely chopped, (optional)
2 cloves garlic, crushed
2 to 3 T. chili powder
½ T. salt
1 t. pepper
1 t. apple cider vinegar

Soak beans overnight in sufficient water to completely cover by 2 inches.

In a Crock Pot, combine all the ingredients, and stir to blend. Cover, and cook on Low heat for 10 to 12 hours. If cook slow cooking on High, 5 to 6 hours will do.

Ms. Heidi Smith
Cincinnati, OH

Flying V
Carl R. Gallagher
Immokalee, FL

TIMES RED CHILI

10 dried red New Mexico chili pods
4 Lbs. beef chunk or pork boneless shoulder, cut into ½-inch dice
1 Lg. clove garlic
Salt to taste
2 C. Boiling water
1 T. vegetable oil

1. Soak the chili pods in cold water for 20 minutes. Do not soak longer or they might become bitter. Drain and remove the stems and seeds.

2. Place the chilies in a blender with the garlic and puree to a smooth paste. Add the boiling water and blend.

3. Heat the oil in a large pot over medium-high heat and saute the meat, in batches, until well browned.

4. Return all the meat to the pot and reduce heat to medium low. Stir in the chili paste and salt, cover and cook for 45 minutes to one hour.

Yield: Eight to 10 servings.

Barry & Roberta Geltner
from New York Times

Barker Ranch
Phoenix, AZ

CHILI MAC OLE'

Add a flavor of the Southwest to your nutritious, delicious Creamettes Macaroni with Hormel Chili No Beans.

2 C. Creamettes' Elbow Macaroni, uncooked
1 (15 oz.) can Hormel Chili No Beans
1 (10 oz.) can tomatoes with green chilies, drained
½ Med. green pepper, finely chopped
3 green onions, sliced
1 t. seasoned salt
¾ C. shredded American cheese, divided

Prepare Creamettes' Elbow Macaroni according to package directions; drain. In medium saucepan heat remaining ingredients (reserving ¼ cup cheese) until cheese melts, stirring frequently.

Arrange macaroni on platter; pour Hormel Chili mixture over; top with remaining cheese. Garnish as desired.

Refrigerate leftovers. 6 servings.

If casserole is desired; combine cooked macaroni and remaining ingredients. Pour into a 2-quart baking dish. Bake in a 350 degree oven for 25 minutes.

Hormel/Creamette recipe

Floppy T Ranch
Carl E. Turner
Harvest, AL

KATHRYN GRAYSON'S ALL-AMERICAN CHILI

'Singing to a pot of chili might improve flavor'

½ Lb. fresh hot chili peppers, about 2½ to 3 inches long
Boiling salted water
3 Lg. onions, peeled
2½ Lbs. lean boneless flank or round steak
2 t. salt
½ t. freshly ground black pepper, more if desired
¼ t. garlic powder
2 eggs, beaten
1 C. unseasoned breadcrumbs
3 cans (15 oz.) tomato puree
2 cans (14 oz.) beef broth, or water
¾ t. oregano leaves, crushed
¼ t. basil, crushed
2 t. ground cumin
2 Lg. bay leaves
¼ C. chili powder
1½ T. brown sugar or catsup, to taste

Rinse chili peppers; place in saucepan. Cover with salted boiling water. Cover and cook over medium heat 10 minutes, or until tender. Drain and split peppers. Remove and discard stem ends and seeds from peppers. Scrape pulp from skin; place in large stock pot. Mince 1½ onions finely and place in stock pot with chili pulp; set aside.

Trim all fat and connective tissue from meat. Cut half the filet into bite-size pieces and set aside. Quarter remaining onions and put through blade of electric or hand grinder along with meat cubes. Season meat mixture as you grind it with 1½ teaspoon salt, half the pepper and garlic powder. Mix with hands. Grind meat second time and divide into two parts.

Add eggs and breadcrumbs to half the ground meat-onion mixture; knead well with fingers to blend. Shape into marble-size meatballs. Broil meatballs a few seconds; set aside.

Add remaining ground meat mixture to stock pot with chili-minced onion mixture. Add tomato puree, stirring to blend, plus beef broth, oregano, basil, cumin, bay leaves, chili powder and remaining salt and pepper. Cook and stir 1 hour over medium heat.

Add meatballs; cook 15 minutes, longer, stirring often. Add filet pieces; cook 30 minutes longer, stirring often. Add sugar and catsup to taste and additional water or broth as needed.

As chili cooks, taste, adding more chili powder or seasonings as desired. Serve hot with cooked rice, macaroni or beans. Serves 12 to 15.

Courier-Post
Cherry Hill, PA

Thrusting W
Agrico Chem. Co.
Pierce, FL

CHILI LOVER'S CHILI

1½ Lbs. ground beef
1 Lg. onion, diced
1 Lg. green pepper, coarse chopped
1 Lg. red pepper, coarse chopped
1 clove garlic, minced
3 T. chili powder
1½ t. salt
½ t. ground cumin
½ t. crushed red pepper
1 can (28 oz.) tomatoes in puree
1 can (17 oz.) whole kernel corn, drained
1 can (15¼ to 19 oz.) red kidney beans, drained
1 can (12 oz.) bottle beer or non-alcoholic beer
3 T. tomato paste
2 T. light molasses

In a large Dutch oven, cook the ground beef, onion, green and red pepper over a high heat. Stir frequently, until vegetables are tender and the meat is cooked. Drain off fat drippings and cooking oil.

Mix in the salt, ground cumin, chili powder and crushed red pepper. Let simmer a few minutes on low. Then mix in the tomatoes with puree, whole kernel corn, kidney beans, tomato paste, molasses and the beer.

Bring the pot to a boil, then reduce to low heat and allow to cook, with an occasional stirring every so often, for 30 minutes.

About 345 calories; 15g fat; 57mg cholesterol; 915 mg sodium per serving. Makes about 8-9 servings.

Judy DeProspo
Merritt Island, Fl

Niihau Ranch
Kawai, HA

CHILI MOLE OLE

2 Lbs. lean ground beef
2 Lg. onions, cut into ½-inch pieces
2 cloves garlic, minced
2 cans (15 oz.) pinto or kidney beans, drained
1 can (29 oz.) tomato sauce
1¼ C. prepared picante sauce
½ C. beef stock
3 T. unsweetened cocoa
2 t. ground cumin
1 t. dried oregano
1¼ t. salt
⅛ t. ground cloves
⅛ t. allspice
1 Lg. green pepper, cut into ¾-inch pieces

In a large saucepan, brown the beef with the onion and garlic. Drain. Add beans, tomato sauce, picante sauce, beef stock, cocoa, cumin, oregano, salt, cloves, nutmeg and allspice, mixing well into beef mixture.

Bring to a boil. Reduce heat to low. Cover, simmer for 40 minutes. Stir in green pepper. Simmer for an additional 20 minutes more.

Ladle into bowls, and if desired top with chopped raw onions, sour cream and/or shredded cheese. Makes 8 servings.

Bernie & Gail Geltner
from Pioneer Press
Rolling Meadows, IL

Mr. & Mrs. Raymond Doherty
Echo, OR

BLACK BEAN ’VEGETABLE CHILI

- 1 Lg. onion, coarsely chopped
- 1 T. vegetable oil
- 1 can (28 oz.) whole tomatoes, undrained, coarsely chopped
- ⅔ C. prepared picante sauce
- 1½ t. ground cumin
- 1 t. salt
- ½ t. crushed basil leaves
- 1 can (16 oz.) black beans, rinsed and drained
- 1 green bell pepper, cut into ¾-inch pieces
- 1 red bell pepper, cut into ¾-inch pieces
- 1 Lg. yellow squash, cut in ½-inch chunks

In large saucepan, cook onion in oil until tender. Add tomatoes, picante sauce, cumin, salt and basil. Cover. Simmer 5 minutes. Stir in beans, bell peppers and squash. Cover. Simmer until vegetables are tender, approximately 15 minutes. Ladle into bowls. If desired, serve with toppings of hot cooked rice, chopped fresh cilantro, sour cream and/or shredded cheese. Makes 8 servings.

Gail Geltner
from Pioneer Press
Rolling Meadows, IL

Bar None Ranch
Robert I. Jackson
Baxter, TN

TIMES GREEN CHILI

8 green New Mexico chilies
2 T. vegetable oil
2 Lg. onions, chopped
1 clove garlic, chopped
4 Lbs. boned chicken thighs, coarsely chopped, or ground beef or pork
2 Lg. tomatoes, chopped
Salt and freshly ground pepper to taste

1. Preheat the oven to 450 degrees.
2. Place the chilies on a baking sheet and roast them, turning often, until well charred. Place the peppers in a large bowl, cover with a damp towel and cool.
3. When cook enough to handle, peel the chilies and remove the stem and seeds. Dice coarsely.
4. Heat the oil in a large casserole over medium-high heat, and saute the onions and garlic until tender, about 10 minutes. Add the chicken and saute briefly, stirring. Add the chilies, tomatoes, salt and pepper and two cups water to just cover the meat. Simmer for 45 minutes to one hour.

Yield: Eight to 10 servings.

Barry & Roberta Geltner
from New York Times

U.S. Indian Brand
Dakota (1882)

NO GAIN CHILI

1 T. olive oil
2 Lbs. very lean beef, chili ground
2 Med. onions, chopped
1 green bell pepper, chopped
1 red bell pepper, chopped
2 cloves garlic, crushed
1 T. chili powder
1 t. dried oregano
1½ t. cumin
½ t. salt
1 can (15 oz.) low-sodium, tomatoes, with juice
2 T. low-sodium tomato paste
1 can (8 oz.) low-sodium tomato sauce

Heat olive oil in large cooking pot. Saute the onions, peppers and garlic until they are done. Remove to a bowl with a slotted spoon, and proceed to cook the meat until it is browned, breaking up with a wooden spoon as it is cooking. Drain as much fat from meat by removing beef with slotted spoon to same bowl with vegetables.

After removing the grease, replace meat and vegetables to large pot. Add all remaining ingredients. Bring the pot to a boil. Reduce heat, and simmer, uncovered for 45 minutes to an hour.

Add tomato juice if it is necessary to thin chili.

Shane T. McCoy
Cincinnati, OH

Mrs. Puna K. Dang
Honolulu, HA

WALK THROUGH THE GARDEN CHILI

2 T. olive oil
2 Med. onions, chopped
2 bell peppers, chopped
4 stalks celery, chopped
3 carrots, chopped
4 cloves garlic, chopped
1 zucchini, chopped
2 yellow summer squash chopped
4 to 5 fresh tomatoes, peeled and chopped
2 T. chili powder
1 t. ground cumin seeds
1 t. dried oregano
1 t. dried basil
1 T. lemon juice
2½ t. salt
½ t. fresh ground black pepper
2 C. tomato juice
1 can (16 oz.) kidney beans

In a large saucepan or kettle, heat the oil and saute the onions, peppers, celery, carrots and garlic until done. Add all remaining ingredients except the beans, and bring to a boil. Reduce heat, uncover, and simmer until the vegetables are tender.

Add the beans and cook an additional 10 minutes to heat them through.

Ben C. Seltzer
Cincinnati, OH

Ms. Atha Deaton
Hamshire,
Jefferon County, TX

CIN-TEX CHILI

The Cincinnati-Texas chili things can be settled with this recipe which was found among old newspapers. I'm sure that it will be taken by all as a good blend between the two chili centers of the country.

- 2 Lbs. beef chuck, ground
- 3 Lbs. beef chuck, chili ground
- 2 Lg. onions, chopped
- 2 Lg. bell green peppers, chopped
- 6 cloves garlic, minced
- 2 cans (15 oz.) tomato sauce
- 2 cans (28 oz.) whole tomatoes, chopped, with juice
- 2 cans (8 oz.) tomato paste
- 4 T. chili powder
- 2 T. ground hot red chile
- 1 T. ground oregano
- 2½ T. ground cumin
- 2½ t. salt
- ½ + t. fresh ground black pepper
- 2 cans (16 oz.) pinto beans, or 4 cups cooked
- 3-4 C. water

In a Dutch oven or other type of large cooking pot, use a little oil and brown the beef. It would be much easier to do the browning in smaller batches than all at once. Drain grease as each batch is done, and transfer to another container. When completely cooked, add all beef to same pot.

Add the chopped onions, peppers, garlic and dry spices to meat, and bring to a boil. Reduce heat to simmer, add tomato sauce, tomato paste and sufficient water to pot, if necessary to thin mixture. Mix pot well to blend the meat and vegetables. Simmer for about 1½ to 2 hours uncovered, stirring occasionally.

Taste and adjust seasonings if desired. Stir in the chopped tomatoes and pinto beans during the last 15 minutes or so of cooking to heat them trough before serving.

Serves 10 to 12.

Sharon Geltner
Boca Raton, FL

Flying M
Michael Partin
Kissinnee, FL

EL PASO CHILI

2 T. salad oil
2 Lg. red onions, chopped
3 Lg. cloves garlic, crushed
3 Lbs. ground beef
2 cans (28 oz.) whole tomatoes
2 Med. green or red peppers, seeded, chopped
1 C. dry red wine
½ C. chili powder
2 t. yellow corn meal or Masa harina
1 T. sugar
1½ t. ground cumin
1 t. salt
½ t. ground red pepper
1 can (16 oz.) red kidney beans, drained
1 can (15 oz.) whole kernel corn, drained

In a large saucepan, heat the oil over a medium-high heat until hot. Add the onions and garlic; saute until they are tender, about 5 minutes. Add the ground beef, and cook until it is browned, crumbling with a spoon to reduce size of meat chunks. Drain off pan drippings and discard.

Stir in tomatoes, and their juice, red pepper, wine, chili powder, corn meal, cumin, salt and ground red pepper, mixing well to blend spices and ingredients with meat mixture. Bring to a boil; reduce heat and simmer uncovered for about 30 minutes. Stir frequently.

Stir in the beans and kernel corn. Simmer 15 minutes longer. For garnish, serve this dish with sour cream, shredded Monterey Jack or Cheddar cheese, and plenty of extra chopped onions.

This recipe makes 10 servings. Per serving, this has: 462 calories, 30 g. protein, 28 g. carbohydrate, 25 g. fat, 91 mg. cholesterol, 802 mg. sodium.

Seena Golden
Cincinnati, OH

Tee Pee Three
Thomas Partin III
Theodore, AL

HORMEL CHILI PIZZA

2 cups baking mix
½ cup very hot water
1 (15 oz.) can Hormel Chili No Beans
1 cup shredded mozzarella cheese
½ cup shredded Cheddar Cheese

1. Heat oven to 450 degrees. Move oven rack to lowest position.

2. Combine baking soda and water; beat 20 strokes.
3. Turn dough onto surface dusted with baking soda. Knead dough until no longer sticky,about 60 times. Roll dough into a 12-inch circle.
4. Place on greased pizza pan. Spread chili over dough. Top with cheese.
5. Bake 12 to 15 minutes or until cheese is melted and bubbly.
Serves 6.

Hormel recipe

Dennis & Cheryl Wong
Kawai, HA

HORMEL CHILI BOATS

- 4 hot baked potatoes
- 1 (15 oz.) can Hormel Chili No Beans, heated
- 4 slices (1 oz. each) Cheddar cheese
- Sour cream (optional)

1. Split potatoes.
2. Top each potato with chili and 1 cheese slice.
3. Broil 2 to 3 minutes or until cheese is melted and bubbly.
4. Top with a dollop of sour cream, if desired. 5. Serve.

Hormel recipe

Mae Davis Durr
Rogers, AR
Jefferson County, TX

The custom of branding animals is an ancient one that was brought to the New World by the Spanish. By 1529 brands were already being registered in Mexico, and by the early 1600's brands were being used in Florida to identify particular herds.

Florida Cowman, A History of Florida Cattle Raising

JAY'S CHILI

I had this recipe for some time, ever since it was sent to me as a namesake recipe. Hope that the "original" Jay isn't offended by me using it.

- 1 T. cooking oil
- 3 Med. onions, finely chopped
- 2 green peppers, cored, seeded, and finely chopped
- 3 stalks celery, finely chopped
- 3 cloves garlic, minced
- 8 Lbs. beef round, chili ground
- 2 cans (20 oz.) tomato sauce
- 2 cans (20 oz.) stewed tomatoes
- 1 can (6 oz.) tomato paste
- 6 C. water
- 1 can (4 oz.) chili salsa
- 1 canned pickled jalapeno pepper, finely chopped
- 6 T. chili powder (the original recipe called for hot and mild chile powder, but this is much easier using)
- 1 T. ground cumin
- 1½ t.dried oregano
- 2 T. salt, or to taste
- Fresh ground black pepper, to taste

In a Dutch oven or other 10-to 12-quart cooking vessel, heat the oil over a medium heat. Saute the onions, green peppers, celery and garlic until the onions are soft and transparent. Do not brown or burn them.

Add the meat, cooking only part at a time so that it is evenly done. Use a wooden spoon to crumble the meat to get rid of large chunks. When the meat is evenly browned, put all in the large pot.

Drain off, either by using a slotted spoon when transferring to large pot, or spooning as much as possible from top of mixture. I try to get as much off as possible.

Blend in the remaining ingredients, bring pot to a boil. Reduce heat to a simmer, and let cook, uncovered, for 2½ to 3 hours. Stir often and taste to adjust seasonings if needed.

Hope 'Jay' enjoys this as much as I.

Jay & Sandy Hatfield
Cincinnati, OH

Keogh Brothers
Idaho (1884)

CHILI CON QUESO PIE with TEX-MEX SALSA

3 T. olive oil
4 fresh Anaheim chile peppers, seeded and chopped
1 to 3 fresh jalapeno peppers, seeded and minced (see note)
1 Med. yellow onion, chopped
3 Lg. ears fresh corn, cut from cob
3 Lg. tomatoes, diced
¼ C. chicken broth
6 Med. flour tortillas
8 Ozs. cream cheese, softened
3 C. (¾ Lb.) shredded Jack cheese

Heat olive oil in a heavy, large skillet. Saute both peppers and onion, stirring, over medium-high heat for 5 minutes.

Stir in corn and cook, stirring for 2-3 minutes.

Add tomatoes and chicken stock and cook over high heat 2-3 minutes more. Remove from heat. Season to taste with salt, if desired.

Spread one side of each tortilla with the cream cheese. Place a tortilla, cheese side up, in a greased 9-inch pie pan. Spoon some of the vegetable mixture over the cheese and sprinkle with some shredded Jack cheese.

Repeat with the remaining 5 tortillas, stacking one on top of another. Pour any remaining vegetable around the edge and save a generous amount of Jack cheese to sprinkle over the top.

Cover and chill until ready to bake.

Bake in a 350 degree oven for 20-35 minutes. (If made ahead and chilled, the maximum baking time will be required.)

Cut into wedges and serve warm. Pass the Tex-Mex salsa to spoon over.

Serve 8 as an appetizer.

NOTE: Number of jalapenos determines spiciness - use only 1 for a mild flavor.

FRESH TEX-MEX SALSA

3 Lg. ripe tomatoes, cored and diced
2 Lg. fresh jalapeno peppers, seeded and minced
1 Med. red onion, finely chopped
¼ cup chopped fresh cilantro leaves
Salt to taste
Pinch sugar

Combine ingredients; stir together. Cover & chill for at least 2 hours.

Cincinnati Enquirer

Luther & Richard Hubbell
Columbia, TN

AVERAGE AWARD WINNING CHILI

32 Oz. canned tomatoes
5 Lbs. round steak (¼" cubes)
Lg. onion, browned & pureed
Lg. red pepper, grilled & pureed
Beef kidney suet (about 4" cube)
20 Oz. beef consomme
4 Lg. garlic cloves, crushed
8 T. Gebhardts Chili Powder
1 T. cayenne pepper
2 T. cumin
1 t. black pepper
1 T. ground oregano
1 T. paprika
3 drops red food color
Sea salt to taste
¼ t. fennel
64 Oz. water
2 bay leaves

Grill Suet and use liquid to brown meat and garlic.
Brown onion and green pepper and puree in blender.
Add all other items to the above and simmer for 2 hours.
Note: add cumin and bay leaves during the last ½ hour of cooking.
Small amounts of cooked beans (al Dente) or pasta shells can be added at serving time but must be cooked separately.

Eight past Champion Chili recipes were "averaged" for this terrific combination. My preference was for a "soupy" chili rather than a "thick" type.

Remember - liquids reduce in cooking so go easy on the soup stock (also reduces salt)

Too much pasta or beans diminish flavor.

Walt Harris
Cocoa Beach, FL

Pierre Wibaux, 1885
French Textile Family
Montana

DE'S VEGETARIAN CHILI

In a large saucepan or skillet:
4 T. olive oil
1 Med. spanish onion
2 carrots
1 head of broccoli
other vegies if desired
1 T. garlic powder
4 T. chili powder

Cook above ingredients over medium-low heat, adding chili powder, and cook until tender.

Add 12 package of diced tofu, and cook for 15 minutes. Add 1 can of tomato sauce, 1 can tomatoes, 1 can tomato paste, and two cans of Bush's Baked Beans (drained) or kidney beans.

Cook for one hour!

Judy DeProspo
Merritt Island, FL

Louis W. Bailey
Chanberlain, SD

MILLER LITE CHILI

(by: Chef-Boy-Hardy)

- 2 Lbs. lean ground beef
- 1 can (28 oz.) kidney beans
- 1 can (16 oz.) tomato sauce
- 1 can (8 oz.) whole tomatoes
- ½ C. whole corn (drained)
- ½ C. chopped onions
- ¼ C. chopped celery
- ¼ C. chopped green pepper
- 1 chopped jalapeno pepper, (include seeds if you like it hot)
- 2 T. chili powder
- 2 T. cumin
- 2 T. minced garlic
- ½ t. pepper
- ½ t. hot sauce

Brown and drain beef in pan. Combine all ingredients in a large sauce pan and simmer, covered for 1 hour. Add beans and simmer for 30 minutes. If chili seems to be too thick ADD MORE LITE BEER!

Serve with the following condiments:

1 bowl of coarse cut onions
1 bowl of diced jalapeno peppers
1 bowl of diced dill pickles
2 boxes of crackers

Plenty of ice cold: "MILLER LITE BEER"

Bill Hardy
Merritt Island, FL

Van E. Coggins
Wartrace, TN

HOT CHILI SOUP

1 T. olive oil
½ + C. chopped onions
½ + C. chopped green pepper
1 clove garlic, minced
1 t. + chili powder
1 t. ground cumin
Dash or two Tabasco sauce
1 can (14 oz.) chicken broth
1 can (16 oz.) stewed tomatoes
⅓ C. uncooked elbow macaroni
Freshly chopped cilantro
1 can (15 oz.) red kidney beans, drained and rinsed

Heat the oil in a skillet over and saute the onion and pepper until tender. Add all ingredients except the macaroni and beans. Cover, and bring to a boil. Reduce heat and simmer for just a few minutes. Add the beans and macaroni and simmer for about 5 minutes, or until the macaroni is tender.

Heidi Smith
Cincinnati, OH

John & Josephine Andrade
Honolulu, HA

HOT CHILI Con QUESO

1 Lb. Velveeta Jalapeno cheese
2 cans (7 oz.) chopped green chile
2 cans mushroom soup
1 small can chopped olives

Place mushroom soup in a pan and let it come to a boil. Slowly add the cheese, cut into small cubes, constantly stirring to avoid sticking. Then add chile and olives. This dip is ready to serve. For a hotter dip, add more chile.

Or try adding some picante sauce. The flavor is incredible.

South of the Border with
Mexican Recipes
by Carol DeSantis-Munoz
El Paso Herald-Post
Carl F. Tarlowski, MD
Los Cruces, NM

McLennan County, TX
Brands from 1800's

CHINA SYNDROME CHILI

2 Lbs. chuck beef, cubed
½ C. vegetable oil
2 onions, chopped
4 cloves garlic, chopped
1 small can, tomato paste
1 small can, tomato sauce
4 chili peppers
1 Lg. pinch cayenne pepper
2 T. paprika
2 t. oregano
4 t. cumin
Salt to taste
2 cans pinto beans

In a large skillet, heat the oil until it's smoking hot. In two batches, brown the beef on all sides and drain the oil from the pan. Cover the beef with water, cover the skillet and simmer over a low flame for 90 minutes. During the entire process, make sure the chili does not come to a boil, or burn.

Add onions; simmer for a half-hour, covered. Following this, add the remaining ingredients and simmer an additional half-hour, uncovered. Top with either homemade or canned pinto beans. Yield: 4 servings.

Bill Hardy
Merritt Island, FL

Corlett Brothers
Wyoming (1884)

HOMINY CHILI

1 C. chili (any cooked you may have)
1 C. hominy
1 Med. onion, chopped
1 C. corn chips, lightly crushed
1 C. shredded Cheddar or Monterey Jack cheese

In a small baking dish, put hominy in a layer. Add a layer of heated chili, with the chopped onions sprinkled evenly on it. Spread a layer of the corn chips, and then finish the dish off with a layer of the shredded cheese.

Bake in pre-heated oven, at 350 degrees for about 25 minutes.

Serves 6.

Ms. Judy Sterling
Cape Canaveral, FL

N M Joined
Nellie M. MacMillan
Delray Beach, FL

CHILE Con QUESO

1 C. Monterey Jack cheese
½ C. Cheddar cheese
¼ C. heavy cream
1 Med.-size fresh tomato, peeled and finely chopped
1 Med.-size sweet onion, finely chopped
¼ C. chopped parched green chilies
1 garlic clove, crushed

1. Melt both cheeses together in a heavy saucepan or double boiler over low heat.
2. After cheese melts, add cream, stirring constantly.
3. Add chopped tomato, onion, green chilies and garlic. Stir to blend all flavors. More cream may be needed; if so, add only a few drops at a time.
4. Serve warm in a chafing dish or a dish set over a candle warmer. Serve with tostados.

Bill Hardy
Merritt Island, FL

Douglas & Tunie Betschart
Rainier, OR

VEGETABLE CHILI

15 oz. tomatoes
Bay leaf
1 apple, chopped
2 t. pickle, chopped
1 t. tomato puree
1 Med. onion, chopped
4 oz. kidney beans
4 oz. peas
4 oz. carrots, chopped
4 oz. potatoes, peeled and chopped
1 t. chili powder
4 oz. vegetable stock

Place all ingredients in a saucepan and cover. Simmer for 1 hour, stirring occasionally. Remove lid and continue to cook until mixture is of a thick consistency. Remove bay leaf. Serve chili on a bed of boiled brown rice. Serves 4.

Bill Hardy
Merritt Island, FL

Thomas M. Fox
Boise, ID

MEXICAN CHILI

2 T. lard or solid shortening (lard will taste better)
2 Lg. onions, coarsely chopped
5 cloves garlic, minced
5 to 6 Lbs. lean boneless beef, cut into ½-inch cubes
2 to 2½ Lbs. fresh, ripe tomatoes, coarsely chopped
1 can (4 oz.) green chilies, chopped
1 t. coriander powder
T. ground cumin seed
C. (or more to taste) puree powder
1 T. oregano
4 C. hot tap water
2 cans (16 oz.) golden hominy, drained
Salt and pepper to taste
Cayenne pepper to taste

Combine lard or solid shortening, onions and garlic in a 7-quart microwave saucepan. Micro 10 minutes on HIGH, stirring once, or until onions are soft. Add beef, tomatoes, green chilies, coriander, cumin seed, chili powder, oregano and water.

Stir well, cover with a lid or wax paper and micro 10 minutes on High. Stir and micro 30 minutes on 50 percent power (MEDIUM). Add Hominy, season to taste and recover. Micro 30 minutes on 30 percent (LOW), or until meat is tender.

Bill Hardy
Merritt Island, FL

John P. Lopes, III
Pearl City, HA

HOT SPICY CHILI

1 Lb. ground beef
1 Med. onion, chopped
2 or 3 cloves garlic, crushed
1 can (16 oz.) tomatoes, cut up
1 can (15½ oz.) red kidney beans, drained and rinsed
1 can (4 oz.) green chile peppers, rinsed, seeded and chopped
1 C. tomato juice
1 t. Worcestershire sauce
2 t. paprika
1 t. oregano
¼ t. cayenne pepper
Salt and pepper to taste
½ t. cumin seeds, ground
½ t. dry mustard
¼ t. celery salt
1 t. sugar
Dash or so of Tabasco sauce

In a large heavy saucepan, brown the beef, onion, and garlic in a little oil. Drain excess drippings and fat from saucepan. Stir in tomatoes, tomato juice, chile peppers, beans, Worcestershire sauce, paprika, oregano, cayenne pepper, cumin, dry mustard, celery salt, black pepper and Tabasco. Add also 1 or so cups water, if necessary for consistency. Cover and simmer for about 30 minutes. Makes 4 to 6 servings.

Carrie Hatfield
Cincinnati, OH

Daryl Ross Thronas
Kawai, HA

CHILI FOR TWO

¾ Lb. lean ground beef
1 T. olive oil
½ C. onion, chopped
½ C. green pepper, chopped
1 clove garlic, crushed
1 small can, tomatoes, cut up
1 can (8 oz.) tomato sauce
1 can, kidney beans, or pinto beans, drained
½ t. oregano
¼ t. cumin
½ t. sugar
1 T. chili powder
Salt and pepper to taste
Cooked rice (optional)

In a large saucepan, saute onions, green pepper and garlic until the onion is transparent but not browned. Add the meat, and cook until it is browned, using a wooden spoon to crumble. After browning, drain off excess oil and grease.

Add remaining ingredients, mixing well to blend with the meat and vegetables. Bring to a boil; reduce heat, cover and simmer for about 30 minutes. Add tomato juice if too thick of a consistency.

Serve in bowls over the rice if desired.

Kelly Haviland
Cincinnati, OH

Habrun's Painted Horses
Millersburg, OH

TEXAS CHILI

40 dried hot chili peppers, or
¼ C. crushed red pepper
3 dried ancho peppers
1½ Lbs. beef round steak, cut into ½-inch cubes
2 T. cooking oil
1 Med. onion, chopped
2 cloves garlic, minced
1½ t. ground cumin
1 can (10½ oz.) condensed beef broth
1 soup can (1⅓ C. water)
½ t. dried oregano, crushed
Hot cooked pinto beans

Crush hot chili peppers. Remove stems and seeds from ancho peppers; cut into 1-inch pieces. Blend peppers in blender until ground. In large saucepan, brown half the meat in hot oil. With slotted spoon, remove meat; and set aside. Add remaining meat, onion, garlic, cumin and ground chili peppers; cook until meat is brown.

Return all meat to saucepan. Stir in beef broth, water and oregano. Bring to boiling; reduce heat. Simmer, uncovered, for 1 to 1½ hours or until meat is tender, stirring occasionally. Serve the chili with hot cooked pinto beans. Makes 6 to 8 servings.

To prepare the pinto beans, rinse 1 pound (2½ cups) dry pinto beans. In a large saucepan or Dutch oven, combine beans and 6 cups of water. Cover and soak overnight. Drain. In the same pan combine drained beans; 6 cups more water, 2 cloves garlic, minced; 1½ teaspoons salt; and ¼ teaspoon black pepper. Bring to boiling; reduce heat. Cover and simmer 1½ to 2 hours or until tender; drain. Makes 6 cups.

Bill Hardy
Merritt Island, FL

The Yellow Rose
Reva G. Yank/Pres./CEO
Liverpool, NY

CINCINNATI "THREE-WAY" CHILI

On its own this chili is great, but Diane says today Cincinnatians love it as a "three-way" — over spaghetti and topped with cheddar cheese.

6 to 8 servings

1 Qt. hot water
2 Lbs. ground beef
1 can (12 oz.) tomato paste
1 Lg. onion, chopped
3 T. chili powder
3 bay leaves
1 T. salt
1 t. cinnamon
1 t. freshly ground pepper
1 t. allspice
1 t. white wine vinegar
½t. cumin
½t. Worcestershire
¼t. cayenne pepper
¼t. garlic powder
1 Lb. freshly cook spaghetti
1 C. grated cheddar cheese

Pour water into large saucepan. Crumble in beef. Add next 13 ingredients. Simmer 3 hours, stirring occasionally. Discard bay leaves. (Can be prepared 1 month ahead and frozen.)

Place spaghetti on serving platter. Pour chili over. Top with cheese. Serve immediately.

Bill Hardy
Merritt Island, FL

A. Sterling Cole
Delano, CA

CHILI

2 T. vegetable oil
2 Lbs. lean beef, chili ground
1 Med. onion, chopped
1 bell green pepper, chopped
2 cloves garlic, minced
1 can (8 oz.) tomato sauce
3 T. chili powder
1 chile pod, ground
1 t. ground cumin
1 t. oregano
Salt and pepper to taste
2 C. cooked pinto beans

In a heavy soup pot, saute the onions and garlic in the oil, until the onions are translucent. Add the meat, and brown using a fork to break it up as it browns. Add tomato sauce and seasonings, cover, and simmer on LOW heat for 45 minutes. Add beans, and cook for 15 minutes longer.

Serve with chopped onions and shredded cheese to be spread on top of each bowl. Serves 8.

Ms. Debra Feder
Cincinnati, OH

Edna Ragan
Creswell, OR

TWO BEAN CHILI

1 Lb. ground beef
1 Med. onion, chopped
1 green bell pepper, chopped
1 Med. carrot, chopped fine
2 stalks celery, chopped
2 cloves garlic, minced
4 slices, cooked bacon, crumbled
2 cans, condensed tomato soup
1 can (16 oz.) whole kernel corn
1 Pkg. (10 oz.) frozen lima beans
1 T. chili powder
1 t. oregano
½ t. dried basil, crushed
Shredded Cheddar cheese

In a skillet, or Dutch oven, brown the beef, onion, green pepper, carrot, celery and garlic until the meat is done. Drain off excess drippings. Add rest of the ingredients, except the cheese. Bring mixture to a boil. Reduce heat, cover, and let simmer on low heat for about 30 minutes, stirring occasionally. Just before serving in individual bowls, sprinkle the bacon bits into chili. Cheese should be added to top of bowls, along with some reserved chopped onions. Makes 6 servings.

Todd Harris
Cold Springs, KY

Gurrentz Inter. Corp.
Pittsburgh, PA

MEXICALE CHILI

1 Lb. beef, chili grind
1 Med. onion, chopped
1 green pepper, chopped
2 stalks celery, chopped
1 can (28 oz.) whole tomatoes, cut up, undrained
1 can (8 oz.) tomato sauce
1 can (6 oz.) tomato paste
1 can (4 oz.) green chiles, rinsed, seeded and chopped
1 T. chili powder
1 bay leaf
2 T. sugar
1 t. oregano leaves, crushed
¼ t. cayenne pepper

In a large skillet or Dutch oven, cook the meat until it is nearly done. Add the vegetables and cook until the onions are tender. Add rest of ingredients, and mix to blend together well. Bring to a boil; reduce heat, cover and let simmer for about 30 to 40 minutes, or till your tasting says that it's done and ready to serve.

Makes 6 to 8 servings depending on added liquid for consistency.

Jeff Alfred
Cincinnati, OH

James & Carl Chandler
Indianapolis, IN

DeSILVA'S CHILI

(Recipe by Woody DeSilva, 1968 tie)

5 Med. onions, chopped
Small amount of cooking oil
Salt and pepper to taste
4 Lbs. chuck beef, coarse chili grind, or chopped into thumbnail-sized pieces
5 cloves garlic, minced
4 T. oregano
2 t. woodruff (an herb)
1 t. cayenne pepper
2 T. paprika
Scant T. to full T. New Mexico chili powder
3 T. ground cumin
Scant t. to full t. chipenos, crushed (also known as chili-piquines and available at stores stocking Mexican groceries)
4 dashed Tabasco sauce
3 cans (10 oz.) tomato sauce
1 can (6 oz.) tomato paste
Water
4 T. flour or masa flour (available at stores stocking Mexican groceries)

In a skillet, brown onions in oil, seasoning with salt and pepper. Place in chili pot. Brown beef in skillet, adding more oil as necessary. Add garlic and tablespoon of the oregano. Add this mixture to the chili pot.

In a paper sack, shake together the woodruff, cayenne pepper, paprika, chili powder, cumin, remaining oregano and jalapenos. Add the blended spices to the chili pot with the Tabasco sauce, tomato sauce, and tomato paste. Add enough water to cover the meat and simmer at least 2 hours.

Cool the chili. Refrigerate overnight. Skim off the excess grease. Reheat the chili to the boiling point and stir in a paste made of the flour and a little water, to thicken the mixture. Stir constantly to prevent sticking and scorching, adding water as necessary for the desired texture.

Bill Hardy
Merritt Island, FL
from Florida Today

A4

Ash Creek Cattle Assoc.
San Carlos, AZ

VENISON CHILI

3 Lbs. coarse ground venison shoulder
¼ C. vegetable oil
1 Qt. soup stock
7 cloves garlic, chopped
2 bay leaves
6 T. chili powder
1½ t. ground cumin
1 t. marjoram
1 t. cayenne pepper
3 t. paprika
2 t. salt
½ t. fresh ground black pepper
1 T. sugar
3 T. flour
6 T. Masa Harina
Cold water

In a heavy chili pot, heat the oil. Add venison and sear, stirring constantly until meat is gray. Add soup, and simmer for about 2 to 2½ hours. Add the remaining ingredients, except the flour and Masa Harina, and cold water. Cook for about 30 minutes or so. Combine the Masa and flour in a little cold water, and add to the chili, stirring constantly. Uncover, and cook for 5 to 10 minutes longer. If necessary to thin the consistency, add a little water. Serves 6.

Ms. June Alfred
Cincinnati, OH

Susan S. Clyne
Elgin, AZ

JAY'S CHILI

(Recipe by Jay Pennington, winner 1977)

1 T. cooking oil
3 Med. onions, finely chopped
2 bell peppers, finely chopped
2 celery stalks, finely chopped
3 garlic cloves, finely chopped
8 Lbs. coarsely ground round steak
2 No. 2 cans tomato sauce
2 No. 2 cans stewed tomatoes
2 No. 2 cans water
1 can (6 oz.) tomato paste
1 can (4 oz.) chili salsa
1 3-inch canned green hot pepper, finely chopped
2 3-Oz. bottles chili powder
1 can (4 oz.) green diced chilies
Dash of oregano
Salt to taste
Coarse-ground pepper to taste
Garlic salt to taste

Put oil in a 10- to 12-quart pot. Add onion, bell pepper, celery, and garlic cloves. Cook until onion is transparent. Add meat gradually, stirring (until redness disappears). Add the remaining ingredients, stirring after each addition. Lower heat and simmer 2½ to 3 hours. Stir frequently to prevent scorching. Serves 12 to 16.

Bill Hardy
Merritt Island, FL
from Florida today

Bruce & Lavon Aldrich
Burns, OR

SWEDISH CHILI

- 3 T. vegetable oil
- 2 Lbs. ground venison
- 1 Lg. onion, chopped
- 2 cloves garlic, chopped
- 1 t. salt
- ½ t. black powder
- 1 can (16 oz.) tomatoes
- 2 T. chili powder, or
- 1 T. chili powder plus 1 jalapeno pepper, seeded and chopped fine
- ½ t. ground cumin seeds
- 1 can (15 oz.) red kidney beans

Heat oil in large skillet or Dutch oven, and saute the onion and garlic until onion is transparent but not browned. Add venison and salt and pepper, and cook until meat is browned. Add tomatoes, chili powder, or the chopped jalapeno pepper if used, cumin and cook for about 1 hour on low heat.

If kidney beans are to be used, add then about 15 minutes before serving, blending well into the chili mixture so that they are thoroughly heated before serving. Serves 6.

(Rengard means Home of The Reindeer)

Mrs. Ragna Berggren
Boliden, Sweden

A.T. Spence
Snelling, CA

CHILI SAUCE

4 Qts. boiling water
18 ripe tomatoes
6 onions, diced
3 green hot peppers
1 C. sugar
2½ C. vinegar
2 t. salt
1 T. cinnamon
1 T. allspice
1 T. ground cloves

Blanch tomatoes by boiling hot water over them, replacing with cold water for a few minutes, and peeling skins off. In a soup pot, add all the ingredients, breaking up the tomatoes with a wooden spoon, and cook on a low heat 1½ to 2 hours until mixture thickens. Stir occasionally to prevent sticking. Makes about 8 pints of sauce.

Ms. Judy Sterling
Cape Canaveral, FL

(GEI)

Genetics Enterprises, Inc
Oklahoma City, OK

BUTTERFIELD STAGE-LINE CHILI

(Recipe by Fred Drexel, 1981 World Championship Chili)

1 can (8 oz.) Budweiser beer
½ oz. Montezuma tequila
2 cans (8 oz.) Hunt's tomato sauce
1 cube Wyler's beef bouillon
2½ cups water
5 cloves garlic, minced fine
½ can (7 oz.) Ortega chilies
⅓ T. Gebhardt's chili powder
5 T. ground cumin
¼ t. dry mustard
¼ t. monosodium glutamate
1½ t. brown sugar
Pinch oregano
5 Lbs. beef brisket in small cubes
1 Lb. ground lean pork
2 Lg. onions, chopped fine
Salt and pepper to taste
4 T. oil

In a large pot, simmer beer, tequila, tomato sauce, bouillon cube, water, garlic, chilies, and all dry ingredients. Brown beef, pork, and onions in a skillet with the oil. Salt and pepper to taste. Add meats to pot. Cover and simmer for at least 3 hours, stirring frequently. Serves 8 to 10.

Bill Hardy
Merritt Island, FL
from Florida today

JM

Morris Brothers
Leesburg, OH

ARTIC CHILLY CHILI

This is a favorite from my hometown of Boliden, Sweden.

2 Lbs. ground sirloin
2 Med. red onions
3 cloves of garlic
1 can (16 oz.) kidney beans
1 can (16 oz.) white beans
1 Lb. fresh tomatoes
1 C. fresh dill
½ C. cognac
Salt to taste
Pepper to taste
1 C. half & half
Banana pepper hot sauce

Brown ground sirloin in frying pan. Add chopped onions and garlic. Bring out your good big pot! Put the sirloin in the pot - add kidney beans and white beans - salt - pepper - let simmer for ½ hour.. so take a break!

Put aside. Add chopped dill - add tomatoes, cut in pretty big pieces. Let it sit on low for 20 minutes. Add the half & half - stir in.

Last but not least, add cognac!

Enjoy the chilly of the Article Circle! It's bound to warm you up!

Osa Berggren
Season Tickets Boutique
Cocoa Beach, FL

Ingle Beefmasters
Ray Ingle
Collierville, Tn

SHEPARD'S CHILI PIE

While viewing a television commercial, I decided to try using mash potatoes, spread lightly over an oven-proof individual serving bowl. The surface of the potatoes was roughed up, but I guess that a squeeze cloth could be used to make it decorative.

The chili was some left over, and was spooned about 1 inch thick, with the potatoes on top.

Baking was for about 25 minutes to get a little browning of the potatoes, and was sufficient time to thoroughly heat chili.

For a garnish, a little shredded cheddar was used on top, but not too much.

Mildred Yost
Merritt Island, FL

Viking Ranch
Lazy V
Richard Morrison
New Paltz, NY

GREEN STEW WITH MOUNTAIN CHILE

1 pound pork for stew, cut into 2-inch cubes
2 (10-ounce) cans Mexican green tomatoes
3 cloves garlic, chopped
6 sprigs fresh coriander (cilantro)
12 canned serrano chiles
1 tablespoon lard or salad oil
Salt
Freshly ground pepper
1 3- to 4-pound chicken

Simmer the pork, covered, in enough salted water almost to cover, for 1 hour. Drain, reserving the stock, and set the meat aside.

Combine the green tomatoes, a little of the liquid from the can, garlic, coriander (cilantro) and chiles in the electric blender and blend to a smooth puree. Heat the lard in a skillet; add the puree, and cook, stirring constantly, over a moderate heat for 2 to 3 minutes. Stir in the remainder of tomato liquid and all the pork stock. Season to taste with salt and pepper.

Place the whole chicken in a large, heavy flameproof casserole (stew pot) with a lid; surround with the pork and pour the sauce over all. Cover, and cook over a low heat for about an hour, or until the chicken is tender when pierced with a fork. Serves 6.

NOTE: 12 serrano chiles will be HOT; try 6.

From "The Complete Book of Mexican Cooking" by Elisabeth Lambert Ortiz.

Florida Today

Little Myakka Ranch
Rudolph Garber, Jr.
Sarasota, FL

FATHER TOM WARREN'S OSO FLACO CHILI

Father Tom Warren is a modern-day mission father at San Buenaventura. His great-grandmother, Laureana Gularte, came around the Horn to California from the island of Rico, in the Azores, in the 1880's. His grandmother was baptized at Mission San Luis Obispo de Tolosa, and married at Mission Santa Ines. At the family ranch at Oso Flaco (Lean Bear) in the Santa Maria Valley, the family has kept the use of cumin, brought from the Azores, in its cooking. Along with this Father Warren makes generous use of cardamon and locally grown and packed chile in his Oso Flaco Chili.

2 cloves garlic, diced
8 Ozs. dried California red chiles, broken up and stems removed
4 T. cumin seed
Water
2 cans (10 oz.) Las Palmas red chile sauce
2 t. dried oregano
½ t. ground allspice
1 t. ground cinnamon
2 T. chili powder
4 T. ground cardamon
Salt to taste
Olive oil
2 Lbs. ground round
Cabernet Sauvignon or other good California dry red wine

Place garlic, chiles, and cumin in a large stewing pot. Fill pot ¾ full of water and let ingredients soak overnight. Next morning, bring to a boil. Add the chile sauce, spices, and salt. Cook over low heat for about 2 to 2½ hours. In a little olive oil, lightly brown ground beef and add to pot. Simmer until seasonings are well blended with meat. To add a little zest, pour some Carbernet Sauvignor into the chili and heat to proper serving temperature.

Bill Hardy
Merritt Island, FL
from Florida Today

Hoven Ranch
Bowdle, SD

SOUTHWEST CHILI GRILL

1 2½ to 3 Lb.) chicken, cut into serving sizes
½ T. salad oil
1 t. chili powder
1 t. cumin
½ t. oregano
1 Pkg. onion soup mix
½ C. sour cream
1½ to 2 T. skim milk

In a small mixing bowl, blend all the ingredients thoroughly, and as the chicken is grilling, baste it with the seasoning mix.

Mildred Yost
Merritt Island, FL

Ronald Wayne Jipp
National City, CA

THE GREAT ONE'S CHILI CON CARNE

There are many reasons why Jackie Gleason, the Great One, will never be forgotten. Now we can add his recipe for chili con carne to the list.

John Tomlinson asked readers to help him find the recipe, which he had clipped from the Herald many years ago.

It turned out the recipe appeared Nov. 14, 1971. Fran Leckie of North Miami sent us a photocopy of the original newspaper clipping, which quotes Beverly Gleason as saying, "The secret of the recipe is the bacon. I serve it with garlic bread and salad."

For the sake of history we're publishing the recipe as it appeared in the original story. No doubt many folks will want to reduce the fat by draining the meat, but that is not the intent of the original.

As to can sizes, all I can do is guess that in 1971 a large can of tomatoes probably meant at least 32 ounces (currently you by 25- to 28-ounce cans of tomatoes, or substitute 2 14- to 16-ounce cans).

The beans are another quandary. I don't know if originally "large" referred to a 16-ounce can or one around 2 pounds, since reference books I checked indicated that 20 years ago you could buy kidney beans in 8¾-ounce, 16-ounce or 27- to 32-ounce sizes. Since I prefer a ratio of less beans than meat in my chili, I simply used 3 14½-ounce cans of beans in testing the recipe. If you like a thick chili, you may want to cook the chili a little longer to reduce the amount of liquid.

1 cup thinly sliced onion
3 tablespoons salad oil
2 large cans tomatoes (see note above)
3 large cans kidney beans
4 tablespoons chili powder
2 tablespoons sugar
Salt and pepper to taste
4 garlic cloves
10 strips bacon
2 pounds ground round steak (see note above)

Saute the onions in the salad oil until tender. Add tomatoes, beans, chili powder, sugar, salt and pepper and garlic. Fry Bacon until crisp. Brown the meat in the bacon drippings. Add the meat to the tomato mixture. Add the crumbled bacon and simmer about 2 hours. Remove the garlic gloves and serve.

(1990 note: This makes about a gallon of chili).

Miami Herald
Barry & Roberta Geltner

//4

Two Slant Bar 4
Philip Virgilio, Sr.
Kissimmee, FL

CAPITAL PUNISHMENT CHILI

(Recipe by Bill Pfeiffer, 1980 winner)

1 T. oregano
2 T. paprika
2 T. monosodium glutamate
9 T. chili powder
4 T. cumin
4 T. beef bouillon (instant crushed)
2 cans Budweiser beer
2 C. water
4 Lbs. extra lean chuck, chili ground
2 Lbs. extra lean pork, chili ground
1 Lb. extra lean chuck, cut into ¼-inch cubes
2 Lg. onions, finely chopped
10 cloves garlic, finely chopped
½ C. oil or kidney suet
1 t. Mexican mole powder (a spice)
1 T. sugar
1 t. coriander
1 t. Durkee's Louisiana Red
Hot sauce
1 can (8 oz.) Hunt's tomato sauce
1 T. Masa Harina flour
Salt to taste

In a large pot, add paprika, oregano, MSG, chili powder, cumin, beef bouillon, beer, and 2 cups water. Let simmer. In a separate skillet, brown 1½ pounds meat with 1 tablespoon oil or kidney suet until meat is light brown. Drain and add to simmering spices. Continue until all meat is added. Saute onions and garlic in 1 tablespoon oil or kidney suet. Add to spices and meat mixture. Add water as needed. Simmer 2 hours. Add mole powder, sugar, coriander, Louisiana Red Hot and tomato sauce. Simmer 45 minutes.

Dissolve flour in warm water until a paste forms. Add to chili. Salt to taste. Simmer 30 minutes. For hotter chili, add Louisiana Red Hot to taste.

Bill Hardy
Merritt Island, FL
from Florida Today

Huehue Ranch
Honolulu, HA

TEXAS CHILI CON CARNE

- 6 dried ancho chilies, plus 8 dried hot red chilies, each about 2 inches long
- 3½ C. boiling water
- ½ Lb. beef suet, preferably kidney suet, cut into ½-inch bits
- 3 Lbs. lean boneless venison or beef chuck, trimmed of excess fat, sliced ½-inch thick and cut into ½-inch cubes
- 3 Med. sized bay leaves, finely crumbled
- 1 T. cumin seeds
- 2 T. coarsely chopped garlic
- 4 t. dried oregano
- 3 T. paprika
- 1 T. sugar
- 1 T. salt
- 3 T. yellow cornmeal
- 1 t. ground red hot pepper (cayenne; optional)
- Freshly cooked pinto beans
- 9 C. freshly cooked rice made from 3 cups long-grain white rice

Under cold running water, pull the stems off the ancho and red chilies. Cut open the chilies and remove the seeds. Remove the large ribs with a small, sharp knife. Chop the chilies into coarse pieces, and place them into a bowl. Pour boiling water, enough to cover them completely, and let them soak for at least ½ hour. Strain the soaked chilies through a sieve, and reserve the liquid. Set the chilies aside.

In a heavy 5- to 6-quart casserole, cook the beef suet over a moderate heat, stirring frequently until the fat has been rendered from it. Using a slotted spoon, remove and discard the bits of suet. Also remove all but ¼ cup of oil from the casserole.

Add the venison or beef cubes, and cook over a moderate heat, stirring constantly until the meat is cooked but not browned. Add 2½ cups of the reserved chili liquid to the meat, and bring to a boil. Add the bay leaves, reduce the heat to low and simmer for 1 hour. Stir the casserole mixture occasionally.

Place the cumin seeds in a small ungreased skillet and, sliding the pan back and forth frequently, toast the seeds over a low heat for 10 minutes. Drop the seeds into the jar of an electric blender and blend at a high speed for about 30 seconds. With the blender off, add the ancho and red chilies, the rest of the chili-soaking liquid, garlic, oregano, paprika, sugar and salt. Blend together at high speed until the mixture becomes a smooth puree.

When the meat has cooked, stir in the puree. Cover partially, and on a simmer, cook for about 30 minutes. After this time, pour the cornmeal into the mixture, remembering to stir constantly to eliminate lumps. This should be brought to a boil as the cornmeal will thicken the chili somewhat.

Serve hot with side dishes of hot pinto beans, chopped onions, shredded cheese and any other accompaniment your use.

Jeffery & Gina Celesti
Cincinnati, OH

E.E. Marvel
Dufur, OR

NEVADA ANNIE'S CHAMPION CHILI

(Recipe by LaVerne Harris, 1978 winner)

3 Med. onion
2 Med. green peppers
1 Lg. stalks celery
2 small cloves garlic
½ or more fresh jalapeno pepper, diced
8 Lbs. lean chuck, coarsely ground
1 can (7 oz.) diced green chilies
2 cans (14½ oz.) stewed tomatoes
1 can (15 oz.) tomato sauce
1 can (6 oz.) tomato paste
2 3-Oz. bottles chili powder
2 T. cumin
Tabasco to taste
1 can (12 oz.) beer, divided into two portions
1 bottle (12 oz.) mineral water
2 or 3 bay leaves
Garlic salt to taste
Salt and pepper to taste

Dice and saute the five ingredients. Add the meat and brown it. Add the remaining ingredients, including ½ can beer (drink the remainder, says Annie). Add water just to cover the top of the mixture. Cook about 3 hours on low heat, stirring often. Serves 24 or more.

Bill Hardy
Merritt Island, FL
from Florida Today

Hawaii Meat Co. Ltd.
Oahu, HA

CARROLL SHELBY'S CHILI

This recipe is made for serving 40 persons.

20 Lbs. coarsely ground round or chuck beef
12 large onions, finely chopped
6 green bell peppers, chopped
6 red bell peppers, chopped
rendered suet or oil
5 cans (15 oz.) tomato sauce
1 gal. water
10 T. chili powder
2½ t. cayenne pepper
5 t. black pepper
5 t. oregano
10 t. ground cumin
20 cloves garlic, finely chopped
Salt to taste
Drained canned kidney beans, (optional), as desired

Brown the meat, onion, and bell peppers in suet or oil. Transfer to a large pot and add the tomato sauce and water. Mix well. Stir in remaining ingredients except the beans.

Let the mixture cook for an hour or two, with an occasionally stirring. Add the kidney beans, if you desire, during the last minutes of the cooking time. Serve the beans hot as a side dish, along with a bowl of chopped onions for those eating who wish to leave beans out of their serving.

Dan Bernert
Cincinnati, OH

JC

S.C. Combs, 1907
Waco,
McLennan County, TX

CHILE RELLENO CASSEROLE

1 Lb. ground beef
2 cans (4 oz.) whole green chilies
½ C. chopped onion
1½ C. grated Cheddar cheese
4 eggs, beaten
1½ C. milk
¼ C. flour

Spray a casserole dish with non-stick cooking spray. Cut green chilies in halves crosswise and take seeds out. Arrange half green chilies in the bottom of casserole dish.

Brown ground beef, drain fat, add Taco Mix, stir to coat meat. Simmer onions with beef.

Top green chilies with a layer of beef mixture, then cheese. Repeat; layers. Beat eggs with milk and flour. Pour gently over layers.

Bake in preheated oven at 350 degrees for 45 to 50 minutes. Let set for about 20 minutes. Top with salsa or picante sauce, if desired.

Spanish rice is a nice accent to this casserole.

Jo Ann Hogan
Merritt Island, FL

Manuel C. Rapoza, III
Honolulu, HA

TURKEY CHILI

- 1 pound ground turkey*
- ½ cup chopped onion
- ½ cup chopped green pepper
- 1 clove garlic, minced
- ¾ cup dried kidney beans, cooked
- 1 cup water
- 3 medium tomatoes, peeled and chopped
- 1 (6 oz.) can no-salt added tomatoes paste
- 1 teaspoon chili powder
- ½ teaspoon dried oregano leaves
- ½ teaspoon ground cumin
- ⅛ teaspoon ground red pepper
- 30 Fat Free PREMIUM Saltine Crackers

* pound lean ground beef may be substituted

In large heavy pot, brown turkey; pour off any excess fat. Add onion, green pepper and garlic; cook 2 minutes, stirring occasionally. Add beans, water, tomatoes, tomato paste, chili powder, oregano, cumin and red pepper; cover. Simmer for 1½ hours, stirring occasionally. Serve hot with crackers.

NUTRITION INFORMATION per serving (1 cup chili;, 5 crackers); 242 calories, 172 mg sodium, 34 mg cholesterol, 8 gm total fat, 3 gm saturated fat.

NABISCO Fat Free PREMIUM
cracker box recipe

Piney River Ranch
Lee R. McCormick
Nunnelly, Tn

TEX-MEX BEANS WITH CHEESE

2 cloves garlic, minced
2 small onions, coarsely chopped
3 T. vegetable oil
1 can (15 oz.) tomato sauce
1 can (6 oz.) tomato paste
1 T. chili powder
1 t. EACH cumin, oregano and sugar
1 can (30 oz.) red kidney beans, drained and thoroughly rinsed
1 can (15 oz.) garbanzo beans, drained
Salt and pepper to taste
1 fresh green chili pepper, seeded and chopped (optional)
8 Ozs. Colby cheese, shredded

Combine garlic, onion and oil in a microwave safe skillet and MICRO 15 minutes on HIGH, stirring once, until onions are completely soft. Add tomato sauce, tomato paste, seasonings (not salt and pepper) and chili pepper. Stir well and cover with a lid or wax paper. MICRO 5 minutes on HIGH, stirring once. Add beans, stir well and recover. MICRO 5 minutes on HIGH, or until beans are very hot. Season to taste with salt and pepper and stir in shredded cheese until cheese is melted. Serve at once.

Bill Hardy
Merritt Island,FL
from Florida Today

Thomas R. Singley, MD
Pascagoula, MS

ISLAND CHILI Con QUESO

2 T. butter
¼ C. finely chopped onion
2 can (8¼ oz.) tomatoes, undrained
1 can (4 oz.) green chilies, drained and chopped
¼ t. salt
½ Lb. Monterey Jack cheese, cubed (sharp cheddar may be used)
¼ C. heavy cream

1. In hot butter in medium skillet, saute onion until tender. Add tomatoes, chilies, and salt, mashing tomatoes with fork. Simmer, stirring occasionally, 15 minutes.
2. Add cheese cubes, stirring until cheese is melted. Stir in cream. Cook, stirring constantly, 2 minutes.

3. Remove from heat and let stand 15 minutes. Serve warm, as a dip with tostaditas (canned tortillas, cut in wedges and dried until crisp) or corn chips.

Bill Hardy
Merritt Island, FL

Alicia S. King
Honolulu, HA

HUNT'S TURKEY CHILI

- 2 T. Wesson Vegetable Oil
- 1 Lb. ground turkey
- 1 C. chopped onion
- ½ C. chopped green bell pepper
- 1 t. fresh minced garlic
- 1 (15-oz.) can Hunt's Tomato Sauce
- 1 (15-oz.) can Hunt's Small Red Beans, undrained
- 2 t. Gebhardt Chili Powder
- 1 t. ground cumin
- 1 t. instant chicken bouillon granules
- ½ t. ground oregano
- ½ t. salt and pepper
- ½ Lb. spaghetti, cooked and drained
- Shredded Cheddar or Monterey Jack cheese

In large skillet, heat oil; saute turkey, onion, green pepper and garlic until turkey is no longer pink. Stir in remaining ingredients except spaghetti and cheese. Simmer, covered, 15 to 20 minutes; stirring occasionally. Arrange spaghetti on platter; top with chili, then sprinkle with cheese, if desired.

Beatrice/Hunt-Wesson, Inc.

Recorded to R. W. Clifford of Ubet, Fergus County, on May 16, 1887.
Appeared on the grey horse in "The Herd Quitter" (1897), "Hooverizin" (1918), "Bronco Bustin" (1895), and a bronze "The Horse Wrangler" (no date).
Also in 1st picture of the "Sunshine " series.
Montana

NOUVELLE CUISINE CHILE

1½ Lbs. ground turkey
2 Lg. cans tomatoes
1 Lg. can tomato puree
2 reg. cans kidney beans
1 C. chopped onion
1 C. Chopped celery
1 C. chopped green pepper
½ C. Hot Pace Picante Sauce
3 T. capers
¼ C. chopped black olives
1 t. chervil
1 t. cinnamon
2 t. chili powder
1-2 T. garlic (to taste)
¼ C. Soy Sauce
3 T. Worcestershire sauce
Red, black and white pepper to taste
4 beef bouillon cubes
2 T. sweet basil
Olive oil

Brown meat in small amount of olive oil using a Dutch oven. Add rest of the ingredients. Simmer on low heat till done.

Sandra Beck
Park Hills, KY

Evans Cattle Co.
Mechanicstown, OH

TEXAS CHILI BY MICRO

Remove gristle, tendons and most extraneous fat (suet) from meat. Cut fat (suet) into small pieces. Dice meat into pieces about ½-inch or smaller. Place suet in 3½ to 4-quart micro-proof casserole. Cook on HIGH (maximum power) 4 to 5 minutes to melt fat. Remove suet particles. Add meat to hot fat and cook on HIGH 11 to 12 minutes or until lightly browned. Stir in garlic and seasonings. Cook on HIGH 2 minutes to blend flavors. Stir 1 cup water into masa; blend until smooth. Stir into meat. Add broth. Cook on HIGH 28 to 30 minutes to bring to a boil, stirring every 5 minutes. Cook at 90 percent power 40 to 45 minutes or until meat is very tender, stirring every 10 minutes. Correct seasonings, if necessary. Skim off unwanted fat.

Serve in individual bowls with mounds of rice.

Bill Hardy
Merritt Island, FL
from Florida Today

Roy A. Merrill, III
Elmore, AL

MEXICAN CHILE DISH

- 2 Lbs. tenderloin tips, cubed
- 1 potato
- 2 tomatoes
- 3 oz. dry red wine
- 4 green chiles
- 4 oz. peas
- 1 green pepper, chopped
- ½ stick butter or margarine
- 1 can, kidney beans

Cut potato Julian style making one-inch lengths. Place in dish with a little lime juice and salt to keep white.

In a hot pan using either butter or margarine, add tenderloin cubes one at a time. Add salt, pepper and flour.

Skin one tomato, quarter, remove center core, and add to meat. Add the wine.

Chop 4 green chiles and add to meat mixture along with the green pepper. Let cook - then add potato lengths and peas.

Add remaining butter or margarine to beans that have cooked for 2 hours. Add 2d tomato and 1 teaspoon of chili powder to beans.

Place meat on platter and beans around edge; top with chopped egg and parsley.

Mary Jo Fairchild
Rockledge, FL

Harry A. Hueu
Maui, HA

SQUASH CASSEROLE with GREEN CHILES

6 zucchini squash
3 slices bacon, minced
1 Med. onion, minced
½ C. tomato juice
4 Saltine crackers, crumbled
1 can green chiles, chopped
Chez Wiz

Cut squash into quarters and cook in salted water until almost tender. Drain well by placing them on paper towels. Brown the bacon, reserving grease, and saute the onion. Add salt and pepper to taste. Mix together the above ingredients, add green chiles, and crumbled Saltines. Put in casserole dish and bake for 30 minutes at 350 degrees. Add Chez Wiz (about 2 tablespoons). Stir lightly after cheese has melted.

Mary Jo Fairchild
Rockledge, FL

Sam R. Parker
Lavergne, TN

BAJA CHILI

6 Lbs. coarsely ground beef (from top round)
Salt, MSG, white pepper
1½ Lbs. pork sausage
2 cloves garlic, finely chopped
1 bell pepper, finely chopped
3 ribs celery, finely chopped
4 onions, finely chopped
½ can (6 oz.) beer
⅓ C. LaVictoria pasilla chili powder
½ C. LaVictoria California chili powder
¼ C. LaVictoria New Mexico chili powder
1 C. (6 oz.) tomato paste
2 C. 16 oz.) stewed tomatoes
1 can tomato sauce with herbs
3 T. powdered oregano
1 T. beau monde seasoning
2 T. Gebhardt's chili powder
2 cans chicken broth combined with:
3 cans water
1 T. cilantro

Brown the beef, adding salt, pepper and MSG to taste. In another pan, brown the sausage along with the garlic, bell pepper, celery and the onions. Drain the fat and rinse the browning pans with the beer, scraping up any brown bits.

Combine the beef and sausage mixtures with the remaining ingredients in a large stock pot. Simmer the chili for two hours.

NOTE: You may have to scour the ethnic markets for some of these brands of chili powder, but the results are worth it.

Bill Hardy
Merritt Island, FL
from Florida Today

XIT

The Capital Freehold Land and Investment Co., Ltd, of Texas recorded this brand on August 11, 1890
Montana

CALIENTA FUEGO DEL RIO CHILI
(Hot Fire Of The River)

5 Lbs. Chuck roast
2 C. beef broth
4 cans (16 oz.) stewed tomatoes
1 C. water
1 C. finely chopped onions
½ C. finely chopped celery
3 T. garlic powder
¼ C. chili powder
3 T. cumin
1 T. salt
2 T. sugar
1 can (15 oz.) pinto beans
2 cans(6 oz.) tomato paste
¾ C. Picante Salsa (Hot)
1 T. red pepper

Trim fat from beef. Cut beef into bite sized pieces. Brown in well seasoned iron skillet - brown well! Do only a few pieces at a time and remove them from skillet.

When all pieces are well browned, put back into the iron skillet with the beef broth. Stir and scrape all little particles of meat from sides and bottom of pan that may have been left from browning.

Add all other ingredients except the beans. Bring to a boil. Boil for about 10 minutes. Reduce heat to a simmer. Simmer until the meat is tender (about 1 hour). Watch water...add if necessary. Stir to keep from sticking.

Puree beans, and add to mixture. Add water (if necessary) to bring to the desired consistency.

Simmer about 10 more minutes. Serve with condiments such as chopped green onions, sour cream, shredded cheese.

Robert Wyllie
Orange Park, FL

Broken Arrow Farm
Blue Rock, OH

TEXAS CHILI WITH RICE

Pot luck supper, church fund raiser, family reunion. And you've been assigned to bring the main course. What to make that can be done ahead and will travel well?

Texas Chili with Rice is perfect. What makes Texas Chili different? Number one... no chili powder; then you use diced beef instead of ground. And... no beans. And to top it all off, it's served over rice!

If this kind of chili is new to you, you'll soon understand why it is so popular in the Southwest. It just plain tastes good! Start with half the amount of ground red chilies if your guests aren't used to "hot" foods. But remember when you're tasting it that it is meant to be served over rice. The bland flavor of the rice cools down the hot chili taste.

- 4 Lbs. boneless beef round or chuck steak
- 6 cloves garlic, minced
- ½ C. paprika
- 2 T. oregano leaves
- 2 T. cumin seed
- 1 to 2 T. ground red chilies*
- 1 T. salt
- ¾ C. masa harina (corn flour)**
- 2 Qts. hot beef broth (or beef bouillon dissolved in water)
- 6 to 8 C. hot cooked rice

Remove gristle, tendons and most extraneous fat (suet) from meat. Cut fat (suet) into small pieces. Dice meat into pieces about ½-inch or smaller. Place suet in Dutch oven or heavy pot. Cook over low heat to melt fat. Remove suet particles.

Add meat to hot fat and cook, stirring often, until lightly browned. Stir in garlic and seasonings. Cook about 5 minutes to blend flavors. Stir 1 cup water into masa; blend until smooth. Stir into meat. Add broth. Bring to a boil, reduce heat and simmer until meat is very tender, about 1 to 1½ hours.

Add water in small amounts as necessary to maintain liquid level. Correct seasonings, if necessary. Skim off unwanted fat. Serve in individual bowls with mounds of rice. Makes 12 servings.

* Or use crushed or ground red pepper to taste

** Or use corn meal

Bill Hardy
Merritt Island, FL
from Florida Today

Hal & John Shook
Kensington, GA

MY CROCKPOT CHILI

1 Lb. ground turkey
1 can (28 oz.) whole tomatoes, in thick puree (reg. or Italian plus tomatoes
1 Med. chopped onion (about 1 scant cup)
⅛ t. garlic powder
1-2 T. chili powder
1 t. salt
1 t. sugar
1 t. oregano
1 t. Worcestershire sauce
1 can (15-16 oz.) kidney beans, drained
1½ C. chopped green peppers

In a skillet, brown ground turkey until it loses it's pink color. Drain. Chop the whole tomatoes in food processor. Combine all ingredients, except the peppers, in crock pot. Stir well. Cook on High 3 to 4 hours. In the last hour add peppers if desired. Makes 4 servings. Serve over rice.

Anne M. Gruce
Stratford, CT

M.E. Carer
Wyoming (1884)

SPICY CHILI TOMATO SAUCE

¾ C. chopped onion
1 clove garlic, minced
3 T. cooking oil
2 cans (16 oz.) tomatoes, cut up
2 cans (6 oz.) tomato paste
1 t. salt
1 t. sugar
1 t. chili powder
½ t. pepper
1 bay leaf

Cook onion and garlic in hot oil until tender but not brown. Stir in the remaining ingredients. Simmer, uncovered, for 30 minutes. Remove the bay leaf. Set aside. Use 1 cup of sauce for another dish, and keep remaining warm until time to serve.

Mary Jo Fairchild
Rockledge, FL

150

Alexander Tindall, 1882
Brevard County, FL

CHILE Con COORS Con CARNE

TODAY Executive Editor Buddy Baker has a penchant for cooking spicy foods. He made his debut in this spot in 1982 preparing ham and bean soup, and followed that in '83 with his special spaghetti sauce. Here, he shares his recipe for chile. We think you'll find it irresistible.

By BUDDY BAKER
TODAY Executive Editor

This recipe is dedicated to the readers who wrote to me after my spaghetti sauce was printed in TODAY. Said he: "My wife was dying to try your spaghetti recipe. She did. She died."

As with my two previous gastronomic challenges--ham & bean soup and spaghetti meat sauce-this one will serve Santa Ana's army. As long as you're in the kitchen, you might as well make enough for a relatively cheap party--or freeze a batch or two for later, right?

Assuming you've got those things marked above with big T's and little t's in your kitchen, the ingredients for this will cost about $11, depending on where you shop and what coupons you might have.

If you've got an old Herb Alpert and the Tiajuana Brass album, put it on.

This one-dish meal will take the largest Dutch oven you've got or fill almost half a corn-boiler, which is what I used.

3½ Lbs. ground chuck
(HERE'S the beef!)
2 Lg. onions
1 stick butter
3 T. corn oil
¼ t. minced garlic
2 cans (8 oz.) tomato sauce
1 can beef broth
5 T. chile powder
2 cans (28 oz.) peeled tomatoes
1 t. celery seed
1 t. ground cumin
½ t. paprika
¼ t. oregano
¼ t. cayenne pepper
2 cans (30 oz.) chile (red kidney) beans
1 Pkg. dry chile seasoning mix
½ bottle Coors beer

Chop two large onions.

Set the stove on medium, put in one stick of butter, 3 tablespoons of corn oil, ½ teaspoon of minced garlic (yes, I used instant minced garlic again!), the chopped onions, and saute that, but not to the extent the onions start to brown. Then add the whole loaf of ground beef and turn 'er up to medium high. (I used chuck but the President of Mexico probably used ground round). When this starts cooking, poke around in it for 20 or so minutes until the beef browns.

End of phase one.

Now add one 8-ounce can of tomato sauce, a can of beef broth (or the equivalent of a can of Campbell's beef broth), two 28-ounce cans of drained, peeled, and quartered tomatoes, 1 teaspoon of celery seed (go ahead and buy some--it's good in Bloody Marys, too), 1 teaspoon of ground cumin (or 1 teaspoon cumin seed), ¼ teaspoon salt and ½ teaspoon paprika. Stir it up, set the stove on barely bubble, cook uncovered, open a bottle of Coors and go turn the record over.

End of phase two.

During the next hour, stir the chile about every 15 to 20 minutes. In between, have a couple of Coors, sing a couple of choruses of La Cucaracha
and pet your chihuahua for luck. If you don't have a chihuahua, at least you'll learn how to spell it.

End of phase three.

Drain excess juice from two 30-ounce cans of chile (or red kidney) beans, then put 'em in and stir. If you bruise a bean or two, don't worry about that either. Time your beer drinking so that you have a half-bottle left and pour it in. Add to this one package of dry chile seasoning mix (I used a 47-cent package of El Paso brand). If you've got masa flour, you can use 2 tablespoons of it instead, but that stuff is hard to find. Set the stove on low and let it cook for one more hour or so and you're done.

Chile should be stocky, not soupy. If you think it's too thin, add another pack of the dry seasoning mix.

If you want to stretch it, add another can or two of beans.

This chile is tangy but it's not so hot it will clear your sinuses. If you're super-sensitive and want mild chile eliminate the cayenne pepper and reduce the chile powder by one tablespoon. Zapata will be ashamed of you, but he's dead--and besides, you paid for it.

Fresh saltines and cold beer are all the complements you'll need.

Although Gerald Ford said Vicki Carr was his favorite Mexican dish, I'm sure the former President has never tried Chili con Coors con Carne. If you don't like it, don't write to me--just have another Coors.

Bill Hardy
Merritt Island, FL
from Florida Today

Wall Ranch Inc.
Honolulu, HA

LUCY'S LOW FAT CHILI CON CARNE

Pam spray for bottom of pan
3½ Lbs. ground turkey
1½ t. salt
2 T. flour
¾ C. chopped onion
4½ loves garlic
2 C. canned tomatoes
3 C. water
1 t. oregano
2 T. chili powder
2 cans red kidney beans
1 t. dried mustard

Spray Pam on bottom of pan. Brown turkey, and flour until brown. Sprinkle meat with salt then cook in onion and garlic for 5 minutes. Add rest of the ingredients (except beans). Simmer for 1½ hours. But stir frequently. Then add beans and simmer for 15 minutes longer.

Eat chili by itself, or serve over white rice.

Children love this chili over buttered noodles.

Lucy Miller
Merritt Island, FL

Kristine Smith
Milesville, SD

CHILI CASSEROLE

1 Lb. ground meat
1 Lg. onion, chopped

Cook the above with a bit of salt

½ C. of green chiles
6 oz. grated Cheddar cheese

Put in baking dish. Beat 4 eggs and ¼ cup of flour. Add 1½ cups of milk. Pour over meat mixture, and bake at 350 degrees for 40 minutes.

Mary Jo Fairchild
Rockledge, FL

Morag Rice
Honolulu, HA

MAVERICK CHILI

2 C. black beans
5 T. vegetable oil
3 yellow onions, chopped
6 garlic cloves, chopped
3 T. chili powder (or to taste)
2 T. dried oregano
1½ T. Cumin
1 T. Paprika
2½ Lbs. pork (center cut with fat trimmed off or substitute chicken) cut into ½-inch cubes.*
3 C. (or more) chicken stock
½ C. Tequila
2 T. (or more) minced, seeded jalapeno chiles
2 T. unsweetened cocoa powder
Freshly ground pepper (or Mrs. Dash Spicy)
2 Lbs. chicken thighs, skinned, boned, cut into ½-inch cubes
Freshly cooked rice
Sliced avocado
Chopped tomato
Chopped red onion
Grated lite Cheddar cheese

Place beans in bowl. Add enough water to cover. Let soak overnight. Drain and rinse beans thoroughly.

Heat 4 tablespoons oil in heavy large pot over medium heat. Add yellow onions and saute until golden, about 10 minutes. Add garlic and saute for 5 minutes. Add chili powder, oregano, cumin and paprika and saute 5 minutes. Remove onion mixture from pot with slotted spoon. Set aside.

*If pork is used add remaining 1 tablespoon of oil in same pot over a medium heat. Add pork (in batches if necessary) and cook until browned. Stirring frequently, about 10 minutes. Pour off fat from pot. Add beans, 3 cups stock, tequila, 2 tablespoons chiles and cocoa powder. Season with Mrs. Dash. Cover and simmer 1 hour and 45 minutes, adding additional chicken stock if chili appears too dry.

*If pork is not used, please use 4½ pounds chicken. Add chicken to chili. Cover and simmer until cooked through, about 15 minutes. Taste and add additional chiles, Mrs. Dash if desired.

Mound rice on platter. Top with chili. Garnish with avocado arranged in pinwheel fashion, tomato, red onion and cheese...serve immediately.

Serves 8.

Sherry Frattarola
Melbourne Beach, FL

Bridle Bit Ranch
Texas (1893)

CHILI SOUP JARLSBERG

1 Lb. round steak, diced
2 T. Oil
2 cans (16 oz.) beef broth
1 Med. green pepper, chopped
1 Med. red pepper, chopped
1 Lg. onion, chopped
1 Lg. clove garlic, minced
3 t. chili powder
¼ t. ground cumin
1 can (16 oz.) tomatoes, chopped and undrained
1 can (16 oz.) dark red kidney beans
1½ C. grated Jarlsberg cheese
Kavli crispbread
¼ C. softened butter or margarine
1 small clove garlic, minced
¼ t. chili powder

In large deep saucepan, brown beef in oil, turning to brown on all sides. Add beef broth and simmer 1 hour. Add peppers, onion, garlic, chili, cumin, tomatoes and beans. Cover and simmer for 30 minutes.

Gradually blend in ½ cup Jarlsberg cheese. Heat just until cheese melts.

Meanwhile, blend softened butter, garlic and chili powder. Spread on 12 slices Kavli. Bake at 375 degree F. for several minutes, to melt butter. Sprinkle with ½ cup Jarlsberg. Heat just until cheese is melted.

Serve soup garnished with remaining ½ cup Jarlsberg. Pass the Kavli.

Makes 6 servings.

Jarlsberg Cheeses
New York, NY

Recorded to Harmon Ranney of Helena on December 19, 1883. Appears in "Men of the Open Range" (1923). Montana

HEARTY CHILI Con CARNE

A menu for a meatless day
By Corydon Ireland
Gannett News Service

No sweat. You can be a vegetarian for a day. And with today being Great American Meatout day, seize the day:

Breakfast - fruit, oatmeal, two slices whole wheat toast with apple butter, herbal tea.

Morning snack - a handful of peanuts, raisins and some tea.

Lunch - a meatless sandwich, either peanut putter or a pita pocket packed with tomatoes, lettuce, sprouts and avocado; tomato soup; fruit.

Mid-day snack - popcorn. No butter.
Dinner - with a leafy green salad and some bread, try:

Hearty Chili Con Carne

1 cup kidney beans
4 cups water
1 cup frozen corn
1 clove garlic, pressed
1 teaspoon salt
1 tablespoon vegetable oil
1½ cups tomato sauce
1½ tablespoons chili powder
1 teaspoon cumin

Saute the onion and garlic; add seasonings, tomato sauce and corn. Add the tomato mixture to heated beans and stir. Simmer briefly.

This recipe is from "Vegetarianism: Answers to the Most Commonly Asked Questions," North American Vegetarian Society.

Florida Today

Rocking Dollar
Shirley Pinder
Okeechobee, FL

SANTE FE CHILI SOUP

1½ C. cooked chicken, with fat trimmed, diced
2 cans chicken broth
1 small onion, diced
1 clove garlic, minced
1 can (28 oz.) plum tomatoes
1 can (15 oz.) garbanzo beans
1 can (16 oz.) pinto beans
1 can (4 oz.) green chilies, diced
2 C. cooked macaroni

Heat the broth with the tomatoes until just the boiling point. Reduce the heat. Add the onion, garlic, and green chilies. Simmer for 1 hour.

Add diced chicken and macaroni,and simmer an additional 20 minutes.

This is good with tortillas, or corn chips.

Steven Seltzer
Cincinnati, OH

Sam S. Hironaka
Honolulu, Ha

BLACKENED VENISON CHILI

1 Lb. venison, cut into ¼-inch cubes
6 Ozs. andouille (Cajun sausage), cut into ¼-inch cubes
1 Lb. (½ Lb. each) mixture of ground beef and aground venison
¼ C. diced yellow onion
¼ C. diced red onion
⅓ C. diced mixture of red, yellow and green bell peppers
2 t. chopped chili peppers
⅓ C. diced fresh tomato
1 t. chopped fresh garlic
2½ C. chicken or venison stock
2½ C. beer (any kind will do)
1 C. tomato paste
2 t. cumin
2 t. chili powder
1 t. oregano
Salt and cayenne pepper to taste
1 C. Blackened Marinade Sauce

Toss venison cubes with Blackened Marinade Sauce; cover and marinate 15 to 30 minutes in refrigerator.

Brown onions, garlic, ground beef and ground venison in a medium pot. Add andouille. Cook, stirring until meat is brown and onions are translucent.

Drain mixture to remove extra fat. Add tomato paste, spices, stock and beer.

In a hot iron skillet, blacken the marinated venison cubes, stirring until well done; be sure not to overcook. Your goal is to sear the meat. In a very hot skillet, this should take about five minutes.

Add blackened venison and remaining ingredients to onion mixture and simmer for 1 to 2 hours, or until meats are tender. Stir occasionally.

Makes 6 to 8 servings.

Test kitchen notes: If you are unable to find andouille in Central Florida, you can substitute chorizo.

This recipe won first place in the corporate category in the 1990 Chili Cook Off at the Sheraton Orlando in Maitland. Proceeds from the event went to United Cerebral Palsy of Central Florida.

Bill Hardy
Merritt Island, FL
from Florida Today

Joe & Iris Doherty
Pilot Rock, OR

SOUTHWESTERN CHILI DIP

Look for pita chips at your grocery store. Or, to make you own chips, split pita bread into 2 single layers. Cut layers into wedges. If desired, brush pitas lightly with oil or margarine for an extra crunch. Bake in a 350 degree oven for 12 to 15 minutes or till crisp and golden brown.

1 Pkg. (8 oz.) low-fat regular shredded Cheddar cheese
1 C. reduced-calorie mayonnaise or salad dressing
1 can (4½ oz.) chopped ripe olives, drained
1 can (4 oz.) green chili peppers, chopped and drained
¼ t. garlic powder
few drops hot pepper sauce
1 medium tomato, chopped
¼ C. sliced green onions
Pita chips (optional)

In a large mixing bowl, stir together the Cheddar cheese, mayonnaise or salad dressing, half of the ripe olives, green chili peppers, garlic powder, and the hot pepper sauce until well blended.

Spread the mixture into a 9-inch quiche dish or pie plate, and bake in a 350 degree oven for about 20 minutes or until thoroughly heated. Sprinkle with the tomato, remaining olives, and green onions into 3 rings.

Serve warm with pita chips.

MICROWAVE DIRECTIONS:

Prepare as directed, except spread the cheese mixture into a microwave-safe 9-inch quiche dish or pie plate. Microwave, uncovered, at 100% power (High) for 4 to 6 minutes or till heated through, stirring twice. Continue preparing as directed.

Dan & Chere Kuller
Cocoa, FL

Frank J. Cabral
Maui, HA

WYNKOOP'S BLACK BEAN CAKES

1 cup raw black beans
1 onion, halved
½ anaheim pepper, seeded, minced
¼ teaspoon cinnamon
1 teaspoon cumin
½ teaspoon chili powder
½ teaspoon salt
2 tablespoons minced, fresh cilantro
1 carrot, scraped
1 stalk celery
1 clove garlic
Pinch oregano
Dash cayenne pepper
2 green chilies or 2 ounces canned green chilies, drained
Pico de gallo*

*Available in Spanish or Tex-Mex sections of markets.

Wash beans and put into deep pot, with water to cover by 1 inch.

Add ½ onion, minced, minced anaheim pepper, ½ teaspoon EACH of cumin, chili powder and salt, and simmer until beans are tender, about 1½ hours. Add water, if needed, to keep beans covered.

Add cinnamon during last 30 minutes of cooking. Process carrot, celery, garlic, and other half onion together in a food processor until very fine. Saute processed vegetables in a heavy, non-stick skillet, adding another half teaspoon cumin, oregano, cayenne and salt. Cook until all liquid is evaporated. Set aside. When beans are finished cooking, spread them on tray to cool, and when cook, mix in minced fresh cilantro. Drain liquid from beans and green chilies, and process together to form a smooth paste. Mix black beans and sauteed vegetables together. Put 1½ scoops of bean mix on a hot, flat griddle and flatten into cakes. Bake until browned on one side, then turn and cook until browned on the other side. Serve cakes with sour cream and pico de gallo (or salsa). Makes 8-10 cakes.

Carroll Jose Edwards
Florida Today

North Country Zebus Farm
Warren & Roberta Stevens
Antwerp, NY

1-2-3 ALARM CHILI

"You can adjust the level of garlic, chili powder and pepper in 1-2-3 Alarm Chili to please just about any taste. Cubed rather than ground beef makes it authentic, tortilla presentation gives it flair and versatile Jarlsberg--the Scandinavian contribution--mellows the flavor while enriching texture".

1½ Lbs. round steak, cut into ½-inch cubes
¾ Lb. pork loin, cut into ½-inch cubes
1 can (16 oz.) tomato sauce
1 to 3 Lg. cloves garlic, minced
2 cans (16 oz.) tomatoes, coarsely chopped
1 can (26 oz.) dark red kidney beans, undrained
½ C. water
½ C. chopped green pepper
½ C. chopped red pepper
1 to 3 chopped jalapeno
2 T. ½ t. oregano, crushed
¼ t. cayenne pepper
2 C. shredded Jarlsberg cheese
Additional oil for frying, optional
6-inch corn tortillas, optional

In large deep saucepan or Dutch oven, brown beef and pork in oil. Add onion and garlic and cook until onion is golden, stirring often. Add next 10 ingredients and simmer 30 minutes, until beef is tender.

Gradually blend in 1 cup Jarlsberg. Heat, stirring often.

Meanwhile, heat 1 inch oil in deep skillet. Add tortillas one at a time and fry until golden on both sides, about 1 minutes. Press each into small serving bowl, keeping one end 2 inches above top of bowl. Serve chili on tortillas and garnish with remaining cheese. Makes 8 servings.

Jarlsberg Cheeses
New York, NY

Lee H. Rice
Oracle, AZ

MELBOURNE FINEST CHILI

2 T. olive oil
4 Lbs. beef sirloin course chili grind
3 Med. onions, chopped
1 red pepper, chopped
1 green pepper, chopped
4 Lg. cloves garlic, minced
1 can (6 oz.) tomato paste
1 can (10 oz.) tomato sauce
2 or 3 T. chili powder
1 T. oregano
¼ t. dried basil
½ t. paprika
1 T. ground cumin
Salt and pepper to taste

In a heavy pot, heat the oil and add meat, using a wooden spoon to break up chunks into smaller pieces. Continue stirring the meat so that it is evenly browned. Stir in all the remaining ingredients. Bring the pot to a boil, reduce the heat to simmer, and allow to cook for 2 to 3 hours with an occasional stir to keep the chili from sticking to the pot.

Taste as you stir and adjust your seasonings if necessary. Serves 8.

Ms. Susan Stolarski
Melbourne, FL

J. T. Williamson, 1897
College Heights,
McLennan County, TX

COLORFUL VEGETABLE CHILI

1 cup chopped onion
½ cup chopped celery
½ cup chopped carrots
1 zucchini, cut in slices
1 medium green bell pepper, chopped
2 garlic cloves, minced
¾ cup oil
1 28-Oz. can stewed tomatoes, undrained
8 ounces picante sauce
1¼ cups water
1 teaspoon low-sodium beef bouillon powder or paste
1½ teaspoon cumin
1 15-Oz. can garbanzo beans, drained and rinsed
1 15-Oz. can spicy chili beans, undrained
2 ounces canned chopped mild green chilies
1 tablespoon cornstarch thinned with 3 tablespoons cold water
Roasted peanuts
Shredded jack cheese
Alfalfa sprouts
Chopped green onion
Sliced ripe olives
Sour cream
1 tablespoon chili powder

In a large saucepot, heat oil, and in it saute onions, celery, carrots, zucchini, green pepper, and garlic until crisp-tender. Add tomatoes with their liquid, picante sauce (hot or mild, as you like), water, water, bouillon powder, and cumin and chili powder. Bring to a boil. Reduce heat, cover, simmer 30 minutes, stirring occasionally. Add green chilies, chili beans and garbanzos. Stir in cornstarch to thicken. Simmer 5 minutes more. Ladle into bowls. Pass small bowls of peanuts, jack cheese, sprouts, green onion, ripe olives, and sour cream as condiments.

Florida Today

Carrol Jose, Florida Today's Food Section, has aided us quite a bit on CHILIMANIA! The following article appeared March 28th, and we thought that it may be of general interest.

'When we were in Denver a while ago, I sampled several interesting dishes in several interesting restaurants. One was located in an old, still-working brewery, and called, appropriately, Wynkoop Brewing Company. A downtown Denver landmark. Wynkoop's offers diners casual atmosphere, reasonable prices, samples of their beers, brewed on site, and such unusual dishes as medallions of caribou, elk steaks, and numble pie, made with venison. One isn't likely to run across many elk or caribou here in Florida, but we can make one dish they are famous for - black bean cakes. Crisp and flavorful. And a boon to vegetarians.

'Yes, well, beans. They've never been real popular, due to something we can call the "flatulence factor." However, now a culinary breakthrough for bean fans (or fans of other veggies of gas-producing ilk) has been make with Beano. Produced by Lactaid Inc., this product will be available in the antacid section of supermarkets, and, if used as directed, is claimed to reduce or eliminate the gas associated with eating beans and such. Since beans and cabbage and broccoli and such are very nutritious, "Beano" should make these items an attractive menu option again. Question for Lactaid: Can one put a few drops of Beano in one's beer, to prevent flatulence? If so, the women of the world may knight the inventors!

'But back to beans. Chef Mark Schiffler of Wynkoop's kindly shared his recipe with me, and I pass it on to you. Bring on the Beano, and scarf up the beans and beer!

222 E.C. "Teddy Blue" Abbott
"We Pointed Them North"
October, 1892, Montana

BANANA RIVER CHILI

2 Lbs. lean ground beef
1½ C. chopped onion
¼ C. chopped celery
2 t. minced garlic
1 C. beef broth
1 can beer
1 can (8 oz.) tomato sauce
2 T. chili powder
2 t. cumin
1 t. salt
½ t. pepper
1 t. hot sauce or to taste
1 can (30 oz.) kidney beans
Shredded Cheddar cheese (optional)

Brown beef and remove from pan. In 2 tablespoons of drippings, saute the onion and celery until the onion is transparent. Add garlic and saute 1 minute longer. Combine all ingredients in large saucepan, except the beans and the cheese. Simmer, covered, for 1 hour. Add beans and simmer 30 minutes. If chili is too thick, add a little more beef broth. Serve in individual bowls. Top with shredded cheese if desired. Serves 4 to 6.

Bill Hardy
Merritt Island, FL
from Florida today

W.F. Cody
Nebraska (1884)

CHOCOLATE CHICKEN CHILI

2 onions, finely chopped
1 T. Vegetable oil
2 t. Liquid Spice Garlic
2 t. Liquid Spice Chili
1 t. Liquid Spice Oregano
1 t. Liquid Spice Thyme
¼ t. Liquid Spice Hot
Red Pepper
2 Lbs. boneless chicken breast, cut into 1-inch cubes
1 C. chicken broth or stock
1 C. dark beer
1 T. tomato paste
Salt to taste
1 Oz. unsweetened chocolate, grated

In a large skillet, cook onion in oil until lightly browned. Add liquid spices. Add Chicken and saute until tender.

Add broth, beer and tomato paste. Bring to a boil and season with salt. Simmer for 10 minutes. Stir in chocolate until melted.

Serve immediately over rice or beans. (Pass Liquid Spice Garlic, Chili and Hot Red Pepper for those who like even zestier flavor.) Serves 6.

NOTE: Chili can be cooked ahead of time and stored in refrigerator overnight.

Dilijan Liquid Spice
New York, NY

Robert & David Brown
Napa, CA

SHERRY'S HOT STUFF CHILI

½ C. chopped red onion
1 Lb. ground turkey or lean ground beef
2 cans Hunt's Garlic and Spice Tomato Sauce
1 can (10½ oz.) tomato soup
½ t. paprika
½ t. cayenne pepper (hot) (mild ⅛ t.)
1 bay leaf
1 T. chili powder (mild) (hot 2 T.)
2 cans (16 oz.) red kidney beans with liquid

If turkey is used,brown it until pink color has disappeared, and drain off liquid. If you use ground beef, use as little oil as necessary to start browning it until it created it's own oil, and also drain off as much liquid as possible. In both cases, break up meats as they brown with a large wooden spoon.

Add the onions to the turkey or beef, and allow to saute. Add the rest of the ingredients except the beans; cover, and simmer for 30 to 45 minutes. Taste and check on seasonings as you gradually the amount of each. During the last 15 minutes of cooking, add the beans with liquid.

Serve hot with diced onions and shredded cheese sprinkled over the servings.

Sherry Frattarola
Melbourne Beach, FL

Walking A
Lynn Anderson
Davie, FL

VEGETARIAN CHILI WITH RICE

1 T. vegetable oil
1 Lg. yellow onion, chopped
1 Med. size carrot, peeled and chopped
3 cloves garlic, minced
1 Med. size sweet green pepper, cored, seeded & chopped
½ C. dried lentils, rinsed and sorted
2 t. chili powder or to taste
1 t. ground cumin
1 bay leaf
⅛ t. cayenne pepper
1 can (1Lb.) low sodium tomatoes chopped with their juices
½ C. cooked & drained chick peas
½ C. cooked & drained pinto beans
½ C. cooked & drained black beans
¾ C. long-grain rice

To prepare:

1) In a heavy 6-quart Dutch oven, heat the vegetable oil over a moderately low heat for 1 minute; add onion, carrot, garlic and green pepper, and cook, covered for 10 minutes or until the vegetables are soft.

2) Add the lentils, chili powder, cumin, bay leaf, cayenne pepper and tomatoes along with a small amount of water if the mixture appears thick. Cover and simmer 10 minutes. Add chick peas, pinto beans and black beans. Cover, simmer for 30 minutes or until lentils are tender.

4) Before the chili is done cook rice following package directions, omitting the salt. Ladle the chili over it and serve with a nice crispy green salad. Serves 4.

Prep time: 15 minutes. Cooking: 51 minutes.

Each serving has:

Cal.	411	Cholesterol	0	Sodium	52mg
Total fat	5g	Protein	17g	Sugar	0
Sat. fat	1g	Carb.	75g	Fiber	7g

Gail Cobb Benedict
Merritt Island, FL

Kenneth R. Sigman II
Homeworth, OH

TEXICAN DEER CHILI

2 Lbs. venison, coarse-ground or diced
4 slices salt pork, chopped
1 can tomatoes (hot with green chilies, if you prefer)
1 Lg. onion, chopped
1 garlic clove, minced
2 jalapenos (canned hot green chili peppers), chopped
2 T. chili powder
½ t. oregano
½ t. ground cumin
½ C. red wine
Pepper
Salt
Water
2 C. cooked red kidney beans

Brown the salt pork in a large, deep iron skillet, frying out all fat as liquid. Add venison and onion, brown quickly and cook 30 minutes at medium heat. Add tomatoes, seasonings, wine, a substantial amount of pepper and a dash of salt. Mix well. Reduce heat and simmer about 2 hours, adding small amounts of water if necessary. Refrigerate overnight and reheat. If beans are desired, add when reheating. Serves 5.

Bill Hardy
Merritt Island, FL
by Bryon Dalrymple

Chas. & John McCarter
Corinth, MS

CHILI-OODLES

1 Lb. lean ground beef
1 cup onion slices
1 cup chopped green pepper
2 cloves garlic, minced
2 cups water
1¾ cups (15 oz. can) crushed tomatoes
⅔ cup (6 oz. can) tomato paste
1 to 2 tablespoons chili powder
2 tablespoons Worcestershire sauce
½ teaspoon salt
9 cups (12 oz.) Light'n Fluffy Wide Egg Noodles, uncooked

In large saucepan, cook meat and onion until meat is almost done, drain. Add green pepper and garlic; cook until green pepper is just tender. Stir in remaining ingredients except pasta. Heat to boiling. Reduce heat; simmer 20 minutes, stirring occasionally. Cook pasta according to package directions; drain. Serve chili over hot pasta. 6 servings (1¾ cups ea.).

Light'n Fluffy
Hershey Foods Corp

Crescent Double A
American Agronomics Corp
Arcadia, FL

BLACK BEAN-TURKEY CHILI

1½ C. dry black beans
1 medium onion, quartered
2 T. olive oil
2¼ Lbs. turkey drumsticks
1 onion, chopped
1 green bell pepper, cut into squares
1 red bell pepper, cut into squares
1 Lg. clove garlic, minced
1 C. chicken broth
2 T. chili powder, or to taste
1 T. ground cumin
1½ t. salt, or to taste
¼ t. black pepper, fresh ground
hot cooked rice, sour cream or yogurt and salsa

Place beans in a large bowl, cover with water 2 inches above beans. Cover and soak overnight. Drain beans and add fresh water, covering the beans by an inch. Push the quartered onion into the beans. Cover, bring to a boil. Lower the heat, and simmer for 45 minutes to an hour, or until the beans are tender but not mushy.

Heat olive oil in a large skillet or a Dutch oven. Saute the drumsticks for about 10 minutes, turning to brown evenly and lightly. Add the chopped onions, squared bell peppers, and the garlic. Saute slowly until the vegetables are tender but do not let them brown.

Add chicken broth, chili powder, cumin, salt and pepper. Cover and simmer 30 minutes, until the turkey is tender. Remove the drumsticks, cool until they can be handled. Cut the meat into bite-size pieces, discarding the skin and bones. Return the meat to the vegetable mixture; stir in the black beans. Simmer for 30 minutes, adding hot water if necessary to keep the chili runny but not swimming in liquid.

Serve hot on rice with a dollop of sour cream or yogurt, and salsa on each serving. Serves 6 to 8.

Post marked:
New Orleans, LA no name

Arrow Head Cattle
Co., Inc.
Visalia, CA

CHILI MEAT SAUCE

2 Lbs. lean, trimmed chuck or beef shank, coarsely ground
1 Lb. kidney suet
4 to 6 cloves garlic, crushed
1 T. cumin seed
2 T. chili powder
1 T. paprika
1 T. salt
1 t. chili caribe (coarsely ground red chile with seeds), or
1 heaping t. of crushed chilipiquins

Saute meat-suet mixture in a heavy pot or skillet until gray. Add garlic, chile caribe (or chilipiquins), and cumin seed and continue to saute, stirring occasionally, until fat is melted.

Add remaining ingredients and mix well. Lower heat and simmer gently for at least 3 hours until all the liquid except the fat is cooked out. The fat will keep it from scorching, but check it regularly anyway.

Pour into a loaf pan or heatproof bowl and let cool. When mixture solidifies, it can be frozen or refrigerated whole or cut into pieces that can be added to a simmering pot of beans, or reheated for chili, as needed.

Ms. Kim Wilking
Cincinnati, OH

Kuykendall & Carr
Wyoming (1884)

ROCKING OPEN A K

Parham Cattle Company,
National Cattlemen's Assoc.
Fresno, California
Established: Nov 1989
Herd: purebred Polled Herefords
Location: Central California

CHILI CHEESE DIP

1 Lb. ground beef (lean)
1 Lb. American Cheese or Velveeta
1 can (8 to 10 oz.) green chilies (Medium)
1 can (8 to 10 oz.) tomatoes
2 T. Worcestershire sauce
½ t. chili powder (to taste)
Dash of hot sauce

Brown ground beef well; drain grease. Put ground beef and all ingredients into a large pot or crockpot. Stir well. Make sure that cheese is cut into small cubes. Cover and cook approximately 1 hour. Stir occasionally until cheese melts. Serve immediately or cook on low heat for serving up to 6 hours.

Recipe may be doubled and seasoned to taste.

Mr. & Mrs. Art Parham
Fresno, CA

QUARTER CIRCLE K R

Kirk & Robinson Ranch
National Cattlemen's Assoc.
Heppen, Oregon
Established: 1947
Herd: Polled Herefords, Salers, Commercial
Location: Northeastern Oregon

OREGON CATTLEMEN'S CHILI

1 Lb. Lean meat, coarsely ground
¾ C. Beef Broth
1 can (28 oz.) tomatoes, crushed
1 T. salad oil
1 Lg. onion, chopped
1 Lg. green bell pepper, chopped
2 stalks celery, chopped
2 Med. cloves garlic, minced
2 T. chili powder
¼ t. dried oregano
1 t. ground cumin
½ t. salt
shake or two black pepper
2 cans (15 oz.) red kidney beans, drained (optional)

In a large pot or Dutch oven, heat the oil and saute the onion, pepper, celery and garlic for a few minutes until they are just about done. Add the seasonings and blend with a spoon. Add the beef, and brown using a heavy spoon to crumble as it browns.

Once the beef is cooked, add the tomatoes and beef broth, bring to a boil. Reduce heat, and simmer for no longer than 30 minutes. Add the beans if desired, about 10 minutes before serving to allow them to be heated thoroughly.

If desired, serve with shredded cheeses, crackers, or other type of side dishes that you like.

PROFESSOR ZACHARIAH BISHOPS MIRACLE CHILI

JH
Jim Akers
P.O. Box 2812
Nashville, TN 37219

This chili is officially known as "Professor Zachariah Bishops Miracle Chili." 1988 Tennessee CASI Open Championship Recipe.

3 Lbs. coarse ground very lean beef
1 C. finely chopped white onion
2 C. chopped, seeded and drained tomatoes
1 C. tomato sauce
⅓ C. tomato paste
2 T. dark chili powder
½ T. paprika
1½ T. cumin
½ T. Mexican oregano
½ T. black pepper
1 t. salt
½ t. brown sugar
2-3 cloves garlic minced
½1 t. Cayenne or Jalapeno pepper
dash Tabasco & MSG
water
1 t. oil
dark red kidney beans (optional) 2 cans
Sazon con culantro y achiote (optional & available in Mexican food store) 2 packs

Brown meat in oil and drain well. Saute onion, garlic and chopped tomatoes in oil until soft and add meat, paste, sauce, paprika, black powder, Tabasco, MSG and cover with water. Add ½ of the following: chili powder, cumin, oregano, Cayenne or Jalapeno. Simmer covered for one hour. Add remaining ½ measure of powder, cumin, oregano, Cayenne or Jalapeno along with salt and sugar. Add water if necessary and simmer one hour more.

If you want beans, drain and rinse them, and add now. Add Sazon and adjust heat with Cayenne and simmer ½ hour. Chili should cook between 2 and 2½ hours.

Regards, Jim Akers
For the team

Brand only: Anvil C
Craig Colflesh
R.D. #1, Box 8020
Grantville, PA 17028

HOME MADE CHILI SAUCE

13 Lbs. ripe tomatoes
2 whole stalks celery
½ T. ground cloves
6 onions, chopped
4 green peppers, chopped
¼ C. salt
¾ T. dried mustard
1 t. ground cinnamon
about 2 Lbs. grown sugar
Cider vinegar

Blanch tomatoes, and cook until nearly done. Save half of the liquid from cooking and discard remaining amount. Add chopped vegetables to the tomatoes, and simmer about 1 to 1½ hours. Put the ground cloves into a small tied packet, and add with the rest of ingredients to the pot, and cook for another 2 hours.

Using sterilized jars, seal the hot sauce, and allow to cool. Makes about 6 pints or so.

Laurie A. Seltzer
Cincinnati, OH

Lawrence E. Jordan
Kawai, HA

CHILI MEAT BALLS

1 Lb. lean ground beef
1 Lb. lean ground pork
¼ C. onion, chopped fine
¾ C. rice, uncooked
½ C. water
1 egg, beaten
1 can (16 oz.) tomatoes, chopped
1 t. salt
1½ t. chili powder

Cook rice as directed on package, and set aside. In a large mixing bowl, combine all ingredients except the tomatoes and water.

Combine the tomatoes and water and bring to a boil. Form meat mixture into balls, and drop into boiling contents. Cover, reduce heat, and simmer for 1½ to 2 hours, stirring gently to move meatballs for even cooking.

This should make about 20 balls. Ladle liquid over meatballs when serving.

Jay & Sandy Hatfield
Cincinnati, OH

Red House Ranching Co.
Angels Camp, CA

THE GARDEN PATCH'S VEGETARIAN CHILI

1 can (36 oz.) Bush's Best Hot Mexican Beans, undrained
1 can (36 oz.) kidney beans, undrained
1 can (30 oz.) tomato juice
1 can (16 oz.) diced tomatoes
1 small onion, chopped
2 green peppers, chopped
1 t. paprika
1 t. oregano
1 t. onion powder
1 t. minced fresh garlic
1 t. sweet basil
2 t. chili powder
1 Med.-size wedge Havartl cheese, chopped

MICROWAVE: To make in the microwave, combine all of the ingredients in a microwave-safe casserole dish. Microwave on High (100%) power for 45 minutes, rotate and stir halfway through the cooking cycle.

STOVETOP: To make on the stovetop, combine all of the ingredients in a large soup kettle or stockpot, simmer for 2 hours, stirring occasionally. Add more liquid if necessary.

Makes about 1 gallon (freezes well).

Bill Hardy
Merritt Island, FL
from Florida Today

James Fergus & Son of Ft. Maginnis purchased this brand from W.W. Welter on Sept. 26, 1890. Montana

CHILI con POLLO

1 Lb. cooked chicken breast, deboned, diced
2 C. cooked salad macaroni
1 can (28 oz.) plum tomatoes
½ t. or less salt
1½ t. chili powder
1½ t. dry mustard
2 cloves garlic, minced
2 cans (15 oz.) red kidney beans

Combine all ingredients except the chicken, macaroni and kidney beans in a soup pot. Simmer for 1½ to 2 hours uncovered.

Add the chicken and beans and heat to it starts to boil. Stir in the macaroni, and serve.

Jerry & Nancy Schwartz
Cincinnati, OH

Kim & Verona Martin
Madras, OR

This recipe was forwarded by the Cincinnati Fire Department on a request for any chili recipes that their fire fighters may wish to contribute to CHILIMANIA!

Chief-

Enclosed you'll find a copy of one of my chili recipes for the gentleman and lady who are writing the Chilimania Cookbook.

I hope that they'll be able to use this recipe and that it may reflect our sincere cooperation with their culinary literary pursuits!

Respectfully submitted,
William M. Donovan
FAO II/Engine 7

DONOVAN'S CODE "3" CHILI

INGREDIENTS:

7 Lbs. Ground chuck or turkey (when using turkey, add 1 cup of vegetable oil)
½ C. Onions, chopped
½ C. Green bell peppers, chopped
3 T. Fresh garlic, diced
5 Ozs. Chili powder
1 T. Garlic salt
1 Lg. can (29 oz.) Tomato sauce
1 Lg. can (21 oz.) Kidney beans
1 C. Catsup
5 T. Jalapenos, seeded & chopped (optional)
2 T. Crushed red pepper
2 T. Ground allspice
3 T. Ground cumin
1 T. Ground white pepper
5-6 C. Water, added according to your desired consistency
3 Whole bay leaves

PROCEDURES:

Brown meat for 15 minutes. Add onions, green pepper and fresh garlic. Cook for another 20 minutes, or until vegetables are transparent. Remove and strain the grease in a colander. Put meat back into the pan. Add remaining ingredients and let simmer for 1½-2 hours or until chili has reduced it a thicker consistency. Add additional water if necessary. Remove the bay leaves and start salivating and start BLOATING!

Serves 10 hungry firefighters

Bill Donovan
Cincinnati Fire Dept. Engine 7

Recorded by the Price Russell Co. on December 30, 1905. This was a partnership between Con Price and Charlie Russell. Montana Territory

TWO-BEAN CHORIZO CHILI

1 Lb. chorizo (Mexican sausage
3 Med. onions, cut into ½-inch pieces
1 can (16 oz.) black beans, undrained
1 can (16 oz.) kidney beans or pinto beans, undrained
1 C. beef broth
1 can (8 oz.) whole kernel corn, drained
¾ C. picante sauce
1 Med. green pepper, cut into ¾-inch pieces
1 Med. red pepper, cut into ¾-inch pieces
Toppings:
Sour Cream
Shredded Cheddar Cheese
Chopped cilantro
Chopped green onions

Remove sausage from casing.

In a large saucepan or Dutch oven, brown sausage with onion until onion is tender; drain.

Add remaining ingredients except optional toppings. Bring to a boil; reduce heat. Simmer uncovered about 15 minutes, stirring occasionally, or until chili is desired consistency. Ladle into bowls; top as desired and serve with additional picante sauce.

Makes 6 servings, about 6 cups chili.

Bill Hardy
Merritt Island, FL
From Florida Today

W.H. Greenwell Ranch
Honolulu, HA

MY CHILI con CARNE

1 Lb. ground round, extra lean
1 med. onion, chopped
1 med. green pepper, chopped
1 can (4 oz.) green chilies, chopped
2 cloves garlic;, minced
½ t. ground cumin
1 T. chili powder, or less to taste, or more if you like it "spicier"
1 t. cayenne pepper
1 can (28 oz.) tomatoes, broken or chopped with knife
2 cans (15 oz.) red kidney beans, with liquid
2 C. salad macaroni, cooked

In a skillet, broth the beef, and saute the onion and green pepper until they are tender. Drain off fatty drippings. Add all remaining ingredients except the beans, macaroni and the chilies; uncover, and simmer 1½ to 2 hours.

Add beans and heat to boiling. Add macaroni a short while before serving, and sprinkle with the chopped chilies.

Gayle Hollander
Cincinnati, OH

James D. Dow
Detroit, MI

GRILLED SALMON WITH CORN SALSA

6 to 8 salmon steaks (6 to 8 ounces each), thawed if necessary

Corn salsa:
- 2 cups canned yellow corn kernels
- ½ cup green pepper, finely chopped
- ½ cup tomato, finely chopped
- ½ cup onion, finely chopped
- 2 tablespoons garlic, minced
- 2 tablespoons olive oil
- 2 tablespoons balsamic (or other red wine) vinegar
- ¼ cup chopped fresh Italian parsley
- Salt and freshly ground black pepper

Mix all salsa ingredients in a small mixing bowl and allow to sit 1 hour.

Place salmon steaks on swell-oiled grill over hot coals. Grill 10 minutes per inch of thickness, measured at thickest part, or until fish just flakes when tested with a fork. Turn halfway through cooking. Serve with corn salsa.

Florida Today

Flying T
Percy & Ruby Thornton
Vero Beach, FL

SIMPLE VEGETABLE CHILI

1 T. olive oil
1½ C. chopped onion
½ C. Chopped celery
1¼ C. chopped pepper
2 cloves garlic, minced
1 to 2 T. chili powder (to your taste)
1 t. cumin
½ t. fresh ground pepper
2 cans (16 oz.) tomatoes, with juice and chopped
1 can (16 oz.) pinto beans, drained
1 can (16 oz.) red kidney beans, drained
1 C. tomato juice

In a large pot or a Dutch oven, saute the first four ingredients in as little oil as possible, until the vegetables are tender. Add the rest of the ingredients except the beans, and bring to a boil. Reduce the heat and add the beans and allow to simmer for a short while before serving. Add more tomato juice if necessary to reach the desired consistency.

Tallahassee, FL
no name

Red Cloud Ranch, Inc.
Bend, OR

CHILI CHEESE BUTTER*

½ C. softened butter or margarine
½ C. shredded Jarlsberg cheese
1 small clove garlic, minced
¼ t. chili powder

In bowl, combine all ingredients until well blended. Spoon into serving dish; cover. Chill until ready to serve. Makes about 1 cup spread.

*This is delicious with your favorite corn bread recipe, too.

Jarlsberg Cheeses
New York, NY

Richard Osswald
Brookville, OH

GATOR CHILI

1 Lb. coarsely ground gator
2 C. chopped onion
¼ Lb. hot ground sasage
½ C. chopped fresh cilantro (corinader) or parsley
2 T. minced garlic
6 C. ham stock *see below
2 C. cooked or canned small red beans
2 C. tomato sauce
Chili powder to taste
Dash ground cinnamon
Louisiana Hot sauce or ground cayenne pepper to taste
Salt to taste

Yields about 6 to 8 servings.

Brown ground gator and sausage over medium-high heat in a large pot. Then saute onions, cilantro, and minced garlic with meat until the onions are tender. Add ham stock, beans, tomato sauce, chili powder, cinnamon, hot sauce, and salt. Stir well.

Bring to a boil, then reduce het to low; cover and simmer for at least 2 hours. Stir often. Serve hot with chopped onions and grated cheese if desired. Also can be served over cooked rice.

*Ham Stock

1 C. dry white wine
Ham trimmings and cracked bones
2 Med.-sized onions, coarsely chopped
1 C. coarsely chopped celery
1 T. coarsely chopped garlic
1 whole cayenne pepper, or ¾ t. ground cayenne pepper
3 Qt. water

Place all ingredients in a large stock pot. Cover; bring to a boil. Reduce to low heat. Cover and simmer for 3 to 4 hours. Remove scum as it forms.

Removing large bones and strain into containers and cover. Remove any unwanted fat after stock has chilled.

(Will keep in refrigerator for 3 or 4 weeks, or can be frozen and kept even longer).

Yields about 1 gallon.

Mark Banks
Cocoa,FL

P Cross Saucer
Polly Alma Rojek
Cocoa, FL

CHILI PIZZA

Prep time: 15 minutes
Cooking time: 15 minutes

- 2 C. prepared Carroll Shelby's Original Texas Brand Chili Mix
- 1 prebaked 12-inch pizza crust
- 1½ C. (6 ox.) Velveeta Shredded Pasteurized Process Cheese Food
- 3 green onion, chopped
- 1 Lg. tomato, chopped
- 1 green pepper, chopped
- ½ C. pitted rip olive slices

Preheat oven to 375 degree F.

Spread chili over crust, top evenly with process cheese food and remaining ingredients.

Bake 10 to 15 minutes or until process cheese food is melted.

Let stand for 5 minutes before cutting.

6 servings.

Microwave: To heat chili, microwave on HIGH 3 to 4 minutes or until thoroughly heated.

Carroll Shelby's Chili Mix

Glenn Johnson
Rebel's Rest Ranch
Springfield, TN

THE BIG DIPPER

The big taste of Hormel Chili No Beans and Ro-Tel Tomatoes & Green Chilies make it the one dip everyone will look up to.

- 1 (15 oz.) can Hormel Chili No Beans
- 1 (10 oz.) can Ro-Tel Tomatoes & Green Chilies (diced), reserving 1 Tbsp (drained) for garnish
- 1½ cups (approx. 8 oz.) pasteurized processed cheese, cubed
- ½ cup sliced green onions
- ½ tsp. cayenne pepper

In saucepan, combine all ingredients. Heat just until cheese melts, stirring frequently. Serve warm with assorted raw vegetable dippers and toasted French bread slices. Garnish dip with reserved tomatoes, red pepper and additional green onions, if desired. Makes 4 cups.

Hormel/Ro-Tel recipe

Princeville Cattle Co.
Kawai, HA

CHILI CON CARNE

1 Lb. chili ground beef
2 T. vegetable oil
1 Lg. onion, chopped
1 green bell pepper, chopped
1 red bell pepper, chopped
2 ribs celery, chopped
2 cloves garlic, minced
1½ t. salt
⅛ t. paprika
⅛ t. cayenne pepper
1 bay leaf
1 to 2 T. chili powder, or to taste and KICK
1 can (15 oz.) either red kidney beans or chili flavored beans
1 can (16 oz.) tomatoes, chopped up some

Saute the vegetables with garlic, in oil until soft but not brown. Drain them from skillet, and brown the beef in the same oil until done. Add tomatoes and seasonings. Cover, and simmer for about 2 hours, adding water if necessary. Just before serving, add the beans so that they are thoroughly heated. Makes about 6 servings.

Katie Furr
Cincinnati, OH

Heine I. Kamai
Honolulu, HA

CHILI-CHEESE SALAD

1 T. gelatine
¼ C. cold water
1 C. dry cottage cheese
½ C. salad dressing
½ t. salt
1 C. chili sauce
1 C. heavy whipped cream

Combine all ingredients in mixing bowl until smooth. Pour into a prepared mold, and chill until firm.

Remove from mold when ready and garnish with vegetables for a very attractive dish when serving.

You can spice up this salad with a bit of added seasonings, and serve with chips or nachos.

Allen Furr
Cincinnati, OH

Gary & Dulinda Moniz
Honolulu, HA

QUEMADA SALSA

"Quemada" literally means "burnt" --and that is what is done to the tomatoes and green onions, giving the salsa a smoky flavor and rich color.

1 pound tomatoes, diced
1 bunch green onions, trimmed and washed
½ bunch cilantro
1 tablespoon vegetable oil
3 serrano peppers, stemmed
1 tablespoon garlic puree, chop and mash fresh garlic into a paste
1 tablespoon lime juice
1 teaspoon salt
½ teaspoon ground white pepper
½ teaspoon ground oregano
1 cup water

Place tomatoes and green onions on a hot mesquite grill (over hot coals, not flames). Pile the cilantro on top, so that it does not touch the grill. Grill the vegetables 10 to 15 minutes or until the peppers are soft.

Place the vegetable oil in a saute pan and heat. Add the serranos and saute until the peppers are soft.

Place the serranos, tomatoes, onion and cilantro in a food processor. Blend until coarsely ground. Remove to mixing bowl and stir until ingredients are evenly distributed. In a separate bowl, mix remaining ingredients until well blended, then add to the ground vegetables and mix thoroughly. Makes about 2 cups.

Nutritional information per tablespoon: 8 calories; 0.2 grams protein; 1 gram carbohydrate; 0.5 grams fat; 46 percent of calories as fat; 0.3 grams fiber; 0 milligrams cholesterol; 68 milligrams sodium.

The Great Chile Book
by Mark Miller
The Miami Herald

Robert Marble
Lamoille, NV

CHILI MEATBALLS

1 Lb. meat-loaf mixture
¼ C. white cornmeal
1 clove garlic, crushed or minced
1 small onion, grated
1 t. ground coriander
1 t. salt
¼ t. pepper
Sauce

Mix lightly all ingredients, except Sauce. Shape in balls about ¾" in diameter. Drop into boiling Sauce, cover and simmer 10 to 15 minutes. Makes 4 servings.

Sauce: Melt 1 tablespoon butter in saucepan; add 1 small onion, chopped and 1 clove garlic, crushed and minced. Cook slowly until lightly browned. Add 1 tablespoon chili powder and 1 can (1 pint 2 ounces) tomato juice; simmer 10 minutes. Season with salt and pepper.

Woman's Day

Robert & Helen Davis
Homedale, ID

PESCOS PASTA

1 Pkg. (7 oz.) Creamettes Elbow Macaroni, 2 cups uncooked
1 T. butter or margarine
1 Small green pepper, chopped
1 Small onion, chopped
2 cans (15 oz.) Hormel Chili with beans
1 can (12 oz.) whole kernel corn, drained
1 t. seasoned salt
⅛ t. pepper
1 C. shredded Cheddar Cheese

Prepare Creamettes Elbow Macaroni according to package directions. Drain. In a large skillet melt butter; add green pepper and onion. Cook until tender, (do not brown). Add Hormel Chili, corn, seasoned salt and pepper. Simmer on low heat 5 minutes. Stir in cooked Creamettes; top with shredded cheese. Cover and heat on low 5 minutes. 6 servings.

Hormel Recipe

O.V. Lynn Jr.
Hurricane Mills, TN

WIFE'S FATHER'S RECIPE CHILI

Brown 1 Lb. Hamburger (drain)
Add 1 small chopped onion
2 small cans sliced mushrooms
1 Lg.can whole tomatoes
1 15 oz. cans kidney beans
chili powder to taste
1 T. sugar

Combine all ingredients with cooked meat, simmer in pot until ready, and eat and enjoy.

Dan Lewis
Orlando, FL

James & Norma Oldenberg
Marcus, SD

CHILI CHEESE DIP

1 can (10 oz.) RO-TEL Tomatoes and Green Chilies (Whole or Diced)
1 can (15 oz.) Hormel Chili
1 Lb. of your favorite Pasteurized Process Cheese Spread

QUICK N EASY

Cut cheese into cubes and melt in a double boiler over low heat while stirring. Stir in Hormel Chili and RO-TEL tomatoes and green chilies. Enjoy.

*MICROWAVE: Cut cheese into cubes and melt in a microwave-safe covered bowl at full power (high) for 3 to 3½ minutes, stirring every minute. Stir in Hormel Chili and RO-TEL tomatoes and green chilies. Serve warm. Enjoy.

SERVING TIPS: Enjoy served warm with tortilla chips, corn chips, or crackers. Makes a great sauce over Mexican food. Leave the cheese out and enjoy a delicious bowl of Hormel Chili.

*Microwaves vary in wattage and power output; cooking time may need to be adjusted.

Hormel recipe

Vera Lee Story
Titusville, FL

CHILI DIP CON QUESO

Prep time: 10 minutes
Microwave cooking time: 7 minutes

1 (8 oz.) pkg. Philadelphia Brand Cream Cheese, softened
2 C. prepared Carroll Shelby's Original Texas Brand Chili Mix
1 (4 oz.) can chopped green chilies, drained
1 (4 oz.) can chopped pitted ripe olives, drained
2 T. chopped green onion
1 C. (4 oz.) Velveeta Mexican Shredded Pasteurized Process Cheese Food

- Spread cream cheese over bottom of 9-inch pie plate.
- Layer remaining ingredients over cream cheese.
- Microwave on HIGH 5 to 7 minutes or until thoroughly heated. Serve with tortilla chips. 8 to 10 servings.

Carroll Shelby's Recipe

Gen. James W. Van Fleet
Polk City, FL

CHILI BRAVO

Win applause for your next rice dish by adding Hormel Chili No Beans.

1 (15 oz.) can Hormel Chili No Beans
1 (6 oz.) can vegetable juice
½ cup chopped onion
3 cups frozen vegetables, thawed, drained
4 cups cooked rice

In large sauce pan, combine chili, vegetable juice, and onion, cook 5 minutes over medium heat. Stir in mixed vegetables. Cover, simmer an additional 4 minutes. Serve over rice. Serves four.

Hormel Recipe

Clarence W. Coelho, Jr.
Kailua, HA

SALSA INGREDIENTS

The following information was contained in The Miami Herald January 9, 1992 along with salsa recipes so indicated, by Mark Miller from his book The Great Chile Book.

'Here's a rundown on some of the common ingredients in salsas. Some can be found in the supermarket; others may require a trek to a specialty foods store. You'll find that names of chilies vary wildly from market to market and source to source.

› Jalapeno peppers: Bullet-shaped hot peppers that are found fresh in the produce department or pickled in the specialty canned goods aisle. Most of the heat is in the seeds and inner stems; use care when handling jalapenos and other hot chilies. May be green or red.

› Cilantro: Also called Chinese parsley or fresh coriander, it's a flat-leafed herb with a distinctive, somewhat soapy taste. Stand the stems, with roots attached, in a glass of water, then cover the tops with a plastic bag and a rubber band. Store this way, cilantro will stay fresh in the refrigerator for days.

› Tomatillos: Commonly referred to as Mexican green tomatoes, these are actually related to the gooseberry. Look for firm, green tomatillos covered with a papery husk in the produce department of big, well-stocked supermarkets. They're also available canned in specialty food markets.

› Fresh green chilies: Look for big, mild chilies labeled Anaheim or long green or New Mexican in the produce section, if you can't find them, canned mild green chilies are available in 4-ounce cans in most supermarkets. Poblano chilies are also big and green, but they're hotter and generally not eaten raw.

› Other Chilies: Other chilies called for in these recipes include ancho peppers (big, mild, red, dried chile) and pasilla (a narrow, dark-red dried chile). You'll probably have to seek out the pasilla in a specialty food store; the ancho peppers are sometimes available in supermarkets.'

The Great Chile Book
by Mark Miller
The Miami Herald

The Graham Company
Miami Lakes, FL

SALSA De TOMATE VERDE COCIDA
(Cooked Green Tomato Sauce)

½ pound tomatillos, chopped
¼ white onion
2 cloves garlic
1½ serrano chilies
2 cups water
2 sprigs fresh cilantro, chopped
Salt to taste

Remove paperlike skin from tomatillos and wash. Bring tomatillos to a boil with onion, garlic, chilies and 1 cup of water. Once water is boiling, remove from heat and allow to cool. Pour contents into a blender and blend to a fairly smooth consistency, adding the last cup of water as needed. Finish by adding salt and cilantro. Makes 1½ to 2 cups.

Nutritional information per tablespoon: 4 calories; 0.2 grams protein; 0.8 grams carbohydrate; trace of fat; 6 percent of calories as fat; 0.1 gram fiber; 0 milligrams cholesterol; 1.5 milligrams sodium.

The Great Chile Book
by Mark Miller
The Miami Herald

Marley Cattle Co.
Phoenix, AZ

SALSA De TOMATE VERDE CRUDA
(Raw Green Tomato Sauce)

½ pound tomatillos, quartered
1 white onion, coarsely chopped
2 serrano chilies
1 clove garlic
½ avocado
1 cup water
Pinch sugar
Salt to taste
2 sprigs fresh cilantro, chopped

Remove skin from tomatillos, then clean and wash them. Cut into quarters. Add chopped onions, chilies, garlic and avocado pulp. (Ingredients should not be chopped too finely). Put in blender with water, sugar and salt and blend thoroughly. Pour into serving dish and sprinkle with cilantro. Makes 1½ to 2 cups.

Nutritional information per tablespoon: 13 calories; 0.3 grams protein; 2 grams carbohydrate; 0.6 grams fat; 39 percent of calories as fat; 0.4 grams fiber; 0 milligrams cholesterol; 2 milligrams sodium.

The Great Chile Book
by Mark Miller
The Miami Herald

Tenderfoot Ranch
Cocoa, FL

MACHO NACHO

Beef up your nachos with delicious beefy, Hormel Chili No Beans.

½ (15 oz.) bag tortilla chips, any flavor
1 (15 oz.) can Hormel Chili No Beans, heated
½ cup shredded cheese (Cheddar, Jack or American)

Spoon chili over chips. Sprinkle with cheese. Heat in microwave oven or broil until cheese melts, 1 to 2 minutes.

Hormel Recipe

Campbell Cattle Co.
Cedarville, OH

EASY CHILI CON CARNE

This is one chili that is easy to prepare, and not hard to eat. Somewhat of a mild tasting dish.

2 T. butter, bacon drippings, or margarine
½ C. chopped onion
1 Med. green pepper, chopped
1 small clove garlic, minced
1 Lb. lean ground beef
1 can (15 oz.) tomatoes, broken up
2 t. to 2 T. chili powder
½ to ¾ t. salt
ground black pepper, if desired

Saute onion, green pepper, and garlic in skillet using any of the first item. After the onions are nearly done but not browned, drain all liquid, and add the ground beef, and brown till done. Again, drain off all drippings.

Add remaining ingredients, cover, and simmer on low for 1 hour. You can add and additional ingredients, or alter those of this recipe to your own personal taste.

Tom & Rita Barnett
Rockledge, FL

Windmill Ranch
Higley, AZ

SALSA BORRACHA
(Drunken Sauce)

This sauce is excellent with steaks and barbecue.

3 ancho peppers, seeded
3 chilies pasilla (dried red chilies, red and long), seeded
1 tablespoon oil, divided
1 white onion, coarsely chopped
4 cloves garlic
½ bottle beer or 1 cup orange juice (or half of each)
¼ cup tequila
Salt to taste
Green olives and grated white cheese for garnish

Fry ancho and pasilla chilies in 1 teaspoon oil, turning them constantly so that they do not burn. When they have turned a lighter color, remove from pan and allow to cool.

Meanwhile, saute the onions and garlic in remaining oil. Remove stems from the cooked chilies and chop chilies in blender with cooked garlic and onions. Blend until a heavy sauce is attained, adding the liquid last. Season with salt, then pour into a bowl, stir in olives and sprinkle with a white cheese such as anejo. Makes 2 to 2¼ cups.

Nutritional information per tablespoon: 14 calories; 0.1 grams proteins; 1 gram carbohydrate; 0.5 grams fat; 28 percent of calories as fat; 0.3 grams fiber; 0 milligrams cholesterol; 6 milligrams sodium.

The Great Chile Book
by Mark Miller
The Miami Herald

Allan L. Peters
Murdo, SD

CHILI CON CARNE

1 C. dried pinto beans
3 Lbs. lean stew beef
¼ C. olive oil
1 bay leaf
2 T. chili powder
1 T. salt
1 t. crushed cumin seed
1 t. oregano
3 T. paprika
3 T. cornmeal
1 T. flour
4 cloves garlic, minced

Cover washed beans with 4 cups water, bring to boil and boil 2 minutes. Cover and let stand 1 hour, then cook until tender. Drain. Cut meat in ½" cubes and sear in hot oil. Add 6 cups water, cover, bring to boil and simmer 1 hour. Add bay leaf and next six ingredients. Simmer ½ hour. Blend cornmeal, flour and cold water to make a paste. Stir into mixture; simmer 5 minutes. Add beans and heat. Makes 6 servings.

Woman's Day

Hard Times Ranch
C.J. & D.J. Van Hoomissen
Baker, OR

In the 1985 motion picture 'Murphy's Romance', James Garner is asked by co-star Sally Field what he wants to do in the future. His reply included "..... write a chili cookbook".

CLASSIC SALSA

This classic salsa starts with fresh tomatoes, but canned tomatoes can be substituted. Tasting as you go is a must, since the heat of jalapenos varies.

- 3 or 4 ripe tomatoes
- 6 to 10 fresh jalapenos
- ½ teaspoon chopped garlic
- Salt and pepper to taste

Using tongs, hold tomatoes over flame of gas burner just until they are softened and the skin blisters slightly. (Or place in a shallow baking pan and broil.) Place in a blender container. Add jalapenos, unseeded, and remaining ingredients. Blend to desired consistency. Makes about 3 cups.

Nutritional information per tablespoon: 2 calories; 0.1 grams proteins; 0.5 grams carbohydrate; trace of fat; 10 percent of calories as fat; 0.1 grams fiber; 0 milligrams cholesterol; 0.8 milligrams sodium.

The Great Chile Book
by Mark Miller
The Miami Herald

Craig & Susan Leister
Dornoch Angus Farm
Columbus, OH

HOME GROWN CHILI SAUCE

16 Qts. (½ bushel) tomatoes
15 Lg. Green peppers, chopped fine
12 Lg. onions, chopped fine
1 C. sugar
¼ C. coarse salt
¼ C. celery seed
2 C. cider vinegar
Salt to taste

Blanch and peel tomatoes. In large cooking vessel, bring to a boil and add chopped onion, green pepper along with rest of ingredients. Boil the contents until it becomes thick. Stir frequently, and taste during the three hours really desired to prepare this sauce, and flavor as desired.

After cooking, allow to set for a short period before bottling. This recipes makes about 4 to 5 quarts.

Mrs. Masuyo Doi
Honolulu, HA

CAROL'S CHILI CON CARNE

2 Lbs. ground beef
2 T. olive oil
2 cloves garlic, minced
1 T. ground cumin
1 Lg. Spanish Onion, diced
½ C. beef stock or bouillon
1 T. minced cilantro (1 t. dried)
3 C. cooked pinto beans or red kidney beans
2 T. minced fresh parsley
3 C. stewed tomatoes
1 T. chili powder, or to taste
½ T. roasted red peppers, chopped
1 T. paprika
¼ t. cayenne pepper, or to taste
3 C. cooked Thai jasmine rice,* or long-grain rice

* Available in Orients markets and some supermarkets.

If using canned beans, drain, rinse and set aside. In a heavy saucepot, heat oil and saute garlic, cumin and onion 1 minute. Add beef and cook, stirring, until beef is lightly browned. Pour off grease. Add all other ingredients, except rice (be cautious with cayenne pepper, unless you like hot chili); stir, cover and simmer 30 minutes. Taste and correct seasonings. Simmer another 10 minutes. Serve in bowls over cooked rice.

Note: Shredded cheese maya be added as a condiment, if desired.

Florida Today

Elfrida F F A Chapter
Elfrida, AZ

TEQUILA SPIKED CHILI

2 T. vegetable oil
3 Lbs. chili ground, lean beef
1 Lg. onion, chopped
1 green pepper, chopped
2 cloves garlic, minced
4 T. mild red chile, ground
1 t. cayenne pepper, more if a hotter taste is preferred
1 T. ground cumin
1½ t. salt
1½ t. oregano
Several good shakes of Tabasco sauce
2 C. tequila
water

In a Dutch oven or large pot, saute vegetables and garlic in oil until soft. Add beef, and cook until browned, breaking up beef with wooden spoon as it cooks evenly.

Drain off excess fat and oil, and all remaining ingredients. Bring to a boil, reduce heat, cover and allow to simmer slowly with a occasional stirring, for about 1½ to 2 hours.

During simmering time, taste and if necessary, add desired seasonings.

Jack Morris
Palm Bay, FL

Edward Thomas Silva
Honolulu, HA

PECK OF CHILI SAUCE

1 peck tomatoes, cut up
3 C. sugar
4 Med. onions, cut fine
2 t. cloves
2 T. salt
2 t. pepper
2 t. cinnamon
1 C. vinegar

In a large vessel, combine all ingredients except the vinegar. Blend all ingredients well, and boil very slowly until mixture thickens. Add the vinegar, bring to a boil and process into cans or jars while still hot.

Barry & Lois Drizin
Ft. Thomas, KY

OH HO Ranch
Coolridge, AZ

SALSA MEXICANA

(Mexican Sauce)

This sauce can be used as a relish with meats, fish or on tacos.

- 1¼ big, ripe tomatoes, diced small
- ½ medium white onion, finely diced
- 1 sprig fresh cilantro, coarsely chopped
- 1 serrano chile, chopped
- ¼ cup cold water
- Salt and white ground pepper to taste

Chop ingredients separately, making sure the tomatoes are not into even cubes. Mix together and add water, salt and pepper. (Note: If you prefer a mild salsa, remove the inner seeds and veins of the chilies before chopping.) Makes 1½ cups.

Nutritional information per tablespoon: 3 calories; 0.1 grams protein; 1 gram carbohydrate; trace of fat; 8 percent of calories as fat; 0.2 grams fiber; 0 milligrams cholesterol; 1 milligrams sodium.

The Great Chile Book
by Mark Miller
The Miami Herald

Duane Schneider
Boise, ID

CHILI CON CARNE

- 1 Lb. ground beef
- ¼ C. onions, chopped
- ¼ C. celery, chopped
- ¼ C. dried pepper
- 1 can (16 oz.) tomato, broken up
- 1 can (8 oz.) tomato sauce
- 1 can (16 oz.) red kidney beans
- ½ t. chili powder
- 4 T. Worcestershire sauce
- Onion and garlic salts to taste

In a large skillet, brown beef. Break up with a spoon. Drain off fat. Add onion and celery and saute for a few minutes. Add remainer of ingredients except the beans. Cover, bring to a boil, reduce heat and simmer and adjust seasonings to your taste.

This can be served over rice, adding chopped onions and shredded cheese if desired for flavorings.

Jay &. Sandy Hatfield
Cincinnati, OH

Clifford L. Freitas
George Freitas Dairy
Kaneohe, HA

MESA VERDE

Fresh green chilies make the best salsa, but if you can't find them, substitute canned roasted green chilies.

- 1 pound fresh green chilies
- 3 tablespoons olive oil
- ½ cup diced onion (¼-inch dice)
- 1 tablespoon salt
- 1 teaspoon granulated sugar (like garlic powder)
- 1 teaspoon dried leaf oregano
- 2 cups water
- 3 tablespoons flour blended with
- 2 tablespoons vegetable oil

To prepare fresh green chilies, roast on a barbecue grill, then peel the skins under running water or by rubbing with a wet towel. Remove stem and seeds before dicing. Puree roasted green chilies and set aside.

Place olive oil in a pan; heat and saute the onion until translucent. Add the spices and reduce heat to medium. Add the green chili puree, then add water. Bring to a slow boil; stirring occasionally.

Add the flour-oil mixture gradually, stirring constantly, until mixture thickens (you may not need to add it at all, depending on the amount of juice in the chilies). Simmer 2 minutes, stirring continually to avoid sticking. Transfer to a covered container and refrigerate. Serve chilled. Makes 1 quart.

Nutritional information per tablespoon: 14 calories; 0.2 grams protein; 1 gram carbohydrate; 1 gram fat; 66 percent of calories as fat; 0.2 grams fiber; 0 milligrams cholesterol; 100 milligrams sodium.

The Great Chile Book
by Mark Miller
The Miami Herald

George P. Cooke, Jr.
Waialua, HA

The use of brands has helped to discourage cattle rustling in Florida, but many cattlemen still do not brand. Some of these older brands are still used and have been passed on from one family to the next with the transfer of herds.

Florida cowman, A History of
Florida Cattle Raising

CHILI FOR A MOB

5 Lbs. lean ground beef
4 T. olive oil
2 Lg. onions, chopped
2 green bell peppers, chopped
4 cloves garlic, minced
2 cans (16 oz.) Tomatoes, undrained
4 bay leaves
1¼ to 1½ t. salt, or to taste
6 T. chili powder
* cayenne pepper, to taste
4 t. ground cumin seeds
2 t. ground oregano
4 T. fresh ground cilantro, or 1 t. coriander
4 T. flour
water

In a large skillet or Dutch oven, brown beef in batches using the oil, breaking up the meat so that it is evenly cooked. Drain off as much of the excess fat and oil.

Using a knife, cut up the tomatoes quite well. After which using several cups of water, add the tomatoes to a pot and cook over a medium heat.

The meat is cooked and drained, add the tomatoes, onions, green pepper, garlic, bay leaves, chili powder, cumin, oregano, salt*. Bring to a boil, reduce heat, and allow to simmer covered, for 1½ to 3 hours depending upon your cooking preferences. Stir occasionally, and add more water if necessary for consistency desired.

*Cayenne pepper can be added with other ingredients if a you wish for a hotter chili. Remember, it is the cayenne pepper that gives this chili or any chili it's "kick", so go cautious.

The cilantro can be added about 30 minutes before serving. With a little cold water, mix the flour using cold water or tomato juice into a paste to thicken the chili if necessary. Stir this flour paste, if used, thoroughly with chili to avoid lumps. Bay leaves can be wrapped in a bit of cheese cloth to locate easier after cooking.

Makes 18 to 20 servings depending upon those invited to partake in this chilihead's delight.

Barry & Lois Drizin
Ft. Thomas, KY

Maverick Cattle Co., Inc.
Peoria, AZ

CHEESY VEGETABLE CHILI

Prep time: 20 minutes   Cooking time: 25 minutes

2 garlic cloves, minced
1 Lg. green or red pepper, chopped
½ Lb. mushrooms,sliced
½ C. chopped onion
2 T. oil
1 can (28 oz.) crushed tomatoes with added puree
1 can (15 oz.) tomato sauce
2 T. chili powder
1 t. ground cumin
2 cans (15 oz. each) kidney beans, drained, rinsed
1½ C. diced zucchini
1 Pkg. (10 oz.) BIRDS EYE Sweet Corn, thawed
½1 C. (6 oz.) DRAFT Natural Shredded Sharp Cheddar Cheese, divided

• Cook and stir garlic, peppers, mushrooms and onions in oil 5 minutes or until vegetables are tender.

• Add tomatoes, tomato sauce, chili powder and cumin. Heat to a boil.

• Reduce heat to low; add beans, zucchini and corn. Simmer 15 minutes or until vegetables are tender. Add 1 cup cheese; stir until melted.

• Spoon into serving bowls. Top with remaining cheese. Makes 8 servings.

KRAFT FOODS

Cantrell Land & Cattle Co.
Cookeville, TN

BESTO'S SALSA

1 Lb. ripe tomatoes, peeled and chopped
2 carrots, parboiled, peeled and finely chopped
2 canned pickled jalapeno chilies (seeds and all)
1 t. oregano leaves
2 T. pickling liquid from canned chilies
2 T. olive oil
1 t. garlic, mashed (optional)

In a large bowl, mix tomatoes and carrots. Season with salt, and add the jalapeno, oregano, pickling liquid, oil and mashed garlic. Let mixture stand for at least an hour so that the flavors will blend together before serving. Makes 3 cups.

Skip & Paulette Busam
Milford, OH

R. A. "Bobby" Roberts
Immokalee, FL

CINCINNATI CHILI

2 Lbs. ground beef
½ C. onion flakes
4 T. chili powder
1 Qt. beef broth
1 t. ground cinnamon
1 6 Oz. can tomato paste
1 t. ground cumin
¼ t. ground allspice
⅛ t. black pepper
½ t. salt
¾ t. instant minced onions
¼ t. ground cloves
1 can (15 oz.)tomato paste
1 bay leaf
2 T. white vinegar
½ Oz. unsweetened chocolate

In a large skillet or Dutch oven, boil the beef broth and slowly add the beef stirring to crumble meat into small pieces. Cover, simmer meat for 30 to 40 minutes. Add the remaining ingredients to the meat; cover and simmer for an additional hour, stirring occasionally.

Remove the bay leaf and discard. Set the chili aside, and skim off as much of the fat as desired. Makes about 8 servings

Starr Fischer
Cincinnati, OH

National Cattlemen's Assoc.
Englewood, CO

PICANTE SALSA

3 fresh serrano chiles, or jalapeno peppers
3 tomatillos or 1 medium-size green tomato, cored
1 bunch green onions, cut into 1-inch pieces
2 Med. tomatoes, cored and cut into eights
½ C. olive oil
15 sprigs of fresh cilantro, or parsley
Juice of 4 limes (about ½ cup liquid)
1 t. garlic powder
1 t. ground cumin
1 t. salt
Pinch of sugar
½ t. allspice

Place chiles or peppers on a baking sheet; broil 3 to 5 inches from the heat, turning often with tongs, until blistered on all sides.

Immediately place chiles in a plastic bag; fastened securely, and let steam 10 to 15 minutes. Remove peel of each chile.

Cut a small slit in side of each chile, and rinse under cold water to remove seeds, (wear rubber or plastic gloves when rinsing and cutting chiles, if you have sensitive skin). Remove stems from chiles, quarter each, and set aside.

Remove husk from tomatillos. Place tomatillos in a small saucepan; add water to cover. Bring the water to a boil; drain, and cut tomatillos into 6 wedges, and set aside.

Combine all of the ingredients in a container of an electric blender or food processor with knife blade. Process ingredients for 10 to 15 seconds or until texture of mixture is achieved. Chill before serving. Makes about 5 cups.

Jacob R. Hatfield
Cincinnati, OH

Charles & Peggy Lou Anderson
Vonore, TN

Chili Secrets from TABASCO®

BRAND PEPPER SAUCE

In our quest chili related recipes, we have corresponded with many manufactures and distributors in hopes of obtaining whatever recipes they may have including their products. Several sent us recipes, while most probably felt that chili was such a small part of their overall business, that it didn't warrant the effort.

The McIlhenny Company, makers of Tabasco sauce, were the exception to the rule and sent the following recipes with their new 7 Spice Chili Recipe, for us to use as we wished.

7 SPICE CHILI RECIPE is a product that is not distributed nationally as yet, but if you see it on the shelf, buy it for a test sampling of a real fine mixture. The RECIPE can be used as a salsa for an altogether different flavor.

You may have already observed, while flipping through the pages of CHILIMANIA!, that many of the recipes do indicate Tabasco as an ingredient, or use another brand hot sauce, as a flavoring for their dishes. The trade name Tabasco is well known internationally and there would be no reason for us not to pass on to you in form of a chapter, their recipes with 7 Spice Chili Recipe.

We are quite sure that you will find some, of not all, to your taste and liking. There are many recipes using Tabasco as an ingredient in CHILIMANIA! This chapter are those using 7 SPICE recipes only.

The only items which we have added to this chapter, is the continued use of cattle brands as recipe dividers, as it may appear that I have somewhat of a hangup over livestock.

BLACK BEAN CHILI

¼ C. vegetable oil
1 T. chili powder
1½ t. paprika
1 t. dried oregano leaves
1 t. ground cumin
2 C. coarsely chopped onions
4 cloves garlic, minced
2 cans (16 oz.) tomatoes in juice, undrained, coarsely chopped
2 C. chopped zucchini
1 C. shredded carrots
2 t. TABASCO pepper sauce
½ t. salt
2 cans (16 oz.) black beans, drained

In a 5-quart Dutch oven or saucepot, heat the oil over medium heat. Add chili powder, paprika, oregano and cumin. Cook on high for 1 minute. Add onions and garlic, stirring frequently. Cook for 5 minutes or until onions are tender. Add the tomatoes, zucchini, carrots, TABASCO sauce, and salt. Stirring occasionally, cook 5 minutes. Add black beans. Bring to a boil. Reduce the heat and simmer for 1 hour.

Serve over shredded Cheddar or Monterey Jack cheese and top with sour cream, chopped tomatoes and cilantro, if desired. Makes 8 (1-cup) servings.

Louis J. Deveggio
Angels Camp, CA

PEPPER CHILI

8 C. water, divided
1 Pkg. (1 Lb.) dried lima beans
1 T. vegetable oil
3 ribs celery, chopped (1½ cups)
2 Med.-sized green peppers, seeded and chopped (1½ cups)
2 Med.-sized red peppers, seeded and chopped (1½ cups:)
1 Med. onion, chopped (½ cup)
1 Med. Tomato, chopped (1 cup)
3 fresh green chili peppers, seeded and chopped
3 T. chili powder
2 cloves garlic, minced
1 t. ground cumin seed
1 Lg. acorn squash, pared, seeded & cut into 1-inch cubes (4 cups)
1 t. TABASCO pepper sauce

In a large bowl, soak the beans in 5 cups, or more to cover by two inches, overnight. Or, in a large saucepot, bring 5 cups of water to a boil; add beans; remove from heat, cover and let stand for 1 hour. In a large saucepot or Dutch oven, heat the oil. Stir in celery, green pepper, red pepper, onion, tomato, chili powder, garlic and cumin. Coo;k for 10 to 12 minutes or until vegetables are tender. Add the remaining 3 cups of water. Bring to a boil; cover; reduce heat and simmer 1 hour. Add additional water if necessary. Add acorn squash and TABASCO sauce. Cook 50 to 60 minutes longer or until beans and squash are tender.

Yield: 10 cups. 215 calories per cup.

Manuel Gomes
Honolulu, HA

CHILI MEXICANA

4 slices bacon
1 C. chopped onion
1 clove garlic, minced
1 Lb. ground beef
2 T. chili powder
1 C. (8 oz. can) tomato sauce
½ C. beer
½ to 1 C. water
2 T. chopped, canned, green chili peppers
1 t. ground cumin
1 bay leaf
¼ t. salt
1 can (15¼ oz.) red kidney beans, drained
½ C. sliced, pitted ripe olives
1 Oz. (1 square) semi-sweet chocolate
½ t. TABASCO pepper sauce

In a large skillet, brown bacon; sauce onion and garlic until soft. Add the ground beef, stirring to break up meat as it browns. Add chili powder; cook, stirring, for 2 minutes. Add tomato sauce, beer, ½ cup water, chili peppers, cumin, bay leaf and salt. Bring to boiling; cover. Reduce the heat and simmer for 1 hour, stirring occasionally. Add kidney beans, olives, chocolate and TABASCO sauce; stir until chocolate is melted. Add ½ cup more water if chili seems dry. Cover, and cook 15 minutes longer. Serve with additional TABASCO sauce, if desired.

Yield: 4 servings.

James & Betty Dunn
Prineville, OR

OLD MEXICO CHILI

1½ Lb. beef stew meat, cubed
1 Med. onion, chopped
1 can (8 oz.) tomato sauce
1 can (6 oz.) tomato paste
1 can (16 oz.) kidney beans
1 T. chili powder
1½ t. salt
½ to 1 t. TABASCO pepper sauce

THE TRADITIONAL WAY

Brown stew meat in 2 tablespoons oil. Add the onion and cook until tender. Add remaining ingredients and ½ cup water; stir. Cover and simmer 1 hour and 30 minutes, or until meat is tender, stirring occasionally. Serves 4.

THE MODERN WAY

Place stew meat and remaining ingredients in an electric slow cooker, mix well and cover. Cook on low for 8 to 10 hours. (High 4 to 5 hours. Serves 4.

THE

Eddie Cuny
Allen, SD

AZTEC CHILI

2 T. salad oil
1 Med. onion, chopped
1 clove garlic, crushed
1 Lb. ground beef
2 t. salt
1 t. paprika
2 t. chili powder
2 cans (16 oz.) kidney beans
½ C. bean liquid
1 can (16 oz.) seasoned stewed tomatoes
1 can (6 oz.) tomato paste
½ t. sugar
¾ t. TABASCO sauce
1 can (12 oz.) whole kernel corn, drained

HOT STUFF

Heat the oil in a large skillet; add onion and garlic, and cook until they are yellow, but not brown. Add ground beef; sprinkle with salt, paprika and chili powder. Cook the meat until brown, breaking up with a fork. Drain kidney beans and discard all but ½ cup of the liquid; reserve beans. Stir in bean liquid, tomatoes, tomato paste, sugar and TABASCO.

Cover and simmer for 30 minutes. Add kidney beans and corn; simmer for 15 minutes longer, stirring occasionally. Serve with rice if desired.
Yield: About 6 servings.

Marion Platt
Palm Bay, FL

TABASCO CHILI

- 3 Lbs. stew beef, cut in 1-inch cubes
- ¼ C. salad oil
- 1 C. chopped onion
- 1 Cloves garlic, minced
- 4 to 6 T. chili powder
- 2 t. salt
- 2 t. ground cumin
- 2 t. TABASCO pepper sauce
- 1 can (4 oz.) green chilies, seeded and chopped
- 1 Qt. water

In a large saucepan, brown beef in the oil. Add remaining ingredients and mix together well. Bring to a boil; reduce heat and simmer, uncovered, 1½ to 2 hours, or until meat is tender. If desired, serve with additional TABASCO sauce.

Other recipes from the McIlhenny Company for CHILIMANIA! As they all contain the ingredient 7 SPICE CHILI RECIPE, which we have used and have found it to be great. All the recipes in folder CHILI SECRETS FROM TABASCO brand are included and are shown.

Robert L. White
Skull Valley, AZ

APPETIZERS

SHRIMP COCKTAIL SAUCE: For a tantalizing shrimp cocktail sauce with a tangy flavor, combine 3(T.) 7 SPICE CHILI RECIPE, 2 heaping (t.) horseradish and 2 (t.) lemon juice. Also a terrific sauce for clams on the half shell.

CHILI 'N CHEESE PARTY DIP: The life of the party! Combine ½ jar "Spicy" 7 SPICE CHILI RECIPE with 8 oz. cream cheese. Blend well. Refrigerate before serving. Great with tortilla chips or as a crudite dip with assorted raw vegetables.

PAPAS EXTRAORDINAIRE: or Potato Skins Supreme...Bake 6 potatoes. Scoop out potato, leaving the skins. Lightly rub skins with oil inside and out. Broil until crispy. Top each with 2 (T.) 7 SPICE CHILI RECIPE and shredded cheddar cheese. Broil or microwave until cheese melts.

ALBONDIGAS TEXICANA: or Tex-Mex Meatballs. Serve as a real stick-to-your-ribs main course, or make mini-meatballs and serve as hearty cocktail canapes. Combine 1 (T.) oregano, 1 lb. ground beef, 1 egg, ½ cup bread crumbs. Cube 8 oz. mozzarella cheese. Place small cube into center of small amount of meat mixture and shape into ball. Cook in sauce made of 1 jar "Original" 7 SPICE CHILI RECIPE, 2 cups tomato juice, 2(T.) lemon juice and a pinch of sugar, mixed together. Serve over spaghetti, if desired, or with toothpicks for cocktail canapes.

Coelho Meat Co.
Taulre, CA

CHILI CHICKEN WINGS: A dinner surprise or party favorite, seasoned to just about anyone's taste. Combine 12 jar "Spicy" 7 SPICE CHILI RECIPE with 2 (T.) horseradish. Spoon over cooked chicken wings. Brown until crispy.

CHILI CHORIZO DIP: The best snack or hors d'oeuvre you'll ever serve! Brown 1 lb. crumbled sausage. Drain well. Add 1 (T.) oregano, 4 oz. cheddar cheese, shredded; 1 clove garlic, minced; 1 jar "Spicy" 7 SPICE CHILI RECIPE; 8-oz. cream cheese. Simmer until cheese is melted and mixture thickens. Serve with crackers. Terrific warm or cold.

John D. Denney
Rafter X Brahamans
Sevierville, TN

BRUNCH OR LUNCH

OMELET PICANTE: Great for a hearty rancher-type breakfast or a light lunch...Top a 2-egg omelet with ¼ cup minced sweet onion, 1 oz. cubed cream cheese, strips of Virginia ham and 3 (T.) 7 SPICE CHILI RECIPE.

HUEVOS BENEDICT: A new taste thrill specially for the brunch bunch. Poach six eggs. Toast six English muffin halves. Top each muffin half with one slice ham, one egg, cheddar cheese. Microwave at Medium 30-45 seconds, until cheese melts. Combine ½ cup 7 SPICE CHILI RECIPE, 1 (t.) sweet basil, 3-4 (T.) lemon juice. Spoon over eggs. Microwave at Medium for 15 seconds more.

PITA POCKET MEXICANA MELT: Tex-Mex meets the Middle East in this flavor-filled sandwich. Combine 1 (T.) 7 SPICE CHILI RECIPE, with 1 (t.) vinegar. Fill pita bread with sliced ham and cheese. Microwave at Medium for one minute. Add sauce and microwave at Medium for 15 seconds more.

SALADS

PASTA SALAD ROJO: A tangy original 7 SPICE CHILI RECIPE salad dressing that perks up almost any salad: Mix ⅓ cup 7 SPICE CHILI RECIPE with ½ cup mayonnaise. Cook elbow or shell pasta according to package directions. Add sliced bell peppers, scallions, olives and shredded cheddar cheese. Add dressing and blend well. Chill before serving. Also a great dressing for green salads or taco salad.

CHILI CHICKEN SALAD: A wonderfully zesty, nutritious lunch. Substitute low-calorie mayonnaise or plain yogurt for mayonnaise for a super diet salad. Cook and cube 2 chicken breasts. Combine with 4 stalks celery, finely minced; 4 (T.) mayonnaise, 2-3 (T.) 7 SPICE CHILI RECIPE, dash of lemon juice, salt and pepper to taste. Mix well. Chill before serving.

ON THE SIDE

TEX-MEX CHILI EGGS: Stuffed eggs with a luscious new flavor. Hard-boil 6 eggs. Slice in half and scoop out yolks. Combine egg yokes, ½ cup 7 SPICE CHILI RECIPE, ¼ cup mayonnaise, salt and pepper to taste. Blend well and fill eggs. Garnish with paprika.

7 SPICE CHILI SPANISH RICE: Substitute 7 SPICE CHILI RECIPE mixed with lemon juice (1 (T.) per cup) next time you make your favorite Spanish rice recipe.

CHILI RIGATONI: Tex-Mex pasta- an incredible flavorful side dish-or a great luncheon entree. Saute 10 oz. fresh mushrooms, sliced, in 2 (T.) butter or margarine. Add 1½ cups light cream, 1 cup finely chopped broccoli, cooked, 1 jar 7 SPICE CHILI RECIPE, 1 (t.) oregano and 1 (t.) basil. Cook 5 minutes. Cook 1 lb. rigatoni according to package directions. Drain and combine with sauce. Season with salt and pepper to taste. Sprinkle with ¼ cup grated parmesan cheese.

MAIN DISHES

TEX-MEX STUFFED PEPPERS: Stuffed bell peppers with a real south-of-the-border accent. Substitute "Spicy" 7 SPICE CHILI RECIPE for the tomato sauce in you favorite stuffed pepper recipe. Pour additional sauce over top. If desired, add shredded Cheddar or Monterey Jack cheese to filling. Or, use filling mixture minus peppers for Porcupine Meatballs. Serve with additional sauce.

MEATLOAF A LA MEXICANA: Delectable version of a traditional favorite. Combine 1 lb. ground beef, 1 cup "Spicy" 7 SPICE CHILI RECIPE, ½ small onion, chopped, 2 eggs, ½ cup bread crumbs. Shape into loaf and bake at 350 degree F. for 50-60 minutes.

7 SPICE PASTA SAUCE: Combine 1 jar "Original" 7 SPICE CHILI RECIPE, 1 cup tomato juice, 3 oz. (half of small can) tomato paste, 1 (T.) sweet basil, 4(T.) lemon juice, 1(t.) sugar. Simmer until thoroughly heated. Serve over spaghetti for pasta a la Mexicana!

7 SPICE PASTA SAUCE is superb over ravioli, sausage, and peppers, or stuffed shells. It's also a great lasagna sauce.

TERNERA PARMESAN: Tex-Mex style Veal Parmesan - a surprise entree chock full of appetite appeal. Lightly grease a casserole dish. Place frozen veal patties (2 per person) in single layer on bottom. Top with mozzarella cheese. Place second layer of patties on top. Sprinkle with salt and pepper. Cover patties with 7 SPICE PASTA SAUCE (recipe above) and sprinkle generously with grated parmesan cheese. Bake at 450 degrees F. for 45 minutes.

TEXAS STYLE CHICKEN PARMESAN: A Tex-Italian favorite. Sprinkle 4 boneless chicken breasts with bread crumbs. Brown on both sides. Pour 7 SPICE PASTA SAUCE over breasts. Add red and green bell pepper slices and chopped onion. Cover and simmer on low until thoroughly cooked. Top each chicken breast with sliced mozzarella cheese and cover until cheese melts.

PHILLY CHILI CHEESE STEAK SANDWICHES: A Philadelphia favorite with a Tex-Mex accent. Add 7 SPICE PASTA SAUCE to your favorite Cheese Steak recipe.

CHILIBURGERS: One of the yummiest burgers you'll ever eat. Add ½ cup 7 SPICE CHILI RECIPE to 1 lb. ground beef or your favorite hamburger mixture. Top each burger with Cheddar cheese, melt, eat and enjoy.

MASHED POTATO CHILI PIE: A colorful dish that will have everyone coming back for seconds. Peel and quarter 8 medium red potatoes, boil until tender. Drain. Mash potatoes, mix with 1 cup sour cream and place in a greased round casserole. Bake 15 minutes at 350 degrees F. Place under broiler until brown top. Combine 1 egg, beaten, 1 jar 7 SPICE CHILI RECIPE, 1 clove garlic, minced and 1 10-oz. package frozen spinach, thawed and squeezed dry. Blend well. Cover potato crust with spinach mixture. Top with 1 cup shredded sharp Cheddar cheese. Bake at 350 degrees F. for 30 minutes.

ESTOFADO HAM: 7 SPICE CHILI RECIPE adds personality to this Tex-Mex version of ham stew. Combine 1 cooked ham steak, cubed; 1 10-oz. package frozen corn, thawed; 1 10-oz. package frozen beans, thawed; 1 jar 7 SPICE CHILI RECIPE, 1 cup tomato juice, 3 oz. tomato paste, 2 (T.) lemon juice; 1 (t.) basil. Simmer 30 minutes. Stir in ½ cup sour cream, if desired. Serve over broad noodles. Yum-m-m!

CHILI FLAM BAKE: 7 SPICE CHILI RECIPE meets flounder and yams in a baking entree everyone's is sure to love. Combine 1 jar 7 SPICE CHILI RECIPE, ½ cup lemon juice, 1 cup water, 1 (T.) basil, 1 (t.) salt.

Peel and thinly slice 4 yams. Thinly slice 1 large onion. Arrange yam and onion slices in a 9"x13" baking dish. Cover with sauce mixture. Bake at 350 degree F. for 20 minutes. Remove from oven. Arrange 2 lbs. flounder filets over top. Spoon additional sauce over filets. Cover dish with foil, return to oven. Bake at 325 degrees F. for 20 minutes. Serves 6.

TEX-MEX POT ROAST: Pot roast with a zippy south-of-the-border flavor. Combine 1 jar 7 SPICE CHILI RECIPE, with 1 can cream of mushroom soup. Top an oven pot roast with mixture before roasting. Great with roasted potatoes and onions.

CHILI CHARTICHOKES: A delicious, daring mixture of artichokes and chicken with the sparkle of 7 SPICE CHILI RECIPE to delight your family and friends. Brown 4 boneless chicken breasts. Add 1 jar 7 SPICE CHILI RECIPE, juice of 1 can artichokes (packed in water, not marinated) and 2 chicken bouillon cubes. Cut artichoke hearts into pieces; add to chicken. Season with salt and pepper to taste. Simmer on low until chicken is thoroughly cooked, about 30 minutes. Serve over rice. (For a change of pace, add minced garlic and one bouillon cube while cooking rice.

SPAGHETTI 'N CHILI PIE: Tex-Mex meets Italy in this tasty blending of flavors. Lightly grease pie pan. Brown 1 lb. ground beef with 1 cup chopped onion. Drain. Stir in 1 jar 7 SPICE RECIPE, 2 (T.) lemon juice, 2 (t.) oregano, 2 (t.) basil, 1 (t.) salt. Simmer 15 minutes. Combine ½ lb. spaghetti, cooked, ¾ cup parmesan cheese, grated and 1 clove garlic, minced. Toss lightly. Press spaghetti mixture into pie plate to form crust. Pour meat mixture over crust. Sprinkle with ¼ cup parmesan cheese, grated. Bake at 350 degree F. for 25-30 minutes. Let stand 5 minutes before serving.

SPICY SPUDS: A nutritious lunch in itself- or a yummy side dish. Wash 6 potatoes, bake as usual and slice each in half lengthwise. Top each half with 2 (T.) 7 SPICE CHILI RECIPE and shredded cheese. Broil or microwave until cheese melts.

JIMOMATE ¡BRAVO!: Stuffed tomatoes with a Tex-Mex accent. Cut tops from tomatoes and remove stems. Hollow out tomato, keeping pulp and discarding seeds and juice. Mix cubed pulp with 4 oz. cubed mozzarella cheese, 4 (T.) 7 SPICE CHILI RECIPE, 2 (t.) vinegar, ½ cup breadcrumbs, salt and parsley. Fill tomatoes, replacing tops and cover holes with filling. Microwave at Medium for 10 minutes.

GAZPACHO OLE: The best gazpacho you've ever tasted, we guarantee. Combine 1 cucumber, cubed; 1 green pepper, minced; 2 celery stalks, minced; 3 scallions, minced; 1 jar 7 SPICE CHILI RECIPE, 3-4 (T.) lemon juice, 3-4 cups tomato juice, pinch of sugar and dash of salt. Chill 3-4 hours before serving.

PESCADO FANTASTICO: Give baked fish a luscious, zingy flavor! Top filets with our Shrimp Cocktail Sauce.

7 SPICE TUNA CHILI 'N RICE: A hearty, nutritious one-dish lunch. Combine 1 can tuna, 1 jar "Spicy" 7 SPICE CHILI RECIPE, 1 (T.) lemon juice, 1-2 stalks celery, chopped. Heat until warm. Serve over rice.

DIET CHILI PIZZA: You won't believe anything that tastes this good could be so good for you! Mix together 1 heaping (T.) 7 SPICE CHILI RECIPE with ¼ (t.) vinegar. Spoon over a rice cake. Top with grated cheddar or mozzarella cheese. Microwave at High for 4 seconds.

VEGETARIAN CHILI PIZZA: Combine 1 jar 7 SPICE CHILI RECIPE, 3 oz. tomato paste, ½ (t.) sugar, 2 (T.) lemon juice, 1 (t.) basil, and 1 (t.) oregano. Simmer for 15 minutes. Spread over your favorite pizza crust. Top with onions, peppers, mushrooms, olives and artichoke hearts. Cover with grated mozzarella cheese and bake as usual.

CLASSIC 7 SPICE CHILI: A basic chili you can eat alone or use a number of different ways (see following recipes). Brown 1 lb. ground beef, drain well. Add 1 jar 7 SPICE CHILI RECIPE, ¾ cup water, beer or tomato juice and 1 can cooked kidney beans (if desired). Heat thoroughly.

Microwave directions: Crumble 1 lb. ground beef evenly into a 2 qt. microwave-safe casserole. Cook at High for 5 minutes or until beef is no longer pink, stirring twice during cooking. Drain. Return beef to casserole. Stir in 1 jar 7 SPICE CHILI RECIPE, ¾ cup water and 1 can cooked kidney beans, drained. Cook at High 5-8 minutes, stirring twice. Let stand 5 minutes.

ULTIMATE CHILI: A ranch-style chili that has no equal. Brown ¾ lb. coarse ground beef and ¼ lb. pork sausage, drain well. Add 1 jar 7 SPICE CHILI RECIPE and ¾ cup beer. Simmer 20 minutes. Top with sour cream and avocado.

CINCINNATI FIVE-WAY CHILI: Cincinnati is a renowned chili city and here's a new version of an old favorite. Brown ½ lb. ground beef, drain well. add 1 jar 7 SPICE CHILI RECIPE and 1 can cooked kidney beans, drained. Pour over spaghetti. Top with grated cheese and chopped onions.

7 SPICE CHILI RECIPE CORN CHIP PIE: Prepare Classic 7 Spice Chili. Cover bottoms of 4 separate bowls with FRITOS Brand Corn Chips. Pour chili over chips. Top with grated cheese. Garnish as desired.

LEGUME CHILI: A glorious protein substitute for a change of pace. In a deep skillet or Dutch oven, heat 1 (T.) oil over medium heat. Add 1 cup sliced carrots, 1 cup sliced celery and 1 cup sliced zucchini. Cook 5 minutes, stirring frequently. Stir in 1 jar 7 SPICE CHILI RECIPE, ¾ cup water and 2 16-oz. cans beans, drained (choose garbanzo, pink, pinto, red or white kidney beans). Bring to boil. Cover, reduce heat and simmer 10 minutes or until vegetables are tender-crisp. Serve over rice if desired.

USE CLASSIC 7 SPICE CHILI FOR:

- A delightfully seasoned bake potato topping, spooned over a blossomed baked potato and smothered with shredded cheese.
- A tasty Mexican salad. Chill and serve with greens, scallions, shredded cheese, corn chips and sour cream.

- A great chili dog. Top a hot dog in a bun with ¼ cup prepared chili.
- A Mexican sloppy joe everyone will relish. Top a hamburger bun with prepared chili.
- Use as a terrific pizza topping, then sprinkle with shredded cheese.
- Tacos, where 7 SPICE CHILI RECIPE will be right at home. Fill each taco shell with ⅓ cup prepared chili. Top with shredded lettuce, diced tomato and shredded cheese.
- A pita pocket sandwich with gusto. Fill pita bread with ¼ cup prepared chili, sliced avocado and shredded cheese.
- A super supper chili muffin. Spoon ¼ cup chili on toasted English muffin half. Top with mozzarella cheese and broil.
- A quick 'n luscious stroganoff. Stir ½ cup sour cream and 1 cup sliced, cooked mushrooms into chili. Serve over cooked noodles or rice.
- Chili lasagna for a great entree or side dish. Use chili in place of meat and spaghetti sauce in your favorite lasagna recipe.
- Zucchini boats that are fun to eat. Spoon ⅓ cup prepared chili into each scooped-out zucchini half. Sprinkle with grated cheese. Bake until cheese melts.

DANGER
UNAUTHORIZED
PERSONNEL ALLOWED
BEYOND THIS POINT

The American Chemical Society has graciously permitted us to use the contents of their chili cookbook from their National Chemistry Day of November 6, 1987, and to the thousands of their members, thanks.

It includes "A Small Dissertation Upon Chili Con Carne with a Recipe Taught to Me by a Gentleman of the Country" by Dr. John K. Crum, Executive Director, American Chemical Society.

A person not too familiar with their type of jargon, might have to take a few moments to understand their terms when it is used with their recipes. In which ever case, we greatly appreciate the use of the cookbook from the Society, and we hereby classify this section of CHILIMANIA! and somewhat, hazardous zone, and extreme precautions should be taken when considering attempting to prepare these recipes.

Mr. E. James Bradford, Ph.D., Program Manager for ACS, in his letter allowing permission to use their cookbook, stated " You have the sincere best wishes of the American Chemical Society as you build your collection of experimental procedures for the manufacture of some of the tastiest combinations of molecules".

"A SMALL DISSERTATION UPON CHILI CON CARNE"

with a
Recipe Taught to Me by a Gentleman of the Country
by

Dr. John K. Crum
Executive Director
American Chemical Society

From the beginning, let me admit that I am not predisposed to the view that chili con carne is the best, or even one of the better, food concoctions on the planet. On the other hand, it probably does not deserve a reputation for being a punishment for the palate, for the ingredients can be adjusted to provide the proper combination of warmth and flavor.

I am a firm believer in the philosophy that the best tasting food flows from the careful selection of the best ingredients. Therefore, if you are of the school that chili is a low-cost food preparation that had its best days in the Great Depression, you might as well stop reading this!

Given its origins and the foodstuffs with which people were forced to be inventive, the culinary development of this dish over the years have has provided a very pleasing result. However, the modern-day cook must use care in the selection of ingredients and in attention to proper cooking techniques.

In this article I will address some of the history of chili con carne (literally peppers with meat) as I see it, then trace down some of the chemistry involved with the ingredients, and finally talk about inconsistencies in preparation and naming of this marvelous dish.

Many Texans assert that beans are an unnecessary (and indeed undesirable) diluent in chili, while others would insist that the size and type of bean is the most important thing to discuss. Some chilies have tomatoes, some do not. Some have garlic, some do not. And so the debate goes on.

The exact origins of chili con carne are probably unknown (one version even has it invented in San Antonio!), but you might assure that the marriage of beef from bovine animals-introduced by the Spaniards after the discovery of America-with the red peppers indigenous to the American continent took place at some time after 1493. In that year Columbus, on his second voyage to America, brought beef animals to Cuba and Hispaniola, from which they were later transported to Mexico and Florida (11).

These were mostly work animals that were only eaten after they had preformed other services, so it is likely that the meat derived from them was tough and stringy, and the resourceful cooks of the day were forced into the use of cooking techniques that would render the meat tender. They probably also took advantage of the spices and other flavorings that the Aztecs had used for a few centuries. The very word chili is most likely a derivation of the Nahuatl (Aztec) "chilli" which the Spaniards picked up after the arrival in Mexico by Captain General Cortez and his brigands in 1519.

How the foregoing was translated into a more general recipe for chili con carne as we know it today has been the subject of much speculation. One story is that an Englishman among the settlers of early Texas in the 1820's used locally available ingredients to come up with a substitute for curry powder with which he had been familiar on an assignment in India (was this the first chili powder?).

Another version is that Canary Islanders who settled around San Antonio de Bejar in the late 1600's, and who had been accustomed to spicy stews and curries, developed forerunners of our present-day chili con carne. It is certainly true that a big boost to chili making came about when William Gebhardt of San Antonio first ground together several chili making ingredients into a readily usable additive. The company he started in 1986 still provides chili powder of the original formula, which is one I have always used in my recipes for Mexican or Southwestern cooking.

THE MEAT

A good quality round steak, trimmed of most fat, is my choice, but any good quality beef, or mixture of beef with lean pork, will make an excellent chili. The matter of whether the meat should be cubed or ground is another great controversy with chili cooks-if you want a more finely divided meat, I would advocate grinding it yourself so that you are more assured of the ingredients. A compromise is to use a grinder with a blade that provides the coarsest cut.

Chemically speaking, you should understand that meat is comprised of protein, fat, and water, along with vitamins, and the taste and texture of the cooked meat will depend upon the amount of fat and water and the types and shapes of the protein molecules. The proteins are embodied in the muscles fibers and connective tissues of the meat.

There is some good science at work here, because whatever you do to meat-cutting, grinding, or pounding-has the effect of breaking down the muscle structure to produce tenderizing. Tenderizing can also be effected chemically by using commercial products that contain papain or other enzymes that digest protein in muscles and connective tissues of the meat. Historically, this chemical procedure was used in even pre-columbus Mexico by wrapping meat of turkeys and other fowl in leaves of the papaya plant before cooking.

Almost all of the recipes for preparation of the meat for chili call for browning the meat first. Why is the meat not merely cut or ground, and dumped into boiling water to cook? The reason is that browning imparts a better flavor to the meat because of some interesting chemistry! Frying (or sauteing) with just enough fat or oil to prevent sticking at a relatively high temperature causes the beat to brown-in very simple terms the proteins at the surface of the meat are converted to other proteins that result in a more intense flavor.

After browning the meat in hot fat and adding it to the other desired ingredients, cooking the meat in water at high temperatures bring into play another interesting aspect of chemistry. Inasmuch as the connective tissue of meat is comprised of three proteins-elastin, reticulin, and collagen-it is possible to make meat more tender when cooking in water, as is chili, by maintaining the cooking temperature near the boiling point of water.

This has the effect of transforming collagen into gelatin, which is a gummy solution that has the effect of making tougher meats more tender, and this is especially important if one decided to use a lower quality of meat for chili than was recommended earlier in this article.

FLAVORINGS

Let us take the most basic of all chili recipes, which would include meat (say either beef or pork, or both) cooked down in water with red peppers and salt. This would provide an edible chili con carne, but would not do much for your lasting impression of what a good chili could taste like.

The most likely other ingredients to be added would be tomatoes, onion, garlic, cumin, green peppers, black pepper, flour or cornmeal or masa harina (for thickening), or perhaps even bay leaves, oregano, or beer. Also, think about red beans. My secret ingredients, discovered years ago, are a touch of sugar to smooth it out (it seems to reduce the tartness), and black coffee with chicory as a flavor enhancer.

There is a lot of chemistry involved, because all of the ingredients in chili mentioned above will, by the method of cooking or preparation used, or by the quantity and quality of flavor introduced, more or less subtly alter the perceived flavor of the final product. After all, taste and smell are referred to as the chemical senses, and red pepper, garlic, and onions are some of the most powerful substances that bring these senses into play. So, there is a reason why chili has such a profound effect on the human system!

As an example, let us think about the startling physiological effects produced on the human body by ingestion of red peppers, the fruit of several varieties of a woody plant Capsicum annum or frutescens. In concentrations just a little too hot we can experience burning sensations, coughing, choking, wheezing, perspiration, and even skin rashes and diarrhea.

THE PEPPERS

As I have indicated earlier, the simplest of chilies could be made from only meat and peppers, and indeed can be made with chili powders commercially available without resorting to procuring, or having an understanding of, the best types of chili peppers that are available for the purpose.

Most of the commercial chili powders (to be distinguished from powdered red chilies) contain cumin, oregano, and garlic, so if they are used it may not be necessary to add these ingredients. Peppers that are used in chili recipes in this country include Serrano, Cayenne, Jalapeno, Poblano, Chilaca, Guero, Habanero, Japones, Tabasco, Anaheim, Fresno, and various New Mexican and Mexican varieties. Some of these have different names when ripened and dried, such as the Jalapeno becomes Chipotle (Nahuatl for chili-pepper + poctli-smoked) and the Poblano becomes the Ancho. The red peppers are rich in vitamins A and C.

Most of the "heat" in red peppers is concentrated in the placental material that bears the seeds. Therefore, peppers that have been roasted and had the skin, seeds, and white lining removed have been "detoxified" to a great extent and will be much more palatable in your chili concoction.

One of the more interesting chemical aspects of capsaicin, a principal ingredient of red pepper, is that it acts as an antioxidant-in this capacity it probably minimizes fat oxidation in the cooking process. This means that release of phospholipid and unsaturated fats from meat muscle tissues may actually be slowed during the heating process, leading to better flavor and a more palatable "left-over" flavor. This is in fact suspected to be the case, because most chili lovers claim that it improves after one or two days, whereas beef fat normally deteriorates on standing.

(See TABLE I, PEPPERS at end of text.)

THE BEANS

If you insist on having the beans, you should at least do them right! The red kidney, Phaseola vulgaris, which originated in Mexico about 5,000 B.C., is usually the bean of choice. The best approach is to prepare the beans in advance and add them into the chili cooking process at the appropriate point. There is reason for this, which as a good chemical background, as is explained in Reference (7).

The bean cell wall hemicellu-loses are more soluble in alkaline conditions, and the experienced chili cook knows that partially cooked beans, when added to the acidic conditions in partially cooked chili, will simply not get any softer as you continue the heating process. Therefore, the beans should be introduced after they have been previously cooked to the desired softness (as in the case of canned beans), and added at a point where commingling of flavors with the meat, peppers, and other ingredients can be accomplished. This also allows you to judge the amount of beans you want to add. I think the best chili is with a very high ratio of meat to beans. Another technique that I have employed is to use the juice from cooking beans to flavor the chili without actually having beans in the finished product.

(See TABLE II, BEANS at end of text.)

TOMATOES

Not all chili recipes call for tomatoes, as is the case with beans, although both were cultivated and widely used as foodstuffs in Central and South America in pre-Columbus times. Both were used in stews and kindred dishes by the Aztecs in the Valley of Central Mexico at the time of the Conquistadors, as is well chronicled by Fra Bernadino de Sahgun from his base at Tenochtitlan (9).

Bernal Diaz del Castillo, in his epic "The Conquest of Mexico," also noted this phenomenon (4) in his account of the costumery, rituals, and traditions of the royal court of Montezuma. (Any comments about the contribution of chili to Montezuma's revenge?)

The fruit of the tomato plant, Lycopersicon esculentum, derives its name from the Nahuatl (Aztec) work tomatl and was widely used in the time of the Aztec empire. The red pigmentation of tomatoes (and red bell peppers) comes from a class of chemical compounds called earotenoids, and the parenchymal cells in the jelly-like material surrounding the seed are rich in vitamin C.

When tomatoes are used in chili it is desirable to remove the skin by plunging the fruit into rapidly boiling water for about one minute to facilitate paring. The tomato should then be chopped coarsely and seeded. Of course, canned tomatoes can be used if you are not a purist (be sure to drain them first).

GARLIC AND ONIONS

Onions and garlic are members of the same family (Allium cepa and Allium sativum, respectively). Both of these ingredients of chili were well known in the Old World; and were extensively used by the Romans

(1,3). It is interesting to note that the name for the allyl group structure used in chemistry was derived from the name of the genus of this family, allium. The flavors and aromas of onions and garlic are generally attributable to allyl sulfides.

When cutting into a pod of garlic, for example, an enzyme already present acts on the amino acid cysteine, which is converted to ammonia, pyruvic acid, and an unstable compound (+)-S-allyl-L-cysteine sulfoxide-which breaks down into diallyl disulfide with its characteristic odor.

(See TABLE III, ONIONS at end of text.)

THE RECIPE

All of the proceeding brings us to the point where we can propose a decent recipe for chili con carne. We will call it National Chemistry Day Chili:

NATIONAL CHEMISTRY DAY CHILI*

Ingredients:

6 pounds lean beef, preferably round steak
1½ pounds lean pork
4 tablespoons avocado oil (or sunflower oil)
2 large yellow onions
6 small scallions, trimmed and cut into small cylinders
1 seeded and chopped red Serrano pepper
2 seeded and chopped Jalapeno peppers
3 ounces (1 bottle) Gebhardt Chili Powder
2 teaspoons cumino powder
3 large cloves garlic, chopped
1 pound dried red kidney or pinto beans
2 large tomatoes, peeled and chopped
½ pound suns-dried tomatoes
2 cups strong black coffee
½ cup masa harina
1 tablespoon brown sugar

Procedure:

Pick over the beans and soak in cold water overnight.
The next day, use a large pot and cook the beans in 3 quarts of water for about 2 hours, until tender.
Reserve beans and liquor for further processing.

Trim the beef, and either cube into ½-inch pieces or grind with the coarse blade of a food chopper (I use 2 pounds of ground beef and 4 pounds of cubed beef). Cube the pork into ½-inch pieces. In a heavy skillet, heat the oil until very hot (the smoke point of avocado oil is 600 degree F), and thoroughly brown the meat and scallions. Pour off excess fat.

Add the meat and scallions to the bean pot (at this point you may use just the bean liquor, and use the beans for other purposes) and bring to a boil. Add the black coffee, chili powder, peppers, cumino powder, yellow onions, garlic, tomatoes, beer, and brown sugar and cook covered for about 2 hours, then cook uncovered until the broth is thicker. Add salt to taste and masa harina (or flour mixed with water into a paste) if further thickening is desired.

In this recipe I have chosen ingredients that are in keeping with our newly enlightened sense of health and nutrition, by calling for ingredients that minimize cholesterol and saturated fats. This chili is a one-dish meal and would be excellent served with a crisp green salad or guacamole, accompanied by a good hearty California cabernet sauvignon. The recipe may be scaled up to serve more, but be conservative with the chili powder when increasing the other proportions.

As an indication of regional and other applications in naming chili, I am including the names of some of the recipes that I have collected over the years:

California Chili (should have Anaheim or Fresno peppers, of course)
New Mexico Chili (very hot peppers)
Presidio Chili
South Texas Road Meat Chili (calls for a can of beer!)
Pedernales River chili
"Bowl of Texas Red" Chili
Hot Pants Chili (??)
Venison Chili
Cincinnati Chili (served over spaghetti, of all things?)

Texas-style Chili (no beans)
Will Roger's Chili and Beans
Jailhouse Chili
Dallas County Prison System Chili
Seven Pepper Chili (you guessed it-seven different peppers?)

Of course, if you are really into gutpunching recipes, I could recommend additions of Tabasco or other hot pepper sauces, such as Crystal's Hot Pepper Sauce (New Orleans), Louisiana Perfect Hot Sauce (New Iberia, La.), and Cajun Sunshine from Gourmet Foods, Inc. (Knoxville, Tenn.), or you may want to use more jalapenos, and the like. Some people like a topping of grated cheddar, finely chopped scallions, even a dollop of sour cream. Whatever your recipe, I can predict that chili con carne will survive for at least the next chiliad!

ACKNOWLEDGEMENTS

I wish to thank the following organizations for promptly providing me with information about their products or services: The International Chili Society, Beatrice Companies, Inc, (Gebhardt Chili Powder), and Out West Publishing Co., (The Whole Chile Pepper Catalog). I also wish to thank Mr. Jeff C. Fried of Beatrice Companies and Ms. Elspeth Davidson of Caliente Chili, Inc. (Austin, Texas) for recipes, Ms. Diane Bender, Dr. Maureen Matkovich, and Dr. Randall Wedin for gathering source information, Ms. Joan Wheeland for formating the tables, and especially Ms. Marlyne Carr for supervision of the project and preparation of the manuscript.

TABLE I. PEPPERS**

TYPE	SIZE	COLOR	STRENGTH	OTHER OR SIMILAR NAMES
Jalapeño[1]	2.5" X 3/4"	Green to Red	V. Hot	Chipotle (R,D,S)(brown) Chipocle Chilpotle
Serrano	1.5" X 0.5"	Med. Green to Scarlet	V. Hot	Serrano Seco (R,D) Chiles Japones (R,D) (Hotter than Serrano)
Poblano	5" X 3"	Dark Green	Hot	Ancho Chile (R,D) (deep red-brown)
Cayenne	3" X 3/8" or larger	Green	V. Hot	
Anaheim	6" X 1"	Light Green	Mild to Hot	Chile Colorado (R,D)(red) Chile Verde California Green Chile
Pequeño	1/4" d.	Red or Green	V. Hot	Piquin (R,D) Chiltepin
Cubanelle	5" X 1-1/2"	Lt. Green to Red	Mild	Italian Frying Pepper
Habanero[2]	1" X 1"	Lt. Green to Orange	Hottest Known	————
Chilaca	6" X 1"	Greenish-Black	Hot	Pasilla (R,D) Brown-Black
Güero	4-1/2" X 1"	Pale Yellow	V. Hot	——

** There are more than a hundred varieties and names of chili peppers. This is just a sampling!

R = Ripened   D = Dried   S = Smoked

[1] Almost all chiles in this Table are <u>Capsicum annuum</u>

[2] This is <u>Capsicum sinense</u>

TABLE II. BEANS

TYPE	DESCRIPTION	USES	SUITABILITY FOR CHILI
Red Kidney	Reddish brown, "Kidney" shaped	Chili, soup, salads, refried beans, Creole recipes, used for canning	Preferred
Red Bean, or Mexican Chili Bean	Reddish-brown, small, peashaped	Red Beans and Rice, salads	Excellent
Pinto Bean	"Kidney"shaped, beige, dappled	Chili, refried beans, cooked with ham and peppers	Good
Pink Bean	Pink, but turns reddish-brown on cooking	Chili, cooked with ham for barbecues	Good
Black Bean (or Turtle Bean)	Small, black, round	All kinds of South American and Caribbean cooking, and in "Nouvelle" California cooking	Good
White Bean (or Navy Bean)	Small, white, round	Boston baked beans	NA
Great Northern	Larger than white beans	Baked beans and casseroles	NA
Lima Bean (or Butter Bean)	Flat, large, greenish	Soups, casseroles, or as a vegetable	NA
Black-Eyed (or cowpea or blackeyed pea)	Black or yellow "Eye" in tan bean	Southern cooking	NA
Garbanzo (or chickpea)	Golden	Soups, marinated salads	NA

TABLE III. ONIONS

TYPE	DESCRIPTION	USES
Sweet Onion	White, with succulent flavor: special varieties available seasonally are: Texas Sweets, Vidalia, and Walla-Walla	Hamburgers, salads, all purposes for raw onions
Yellow Onion	Large (3-5.5 in. in diameter)	For all purposes: very good for making chili con carne
White Onion	Small, with a "silvery" skin	Good for soups or eating as a vegetable (as creamed onions)
Red Onion	Dark red in color, about same size as the Yellow Onion	Suitable color enhancer for many dishes
Green Onion or Spring Onion		Excellent for chili con carne when cut into small cylinders; also can be used raw as a topping with grated cheddar cheese or sour cream
Spanish Onions	Mild in flavor, about 4-5 inches in diameter	A good "all-purpose" onion

Prehigh School Chili

Q.: What's the Weather? A.: Chili Today!

You'll REALLY need your adult partner for this activity! Remember, cutting with sharp knives and cooking on the stove can be dangerous. But this doesn't mean you only get to watch! Your jobs will be measuring, opening cans, and stirring. Measure well, 'cause I LOVE good chili!

YOU WILL NEED UTENSILS
Measuring spoon and cup
Can opener
4 quart pot with lid
wooden spoon
knife
1 quart bowl
metric ruler
pencil
pot holder

INGREDIENTS
1 pound of stew beef
2 cups of canned tomatoes, chopped
2 medium cans of dark kidney beans
1 large can of pork and beans
½ cup of green pepper, chopped
1 small can of chopped green chili peppers
1 tablespoon chili powder
1 teaspoon salt
¼ teaspoon black pepper
1 cup of chopped onion
1 teaspoon of chopped garlic
4 strips of bacon, chopped

1. Get all your ingredients ready first. Have your adult partner do all the chopping. If you open the cans, let your partner lift up the lid. The edge is VERY sharp!

2. Have your partner put the bacon in the pot and cook it slowly until it is almost crisp. The bacon is then taken out of the pot and set aside in the bowl for later.

3. Your partner should then cook the pepper (both kinds), onion, and garlic in the bacon fat until all these ingredients are soft. If you are VERY careful, and your partner stands right next to you, then you may be allowed to help stir.

4. The pan should be taken off the heat, and the onion mixture added to the bowl with the bacon. (Leave the bacon fat in the pot!) Your partner should then add the stew beef to the bacon fat in the pot and brown the beef over medium heat. (Let your partner do the stirring this time, as the meat sometimes splatters when it cooks.)

5. When the meat is brown all over; the bacon and onion mixture, the tomatoes, the beans, and the seasonings should all be added to the pot with the meat. It's best to do this off the heat. You may be allowed to help stir this all together with your partner's permission. (Remember, the pot is still hot! Be Careful!) What should the chili look like now? (Describe the colors of the ingredients, the amount of liquid present, and the smell of the chili. Also, measure and record the height of the chili from the top of the pot.) Record your observations in the chart below.

6. Have your partner put the pot back on the heat, and bring the mixture to a boil while stirring. The heat should then be reduced to LOW, and the chili should be allowed to cook for two and a half hours, partially covered. Be sure to have your partner stir the chili from time to time, as the beans are very starchy and will stick to the bottom of the pot. Every ½ hour, with your partner's help, look at the chili and record your observations in the chart. Be sure to ask your partner to measure the height of the chili from the top of the pot. Does this height change? In which way?

7. After the cooking time is up, have your partner taste the chili to see if the seasoning is right. (Usually, the chili will need more salt.) Your chili is done! It can be ladled into bowls and enjoyed with chips, corn bread, or rice. Some people like to put sour cream or cheese on top of chili. What do you like best with your chili?

8. Look at your CHILI CHART below and talk these questions over with your partner. How did the appearance of the chili change over time? What sort of energy was applied to the pot of chili that could have caused the changes? What did you think would have happened if the chili were never stirred for the whole 2-½ hours? Why?

How did the level of the chili in the pot change over time? What do you think could have caused the change? Where did the missing chili go? (Be sure to look at the inside of the chili pot lid when you think about this question.) How could you have caused the chili level to change more rapidly? More slowly?

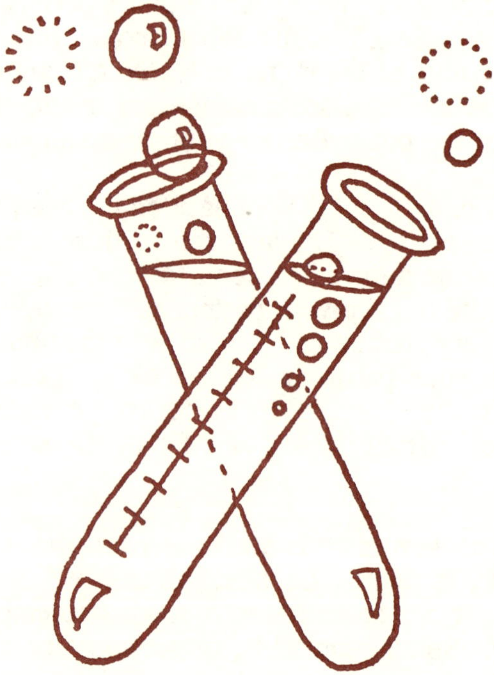

CHILI CHART

TIME (MINUTES)	HEIGHT OF CHILI FROM TOP OF POT	APPEARANCE OF CHILI (COLOR, SMELL, ETC.)
0		
30		
60		
90		
120		
150		

The three basic food categories are proteins, carbohydrates, and fats. Which ingredients in your chili fall in which of these categories? Talk this over with your adult partner and make a list in the proper columns below. Let's see if your chili is a balanced dish.

PROTEIN	CARBOHYDRATE	FAT

Submitted by: Society Committee on Education
Subcommittee on Precollege Activities
Prehigh School Program and *WonderScience*

FOR DELAYED ACTION

EL GRANDE CALIENTE CHILI

The Committee on Constitution and Bylaws petition that Bylaw III, Sec. 3 (d) (1) (F) be amended by adding the following paragraph 9 (additions underlined; deletions in brackets):

BYLAW III, Sec. 3 (d) (1) (F)

9. preparing the following Chili recipe for the Chemistry Week Chili Cookoff.

2 Lb coarsely ground (lean) beef
½ to 1 lb. (boiled, freshly shucked armadillo) venison, finely chopped
1 tbsp. (fresh) garlic, finely chopped
1 large white onion, chopped
½ cup green onion stems, cut in (10 mm) 5 mm lengths
1 cup chopped celery, optional
2 cans (8-oz.) tomato paste
1 tbsp. salt
3 cups water
1 tsp. cayenne pepper
2-3 tbsp. chili powder (to taste)
½ tsp. ground allspice
(2 dashes ground pepper) ¼ tsp. chopped ginger root
(2) ½, or exclude, flat dry, oak-leaf shaped, Mexican peppers, WITH SEEDS REMOVED, finely chopped. These peppers make the chili too hot for most humans to handle
about 1 tbsp. Masa Trig corn meal, to thicken if desired
1 bottle tequila

Brown beef and (armadillo) venison in a (large rusty cast iron) oven proof glass Dutch oven. The mexican peppers will dissolve a cast iron pot. Check the tequila for quality. Add garlic, onions, and celery and cook until transparent (about two shots of tequila). Stir in remaining ingredients, except for Masa Trig and tequila, and (simmer) reflux gently, covered, for 1 and 1½ to 2 hours, stirring occasionally, and sipping tequila as needed. (When completely stewed) When the stewing is complete, thicken mixture with Masa Trig if (you can) desired. Serve hot (an understatement if you used the Mexican peppers) with Jalapeno, corn bread and (the rest of the 'quila) the remaining tequila.

Explanation

The Committee on Constitution and Bylaws has noted that, while the SOCIETY'S documents delineate procedures which complicate almost every aspect of life with significant and picky bureaucratic detail, nowhere in the Chapter, Constitution, Bylaws, and Regulations of the SOCIETY are culinary responsibilities assigned.

Signed: Paul R. Jones, for the Committee on Constitution and Bylaw

(This petition has been referred to the Committee on Gastronomical Purity, the Committee on Environmental Disasters, the Committee on Budget and Finance, the Committee on Constitution and Bylaws, and the Circular Fine.)

STATEMENT OF FINANCIAL IMPACT

The Committee on Budget and Finance has examined this petition and finds that venison is too expensive.

PRELIMINARY REPORT OF THE COMMITTEE ON CONSTITUTION AND BYLAWS

The Committee on Constitution and Bylaws, after consultation with the Committee on Chemical Safety and the Division of Medicinal Chemistry, has prepared a revised version of the petition. Although the Committee finds the petition to be legal and consistent, it may have an adverse effect on the Constitution of the Society. Several members have expressed the opinion that the amendment may be inconsistent with Constitution Article II, Section 1, "The objects of the AMERICAN CHEMICAL SOCIETY shall be...fostering public welfare ... and adding to the material prosperity and happiness of our people." Despite these reservations, the Committee recommends adoption of the amendment by majority vote of Council, provided that the amount of tequila is increased.

Submitted for: Charles B. Lindahl, Chairman
Committee on Constitution and Bylaws

Olympiad Chili

1 ¾ lbs. chopped lean beef
1 tablespoon vegetable oil or ½ strip bacon
2 small onions minced
1 (16 oz.) can tomatoes
1 large (6 oz.) minced sweet green pepper
1 (2 oz.) can pimento, chopped
1 (10 oz.) can pinto or red beans
½ tablespoon chili powder
½ teaspoon thyme
½ teaspoon dry mustard
1 teaspoon brown sugar
¼ teaspoon (red or white distilled) vinegar
2 tablespoons celery seeds
2 sections garlic cloves, minced

Brown beef and onion at moderate temperature (300 degree F.) in vegetable oil or bacon. Stir often. Add next four ingredients. Stir in chili powder well. Blend in thyme, dry mustard, brown sugar, and vinegar. Sprinkle celery seeds over cooking chili. Add minced garlic and stir gently.

Cook 35 to 45 minutes at 300 degree F. Serve over steamed white rice. Garnish with endive, parsley or hot pepper. Serve hot.

Submitted by: U.S. National Chemistry Olympiad Subcommittee
David Lavallee and Martha K. Turckes

Texas Style Chili (from Georgia)

3 lbs. ground chuck
1 lb. hot bulk sausage
3 medium onions, chopped
4 cloves garlic, minced
¼ cup chili powder
2 tablespoons all-purpose flour
1½ tablespoons sugar
1 tablespoon oregano (ground)
1 tablespoon salt
2 (28 oz.) cans whole tomatoes, undrained & chopped
3 (16 oz.) cans kidney beans, drained

Combine ground chuck, sausage, onion and garlic in Dutch oven, cook until meat is browned, stir to crumble. Drain. Stir in next six ingredients. Cover and simmer one hour, stirring occasionally. Add drained beans, simmer an additional 20 minutes.
Enjoy!

Submitted by: The Georgia Local Section
Ann Ware (Lawrenceville, GA)

Louisiana Chili

2 lbs. ground hamburger finely chopped
1 large onion (¾ to 1 lb) sliced and separated into rings
1 lb.)can dark red kidney beans
(1 lb.) can light red kidney beans
(1 lb.) blackeye peas, drained
4 oz. can mushroom stems and pieces, drained
½ cup onion bits barbecue sauce*
½ cup of hot barbecue sauce*
½ cup hickory smoked barbecue sauce*
½ cup of catsup

* Kraft barbecue sauces were used

Thoroughly brown hamburger in a 12-inch skillet. Mix in onion rings and cook until thoroughly softened but not brown. Pour off all excess grease.

Add hamburger and onion mixture to 3 qt. (or larger) saucepan containing the contents of the dark red kidney beans, light red kidney beans, blackeye peas, and mushroom stems and pieces. Thoroughly mix the ingredients and heat to a gentle boil. Add onion bits barbecue sauce, hickory smoked barbecue sauce, hot barbecue sauce, and catsup. Thoroughly mix and simmer for 10 minutes.

Submitted by: Oliver D. Dailey, Jr.
Louisiana Local Section

Sandra's California Chili Con Carne & Beans

1 large garlic bulb (10-12 cloves)
2 tablespoons olive oil
1 lb. pinto beans (soak for 24 hours or overnight) and cooked for 1 hour
2 large brown onions (about 3 cups chopped)
3 tablespoons of chili powder (more if you like it hot)*
1 tablespoon paprika
1 tablespoon dried cumin
1 tablespoon dried oregano leaves
1 lb. boneless lean beef chuck, cut into ½-inch cubes (about 2 cups)
1 lb. boneless lean pork shoulder, cut into ½-inch cubes (about 2 cups)
1 pound of sweet Italian Sausage, casings removed**
2 cups chopped celery
2 cups chopped green peppers
2 cups chopped carrots
2 4 oz. cans Ortega Green Chiles
1 7 oz. can Ortega Green Chili Salsa
3 oz. sun ripened, dried tomatoes, blanched in boiling water and soaked in 1 cup hot water overnight
1 28 oz. can of whole Roma tomatoes, or one pound of fresh peeled tomatoes
1 bunch cilantro (coriander or Chinese parsley), half of it chopped, (about ½ cup)

* If you prefer it hotter, add 1 medium chopped jalapeno and cayenne.
** Use hot sausage for hotter chili.

Pound garlic cloves with heavy knife, peel and chop. Heat olive oil in heavy iron 6-8 quart covered pot, add chopped garlic and onions and saute for about 15 minutes until transparent. Add chopped beef and pork and brown with paprika, chili powder, oregano and cumin for about 15 minutes.

When all the meat is well browned on all sides, add chopped sausage, celery, bell peppers and carrots and cook for 15 minutes more. Then add dried and canned tomatoes with liquid and salsa along with chiles and chopped cilantro (reserve the unchopped part for garnish) and simmer for one hour on medium heat. Add drained, cooked chili beans and cook for another half hour.

This dish improves with age. However, bring it just to the simmer when reheating or the beans will become mush. Another method of preparation is to store the chili without beans in the refrigerator for a day or two, or freeze for longer periods. Then add beans to the defrosted chili and heat for half an hour.

This chili is good served with chopped onions and chopped cheddar cheese. Garnish with fresh cilantro leaves for heavenly smell and a bright green highlight. For a real California touch, (and a lot more calories) serve with sour cream and chopped avocadoes and/or chopped black olives.
Enjoy!

Submitted by: Sandra Lamb
Southern California Local Section

Low Fat/No Infringement Chili

1 pound ground turkey
1 medium onion, chopped
2 tablespoons chili powder
1 can (10-¾ oz.) tomato soup
1 cup chopped celery
½ cup water
2 cans (15-½ oz. each) kidney beans, not drained

In a skillet, brown turkey pieces. Add celery and onion and cook until tender. Add chili powder, soup, water, and beans. Cook over low heat for 20 minutes, stirring occasionally. Serve with crackers. Makes 6 1-cup servings.

WARNING! WARNING! WARNING!

Duplication of this recipe (with attribution) is expressly encouraged. All methods of duplication (including photoreproduction, electronic reproduction, and oral communication) are covered under this warning.

Submitted by: Lydia E. M. Hines
Committee on Copyrights

Milwaukee Section Dairy State Chili

2½ cups canned chili beans
1 large onion, chopped
1 green pepper, chopped
1 sweet red pepper, chopped
2 tablespoons butter or margarine
1 pound ground beef
2 one-pound cans of peeled tomatoes
1½ tablespoons chili powder
1½ teaspoon salt
3 whole cloves
1 bay leaf
⅛ teaspoon cayenne pepper
⅛ teaspoon paprika
½ bottle beer (the Milwaukee Section prefers to use Lowenbrau)
5 or 6 chives, chopped
1 pint sour cream
8 oz. shredded Wisconsin cheddar cheese

Brown onion, peppers, and meat in melted butter. Add tomatoes, seasonings and beer. Simmer 2 hours; add more beer or water if necessary. Add beans; heat thoroughly. Serve in large bowls with garnish of sour cream, chopped chives and cheese. Serves 6.

Submitted by: Michele Clarke
Milwaukee Local Section

Dr. Strangebuds' Chili Alkahest

Take one freshly run-over armadillo, undressed and cubed (cubes 0.7 cm on a side), 1 kg. For those in areas were freshly-harvested armadillo is not readily available, take instead 1 kg. chili beef (coarsely ground). Brown in frying pan. Pour off all grease. Place meat in 4 liter wide-mouthed reaction vessel fitted with stirrer and reflux condenser (or use 4 qt. pot with lid and manually-driven wooden spoon if the former are not available).

Add: two 8 oz. cans Hunt's tomato sauce, three tomato sauce cans of water, one medium minced (grated) yellow onion, one minced garlic clove, five heaping teaspoons of green chile salsa (no, not chili sauce; Mission Brand was employed). Reflux gently for one-half hour, stirring frequently.

Then add:

8 tsp. (rounded) Gebhardt Eagle Brand chili powder
3 tsp. ground cumin
1 tsp. powdered coriander seed
1 tsp. powdered oregano
1 tsp. paprika
2 tsp. garlic NaCl
2 tsp. McIlhenny's tabasco sauce

Reflux for an additional one-half hour with frequent stirring. Remove reflux condenser (or lid) and fit for distillation (or use wire mesh splatter-shield) and distill with frequent stirring until the chili alkahest has reached the desired consistency (the distillate is not collected; caution: the distillate is a chemical!) Yield (residue): 84%, or three bags full. (1,2)

Cook to ca. 65 C. Eat. If you cannot eat it all at one sitting (both likely and advisable), freeze remainder for later use.

Disclaimer: Ars est celare artem!

----

1. Anon., "Old Fashioned Mother Goose Nursery Rhymes", Albert Whitman & Co., Chicago (ca. 1935), p. 161.
2. Sandwich-size ziploc bags.

Submitted by: Gerald R. Dodson
Dallas-Ft. Worth Local Section

Brazosport Chili

3 lbs. diced beef
¼ cup olive oil
2 cans (8 oz. each) tomato paste
1 can (14.5 oz.) whole tomatoes
water
6 tablespoons chili powder
2 teaspoons salt
8 cloves of finely minced garlic
1 teaspoon cumin powder
10 dashes hot pepper sauce (Tabasco)
1 tablespoon sugar
1 onion chopped very fine
2 tablespoons paprika
½ cup masa flour

Heat olive oil in a heavy 6 quart pot. Add the meat and sear over high heat, stirring constantly until the meat is gray, not brown. Put tomato paste and whole tomatoes together in a separate container. Add enough water to make one quart liquid volume. Pour the tomato, water mixture over the meat. Add the onion. Simmer for 1.5 hours. Stir every fifteen minutes.

Skim off any fat. Add all the remaining ingredients, except the masa flour. Simmer for another thirty minutes. Mix the masa flour into one cup of warm water. Add the flour plus water to the chili. Stir vigorously. Cook with stirring for 15 additional minutes. For bean lovers, pinto beans may be cooked separately and added after the initial 1.5 hour simmering.

Chili should be served with Fritos.

Submitted by: Wanda Golding
Brazosport Local Section

Recipe for Cleveland Chili

½ cup dried red kidney beans
2 cups water
2 teaspoons salt
1 tablespoon chili powder
1¼ pounds lean ground chuck
¼ cup Mott's natural apple juice or apple cider
1 cup Bennett's chili sauce
1 teaspoon cayenne red pepper
1 teaspoon liquid hickory smoke

I. BEANS

The ½ cup of dried beans are rinsed with water, drained and place in a sauce pan. Two cups of water are added to cover the beans and heated to a boil. After one minute, the pan is covered, the heat is turned off, and the beans are allowed to soak for one more hour.

II. MEAT SAUCE

The salt and the tablespoon of chili powder are blended together in a little dish or shaker. A clean, dry, heavy skillet is heated very hot. The 1¼ pounds of ground chuck is formed into a large slightly flattened pattie.

The ¼ cup sesame oil is poured into a shallow bowl and the beef pattie is coated on both sides by dipping it into the oil. The beef pattie is then coated with spice by sprinkling with the salt and chili powder mixture.

The coated beef pattie is place into the very hot skillet and browned on both sides very dark. The meat is then broken up crumbled into small pieces with a wooden spoon. The heat reduced to low and the beef is sauteed until the redness is gone. The next four ingredients are added and the mixture is stirred gently and simmered for 5 minutes.

III. BAKING

The meat sauce is transferred into a casserole or deep baking dish. The excess liquid is drained from the beans and the beans are added to the meat sauce. The beans are stirred into the sauce, the baking dish is covered and placed into a 300 degree oven. The chili is baked for 2 hours, stirring it one time after about one hour.

Submitted by: Tom Flechtner
Cleveland Local Section

Three Bean Chili

½ lb. lean pork
1 green pepper, diced
1 can (16 oz.) pinto beans
1 can (15 oz.) chili beans
5 oz. sliced mushrooms
4 yellow chiles, seeded
3 jalapeno peppers, seeded

½ lb. lean beef
29 oz. Italian stewed tomatoes
16 oz. tomato sauce
1 white onion, diced
9 cloves garlic
3 green chiles, seeded
1 teaspoon salt

Dice the pork and beef. To a hot skillet, add one tablespoon of vegetable oil and the diced meat. Sear the meat until tender. Cover and let sit. Puree the stewed tomatoes for a few seconds and add to a large pot. Blend the tomato sauce, 6 cloves of garlic, chiles, and jalapenos together and add to the pot.

Dice the remaining 3 cloves of garlic and add to the pot along with the green pepper, onions, salt, mushrooms, and meat (along with pan drippings). Drain the beans and add to the pot. Simmer until the beans are tender. Serve with Tabasco sauce and/or diced black olives as desired. Serves approximately 6-8.

Submitted by: Edward Brewer
Eastern New York Local Section

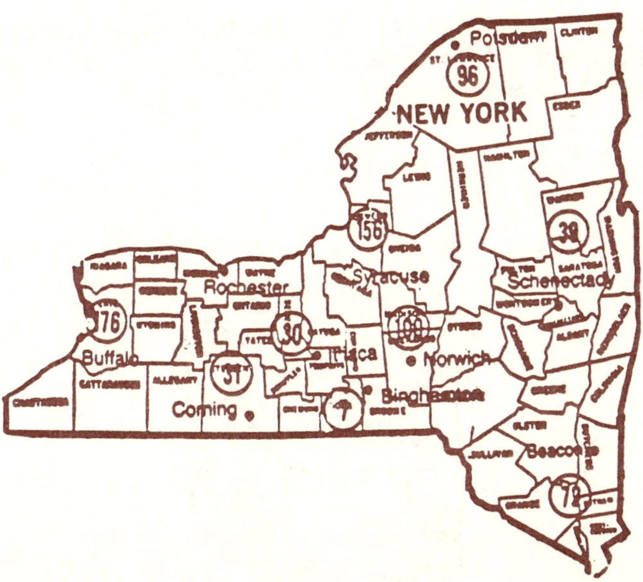

Dayton Chili

1 pound coarse ground beef chuck
⅓ cup chopped red onion
1 clove garlic, diced
2 tablespoons bacon drippings
½ cup beef stock
1 cup chicken stock
1 cup tomato, chopped
1 cup tomato sauce
1 teaspoon paprika
1 teaspoon oregano
½ teaspoon cumin
½ teaspoon coriander
6 tablespoons ground red chili
cayenne red pepper (to taste - ½ tsp. = HOT)
salt (to taste)
corn flour paste (1 tablespoon with equal parts water)
seasoned black iron pot (optional)

Brown meat and set aside to drain well. Saute onion and garlic in bacon drippings. Add beef and chicken stocks, tomato sauce, and spices. Bring to simmer. Add browned meat. Simmer covered for 30 minutes. Add chopped tomato. Simmer covered for additional 15 minutes. Stir in corn flour paste. Simmer uncovered for 10 minutes.

Serving suggestions: goes well over steamed white rice or garnish to suit taste with cooked red kidney beans, chopped red onion, or shredded cheddar cheese (cheddar or Colby).

Submitted by: Mathias G. Schneider, Jr.
Dayton Local Section

Hearty Northern Chili

2 lbs. hamburger
1.25 cup chopped onions
1 large chopped green pepper (¾ cup)
3 pints canned whole tomatoes
1 can tomato paste (6 oz.)
1 40-48 oz. can kidney beans (drained)
2.5 teaspoons sugar
1.5 teaspoons salt (or more to taste)
2 cloves finely chopped garlic
3 whole cloves
3 tablespoons chili powder (dissolved in similar quantity cold water)

In large pan, very lightly brown hamburger to generate fat. Add onions and green pepper to the hamburger and saute until the onions and green peppers are tender. Drain off liquid and add the rest of the ingredients except the kidney beans. Bring to a gentle simmer, cover, and cook 1.5 hours. Stir periodically.

Submitted by: Rick & Helen Herman
Lehigh Valley ACS Section

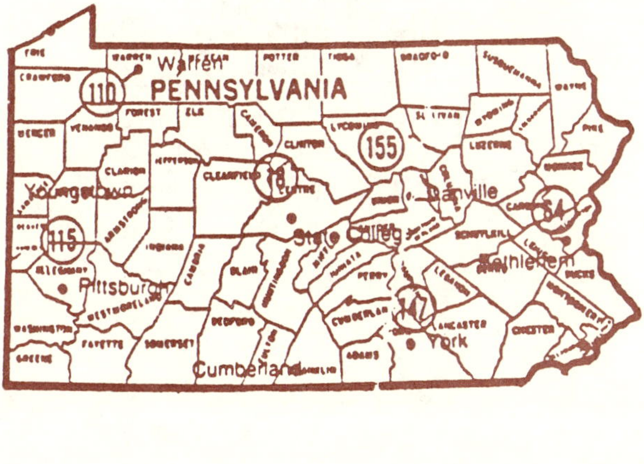

Reach the Public Chili

2 lbs. of coarse ground beef (chili grind)
2 medium onions, chopped
2 cloves garlic, crushed
2 teaspoons cumin
6 tablespoons or more chili powder (Gebhardts)
1 teaspoon salt
2 cans (16 oz.) tomatoes
¼ teaspoon ground red pepper
1 tablespoon sugar
Add enough vinegar so that you can smell it

Saute onions in vegetable oil. Add the garlic, meat, and seasonings and brown. Add the tomatoes, cover and simmer 2 hours.

Submitted by: Eric Leber, Smithsonian Fellow
Hall of American Science

Smithsonian Institution
Washington, D.C. 20560
U.S.A.

Chili Manana
(For frugal cooks)

2 cups shredded roast beef (left over)
1 cup minced onion
1 tablespoon salad oil
2 cloves garlic, peeled and minced
2 medium cans tomatoes with chilies
1 teaspoon chili powder
¼ teaspoon basil
¼ teaspoon cumin
Salt and pepper

Saute beef and onions in oil over medium high heat until onion is tender. Add remaining ingredients, season with salt and pepper, and simmer for 15 minutes.

Serve with warm flour tortillas.

Submitted by: Katherine Weissmann
Society Committee on Education
Task Force on Two-Year colleges

CRITICAL ISSUES IN TWO-YEAR COLLEGE CHEMISTRY

Consultants' chili

1 lb. ground turkey (or chicken)
2 tablespoons salad oil
1 cup finely chopped onion
2 cloves garlic, peeled and chopped
1 quart tomatoes or tomato juice
1 6 oz. can tomato paste
1 7 oz. can diced green chilies
¼ teaspoon basil
¼ teaspoon cumin
¼ teaspoon tabasco
1 (1 lb. 4 oz.) can cannellini (white kidney beans)
1 tablespoon lime juice
Salt and pepper

Recommendations:

Cook ground poultry meat in oil until just beginning to brown. Remove with slotted spoon and set aside. Add onions and garlic to pan and saute until softened. Stir in tomatoes, tomato paste, green chilies, basil, cumin, oregano, and tabasco sauce. Bring to boil, reduce heat, and simmer about 15 minutes. Return meat to pan along with drained beans and simmer about 10 more minutes.

Add lime juice and season with salt and pepper to taste. May be served with dollops of sour cream, chopped red onion, jalapenos, and/or shredded yellow cheese.

Submitted by: Katherine Weissmann
College Chemistry Consultants Service

North Jersey Chili

3 tablespoons butter or olive oil
1 medium onion, chopped
2 cloves garlic, minced
1 pound chopped beef
1 large can of tomatoes
1 can kidney beans
½ green pepper, minced
½ teaspoon celery seed
¼ teaspoon cayenne pepper
1 teaspoon cumin seed, crushed
1 bay leaf
2 tablespoons chili powder
⅛ teaspoon basil
1 teaspoon salt

Heat butter in skillet, add onion, saute until golden. Add meat and brown. Add other ingredients and simmer, adding water as necessary to keep moist. Add kidney beans and simmer for an additional half hour. This chili can be made spicier by simmering for three hours.

Submitted by: Dorothy Lehmkuhl
North Jersey Local Section

Campaign Kickoff Chili*

MATERIALS

2.5 Kg ground beef steak
1 large Vidalia onion
3 sweet green peppers
1 Kg shredded roast beef
1 #10 can whole tomatoes
1 #10 can kidney beans
2 Liters tomato juice
20 g (2 tablespoons) chili powder
20 g red peppers
20 g oregano
20 g bay leaves, crushed
20 g salt

METHOD

Brown ground beef steak, pepper and onion in a minimum of safflower oil. To a large kettle, add tomatoes, beans (and their juices), and the shredded beef. Bring to a slow boil and add in the browned beef, pepper, and onion. Reduce heat and simmer for at least five hours, adding water as needed.

RESULTS*

This Campaign for Chemistry Kickoff Chili, when supplemented by French bread, tossed salad, and desserts (all free, of course), was able to attract many members of the St. Joseph Valley Local Section to the introduction of the Campaign's member solicitation project.

SUMMARY AND RECOMMENDATIONS

This remarkably successful chili may be used to good advantage by other local sections seeking volunteers. For reasons not yet fully understood, this chili put people in a very cooperative and philanthropic mood.

Submitted by: Helen Free
St. Joseph Valley Local Section

Jo's Chunky Kentucky Chili

2½ lb. extra lean ground beef
2½ lb. boneless chuck roast, trimmed and cut into 1 inch cubes
1 40 oz. can red kidney beans and juice
2 8 oz. cans mushroom pieces and juice
2 6 oz. cans large pitted black olives, sliced
2 28 oz. cans crushed tomatoes in puree
2 6 oz. cans tomato paste
5 stalks celery with leaves, coarsely chopped
2 medium-sized green peppers, coarsely chopped
4 medium-sized onions, coarsely chopped
10 cloves garlic, coarsely chopped
20 to 30 jalapeno peppers, coarsely chopped
8 oz. chili powder
5 bay leaves
2 tablespoons cumin
5 tablespoons tabasco
3 tablespoons black pepper
1 teaspoon salt
1 can beer

Brown ground beef in large skillet, drain and transfer to a large stock pot. Repeat with beef chunks. Saute onions, peppers, celery, garlic, and jalapenos until onions are transparent. Add this mixture to meat in pot. Add tomatoes, tomato paste, beans, mushroom, and olives along with all of their juices. Stir and bring to simmer over medium heat. Add all other ingredients during this heating period. Simmer for four or five hours, stirring often and scraping the bottom of the pot.

Submitted by: Jo Ann McConnell
Louisville Local Section

Magnanimous Chili

CONTRIBUTE two Tablespoons bacon drippings to a large pot, heat over medium heat.

DONATE one large onion, coarsely chopped, and heat until onions are transparent.

PLEDGE four pounds of beef round, coarsely ground, to the pot.

COMMIT three cloves of garlic, finely chopped.

ENDOW the pot with four Tablespoons of chopped jalapeno peppers.

BESTOW on the concoction three Tablespoons cayenne pepper, one Tablespoon cumin, two teaspoons salt, and one teaspoon dried oregano.

GRANT sixteen ounces of tomato sauce and one tin cup of water.

GIVE the pot one minute to boil and one hour to simmer.

VOLUNTEER, if you wish, a little parsley.

BEQUEST ½ cup masa harina and cook ten minutes longer.

SERVE the chili and the American Chemical Society.

ENJOY the chili and the good feelings that come from helping your professional society.

Note: This chili is best when served with...Champagne for Chemistry!

Submitted by: Kay Burch
Campaign for Chemistry

CAMPAIGN
FOR
CHEMISTRY

Chili In The Abstract

1½ cans dry red or kidney beans
1 large onion, diced
1 large green pepper, diced
1 pound ground chuck roast
2 cans tomatoes, diced
1 8 oz. can tomato sauce
2 teaspoons chili peppers
1½ tablespoons chili powder
1 bay leaf

Brown green pepper, onion, and meat. Drain and rinse beans. Add beans and other ingredients to pot. Simmer one hour. Eat.

Submitted by: Richard Sutton
Columbus Local Section

Ozark Chili

1 pound hamburger
1 cup onion, chopped
2 cloves garlic, crushed
16 oz. can whole tomatoes
1 cup celery, sliced
½ medium green pepper, chopped
3 tablespoons chili powder
1 teaspoon cumin seed
2 teaspoons salt
1 teaspoon Worcestershire sauce
½ teaspoon red pepper sauce
1 teaspoon sugar
15 oz. can kidney beans

Cook, with stirring, hamburger, onion, and garlic in a 3 quart pot until hamburger is brown. Drain and then stir in all items except kidney beans. Heat to boiling and then simmer for one hour covered. Add beans, heat to boiling and simmer for 20 to 30 minutes.

Submitted by: Vernon Thielman
Ozark Local Section

Houston Chili

3 pounds of Texas chili meat
2 large onion, finely chopped
15 oz. can tomato sauce
1 cup water
1 teaspoon tabasco sauce
4 heaping Tablespoons chili powder
1 heaping Tablespoon oregano
1 teaspoon cumin
3 cloves garlic, pressed
black pepper, to taste
1 oz. fine whiskey (optional)
1 teaspoon cayenne pepper
1 level teaspoon paprika
1 dozen red peppers, chopped
4 or 5 serrano peppers, chopped
¼ teaspoon food-grade xantham gum (or 2 Tbsp. flour)

Sear meat and onions until meat is brown. Add tomato sauce and water. Stir and add the rest of the ingredients except for the xantham gum (or flour). If you want milder chili, remove the seeds from the peppers before adding them. Simmer for an hour and a half. Add thickener (mix the gum in a blender) and add to the chili, simmer for 30 minutes.

Submitted by: John Bell
Southeast Texas Local Section

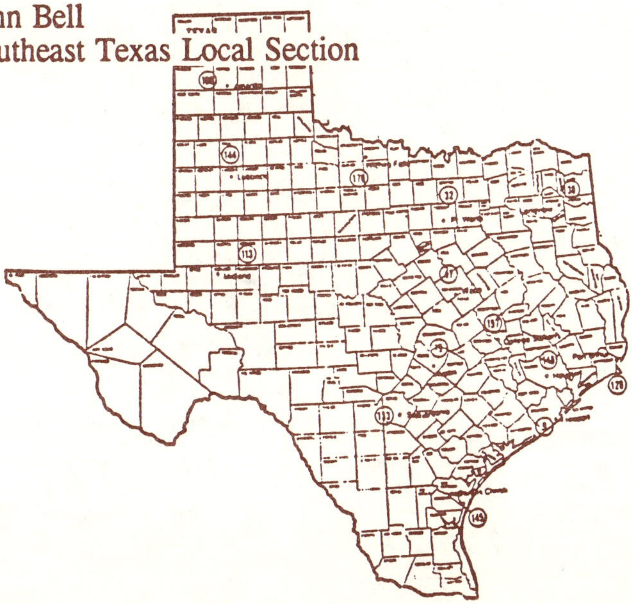

Silicon Valley Chili for Lots of Chemists

10 pounds of beans, mixed red and pink
4 large yellow onions
12 pounds of ground turkey
5 #2 cans of tomato sauce
5 #2 cans of whole tomatoes
4 jalapeno peppers
5 or 6 small chili peppers
3 cloves garlic

Wash the beans two or three times, discarding the water. Soak beans overnight in water then cook the beans in the soak water. Chop onions, peppers, and garlic and saute in olive oil until brown. Add these to the bean pot. Add tomato sauce and finely chopped tomatoes. Brown the turkey in olive oil and add to the bean pot. Simmer for six hours, adding water as needed.

Submitted by: Jack Riley (from Floyd Hobbs' recipe)
Santa Clara Valley Local Section

Really Safe Chili

1 pair safety glasses
1 large reaction shield
1 fire extinguisher
1 pair alkali-resistant gloves
1 pound ground beef
1 large onion
1 large can red kidney beans (with juice)
½ medium can whole tomatoes
1 tablespoon chili powder
2 tablespoons ground cumin
2 tablespoons dry parsley
1 tablespoon salt
1 tablespoon black pepper
2 tablespoons paprika
1 teaspoon garlic powder
½ teaspoon red pepper flakes
4 ounces liquid antacid

Put safety glasses and gloves on face and hands, respectively. Install reaction shield between reaction vessel and experimenter. Place fire extinguisher nearby (read the operating instructions now: when there is a fire is not the time to read the instructions). Read MSDS included in this publication.

In a NIOSH/OSHA/EPA/ACS-approved fume hood, place beans in a large vessel (pot) and heat to simmer. In a heavy Fe (iron) skillet, saute beef and onions until onions are translucent and beef is brown (WARNING: onions are lachrymators and will cause irritation of the eyes and nasal passages). Add beef and onions to beans in pot. Place tomatoes in skillet and heat to boiling, mashing as they cook. Add tomatoes to beans and beef land add all dry ingredients. Simmer and stir for at least ½ hour.

Swallow antacid and eat chili with corn bread.

In case of violent reaction, notify the Chemical Health and Safety Referral Service at 202/872-4515.

Submitted by: Helen Adams for
Committee on Chemical Safety

ACS Staff Chili

6 pounds lean beef, preferable round steak
1½ pounds lean pork
4 tablespoons avocado oil (or sunflower oil)
2 large yellow onions
6 small scallions, trimmed and cut into small cylinders
1 seeded and chopped red Serrano pepper
2 seeded and chopped Jalapeno peppers
3 oz. (1 bottle) Gebhardt Chili Powder
2 teaspoons cumino powder
3 large cloves garlic, chopped
1 pound dried red kidney or pinto beans
2 large tomatoes, peeled and chopped
½ pound sun-dried tomatoes
2 cups strong black coffee
1 can beer
½ cup masa harina
1 tablespoon brown sugar

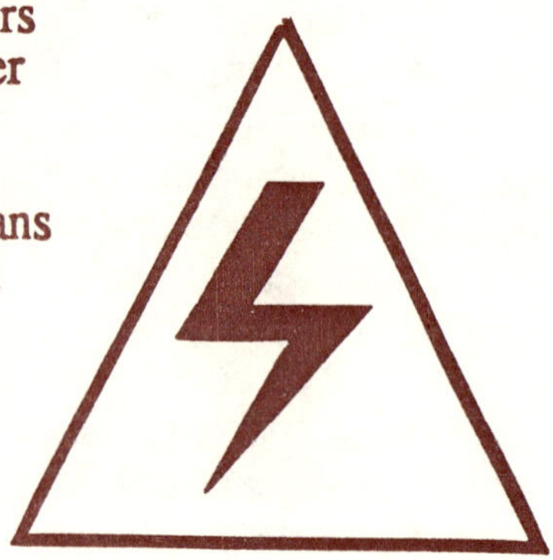

Pick over the beans and soak in cold water overnight. The next day, use a large pot and cook the beans in 3 quarts of water for about 2 hours, until tender. Reserve beans and liquor for further processing.

Trim the beef, and either cube into ½ inch pieces or grind with the coarse blade of a food chopper (preferably 2 pounds of ground beef and 4 pounds of cubed beef). Cube the ;pork into ½ inch pieces. In a heavy skillet, heat the oil until very hot (the smoke point of avocado oil is 600 F), and thoroughly brown the meat and scallions. Pour off excess fat.

Add the meat and scallions to the bean pot (at this point you may just use the bean liquor, and use the beans for other purposes) and bring to a boil. Add the black coffee, chili, powder, peppers, cumino powder, yellow onions, garlic, tomatoes, beer, and brown sugar and cook covered for about 2 hours, then cook uncovered until the broth is thicker. Add salt to taste and masa harina (or flour mixed with water into a paste) if further thickening is desired.

Submitted by: John K. Crum
ACS Staff

When ACS changed its logo,
what happened to the old phoenix?

You guessed it!

Budget and Finance Three-Bean Chili

2 teaspoons each virgin olive oil and safflower oil, mixed
3 cups yellow onions, chopped
8 cloves garlic
2 pounds lean round steak, chopped (not ground)
½ cup amontillado sherry
¼ cup Guinness stout
1 red bell pepper, seeded and chopped
1 cup chopped celery
3 Anaheim chili peppers, seeded and chopped
1 Poblano (or Jalapeno) pepper, seeded and chopped
*Wear gloves while working with chili peppers!
2 cups each cooked black, pinto, and red kidney beans (with liquids)
2 cups chopped plum (Italian) tomatoes
1 can tomato paste
4 teaspoons ground cumin
8 teaspoons chili powder
½ teaspoon allspice
1 teaspoon cinnamon
½ cup corn meal

Procedure

1. In a large, heavy pan, heat the mixed oils and saute the chopped onions until it is soft but not browned. Add the garlic and continue heating for 1-2 minutes.

2. Remove garlic and onion to a large pot which will be able to hold all of the ingredients (a crock pot is especially useful).

3. To the pan used for heating the onion and garlic, add the meat and cook until it is just browned (approx. 5 minutes). Drain most of the fat off, if necessary. Add the cooked meat to the pot containing the onion and garlic.

4. Add the sherry, stout, bell pepper/celery to the pan used for the meat. Simmer for 5 to 10 minutes or until the vegetables are softened.

5. Add the hot peppers to bell pepper/celery mixture and continue heating for an additional 10 minutes.

6. Transfer the above mixture to the large pot and add all remaining ingredients except the corn meal. Mix well and simmer covered for 2 hours or longer to thoroughly marry the flavors. Remove the cover and add corn meal to thicken the chili (if desired).

This recipe will serve 10 to 12 persons, but like the Society's resources, there is never enough to go around!

Submitted by: Paul H. Walter
Committee on Budget and Finance

Singles Seven Course Chili Dinner

2 cans Hormel Chili with Beans (hot)
1 jar of Old El Paso Salsa (hot)
1 can stewed tomatoes
6 cans beer

Combine chili, salsa, and tomatoes in a clean glass pot. Microwave on high for four minutes. Stir and eat from pot. This recipe serves one person twice, or--if you can get a date--two people once.

Submitted by: "Lonesome" Avogadro
Single Chemists Club

6.02×10^{23} nights without a single date!

U.S. DEPARTMENT OF LABOR
Occupational Safety and Health Administration

Form Approved
OMB No. 44-R1387

MATERIAL SAFETY DATA SHEET

Required under USDL Safety and Health Regulations for Ship Repairing, Shipbuilding, and Shipbreaking (29 CFR 1915, 1916, 1917)

SECTION I

MANUFACTURER'S NAME	EMERGENCY TELEPHONE NO.
ACS Committees / Sections / Staff	202/872-4600
ADDRESS (Number, Street, City, State, and ZIP Code)	
CHEMICAL NAME AND SYNONYMS: Chili	TRADE NAME AND SYNONYMS: Chili con Carne, Hot Stuff.
CHEMICAL FAMILY	

See other sheets for: 1602 . . . 1701, 1201, 1202 - 1905, 1614, 2107, 2400 Flat Black Metallic Colors High Heat Paint Colors

SECTION II · HAZARDOUS INGREDIENTS

PAINTS, PRESERVATIVES, & SOLVENTS	%	TLV ppm	CAS Number
PIGMENTS Red, brown, green			
VEHICLE H_2O			
SOLVENTS H_2O, $CO_{2(aq)}$, CH_3CH_2OH			

SECTION III · PHYSICAL DATA

BOILING POINT (°F.)	215°F	SPECIFIC GRAVITY (H_2O=1)	1.15
VAPOR PRESSURE (mm Hg.)	770	PERCENT, VOLATILE BY VOLUME (%)	4.40
VAPOR DENSITY (AIR=1)	unknown	EVAPORATION RATE	unknown
SOLUBILITY IN WATER	unknown		
APPEARANCE AND ODOR	V. Strong		

SECTION IV · FIRE AND EXPLOSION HAZARD DATA

Decomposition products have been reported to be explosive.

Do not use near fire or flame or while smoking. Do not smoke, anyway.

(Continued on reverse side)

SECTION V · HEALTH HAZARD DATA

THRESHOLD LIMIT VALUE	Two servings
EFFECTS OF OVEREXPOSURE	Listlessness, flatulence, future moderation
EMERGENCY AND FIRST AID PROCEDURES	Treat victim with antacids and kindness.

SECTION VI · REACTIVITY DATA

STABILITY	UNSTABLE	X	CONDITIONS TO AVOID: Social situations
	STABLE		
INCOMPATABILITY (Materials to avoid)	other spicy foods.		
HAZARDOUS DECOMPOSITION PRODUCTS	Definitely!!		
HAZARDOUS POLYMERIZATION	MAY OCCUR	X	CONDITIONS TO AVOID:
	WILL NOT OCCUR		Unknown -- caution

SECTION VII · SPILL OR LEAK PROCEDURES

STEPS TO BE TAKEN IN CASE MATERIAL IS RELEASED OR SPILLED: Immediately remove all animals and children from spill area.

WASTE DISPOSAL METHOD: Contact Chili Makers Anonymous (CMA) for disposal instructions.

SECTION VIII · SPECIAL PROTECTION INFORMATION

RESPIRATORY PROTECTION (Specify type)	NIOSH/MSHA Full-face respirator
VENTILATION	
PROTECTIVE GLOVES	Sure, why not?
EYE PROTECTION	Goggles (not visitors' specs!)
OTHER PROTECTIVE EQUIPMENT	Reaction shield.

SECTION IX · SPECIAL PRECAUTIONS

PRECAUTIONS TO BE TAKEN IN HANDLING AND STORING:
Do not brag about your own recipe.
Do not store in aluminum vessels (seriously!)

OTHER PRECAUTIONS:
Do not discuss religion or politics.
Look both ways before crossing a street.

PAGE (2)

Prepared by: Some wise science guys

Form OSHA-20
Rev. May 72

DISCLAIMER

This data sheet is not part of any contract of sale: The information contained herein is believed to be correct or is obtained from sources believed to be generally reliable. However, it is the responsibility of the user of these materials to investigate, understand and comply with law and with procedures applicable to the safe handling and use of these materials. Borden, Inc. shall not be liable for any loss or damage directly or indirectly arising from the use of the product, and Borden, Inc. assumes no obligation or liability for reliance on the information contained herein, or omissions herefrom.

CATTLE BRANDS

DE TAVRO.

To start, 'Brave Men & Cold Steel: A History of Range Detectives and Their Peacemakers', by the Texas and Southwest Cattle Raisers Foundation, 1984, has a short history of the 50 more prominent Southwestern brands, Chapter 7, Legends of The Brands.

'Texas and Southwestern Cattle Raisers Foundation, in the pursuit of education, published this book in order to inform the public about the colorful and lively background of the association's force of brand inspectors, who used Colt .45's as symbol of their law enforcement status to defend the property rights of cattlemen against the lawless element.'

Brave Men & Cold Steel.....

This is a very interesting booklet on brand inspectors, and the guns that were an intricate part of their existence in handling cases of stolen cattle.

(A F Connected) Frates Seeligson, San Antonio, Texas. TSCRA President, 1982-84. Brand used on registered and commercial Santa Gertrudis cattle in Gonzales and Guadalupa counties, Texas, and Chaves County, New Mexico.

(J) John M. Shelton III, Amarillo, Texas. TSCRA First Vice President, 1982-84. Brand used on commercial Hereford x Angus cattle in Oldham County, Texas. Brand was first used as a Lazy J by his grandfather, John M. Shelton, beginning about 1900 in Hartley, Wheeler, Dallam and Oldham counties.

(Hip O) J.E. Birdwell II, Lubbock, Texas. TSCRA Second Vice President, 1982-84. Started using brand in 1940's on cattle throughout West Texas and the Panhandle. Presently used on registered and commercial Hereford cattle in Bailey County, Texas. Brands on left hip.

(K L) Don C. King, Forth Worth, Texas. TSCRA Secretary-General Manager, 1966-present; TSCRA Special Assistant, 1965-66; TSCRA Field Inspector 1962-65. Brand used on registered Hereford cattle in Jack County, Texas.

(T) Bryant Edwards, Henrietta, Texas. TSCRA Past President, 1948-50. Brand used on Hereford cattle in Clay and Briscoe counties, Texas. This type of brand is sometimes called "Winged T."

(N Bar) Norman Moser, DeKalb, Texas. TSCRA Past President, 1958-60. Brand used on commercial cattle and yearling steers in Bowie and Red River counties, Texas, and McCurtain County, Oklahoma.

(Six) Dolph Briscoe Jr., Uvalde, Texas. TSCRA Past President, 1960-62. Brand used on registered and commercial Santa Gertrudis cattle in Uvalde, Webb, and Dimmitt counties, Texas.

(J F) Leo Welder, Victoria, Texas. TSCRA Past President, 1962-64. Brand used on Hereford-Brahman cross cattle in Goliad, Refugio, San Patricio and Duval counties, Texas.

(T U) Fred Wulff, Brady, Texas. TSCRA Past President, 1964-66. Brand used on commercial Angus cattle in McCulloch County. Texas.

(Three C) Ben C. Carpenter, Irving, Texas. TSCRA Past President, 1966-68. Brand used on commercial crossbred cattle in Dallas, Navarro, Anderson, Kaufman, Ellis, Freestone and Henderson counties, Texas.

(T L) T.L. Roach, Jr., Amarillo, Texas. TSCRA Past President, 1968-70. Brand used on commercial Hereford cattle in Donley County, Texas. Brand was started by Roach's father, T.L. "Jack" Roach, about 1930, and was used in a number of Panhandle counties through the years. In the early years, TL was reserved for "keeper" cattle, and other brands used for yearling and sale cattle. Now TL is used exclusively on all cattle.

(H Crook) Frank H. Lewis, Bay City, Texas. TSCRA Past President, 1970-72. Brand used on registered Brahman and commercial crossbred cattle in Matagorda County, Texas. The H Crook brand was originally registered in 1866 in Matagorda County under the name of J.B. Hawkins.

(Lightning) William C. Donnell, Marathon, Texas. TSCRA Past President, 1972-74. Brand used on registered and commercial Hereford cattle in Brewster, Presidio and Zavala counties, Texas. The Lightning brand was originally registered in 1886 and 1890 by Alfred S. Gate.

(J F D) Hilmar G. Moore, Richmond, Texas. TSCRA Past President, 1974-76. Brand used on commercial and registered Santa Gertrudis cattle in Brazoria, Fort Bend and Wharton counties, Texas. J F D brand originally designed by J.F. Dyer who recorded it in Fort Bent County on Oct. 3, 1839.

(Turkey Track) J.A. Whittenburg III, Amarillo, Texas. TSCRA Past President, 1976-78. Brand used on commercial Hereford cattle and yearling steers in Ochiltree, Dallam, Sherman, Randall, Hutchinson, Hansford, Potter, and Carson counties, Texas. Brand was originally run by C.W. Word and used by a man names McNulty on Moors Creek in Hutchinson County. Reinstated on original Turkey Track headquarters in 1916 by Whittenburg's grandfather, W.T. Coble, a former TSCRA president from 1934-36.

(Five Points) John B. Armstrong, Kingsville, Texas. TSCRA Past President, 1978-80. Brand used on registered and commercial Santa Gertrudis cattle in Cameron, Starr, Kenedy, Kleberg, Jim Wells, Brooks, Duval, Nueces and Jim Hogg counties, Texas.

JS

(J S) John S. Cargile, San Angelo, Texas. TSCRA Past President, 1980-82. Brand used on commercial cattle in Irion and Tom Green counties Texas.

NUG

(N U G) J.C. Loving, Jermyn, Texas. The first TSCRA Secretary, 1877-1902. Loving was born on Jan 6, 1836, in Hopkins County, KY., to Oliver and Susan D. Loving. In 1867 he took over the family cattle operation after his father was killed by Indians.A founder of TSCRA, he served as its first secretary until his death in 1902. He established the first association brand book. The N U G brand was started in Jack and Young counties, Texas, by the Loving Cattle Company in 1865. It was designed by a man named Dave Terrell because it was his girlfriend's initials.

ᗡ

(Backward D) W.T. Waggoner Estate, Vernon, Texas. This Brand was first used about 1950, and today is run in Archer, Baylor, Foard,Knox, Wichita and Wilbarger counties, Texas, on about 10,000 head of primarily Hereford cattle. The forerunner of this brand, Three Backward D's, was begun about 1849. In 1871 it was registered in Wise and Clay counties, and a little later in Wilbarger County.

O

(Circle O) Charles Goodnight and Oliver Loving, both traildrivers. Loving and Goodnight, after the civil war, sought better markets for their cattle than Reconstruction Texas. In 1866 they established a new route from Fort Belknap, Texas, to Fort Sumner, N.M., called the Goodnight-Loving Trail. Loving was killed by Indians on the third trip. Goodnight continued to drive cattle into New Mexico for three more years after joining forces with John Chisum in 1871. The Circle brand was Goodnight and Loving's road brand, and was burned only on cattle destined for the trail.

5

(Five) Scharbauer Cattle Co., Midland, Texas. This brand ispresently used on cattle run by Scharbauer Cattle Company and Scharbauer Bros. and Company, which together comprise eight cattle ranches in West Texas, the Texas Panhandle and southeastern New Mexico. Other versions of the Five brand were started by Baily Dougherty in Kaufman County in 1860, by Capt. L. W. Burrell in Medina in 1880, and by George Crosson who used it in 1866 in Bexar County, in 1871 in Davis County, and in 1884 in Presidio County. Crosson received the brand from his father who had used it on sheep in Ireland in the early 1800s.

(Four Sixes) Burnett Ranches, Inc., Fort Worth and Guthrie, Texas. A common myth is that the Four Sixes brand was chosen to honor a winning poker hand once held by Samuel Burk Burnett, the founder of today's BurnettRanches, Inc. However, that is incorrect. Burnett bought the brand in 1871 along with 100 head of cattle in Denton County. Burnett, an original organizer of TSCRA, registered the brand in Wichita County in 1885, in King County in 1903, and in Carson County in 1908. TSCRA Director Anne Sowell is the Great-granddaughter of S.B. Burnett and is owner and president of Burnett Ranches, Inc., which lies in King and Cottle counties. J.J. Gibson, a TSCRA director, manages the Four Sixes Ranch.

(Frying Pan) Glidden and Sanborn, Texas Panhandle. The brand was begun in 1885 and 1886 in Oldham, Potter and Randall counties by Glidden and Sanbornwho had 250,000 acres adjacent to the XIT Ranch. BillScarborough also registered the Frying Pay brand in 1897 in Motley County and from 1909 to 1912 registered in Winkler, Loving and Andrews counties, Texas and Lea County, N.M.

(Half Circle or "Quien Sabe") Henry M. Halff, Midland, Texas. Thebrand was started in the Big Bend country and given to Halff by his father. Halff used it on Hereford cattle in Midland, Upton and Glasscockcounties. For many years, Halff had one of the best known Hereford herds in the Southwest. The brand was made by two half-circles branding irons. It was also known as the "Quien Sabe?" brand since legend has it that whenever a visitor asked the Mexican cowhands what the brand was they would reply "Who Knows?" in Spanish. The brand is often used in other configurations of the two half circles.

(Half Circle 10) George Saunders, San Antonio, Texas,cattleman, traildriver and founder of the Trail Drivers Association. Saunders entered the cattle business in his early teens when he managed his parents ranch after his father and brothers left to fight in the Civil War. In 1871, Saunders began driving cattle to Kansas, going up the trail nine times in 15 years. In 1888 he started the George Saunders Commission Company and later founded the Union Stockyards, both in San Antonio. His brand was given to him on his tenth birthday by his father, Thomas Bailey Saunders.

(Hashknife) Ernest Hunt, Olney, Texas. Hunt's father bought the brand in 1928 from a man named Anderson who had the Hashknife Ranch near Megargel along the Brazos River. It is the oldest brand registered in Baylor and Throckmorton counties, being first recorded in 1882. At present the brand is used on Hereford cattle in Young, Baylor, Throckmorton, Knox and Archer counties. Another Hashknife brand was run in Taylor County beginning in 1872 by Couts and Simpson. It was sold in 1881 to Continental Land & Cattle Company of St. Louis. Continental sold out to Johnson Brothers in 1893.

(Horsehead or R) Jim Reno, Kerrville, Texas. Reno, sculptor of the life-size bronze, "The Brand Inspector" which stands in frontof the TSCR Foundation building in Fort Worth, registers his brand in Kerr County.

(J A) M.G.W. Ritchie, Claredon, Texas. Col Charles Goodnight selected the JA brand in 1876 in honor of his partner, John Adair, with whom he was running cattle in Randall, Swisher, Briscoe, Donley, Armstrong and Hall counties. Adair died in 1885, and his widow continued the partnership until 1887 when the property was divided. Mrs. Adair retained the JA brand and ranch. Today M.H.W. Ritchie, the grandson of Mrs. Wadsworth

Ritchie Adair, uses the brand on commercial Hereford and crossbred cattle in Armstrong, Donley, Briscoe and Hall counties.

(J Y) Masterson Ranch, King and Knox counties, Texas. FrankCollinson, the old buffalo hunter who first established the ranch on the Tongue River thatwould eventually become Matador Land & Cattle Company, sold the JY brand to R.B. Masterson, who registered it in 1896. By 1936 T.B. Masterson was using the brand on 100,000 acres and 6,500 head of Angus cattle - the largest Angus range operation in the world at that time. R.B. Masterson was also using it in the Panhandle.

(Long S) C.C. Slaughter, Dallas, Texas. Rancher and foundingfather of TSCRA, 1877. TSCRA Past President, 1885-1886. Slaughter become involved in the cattle industry in 1849 at the age of 12. By 1856 he was ranching inPalo Pinto County. In 1868, he begandriving cattle from Texas to Kansas, and in 1871 he brought Shorthorn bulls from Kentucky to improve the native Longhorns. In 1898 he brought Sir Bredwell, the first $5,000 Hereford bull,to Texas. The Long S brand was started in September 1879 by Slaughter.During his lifetime, the brand was used in Howard, Martin, Dawson, Borden, Cochran, Hockley and Hale counties, Texas.

(Long X) Reynolds Cattle Company, Fort Worth, Kent and Dalhart, Texas. The brand originated about 1882, and gave the Reynolds' 225,000-acre ranch in Jeff Davis County its name. Reynolds Cattle Company also used the Long X on its 64,000-acre ranch near Dalhart. Through the years the company has used the brand in Culberson, Jeff Davis, Hartley and Dallam counties. In the early days, it was used primarily on Hereford cattle, but more recently is used in the company's crossbreeding operation. The Reynolds, an early Texas ranching family, were instrumental in organizing TSCRA in 1877.

(M O) Watt Matthews, Albany, Texas. TSCRA Honrary Vice President. The M O brand was begun by Matthews' father, JohnAlexander "Bud" Matthews, in the 1870s. Later when Matthews and Reynolds Company was formed in 1880, the M O brand was used on all commonly held cattle. After the company broke up the brand was discontinued and was not reused until 1967 when Watt Matthewsand some of his nieces and nephews began the M O Cattle Co. Today the brand is run in Throckmorton and Shackelford counties. Matthews also manages the J. A. Matthews Cattle Company at Albany, Texas, which has branded the A V (open A and lazy V) since 1885.

(M Six) J.A. McFaddin Estate, McFaddin, Texas. William McFaddin, a veteran of the Texas War for Independence and the Battle of NewOrleans, originated the brand in 1877. He used it first in Chambers County near Beaumont. Later, he joined his son, W.P.H. McFaddin in the cattle business in Victoria County and they burned M Six on 6,000 head of cattle. W.P.H. McFaddin's son, J.A.

(Mashed O) Halsell Cattle Co., Muleshoe, Texas. W.E. Halsell adapted the Mashed O from a circle brand that he and Glen Hasell used in 1889 in Cosweescoowee District, Indian Territory. After the partnership was dissolved, Halsell flattened the circle into a "Mashed O." In 1901 Halsell bought land in Lamb County, Texas,from XIT and added an additional 50,000 acres in Bailey County. The Mashed O brand was also used by L.P. Powell in the 1910s in New Mexico. He brought it with him in 1917 when he began ranching in Reagan County and registered it in Schleicher County in 1936. His son Virgil J. Powell used it. And today it is the brand of his son TSCRA Director James L. Powell of Fort McKavett, who burns it on Hereford and crossbred cattle in Schleicher, Sutton, Edwards, and Tom Green counties. From 1943 to 1958, the West-Pyle Cattle Company of Sanderson, Texas, owned by J.M. West and Buck Pyle, used the Mashed O on as many as 15,000 head of cattle at one time in Pecos, Brewster, Culberson, Hudspeth, Webb, Maverick, Dimmitt, Harris and Galveston counties, Texas, and Socorro, Pecos, Valencia, Quay and Union counties, N. M. The company branded the horizontal Mashed O on the left hip and the vertical Mashed O on the left thigh.

(Matador V) Matador Land and Cattle Company, Motley County, Texas. In 1879, John Dawson sold a herd of cattle wearing the "V" brand to Matador Ranch. The next summer when working cattle the ranch adopted the brand as its own. When Matador Land and Cattle Company, Ltd., the Scottish company, bought the ranch in 1882, the brand went with it. At that time the ranch had 60,000 cattle on 300,000 acres in Motley, Dickens, Cottle and Floyd counties. Murdo MacKenzie, TSCRA president from 1901 to 1903, became manager of the ranch in 1891. By 1936 the brand was run on 861,000 acres and 50,000 Hereford cattle. The ranch was sold in 1951. Fred C. Koch bought the Matador headquarters and four large tracts of land in Motley County in 1952. The ranch today is run by Matador Cattle Co., Wichita, Kan., Larry Angell, president.

(Media Luna or Half Moon) Armstrong ranch, Armstrong, Texas. TheMedia Luna or Half Moon was first used by Armstrong Ranch as a holding brand for cattle that the ranch has bought. The brand is still used by TSCRA Director Tobin Armstrong on Armstrong Ranch's registered and commercial Santa Gertrudis operation in Kenedy County. A Media Luna brand was also recorded by Col.Dillard Rucker Fant, a Civil War veteran and early traildriver, in Hidalgo and Cameron counties. Fant bought the brand and a ranch called Santa Rosa from a man named parker. Fant later sold Santa Rosa to the Magill Brothers of Alice, Texas.

(Mill Iron) Mill Iron Ranches, Texas Panhandle. Col. Wm. E. Hughes, a Civil War veteran, organized the Continental Land and Cattle Company and began purchasing land in Hall, Collinsworth and Hughes counties. In 1870 the company registered the Mill Iron brand. Before the 1900s, the company boasted 900,000 acres in Cottle, Motley, Hall, Collinsworth and Wheeler counties, but sold off much of the land in 1914. In 1949, the Mill Iron ranch was under the management of Lafayette M. Hughes of Denver, Colo., and for many years was one of the best known registered Hereford operations in the country.

(Muleshoe) Muleshoe Cattle Co., Howell E. Smith, TSCRA Honorary Vice President, Jolly, Texas. Smithy received the Muleshoe brand when he was in partnership with Pete Richardson in Henderson County. Richardson's father was William Richardson, one of the biggest cattlemen in Henderson County in the 1880s, who branded the Muleshoe on the left hip. The brand was also used by Smith in partnership with G.D. "Nig" London, Throckmorton, Texas from 1950 to 1976. London Continues to use the brand in a "lazy" position on his operations in Throckmorton, Baylor and Foard counties. Legend has it that Dan Waggoner also once used the brand when he made two cast-off muleshoes serve as the iron he forgot to bring. This popular brand is also currently used by Trammell-Swanson Ranch of Breckenridge operated by Mr. and Mrs. Howard Swanson. The ranch runs registered Hereford cattle in Stephens County.

(O Six) H.L. Kokernot Ranch, Alpine, Texas. The O6 was registered in Calhoun County as early as 1837. In the 1850s, Captain W.E. Jones registered the brand in Gonzales County, and in 1872 it was bought by J.W. Kokernot. In 1883, Kokernot and his brother, L.M., leased land from the state in the Trans-Pecos region and began running cattle. They registered the brand in Jeff

Davis County in 1889. In 1896, the brand ownership transferred to L.M. Kokernot, who bequeathed it to his son, H.L.Kokernot Sr., TSCRA president from 1924-26, who began expanding the ranch by purchasing land. In 1920, management of the ranch was turned over to H.L. Kokernot Jr., who is presently a TSCRA honorary vice president. Today, his grandson, Chris Lacy Jr., a TSCRA director, manages the sprawling O6 holdings, which lie between Alpine and Fort Davis.

101

(One Hundred One) 101 Ranch, Lamont, Okla. Colonel George Washington Miller, a Confederate officer, began ranching on the Salt Fork of the Arkansas near Lamont in the 1870s. Soon afterwards, he began branding his cattle with 101. Legend has it that he got the brand from a saloon near San Antonio called the 101. Miller's men wrecked it, and the colonel paid the damages, but he branded his cattle with the saloon's name to remind them of what had happened. The ranch also at one time had 101,000 acres. Miller passed the ranch on to his three sons, and by 1932 their debts caused them to close it down. R.S. Guthrie registered the "Hundred and One" brand in Brewster and Presidio counties, Texas, in 1886 because of his friendship with Colonel Miller. Two irons, the O and 1 are used to make the brand with the Oplaced on the hip bone.

(Pitchfork) Pitchfork Land & Cattle Company, Guthrie, Texas. Norman Savage of Matagorda County first registered the Pitchfork brand in 1843. It was used upside down and did not have a middle prong. But in 1879, a man named Jerry Savage (not related) ran cattle near the headwaters of the Wichita River using the Pitchfork brand upright and with a middle prong. In 1881, Savage's cattle and brand were purchased by D.W. Godwin and D.B. Gardner, one of the organizers of TSCRA in 1877. The ranch was incorporated as Pitchfork Land & Cattle Company, in 1883. Today the Pitchfork brand is used on primarily Hereford cattle and some crossbred cattle and steers on 165,000 acres in Dickens and King counties, Texas, on 32,000 acres in Wyoming and on 4,000 acres in Kansas. TSCRA Director Jim Humphreys is presently serving as the sixth Pitchfork manager.

(Rocking Chair) Rocking Chair Company, Ltd., Collingsworth and Wheeler counties, Texas. The Rocking Chair brand came to Collingsworth County from the area around the Llano River about 1879. The brand was acquired by John T. Lytle on Medina County in 1881 and he registered it at Mobeetie. Lytle lost interest in the area and sold the brand, land and cattle to John Drew in 1883. Drew, an Englishman, promptly resold the property to two countrymen, and he remained as manager. However, he was discharged for poor management and was replaced by Texas Ranger Captain George W. Arrington in 1882. Arrington, who had come to the area to rid it of cattle thieves, was also elected sheriff of Wheeler County and the 14 counties attached to it. Arrington resigned in 1891, but kept the Rocking Chair brand. Today, two ofhis descendants, Bill and George Arrington, continue to use the brand in Carson, Gray and Hemphill counties. Another version of the Rocking Chair brand is run by L.C. Whitehead of Dallas, president of the Texas Hereford Association in 1983. Whitehead's Rocking Chair Ranch is at Fort McKavett, and his brand is registered in Tom Green and Schleicher counties.

(Running W) King Ranch, Inc., Kingsville, Texas. Captain RichardKing in 1852 bought a Spanish land grant of 75,000 acres on Santa Gertrudis Creek in Nueces County. In 1860, his steamboating partner Mifflin Kenedy joined him and the land holdings swelled. They dissolved their partnership, but King held on to the Santa Gertrudis and other acreage and in 1885 his holdings amounted to 500,000 acres. The Running W brand appeared as the official brand of the King Ranch in the 1860s. The brand has been burned on the sides of thousands of cattle through the years including Mexican cattle, native

Longhorns, Shorthorns, Herefords and Brahmans. Butsince about 1950 the main breed of cattle to wear the Running W has been the Santa Gertrudis breed, which was developed on the ranch by then-ranch manager R.J. Kleberg Jr. TSCRA Director J.H. Clement serves as president, TSCRA Past President John B. Armstrong serves as executive vice president, and TSCRA Director Stephen (Tio) Kleberg is secretary of King Ranch, Inc.

(Seven Up) Used by several cattlemen through the years. The first recorded use was by Frank Wilson in Virginia whose son brought it to Polk County, Texas, in the 1830s. It stayed in the family for more than a century and was recorded in Leon County. The brand was also registered in 1876 in Van Zandt County by H.N. (Doc) Williams. It was commonly believed that he selected it because he was a fan of the card game "Seven-Up". There is one recorded instance of the same game actually earning someone a ranch and cattle. J.W. Carter bet his cattle to his wife Mrs. Ellen Carter in a game of Seven-Up. Mrs. Carter won and Carter designed the brand in honor of the game which won here the cattle. It was used in 1886 and egistered in 1891 in Castro County. Mrs. Carter's operation ceased running in 1920. Henry Rompel Jr. has also use the Seven Up brand since 1943. He registered it in Comal and Hayes counties.

(Seven Six) Welder-McCan Partnership, Refugio County, Texas. When James F. Welder Jr. and Claude McCan, a former TSCRA president from 1942-44, entered a partnership in 1933, they leased their land and bought their cattle. But when they were getting ready to brand that first year, they forgot to bring along an iron. So they turned a year brand with the number 2 over, which made it a connected 7 and 6. today the Welder-McCan Partnership is run by Leo J. Welder of Victoria, a former TSCRA president from 1962-64, and TSCRA Director Kerry McCan Jr. The Seven Six brand is burned on crossbred cattle in Refugio, Victoria, San Patricio, and Bee counties.

(SMS) Ranches, Stamford, Texas. Svante Magnus Swenson, an immigrant Swede, came to Texas in 1836 and prospered in the mercantile business and banking. His wealth enabled him to acquire vast acreage in the Texas Rolling Plains. His sons, Eric and S.A. Swenson, began to develop this land for ranching and in 1882 ran cattle on 500,000 acres. They selected their father's initials as the ranch's brand. Legend says that the S's were branded backwards after a blacksmith mistakenly forged an iron that way. It was first run in the spring of 1882 in Jones, Haskell, Stonewall, Throckmorton and Shackelford counties. In recent years the ranch was divided among the heirs. One of these divisions, owned by the Swen R. Swenson Cattle Co. of Dallas and managed by Gary Mathis of Stamford, continues to use the brand in Jones, Stonewall, Haskell and Throckmorton counties.

(Spade) Spade Ranches, Colorado City and Lubbock, Texas. Isaac L. Ellwood, one of the inventors of barbed wire, bought the 130,000-acre Renderbrook Ranch in Lamb, Lubbock, Hockley and Hale counties in 1889. He stocked it with cattle bought from J.F. "Spade" Evans. The cattle carried the Spade brand. Evans had designed the brand based on the suggestion of his friend Dan Cummins and had registered it in Donley County in 1880. Ellwood continued to use the Spade on all his cattle. Today Spade Ranches consists of Renderbrook-Spade, Chappell-Spade, Borden-Spade and Wagon Creek-Spade ranches. The Spade is branded on the ribs of the ranch's registered Hereford, Simmental and crossbred cattle in Mitchell, Sterling, Coke, Borden, Throckmorton and Palo Pinto counties, Texas, and San Miguel County, New Mexico. TSCRA Director William J. "Dub" Waldrip, 1983 president of the National Cattlemen's Association, manages the ranches.

(TC) O'Connor Bros., Victoria, Texas. Thomas O'Connor began using the brand in 1837 in Refugio, Goliad, Calhoun, Victoria and San Patricio counties. He first registered it in Refugio County on April 18, 1848. The brand is still used by O'Connor Bros. in Refugio, Victoria and Goliad counties.

(Turkey Track) Olive Loving & Son, Jermyn, Texas. This brand has been used since about 1900 in Jack and Young counties. Two irons, a half circle and a bar, are used to make the Turkey Track brand. Olive Loving III of Jermyn continues to use the brand on cattle in Jack and Young counties today.

(XIT) XIT Ranch, Texas Panhandle. When the Chicago firm of Taylor, Babcock and Co. (the Capitol Syndicate) received from the state 3,050,000 acres for construction of the Texas Capitol building in 1885, the owners formed an english company and stocked the ranch with cattle. The first cattle were brought to the area by Abner Blocker, who is generally credited with having devised the XIT brand. It was known throughout cattleland as one of the hardest brands for a thief to alter. In the early years, the brand was carried by as many as 150,000 Longhorn cattle. The ranch began to slowly improve the native cattle by infusing blood of Hereford, Shorthorn and Angus breeds. The XIT brand was registered in Dallam, Hartley, Oldham, Jeff Smith, Parmer, Castro, Bailey, Lamb and Hockley counties. In 1901, the ranch began selling some of its land, and by 1912 the last of the XIT cattle were sold.

(Y O) Y.O. Ranch, Mountain Home, Texas. Captain Charles Schreiner, after he left the Texas Rangers, made a fortune in the mercantile business in Kerrville, Texas. This money enabled him to purchase more than 600,000 acres stretching from Kerrville to Menard by 1900. He first registered the Y brand in 1887 in Kerr, Kimball, Mason, Bandera, Edwards, Gillespie and Kendall Counties. in 1919 the ranch was divided and the brand went into the possession of Gus F. Shcreiner, Charles Scheriner III, who has managed 60,000 acres of the original ranch from 1949 to 1976,began using the Y.O. brand in 1949. It was also the name of the ranch that is famous for its Texas Longhorns, crossbred cattle, Angora goats, Rambouillet sheep, Quarter Horses and exotic animals from four continents.

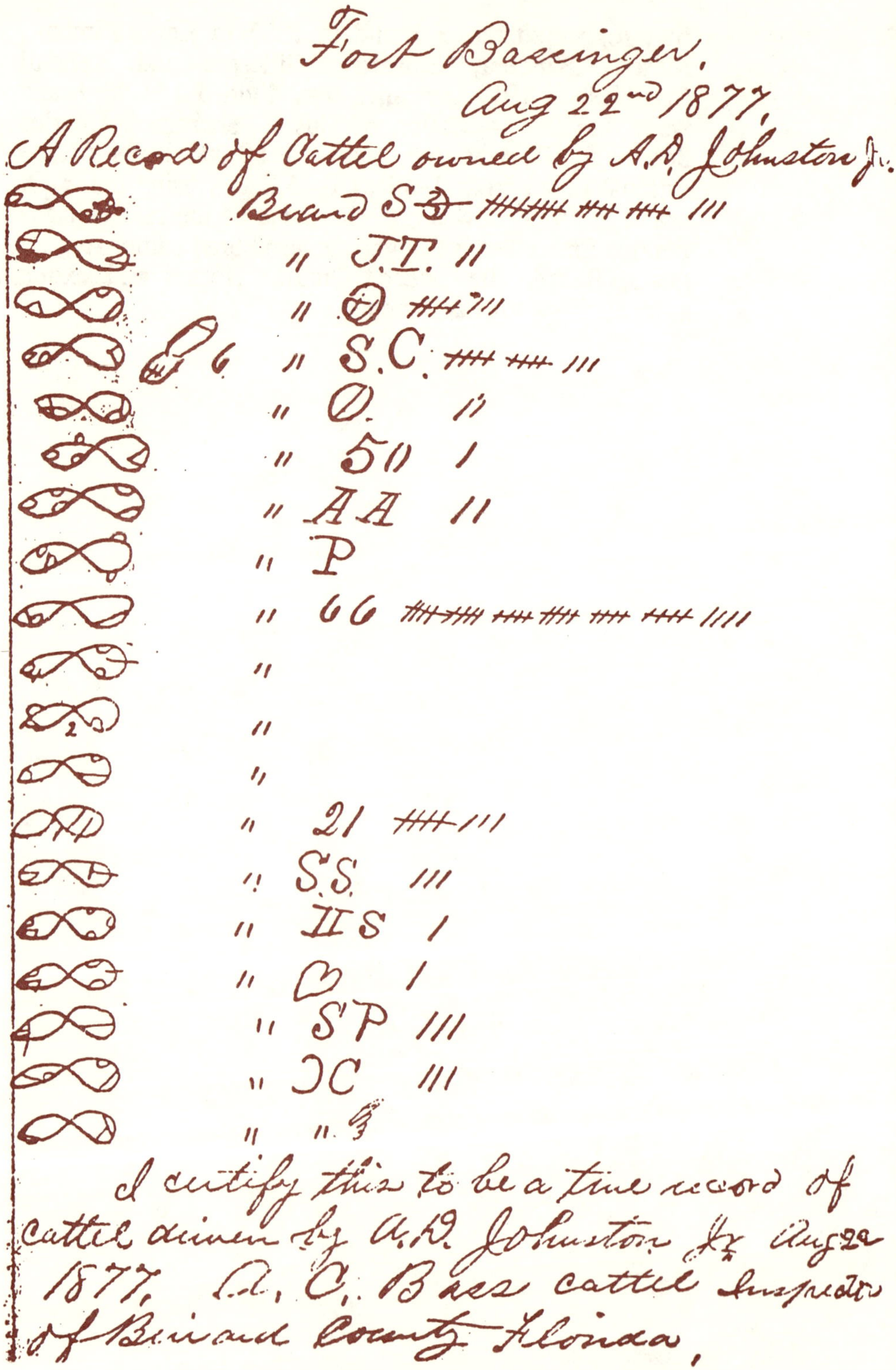

Fort Bassinger.

Aug 22nd 1877.

A Record of Cattel owned by A.D. Johnston Jr.

Brand S3

" J.T.

" O

" S.C.

" O.

" 50

" AA

" P

" 66

"

"

"

" 21

" S.S.

" IIS

" ♡

" SP

" JC

" " 3

I certify this to be a true record of cattel driven by A.D. Johnston Jr Aug 22 1877. A. C. Bass cattel Inspector of Brevard County Florida,

Historical Records, Courtesy of Brevard County, Florida

'In the FIRST HALF of the 16th century the Spanish Conquistadors under HERNAN CORTES and FRANCISCO PIZARRO built an empire from Mexico to Peru. Cattle were shipped in from Spain for breeding in these waste lands, and cattle breeding became a pillar of wealth on this new continent.

The Spaniards brought along the medieval custom of putting their family marks on everything they owned. They branded their cattle with the sign of the breeder. From then on branding became an American heraldry.

The early cattlemen of the last centuries were the rough knights of the frontierless open spaces of the American continent. Their cattle brands are the escutcheons of a trail blazing period'

Various brands symbols have been around for a long, long time. Many are the symbols which, in one way or another, you have contact with every day. They are the marks that tell you in an instant the name of a certain product such as a package of chili mix, a can of beans, frozen vegetables or any one of a million other items. The manufacturers' name is readily identified, not by actual name, but by a specific character you know.

They are the brand marks you have easily associated to items you trust, or those that are strictly hands off. It is the same with livestock brands. Brand officials whose job it is to know brands, can identify thousands upon thousands of brands, even tell you the owners, where the ranch is locations, and in general, if necessary, a history of each.

CHILIMANIA!, may expose some readers to their first contact to what livestock brands are. The slight change in altering of single letters' shape can easily indicate the difference between one owner's brand and another. Each state regulated brand registration within their state only, but the transportation of livestock interstate, requires knowledge of many brands from out-of-state breeders.

An example of using brands are the nomadic people of the Sahara, who for thousands of years have been using a simple hot iron bar to mark and identify their camels and goats. Their symbols are basically those of straight lines. Some lines being long, other short. To these lines were added additional lines forming branches. The various final lines and branches are sufficient to identify one family from another. A youngster among these people is expected to know thousands of markings and be well versed in how to apply the markings on their own animals. As livestock have the ability to wander and mix with other stock, it is necessary to identify each animal and it's owner.

From comments we have received from cattle raisers, CHILIMANIA! has presented the widest coverage of assorted brands from many sources as yet to be in one book. From the thousands of brand symbols received from States and organizations who were interested in the scope of our project, we have attempted to use a cross reference of designs. Livestock, whether they be cattle, horses sheep or hogs, is a very important segment of our past. A past that is now our present, and livestock is an industry that is a very important part of our future.

Incorporating the use of brands in CHILIMANIA! was an after thought. It came about in trying to determine what to use to separate recipes. We believed that this book was one that did not need the use of flowers, fancy curly lines, etc. The normally proliferated recipe dividers found in general cookbooks, we felt, did not suit this book.

What better way of honoring the cowboys and ranchers of years gone by then by using brands. And since chili first made it's appearance on the ranges of the Southwest, we believed that the use of livestock brands as separators, would fit in to a T.

Various ranches, and their brands have been passed down through generations. In many instances, brands used by previous owners were, at times, more important than the actual value of the ranches or even the livestock. The prestige of owning a particular brand was of great significance. Brands were at times, and to some extent, remain a status symbols which has set one herd above another, one ranch above the next.

Today, branding is still maintained, but not on a scale as it was done in yesteryears. As previously mentioned, branding was done to identify one's property from anothers.

There were those, as there are some who feel that everything is their's, and everyone else owes them a living. The rustling, or thief of livestock has been a problem as long as easy money was available. And money in one form or another, has been around as long as cattle have been raised. During the early years of cattle raising, being found with a running iron (a straight iron rod, heated and used to alter a brand into another symbol), a fire, and a bound animal was a sure way of getting one's neck stretched. It was known as range justice.

With the modern trend displayed in today's legal system, the penalty for stealing cattle, as are the cases of any theft, may generally be a slap on the wrist by a judge. A judge who probably wouldn't know the front end of a cow from it's rear. He would also think that all beef comes pre-packaged directly from the grocery. The offender may even be given a warning not to do it again, well, not for at least 24 hours, but if you do it, don't get caught.

If you happen to see any "midnight raiders" ripping off cattle from a pasture along a dark country road in the middle of nowhere, give the cattleman a break. Reach the nearest phone and notify the closest authority. It will not only be appreciated by the one who's cattle are involved, but livestock raisers everywhere who depend upon their stock getting to market for their livelihoods.

We hope CHILIMANIA! has increase your interest in an aspect of Americana that goes back many years, and in some ways, is quite historic. It is a way of life that is centuries older than the United States. It is in one way, it's a life-style that is gradually fading further and further into the past. As foreign firms purchase and operate huge ranches for raising cattle to self-supply their own countries, it is destroying a part of Americana.

The lost of business by this Nation's livestock breeders, has forcing many old ranches to go under. More and more of what was once a proud way of American life, is rapidly going down the tubes.

If anyone happens to see a Japanese brand on a steer, we would really appreciate a picture of it.

'Before the Wild West saw its first gunfight, before a Texas cowboy roped his first steer, there were cowboys in Florida.

Salty, rawboned cowboys drove red-eyed longhorns through the pastures and swamps of Florida; Fort Pierce and Okeechobee and Basinger were booming cattle towns replete with gaudy saloons, boardwalks, dusty streets and one-on-one shootouts that equaled any of the Old West.'

'Perhaps the most underestimated of cowhands, a ranch dog is a work dog, a highly disciplined animal who knows how to corral cattle, when to bark at a steer, when to snap and when to bite. And when not to. Often, the cowboy need to no more than turn his dogs on the recalcitrant bull. They'll take care of the rest.

'History has dealt Florida's cowboys a bust hand. They've been left out of the book, shut out of the movie deals. Even when Florida did get notice, the reviews were negative. Frederic Remington, known for his paintings depicting Western cowboys life, toured Florida cow country in 1895 and sniffed: "Not a country for a high-spirited race or moral giants."

Florida cowboys, said Remington, "lack dash and are indifferent riders, but they are picturesque in their unkempt, almost unearthly wildness."

"The Wild, Wild East"
by Bill Rose
The Miami Herald, Feb. 1991

The Branding Iron used by the Lewis & Clark Expedition. An iron of this type would have been used to mark packing crates, etc. rather than livestock.
Montana

BRAND ACKNOWLEDGEMENT

We wish to thank the following for their assistance in furnishing brands and information from their states and organizations, and most of all, the livestock raisers from around the United States for our using their brand symbols.

The libraries of Brevard County: Merritt Island branch, and the Main Office in Cocoa for their valuable assistance in heading us in the right directions in locating the sources for the material we needed.

The American Angus Association, Mr. Kieth E. Evans, Director

Arizona Department of Agriculture, Ms. Helen Jenkins, State Brand Clerk

California Bureau of Livestock Identification, Mr. Patrick J. Taylor, Brand Inspector/Registrar

Coastal Cattle Association, Inc., 1946, Beaumont, Texas Jefferson County Library System

Florida Division of Library and Information Services, Tallahassee, Ms. Karen Southwell, Reference Librarian

Hawaii Dept. of Agriculture

Mclennan County, Texas, Mr. Frank Denny, County Clerk,

Montana Dept. of Agriculture

New York Dept. of Agriculture and Markets, Albany, NY

Ohio Dept. of Agriculture, Reynoldsburg Laboratory Divisions

Oregon Dept. of Agriculture

South Dakota Dept. of Agriculture

Tennessee Dept. of Agriculture, Ellington Agricultural Center, Nashville, TN

Texas And Southwestern Cattle Raisers Foundation, Ms. Carol Williams, Foundation/Museum Coordinator

Texas Dept. of Agriculture, Mr. Rick Perry, Commissioner

BIBLIOGRAPHY

Symbols Signs & Signets, Ernst Lehner, 1950, Dover Publications, Inc. Brand symbols from Central America and Western ranches shown with dates, as well as the De Tavbro Bull in Cattle Brands, are from this publication.

Florida Cowboy, a History of Florida Cattle Raising, The Florida Cattlemen's Association, Kissimmee, FL.

Cattle & Men, Charles Wayaland Towne/Edward Norris Wentworth, University of Oklahoma Press, 1955.

Irons in the Fire, Oren Arnold, Abelard-Schuman, NY, 1965.

Four Centuries of Florida Ranching, George H. Dacy, Pritt Prtg, Co., St. Louis, 1940.

Cattle Brands, Jefferson County, Texas, Coastal Cattle Association, Inc., Beaumont, Texas, 1946.

World Book Encyclopedia, Vol. 16, 1991.

FINAL RECIPE ROUND-UP

HUNTSVILLE'S CHILI

Here's a recipe that's healthy and good:

2 Lbs. ground turkey
1 C. chopped onions
1 can (16 oz.) tomatoes
4 T. chili powder
2 cans (16 oz.) dark red kidney beans, drained
2 cans (8 oz.) tomato sauce
2 green peppers, chopped
3 jalapenos, finely chopped including seeds (remove stem and discard)
1 bay leaf

In a heavy skillet, cook meat and vegetables, until meat is lightly browned and vegetables are tender. Stir in remaining ingredients, cover, and simmer for approximately 90 minutes. Remove bay leaf. Serve over warm wheat toast, crackers, or just plain. Serve with whole jalapenos, Tabasco sauce, and a lot of water!!

Lisa & Bob Wilson
Huntsville, AL

Doyle E. Lightsey
Bar Arrow Thru L
Brandon, FL

PEPPERONCINI & ZUCCHINI CHILINI

3 T. olive oil
2 Lg. cloves garlic, crushed
1 Lg. onion. chopped
1 Lg. green pepper, chopped
1½ C. mushrooms, chopped
2 cans (28 oz.) whole tomatoes, lightly drained and chopped
1 can (15 oz.) tomato sauce
6 Med. pepperoncini salad peppers, drained and chopped
2 cans (15 oz.) chili beans, drained
2 T. chili powder
1 t. ground cumin
¼ t. curry powder
1 Pkg. frozen corn, thawed and drained
1½ C. zucchini, chopped

Saute; garlic, onions, green pepper and mushrooms in olive oil until tender. Place in a 3 to 4 quart pot with the tomatoes, tomato sauce, pepperoncini, beans, spices and corn; bring to a boil. Reduce heat and simmer for 15 minutes more. Serve in bowls with cornbread. Makes 12 servings.

Mark E. Moffitt
Nancy Hoffman
Cocoa Beach, FL

Thomas V. Hawk
St. Francis, SD

RENEE'S FAST & EASY TOFU CHILI

1 t. vegetable oil
1 Med. onion, chopped
1 t. minced garlic
1 can (16 oz.) tomato sauce
1 can (30 oz.) kidney beans with liquid
1 can (30 oz.) spicy chili beans with liquid
1 can (10 oz.) diced tomatoes with green chilies
1 Pkg. (9 oz.) Marion brand, tofu crumbles (vegetarian hamburger)

Cook garlic and onions in oil until the onions become translucent. Add remaining ingredients, except the tofu. Simmer, uncovered for 25 minutes. Then simmer covered for an additional 25 minutes. Add tofu and heat for approximately 5 minutes. Served topped with chopped onions, cheese or avocado. Makes about 8 medium-hot chili servings.

Renee Ann Conwell
Cocoa, FL

Blackbear Cattle Co.
Richard, OR

CHICKEN CHILI

This dish stretches two pounds of chicken breasts with enough vegetables and black beans to feed a crowd. It's a soupy chili that wants to be ladled into bowl or over brown rice. Bring containers of shredded Cheddar, chopped onion, chopped pickled jalapeno peppers and sliced black olives to offer on the side. Recipe makes 12 servings.

3 T. olive oil
2 Med. onions, chopped
2 garlic cloves, finely chopped
2½ T. chili powder
2 t. ground cumin
1 t. dried oregano leaves, crushed
¼ t. cayenne ;pepper, or to taste
1 14⅔ ounce can reduced-sodium chicken broth
1 28-ounce can Italian peeled tomatoes, chopped, with juice
1½ cups amber beer or water
1 t. sugar
1 t. salt
1 bay leaf
1 T. yellow cornmeal
2 pounds boneless, skinless chicken breasts, cut into 1-inch chunks
2 Med. zucchini (1 to 1¼ pounds), cut into 1-inch cubes
1 15-16 ounce can black beans rinsed and drained (white beans may be substituted)
1 11-ounce can whole-kernel corn, drained

In stockpot with cover heat olive oil over medium heat. Add onions, cover and cook 5 minutes. Uncover and continue to cook, stirring occasionally, another 8-10 minutes or until onions are pale golden and just beginning to brown. Add garlic, chili powder, cumin, oregano and cayenne. Cook, stirring, 1-2 minutes to toast spices lightly, but do not burn. Stir in chicken broth. Add tomatoes and juice, beer or water, sugar, salt and bay leaf. Bring to a boil over high heat, reduce heat to low and simmer, partially covered, 40 minutes.

Remove bay leaf. (Recipe can be prepared to this point up to two days ahead and refrigerated. When ready to finish, return chili base to gentle boil.) Slowly dust cornmeal over surface and stir to blend with liquid without forming lumps. Add chicken and zucchini, bring to boil; reduce heat and simmer 5 minutes; add beans and corn, simmer 5 minutes more or until heated through.

Nutrients per 1½ cup serving: calories 389, protein 40g, carbohydrates 28 g, fat 10g, dietary fiber 8g, cholesterol 878mg, sodium 645.

Modern Maturity

James L. Gardner
Christmas, FL

CHEAP CHILI

- 1 Lb. hamburger
- 2 C. spaghetti, cooked (break strands into several pieces before cooking)
- 1 Lg. onion, chopped
- 1 can (15 Oz.) kidney beans or chili beans
- 2 cans (6 Oz. each) tomato paste
- 2 cans (15 Oz.each) Hunt's Special Sauce (with tomato bits, onions, celery and green peppers), plus
- 1 -2 cans water, depending how thick you like your chili
- 2 Packets Bueno Vida (Frank's) Chili Powder or more, depending on how spicy you want it
- ½ t. garlic salt
- ½ t. salt
- ½ t. pepper
- ¼ t. cumin, optional

Put ground beef with onions in skillet. Drain off excess fat. Put cooked spaghetti in large saucepan. Add ground beef, onion, kidney beans, tomato paste, Hunt's sauce and 1-2 cans water, chili powder, garlic salt, salt, pepper and cumin, if necessary. Cook about 30 minutes over low to medium heat. Serve with saltines. Serves 8.

Cincinnati Enquirer

Steer Inc.
Bismark, ND

Some like it hot, but we say to have it Fresh! While tomatoes are still rolling in from the area farms, consider this fresh tomato salsa. It's great with tortilla chips, tacos or you own freshly made fajitas.

FRESH TOMATO SALSA

1 Lb. ripe tomatoes (about 2 large)
½ C. finely chopped green onions
1 t. minced garlic
1 - 2 T. finely chopped hot pepper
¼ C. chopped fresh cilantro
½ t. salt
juice from 1 lime

Halve tomatoes, remove seeds and finely chop. Drain excess juice. Combine with other ingredients. The "heat" of the salsa depends on the type and amount of hot pepper you choose. Makes about 2 cups.

Each ¼ C. (4 T.) contains 14 calories, no fat or cholesterol, 1g. fiber, and 106 mg sodium.

Wegmans Food Markets
Rochester, NY

C/B

Ronald & Marjorie Cowdrey
Christmas Valley, OR

DOMESTIC GODDEST CHILI

Roseanne (Barr) Arnold

When Roseanne's gang quits fighting about whose turn it is to set the table, they chow down on this.
Prep time: 10 minutes Cooking time: 20 minutes

2 Lbs. ground beef
2 C. chopped onions
¼ C. chili powder
2 t. minced garlic
2 cans (15 oz.) tomato sauce
2 jars (8 oz.) mild or medium taco sauce
2 cans (15 oz.) kidney beans, drained and rinsed
Shredded Cheddar cheese and tortilla chips

Cook beef in Dutch oven over high heat, stirring to bread up meat, until no longer pink, 3 minutes. Add onions and cook, stirring, until transparent, 2 minutes. Stir in chili powder and garlic; cook 1 minute. Stir in tomato sauce and taco sauce; bring to boil. Reduce heat and simmer uncovered 10 minutes. Stir in kidney beans and heat thoroughly. Serve with cheese and chips. Makes 10 servings.

Nutrition info per serving: 415 calories, 21 gm protein, 31 gms fat, 28 mgs carbohydrates, 1,254 mg sodium, 77 mg cholesterol.

Ms. Cheryl Haat
Ontario, NY

Larry Joseph
Waianae, HA

THREE-BEAN BARBECUE-CHILI

2 T. vegetable oil
1 Med. onion, chopped
1 t. chili powder
1 can (14½ to 16 oz.) stewed tomatoes
1 can (15 to 16 oz.) black beans
1 can (15½ to 19 oz.) red kidney beans
1 can (16 to 19 oz.) white kidney beans (canellini)
1 pkg. (10 oz.) frozen mixed vegetables
1 can (4 oz.) chopped mild green chilies
¼ C. bottled barbecue sauce

In a 5-quart Dutch oven heat the oil on medium-high heat. Saute the onions until transparent but not browned. Adds the chili powder and blend together. Add the stewed tomatoes mixing with the onions and chili powder.

Reduce heat to simmer, and cook, uncovered for 10 to 15 minutes. Drain liquid from beans, and add to mixture along with remaining vegetables, chilies, barbecue sauce and ½ to 1 cup of water depending on thickness desired. Bring to a boil. Reduce heat to simmer, and cook uncovered for about 15 minutes.

John Whitacre
Cincinnati, OH

Wedgworth Farms, Inc.
Belle Glade, FL

FOUR-BEAN BARBECUE CHILI

2 T. salad oil
1 Med.-size onion, chopped
1 t. chili powder
1 can (14½ to 16 oz.) stewed tomatoes
1 can (16 oz.) garbanzo beans
1 can (16 to 19 oz.) white kidney beans
1 can (15½ oz.) red kidney beans
1 can (15 oz.) black beans
1 can (4 oz.) chopped mild green chilies
1 pkg. (10 oz.) frozen mixed vegetables
¼ C. bottled barbecue sauce
dash or two Tabasco hot sauce, optional

In a Dutch oven, over a medium-high heat, cook the onions until quite tender in the salad oil. Drain off excess oil before mixing in the chili powder. Simmer for a few minutes, then add the tomatoes and bring to a boil. Reduce the heat and simmer for about 10 minutes, uncovered.

Drain all the cans of beans completely of their liquid, and add to the tomatoes mixture. Mix in the frozen vegetables, chilies with the liquid, barbecue sauce. Add a little tomato juice to make a desired consistency, and bring to a boil. Reduce heat and blend flavors by simmer for 10 to 15 minutes. Makes four main course servings.

Mick & Helen McConkey
Cocoa Beach, FL

RAC
Rea Ag Corporation
Milton-Freewater, OR

FOX RUN'S CHILI OLE' APPETIZER

Ingredients:

2 - 8 oz. packages cream cheese
2 cans Dixie Chili
1 Pkg. shredded cheese (more if desired

Line baking dish with all cream cheese, pour Dixie chili over cream cheese. Sprinkle cheese over top. Take at 350 degrees for 15-20 minutes. Let Stand 1-2 hours. Serve with Tortilla chips. Best made ahead of time; the longer it stands, the better it is.

Jim & Tori Fogler
Cincinnati, OH

S.A. Tucker, Jr.
Gallatin, TN

QUICK FIX CHILI

½ Lb. ground beef
1 small onion, chopped
¼ C. chopped green and sweet red peppers, combined
1 small clove garlic, minced
1 t. chili powder, optional
1 can Campbell's Chili Beans in zesty sauce
1 C. Campbell's Tomato Juice or V8 vegetable juice

1. In 2-quart sauce pan over medium heat, cook ground beef, onion and pepper with garlic and chili powder until beef is browned and vegetables are tender, stirring to separate meat.
2. Add beans and tomato juice. Heat to boiling. reduce heat to low; simmer 15 minutes, stirring occasionally. Makes 3½ cups or 4 servings.

CAMPBELL'S Recipe

James & Mary Ann Dowsett
Waipahu, HA

NOTES FROM THE DUTCH OVEN

This section of CHILIMANIA! contains dibs and dabs of probably utterly useless material and information about nothing in particular, but something that will add a page or two more to this book. It may be informative to some, and not to others. So if after you go through it and find the copy it of no interest, just forget that you've gone through it.

Mr. Bill Hardy of Merritt Island was generous in offering his collection of notes and clippings on chili. Some items are from others, and have been dropped into the pot as well. Some scraps of info were inserted elsewhere, and can be found somewhere within the pages.

from USA Weekend

"One man's chili is another man's axle grease. If a guy wants to toss in an armadillo, I don't argue - I just don't eat with him".

-Carroll Shelby
International Chili Society

A Chilihead's Compendium

First, There Was The Chili Pepper: Texans claim chili con carne originated in the 1800's. One story has jail cooks using chili powder to mask the odor of bad meat. Another tale comes from San Antonio, where lavanderas (washerwomen) for Republic of Texas soldiers not only washed clothes in their tubs but made chili in them, too. The Chili Queens set up temporary sidewalk cafes in the military plaza before being put out of business by the health department around World War II.

How The Debate Began: Cheap and filling, chili attained national popularity during the Depression. But it wasn't until 1951, when the Chili Appreciation Society International was founded, that it reached cult status. The true mania began in 1966, when Midwestern H. Allen Smith wrote a piece called "Nobody Knows More About Chili Than I Do' for Holiday magazine. That stirred up the first international Chili Cook-off in the West Texas town of Telinqua in 1974. There, Smith faced off against Wick Fowler,the Lone Star's legendary chilihead. The contest ended in a draw.

Topping Bar: What do people put on-on under-chili? Grated cheese, chopped black olives, lime juice, red pepper flakes, chili-pepper vinegar, fresh or pickled jalapeno, guacamole.

Long-Distance Chili Fix: The award has to go to Chasen's, the Los Angeles beanery beloved by Hollywood. Elizabeth Taylor, while filming Cleopatra in Rome, wired the restaurant to fly in some chili. A week later, Chasen's received another telegram; "The chili is so good. All gone now. Please send 10 quarts in dry ice to 448 Via Appia, Pignatelli. Love and kisses."

THE REAL CHILI STORY

by Dianne Conroy
TODAY, Gannett News Service

"The great debate, it seems, is not limited to whose chili is best. Even more heated is the argument over where the first bowl was made and by whom. Estimates range from 'somewhere west of Laramie,' in the early nineteenth century-being a product of a Texas trail drive-to a grisly tale of enraged Aztecs who cut up invading Spanish conquistadors, seasoned chunks of them with a passel of chile peppers, and ate them.

"Never has there been anything mild about chili."

"The Official Chili Cookbook"

The first time that a chili-loving relative of mine was in Mexico, he could not wait to get a bowl of the concoction. In a small restaurant in a border town, he confidently ordered chili and was serve chile, the hot peppers.

When he tried to make himself better understood and ordered chili con carne, he got a mixture of peppers and meat. It took awhile, but he finally got the message. That soup-like concoction that is the passion of so many Americans in the Southwest, in particular--is not a Mexican dish.

While the red hot peppers and other spices of Mexico and the American Southwest helped inspire the creation of chili, it is essentially an American creation. The die-hard chili aficionados of Texas will tell you that Texas is not only the home of chili but that the best chili is made in Texas.

In "The Official Chili Cookbook," the authors say that chili was a staple on cattle drives. The most romantic of tales about the origins and popularization of chili claims that a range cook planted gardens along the trails so that he would always have a supply of some of the necessary ingredients-oregano, chile peppers, garlic and onions. He used whatever meat was handy-beef, buffalo, rattlesnake, jack rabbit or armadillo.

The raging debates over the origins of chili and who makes the best are not easily settled and, in fact, probably never will be.

One of the wackiest annual cooking contests in the country got its start because of who-makes-the-best debate.

In 1967, writer H. Allen Smith wrote tongue-in-cheek article for Holiday magazine in which he touted his abilities as the chili cook. The title of the article claimed "Nobody Knows More About Chili Than I Do."

Some Texans took good-natured xxxx and challenged Smith to pit his chili against of that of an Austin, Texas, newspaperman named Wick Fowler, who represented the Chili Appreciation Society International. The Smith-Fowler cook-off was to be the first, last and only chili cook-off but one of the judges, with searing taste-buds, declared a tie which he suggested could be settled the following year.

And that was the informal beginning of the International Chili Society's annual World Championship Chili Cook-off.

"There are as many ways to make chili as there are cooks... Every cook swore by his own chili makin's and the best thing one of 'em would say about some other cooks' chili was, Mmmm that's purty near chili!!"

BICARB BLAST

STOMACH RUPTURES AFTER BAKING-SODA USE

New Brunswick, N.J. -- An editor whose stomach ruptured after taking bicarbonate of soda got little relief from a jury.

In his suit against Arm & Hammer baking soda, William Graves, 64, editor of National Geographic, said he drank bicarb in a glass of water after downing a bowl of homemade chili, two martinis, and a glass of wine. His stomach ruptured, leading to seven operations.

A Superior Court jury here found the labeling defective in not warning of stomach rupture. But it awarded no damages, saying his indigestion would have overridden any reasonable warning. Yet Graves claims a Pyrrhic victory (a victory won at excessive cost): the label now warns of a hazard of an over-full stomach.

--Malcolm Manber

A chili with sugar? Yes, and more
By Barry Cheek
TODAY-Gannett News Service

Listen up, chili heads of the world: Now we've really got something to get burned up about.

It's an objective book about chili. That's right, objective, for crying out loud. A book that gives equal time, and credence, to chili from Cincinnati or Dallas. A book with chili recipes incorporating such miscegenations as sugar, applesauce, peanuts, cocoa, bay leaves, tequila, Cabernet Sauvignon and sauerkraut. A book that recognizes - and thereby legitimizes - the existence of canned chili. Wuf.

The Great American Chili Book by Texan-turned Californian Bill Bridges is a slap in the face of the great American chili tradition. More than any other food, even barbecue, chili incites ferocious regional chauvinism and selfrighteous loyalties. Anyone who know beans about chili knows there is only one legitimate way to make it - his own.

Any self-respecting Texan confronted with a bowl of olive-infested California chili would do the honorable thing and shoot it. A Californian on a chili odyssey would find the Texas or New Mexico versions about as much fun as dynamite.

However, the author's appalling broad-mindedness is what makes the Great American Chili Book worthwhile - for some people. Advanced chili heads wouldn't be caught dead with it, but the neophyte who's just beginning to explore the world of chili will find useful and intriguing ideas in it.

It's nothing if not complete. There's an exhaustive chapter on chili's origins that patiently explore 11 different theories. The one about the Hungarian shepherd will be new even to veteran aficionados.

There's a list of chili publications and a directory of mail-order supplies of ingredients, for chili freaks marooned, say, in St. Cloud, Minn. There are visits to many chili parlors, famous and obscure alike, such as Chili John"s, the oldest restaurant in Green Bay, Wisc.; or Frank Tolbert's Texas Chili Parlor in Dallas. Bridges even claims to have located acceptable chili in Paris. Finally, there's the real meat of the book - 100 chili recipes, ranging from the classic Texas Prison Chili to the funky Anchor Steam Beer Chili. Most of them seem longer on imagination than plain ol' hellfire, which is curious.

There are some good ideas that the selective chili book can pluck from these recipes and incorporate, but one still wishes that the author has switched on his folly filter when compiling them. No chili recipe that use - gaaaack - sugar be allowed to see the light of day, and there are at least 10 or 12 of those.

I often wondered at cooking contests what is being judged - the quality of the food or the capacity of the judges.

When I sat out for Agoura, a small town about 30 miles north of Los Angeles, it was with no little trepidation. I was to help judge the International Chili Society's annual World. Chili Cook-off, where there would be about 50 finalists.

Fifty bites of any food is no means volume of food - but of chili?

I carried along a supply of Alka-Seltzer and made a silent promise to take very dainty bites.

What makes a winner?

Flavor first, of course. Not an eye-watering, palate-parching overabundance of chili powder, but a balanced blend that still allows the flavor of the meat to come through.

Consistency also is important. Grainy, gritty chili, with a half-inch-thick layer of grease floating on the top didn't make it. Some or all of the meat should be hand chopped in consistent pieces. Vegetables such as celery or green pepper should flavor the chili, but not float around in big chunks.

Color should be that bright red-brown, brick hue.

Marjorie Rice
Special to TODAY

"We heed old proverbs, but who said what first?" One..Too many cooks spoil the broth: Origin: Too many cooks spoil the broth. Sir Balthazar Gerbier, "Principles of Building," 1662.

"Absolutely. Most likely, 99.9 percent of the time the broth will spoil."

So says Chef Frederic Sonnenschmidt, certified master chef and culinary dean at the Culinary Institute of America in Hyde Park, N.Y.

"It doesn't matter how many people you have to do something. Without a leader, they can't function. You can have 20 people in the kitchen -- each with ideas about how to make the meal taste better. But if there are too many cooks but no chef, the broth will spoil by the time they make a decision," he says.

Doesn't this sound too familiar when the subject of putting together a special pot of chili for a group.

Malinda Reinke
Gannett News Service
Florida Today 8/2/91

On two occasions, we've applied for inclusion into the Guinness Book of Records. But we were informed on both attempts that the nature of the book is "too specialized from our point of view."

From the wide use of non-specialized records in the Book, CHILIMANIA! might well be better than some used. Is there a record for ways to prepare Fish 'n Chips?

HG

In the search for recipes, we turned to a Director of a specific Southeastern university press, whom we were told had some terrific recipes. The following was part of his reply: "P.S.: I note in the piece from the El Paso Times that you are from Cincinnati. Surely you will not include the recipe from that abomination that goes by the name 'Cincinnati Chili'"?

I'll bet our worst chili against his best that the owners and operators of the Cincinnati chili parlors end up with a larger check at the end of the month than he does.

As we've stated before, others may not care for ours chili, just as we may not like someone else's. As chili becomes very personal to some, no matter what it tastes, appears to be, or the flavor or aroma it releases, it is the way others like it. This would not be much of a cookbook if it only contained our recipes, or those prepared with specific ingredients.

CHILIMANIA! is a consensus of chili of many people between two covers, and that is all we have intended it to be.

H&CG

Chili peppers. Capsaicin is the element in the chili that holds the curative powers. It thins the mucus in the lungs, helping to clean up respiratory ailments. On the other hand, hot peppers can aggravate ulcers and hemorrhoids.

Ellen Carlson
Knight-Ridder Newspaper
The Boca Raton News, Mar. 1992

Many cities claim credit for chili. Cincinnatians call the Queen City's version preeminent in the world of chili. Texans and southwesterners would argue that theirs is best. San Antonio is said to have the earliest recorded chili recipes. (Not surprisingly. Texas has also been a leader in heart disease research).

Florida Today
Gannett News Service
Sept. 1989

PEPPERS

Bland To Blistering

Ten of the most popular varieties of peppers:

Bell Pepper
Sweet, mild. Also in red, blond, yellow, orange, violet.

Anaheim
Best when roasted, stuffed or in stews.

Poblano
Smoky, earthy flavor when roasted; when dried, called 'ancho' and tastes sweeter.

Jalapeno
Most widely eaten hot chile in U.S. Often pickled.

Serrano
Hottest chile commonly found in U.S.; used in salsas.

Thai
A staple of Southeast Asian cooking.

Cayenne
Pungent, tart. Usually powdered.

Scotch bonnet
Fruity, smoky. Found in Caribbean cuisine.

Tabasco
Sharp, biting. Basis for the McIlhenny Tabasco sauce.

Habanero
Hottest of all chiles. Found in bottled condiment sauces.

Florida Today
From The Great Chile Book
by Mark Miller

Peppers Are Hot On Palate
...And On Trendy Menus
by Jane Harvey
Gannett News Service

Chile peppers - the atomic seasoning long a staple in equatorial cuisines - are igniting mainstream U.S. taste-buds as never before.

Chile fever has inspired an explosion of products, from chile-patterned boxer shorts to heaps of new sauces.

"Americans are just beginning to realize the variety of hot and spicy foods available," says Dave DeWitt, editor of Chile Pepper magazine, which has a circulation of 65,000.

Changing immigration patterns play a big role in boosting the popularity of hot foods, DeWitt says. Today's immigrants are more likely to be from Asia, Africa, the Caribbean, Mexico and Central America, and they're introducing new dishes.

"The result is an American public that's willing to take more chances with food flavors," says DeWitt, who notes that an estimated 75 percent of the world's population eat chile daily.

RECIPE INDEX

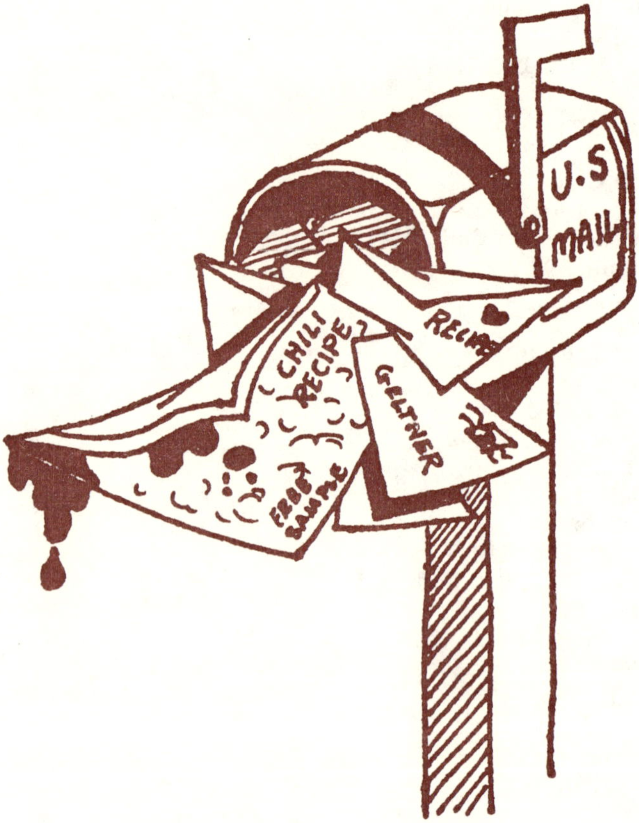
U.S
MAIL
CHILI
RECIPE
FREE
SAMPLE
RECIPE
GELTNER

CONTRIBUTORS' INDEX

RANCHERS/BRANDS' INDEX

ORDER FORM

Use this form or make a photocopy

Please send me ..... copies of CHILIMANIA! @$17.95 (price includes $14.95 + $3.00 shipping and handling). For additional books, add 75¢ each for shipping.
Floridians: Add 6% sales tax.

NAME ....

ADDRESS ....

CITY..........................STATE.....ZIP CODE ....

Make checks payable to ***G.S.C. Books***, and mail to:
G.S.C. Books, P.O. Box 2333, Merritt Island FL 32954-2333
Your satisfaction is Guaranteed.

☐ Enclosed are chili recipes for CHILIMANIA!II
☐ Yes, add my name to CHILIMANIA!II mailing list

CHILIMANIA! would make a wonderful gift to relatives and friends.

* *

ORDER FORM

Use this form or make a photocopy

Please send me ..... copies of CHILIMANIA! @$17.95 (price includes $14.95 + $3.00 shipping and handling). For additional books, add 75¢ each for shipping.
Floridians: Add 6% sales tax.

NAME ....

ADDRESS ....

CITY..........................STATE.....ZIP CODE ....

Make checks payable to ***G.S.C. Books***, and mail to:
G.S.C. Books, P.O. Box 2333, Merritt Island FL 32954-2333
Your satisfaction is Guaranteed.

☐ Enclosed are chili recipes for CHILIMANIA!II
☐ Yes, add my name to CHILIMANIA!II mailing list

CHILIMANIA! would make a wonderful gift to relatives and friends.